The Associations of Classical Athens

The Associations of Classical Athens

The Response to Democracy

Nicholas F. Jones

New York   Oxford
Oxford University Press
1999

Oxford University Press

Oxford   New York
Athens   Auckland   Bangkok   Bogotá   Buenos Aires   Calcutta
Cape Town   Chennai   Dar es Salaam   Delhi   Florence   Hong Kong   Istanbul
Karachi   Kuala Lumpur   Madrid   Melbourne   Mexico City   Mumbai
Nairobi   Paris   São Paulo   Singapore   Taipei   Tokyo   Toronto   Warsaw

and associated companies in
Berlin   Ibadan

Library of Congress Cataloging-in-Publication Data
Jones, Nicholas F.
    The associations of Classical Athens : the response to democracy /
Nicholas F. Jones.
        p.   cm.
    Includes bibliographical references and index.
    ISBN 0-19-512175-9
    1. Associations, institutions, etc.—Greece—Athens—Political
aspects.   2. Athens (Greece)—Social life and customs.   3. Political
participation—Greece—Athens—Societies, etc.   4. Greece—
Civilization—To 146 B.C.   5. Democracy—Greece—Athens.
I. Title.
DF277.J66   1998
938—dc21   97-46502

DF277
.J66
1999

9 8 7 6 5 4 3 2 1

Printed in the United States of America
on acid-free paper

To Marilyn
and our children
Nathaniel, Emily, Deborah, and Alice

Preface

Comprehensive study of the association in ancient Greece has lagged well behind the stupendous progress made in recent decades in our understanding of Greek public life and especially, where the present study is concerned, the institutions of Classical Athens. The reasons are not hard to discover. For one thing, the "association" in its ancient Greek context is an intractable phenomenon, difficult to define and, once defined, difficult to study owing to the scarcity and peculiar characteristics of the primary evidence. Those groups, furthermore, that we can satisfy ourselves are adequately labeled "associations" bear little resemblance to the groups that go by that name in more recent historical or living societies. Some, indeed the most important by far, are not, as one might expect, freestanding, independent private organizations but rather the internally organized segments of the state itself, as in the case of the deme association, the "constitutionalized" village of Kleisthenic Athens. Others bear signs of a strong kinship orientation, with membership sometimes confined to a few closely related families, new members added not by recruitment but by descent in the male line. Thus the expectations awakened by the modern notion of "voluntary association" have very little application to the ancient Greek, and certainly to the ancient Athenian, case. So, difficulty in coming to grips with this slippery subject may, I suggest, help explain why the only two existing inclusive studies of Greek associations date to around the turn of the twentieth century and, more pertinently for the present case, account for the total absence of a comprehensive examination of the subject matter of this book—the associations of classical Athens.

The time is ripe for a work of this kind. The last twenty years have witnessed the appearance of several exemplary publications devoted to some of the individual "associations" comprehended within the scope of this study. While the authors and titles of these (and other) studies all appear among the overview of the secondary literature at the close of the Introduction, it is appropriate that I acknowledge here my particularly great debt to the two monographs (1975 and 1986) of John S. Traill dealing systematically with the organization of Attica, to the comprehensive political and social study of the demes by David Whitehead (1986), and to the even more recent general treatment of the phratry by S. D. Lambert (1993). Were it not for the existence of these fundamental works, any attempt to grasp the "big picture" would not have been possible. At the same time, furthermore, since, as the subtitle of my book indicates, my goal is to examine for the first time the Athenian associations with respect to their "response to democracy," it is most fortunate that we now possess so much better an understanding of that democracy, particularly in respect to those features of the government with which, I will argue, the associations stood in a responsive or sort of dovetailing relationship. Here, too, I must acknowledge a specific debt by name—to both the more specialized and the more exoteric writings on the Athenian government by Mogens Herman Hansen.

The project was launched at the Institute for Advanced Study in Princeton, New Jersey, where, with the status of visitor, I spent the 1984–1985 academic year on leave from my post at the University of Pittsburgh. It was at the Institute that I commenced the usual spadework required by a project of this kind and, more crucially, conceived in embryonic form the ideas that were eventually to underlie the design and ultimate purpose of my investigations. That the thesis of the study should have begun to emerge at so early a stage was in part due to a lucky coincidence. Some of my time was devoted, in the hope of gaining a wider context for my study, to reading some of the more recent secondary literature dealing with the associations of nonclassical historical and living societies. Among other revelations, it became increasingly clear that in advanced societies associations, voluntary and otherwise, often bear a significant, indeed an organic, complementary relationship with the central government and its functioning. Concurrently, in the course of an effort to catch up with the most recent scholarship on the Athenian democracy, my readings of Hansen's groundbreaking articles on the Athenian democratic government — especially those concerning aspects of participation—made clear the low level of involvement by the citizen body in this nominally inclusive and egalitarian regime. At once, I began to explore the hunch, prompted by the nonclassical evidence, that low participation in the democracy was somehow counterbalanced by the engagement of the de facto disfranchised in their associations. Methodologically, the investigation was put on a sounder footing when I realized that the phenomenon of association could be defined by the usage of the ancient Athenians themselves, exemplified in a law of Solon and in certain key passages in Aristotle's writings. Over time, too, the simple fact of nonparticipation expanded to include other modes of estrangement or dissatisfaction originating in the distinctive features of the democracy—its egalitarianism, direct rule, and, beyond the citizen class, total exclusion of all but the adult male lineal descendants of the citizen caste. Eventually, the associations taken as a whole, despite their variations in origin, structure, and composition, all seemed to share in common a feature or features shaped by some perceived deficit of the *demokratia*. Now, a decade later, the book bears the subtitle "The Response to Democracy."

Debts of gratitude have been incurred in the course of my work, not the least of which is an institutional one. To the National Endowment for the Humanities, and ultimately to the taxpayers of the United States of America, I am thankful for the award of the senior fellowship that made possible my full year of study at the Institute. Since this book—the end-product of the research supported by the fellowship—aims to shed new light on the democracy from which our own form of government descends, I sincerely hope that my fellow Americans will think that they have received not only a good but an appropriate return as well on their investment.

At the Institute, Christian Habicht sponsored my year in residence at the School of Historical Studies (and, again, a brief return visit in the summer of 1994) and generously shared his knowledge on a number of topics as well as offering helpful advice and extending cordial hospitality. To Homer Thompson I am grateful for searching explorations of several subjects relating to the Athenian Agora, for friendly comraderie and encouragement, and for giving up some of his leisure time to introduce my wife and me to the historical sites and monuments of the Princeton area. Special thanks to a visiting member, Malcolm Errington, of Philipps-Universität in Marburg, Germany, for productive conversations in the epigraphic library, for interest in my project, and for making possible happy gatherings of our two families. During the year, I also profited from contact with the School of Social Science through exchanges with faculty and visiting members and attendance at various presentations. I am particularly grateful to the School and to the facilitator of its luncheon seminar at that time, Clifford Geertz, for the opportunity to present a paper entitled "The Role of Associations in the Athenian Democracy" in the spring of 1985.

Since my stay at the Institute, I have delivered presentations on various aspects of the topic to the general meeting of the American Philological Association and, back at the University of Pittsburgh, to the Department of History, the local chapter of the Archaeological Institute of America, and the Department of Classics. Audiences on each of those occasions are here thanked for any productive questioning or helpful comments offered in response to my presentation. Anonymous readers provided valuable corrections (notably concerning the chronology of certain documents of the *orgeones*), references to recent or forthcoming publications of relevance, and, no less valuably, an advance inkling of the reception my ideas may receive. With regard to the last point, while it is clear that others might have approached my subject differently, if the ultimate outcome of the publication of my book, even if that outcome includes controversy, proves to be a significant advance in our understanding of ancient Greece's first city, I will have achieved my purpose.

To mention a far more remote, but no less important, debt, I would be remiss if I failed to acknowledge the formative impact on this book of my two academic years' study in Greece under the auspices of the American School of Classical Studies during the 1970s. Were it not for my travels throughout Greece, my extended stay in Athens, and my residence in the village of Herakleion in the Argolid as a field excavator with the University of California, Berkeley, expedition to Nemea, this project could not have been conceived, much less brought to completion. While it is not possible here to catalog the names of all those to whom I am indebted for helping me in my efforts to understand the land, monuments, and people of Greece, I will mention a particular event that well exemplifies the mutually enlightening interplay of archaeology, topography, and epigraphy characteristic of this field of study —a "Saturday Walk" to the demes of the Marathonian Tetrapolis led by Eugene Vanderpool, the American School fellowship in whose name I was honored to hold during the academic year 1974–1975.

Chapters 5 and 6 together represent a slightly altered version of my article "The Athenian Phylai as Associations: Disposition, Function, and Purpose," *Hesperia* 64 (1995) 503–542, reprinted here courtesy of the American School of Classical Studies at Athens. Chapter 9 is a more substantially reworked version of my article "The Organization of the Kretan City in Plato's *Laws*," *Classical World* 83 (1990) 473–492, reprinted here with permission of the editor. For valuable assistance in procuring the illustrations, I am particularly indebted to H. Anne Weis here in Pittsburgh and to William R. Biers in Columbia, Missouri.

From 1989, nearly all the thinking, reading, and writing that have gone into this book were carried out in my home in Hampton Township, Allegheny County, Pennsylvania. My work has flourished amidst the invigorating hustle and bustle created by six people simultaneously engaged in carrying their several tasks to completion. My thanks to my wife and our children for setting so fine an example by their enthusiasm, industry, and accomplishments, but especially to Marilyn who, while never losing sight of her own mission in life, has stood by me all these years "in sickness and in health."

Pittsburgh, Pennsylvania   N. F. J.
August 1997

Contents

Figures

Abbreviations

Given below are the full particulars regarding general scholarly publications referenced throughout this book in abbreviated form. Excluded here are all publications dealing with the substance of my topic; for the full references to these the reader should consult the Bibliography at the end of the volume.

Periodicals

The abbreviations used throughout are those adopted in the most recent volumes of *L'Année philologique*, with the exception of the few easily recognized cases where English usage is not in agreement with the French, *CP* for *CPh*, *PCPS* for *PCPhS*, and so on.

Dictionaries and Encyclopedias

DarSag Ch. Daremberg and E. Saglio, *Dictionnaire des antiquités grecques et romaines d'après les textes et les monuments*, Paris 1877–1919

Frisk Hjalmar Frisk, *Griechisches Etymologisches Wörterbuch*, Heidelberg, vol. 1 (1960), vol. 2 (1970), vol. 3 (1972)

KlPauly *Der Kleine Pauly*, 5 vols., Stuttgart 1964–1975

LSJ⁹ H. G. Liddell and R. Scott, *A Greek-English Lexicon*, 9th edition, revised by H. S. Jones, Oxford 1940

OCD²,³ *The Oxford Classical Dictionary*, 2d edition, edited by N. G. L. Hammond and H. H. Scullard, Oxford 1970; 3d edition, edited by Simon Hornblower and Antony Spawforth, Oxford 1996

RE   Pauly-Wissowa, *Real-Encyclopädie der classischen Altertumswis-senschaft*, Stuttgart and München, 1893–1978

Non-Epigraphic Ancient Greek Texts

Names of authors are given in transliterated, Greek form, except for a few familiar Latinized or Anglicized spellings, such as Thucydides and Homer. Abbreviations of writings follow the conventions used in *OCD*³, pp. xxix–liv. All texts quoted are from the most recent Oxford Classical Text (*OCT*) or Teubner edition unless otherwise specified.

Fragments of historical writers are cited according to the edition of F. Jacoby, *Die Fragmente der griechischen Historiker*, Berlin and Leiden 1923–1958, in the form Krateros, *FGrH* 342 F 4. Where Jacoby fails, occasional reference is made to C. Müller, *Fragmenta Historicorum Graecorum*, 3 vols., Paris 1841–1870 (abbreviated *FHG*).

For the fragments of Athenian comedy, I provide references to the thus-far completed volumes of *Poetae Comici Graceci (PCG)*, edited by R. Kassel and C. Austin, Berlin and New York, from 1983. Otherwise, I cite *Comicorum Atticorum Fragmenta (CAF)*, edited by Th. Kock, 3 vols., Leipzig 1880–1888, and, occasionally, J. M Edmonds, *The Fragments of Attic Comedy after Meineke, Bergk, and Kock (FAC)*, 3 vols., Leiden 1957–1961.

The texts and translations of the *Loeb Classical Library*, Cambridge, Mass., and London, various dates, are referenced as "Loeb" accompanied by the translator's name and volume number.

Epigraphic Collections and Other Works, Prosopographies, and Archaeological Publications

Agora 3   R. E. Wycherley, *The Athenian Agora*, vol. 3, *Literary and Epigraphic Testimonia*, Princeton, N. J., 1957

Agora 14   H. A. Thompson and R. E. Wycherley, *The Athenian Agora*, vol. 14, *The Agora of Athens*, Princeton, N. J., 1972

Agora 15   B. D. Meritt and J. S. Traill, *The Athenian Agora*, vol. 15, *The Athenian Councillors*, Princeton, N. J., 1974

Agora 16   A. G. Woodhead, *Inscriptions: The Decrees*, Princeton, N. J. 1997

APF   J. K. Davies, *Athenian Propertied Families 600–300 B.C.*, Oxford 1971

IG   *Inscriptiones Graecae*, editio minor, vol. I, edited by F. Hiller von Gaertringen, Berlin 1924; vols. II–III, edited by J. Kirchner, Berlin 1913–1940; editio tertia, vol. I, edited by D. M. Lewis et al., Berlin and New York, fasc. I, 1981; fasc. II, 1994

M–L   R. Meiggs and D. M. Lewis, *A Selection of Greek Historical Inscriptions to the End of the Fifth Century B.C.*, Oxford 1969

Michel   C. Michel, *Recueil d'inscriptions grecques*, Brussels 1900

PA   J. Kirchner, *Prosopographia Attica*, Berlin, vol. 1, 1901 and vol. 2, 1903

PECS   *The Princeton Encyclopedia of Classical Sites*, edited by Richard Stilwell et al., Princeton 1976

SEG   *Supplementum Epigraphicum Graecum,* vols. 1–43, covering epigraphic publications through 1993, various editors (since vol. 26 for 1976/1977, H. W. Pleket, R. S. Stroud, et al.)

Threatte, *GAI*   Leslie Threatte, *The Grammar of Attic Inscriptions*, Berlin and New York, vol. 1, *Phonology,* 1980; vol. 2, *Morphology,* 1996

The Associations of Classical Athens

Introduction

The Subject

The subject of this work is the associations of ancient Athens during the so-called classical period, more precisely under the democracy of free Athens from its foundation by Kleisthenes in 508/7 down to the Macedonian takeover in 321 B.C. A further limitation of the subject is indicated by the subtitle, *The Response to Democracy*, for our goal will not be to provide a complete accounting of all associations during our period, but rather to investigate the contemporary association in its relation to the central government and to the state of Athens as a whole. The result, it is hoped, will extend beyond an enhanced appreciation of some important aspects of the associations in question to a new way of looking at the whole of the Athenian democratic polity, at least in institutional terms.

In chapter 1 sustained attention will be given to the thorny problem of defining the meaning of the concept "association" in relation to contemporary Athenian language, usage, and law. The definition eventually accepted will be based upon certain key passages in the writings of Aristotle, and the implications of those passages will be found to be in accord with the only inclusive legal text that has come down to us, Solon's statute on associations. But for the moment, it may be helpful to the reader if I provide a more specific and concrete idea of the contents of this study by simply listing, in accordance with that analysis in chapter 1, the various groups so identified by these two sources: Aristotle's roster of examples, embedded in two generalizing statements (neither of which purports to be complete or uniquely Athenian), embraces *phyletai*, *demotai*, *phrateres*, *orgeones*, *eranistai*, *thiasotai*, soldiers, sailors, "business partnerships," and travelers.[1] From Solon's law, once correctly emended and inter-

---

1. The passages are *Eudemian Ethics* 7.9.3 (1241b) and *Nichomachean Ethics* 8.9.4–6 (1160a). See "Aristotle on *Koinoniai* and a New Definition," in chapter 1.

preted, come the deme, *phrateres, orgeones, naukrariai,* "messmates," burial societies, *thiasotai,* "pirates," and "traders."[2] Very broadly characterized, these groupings comprise the internally organized segments of the public organization (namely, deme and phyle as well as the pre-Kleisthenic *naukraria*), the quasi-public phratry, and a wide spectrum of what might now be called "voluntary associations." To these will be added from other classical sources, with due explanation for their absence in Solon and Aristotle, the *hetairiai,* philosophical schools, regional associations, and *genê.*

Under the classical democracy, membership in these organizations was largely confined to the citizen class, but over time was gradually extended to various "outsiders," notably foreigners and women. Presumably all citizens (and only citizens) belonged out of necessity to a deme association and phyle association; and they, and eventually all other adult residents of Attica, seem to have enjoyed the option of joining still other groups according to their social and economic status, cultic interest, membership in a military unit, occupation, and so forth. Thus, even from this sketchiest of summaries, it is obvious that the potential involvement of the people of Attica was immense. But, as it happens, the actual coverage of the topic announced by my title will, owing to circumstances regarding the evidence, be significantly restricted.

Limitation of the Subject: Quantity of Evidence and Chronology

The first factor concerns quantity of evidence. As a whole, the Athenian associations are not abundantly documented, and in several cases the surviving traces are exiguous to the extreme. For example, the associations based upon the intermediate units of the state's public organization, the *trittyes,* although enough evidence survives to prove their existence, have left very little trace of their activity (if, indeed, they were ever significantly active).[3] The "burial societies" mentioned in the Solonian statute are elsewhere exampled by only a single noncommunicative phrase of a fourth-century forensic speech.[4] Athenian cleruchs, when acting as a record-producing collectivity, are represented by only two documents of the classical era.[5] The epigraphic record of the Paraloi is confined to two decrees and a dedication.[6] The closest that the classical period comes to a workers' guild is a single unilluminating dedication by a number of servile or freed fullers.[7] It is obvious that, since the ex-

2. *Digest* 47.22.4. For the emendation and close analysis of the text, see appendix 2. For my interpretation, see "Solon's Law on Associations," in chapter 1.

3. For what few traces there are of the associational organization of the Kleisthenic trittyes, see Jones 1987, ch. 1, sec. 1.33, pp. 60–61.

4. Demosthenes 57, *Against Euboulides,* §67. See, for the text and discussion, appendix 2.

5. *AJA* 60 (1956) 172–174 (= *Hesperia* 4 [1935] 174–175, no. 39 + *IG* II² 1952; *SEG* 15.129; ante med. s. IV), a catalog of cleruchs of unknown destination; and *IG* II² 1222 (fin. s. IV), a decree of the cleruchs from Hephaistia on Lemnos. Cf. the later such decrees, *IG* II² 1225 (cleruchs from Salamis; *SEG* 19.118, 28.105, 41.80; ca. 250), 1226 (Salamis; s. III), 1223 (Hephaistia; post 167), 1224 (Myrina on Lemnos; *SEG* 28.104; ca. 148/7-135/4), 1227 (Salamis; 131/0), and 1228 (Salamis; *SEG* 13.44; 116/5).

6. The decrees: *IG* II² 1254 (post med. s. IV) and *REG* 44 (1931) 296–301, no. 2 (ca. 300; *SEG* 37.102); the dedication: *IG* II² 2966 (med. s. IV).

7. *IG* II² 2934 (med. s. IV). The dedicators, who are both male and female, call themselves οἱ πλυνῆς (line 1). Compare, from a later period, *IG* II² 2941 (268/7), a dedication by parties "[crowned] ὑπὸ τοῦ κοινοῦ τῶν ἐργαζ[ομένων---]" (lines 1–2).

amination not merely of an association but of that association in its relation to the central government and to the state as a whole requires a fairly full record of evidence, little or no headway can be made in cases such as these.

The second limitation is that imposed by the chronological parameters of the study. The upper limit poses little difficulty since all organizations, including those attested by Solon's law in or around the year of his archonship in 594, may be presumed, barring negative indications, to have remained in existence under the later *demokratia*.[8] My policy, accordingly, has been to include, or otherwise account for, all associations attested from the earliest historical times down to the suppression of the free government in 321 (and, wherever appropriate, to trace their continuing functioning into later periods). But many Athenian associations do not come into prominence until after this epochal year. The problem is whether such associations should or should not be included, since obviously a cultic organization, say, known primarily from Hellenistic epigraphic sources might in fact have flourished in an earlier era. Is the argument from silence to be accepted in this instance? Two lines of approach, I think, are open to us. First, considerable respect must be accorded the failure of an association to be recognized by either Solon or Aristotle, in the former case because, as I argue, his law's roster of organizations appears to have been complete for his day,[9] and in the latter because the writer's voluminous comment upon Greek, and specifically Athenian, society presented innumerable opportunities to mention any *koinoniai* in existence at the time of writing. Accordingly, the absence in either the law or the Aristotelian corpus of a given class of association must be regarded as severely prejudicing the likelihood of its existence in 594 or toward the end of the classical democracy, respectively.

Another line of approach, more limited in focus than the preceding, is addressed to those several types of association that first appear in our records at about the time of or shortly after the end of the classical era. Do these groups belong to the present study or not? My position rests on the contention that the surviving epigraphic record is a reliable index of associational activity, at least where the closing years of the classical democracy are concerned. For as it happens, the half-century ca. 350–300 is the most abundantly documented such period, at least as regards associations, in all of Athenian antiquity. To take the most straightforward example, over 40 percent of all the approximately 157 documents of the deme associations fall within these limits despite the fact that these organizations collectively enjoyed an active existence of approximately three centuries, from 508/7 to ca. 200.[10] The implication is that, if an association known to have left inscribed records from the postclassical era was in existence in the decades immediately preceding (as well as following) the end of the classical democracy, some trace of that existence would

8. As is well known, at least one of the pre-Kleisthenic phylai and one of its *trittyes* were still functioning around the end of the fifth century (for their citation in the law code of Nikomachos, see *Hesperia* 4 [1935] 5–32, nos. 1 and 2, at p. 21, no. 2, lines 35–37). For all we know, the same may have been true of the similarly pre-Kleisthenic *naukraria*, a reference to which I have restored in the *Digest's* text of the statute: see appendix 2.

9. See appendix 2.

10. For the breakdown, see chapter 4, with note 68. Actually, if the full truth were known, the percentage might be appreciably higher since the categories "med. s. IV" (15 texts) and "s. IV" (3 texts) undoubtedly include inscriptions belonging to the second half of the century.

have survived. The *argumentum e silentio*, in short, is in this instance a valid one. The possible objection that an association might function without producing inscriptions would be difficult to make, if, first, that association produced such texts at a later date and since, second, to judge from the extraordinary variety of record-producing bodies, the practice seems to have been universal, or nearly so.[11]

By this latter criterion we must eliminate from our study the following: societies of *eranistai*, independent *thiasotai*, cultic associations going by various names, groups of foreigners and others identified by common ethnicity, professional or commercial organizations, groups of women, and the unidentifiable groups responsible for a large volume of fragmentary epigraphic records.[12] These bodies correspond more or less to the well-known phenomenon of the "Hellenistic association." If a new point is being made here, it is that these associations (as opposed to those others surviving from the classical era) did not, if I am right, exist or, if they existed, functioned only to an insignificant degree, prior to the demise of the free democratic government. Thus the rise of the Hellenistic association is potentially a product of the organic engagement between government and association being explored in this investigation of the preceding democratic era. At the close of our study, in chapter 10, we shall return to this topic and ask ourselves why the demise of the classical *demokratia* should have been attended in short order by the sudden emergence of these new organizations.

The upshot of the operation of these limiting factors is the concentration of our efforts upon no more than eight or so well known and already intensely studied groups. What will set our study apart from all previous work will be, first, the strategy of marshaling under a single rubric "association" a number of organizations that thus far for the most part have been examined only in isolation from each other and, second, pursuant to achieving the primary goal of the project, to do so in the light of their varying interdependent or even symbiotic relationships with the democracy. These organizations are: the deme association, including groups of soldiers encamped within their boundaries (chapters 2, 3, 4); the phyle association (chapters 5 and 6); the phratry (chapter 7); "clubs" (the *hetairiai*), "schools" (the philosophical installations in the gymnasia), regional associations, and the cultic *genê* and *orgeones* (chapter 8). These groups, though falling short of the full roster of the types of association that eventually were to come into existence in ancient Athens, include, as the informed reader will perhaps already realize, the groups of real importance under the democracy; and in the end it will be possible, on the basis of the examination of them alone, to reconstruct in its main lines the web of associations that, I hope to show, were organically intermeshed with, or at least acquired their distinctive characteristics in response to, the key organs of the central government. Next, with the completion of our examination of the primary record, in chapter 9 we shall turn to an examination of the quasi-utopian community created by Plato in the *Laws*, with a view to discovering in the institutional design of his "Cretan City" at least partial confirmation of our thesis. Chapter 10, finally, will look back over our efforts and attempt to weave together the loose threads of our individual studies into

---

11. Examples of nonrecord-producing societies would include the indubitably active *hetairiai* and philosophical schools, but there were few, if any, others.

12. For the detailed justification of this claim, with full reference to primary sources, epigraphic and otherwise, see appendix 1.

the fabric of interrelated institutions—characterized above all by a responsive, dovetailing relationship between central government and associations—that was classical democratic Athens and Attica.

Ancient Sources for the Associations of Classical Athens

Were this study devoted to a comprehensive treatment of all aspects of a particular association or associations, it would be appropriate, indeed necessary, to offer a comparatively complete accounting of the relevant primary source materials. By now, however, it should be clear that the restricted focus of my investigation obviates the necessity for any such accounting. Nonetheless, it is always desirable on general grounds to have in mind at least a rough idea of the kinds and quantities of source materials that comprise the ultimate evidentiary base alternately justifying, qualifying, or potentially refuting every claim to fact contained in a work of this kind. Beyond that, certain general features of the source materials, once brought to light, may, quite apart from their specific content, tend to offer support for, raise questions concerning, or even seriously call into question, the hypothesis under review. This seems to be the case with regard to the present study, for, while it will be argued throughout this work that under the democracy the associations enjoyed a complementary, even symbiotic, relationship with the central government, the sources for these same associations, despite the enormously important role being ascribed to them, are either very few in number or, where they do exist in quantity, silent regarding any such relationship with the state.[13]

Let us take up, first, the easier question of the simple existence or nonexistence of primary source materials. If it is legitimate to have an expectation in such matters, that expectation would be, I should think, that associations such as those described above, irrespective of their relationship with other entities (including the central government), would be relatively well documented. After all, ancient Greek associations, as their denominators indicate, cover a very wide spectrum of human activity, indeed virtually all extradomestic occupations or pastimes. At Athens, if the internally organized segments of the state are counted (as they properly are in this work), the associations open to citizens alone numbered in the low hundreds, with any given son of citizen-class parents eligible to become a member of a half-dozen or more different organizations.[14] The potential for associational activity, and

13. With respect to later Greek antiquity, the paucity of nonepigraphic sources was noted by Tod in his *OCD²* article on "clubs, Greek," p. 254: "Despite the large number and great popularity of clubs in the Greek period, both in the Hellenistic and Greco-Roman world, literature makes surprisingly few references to them, and the available evidence consists almost entirely of inscriptions and, in the case of Egypt, papyri." No attempt at an explanation for this major fact, however, was made, either here or in the later 1996 version of the article at *OCD³*, s.v. "clubs, Greek," p. 351.

14. Every citizen, by virtue of his citizenship, necessarily belonged to a phyle, trittys, and deme (not counting the phylai and the trittyes, and possibly the *naukrariai*, of the pre-Kleisthenic organization known from classical sources to have survived the creation of the democracy) and almostly certainly belonged to a phratry. Many, if not all, aristocrats, were members of *genê*. To these affiliations others, depending upon the individual case, could be added from the remaining roster of groups mentioned at the head of our discussion.

for the production of documentation of that activity, is accordingly enormous. But the bulk of such material reaching us is in fact on any accounting sadly disappointing. This is a major fact about our study requiring explanation, if not through item-by-item analysis, then at least in terms of any pronounced trends affecting the production or survival of that material.

It is appropriate to begin with the records of the associations themselves, the *epigraphic record*. A wide range of different types of association chose to inscribe their acts on stone—the demes and phylai, the phratries, the regional associations, the cultic *genê* and *orgeones*, bodies of encamped soldiers, and so on. Even so, the corpus of preserved inscriptions, given the range and number of potentially inscription-producing bodies, is not at all large. For instance, approximately 157 documents of the deme associations survive, representing 48 of the original 139 village associations—meaning 91 are not directly documented at all by stone inscriptions.[15] The phylai, originally ten in number and eventually totaling 15 (with a maximum of 13 in operation simultaneously at any one time), are documented by a small body of texts, about 65 in number, with the decrees distributed over the entire career of the Kleisthenic and post-Kleisthenic associations numbering only 48.[16] Lambert's catalog of phratry documents numbers only 36 items even after "possible phratries" are included.[17] From these three easily cited examples it is at once clear that, if these groups were playing the vitally important roles ascribed to them in the present work, they have left surprisingly little evidence of their activity.

Naturally, the usual explanations are ready at hand. Perhaps many acts of associations were never written down, even on papyrus, much less inscribed on stone. Those that were inscribed may not have survived or may still remain undiscovered. Another approach to explanation, however, is suggested by the uneven distribution of *types* of inscribed document. To take the best documented and so best understood case, that of the deme, the 157 texts just mentioned include decrees, leases, sacrificial calendars, so-called *leges sacrae*, *horoi*, and dedications. But of this heterogeneous lot, a large portion—something over 100 or about two-thirds—are recognizably decrees; and of the decrees, about 69 percent are recognizably honorary decrees.[18] Similarly, the great bulk of the phyle inscriptions are decrees, and of the 48 surviving examples, 45 or 94 percent are honorary.[19] Were the records of other types of association plentiful enough to make tabulations of this kind significant, we might well find the same pattern prevailing—at least there is no reason to preclude

15. For rosters of the documents of the demes, see Whitehead 1986, app. 3, pp. 374–393; and Jones 1987, pp. 67–72. For more recent finds, and for the details on my count, see chapter 3 of the present work, with note 54.

16. For the list of documents of the phyle, see appendix 3. For discussion of the honorary decrees, see chapter 6.

17. See Lambert 1993, app. 1, "Phratry Documents," pp. 279–370. The texts of the "possible phratries" are nos. 27–36, pp. 363–370.

18. For the roster of deme documents on which these figures are based, see, again, chapter 3, with note 54. To the honorary decrees should be added at least nine dedications reflecting the previous passage of an honorary decree. Naturally, both categories (decrees and specifically honorary decrees) would undoubtedly be swollen were it possible to identify the character of several fragmentary texts of uncertain content.

19. See "The Honorands of the Decrees," in chapter 6.

its operation elsewhere. Publication of the acts of an association in permanent form, therefore, may be closely—and disproportionately—linked to the process of conferring honors. Monumentality and permanence were undoubtedly regarded as part and parcel of the substance of the accolade. If at some future date a question should arise about that accolade's specific content, an inscribed stone, unlike a perishable sheet of papyrus, would presumably be available to be checked. And, to make a vitally important point, an inscribed stone could serve as an advertizement of an association's attitude regarding its benefactors and, if (as often) the text contained the promise that similar honors would be bestowed upon future benefactors, might usefully encourage others to promote the interests of the association.[20]

The point is that, since the engraving on stone of the high proportion of surviving texts, namely the honorary ones, was probably prompted by these extraneous concerns, the relatively low survival of inscriptions from our associations need not be taken as a necesssary indication of any lack of importance or vitality on their part. Nor, to add another, quite different consideration, should any particular significance be attached to the rather restricted chronological range of this epigraphic record. Specifically, while the classical democracy, by the upper and lower limits of which our study is limited, was founded in 508/7, only a thin scattering of documents from the associations can be dated before 400, leaving the greater part of our period entirely unrecorded. Again, to illustrate the trend, it is necessary only to appeal to our few better documented associations. Of Lambert's catalog of 36 phratry documents, none is dated to a single year earlier than 396/5.[21] Of the 157 deme documents, only about a dozen are certainly or probably assigned to the fifth century.[22] For the phylai, only one text, a dedication dated on epigraphic criteria, is likely to have antedated the turn of the century.[23] What is the explanation? The answer, may I suggest, is to be found in the widely acknowledged exemplary role played by the central government with respect to its segmental units. As the *polis* went, so went the phratry, deme, phyle, and the rest. Certainly the institutional arrangements of the associations (leaving the form of their documentation out of it) contribute strongly to such an impression.[24] In the main, they resemble their analogous counterparts in the urban center. Since, accordingly, the state did not begin to engage in

20. See, for example, the several instances of such language in the honorary decrees of the phylai: chapter 6, with note 89.

21. The so-called decrees of the Demotionidai, *IG* II² 1237.

22. Viz., *IG* I³ 251 (= I² 183; Eleusis; ca. 445); *SEG* 12.52 (Halai Aixonides; fin. s. V); *IG* I³ 253 (= I² 186; Ikarion; ca. 450–425); I³ 254 (= I² 187; Ikarion; ca. 440–415?); I³ 256 (Lamptrai; ca. 440–430); I³ 243, frag. 10 (Melite; ca. 480–450); I³ 250 (Lower Paiania; ca. 450–430); I³ 242 (Peiraieus; ca. 490–480); I³ 258 (= II² 1172; Plotheia; ca. 425–413); I³ 248 (Rhamnous; ca. 450–440); I³ 244 (= I² 188; Skambonidai; ca. 460); and I³ 245 (= I² 189; Sypalletos; ca. 470–460).

23. *Hesperia* 11 (1942) 341–343, no. 1 (fin. s. V), phyle Pandionis. The earliest text dated internally to a specific single year is the decree of the same phyle, *IG* II² 1140 (386/5).

24. With regard to the internally organized segments of the city-state—e.g., at Athens, the phyle, trittys, and deme—the point can be appreciated by a glance at the third analytical index at the back of Jones 1987, pp. 396–403. To be sure, differences in nomenclature or detailed procedure are met at every turn, but the basic apparatus of assembly, officers, the honoring of benefactors, financial administration, cultic installations and functions, etc. is unmistakably a replication of the arrangements of the central government.

the regular promulgation of its acts in the form of lapidary inscriptions until well into the fifth century, with honorary texts (for our purposes, the most significant item) following at an interval after that,[25] it is to be expected that the practice would not be imitated at the associational level until appreciably later. So, as with the matter of documentation in general, the relatively late first appearance of our associational inscriptions need not in any way be taken as reflecting upon the possibility of a significant relation between association and state. For all we know, any structural accommodation between central government and associations may have been, at least in its nascent form, the work of the founder of the *demokratia* himself.[26]

With *nondocumentary texts* the relative silence is even more profound, particularly if one takes into account the comparatively large bulk of such materials. In the case of poetry, of course, silence about our subject is to be expected. Works of fiction, particularly if their setting is an otherworldly time and place, are unlikely to reflect, however indirectly, anything so mundane as a contemporary burial society or bivuoac of soldiers. Besides, the focus of tragedy, the most plentifully preserved of classical Athenian verse, tended to vacillate between the individual and the state, with little attention to intermediate tiers of social organization. If the immediate setting of a tragedy was a household, it was the conjugal household of parents and children, without a hint of the existence of the phyle association or phratry or cultic organization to which such a household (in the real world of classical Athens) would likely have belonged. Comedy, and particularly Old Comedy, however, is another matter altogether. Its frequent recognizable setting in Athens, its representation of living Athenians, and its pervasive topicality of theme and ambience all contributed to make the genre a particularly promising source of information, or at least of impressions, about our subject. Two suggestive examples are the titles of lost works about a *genos*, Kratinos's *Euneidai*,[27] and about *phrateres*, Leukon's comedy by that name.[28] As it turns out, however, it is the deme alone that is mentioned or alluded to with sufficient frequency to make a significant contribution to the present study. When, in chapter 3, we turn to the question of the isolation of the extra-urban demes, we shall find partial corroboration of our thesis in a pattern of references to the demes discernible over the entire expanse of Old, Middle, and New Comedy.

Like comedy, historical narratives deal with the real world, although, unlike comedy, not necessarily with the real world of the present. Nonetheless, the surviving writings of Herodotos and of the Athenians Thucydides and Xenophon, to mention only the principal representatives of the genre, would seem to afford ample opportunities to preserve something of importance about Athenian associations, even if in a context only tangential to the subject at hand. But any such expectation goes largely unfulfilled. Herodotos's text incorporates some of the vocabulary denoting classical Athenian associations, but only seldom with reference to the actual organi-

---

25. Of the nineteen honorary decrees earlier than 403/2 collected in the third edition of *IG*, viz., nos. 155–183, the earliest are 155 (ca. 440–430), 156 (ca. 440–425), and 157 (ca. 440–410).

26. For speculations, with some supporting evidence, along these lines, see chapter 10.

27. *PCG* IV, Cratinus, 71–72.

28. *PCG* V, Leuco, 1–5.

zations under review in this book.[29] A scattering of references to the predemocracy era includes a rare, and problematic, mention of the "prytaneis of the *naukraroi*,"[30] though any ascription of an associational development of the *naukraria* is entirely lacking. Additionally, the author in several passages refers to phylai, but in only three cases are they the phylai of (post-Kleisthenic) Athens, and in none of the three passages is the internally organized association in question.[31] Among many uses of the term *demos* in connection with classical Athens, while some seem to bear the sense of "village" in its nonconstitutional sense,[32] three others clearly refer to the formal constitutional entity.[33] Even so, again, in none of the three latter passages is there any hint of the existence of the deme association. Exceptionally, an isolated mention is made of the *hetairia* of Cylon, and it may be that the author has retrojected a term current in his own day to this much earlier time.[34] With Thucydides, a similar pattern, equally lacking in illumination, is in evidence. His few mentions of the Athenian phylai concern only their statewide roles,[35] and only twice does he make passing reference to the Athenian demes, in both instances in their territorial dimension.[36] By contrast, his references to *hetairoi* are not infrequent,[37] and in a famous passage he acknowledges the critical role played by the "sworn conspiracies" in the overturning of the Athenian democracy.[38] Xenophon, like Herodotos, evidences some associational vocabulary, but its uses are mostly nontechnical. The few occurrences of *phyle* (and of the personal *phyletes*) occasionally concern Athenian arrangements, but never with reference to the phyle association.[39] Surprisingly, too, the word *demos* in this Athenian author never denotes a deme; and the people called *demotai*, analogously, are not the members of the constitutionalized village but, in accord with popular usage, "commoners" or "plebeians."[40] *Thiasos* is once used of a cult society of some kind,[41] and once he writes loosely that "we are all *thiasotai* of Eros."[42] Among the words never found in his voluminous corpus are *gennetes*, *eranistes*, *orgeones*, and *phrateres*. It hardly matters, then, that *hetairos* and *hetairia* are not seldom found in the senses of comrade or faction. As for Herodotos

29. For example, his two uses of δημότης refer to "commoners" in Egypt (2.172.2 and 5) and Persia (5.11.2), his single mention of a phratry to Persian society (1.125.3).

30. 5.71.2.

31. 5.69.2; 6.111.1 and 131.1.

32. 1.60.4, 62.1; 5.74.2. In the third example, the fact that Hysiai (in parallel construction with the established Kleisthenic deme [Aiantid] Oinoe) is so designated is proof that the intended sense is nonconstitutional, since no deme by that name existed.

33. 5.69.2; 9.73.1 and 74.1.

34. 5.71.1. Compare his use of προσεταιρίζομαι at 3.70.2 and 3 and, with respect to the Athenian Kleisthenes, at 5.66.2.

35. 2.34.3; 6.98.4; 7.69.2; and 8.92.4. Cf. 3.90.2 (Messene) and 6.100.1 (Syracuse).

36. 2.19.2 and 23.1. In the former passage, the author's explanation for Acharnai as "the biggest settlement of Attica of the so-called *demoi*" reveals his effort to reach a non-Athenian audience.

37. 6.30.2; 7.73.3, 75.4; 8.48.4, 65.2, and 92.4. Cf. 3.82.5 (*hetairia* at Corcyra).

38. 8.54.4.

39. For the Athenian phyle, see, e.g., *Poroi*, 4.30; *Memorabilia*, 3.4.5; for *phyletai* as the members of a cavalry regiment, *Hipparchikos*, 2.5.

40. *AthPol*, 1.4; *Memorabilia*, 1.2.58; *Cyropaedia*, 2.3.7 and 3.15; 8.3.5.

41. *Memorabilia*, 2.1.31.

42. *Symposium*, 8.2.

and Thucydides, the "association" as understood in the present work is scarcely to be found in the pages of this, at first glance, promising source of information.

The explanation for the general silence on the part of the historians is simply that, as a consequence of their substantive concern with events affecting the whole of Greece or, within Greece, matters of inter-state relations, they treat the entirety of the *polis* rather than its individual component parts. Where, as we have just seen, one of those parts, a phyle or deme, *is* mentioned, it is in respect to its statewide role rather than to its internally organized mode as an association. Nonpublic associations, the phratry, *hetairia*, or *thiasos*, and others, since they were devoted largely to domestic or civilian peacetime pursuits, naturally only very rarely met the ancient Greek historian's criteria of relevance. All the more reason, therefore, to approach with high hopes a body of writings devoted in large part to just those pursuits — contemporary Athenian *forensic oratory*.

The rich fund of information provided by these legal briefs may, despite its bulk and (as our discussions will repeatedly affirm) transcendent importance, be briefly categorized and characterized. My first observation concerns lost evidence. We know from the titles of speeches preserved in later, chiefly lexicographical sources that several litigations at various times involved the members of Athenian associations. True, a classical Athenian association never attained, so far as we know, the status of a legal person, and therefore could not sue or be sued.[43] But nothing prevented the *members* of that same association from figuring as parties to a legal proceedings, and this may have occurred with some frequency. The behind-the-scenes shenanigans of the "clubs" in influencing the outcome of litigation are of course well known.[44] But even more impressive is the evidence for the actual appearance of members of associations in courts as principals in various legal proceedings. Evidence for the demes, to judge from the traces of lost briefs attributed to Isaios[45] and Dinarchos,[46] shows that the conspicuous role played by the demesmen of Halimous in Demosthenes' brief *Against Euboulides* (57) was not an isolated phenomenon. A lost speech of Isaios, *Against the Orgeones,* argued a case regarding a piece of land.[47] *Orgeones* also figure in an inscription of the mid-third century, *IG* II² 1289, recording the arbitration by *dikastai* of a dispute among members of the society concerning its internal financial affairs. According to the *Athenaion Politeia*, the archon basileus had jurisdiction over all disputes about cult matters involving *genê* (and priests).[48] Actual examples of proceedings involving *genê* are provided by a

43. For the view that "the modern institution of the juristic person was largely unknown in the Greek cities," see Finley 1985, p. 89. For similarly skeptical opinion regarding the association as legal person, see Harrison 1968 and 1970: vol. 1, p. 242; vol. 2, p. 22; and Rhodes 1981, p. 586 (on *AthPol* 52.2).

44. The subject is fully treated by Calhoun 1913, pp. 40–96.

45. Speeches VI, p. 188 Thalheim (Πρὸς Βοιωτὸν ἐκ δημοτῶν ἔφεσις) and VII, no. 4, pp. 188–189 Thalheim (Πρὸς τοὺς δημότας περὶ χωρίου). Cf., in a preserved Isaian speech, the suit brought against the deme and demarch (12.11).

46. Speeches XX, nos. 1–2, p. 105 Conomis (Διαδικασία Φαληρέων πρὸς Φοίνικας ὑπὲρ τῆς ἱερωσύνης τοῦ Ποσειδῶνος) and XXXIV, pp. 111–112 Conomis (Διαδικασία Ἀθμονεῦσι περὶ τῆς μυρρίνης καὶ τῆς μίλακος). For discussion, see Haussoullier 1883, pp. 99–102.

47. Speech XXXV, nos. 26–27, p. 198 Thalheim.

48. 57.2. For the text, see Rhodes 1981, pp. 639–640; for the interpretation, Harrison 1971, vol. 2, pp. 8–9.

lost speech of Lykourgos[49] and by no fewer than four titles of briefs ascribed to Dinarchos, three of them *diadikasiai*.[50] Specific suits apart, and a further indication of the magnitude of the never recorded or lost material, certain courts in classical Athens were specifically dedicated to cases involving *eranoi* and *koina*.[51] There is no mistaking that a great deal of valuable information regarding our subject has perished. Nonetheless, the evidence of lost sources speaks emphatically to the point of the present work's substantive concerns. Associations had become, by accident or design, subject to the workings of the central government's legal system (rather than, to mention a competing strategy, being left to pursue their claims through self-help). This is a matter to which we shall repeatedly return in our efforts to gauge the nature and extent of the democracy's regulation of contemporary *koinoniai*.

Secondly, a cursory examination of forensic texts preserves, even with the loss of briefs explicitly and directly addressed to the affairs of associations, a wide range of information about their structure, function, and dealings. The "Attic Orators," collectively, and consistently with our earlier preliminary observations regarding Solon's law and Aristotle, reflect the contemporary presence in Athens of the phyle and deme associations, the phratry, *genos*, *orgeones*, and *hetairiai*. Negatively, those associations that first appear in the epigraphic record just before or around the time of the Macedonian seizure are either entirely absent or only scarcely recognized,[52] thereby partially confirming the speculations about their non existence under the classical democracy offered earlier. But it is the positive record that interests us here, though it must be admitted that much of it consists of detail—and repetitious detail—only incidental to the case before the jury. To attempt a characterization of the content of many scores of individual passages scattered over the ten orators, the prevailing subjects include: mention of the statewide roles (for example, on boards, in the military, or as *choregoi*) played by members of deme or phyle; references to meetings, votes, crownings, and other activities of deme and phyle assemblies; acceptance by and enrollment among the memberships of deme, *genos*, or phratry; associational events (such as the staging of a wedding feast for one's *phrateres*); the service as witnesses by *demotai*, *orgeones*, and *phrateres*, and their consequent testifying before a court; and so on. Notably, and negatively again, little of this information bears directly upon the principle preoccupation of the present work with the place of the association within the larger framework of the Athenian polity.

For that, we must turn, thirdly, to the substantive content of the briefs, and here our general expectations about the prominence of the association in ancient Athe-

---

49. Speech VII, nos. 1a–6, pp. 105–107 Conomis (Περὶ τῆς ἱερωσύνης Κροκωνιδῶν διαδικασία πρὸς Κοιρωνίδας).

50. Speeches XX, nos. 1–2, p. 105 Conomis (Διαδικασία Φαληρέων πρὸς Φοίνικας ὑπὲρ τῆς ἱερωσύνης τοῦ Ποσειδῶνος); XXXI, p. 109 Conomis (Κατὰ Κηρυκῶν); XXXVIII, p. 114 Conomis (Διαδικασία Εὐδανέμων πρὸς Κήρυκας ὑπὲρ τοῦ κανοῦ); LXXXIV, nos. 1–2, p. 138 Conomis (Κροκωνιδῶν διαδικασία).

51. *AthPol* 52.2.

52. Thus, though the Greek term *eranos* is often used in the sense of contribution or friendly loan, no trace is to be found of the *eranos* association (or of *eranistai*). Greek *thiasos* seems usually to refer to informal "routs" or "gangs" of Bacchic revelers (e.g., Demosthenes, 18.260; 19.199 and 281). The *thiasotai* of Herakles at Isaios 9.30 need not have been an association. The terms *thiasos* and *thiasotai* are not found in Aischines, Andokides, Isokrates, and Lysias.

nian life are richly rewarded. To illustrate the point it will suffice to mention a few of the forensic texts that will loom large in the following chapters: the short brief composed by Lysias regarding the defendant's disputed membership in a distant rural deme;[53] the narration of a meeting of the members of the deme Halimous embedded in a speech of Demosthenes;[54] the illuminating references to "the women of the *demotai*" in a speech of Isaios;[55] and (an example directly addressed to the matter of the state's relations with the associations) Aischines' mention and discussion of a decree of the legislature prohibiting the demes and phylai from making announcements of honors before general audiences at the tragic competitions of the City Dionysia.[56] These passages preserve information, and angles on the interpretation of that information, unobtainable from any of the other source materials mentioned to this point. The fact that all the briefs are of Athenian reference, composed by Athenians (or, in Lysias' case, a metic resident in Athens) for Athenian litigants in trials before Athenian courts, and their contemporaneity with the epigraphic documentary record together place them among our most valuable and informative testimonies.

Forensic oratory is valuable because the speaker before a panel of jurors is ostensibly presenting an account against the backdrop of some aspect of contemporary Athenian life. To be sure, the tendency to falsify the facts was undoubtedly in many cases a strong one, but it remains true that that tendency would be checked by the speaker's knowledge that his audience, on whose vote the outcome of the proceedings entirely depended, was in the main presumably thoroughly conversant in the structure and workings of Athenian society. The fact that they were all citizens and at least thirty years of age by itself practically guaranteed as much. Accordingly, the litigant before an Athenian court, when addressing a matter so familiar and mundane as the very associations of which so many, if not all, of the jurors were themselves members, may be assumed to provide a tolerably accurate account of the facts, unless contrary indications suggest otherwise.

Even with the full acceptance of the forensic record, however, there may yet be a more valuable source of information, at least where the present work is concerned —*political theory*. Inscriptions and legal briefs may provide us with the raw materials, the data base, of our investigation, but it is to the theorizing of the philosophers that we must look if there is to be any hope of uncovering confirmation of larger, more speculative claims, specifically those regarding the unique relationships between central government and associations alleged throughout our studies.

Plato's speculative works might not at first be thought promising in this regard, but in his case initial appearances are deceiving. True, the specific arrangements of the visionary commonwealth set out in the *Republic* fly in the face of the basic principles on which virtually every ancient Greek social and political order, certainly including the Athenian, was founded, and so, even if one were to find a seeming point of agreement with the model of Athens advanced in this book, it would be a fortu-

---

53. See "Pankleon, Dekeleia, and the Isolation of the Rural Demes," in chapter 3.
54. See "*Agorai*," in chapter 3.
55. See "The Women of the *Demotai*," in chapter 4.
56. See "The *Agorai*: . . . Location and Schedule," in chapter 5.

itous and groundless coincidence devoid of meaning. But the same negative characterization may not apply, as already suggested, in the case of the philosopher's later, and far more realistic, utopian order, the Cretan City described in his final, massive dialogue, the *Laws*. That commonwealth, arguably constructed in large part on the basis of observation of the actual arrangements of historical centers in contemporary Greece, does seem, by virtue of its detectable relevance to Plato's own Athens, to possess the capacity to either confirm or refute the reconstruction of the classical Athenian polity under consideration in this work. But the required examination of Plato's dialogue will demand greater attention than can comfortably be accommodated within the brief compass of this Introduction. For this reason, full consideration of the Cretan City will be reserved for separate treatment in chapter 9.

Aristotle's approach, or approaches, to describing and understanding the Greek city-state involve two quite different perspectives. First, at the level of description and close analysis, the empirical data-gathering carried out by the school and embodied in the 158 *Constitutions*[57] led, in the case of Athens, to the creation of a work that, in both its historical diachronic and contemporary synchronic dimensions, preserves several, and in a few cases valuable, traces of associational arrangements in Aristotle's adopted city. The small dossier of passages may be briefly enumerated. Historically, the intact text of the *Constitution* records the existence in the time of (and even before the time of) Solon of the four phylai (and *phylobasileis*), of three constituent trittyes in each phyle, and of *naukrariai*, apportioned twelve to each phyle (8.3). The famous story of Peisistratos's second tyranny brings into play the woman Phye of the "deme" of the Paianieis (14.4), and Aristotle ascribes to the third tyranny the institution of *dikastai kata demous* (16.5), but at this early date, a half century before Kleisthenes, the demes had not yet achieved official, constitutional status[58] and so on these, as well as on strictly chronological, grounds, these predemocracy village communities do not fall within the scope of our study.[59] Kleisthenes' rise to power and the creation of the *demokratia* occasion the valuable description of the new organization of ten phylai, thirty trittyes, and the demes, with its explanation of the "mixing up" of the population achieved by assigning a trittys of demes from the city, another of demes from the coast, and a third of demes from the inland region to each phyle (21.2–4). But, in contrast with this mere acknowledgment of the units of the statewide organization, it is the remark that Kleisthenes "made those living in each of the demes *demotai* of each other" (21.4) that seems to acknowledge the existence of a deme association, and indeed ascribes the creation of that association to the founder of the democracy himself.[60] Equally, though differently, illuminating is the ensuing comment that Kleisthenes (in implied contrast with his innovations regarding the phylai) "allowed each person to keep their *genê* and phratries and priesthoods in accordance with ancestral custom" (21.6). This

57. For the number, see Rhodes 1981, pp. 1–2.

58. For the evidence pertaining to the demes before Kleisthenes, see Whitehead 1986, pp. 5–16. I concur with his rejection of the putative indications of "the idea of officially recognized demes" in the time of Solon or of Peisistratos and his sons (op. cit., p. 14).

59. For the possible significance of the occurrence of the term δῆμος in Solon' s law, dating to nearly a full century before the creation of the democracy, see appendix 2.

60. In the concluding chapter 10, I shall return to this point.

seemingly innocuous remark will, as we shall see in chapter 10, play a significant role in the reconstruction of the state's evolving engagement in the affairs of the Athenian associations. Except for these two fleeting comments, however, the account of the "changes" undergone by the constitution draws to a close with little more to offer than a few perfunctory acknowledgments of the normal apportioning of statewide functions *kata phylas.*

In the second half of the *Constitution,* the description of the democracy in Aristotle's own day—that is, near the end of the free government—and the very place where one would expect to find recognition of any role of significance played by the associations, if such existed, our disappointment is even more acute. At 48.4, early editors once believed that the text made mention of the *agorai,* or meetings, of the (internally organized) phylai, but modern commentators favor a quite different interpretation entirely unrelated to the phylai or their associations.[61] That leaves the assignment to Athenian courts of suits involving "friendly loan societies" (*eranoi*)[62] and "associations" (*koina*) (52.2). Over and beyond the writer's acknowledgment of the existence of "societies" and "associations," the centralized administration of suits concerning such groups serves as well to illustrate the point, important for my thesis, that the democratic government eventually became directly involved in the regulation of even private associations. All remaining references to our groupings merely testify to their statewide role of providing the basis for the apportioning of duty and privilege, the one exception being a reference to the misconduct on the part of demes (more exactly, members of deme associations) who had resorted to the "selling" of the offices apportioned to them (62.1). Again, as in the previous examples (regarding the pre-Kleisthenic *genê* and phratries and the suits just mentioned), regulation (or its absence) of an association appears to be at issue. But as important as these particulars are for our purposes, how are we to explain the *Constitution*'s general silence on the matter of the place of associations in the Athenian polity?

An answer is at hand. But before we turn to it, let us first address the evidence provided by other Aristotelian writings about the city-state, above all the *Politics* and the *Eudemian* and *Nichomachean Ethics.* These works are of course, in contrast with the *Constitutions,* general expositions of theory, and although they are grounded in and occasionally illustrated by the historical experience or current practice of particular Greek city-states, they obviously cannot be taken as descriptions or analyses, even in general terms, of any one of them, Aristotle's own place of residence, Athens, included. But even a superficial reading of this material offers encouragement. For one thing, scattered references are to be found to associations of several different types that were demonstrably in existence in Athens in or around the time of Aristotle. Examples include the deme (or *demotai*),[63] *eranistai,*[64]

---

61. For discussion of this point, see chapter 5, "The *Agorai:. . .* Agenda and Purpose."

62. For the view, however, that the development of the *eranos* as an association is postclassical, see appendix 1. Accordingly, the *AthPol*'s *eranoi* are probably merely "friendly loans."

63. E.g., *Eth. Nic.* 8.9.5 (1160a); *Poet.* 3.1448a37; *Pol.* 4.12.11(1300a), frags. 412 Rose (1540a41), 414 Rose (1540b19), 453 Rose (1546b35).

64. E.g., *Eth. Nic.* 8.9.5 (1160a), cf. 4.2.20 (1123a).

hetairia,[65] *orgeones*,[66] phratry (or *phrateres*),[67] phyle (or *phyletai*),[68] *syssitia*,[69] and *thiasotai*.[70] To some of these and to other, similar groups, Aristotle attaches the generic term *koinonia* in a valuable passage of the *Nichomachean Ethics*, shortly to be discussed in chapter 1. Now, as it turns out, the little particular information he imparts about these demes, phratries, phylai, and other associations does not shed much light on their history, structure, or function. But it is clear that the writer knew something about these groups, and it is a sound inference that that knowledge may have played a role in his theorizing about the relation to the whole of a state of its constituent parts.

The gist of that theorizing may, with the guidance of Mulgan's helpful study, be pieced together from the philosopher's rather disjointed presentation.[71] At bottom, Aristotle contends that the impulse is present in all people to enter "into *koinonia*" —into partnership, association, or community (*Politics* 1.1.12: 1253a). By my multiple renderings, I underscore the ambiguity and elasticity of our critical term, for it in fact is capable of a wide range of specific applications. To mention one, for Aristotle the *polis* itself is "a kind of *koinonia*"—the assertion with which he opens the *Politics* (1.1.1: 1252a). That is, it is a whole comprising constituent parts. But that "whole," as Mulgan explains, is not a mere "heap" or "aggregate" of unrelated elements accidentally brought into proximity with one another. Rather, the parts share a unity of "form"[72] or, to gloss the philosopher's concept with a more familiar synonym, purpose. Even so, the parts are still discernible as parts; indeed they may be quite dissimilar in function, despite the existence of the "form" imposing a unity upon them.[73]

It is obvious that this formal model is applicable to the subject of our study. Aristotle himself declares in the opening of the *Politics* that the *koinonia* of the *polis* embraces all the other *koinoniai* (1.1.1: 1252a), and in the *Ethics* all *koinoniai* are said to be parts "of the *polis*" (8.9.6: 1160a).[74] Furthermore, with regard to the point about purpose, the *polis* is said to be the "end" (*telos*) of "(all) the other *koinoniai*" (*Politics* 1.1.8: 1252b). Thus the specific historical associations mentioned here and there throughout Aristotle's general writings (and, as well, in the *Constitution of the Athenians*) may, on the philosopher's model, be brought into relation with the *koinonia* constituted by the *polis*. And, in contrast with the latent assumptions of previous modern scholarship, the Athenian associations are not, if Aristotle were to be

---

65. E.g., *Pol.* 5.5.5 (1305b), 5.5.9 (1306a), 5.9.2 (1313b).

66. E.g., *Eth. Eud.* 7.9.3 (1241b).

67. E.g., *Eth. Eud.* 7.9.3 (1241b), *Pol.* 2.1.10 (1262a), 2.2.11 (1264a), 3.5.14 (1280b), 4.12.11 (1300a), 5.7.11 (1309a), 6.2.11 (1319b), and frag. 385 Rose (1536b7, 1, 13, 18).

68. E.g., *Eth. Nic.* 8.9.5 (1160a), *Pol.* 2.1.12 (1262a), 2.2.11 (1264a), 4.11.3 (1298a), 4.12.11 (1300a), 5.3.7 (1304a), 5.4.6 (1305a), 5.7.11(1309a), 6.2.11 (1319b); cf. *Eth. Nic.* 8.12.1 (1161b), *Soph. El.* 1.164a27, and frags. 385 Rose (1536a48 and b6) and 387 Rose (1537a2).

69. E.g., *Pol.* 2.2.11 (1264a), 5.9.2 (1313b).

70. E.g., *Eth. Nic.* 8.9.5 (1160a); cf. [*Oec.*], 2.1346b15 and 17.

71. Mulgan 1977. Particular relevant and valuable are the discussions in ch. 2, "The Polis," pp. 13–37.

72. Mulgan 1977, p. 28, citing passages from the *Metaphysics*.

73. See *Pol.* 2.1.4 (1261a) on the necessity that the components that make up a whole differ in kind.

74. For the discussion of the passage, see "Aristotle on *Koinoniai* and a New Definition," in chapter 1.

our guide, analyzable as merely "heaped" together within the territorial limits of Attica. Rather, they may, upon closer investigation, be found to be organically related to one another and to the commonwealth as a whole. Again, though the functions of those associations may appear diverse, they might be found to complement one another; and, if so, the constituent associations would thereby share in the "form" or purpose of the state. Taken together, associations and state would comprise an integrated whole—the whole of the state in the broader sense of that term.

By this last clause, however, an important point regarding the philosopher's conceptual vocabulary, so far not acknowledged, is made. By "state," at least in contexts relevant to our concerns, Aristotle seems to mean the whole of society, including both the central controlling institutions *and* those other constituent "communities" that they control.[75] Yet, by understanding the *polis* in this wider, "inclusive" sense, the philosopher implicitly blurs the distinction between the all-encompassing monolith of the state and the "state" in its narrower, "exclusive" sense as the central authority—in the case of classical Athens, the democratic government. This distinction is fundamental to the thesis under review, for it will be maintained that the Athenian associations are in a condition of "response" to an "exclusive" central government, and that it was out of this process of response that emerged the "state" of Athens in its wider "inclusive" sense. Aristotle's model, however, eliminates automatically the possibility of such an intermediate stage of development.

Beyond the question of the meaning attached to the term "state," there is the theoretical issue signaled by Aristotle's use of the concept of "form," glossed above by the verbal synonym "purpose." In contrast with the Aristotelian model, the present study does not proceed on the assumption that the associations, simply because they are organically related to the whole of Athens in the "inclusive" sense, necessarily partook of a putative *teleological* character of that whole. Even if we leave aside any organizations whose function is incidental to the operation of the state at any level (it is to such cases that Aristotle's remarks about "heaps" and "aggregates" pertain), a constituent association integrally involved in the institutional life of Athens may nonetheless, on my reconstruction, be fundamentally at odds with the central government and indeed with the whole of the remainder of Athens, inclusively defined.[76] Not a unified "form" or purpose, but rather stability, or the attainment of equilibrium among competing forces, are the concepts, as suggested in the final chapter, with which one may characterize the constitutional and institutional order urged on the reader by our studies.

So our agreement with the model of government-association relations presented by Aristotle appears to go no further than a structural similarity, devoid of any deeper similarity in underlying principle or dynamic. But the point, even so, is

75. See Mulgan 1977, pp. 16–17, on the "ambiguity" between the exclusive and inclusive senses of "polis," with the statement on the inclusive state at p. 17: "In this case Aristotle is considering the *polis* or political community not as one aspect of city-state society but as the whole of that society, including both controlling 'political' institutions [i.e., the *polis* exclusively defined] and the other communities which they control." For a recent exploration of "the polis as society," see Ober 1996, pp. 161–187.

76. Take, for example, the phyle associations, to which, in chapter 6, I attribute a representative function that essentially pitted the minority membership of the phyle against the remaining nine-tenths of the citizen population.

an important one, for it gives rise to an unsettling question. If Aristotle saw the *polis* as a whole comprising parts, and those parts as including "associations," why does he not provide the sorts of specific factual material or even more pointed generic descriptions of the behavior of associations whereby the abstract model might be corroborated or at least illustrated? Especially if, as suggested, he views the *koinoniai* not as merely "heaped together" but rather organically interrelated within the *koinonia* of the inclusive state? The question is particularly germane in the case of the *Constitution of the Athenians*, which we left with a query regarding its silence on the place of associations in Athenian society. A possible answer, of course, is that such evidence did not exist, that, therefore, the ancient theorist's formal model is without empirical basis, and that, therefore, the structurally similar reconstruction under review in the present work may be similarly baseless.

Fortunately, an alternative explanation, or rather explanations, are at hand for Aristotle's silence on the subject of government-association relations, whether they are the specific relations suggested to have existed in this study or relations of any description. Briefly put, while Aristotle may have entertained such a belief, it is highly unlikely that he had access to the sorts of factual data needed to flesh out a formal model of this kind. Three areas of evidence are in question.

The Central Government. Some of the functions of, or patterns of participation by citizens in, the central government may have lain outside the reach of Aristotle's fact-gathering or observation. Particularly to the point, as I will suggest in chapter 1, is what is now known to have been the fact of minority citizen participation in the organs of government, especially the Assembly. Aristotle knew the quorum to be 6,000 citizens in attendance, but did he know, since he was not a citizen himself and so could not attend the Assembly as a voting participant, that this number was *also* the approximate seating capacity of the Pnyx,[77] a fact that made minority participation a foregone conclusion? And did he have an idea of the total citizen population of Athens at the time he wrote, a datum without which the significance of the size of the minority of 6,000 could not be gauged? The fact that the first known census of Athens was not carried out until the reign of Demetrios of Phaleron, 317–307, a few years after Aristotle's death, suggests that he did not.[78] Questions of a similar kind may be raised concerning the Council of Five Hundred on the points of absenteeism and whether councillors with rural demotics actually resided in the deme of their affiliations or were city-dwellers, and concerning the many boards of magistrates constituted *kata phylas* whether urban demes, or rural demesmen resident in the city, were disproportionately represented. In short, if the central government was dominated by an urban minority, could Aristotle have been aware of this fundamental fact?

77. See Hansen 1976, pp. 130–131. For Pnyx I, ca . 500–400, Hansen estimates the maximum capacity at 6,000; for Pnyx II, ca. 400–330, at 6,500.

78. The same argument is advanced with reference not to Aristotle, but to "the Athenians" by Hansen (1985, pp. 13–16). Among possible sources of demographic data available under the democracy, he cites the *lexiarchika grammateia*; the *pinax ekklesiastikos* (both physically housed in the local deme centers); and the 42 bronze stelai, one for each age class, listing those aged 18–59 and eligible for military service (set up before the Council House in the Agora). Of these, only the first, the deme registers, will necessarily have recorded *all* citizens (including many not actually resident in Attica), but there is no reason to believe that anyone at any time—including Aristotle!—ever attempted a compilation of all 139 registers.

The Acts of the Associations. Any theory ascribing significance to the roles played by the associations of a polity must inevitably take into account the functioning, whether official or behind-the-scenes, of those associations. At the minimum, the metic Aristotle was disqualified from membership in the segmental associations of the citizen society—phyle, trittys, and deme—and so, inter alia, could not attend their meetings or serve as an officer, and so on. Whatever records were produced by associational activity, too, may have been out of reach if deposited (in the case of a papyrus) or displayed (in the case of a stone inscription) in or near a private shrine or distant rural village center.

Preexisting Research on Attica or on Athenian Associations at the Time of Aristotle's Activity. It is a striking fact that virtually all the evidence for research of these kinds points to a time later than Aristotle. The fragments of the earlier Atthidographers, on whom the author of the *Constitution of the Athenians* is widely believed to have been significantly dependent, reveal very little trace of interest in the subjects germane to associations or their relations with the state.[79] The earliest known topographical studies of Attica (which, presumably, would have dealt with aspects of the deme associations) are those of Hegesias of Magnesia (mid–third century)[80] and of Polemon of Ilion (early second century).[81] "The *Horismoi* of the Polis," a scholarly work possibly dealing with the boundaries of the demes, is known only from a scholion on Aristophanes and so may be similarly late.[82] Although study of the Athenian *genos* may have begun in the fifth century with Hellanikos's *Atthis*, Hellenistic and later times witnessed the appearance of at least four additional such studies.[83] It is difficult to escape the conclusion that detailed information on such subjects, because it remained to be collected, had not previously been available to Aristotle and his coworkers.

These considerations are, taken collectively, adequate to explain how Aristotle—who maintained, anticipating the basic structural relation between association and state advanced by the present study, that the *polis* constituted an organic unity of di-

79. True, the pre-Kleisthenic *naukrariai* were alluded to in one connection or another by Androtion, *FGrH* 324 F 36, and by Kleidemos, *FGrH* 323 F 8, but in both cases the point is made with reference to much later developments and neither passage, respectively concerned with "the naukraric fund" and Kleisthenes' new public organization, addresses the internal, associational aspect of the *naukraria*. For a brief appreciation of the question of the *Athenaion Politeia*'s possible dependence upon the Atthidographers, see the discussion of the sources of the first half of the *AthPol* by Rhodes 1981, pp. 15–30. On the (Solonian) naukrary laws, see Lambert 1993, app. 4, pp. 385–388.

80. For the excerpt from Hegesias, preserved in Strabo (9.1.16: 396), see *FGrH* 142 F 24. Hegesias's work is characterized by Traill (1975, p. 97, n. 86) as a "cursive account of Attica."

81. Polemon "the Periegete's" four books are referenced, again, by Strabo (9.1.16: 396), writing in the following century or later. For the fragments, see *FHG* III 108–148.

82. See chapter 2, with note 87.

83. Hellanikos, who was still alive in 406, devoted a section of the second book of his *Atthis* to the *genos* of the Hierophants (see *FGrH* 4 F 45). In the second century B.C., Apollodoros of Athens, *FGrH* 244 F 101(9), composed an excursus on the *genos* of the Hesychidai. To about the same time belongs Drakon's "On *Genê*," *FGrH* 344 F 1; and perhaps in the next century comes Theodoros of Athens' "On the *Genos* Kerykes," *FGrH* 346 F 1. Jacoby conjectures a second century A.D. date for Meliton's "On the *Genê* at Athens," *FGrH* 345 F 1.

verse *koinoniai*—might have been unable, had he made the effort, to assemble the evidence needed to corroborate such a thesis.

Thus far our account of the sources available to us has addressed the matter from the perspective of the associations themselves. But obviously, if our plan is to investigate the relation of those associations to the central government (and their place within the polity of Athens at large), it is natural to ask whether *the records of the acts of that government* itself might not preserve illuminating indications. As a matter of fact, they do. Mention was made above of a state decree preserved in a speech of the orator Aischines (3.41–45) regarding the announcements of the phy-lai and demes at the tragic competitions. To this decree may be added a handful of other contemporary acts of the state affecting a particular association or associa-tions in general; these, as well as Aischines' evidence, will be discussed in detail in chapter 1. At the level of legislation, relevant central governmental acts or policies affecting associations include the much-discussed law about admission to the phra-tries preserved in a fragment of the Atthidographer Philochoros (*FGrH* 328 F 35a and b) and a brief allusion in a brief of the forensic orator Hyperides (4.8) to a law prohibiting the formation of *hetairika* "for the purpose of overthrowing the democ-racy." More fundamentally, the Roman *Digest* (47.22.4) preserves a text of a law as-cribed to Solon and fairly described as a general statute on "associations." This law is minutely examined in appendix 2 and, on the basis of our corrected and emended text, interpreted more broadly in chapter 1. Taken together, these testimonies are not impressive in their quantity or bulk, but they are explicit and speak directly to the point of government-association relations. In the end, they will prove adequate, I believe, to help tip the scales in favor of acceptance of the thesis of this book.

Secondary Literature on the Associations of Classical Athens

In order to place my investigation, as is necessary, within the context of existing scholarship, I shall mention with the briefest possible comment the more important major studies devoted specifically to the associations of classical Athens.

Two comprehensive studies of ancient Greek associations—where "associa-tion," in contrast with the more inclusive scope of the present work, excludes the in-ternally organized public units phyle, trittys, deme, and so on—are in existence. These are Erich Ziebarth, *Das griechische Vereinswesen*, Leipzig 1896; and Franz Poland, *Geschichte des griechischen Vereinswesens*, Leipzig 1909. Strictly limited to the religious organizations is the still older work of P. Foucart, *Des Associations re-ligieuses chez les Grecs, thiases, éranes, orgéones*, Paris 1873. Though all three works have been rendered obsolete by the subsequent discovery of inscriptions throughout Greece, and particularly in Athens, they remain valuable repositories of the ancient evidence known at the time of their composition.

Less sweeping in scope is D. Roussel's *Tribu et cité*, Paris 1976, a revisionist work devoted to the historical study of the genos, the phratry, and the phyle, with a sustained focus on the alleged "primitive" origins attributed to these bodies by ear-lier scholars. Nicholas F. Jones's *Public Organization in Ancient Greece: A Docu-*

mentary Study (Philadelphia 1987) surveys the units of public administration over the whole of Greece. Jones's functional definition of a "public" unit excludes most associations, while including, at Athens, the phyle, trittys, and deme, as well as the similar organizations of about 200 other city-states. Jones also studies these public units in their associational mode, but the discussion of the phyle and deme associations in Kleisthenic Athens is skeletal at best.

Modern detailed scrutiny of arrangements at Athens involves work in the allied fields of topography, epigraphy, prosopography, and constitutional, political, and social history. Eugene Vanderpool, long the Professor of Archaeology at the American School of Classical Studies at Athens, personally and through his influence on numerous students, greatly advanced our knowledge of the Attic demes. A partial treatment of the subject largely confined to matters of topography is C. W. J. Eliot's *Coastal Demes of Attika: A Study of the Policy of Kleisthenes* (Toronto 1962). John S. Traill's *The Political Organization of Attica: A Study of the Demes, Trittyes, and Phylai and Their Representation in the Athenian Council* (Princeton 1975) incorporates much valuable work on the topography of the demes; his more recent *Demos and Trittys: Epigraphical and Topographical Studies in the Organization of Attica* (Toronto 1986) carries the concerns of the earlier study still further. The demes received their first modern comprehensive examination in David Whitehead's detailed and exhaustively documented *The Demes of Attica 508/7-ca. 250 B.C.: A Political and Social Study* (Princeton 1986). To Whitehead we are indebted for a thorough study of what in the present work is called the "deme association." While the trittyes remain for want of evidence an enigma, the possibility of an important statewide military role was explored by P. Siewert in *Die Trittyen und die Heeresreform des Kleisthenes* (Munich 1982). The ten phylai, demonstrably the dominant units in the administration of statewide business, were also well developed as associations, although, surprisingly, the relevant inscriptions and other evidence have remained unexamined. Chapters 5 and 6 of the present work are devoted to remedying this deficiency.

Among cultic associations, the *genos* long suffered under the misunderstanding that it was the relic of an inherited "kinship" group that, paralleling the Roman *gens*, played a decisive role in early Greek politics. The misunderstanding remained alive in Paul MacKendrick's *The Athenian Aristocracy 399 to 31 B.C.* (Cambridge, Mass. 1969), the preface of which alluded to "interesting analogies in Scots clans and Iroquois Indian tribes" (p. vii). But the traditional view was exploded by F. Bourriot's 1400+ page Lille dissertation *Recherches sur la nature du génos: étude d'histoire sociale Athénienne. Périodes archaïque et classique*, 2 vols. (Lille 1976), which left as genuine Athenian associations the "sacerdotal families" discussed in chapter 8. By contrast, the phratry was early on put on a sound footing by Margherita Guarducci, *l'Istituzione della Fratria nella Grecia Antica e nelle Colonie Greche d'Italia* (Rome 1937). For Athens, the principal epigraphic text has recently been reedited and interpreted by Charles W. Hedrick, Jr., *The Decrees of the Demotionidai* (Atlanta 1990), and the entire body of evidence has been acutely handled by S. D. Lambert, *The Phratries of Attica* (Ann Arbor 1993). The record of the *orgeones* was masterfully studied by W. S. Ferguson, "The Attic Orgeones," *Harvard*

Theological Review 37 (1944) 61–140; and "Orgeonika," in *Commemorative Studies in Honor of Theodore Leslie Shear, Hesperia* Supplement 8 (Princeton 1949), pp. 130–163.

The *hetairiai* are the subject of G. M. Calhoun's study *Athenian Clubs in Politics and Litigation* (Austin, Texas 1913). A more recent treatment is that of F. Sartori, *Le eterie nella vita politica ateniese del Vi e V secolo a.C.* (Rome 1957). John P. Lynch's *Aristotle's School: A Study of a Greek Educational Institution* (Berkeley 1972) clarifies the associational nature of the philosophers' arrangements at the Lyceum and elsewhere. In the military sphere, although the inscriptions recording the acts of groups of soldiers encamped throughout Attica have never received separate treatment, the organizations of "young men" of the Hellenistic and Roman periods were examined by Clarence A. Forbes, *Neoi: A Contribution to the Study of Greek Associations* (Middletown 1933).

From this brief survey it is clear that, since the appearance of the synoptic German studies at the turn of the century, research has been conducted on a piecemeal basis, each such investigation being devoted to a particular segment or association. Admittedly, compartmentalization or, to look at the phenomenon from a different angle, division of labor of this kind is both necessary and desirable. But there may also be unwelcome consequences, and in the present case two such consequences are painfully evident: (1) that, because deme, phratry, "club," and so on have been investigated largely in isolation from each other and from other such organizations, the possibility that all might usefully and meaningfully be subsumed under an umbrella concept of "association" has gone unexplored; and (2) that, as a consequence of this failing, it has of course not been possible to investigate how such "associations" in the aggregate might have been related, in structure and purpose, to the democratic government (although, to be sure, there has been no dearth of attention as to how the deme or phratry or philosophical school, in its individuality, interacted with the central authority).

It is time, I think, to challenge both these unspoken yet formidable barriers impeding further progress in our efforts to understand the public life of classical Athens. Accordingly, in chapter 1 we shall commence our study by attempting to formulate a definition of "association," based on ancient Athenian sources, adequate to allow us to think and argue meaningfully about phylai, regional associations of demes, cultic organizations, and the others as superficially differing instances of a single societal entity. From this basis, it will then be possible to address the second of my two concerns, by, in the succeeding chapters, individually investigating each association's distinctive "response" to the realities of the Athenian democracy. These discussions, taken together, will realize the goal of a synoptic study of the relations between Athens's democratic government and the instutionalized associations, public and private, of all of greater Attica.

As it happens, I have been preceded in the larger aspect of this enterprise by Robin Osborne in his 1985 book *Demos: The Discovery of Classical Attika*. Osborne set out to show "how the polis as a whole worked" (1985b, p. xii). But the selection of evidence, though ranging widely over the demographic, economic, and political spectrum, does not, except for the deme association, explore the roles possibly played by various types of association in that "whole." Nonetheless, the fact is that these institutions represent, as I hope to show, a vital component of the complex society which Osborne's study has done so much to illuminate. At the end, when I have established just what it is that the ancient evidence tells us about our associations, I hope that the reader will agree that my study has shed new light on the problem of "how the polis as a whole worked."

ONE

"Associations," Solon's Law, and the Democracy

The Definition of "Association"

The Nature of the Problem

The title of this work identifies as its subject the associations of classical Athens. It is of course incumbent upon us, as a preliminary to our investigation, to define the meaning of the term "association." As it turns out, this is not as easy a task as it might at first seem. For one thing, any naive philological approach involving the isolation of a Greek synonym for the English "association" must be ruled out as a possibility. To be sure, several Greek terms are used on occasion with something like this meaning. Some, such as *koinonia*, *homilia*, and *synousia*, often possess an active, strongly verbal connotation of being together, social intercourse, or interpersonal dealings, but carry no necessary implication of the existence of an organization possessing a structure or unified purpose. If "association" in this latter sense is what we are searching for, the field is quickly reduced to two candidates, namely, *koinonia* (again) and its more concrete cognate *koinon*. Both are sometimes used to denote well-defined and more or less enduring groups.[1] The former, as we shall soon see, is the term employed by Aristotle in the only substantial generalizing statement about associations that has come down to us from classical Greek antiquity; the latter is occasionally found in documents relating to what are, by any other

---

1. For discussion of both terms, see Poland 1909, pp. 163–167; Kornemann 1924, coll. 914–941; and Endenburg 1937, passim.

reasonable criteria, indubitable examples of associations. However, at the same time, as the perusal of the appropriate dictionary articles will show, both terms possess other senses as well, reflecting the ambiguities of the basic concept "common." What this means, again, is that we are not at liberty to design our investigation on the basis of a traditional word-study of the Greek terms for "association," *koinonia* and *koinon*, collecting and examining all phenomena designated by these terms and neglecting or discarding the rest.

For the most part, and certainly in the case of classical Athens, the groupings in which we are interested and which intuitively satisfy any definition of an association are designated not as *koina* (or *koinoniai*), but by a generic class term (e.g., the personal plurals *phyletai*, *phrateres*, *thiasotai* or, far less commonly, the collective substantives *phyle*, *phratria*, or *thiasos*) or sometimes by a masculine plural specifically denoting the individual members of the organization (e.g., the deme associations Eleusinioi, Rhamnousioi, or Thorikioi). At a more fundamental level, these facts open up the possibility that a universalizing notion of "association" encompassing all its particular manifestations may not even have existed, at least not in the minds of the active participants of the Athenian associations responsible for the texts and records that have come down to us. People may well not have sensed an essential similarity shared by demes, phratries, "clubs," cult societies, and philosophical schools. Such in any case seems to have been true, as we shall soon see, early on, in the time of Solon, to whom is attributed the only known comprehensive law concerning the associations of the city of Athens.

Alternative kinds of definitions are of course possible. An at first attractive candidate is the functional definition. In my *Public Organization in Ancient Greece* (1987), where, as here, no comprehensive terminology corresponding to the subject matter of the study was at hand, I defined the "public organization" as "that apparatus of units, whether of territory or population, through which the state conducted its business."[2] But this approach will plainly not work in the present case. The purpose of the earlier study was to examine the structure, composition, roles, and history of organizations possessing a known, and *given*, function (namely, participation in public business). In the present study, the determination of function, whether acknowledged or merely latent, is, by contrast, not a given but, rather, the primary goal of the investigation. For this reason, no assumptions about the presence or identity of any function of our classical Athenian associations (whatever they turn out to be) can be built into the definition of the subject matter to be studied.

Another approach, not uncommon in works of this kind, might be termed stipulative. The investigator imposes upon the subject a definition of external origin— perhaps one based on a priori assumptions, perhaps one derived from the experience of another society or societies—not necessarily without awareness of the differences between the "model" and the problematic "unknown" requiring explanation but in the hope that the definition so stipulated will prove to possess heuristic or explanatory power. Take, for example, the definition with which Tod opens his article on Greek clubs in the second edition of the *Oxford Classical Dictionary*: "The clubs here discussed may be defined as voluntary associations of persons more or less

2. Jones 1987, p. 1.

permanently organized for the pursuit of a common end, and so distinguishable both from the State and its component elements on the one hand, and on the other from temporary unions for transitory purposes."[3] From a modern European or American perspective, such a formulation might be thought to make very good sense. But cursory examination of the record will reveal its extreme arbitrariness with respect to ancient Greek, and specifically Athenian, practice. As will soon become apparent, no substantive grounds exist for so distinguishing "voluntary associations" from the other sorts of groups and unions alluded to in Tod's statement and then according to them alone the status of "club." So much will become clear as we progress. At all events, a definition of this kind would be necessary only in the absence of an equally satisfactory formulation derived from, or based on, ancient Greek sources themselves. As it happens, such a formulation is forthcoming, from two sources in fact, the first of which is Aristotle's speculative writings on social and political theory.

Aristotle on Koinoniai and a New Definition

Aristotle, as we saw in the Introduction, conceptualizes the *polis* as a kind of *koinonia* and further asserts that all other *koinoniai* are "of the *polis*." The task at hand is to attempt to elicit from Aristotle's notion of *koinonia* a serviceable definition of "association," which may then be applied to the limitation of the subject with respect to historical classical Athens.

Aristotle addresses the "association" of the *polis* more particularly in book 3 of the *Politics* where he declares that the state is "the *koinonia* in the good life of households (*oikiai*) and lineages (*genê*) for the sake of a full and independent life" (3.5.13: 1280b); and, shortly thereafter, that it is "the *koinonia* of lineages (*genê*) and villages (*komai*) in a full and independent life" (3.5.14: 1281a). Since elsewhere the village (*komê*) is identified as a *koinonia* of several households (*oikiai*) (1.1.8: 1252b), it is clear that the two formulations are fundamentally identical in content. Far less clear, however, is the status (for Aristotle) of the two terms "lineage" and "village," especially the former;[4] and, however the two terms are to be defined, it is puzzling that both are absent from the seemingly more inclusive statement about the *koinoniai* of the *polis* shortly to be discussed. Fortunately, neither problem need retard our progress since two attractive interpretations of Aristotle's meaning are at hand. One, which might be labeled genetic or evolutionary, is that the writer may be giving a concise account of the development of the *polis* out of prehistoric communities. Such a conception is reflected in Aristotle's statement elsewhere in the *Politics* that the *komê*, the partnership of several households, is "a colony of an *oikia*" (1.1.7: 1252b). So, his meaning in book 3 may be that the *polis* arose out of entities of these kinds, respectively social and territorial, without necessarily implying anything regarding the structure of the contemporary city-state. Two, and speculatively with a look ahead to one of the primary concerns of this book, Aristotle may be broadly differentiating, without any specific "associations" in mind, between the

---

3. *OCD²*, p. 254. The third edition (*OCD³*, p. 351) reproduces the earlier definition word for word except for the substitution of "ephemeral" for "transitory."

4. See, on the senses, associational and otherwise, of the term *genos*, "*Genê*," in chapter 8.

personal and spatial segmentation of the *polis*, represented respectively by the "lineage" and the "village." It will become obvious from the records of classical Athens that neither type of segmentation could in isolation from the other provide a sufficient account, evolutionary or static, of the segmentation of the state.[5] Either way, it is no longer incumbent upon us, on Aristotle's evidence, to find a place for the *genos, oikia,* or *komê* in an Aristotelian (or other) account of the associations of classical Athens.

No such difficulties, fortunately, beset Aristotle's explicit accounts of the *koinoniai* of the *polis* in other contexts. At *Eudemian Ethics* 7.9.3 (1241b), it is stated that "the other types of *koinoniai* [that is, other than soul and body, craftsman and tool, master and slave, etc.] are a part of the *koinoniai* of the *polis*, such as (those of) *phrateres* or *orgeones* or business partnerships."[6] But most detailed and informative of all is the oft-cited passage from book 8 of the *Nichomachean Ethics* (8.9.4-6: 1160a):

> (4) But all *koinoniai* resemble parts, as it were, of the *koinonia* of the *polis*. For people travel for some advantage and to secure some of the necessities of life. And the *koinonia* of the *polis*, too, it seems, was originally formed and continues to endure for the sake of advantage. For it is at this that lawmakers take their aim; and they say that justice consists in what is advantageous to the community. (5) Now, the other *koinoniai* aim at some particular advantage: for example, sailors at what is advantageous on a voyage for income from goods or some such thing; fellow soldiers for what is advantageous in warfare, whether money or victory or the seizure of a city; and likewise *phyletai* and *demotai*. [And some *koinoniai* seem to come into existence for the sake of pleasure—*koinoniai* of *thiasotai* and *eranistai*. For these (are organized) for the sake of sacrifice and social intercourse, respectively.] And all these *koinoniai* seem to be subordinate to the *koinonia* of the *polis*. (For the *koinonia* of the *polis* aims, not at the immediate advantage) but (at the advantage) for the whole of life * * (people) holding sacrifices and gatherings centering on them, bestowing honors on the gods and providing for themselves leisure activities (combined) with pleasure. . . . (6) So all the *koinoniai* seem to be parts of the (*koinonia*) of the *polis*. And the friendships of such kind will correspond to *koinoniai* of such kind.[7]

5. See, for example, chapter 2, where my case is made for two different definitions of the Athenian deme, one personal (the constitutional), the other territorial (defined by precise boundaries).

6. Αἱ δ' ἄλλαι κοινωνίαι εἰσὶν μόριον τῶν τῆς πόλεως κοινωνιῶν, οἷον ἡ τῶν φρατέρων ἢ τῶν ὀργέων (ὀργεώνων Dietsche) ἢ αἱ χρηματιστικαὶ [ἔτι πολιτεῖαι].

7. Aristotle, *Nichomachean Ethics*, 8.9.4–6 (1160a): (4) αἱ δὲ κοινωνίαι πᾶσαι μορίοις ἐοίκασι τῆς πολιτικῆς· συμπορεύονται γὰρ ἐπί τινι συμφέροντι, καὶ ποριζόμενοί τι τῶν εἰς τὸν βίον· καὶ ἡ πολιτικὴ δὲ κοινωνία τοῦ συμφέροντος χάριν δοκεῖ καὶ ἐξ ἀρχῆς συνελθεῖν καὶ διαμένειν· τούτου γὰρ καὶ οἱ νομοθέται στοχάζονται, καὶ δίκαιόν φασιν εἶναι τὸ κοινῇ συμφέρον. (5) αἱ μὲν οὖν ἄλλαι κοινωνίαι κατὰ μέρη τοῦ συμφέροντος ἐφίενται, οἷον πλωτῆρες μὲν τοῦ κατὰ τὸν πλοῦν πρὸς ἐργασίαν χρημάτων ἤ τι τοιοῦτον, συστρατιῶται δὲ τοῦ κατὰ τὸν πόλεμον, εἴτε χρημάτων εἴτε νίκης ἢ πόλεως ὀρεγόμενοι, ὁμοίως δὲ καὶ φυλέται καὶ δημόται. [ἔνιαι δὲ τῶν κοινωνιῶν δι' ἡδονὴν δοκοῦσι γίνεσθαι, θιασωτῶν καὶ ἐρανιστῶν· αὗται γὰρ θυσίας ἕνεκα καὶ συνουσίας.] πᾶσαι δ' αὗται ὑπὸ τὴν πολιτικὴν ἐφίεται, ἀλλ' εἰς ἅπαντα τὸν βίον * * θυσίας τε ποιοῦντες καὶ περὶ ταύτας συνόδους, τιμὰς ‹τε› ἀπονέμοντες τοῖς θεοῖς, καὶ αὐτοῖς ἀναπαύσεις πορίζοντες μεθ' ἡδονῆς. . . . (6) πᾶσαι δὴ φαίνονται γίνεσθαι αἱ κοινωνίαι μόρια τῆς πολιτικῆς εἶναι· ἀκολουθήσουσι δὲ αἱ τοιαῦται φιλίαι ταῖς τοιαύταις

The basic assumptions regarding Aristotle's conception of the internal segmentation of the city-state noted in the Introduction are here explicitly applied to the subject of our study. The *polis* is itself a *koinonia*, and so are its component parts, the various *koinoniai* corresponding in several cases to the historical organizations of classical Athens. And what are the characteristics of the Aristotelian *koinonia* that emerge from the particular illustrations adduced? Note, first of all, the fundamental ambiguity of the senses of the term *koinonia* evidenced by those examples: it vacillates, in conformity with the general Greek usage already noted, between the active, verbal process of mutual dealing (as exemplified by business people, travelers, sailors, and soldiers temporarily cooperating in pursuit of their advantage) and, in the organizational sense, the well-defined and enduring structures characteristic of the *phyletai* and *demotai*. All *koinoniai*, furthermore, as explicitly indicated in the majority of instances, possess a purpose, a purpose expressly identified as appropriate to the shared goals of the members constituting each organization. From this observation follows the vital point not at all self-evidently true in the cases of the statewide administrative segments, the phyle and deme, that Aristotle is viewing all these partnerships in their internally focused, associational dimension. When he mentions *phyletai*, in other words, he does not have in mind merely the administrative unit that fielded a battalion or served as a board of *prytaneis* in the Council of Five Hundred. Rather, his subject is an association with a shrine of its eponym on the Akropolis and which met on occasion to perform sacrifices for the exclusive benefit of its membership.

The absence in these two sources, and particularly from the lengthy stretch of text from the *Nichomachean Ethics*, of certain types of groups is striking. No mention is made of any *koinonia* founded on intimate ties of blood relation, marriage, or affection. To put the matter in terms of the sociologist Tönnies' classic formulation,[8] much of the Gemeinschaft end of the associational spectrum is missing; instead, most of what Aristotle gives us is organizations of the Gesellschaft variety. This cannot be accidental, above all since Aristotle, as illustrated by the two passages from book 3 of the *Politics* at the head of this discussion, does acknowledge the household (*oikia*) and lineage (*genos*) as constituent members—perhaps, as I suggested, in some historical or else vague, generalizing sense—of the *koinonia* of the city. Plainly, it is with deliberate intent that Aristotle does not place the household or lineage on the same footing with the *koinoniai* assembled in the *Eudemian* and *Nichomachean Ethics*, although his reasons for doing so remain obscure. Perhaps he sensed, even if did not explicitly formulate, a distinction corresponding to Tönnies' Wesenwille ("natural will," Gemeinschaft) and Kürwille ("rational will," Gesellschaft), and so distinguished various associations on the basis of a fundamental difference in internal motivation.

κοινωνίαις. The text reproduced here is that of the *OCT* of I. Bywater (1894). The square brackets in section 5 signify, according to the apparatus criticus, that these words, in the editor's judgment, should perhaps be transposed to the lacuna marked by the asterisks a few lines below. But the content of the bracketed words does not itself seem to be under suspicion.

8. Tönnies 1988, with Charles P. Loomis, "Notes on Tönnies' Fundamental Concepts," pp. 261–270.

Even with this limitation of the subject, however, striking variations in mode—orientation, membership status, duration of existence, and purpose—are nonetheless noticeable among the numerous examples of *koinoniai* pressed into service to illustrate the analysis. An association may be public in orientation (like the phyle or deme) or private (such as the *thiasotai* and *eranoi*). Members may join voluntarily (as with *thiasotai* or *eranistai*) or nonvoluntarily (as with the phyle and deme).[9] An association may endure only for the duration of a trip (travelers), voyage (sailors), or campaign (soldiers) or may, as in the case of the segments of the state, be temporally coterminous with the birth, duration, and extinction of the state itself. *Koinoniai* are alternately expressive (as when *thiasotai* and *eranistai* are formed for sacrifices or social intercourse) or instrumental (when sailors and others cooperate in pursuit of some external end).

These last few examples show the extraordinary variety of aspect expressly attached to, or implicit in, the examples of *koinoniai* adduced by Aristotle. For the most part my characterizations are fully justified by the evidence provided by Aristotle himself. In other cases, as with the phyle and deme, the characterization expressed here depends upon common information no less accessible to Aristotle than to ourselves (with the benefit of our copious dossiers of documentary and textual evidence). The point is that this framework of concepts, although such terms as "expressive" and "instrumental" are of modern coinage (at least with the respect to the present subject matter), is in fact Aristotle's to the extent that his selection of particular *koinoniai* exemplifies each of those concepts (and corresponding terminology). On this basis, accordingly, I propose that the analysis depart, not from a list of positively identified "associations" (already found to be, on terminological grounds at least, an impossibility) but rather from, and on the basis of, a series of scales reflecting these characteristics of the groups implicit in Aristotle's roster of *koinoniai*. But before we proceed further, each of the scales requires additional specification and illustration.

Public versus Private. My previous work, as already noted, identified the units of the public organization according to function, that is, in accordance with a record of the performance of public business (or absence of same). What this definition (and my use of that definition) did not do is to generalize and reify the public function so as to result in the labeling of some units (including associations) as exclusively "public" and others as exclusively "private." To take two simple illustrations, the phyle, a segment of the city-state to which one-tenth of most governmental business was apportioned under the democracy and therefore a preponderantly "public" entity, was nonetheless capable of functioning like a private association. Thus a decree of a phyle from the early third century records the group's decision to assume care of the *epikleros* daughter of one of its members, presumably upon his death.[10] Conversely, the phratry, essentially a cultic social organization with no substantial governmental functions, nonetheless served in a public capacity through its crucial gate-

9. Vinogradoff is in error when he asserts (1922, p. 119) that Aristotle is here thinking primarily of "voluntary associations."

10. *IG* II² 1165 (ca. 300–250), lines 30–38. The phyle is Erechtheis. For additional discussion, see "The Solidarity of the Phyle as Association," in chapter 5.

keeper role in the admission of young Athenians to citizenship and, probably as an outgrowth of this role, as one of the units (along with the phyle and deme) into which new citizens were enrolled according to the so-called enrollment clauses in decrees of naturalization.[11] So the phyle, though preponderantly public, and the phratry, though preponderantly private, both partook of elements of the opposing orientation. These examples suggest that we should think of "public" and "private" not as mutually exclusive "either/or" alternatives but rather as opposing extremes on a continuum possessing infinite intermediate gradations.[12]

Voluntary versus Nonvoluntary. This brace of terms will be used in a somewhat different sense from that encountered in the study of nonclassical societies, to the extent that a continuum rather than strictly dichotomous, mutually exclusive categories seems again to be the required model. Take, to illustrate the point, first, the phyle, trittys, and deme complex. Membership was nonvoluntary, given the assumption that all legitimate sons of citizens themselves normally succeeded in becoming citizens in combination with the fact that the young citizen-to-be was required, as a preliminary to enrollment in the citizen body, to be accepted by his father's deme and only by that deme. If you entered the citizen body, in other words, you perforce joined a deme, and only one deme (of 139 or 140) was open to you—your father's. Membership in a particular deme determined, furthermore, membership in a particular trittys and phyle. At the opposite extreme, no one was compelled to join a *thiasos*, *eranos*, or philosophical school as a precondition of citizenship or of any other necessity of public (or even private) life, and there is no reason to believe that, if a person wished to enter an association of this type, that one and only one (say, one's father's) was open to him for admission. But other groups, such as the cultic societies called *orgeones*, occupied middle ground, voluntary in that no one was legally or for all practical purposes required to join (though social pressure may have been considerable), nonvoluntary in that the factor of descent sometimes seems to have limited the field to a single organization.

Temporary versus Permanent. Aristotle writes of associations of travelers, sailors, and soldiers dedicated to the pursuit of immediate goals and presumably, once the temporary partnership had expired, allowed to lapse. His point is splendidly illustrated by the decrees of encampments of ephebic recruits or soldiers in garrisons situated in several of the Attic demes, the decrees (and their specific language) revealing a genuine degree of association. But once the encampment of soldiers was disbanded, that association of necessity ceased to exist.[13] Contrariwise, the segments of the Athenian state came into existence with the creation of the democracy

11. See "The Public Role of the Phratries," in chapter 7.

12. This brief formulation may be evaluated against the wider background of "public and private" interests discussed by Humphreys (1977/78, pp. 97–104). Particularly germane here is her instancing the "subordinate segments of Athenian society, demes and phratries," which, though they had borrowed "all the forms of public procedure in the assembly," remained often "under the sway of private resources and private interests" (p. 98). Given this situation, it would obviously be pointless to continue to categorize some such segments as "public" and others as "private."

13. For my discussions, see "The Rise of the Territorial Deme" and "The Decline of the Constitutional Deme," in chapter 4.

and in some cases are still functioning as bona fide associations in the second century B.C., despite the fact that the central government had long before suffered loss of its autonomy and of many of its democratic functions. For all intents and purposes, the associations of the phylai and demes (the trittyes seem to have become extinct at an early date) were permanent, outliving any cohort of members or any immediate and transitory purposes. Between these extremes, cultic groups, philosophical schools, and social organizations (including the aristocratic *hetairiai*) come and go in our record of documents, probably in many cases in response to the waxing or waning fortunes of the Athenian economy, political developments, and cultural trends.

Expressive versus Instrumental. It is on this distinction, when applied to the associations of classical Athens, that the argument of the present work turns. Expressive orientation is illustrated not only by Aristotle's *thiasotai* and *eranistai*, respectively dedicated to "sacrifice and social intercourse," but as well by the diverse activities of Athenian cultic associations, descent groups, elite societies, and (to no less a degree) the internally organized segments of the citizen body, above all the demes. So much is, I trust, agreed by all. But the thesis of this book centers on the question of the extent to which, and in what particular ways, the classical Athenian associations, individually or collectively, served an *instrumental* purpose. Individually, I shall argue throughout, particular associations underwent various adaptations and functioned in response to specific features, to be characterized from the associations' perspective as failings, of the democratic central government. To take the phyle as an especially clear example, it will be argued that, in response to the prevailing absence of representative mechanisms in the organs of the Athenian democratic government, the phyle association evolved into an instrument of representation whereby the desires of the membership could be relayed to the arena of the central government. Comparable compensating functions will be detected in the records of other associations. Collectively, the body of classical Athenian associations as a whole will have served, I shall conclude, to counterbalance the generally severely restrictive, and therefore destabilizing, tendencies generated by this and several other features of that government. It is in the instrumental aspect, I think, that readers will correctly situate the problematic element of the burden of the present study.

These four defining scales open the door to a new, and potentially far more enlightening, way of studying our subject. That subject, again, is Aristotle's *koinoniai* —a term, as illustrated by his multifarious farrago of examples, so loose and imprecise as to permit a rendering no more exact than "communities" (a vague word significantly echoing the Greek term's derivation from *koinos*, "common"). By defining our associations (or "communities") in terms of the four scales, we shall reap considerable benefits. We will be freed of the unwelcome (and unachievable) task of defining the term "association" and then having to decide which groups did or did not satisfy that definition. Nor need we any longer fear we are committing a "category error" when we conjoin under a single plan of analysis the "public" phyle and the "private" phratry, or an ephemeral coalition of traders and a centuries-old village association, or an ideologically driven political action group and a philosophical school, and so on. Indeed, Aristotle's own juxtaposition of such pairs or trios of "apples and oranges"[14] should already have made clear that these categories of modern invention—"public" and "private," "voluntary" and "nonvoluntary"—though absolutely necessary analytical tools, do not stand in one-to-one relationship with the societal realities of ancient Greece. Rather, any more or less organized "community" (again, as prompted by Aristotle's presentation) is fair game (although, in line with the announced thesis of this book, not all will receive equally intense attention). And each such group, rather than being given some arbitrary label or consigned to some inflexible category, may be defined or characterized by measuring it along the scale indicated by each of our four sets of criteria. Thus, to take a familiar example, the orientation of a phratry falls toward the private end of the public versus private scale; the status of its members is closer to the nonvoluntary end of the voluntary versus nonvoluntary scale; its duration approaches permanence on the temporary versus permanent scale; and its functions, though largely expressive, did contain important instrumental elements. Nor should even this multifaceted characterization be allowed to harden into a fixed description or definition. One phratry may, for all we know, differ from another; and any or all phratries may undergo substantial transformation over time.

With these preliminaries in mind, we turn back to our thesis and to the instrumental functions, both immediate and larger-scale, of classical Athenian associations. Perhaps the reader suspects, despite the disclaimer in the Introduction, that this preoccupation with instrumentality was prompted by Aristotle's characteristically teleological representation of his *koinoniai*. After all, no fewer than a half dozen times in the passage from the *Ethics* at the head of the present discussion he identifies some expressed or implicit external "advantage" to the securing of which the *koinonia* in question is dedicated. But this is not true; the thesis under review is not dependent upon, nor was it even prompted by, Aristotle's discussion. Rather its basis will be seen to emerge from the nonspeculative evidentiary record. That said, let us now begin the investigation of that record by turning to the single most important piece of testimony we possess regarding the legal position of our "associations" in the classical Athenian state, the so-called law on associations ascribed to Solon.

Solon's Law on Associations

The Text and Its Meaning

The *Digest* at 47.22.4 preserves a passage from Gaius's commentary on the Twelve Tables, the archaic Roman legal code. Gaius adduces *ex lege Solonis* a statute that, on the face of it, might aptly be characterized as a "law on associations." Difficulties arising from the transmitted text are dealt with in detail in appendix 2. My final version of the law reads as follows:

---

14. For example, from the *Politics: phrator* or *phyletes* (2.1.12: 1262a); messes, phratries, and phylai (2.2.11: 1264a); phratries, *thysiai*, and *diagogai* (3.5.14: 1280b); *genê* and *komai* (3.5.14: 1281a); phylai, demes, and phratries (4.12.11: 1300a); phratries, *lochoi*, and phylai (5.7.11: 1309a); and phylai and phratries (6.2.11: 1319b).

Ἐὰν δὲ δῆμος ἢ φράτορες ἢ ‹ὀργεῶνες› ἢ ‹ναυκραρία› ἢ σύσσιτοι ἢ ὁμόταφοι ἢ θιασῶται ἢ ἐπὶ λείαν οἰχόμενοι ἢ εἰς ἐμπορίαν ὅ τι ἂν τούτων διαθῶνται πρὸς ἀλλήλους κύριον εἶναι, ἐὰν μὴ ἀπαγορεύσῃ δημόσια γράμματα.

If a deme or members of a phratry or of a ritual society or of a ship-command or messmates or members of a burial society or revelers or people going abroad for plunder or for commerce make an arrangement concerning these matters (i.e., matters appropriate to their organization) among themselves, it is to be valid unless the written statutes of the People forbid.

This is the text of the law on associations purporting to be the work of the Athenian arbitrator Solon, whose archonship and therefore presumably some or all of whose legislative activity is traditionally assigned to the year 594. The fact that the *Digest* was not compiled until the early sixth century A.D., over a thousand years later, permits a healthy skepticism regarding not only the specific wording but even the general import of the text that has come down to us. Nonetheless, three general observations, to open our discussion, would seem to be in order. First, as argued in appendix 2, it is likely that, given a date of composition in the early sixth century B.C., the received text represents an attempt to assemble a more or less complete catalog of associations in existence at that time. Secondly, and reflecting the first point, it is patent that, if a single word or phrase meaning anything like "association" was in use in Solon's time, it was not used. This suggests, importantly for our thesis, that the general notion had not yet been abstracted from the particular instances of such groups and that, on this basis, the lawgiver was very likely breaking new ground, legally and constitutionally speaking, when he formulated this statute. It is to the question of the original, and especially the later developing, purpose of this innovating intervention in the functioning of the Athenian associations that the central thesis of this book will provide an answer.

But before passing to the adumbration of that thesis, a third point, regarding the content of the notion of "association" as evidenced in our text, must be made. At the level of specific detail, it is striking that the specific groups named in the law to a marked degree conform, in name and type, to those mentioned by Aristotle. More fundamentally, it is no less striking that Solon's specific assortment of groups illustrates a similar extreme variation along the four scales just named and briefly described: public versus private, voluntary versus nonvoluntary, temporary versus permanent, and expressive versus instrumental.[15] Though Solon lacks a single, universalizing notion corresponding to Aristotle's *koinonia*, it is clear that the "associations," both individually and in the aggregate, found by the lawgiver and by the Peripatetic were essentially similar. It is this fundamental agreement between Solon's law, composed nearly a century before the birth of the democracy under Kleisthenes, and Aristotle's formulation, written not many years before that same government's suppression by the Macedonians, that prompts an inference of great value for our study: that in the interim of some two and three-quarters centuries the

---

15. Similarly, Vinogradoff comments upon the "varieties of social combination" evidenced by the groups mentioned in the law (1922, pp. 120–121).

phenomenon of the association and its place in Athenian society had undergone, except for the innovations introduced by the democracy, little significant development or other change. It would be reasonable, therefore, to explore the possibility that, in the absence of contrary indications, Solon's law remained in force throughout the entire lifetime of the free government and that, despite the likelihood that it was put to uses not intended or even conceived of by the legislator, it provided the legal instrument for the management—and profitable exploitation—of the association within the larger framework of the Athenian state.

To proceed along this line of investigation, it is necessary as a preliminary to all further speculation to try to determine just what was the more immediate purpose of the law, at least at the time of its initial formulation. Writing in 1910, Max Radin, in his Columbia University dissertation entitled *The Legislation of the Greeks and Romans on Corporations*, undertook this very task.[16] Turning, at the close of his analysis of Solon's law, to its "effect and meaning," he began by dismissing the (even at that time) old view that the law was a " 'general corporation statute,' under and by virtue of which artificial persons are created."[17] Subsequent research has confirmed his judgment on this head. Indeed, one can go much further, for there is general agreement that at no time, certainly at no time prior to the end of the classical period, did Athens witness the emergence of the notion of an association as a "legal person."[18] Radin's own efforts were directed at the received text of the law with a view to determining which of its elements (following the enumeration of particular "associations") marked the *innovating* content of the statute. The choices, as he saw it (basically correctly, I believe) were two: either (1) the words "If . . . (they) make an agreement among themselves . . . it is to be valid" (ὅ τι ἂν τούτων διαθῶνται πρὸς ἀλλήλους κύριον εἶναι) or (2), the final clause, "unless the written statutes of the People forbid" (ἐὰν μὴ ἀπαγορεύσῃ δημόσια γράμματα). Abstractly put, the choice came down, for Radin, to whether one sees the law (to introduce my own terms) as essentially *validating* or *regulatory*, respectively. Viewed as validating in intent, the law would have both formally recognized and empowered associations by guaranteeing the validity of their agreements within the scope of their proper activity (the final point being signaled by the word τούτων).[19] Viewed as regulatory in intent, the law assumes the validity of the agreements *but only so far* as those agreements are not in conflict with the higher law of the Athenian state. For Radin, it was a question of which of these two alternatives was to be preferred.

It was self-evident, thought Radin, that the law was not validating (although he did not actually use this term to characterize the interpretation). "For as to the [phrase]

16. Still earlier discussions include that of Foucart 1873, pp. 47–50. Except for a note in Ferguson's study of the *orgeones* (1944, p. 64, note 5 [pp. 64–65]), surprisingly little attention has been given to this text: no discussion is to be found, for instance, in either of the standard recent treatments in English of Greek law, Harrison (1968 and 1971) and MacDowell (1978). Brief comment may, however, be found in Vinogradoff's *Outlines of Historical Jurisprudence* (1922, pp. 120–121) and Jones's *The Law and Legal Theory of the Greeks* (1956, pp. 160–161). With Vinogradoff, in particular, I find myself in agreement on more than one point.

17. Radin 1910, pp. 50–51.

18. See the Introduction, with note 43.

19. For my argument supporting this interpretation, see appendix 2.

κύριον εἶναι," he wrote, "the law is simply declaratory. Demes and phratries and mystic cults, even people united by voluntary agreements as to common burial, meals or religious ceremonies, had undoubtedly made and enforced rules for their common government before Solon."[20] But this is pure surmise. By no means is it self-evidently true that associations, having "made" rules, could necessarily "enforce" them. A strong hint, from the later period, that they could *not* always do so is the recognition by the later fourth century of suits involving *eranoi* and *koina* reported by the Aristotelian *Constitution of the Athenians*.[21] The purpose of such litigation will presumably have been, at least in part, to enforce the agreements of an association in the face of recalcitrance on the part of its own membership.[22] If such suits were necessary in Aristotle's time, it would be rash to assume that they, or some other form of intervention, were not similarly necessary early in the sixth century.

For Radin, the law was manifestly regulatory. "But in the [words] ἐὰν μὴ ἀπαγορεύσῃ δημ. γρ. we have a new element. Certain statutes or parts of statutes shall be void. Not in every case will the state guarantee the binding obligation of corporate rules. They are enforceable only if, and to the extent that, the state νόμοι do not rescind them, either in advance or retroactively. The corporations are accepted as portions of the state, but the law will not hold its members to their promises or oaths in this connection where the safety of the state is concerned."[23] From this intuitively probable characterization, Radin goes on to search for an occasion for such a provision but does no better than to suggest "[t]he political irregularities, both of the nobility and the groups of men aiming at τυραννίς."[24] This conjecture, though provided with no specific illustration, is certainly not entirely lacking in merit. After all, the regional conflicts leading to the eventual rise and domination of Peisistratos lay only a generation in the future. No one is in a position to say that "associations" of some kind could not have been involved in these disturbances or that the beginnings of such factional conflict could not have been detected or foreseen in the time of Solon. Besides, to appeal again to later conditions in support of our interpretation of the earlier, the law reported by Hyperides prohibiting the formation of an *hetairikon* for the purpose of overthrowing the democracy[25] illustrates the regulation of associations formed for just such a political purpose. (And, incidentally, the fact that Solon's text makes no mention of *hetairiai*, presumably because they did not exist or, if they did, because they were thought to be of negligible importance, may explain, even on the assumption that the Solonian statute had remained, as I believe, in force, why such a law limiting the activities of *hetairika* was

20. Radin 1910, p. 51.

21. *AthPol* 52.2.

22. Rhodes (1981, p. 586), comments negatively (and correctly) on the point about the association as a legal person, but even if an association were not such a person, its several *members* might still, under the terms of Solon's law, appeal to a court for enforcement of its arrangements. As a possible positive example, the association named Eikadeis became involved in litigation according to an inscription of the year 324/3, *IG* II² 1258. Vinogradoff, however, seems to have believed that the court in question was that of the association itself (1922, p. 125).

23. Radin 1910, p. 51.

24. Radin 1910, p. 51.

25. Hyperides 4, *In Defense of Euxenippos* (ca. 330–324), §8.

necessary.) Nonetheless, to register a second objection to Radin's analysis, there is no reason to think that, if the law was regulatory, the suppression of organized seditious political activity *alone* exhausted that regulatory function. According to the thesis argued in this book, the regulation of associations went far beyond so narrow a concern, however real and justified by the evidence that concern might have been.

But before we can explore the wider dimensions of the law's use, we must confront, and then dismiss, a methodological assumption underpinning Radin's analysis: that, of the two possible meanings of the law, validating and regulatory, it could possess *only one* to the exclusion of the other. This assumption is utterly without foundation. No linguistic feature of the text, no known legal principle, no known or suspected fact about the constitutional or political setting of the law can be adduced in support of such an either-or approach. We must leave open the possibility that the law on associations was *both* validating *and* regulatory. By way of corroborating the notion of a dual (yet, as we shall see, nonetheless integrated) function for the law, I shall undertake a brief rehearsal of later Athenian legislation involving or otherwise relating to associations. Radin himself made a beginning in this direction, adducing a total of four texts, three inscriptions and a forensic passage.[26] Improvement over the findings of the 1910 study appears within reach. At the level of documentation, a few more texts can be added to the discussion. More importantly, it is apparent, if only from the arrangement of his discussion, that Radin tacitly sundered these "later" acts of legislation from the Solonian law, both narrowly with regard to the latter's specific content and more generally in respect to what might be tritely termed the "spirit" of that law. It is this tacit feature of the plan, and execution, of Radin's analysis that I also wish particularly to question. For, as the arrangement and brief analysis of the texts below illustrate, they can all be brought under the general headings of "validation" and "regulation"—precisely the two modes at work, as we are seeing, in the text preserved by the *Digest*. While it is impossible to determine whether the Solonian law was still in force, say, two hundred and fifty years afterward during the lifetime of one of our sources, the forensic speaker Aischines, there may nonetheless be value in detecting the continuing operation of that statute's basic principles, even if in the form of more recent legislation or decrees addressed to particular contemporary situations.

Validating Legislation on Associations

It goes without saying that, if the Athenian people (as I believe) hoped to put associations to use in order to achieve certain goals of statewide administration, they could not do so unless these associations were capable of enforcing their wills upon their own memberships. Arguably to such an end, as already mentioned, by the time of the Aristotelian treatise on the constitution, suits involving *eranoi* and *koina* were accommodated by the state's judicial machinery. To these institutional arrangements may be added, with varying degrees of certainty, three documented legislative incidents.

The earliest example is provided by *IG* II² 1177, an acephalous decree of the

---

26. Radin 1910, ch. 5, "Later Athenian Legislation," pp. 52–55.

demesmen of Peiraieus dated epigraphically to the middle of the fourth century. Generally speaking, the decree is concerned with the question of access to, and the use of, the sanctuary called the Thesmophorion, presumably situated within the deme. Following a fragmentary reference to "the priestess" and "the Thesmophorion" (lines 1–2), a purpose clause reads: " . . . in order that no one release people at large or bring together *thiasoi* or set up *hiera* or practice purifications or make approaches to the altars or the *megaron* without the priestess other than when the festival of the Thesmophoria and the Prerosia and the Kalamaia and the Skira [take place] and if on any other day the women come together in accordance with ancestral custom" (lines 2–12). With the declaration of this purpose, the text continues: "decreed by the Peiraieis, if any one acts contrary to these terms in any respect, the demarch, imposing a fine, is to introduce (the matter) to the *dikasterion,* appealing to the laws which are established on these topics" (lines 12–17). At the end is appended a clause concerning a specific item of concern: "And regarding wood-gathering of the *hiera*, if anyone gathers wood, the ancient laws that are established relating to these matters are to be valid" (lines 17–21).

What this decree amounts to is the demesmen's decision to appeal to the state, through the medium of their demarch, in order to enforce their own internal regulations. The *dikasterion* is the court, not of the deme, but of the central government;[27] and the go-between role being played by the demarch comports well with other instances of his function of interfacing between deme association and the statewide authority.[28] The "laws" regarding access to the sanctuary and regarding wood-gathering, except for the fact that the latter are identified as "ancient," are not more precisely defined. Two interpretations are open. Should one set or the other, if the truth were known, prove to be laws of the deme association, the proposed interpretation would fit neatly, since Solon's law on associations ordained that "arrangements made concerning their own proper business" (or the like) be "valid." In the present case, the arrangements in question would be the deme's own laws, and, in accordance with the Solonian statute, the provision for validating those arrangements would consist in granting access to the state's *dikasterion* in order to enforce those laws. If, on the other hand, the laws are state laws, the fit with Solon's text would not be as tight, but even so the state would remain in the position as guarantor of the association's—the deme Peiraieus's—internal arrangements.

This deme's case must not, of course, be regarded as at all typical. The port city was home to a large noncitizen population, including above all a sizable metic component.[29] These non-*demotai* may have exerted considerable pressure upon the services and facilities provided to the association's membership but not, so long as the rule of citizen exclusivity was maintained, open to themselves. It is easy to imagine

27. For a full accounting of the evidence for the presence of deme associations in the statewide courts in Athens, see Whitehead 1986, pp. 128–130. The instances are of sufficient number as to leave no doubt about the nature of the situation in our decree from Pieraieus. For the sole instance of a deme (as it happens, Aixone) providing its own court of law (in this case, its assembly), see Whitehead 1986, pp. 113–114.

28. For this role, see Whitehead 1986, pp. 130–139, "The Demarch as Agent of the State."

29. According to Whitehead's tabulation (1986, pp. 83–84), 69, or almost 19 percent, of the 366 metics whose deme of residence was known to him, were from Peiraieus.

how such a decree concerning access to and use of a deme sanctuary might have been thought necessary. But the central point is that the state is found here ensuring the integrity of the deme association.

A second legislative incident occurs somewhat later, near the turn of the century, placing the state's stance with regard to associations again at issue. In the year 307, the Athenians, acting on a bill proposed by one Sophokles of Sounion, passed a decree whereby it was made illegal for any philosopher to be appointed head of a school without first having been approved by the Council and Assembly. Apparently voluntarily, the philosophers soon thereafter departed from the city. Subsequently, one Philon, a pupil of Aristotle's, indicted Sophokles on the charge of having made an illegal proposal (that is, under the *graphê paranomon*). This counterattack proved successful, for not long afterward the philosophers, including the head of the Peripatos, returned to Athens.[30] The question we have to ask, and to answer, is whether the successful counteraction had anything to do with Solon's, or any other Athenian, law protecting (or "validating") the arrangements made by an association.

Wilamowitz had argued that the philosophical schools were technically and legally *thiasoi*, although, paradoxically, he did not connect this supposed finding with the language of Solon's law in the *Digest*, where, as we saw, the association called *thiasotai* is specifically mentioned. But that makes little difference now that Lynch has demolished Wilamowitz's characterization of the schools as *thiasoi*.[31] Nor does any other explicit link with the law appear tenable in view of the occasional but consistent references to the schools as either *scholai* or *diatribai*— neither a term cited in the text of the *Digest*. Nonetheless, in chapter 8 I shall make a case for regarding the schools as a form of association[32] and so potentially subject to the terms of Solon's law. Philon's successful overturning of the decree moved by Sophokles could then be understood on the assumption that additional terms for associations (such as *scholê* or *diatribê*) had been added to the law or, given an unchanging text, that it had come to be applied in a looser, more inclusive fashion. Either way, the object of the law's application will have been to "validate" the schools qua associations by upholding their proper internal arrangements.

A third instance is provided by an inscription of the middle of the third century recording the result of an arbitration by *dikastai*, *IG* II² 1289. Given the correct restoration of the text, two parties of the *orgeones* of "the goddess" had quarreled about the disposition of the association's properties. The arbitrators decided that the properties belonged to "the goddess" and that no one was to sell or to mortgage them, but that the priest henceforth should use the income therefrom to conduct the sacrifices with the *orgeones* in accordance with ancestral custom (lines 4–8). These rulings of the arbitrators were then reaffirmed by the goddess and by one of the association's officers through a series of clauses forbidding any such sale or mortgage of the goddess' property (lines 9–21).

---

30. The ancient sources are Diogenes Laertius, 5.38; Pollux, *Onomastikon* 9.42 Bekker (pp. 368–369); and Athenaios, 13.610–611. For a modern discussion, see Lynch 1972, pp. 103–104, 117–118.

31. See "Philosophical Schools," in chapter 8.

32. Ibid.

Appeal to private arbitrators was merely the initial stage of the state's legal process but it was part of that process nonetheless.[33] And although the state's judicial machinery is not yet engaged, the guiding principles of the Solonian law are discernible in the background. At issue was the use, appropriate or otherwise, of the association's assets, and the dicasts' ruling has the effect of validating the appropriate internal arrangements made by the members of an association amongst themselves. An association's funds should be used, according to the ruling, only to promote the proper activities of that association and for no other purpose.

Regulatory Legislation on Associations

That Solon's law on associations served to limit the activity of associations is beyond dispute. The final clause, qualifying the validation of an association's arrangements by the proviso "unless the written statutes of the People forbid," expressly subordinates the act of a part of the state to the will of the whole. As it happens, the Solonian law is by no means the only surviving evidence of the imposition of limitations upon associational activity. Above, mention was made of the law preserved in a speech of Hyperides prohibiting the formation of *hetairika* for the purpose of overthrowing the government. Another such specific restriction was believed by Ziebarth to be contained in the decree of the Peiraieis examined above, wherein the purposes of the decree include [ὅπως ἂν μ]/[ηδ]εὶς . . . μηδὲ θιά[σο]/[υς] συνάγει . . . ("that no one . . . bring together *thiasoi* . . .").[34] But Radin was surely correct in objecting that the clause, far from prohibiting the formation of *thiasos* associations, was rather intended to prevent *the convening of a meeting* of an already existing association under the stated circumstances.[35] Nonetheless, four or five relatively bona fide documented instances remain of the state's regulatory intervention.

First, according to Aischines' speech *Against Ktesiphon* (dated to the year 330), Demosthenes had in the year 337 made a motion before the People that on the second and third days of Skirophorion the phylai hold assemblies and that at those assemblies there be chosen from each phyle superintendents for work upon the city walls and treasurers by whom an accounting of the expenses incurred would be rendered (§27). The motion, once approved in the form of a decree, would technically constitute δημόσια γράμματα, thereby bringing the phylai under the regulatory terms of the Solonian law. It is obvious, as will be acknowledged at the conclusion of our discussion, that what initially resembled a passive monitoring by the state of the associations' independent undertakings has by this time evolved into something quite different.

Next, *IG* II[2] 337, dated 333/2, records the decree of the Boule (lines 6–25) and of the Demos (lines 26–45) regarding a request by the People of Kition (lines 9–10, 20–21), later narrowed to the *merchants* of Kition (lines 33–34, 39–40), for

---

33. For the (state's) arbitration by *diaitetai*, see *AthPol* 53.2 with Rhodes's comment (1981, p. 589), citing Harrison 1971, vol. 2, pp. 64–68 and examples of private arbitrations.

34. *IG* II[2] 1177, lines 2–4.

35. Radin 1910, p. 54.

permission to erect a shrine dedicated to Aphrodite on Attic soil. Actually, as the document taken as a whole reveals, the request comprises two elements: the request for *enktesis choriou* (lines 36, 40–41, decree of the Demos), namely, the privilege (otherwise legally not extended to noncitizens) of ownership of land at Athens; and *hidrysis* (lines 10, 21–22, decree of the Boule; cf. lines 37, 41, 44–45, decree of the Demos), the privilege of building on Attic soil (likewise not normally extended to noncitizens). Both the legal capacity to own land and the legal capacity to erect a structure upon that land were needed to establish the shrine. Now, if this is all the decrees are about, where does the state's regulation of associations come in? Two questions are involved.

First, are we dealing with an *association*? The decree of the Boule refers alternatively to "the Kitians" (lines 9–10) and to "the Demos of the Kitians" (lines 20–21). But the following decree of the Demos specifies, again, "the Kitian *emporoi*" (lines 33–34) or "the *emporoi* of the Kitians" (lines 39–40) and, the clinching point, cites the merchants' "decree" (ἔδοξαν, line 34). A body of merchants making a formal decision amongst themselves easily satisfies any Solonian (or Aristotelian) definition of an "association."[36]

The second point, the point about regulation, turns on the question of the referent of a single word that occurs in the decree of the Demos: "... concerning which matters the Kitian merchants resolved lawfully (ἔννομα) to request, asking the Demos for *choriou enktesis* for a piece of land on which they will erect a shrine of Aphrodite, decreed. . . ." (lines 33–38). To what aspect of the request does the word "lawfully" refer? Several replies have been ventured in the literature:

- That the question of legality (taking the text very loosely) somehow concerned a request by the merchants to found, or gain recognition of, a formal association.[37] The easy reply (with Radin) is that no such request is indicated or implied by the preserved text.[38] Another, more fundamental, point is that our sole legal authority on associations, the law of Solon, states or implies nothing regarding the establishment of new (or, for that matter, the recognition of existing) associations. Rather, as we have argued, the burden of that law has to do with the validation and regulation of the acts of associations alone, quite apart from the circumstances of their creation.
- That the legal issue (again, reading the text very loosely) involved the seeking of permission to found a cult of a divinity not officially recognized by the Athenian state.[39] To this suggestion it was rejoined by Radin that there is no evidence that it was ever necessary, at least for foreigners, to obtain permission to establish a "foreign worship" in Athens. Acts of impiety punishable by law rather included the denial (by citizens) of the official gods of the state or else the substitution of *kaina daimonia* in their place.[40] Neither is at issue here.

36. Viz. Solon's ... οἰχόμενοι ἢ εἰς ἐμπορίαν and Aristotle's αἱ χρηματιστικαί (sc. κοινωνίαι) at *Eth. Eud.* 7.9.3 (1241b).
37. Ziebarth 1896, p. 168.
38. Radin 1910, p. 52.
39. Foucart 1873, pp. 83, 127–137, especially 128–131; Ziebarth 1896, p. 168.
40. Radin 1910, pp. 52–53, with approving citation of Wilamowitz at p. 53, note 5.

- That, with Radin, the legal point turns on the grant of *enktesis*. Since, he argues, the merchants had not done anything, namely, benefited the state of Athens, that would have motivated and therefore justified an exception to the normal exclusion of foreigners from the ownership of land ἀρετῆς ἕνεκα, the request could not have been "lawfully" made in the sense that such benefaction to the state (had it occurred) *entitled* them to the grant(s). Rather, he concludes, the text itself provides the answer: the merchants had resolved to request "enktesis *of land on which they will establish a shrine of Aphrodite*" (lines 36–38; cf. lines 40–45). That is to say, if the italicized words are taken closely with, and as limiting, the grant of *enktesis*, the implication is that the request was lawful "*because* the purpose for which it was demanded was the erection of a temple to the Cyprian Aphrodite, not trade or residence."[41]

Radin's analysis is, I believe, a strong one, or at least the strongest justified by the words of the inscription. Furthermore, that the decrees, so conceived, amount to a form of regulation is self-evident, for without them the merchants could not have proceeded with their plans. Such regulation, it may be conjectured, might well have been authorized by Solon's law—the νόμος to which the word ἔννομα conceivably refers. True, the association in question is an association of foreigners, but, as we progress, we shall see that it is precisely with respect to associations of noncitizens (or other outsiders) that the Solonian law was to prove such a powerful administrative instrument.

Still another instance of the state's regulatory intervention is recorded by Aischines, once more in the *Against Ktesiphon*. According to his text, a decree of the People prohibited both phylai and demes from announcing their award of crowns "at the tragedies"—that is, in town before the audiences assembled for the dramatic productions of the City Dionysia (3.41–45 passim). The text is explicit as to the motive: the phylai and demes were felt to be engaging in unfair competition with the state; the persons crowned by them, the speaker declares, were receiving greater honors than those crowned by the People (§43). But, leaving the element of jealousy out of it, an additional supporting consideration, although not one actually acknowledged by Aischines, would have been that these phylai and demes possessed *agorai* of their own and that, as we learn from the surviving epigraphic record, these associational meetings would have provided, and did provide, adequate opportunity to announce the crownings to the association's membership.[42] Given this assumption, the announcements "at the tragedies" could have been portrayed not only as redundant but as inappropriate repetitions as well of the associations' already established internal procedures. A phyle or deme, therefore, could not have justified its claim, qua association, to access to the extra-associational audience drawn from the general population. Perhaps, then, one could legitimately suppose that the associations' excesses had brought them into conflict with the principle that an association's arrangements could be validated only when those arrangements remained within the sphere of its proper activity, the principle arguably signaled in

41. Radin 1910, p. 53.
42. For the *agorai* of the demes, see Whitehead 1986, pp. 86–120; for those of the phylai, see "The Agorai: Location, Schedule, Agenda, and Purpose," in chapter 5.

Solon's law by the word τούτων.[43] By the state's decree, δημόσια γράμματα were created with which, furthermore, those extra-associational acts were now in violation. So reconstructed, the incident may be seen as a paradigmatic example of the regulatory role envisioned by our text of the Solonian law on associations.

Fourthly, *IG* II² 1283, dated epigraphically to the middle of the third century, concerns two associations of Thracian *orgeones* devoted to the worship of the goddess Bendis.[44] The older group, established at Peiraieus, had previously observed the worship of the goddess through various rites in the harbor town. More recently, other *orgeones* have organized themselves in the *asty* for similar purposes. With reference to both groups, the decree's preamble notes that "the People of the Athenians has granted to the Thracians alone of the *ethnê* the right to own land and the right to establish a sanctuary in accordance with the oracle of Dodona and (the right) to send a procession from the hearth in the Prytaneion" (lines 4–7). Now, the text continues, those who have chosen to establish a sanctuary in the *asty* think it necessary that the two groups, the one in Peiraieus and the one in the *asty*, establish cordial relations (lines 7–9). The motivating clause provides the first explicit indication of the state's crucial role: "In order that the *orgeones* also be seen to obey the law of the city that orders the Thracians to dispatch the procession to Peiraieus and (be seen) to be kindly disposed towards the *orgeones* in the *asty*" (lines 9–13). Then the main body of the decree, in the name of "the *orgeones*" (that is, of both groups acting jointly), calls for the *orgeones* of the *asty* to process from the Prytaneion as they see fit (lines 13–16) and for the *epimeletai* in Peiraieus to receive them in appropriate fashion (lines 16–20). Ensuing lines call for the rites to be conducted "in accordance with the ancestral customs of the Thracians and with the laws of the city" (lines 25–26). Thus for a second time explicit acknowledgment is made of Athens' intervention in the form of the enforcement of its laws.

The difficulty involved here is, once again, a thorny one. Just what is the scope of the Athenian laws cited on two occasions in the text? Did they institute the rites *ab ovo* and, having instituted them, ordain that they be carried out in accordance with a specific plan? Or were they, given the previous existence of the rites, concerned only with details, specifically with the procession linking the *orgeones* of the *asty* with those of the harbor community? It is impossible to decide once and for all, but it can at least be ventured that the law, whatever its scope, *did* specifically address in some form the matter of the town-to-harbor procession, for it was by that means that the two groups, both of Thracian origin and ethnicity, could be united (or reunited), at least ceremonially and symbolically, as a single entity. That this was the People's underlying goal is explicitly signaled by the decree's twice instancing the harmony or welfare of "all the *ethnos*."[45]

A final instance of the state's regulatory intervention belongs to a far later period. *IG* II² 1012, dated 112/1, records that an Athenian citizen, the treasurer of "the

---

43. On this point, see appendix 2.

44. For additional discussion of this text, see "Orgeones of Bendis," in chapter 8.

45. Line 23: ὁμονοοῦντος παντὸς τοῦ ἔθ[νους (a genitive absolute construction embedded within the purpose clause and therefore partaking of its purposive character); and line 26: καὶ ἔχει καλῶς καὶ εὐσεβῶς παντὶ τῶι ἔθν[ει (the second member of the compound purpose clause beginning at line 22).

naukleroi and *emporoi* paying dues to support the synod of Zeus Xenios," had reported to the Council that the synod wished to set up a statue of its *proxenos* (who had also been elected epimelete of the harbor) in his (the epimelete's) office and had called upon the body to validate a *psephisma* for him. By its decree, the Council responded affirmatively to the request. The question then arises: Why does the association, through its treasurer's request, go to the trouble of asking the permission of the Council? Radin's answer was that permission was necessary because it was in a public building that the statue was to be set up.[46] Whether or not we grant the correctness of this plausible surmise, it is patent that the state is exercising a regulatory authority over one of its own, apparently at least in part foreign,[47] associations.

We began with the two discernible legal features of the Solonian law on associations, namely the validating and regulatory functions that it vests in the state. We have attempted to trace the operation of the law, or at least of its two guiding objectives possibly embodied in later laws or acts of the legislature, in a number of more recent documented interactions between associations and the state. The search has not proved entirely fruitless. In several instances, possible vestiges of the application of the law on associations as we have it in the *Digest* have been detected, although it would be rash to suggest either that the lawgiver's original text underwent no modification in the two and a half centuries before our earliest example or that our received text is exactly that in operation throughout the lengthy period of its suggested applications. Still, are we not entitled to conclude that the essence of the law, its validating and regulatory purposes, continued to govern, and to justify, the state's posture toward associations of all types, public or private, cultic or commercial, citizen or foreign, and the like?

"Validation" and "regulation" (in the form in which they are indicated in Solon's law) are, however, broad concepts capable of considerable ambiguity and elasticity, undoubtedly by design. After all, the variation in type of association was, as we saw, virtually limitless. Thus the applications of the "validating" role of the law have been seen to range from the deme Peiraieus to the philosophical schools to an organization of cultic *orgeones*. In each instance the state (or private arbitrators, anticipating the state) intervened in order to preserve what might be called the integrity of the association in question. These organizations might have been allowed to be overrun or fall into disarray, but the Athenians preferred to preserve their original configuration and to ensure their vitality and survival.

With the regulatory role, however, still more variety and a pronounced development away from the original Solonian formulation are in evidence. To mark the initial mode of regulation, we might characterize the state's stance in the text preserved in the *Digest* as passive and noninvolved. Associations, so long as they remain within their proper sphere of activity, do as they wish, provided they do not run afoul of the laws and decrees of the central government. But from these innocuous beginnings, the regulatory function develops along three distinct routes of intervention.

46. Radin 1910, pp. 54–55.
47. As noted by Radin, the fact that the association has a *proxenos* shows it was wholly or largely composed of foreigners (1910, p. 55).

Regulation as Checking. Aischines' evidence regarding the restriction on announcements by the phylai and demes (3.41–45) provides an unambiguous example, but the late edict of the Council regarding an association's placement of a statue (*IG* II² 1012) may reflect conditions in earlier times as well. Both episodes, let it be noted, involved access to public spaces.

Regulation as Enabling. Grants of *enktesis* and *idrusis* to the merchants of Kition made possible a cultic installation otherwise illegal under Athenian law (*IG* II² 337). A similar motive appears to be at work in the decree mentioning the laws of the state instituting (or specifying) the joint religious rites of the two Thracian societies of *orgeones* (*IG* II² 1283). Both these interventions served to promote the health of the *koinonia(i)* in question.

Regulation as Directing. The decree ordering the phylai to convene *agorai* for the conduct of state business (namely, the construction of city walls) (Aischines, 3.27) illustrates a manipulation of associations above and beyond merely enabling them to undertake or to maintain their internal functions.[48] If the state benefits indirectly from the other two modes of regulation, in this instance the benefit is patently direct.

These examples, taken collectively, illustrate, however sketchily, various modes of the Athenian state's official interaction with a scattering of different types of association. Those modes of interaction range from mere maintenance to promotion, control, and even the direction of the functioning of an organization. This seems to be a sufficient basis for extending the inquiry further, specifically with a view to determining the purpose or purposes lying behind and driving such intervention. With this goal in mind, let us now widen the investigation by going beyond decrees and the specific applications of Solon's law to consider the place of associations under the Athenian democracy.

Democracy and Associations

Although the general subject "Democracy and Associations" has never been the topic of a thorough investigation in its own right, considerable attention has been given by ancient Greek historians to specific links between the Athenian state and particular classes of association. It will be convenient, as a preliminary to framing the thesis being put forth in this book, to briefly rehearse some of what we already know. In each case I shall attempt to abstract from the isolated particulars a general formulation of the relation, with a specific instance or two offered exempli gratia to illustrate the various kinds of link between *polis* and *koinonia*:

Most generally, associations may be said to mediate the relations between the state and individuals. The association acts as a go-between or intermediary, thereby at once representing the interests of the individual before the central government and, conversely, serving a bureaucratic purpose in the state's interest by implement-

48. Such uses by the state of the *associations* of the segments of the state are, of course, to be distinguished from the common and unexceptionable statewide functions regularly carried out by those same units.

ing its statewide policies. To illustrate the individual-to-state link, let me anticipate my discussion of the phyle associations in chapters 5 and 6, where it will be argued that the association served to represent the wishes of its individual members in the arena of the city of Athens. As for the state-to-individual link, the deme and phratry provide clear-cut, well-documented examples. The demarch, though nominally merely the head of the deme association, also served, to use the phrase introducing Whitehead's discussion of the phenomenon, as "agent of the state" in various capacities.[49] The phratry, too, through its maintenance of stringent standards for admission to membership, facilitated the state's evaluation of candidates for Athenian citizenship. If, that is, a young Athenian could clear the hurdles obstructing his entry into his (citizen) father's phratry, the Athenian People would have little reason to doubt his qualifications for admission to the citizen body.

Paralleling these essentially procedural mediations between the whole and units of the Athenian polity, the associations also may have served in an informal way to facilitate movement from the lower to the upper echelons of the social or political order. It is easy to imagine, but hard to document, the "little society" of a dining, cultic, or village association functioning as a sort of training ground where neophytes honed their skills—social, political or otherwise—in preparation for entry into the "big time" society of Athens. A notable attempt to establish just such a path of upward mobility was Haussoullier's portrayal of "La vie municipale"—by which he intended the "life" of the deme association—as "une école de la vie publique, de la vie politique," etc.[50] But Whitehead's incisive examination of the hypothesis revealed a far more complex situation than Haussoullier had imagined. If by "school of public life" it is understood that the deme served to launch its members, once seasoned in the magisterial setting of the local association, into higher elective office or other prominent role in the city government, the evidential record offers little support. Whitehead found that "those active at deme level and at city level were, broadly speaking, different people."[51] A deme office did not serve as a stepping-stone to the generalship or to the leadership of a faction. Nevertheless, despite this negative finding, it remains arguable that the deme, and as well the phyle and other associations, could serve as "a fairly gentle introduction" (to quote from Whitehead's assessment of the case of the deme) to the workings of the democratic government of Athens.[52] Within the secure setting of the deme or phratry, mistakes could harmlessly be made, administrative talents developed, rhetorical skills polished, and so on. So, in this larger sense an association could indeed facilitate upward mobility into the arena of statewide political activity.

A different, indirect involvement of certain associations within the larger setting of the Athenian *politeia* might be conveniently termed integrative. An association could serve to bring together individuals or groups within the state which, except for the presence of the association, would remain isolated from one another. The state may be said to be indirectly involved to the extent that the associations

49. Whitehead 1986, pp. 130–138.
50. Haussoullier 1884, p. i.
51. Whitehead 1986, p. 319.
52. Whitehead 1986, p. 324.

are facilitating a social and political function in the interest of the state but one which, if only because of the immense expanse of Attica and the relatively large size of the population, the state was itself inadequate to perform. The clearest example is the celebrated *anamixis* or "mixing up" of city, coast, and inland regions brought about by Kleisthenes' adoption of the innovating trittys arrangement of the phylai. Similarly, on a vastly reduced scale, the state's intervention in the affairs of the Thracian *orgeones* of Bendis seems, as I argued above, to have been designed at least in part to unify two widely separated groups of co-national cultists. In the vertical dimension, deme associations cut across all divisions of status or class, bringing into a single organization the entire spectrum of citizen society. At a later time, postclassical private associations will be found accommodating male and female, Athenian and foreign, free and slave, within the confines of a unified cultic *koinonia*.[53] The integrative role, in short, seems well established.

These three categories of evidence are probably typical of the sorts of relations obtaining between a central government and the individual person in a relatively advanced society such as classical Athens. Associations mediated between government and citizen, afforded opportunities for upward mobility, and played various crucial integrative roles. The obvious utilitarian value to the state of such organizations could not have escaped, and in the case of classical Athens manifestly did not escape, the attention of the central authority. It is here that we are to find a wider context of purpose for the specific interventions, grounded in the validating and regulating instruments built into Solon's law, already surveyed. Plainly, the Athenian state had a vested interest in maintaining in good health the vast and complex network of associations that will unfold in this work.

It is the purpose of my study to build upon, and to add specificity to, this general characterization of the relations between central government and association in respect to Athens under the classical democracy. My central claim is that the major known associations of the classical era—the demes, phylai, phratries, "clubs," philosophical schools, regional associations, *orgeones*, and others—acquired certain of their specific configurations, regional dispositions, and functions in response to the distinctive features—a pessimist might call them failings—of the contemporary *demokratia*. To put the situation I envision another way, it might be said that, if the theory argued in this book is valid, one can make sense of a deme or phyle or phratry only by considering it in relation to the nature and functions of the central government. As a final preliminary to our detailed discussion of the associations, therefore, let us note just what those distinctive features of the democracy are.

Egalitarianism. The dominant ideology of the democracy manifested itself in various ways. Sortition is the most obvious such manifestation, for, even if the purpose of allotment was essentially political (for example, in order to eliminate the conflict occasioned by elections), the random selection of magistrates or councillors from a pool of candidates nonetheless rested on the assumption that all citizens were ade-

---

53. Cf. Tod's succinct formulation in *OCD²*, s.v. "clubs, Greek," pp. 254–255: "they [i.e., clubs] appear to have played a valuable role in uniting in a common religious and social activity diverse elements of the population—men and women, slaves and free, citizens and aliens, Greeks and 'barbarians.'"

quately qualified for government service. The same leveling tendencies had also in well-known ways affected adversely the earlier aristocratic domination of the military, religion, the judicial system, and other arenas of public life.

The continuing existence and eventual decisive political activities of elite "clubs" afford only the most obvious manifestation of the aristocratic "response" to egalitarianism. Cultic organizations of less obvious ideological orientation such as the *genê* and *orgeones* (chapter 8) provided small-scale intimate and exclusive retreats from the massed gatherings of the People. And even the segments of the state itself, the numerous and universally accessible phyle and deme associations, in less striking—and lawful—ways provided opportunities for differentiation on the basis of ability, energy, or other personal attainment (chapters 2–4, 5–6). Men of talent, resources, and modest ambition could and did rise to positions of authority and responsibility in the local *koinonia*.

Direct Rule. It is generally maintained, or more often assumed, that the Athenian democracy was a direct democracy, in implied or implicit contrast with the more familiar representative model. There can be no question but that direct rule characterized voting in the Assembly, ostracism, the courts, and elections. The universality of the practice may help account for the fact that no ancient authority, Aristotle in particular, ever explicitly characterizes the Athenian democracy as "direct." Indeed, there is no Greek word or phrase that means "direct" (or, for that matter, "indirect") or anything like it. In view of these circumstances, are we not entitled to search for a "response" to direct rule in the form of a mechanism or mechanisms of representative government?

By the term "representative," it must be emphasized, is intended here the conveying of the will of a constituency to the central government by an elected or appointed member of that constituency. "Representative" is *not* used here in the sense sometimes encountered in discussions of the Athenian Council of Five Hundred, the composition of which was tied to the individual demes by a system of quotas based on population. The Council thus "represented" the demes in the sense that each and every deme sent to Athens a member or members in proportion to the number of its citizen population. But no one has ever been able to demonstrate that the Council was a "representative" body in the technical sense that will be under consideration in this work.

In chapter 6 it will be argued that, in response to the absence of a mechanism for true representation, the phyle associations eventually evolved into organizations capable of transmitting the will of their memberships to the central government.

Minority Citizen Participation. No one has ever seriously suggested that all Athenian citizens regularly participated in the Athenian democratic processes. As in any democratic polity, a certain number of the enfranchised will always, by choice or out of necessity, fail to cast their vote, run for office, sit on a jury, etc. But, in the Athenian case, what was not appreciated until relatively recently is that rule by a minority was literally built into certain of the organs of the democratic government.

The most telling case is that of the Assembly. It is of course known from ancient sources that the quorum of this body was 6,000. But it was shown in a convincing paper by M. H. Hansen[54] that 6,000 was *also* the seating capacity of the meeting place of the Assembly, the slope of the Pnyx in its contemporary period of construction. Thus, once the quorum was attained (signaled by the fact that the seats had been filled), no additional citizens could be accommodated. Hence, at the time when the citizen body numbered 30,000, a maximum of about one-fifth of the citizens made decisions in the name of the entire state.[55] This finding is balanced, but not negated, by the evidence for much higher participation in the Council of Five Hundred and in the many boards of magistrates (considered collectively). The voice of the sovereign body of the Athenians was of necessity the voice of a minority, and a small minority at that.

A skeptic might attempt to avoid this result by invoking the principle of rotation, maintaining that on each occasion the Assembly was filled by *a different set* of 6,000 Athenians. But this approach will not wash. Participation at various levels was also conditioned by numerous de facto constraints, such as wealth, agricultural or other schedule, degree of education, access to political contacts, but most of all, and most fundamentally, by the location of one's residence with respect to the seat of government in the urban center. In chapter 4 it will be argued, against certain other scholars, that the residents of distant rural demes did not regularly journey to the town in order to exercise their constitutional prerogatives. So, above and beyond the unalterable physical constraints imposed by the seating capacity of the Pnyx, dwellers in outlying districts were in any case de facto disfranchised by reason of their remove from the seat of government.

What makes this finding particularly significant for our study is the fact that the Athenian citizen body as a whole must have been highly conscious of its potential for participation in constitutional functions. All or most of Attica had been politicized by the regional conflicts attending the rise of the Peisistratid tyranny; all citizens were made continually aware of their status as Athenians by the addition of the *demotikon* to their "official" names; the deme associations, through the activities of the demarch in particular, transmitted to the local villages, as noted earlier, the policies and edicts of the central government; unavoidable statewide activities such as military training and service regularly forced all citizens to play a part in the operation of the state; and so on. Whatever else may have been true of them, these practically disfranchised Athenians were not apathetic in the sense that they were unaware of their eligibility to play a part in the functioning of the central government.[56]

54. Hansen 1976, pp. 115–134 (= 1983a, pp. 1–20, 21–23).

55. According to the numbers of the well-known census conducted by Demetrios of Phaleron (317–307), the Athenian citizen body stood at only 21,000. Hansen, however, in his 1985 study of Athenian demography came to the conclusion that in the age of Demosthenes the actual number was "no less than ca. 30,000 adult men" (1985, p. 5, with conclusion at pp. 65–69). Hansen's found that the higher figure makes more acceptable the evidence for the relatively very high level of participation in the democratic government (p. 5). Yet, by the same token, it remains an astonishing fact that, on this same evidence, at no time could more than one-fifth of the citizen body take part in a meeting of the Assembly.

56. For a discussion of politicization in fifth-century Athens, see Mion 1986, pp. 219–238. Mion asserts that politicization existed to an "intense degree . . . in the sense that the political was dominant and pervasive in all areas of life" (p. 225). The "primacy of politics" in Classical Greece has also been addressed by Rahe (1984, pp. 265–293). I shall return to this point in our conclusion in chapter 10.

Thus minority rule constitutes a third feature (or failing) of the democracy to which we might expect to find a response in the nature, configuration, or orientation of the associations. It is to this point that our discussions of the Kleisthenic demes in chapters 2, 3, and 4 will be in large part directed. In these typically isolated and introverted village associations will be found the alternative, and compensating, forum of political activity available for those citizens excluded from city life by the accident of their place of residence. The same characterization will also be found to apply to the less well-understood cases of the phratry (chapter 7) and the so-called regional associations (chapter 8).

Exclusion of Noncitizens. The absolute exclusion of all but adult male sons of citizen parents from the citizen caste is so widely and consistently documented as to require no demonstration. Minors, women, metics, and of course slaves were without exception denied access to the democratic constitutional processes. It is self-evident that so large a segment of the population of Athens, living in such close proximity with members of the citizen elite, might be stirred to find or devise forms of group activity to compensate for their exclusion from the numerous collectivities, both public and private, formally open only to the fully enfranchised.

This is the most obvious of the distinctive features (or failings) of the Athenian democracy and, of the four, the one that provides the most obvious opening for the development of associations of a compensating composition and orientation. The detailed exposition of the gradual emergence of noncitizen (or at least nonmember) participation in citizen groups and eventually of associations in significant part accessible to outsiders will constitute a major thread running intermittently through much of our study. As it happens, it will be in the territorial bounding of the deme that we shall find perhaps the earliest and most important "response" to the democracy. It is appropriate, therefore, that we begin our investigation by addressing the fundamental problem of the definition and membership of that association.

TWO

The Demes

Definitions and Membership

Like its predecessor, the new public organization created by Kleisthenes comprised three tiers of units: phylai, trittyes, and demes. At each of the levels, the units, as varying types and quantities of contemporary evidence reveal, were internally organized as more or less independent associations. The phyle associations will be treated at length in chapters 5 and 6. The trittys associations, as noted in the Introduction,[1] have left only a few traces of their existence in the epigraphic record. So, we shall begin our investigation with the deme associations, the building blocks of the Kleisthenic organization and, as we shall see, entities that, in various ways, bear the stamp of a "response to democracy."

The Deme as "Natural Community"

Whitehead's Formulation

Among the topics addressed by Whitehead in his comprehensive *The Demes of Attica* is the extent to which, if any, and in what ways, if any, Kleisthenes modified the already existing village communities of Attica when he created his system of demes. This part of his investigation involved collecting what particulars have survived regarding the early communities and comparing these data with the much fuller record of the demes following the establishment of the new system. White-

---

1. See the Introduction, with note 3.

head concluded that there was little disturbance of existing arrangements and that the ancient settlements, including even some within the walls, were carried into the fledgling organization without discernible significant interference.[2] This result was achieved through the particular procedure employed by Kleisthenes in the initial formation of his new demes. Whitehead follows Thompson in supposing that the reformer created the demes by ordering each Athenian citizen to register in his "home village."[3] Thereby village affiliations at the time of the creation of the democracy were permanently enshrined for all time. To put it negatively, and to mention the main competing hypothesis preliminary to its full consideration below, what Kleisthenes did *not* do, on Whitehead's argument, was to create a new deme by the drawing of territorial boundaries such that every Athenian, regardless of his previous community affiliation, who happened to reside within those boundaries thereafter was to be a member of it. The original distribution of population among the old settlements was thereby in the main preserved.

The basic qualities of the Kleisthenic demes, furthermore, reveal the conservative tendency at work in various aspects of the new organization. The number of demes, on Traill's count 139 (or possibly 140 if, as he later suspected, Acharnai was split into two demes)[4], is arbitrary when compared with the exact decade of phylai and their uniform segmental triads of trittyes. Such a number is less likely to have been the product of a thoroughgoing redrawing of the map of Attica than of the retention of an existing status quo.[5] Similarly, the sizes of the demes vary wildly; one need only mention the variation of the bouleutic quotas of the demes between one and sixteen councillors.[6] Would a reformer, starting ab ovo, have deliberately created units of such marked difference in size? And the demes's names, too, betray the same conservative tendencies, for many are demonstrably of great antiquity.[7] Thus Whitehead sums up the situation well when he characterizes the Kleisthenic deme network as "an essentially natural one."[8]

The general correctness of Whitehead's observation is undeniable. It receives still further confirmation from the variety of institutional arrangements, and of nomenclature used to describe those arrangements, displayed by the demes in their fully developed form.[9] To adequately appreciate the point one need only consider

2. Whitehead 1986, pp. 5–16 ("A. The Demes before Kleisthenes"), pp. 16–38 ("B. The Kleisthenic Demes"). For the conclusion regarding the "natural" character of the new demes, see especially pp. 25–26, 30–31.

3. Whitehead 1986, pp. 27–30, at p. 29 citing Thompson 1971, p. 74.

4. Traill 1986, pp. 133–134, s.v. "Acharnai," with cross-reference to pp. 142–144 (Agora 15, no. 68), where fuller citation of the evidence and literature will be found.

5. Whitehead 1986, pp. 17–23.

6. Whitehead 1986, pp. 23–24. For Traill's most recent tabulation of the quotas, see the "Conspectus of Deme Quotas and Locations," in Traill 1986, pp. 125–140. If Acharnai is split, its quota is reduced from 22 to seven or six (city trittys part) and 15 or 16 (inland trittys part) (Traill 1986, pp. 133–134). Aphidna with certainty had a quota of 16 (op. cit., p. 138).

7. Whitehead 1986, pp. 24–25.

8. Whitehead 1986, p. 25.

9. See, in general, Jones 1987, pp. 61–65. For perhaps the clearest example of the tendency, the marked variation in the titles of the deme's internal officers from one deme to another, see the discussion of Whitehead 1986, pp. 139–144, on "other officials" (i.e., other than the demarch). More recently, the point has been underscored by the publication in 1989 of the new joint decree of Kydantidai and Ionidai

the near total uniformity of the urban-based structures of the associations of the ten phylai.[10] Meanwhile, the demes, reflecting the widely scattered distribution of their historical centers over plain, shore, and hill, continue to evidence the individuality that had characterized them at the time of their institutionalization by Kleisthenes.[11] They had not in fact been subjected to any "unnatural" leveling or homogenization that might have placed the stamp of uniformity upon them.

The purpose of such observations is to demonstrate that the preexisting communities were brought into the new organization by Kleisthenes with relatively little disturbance. The new demes were not artificial products of reform, like the new trittyes or phylai, not to mention the units of dozens of innovating organizations throughout historical Greece. But a question remains. Was the Kleisthenic deme in the time of our documentation in any substantial sense really a "natural" community? Numbers of demes, variable size of demes, inherited names of demes, and archaic posts and terminology merely demonstrate an absence of tampering with preexisting conditions. In fact, I wish to suggest, the Kleisthenic deme, as traditionally understood, was subject to such deficiencies that, except in the more limited respects in which the term was introduced by Whitehead (and repeated by others), it appears inadvisable to continue to describe it as a "natural" community.

Exclusivity and the "Natural Community"

Succinctly put, the Kleisthenic deme association was the exclusive domain of the citizen *demotai*. Normally, only one route to membership lay open. The son of a *demotes*, having reached his eighteenth year, and having passed to the satisfaction of the assembled *demotai* the twin tests of majority and legitimacy, was enrolled "among the *demotai*."[12] The only alternative paths were provided by adoption and naturalization, whereby the prospective member joined the deme of his adoptive father[13] or of the citizen sponsoring the decree of naturalization.[14] The operation of the rule of descent, in short, had closed the door to all attempts at penetration.[15] That the deme, in this its *constitutional* aspect, was so defined is an incontrovertible fact. But is it fair to characterize an *association* so constituted and sustained as "nat-

(*SEG* 39.148; 331/0). Against the editor Matthaiou's contention that the officers called *kolokratai* mentioned at lines 4 and 12–13 are the well-known city magistrates the *kolakretai*, Whitehead has persuasively argued in favor of identifying them as yet another unique board of "local officials" of the deme(s) (1993, pp. 159–162).

10. See Jones 1987, pp. 58–60. The officers of the phylai are discussed in greater detail, with the same result, in *"Epimeletai* and Other Officers," in chapter 6.

11. For the point, see Jones 1987, p. 61 (particularism of demes, their independent origins, and continuing isolation).

12. *AthPol* 42.1–2, with Rhodes's comments, 1981, pp. 495–505.

13. With Isaios 7.27–28 and [Demosthenes] 44.39, see Rhodes 1981, p. 252.

14. On the law and practice of naturalization in Athens, see the definitive account of M. Osborne, 1983, vol. 4, pp. 139–221, with pp. 172–173 on the determination of the honorand's deme.

15. The point acquires still greater significance when one considers the alternative definitions of citizenship that might have been, but were not, adopted. For these, with valuable discussion, see Davies 1978, pp. 105–121.

ural"? My hunch is that, on further inquiry, it would be found not to be a fair characterization. But in order to avoid becoming entangled in the semantics of the English word "natural," let me attempt to justify this hunch by airing some reasons for believing that the Athenian demes qua associations might in fact have been something more than, or at least something different from, the closed, exclusive organizations defined by rule of descent—reasons, that is, for believing that a truly "natural" village association did in fact exist.

There is, first, the general consideration that the term δῆμος" ("deme") itself, in distinction from its constitutionally exclusive derivative *demotes*, "demesman," appears to possess an *inclusive* meaning. Etymology suggests as an original denotation a parcel of arable land, later extended to include the people occupying that land. A *demos* is a village, in both its territorial and human aspects. Thus, if prehistoric antecedents count for anything, the word appears destined to become an all-embracing denominator of the community's holdings and inhabitants, citizen or otherwise.[16] As it worked out, the word, presumably already possessing its inclusive connotations, was in use in Attic Greek prior to the time of Kleisthenes.[17] And Kleisthenes himself? If his intention had been to create, and appropriately to identify, an exclusively adult male citizen membership, he might have coined a neologism bearing such a meaning. But, in contrast with the practice of reformers in other Greek city-states, he did not.[18] The same goes for such inherited toponyms as Eleusis, Peiraieus, and Thorikos (as opposed to the plural demotics Eleusinioi, Peiraieis, and Thorikioi); they are the names, not of citizen elites, but of entire communities, of settlements necessarily embracing the entire human population. Now, does Kleisthenes' use of the traditional term (and of the traditional toponyms), and their continued currency in later times, not tell us something about the possible definitions of the democratic "village"? That Kleisthenic did not innovate in his choice of terminology (and of place names) opens up the possibility that he retained the old term (and names) precisely because, among other considerations, of their inclusive character.

A second consideration has to do with the purposes that many historians, following Lewis,[19] believe animated Kleisthenes to mold the new organization in the

---

16. Etymologically, the word δῆμος seems to denote not people but territory. *LSJ*[9], s.v., adduces Sanskrit *dáti* ("reap"), δαίομαι ("divide"), and δατέομαι (again "divide"); these possible cognates suggest as an original meaning a segment of land, specifically agricultural land. The word's earliest attested uses in Greek occur in the Linear B tablets, Ventris and Chadwick assigning the meaning "an entity which can allocate holdings of land, probably a village community" (1973, p. 538). So by this time a transference from the land to the people occupying the land has occurred, but without any discernible indication of an exclusion of any segment of that population. The politically loaded sense "the commons, common people" (*LSJ*[9], s.v., II), which is very rare in Homer, is a much later development (see Whitehead 1986, app. 1, pp. 364–368, especially 365 and 367) and is, in any case, the only attested noninclusive use of the word. For additional bibliography, see Frisk 1972, vol. 3, s.v., pp. 72–73.

17. Thus Peisistratos's circuit judges were called the δικασταὶ κατὰ δήμους (*AthPol* 16.5) and, as Whitehead noted (1986, p. 366), Herodotos, when relating Athenian history before the democracy, uses the term to denote an individual village community (e.g., 1.60.4).

18. For the roster of Greek terms recognizably denoting territorial segments of the public organization at Athens and elsewhere, see Jones 1987, index I, B, 2 (p. 388). Of the nine, possibly ten, examples, several appear to be later innovations, e.g., ἄμφοδον, κωμαρχία, οἴη, πύργος, τόνος, and ὠβά.

19. Lewis 1963, pp. 22–40.

specific form that we find it. The new phylai, trittyes, and demes, but especially the demes, it is argued, were set up as rivals to an already existing network of regionally based aristocratic cultic associations. The democratic units were meant to bypass, divide, duplicate, or otherwise neutralize their aristocratic predecessors. Thus, to cite Lewis's own strikingly apt (but not easily paralleled) example, Kleisthenes' deme Boutadai was intended to put out of business the aristocratic *genos* Boutadai. (The aristocrats' response, as though to confirm Lewis's thesis, was to rename themselves the Eteoboutadai, the "true" Boutadai.)[20] My point is that these aristocratic associations were certainly anything but exclusive "men's clubs." The principal reason for so thinking is their fundamentally cultic orientation in combination with the well-known fact that the womenfolk and children of Athenians normally participated alongside adult males, or even on their own, in a wide range of religious functions. Accordingly, to compete successfully, the democratic rival units would have to replicate the more inclusive character of their elitist predecessors. Lewis's thesis, once accepted, in other words, prompts the opening up of new possibilities for the definition of the Kleisthenic deme. No one, of course, has ever denied that a demesman's family members participated in deme association cultic activities, but it seems to me that more remains to be said on this head.[21]

Finally, and less concretely, there is the question of the long-range survivability of a group that, though nominally embracing an entire community, in fact restricts participation to only a small fraction of that community. For how long could so small a minority speak and act in the name of the unrepresented majority? Might not the excluded parties set up competing organizations of their own? Nothing prohibited or even discouraged the creation of new associations; only the minimal conditions of Solon's law had to be met. That this is more than just a theoretical possibility is illustrated in Athens at a later date by the attested membership in associations welcoming women, foreigners, and even slaves.[22] Expansion of the circle of the eligible is an established fact. The question is, how far back toward, or into, the period of the classical democracy can the phenomenon be pushed. The position to be taken here is that a more inclusive definition of the deme was in place from an early date, perhaps from the very inception of the democracy.

At all events, the demes of the classical democracy were in fact, as we shall see, subjected to such pressures by outsiders resident within the deme but not formally enrolled within it. In a few (admittedly exceptional but for our present purpose diagnostic) cases, *demotai* were compelled to share the privileges of membership with Athenian soldiers encamped within their territories. Yet even so drastic a concession did not suffice, for in later times these soldiers struck out on their own, bypassing altogether the organization of the deme of their encampment. It would not be unrealistic to suppose that awareness of the consequences of ignoring the pressures exerted by large numbers of nonmembers resident within the territory

20. Lewis 1963, p. 26.
21. See especially my discussion in "The Women of the *Demotai*," in chapter 4. The upshot of that discussion is to elevate demeswomen to a higher, and more formally defined, status than scholars have previously acknowledged.
22. See "*Orgeones* of the Mother of the Gods," in chapter 8.

would have been felt much earlier, in the classical era. We have every reason to press our search for symptoms of an enlarged circle of participation in the deme.

The Disposition of the Deme: People or Territory?

The Problem

Among the uncertainties surrounding the nature of Kleisthenes' reforms is the question of how the demes were defined, both initially by Kleisthenes and in later times. Broadly speaking, two fundamentally opposed views have emerged. According to what might be called the standard view, it was until relatively recently widely believed, or rather assumed, that a Kleisthenic deme was defined by precise territorial boundaries and that the entire expanse of Attica (save neutral areas such as the Akropolis, Agora, and the pan-Athenian sanctuaries) was therefore composed of contiguous blocks of land, namely, the demes, and the trittyes and phylai of which the demes were segmental components. Accordingly, a map of Attica would have resembled that of the states or provinces of a modern nation.[23] Such a model was at least consistent with the *Athenaion Politeia*'s statement (21.4) that Kleisthenes "distributed the land (*chora*) by demes (into) thirty parts" (that is, the trittyes)[24] and was favored by the frequent use of the names of the demes to mark the location of properties, buildings, and so on.[25] However, this position—perhaps partly because till that time it had never been subject to an attempt at rigorous demonstration—was seriously challenged in 1971 by Thompson in a short but seminal paper.[26] Simply stated, his claim was that the demes, while "unquestionably local units," were not necessarily for that reason defined by boundaries. Kleisthenes, he argued, "dealt with the demes as a series of isolated villages, not as blocks of territory."[27] Both the passage from the *AthPol* (21.4) and the use of deme names to mark locations were, he observed (in my estimation, incorrectly), consistent with this new way of looking at the deme. A deme might be shown on a map, not as a block of territory contiguous with other such blocks, but as a point in the near vicinity of which the citizens who belonged to that deme were domiciled. Kleisthenes, in short, thought of his demes, though locally based, not as land or territory but rather (to cite his approving quotation from Lewis) as "the group of people living in that territory."[28]

Since the publication of Thompson's paper, the theory has received a measure of acceptance but not in the context of a thoroughgoing reconsideration of the prob-

23. Among recent works, this assumption underlies Eliot's study of the coastal demes (1962). This work was published the year preceding the date of Lewis's revisionist article.

24. Although my position on the matter of boundaries is, as will be seen, generally in agreement with Langdon's article, I dispute his statement that the *AthPol*'s sentence is "not decisive, because it could apply equally well to demes as people or as land" (1985b, p. 7). The use of the term *chora* hardly leaves any doubt that the author's point concerns the division of territory, not of population.

25. On this point, see below on localizing properties with reference to a deme.

26. Thompson 1971, pp. 72–79.

27. Thompson 1971, p. 72 (both quotations).

28. Thompson 1971, p. 74, citing Lewis's review of Eliot 1962 at *Gnomon* 35 (1963) 724.

lem.[29] And when such a reconsideration was undertaken in 1985, by Langdon, it resulted in a reaffirmation of the doctrine of territorial demes.[30] Whitehead had of course, in *The Demes of Attica*, published in 1986, revisited the question, but without the benefit of Langdon's study. His conclusion turned out to be a compromise between the two positions. While accepting Thompson's account of the creation of the demes by Kleisthenes, he was compelled to acknowledge the existence, and evident significance, of certain inscribed markers generally maintained by scholars to have defined the boundaries of demes but all of which dated to the fourth century. To reconcile the Thompsonian account of the demes' origins with the palpable import of the markers, he suggested that the exact boundaries were a development of the later classical period, possibly created in response to boundary disputes.[31]

It is not possible, I shall maintain, to argue away the evidence for either the personal or the territorial disposition. Already, Langdon has observed that the developed deme manifests elements of both orientations.[32] My first central contention, seconding Langdon's belief that Kleisthenes entertained two conceptions of the deme, is that a Kleisthenic deme, very likely from the moment of its creation, was neither merely an "isolated village" nor a "block of territory," but both. Furthermore, and to carry the dual conception of the deme beyond the point at which it was left by Langdon, I will argue that to each of the two demes corresponded a discrete set of members. The "isolated village" will be identified as the "constitutional" deme, the exclusive community of citizen male *demotai* organized personally on the basis of hereditary inheritance of the *demotikon*. The "block of territory," by contrast, will emerge as a wider, more inclusive organization embodying all free persons —demespeople, non-*demotai* citizens, and resident aliens—and perhaps even slaves, residing within its boundaries. Now, Whitehead broached the possibility of two memberships when he wrote of "the two interlocking and competing 'definitions' of a deme," glossed as "its true members" on the one hand and "its actual (citizen) population" on the other.[33] But no mention was made in his discussion of the possibility that the two definitions might be brought into relation with the two competing conceptions of the deme as alternatively a community of people or a precisely bounded parcel of land. It will be the primary burden of this chapter to attempt to establish a substantive connection between these two sets of ideas. Let us begin by rehearsing briefly the case for the exclusive, "citizen" deme of the *demotai*, and, with that familiar conception as background, attempt to strengthen still further the case for its more problematic counterpart, the deme as a "block of territory."

29. Most notably by Rhodes 1981, on 21.4, pp. 251–252.

30. Langdon 1985b, pp. 5–15.

31. Whitehead 1986, p. 29.

32. Langdon 1985b, p. 10: "In sum, the reforms of Kleisthenes should be seen as built around two elements." He then goes on to contrast "the deme centers, where the majority of the citizenry lived" with "the land associated with these centers." Implicitly denying Whitehead's compromise position opposing the act of creation in 508/7 with the later developments of the fourth? century, Langdon ventures "Kleisthenes had both in mind when he set about his reforms."

33. Whitehead 1986, pp. 76–77. The remark was motivated by consideration of a decree of the deme Ikarion, *IG* I³ 254, lines 3–4, in which it is ordained that tragic *choregoi* be drawn not only from the *demotai* but also from "the people living in Ikarion." This text will be discussed in detail below.

The Citizen Deme: The Demotai

It is one of the solid facts of the Athenian democracy that once a citizen's deme affiliation was established, it remained unchanged for life and was transmitted in the male line to his descendants. The hereditary principle was extended to cases of adoption, since the adopted son's affiliation (inherited from his male parent) was, upon adoption, if different, changed to that of the adoptive father.[34] The portability of the *demotikon* is illustrated by the many cases of citizens who maintain their inherited affilations while visiting or residing in, and occasionally playing a role in the organizational activities of, a deme other than that of their membership.[35] Despite, however, an accumulation of isolated particular instances, the evidential record has always seemed inadequate to permit any meaningful generalizations, with commentators as a result resorting to the citation of piecemeal data.[36] But more recent studies of tombstones bearing the names of Athenians accompanied by the *demotikon* have brought to light the seeming overall trends: considerable movement from country to town, little movement between rural communities, and scarcely any movement from town to country.[37] Finally, on a vastly larger scale, the *demotikon* also traveled to overseas cleruchies and possessions, in the official documents of which the *tria nomina* of Athenian *demotai* are frequently recorded.[38] Thus the constitutional deme, despite its continuing strong local orientation, experienced a gradual loosening of its original territorial integrity. In short, the Kleisthenic deme had since 508/7 been transformed from a cohesive village-based community into a spatially distended "group of people."

It is to these organizations of *demotai* that the great bulk of our documentation relates. The *demotai* make up the deme assemblies, act on admissions to their membership, occupy all deme magistracies, represent the deme in the Council of Five Hundred, form contingents in the Athenian military organization, and so on. Most importantly, virtually they alone authorize the decrees and other documents that constitute our dossier of primary evidence—the great bulk of our evidence on the demes. No wonder that, except for the suggestions, left unpursued, of Langdon and Whitehead alluded to above, current thinking recognizes the deme of the *demotai* as the sole manifestation of the constitutionalized village instituted by Kleisthenes.

The Territorial Deme: The Case for Precise Boundaries

The case for this "second," territorial deme involves two steps of argumentation. First, and (I should think, in the light of the evidence assembled below) less controversially, one must establish that, as was believed or assumed until Thompson, the

---

34. See above, with note 13.

35. For some examples, see "Deme vs. Deme Relations," in chapter 3.

36. See Whitehead 1986, pp. 352–358, where are cited exempli gratia a dozen instances of "migrators" (353, note 14) and another dozen of Athenians still living in their ancestral demes in the fourth century (353–354 with note 15 [354]).

37. Damsgaard-Madsen 1988, p. 6.

38. Athenian demotics are attested epigraphically for the following cleruchies or possessions: Salamis; Aigina; Imbros, Lemnos, Skyros, Peparethos, and Skiathos; Samos; Melos; and Poteidaia. For the sources, see Jones 1987, index I. A. 3. s.v. "Athens" (p. 387).

demes in fact were defined by more or less precise boundaries. The second, more difficult, step requires the demonstration that this territorial deme actually played an official role in the associational lives of those who dwelt within it. Boundaries that merely sit and serve no purpose save to mark the location of a building or mining operation are of no significance for our study. We must demonstrate their application to the public activity of a membership in order for the territorial deme to qualify as an organ of Athenian public organization. Let us first assemble *seriatim* the various bits of evidence favoring the assumption of precise boundaries. Some of this material, (namely, that concerning the *horoi*, localizing properties with reference to a deme, and the *enktetikon*) has previously received attention in this connection, although, as we shall see, in each instance something new remains to be said. The remaining four items, assembled below, are now for the first time brought to bear on the question.

The Horoi. Thompson argued that, if the demes were really blocks of territory, we should expect to discover boundary stones that served to define them. Since such *horoi,* marking the Agora, sanctuaries, silver mines, roads, and so on, have come to light in significant numbers, it is reasonable to suppose, he argues, that, had similar monuments defined the limits of the demes, some of them would have survived.[39] After all, it would have taken a great many markers adequately to define the 139 or so Kleisthenic units. So Thompson, proceeding on the assumption that, if precise boundaries existed, they had to have been marked, found significance in the fact that no such stones appeared to have been discovered.

Yet, as Whitehead noted,[40] Thompson had failed to mention *IG* II² 2623, printed by Kirchner as follows: ὅρος Π[ει]/ραέων [χώ]/[ρ]ας, with the evident meaning "boundary stone of the countryside of the people of Peiraieus." This is, as Whitehead realized, pertinent evidence. But further progress with this text can be made. The squeeze on file at the Institute for Advanced Study in Princeton shows the remains of a horizontal stroke in the upper part of the third to last stoichos of the third line.[41] While definitely eliminating Kirchner's *rho*, these remains are consistent with the reading γᾶς. In combination with the deletion of the restoration at the end of the preceding line, the new reading would yield the sense "boundary stone of the *land* of (the) people of Peiraieus." Besides being more faithful to the remains on the stone, the new restoration would also remove the problem posed by the unexpected use of the term *chora,* which commonly is used in explicit or implicit contrast with an *asty* (and so translated above "countryside"). But even on Kirchner's restoration, the stone can only have marked a boundary of the deme's territory or some fraction thereof. To be sure, it is a single, isolated example, yet it proves that in the fourth century[42] there could be such a thing as a boundary line of a deme. And it is that principle that is here under scrutiny.[43]

---

39. Thompson 1971, p. 73.

40. Whitehead 1986, pp. 28–29.

41. The squeeze was examined during a visit to the Institute during the summer of 1994.

42. For the date, see Kirchner on *IG* II² 2512: "Hic et qui sequuntur termini fere omnes ad saec. quartum a.Chr. referendi sunt."

43. It is pertinent to add that structures and spaces in this particular deme were frequently marked by *horoi*. For a complete listing of the Piraeus boundary markers, with references to place of publication, see Garland 1987, app. 1, pp. 225–226, nos. 1–24 (with the "trittyes markers" appended on

Furthermore, besides the formal pillarlike engraved posts called *horoi*, additional physical evidence of the marking of the boundaries of demes is now available in relative abundance. I refer to the so-called rupestral inscriptions, carved on living rock surfaces, found in various locations throughout Attica. Discovered in some cases quite some time ago but with increasing frequency in recent decades, with new finds undoubtedly still to be made, these *horoi* are sufficient in number to permit some definite conclusions.

Traill, in his 1986 publication *Demos and Trittys*, assembled and set out in tabular form the texts that had been published by that date.[44] While a few others have come to light since then,[45] Traill's tabulation will provide an adequate basis for the present discussion. The "Table of Attic Rupestral Deme Horoi" catalogs six assured series of texts (ranging from two to seven texts each) from six different locations and six "Other Possible Deme Horoi" (in five instances, single texts; in the other, a series of two).[46] All have been, or may be (in Traill's estimation), dated to the fourth century. Typically, the texts are found on land uninhabited in antiquity and often far removed from ancient population centers. This circumstance suggested to Traill that the *horoi* were placed at the borders of demes and, accordingly, must have served to mark those demes' boundaries. But the argument is taken further. Beyond the general need for the definition of boundaries, Traill suggests, on the basis of six of his twelve series of markers, that the *horoi* had come into existence in the train of the reorganization of 307/6 whereby a large number of demes, including those whose boundaries were marked by some of the six series, were taken out of their Kleisthenic phylai and assigned to one or the other of the two new "Macedonian" phylai, Antigonis and Demetrias.[47]

Two points regarding this analysis are in order. The first concerns the markers'

---

p. 226 as items a–e). None of these examples, however, is to be associated with a boundary of the deme itself. For the three *horoi* of the Kerameikos (the Potters' Quarter), *IG* II2 2617–2619, misinterpreted as pertaining to the deme Kerameis by Lauter 1982, p. 300, see Whitehead 1986, p. 29, note 109.

44. Traill 1986, pp. 116–122.

45. These include *IG* II2 13246 and 13247, reinterpreted by Langdon as marking a boundary between two properties (Langdon 1983, pp. 68–69). Four *horoi* of Roman imperial date from Mt. Hymettos published by J. Ober and interpreted as defining an apiary (Ober 1981, pp. 68–77) were referred instead by Langdon to the sorts of "public mountains" attested by *IG* II2 1035 (with line 58 mentioning Hymettos) (Langdon 1985a, pp. 257–260). The same inscriptions, however, had been suggested by Lauter to have marked a deme boundary (1982, p. 314). Also from Hymettos, three rupestral inscriptions, one reading ΟΡΟΣ ΔΙΑΝΟ, were identified by Eugene Vanderpool as markers for a conduit, the text being filled out as ὅρος διανό(μου) (Langdon 1985a, pp. 260–263, with supporting documentation). For still another *horos* from Hymettos, in this case from Hill 411.2, see Langdon 1985a, pp. 264–266. *Horoi* of Hadrianic or Antonine date from Vari were interpreted by Langdon to have marked the lands of the Zoterioi and of a certain "royal" property (Langdon 1988b, pp. 75–81). In none of these cases is a connection with deme boundaries sufficiently established to bear one way or the other on the findings of Traill's 1986 discussion (or upon my response to that discussion).

46. Traill 1986, p. 117.

47. For all the above points, see Traill 1986, p. 118. The six series involving demes moved to Macedonian phylai are nos. 1,2, 3, 4, 9?, and 10? Numbers 6 and 8, however, are positively excluded, while the four others remain doubtful.

specific locations. Traill noted that all of the series, with two exceptions, are situated on ridges and/or saddles in hilly terrain—and, so, he concluded, "they clearly served to mark boundaries."[48] Such a situation, however, seems to me a contradiction in terms. Are not ridges and saddles the very sorts of conspicuous, well-defined topographical features that, if they constituted a boundary between demes, would *not* have to be marked? The pattern of distribution becomes all the more unsettling when one considers the general absence of surviving markers of any kind from those areas—for instance, where a boundary presumably cut across a flat plain—lacking natural features of these kinds. But an explanation is at hand. Possibly the use of cairns, broached already by Langdon[49] and by Traill himself,[50] prevailed where no exposed horizontal surfaces of living rock were available. A loose pile of stones would stand little or no chance of surviving intact from antiquity to modern times. But the original unsettling paradox remains. Why mark a boundary that, in comparison with other (presumed) boundaries, seemingly required no artificial demarcation?

There is attraction to the view that, although these *horoi* may indeed have marked boundaries between demes, they were cut in those places only when special circumstances required them.[51] Stanton makes the attractive suggestion that the *horoi* were designed to demarcate grazing lands, but only on rare occasions when disputes arose.[52] The same principle could apply in any case where a citizen whose land was bounded by the limits of his (or of another) deme wished to mark that boundary. So, even in places where the boundary between demes was defined by a conspicuous topographical feature and there would normally have been no need for markers, such unusual conditions might well have required a more exact or more visible indication of the location of the line. But it is the underlying assumption that interests us here. Even the occasional or sporadic markings of boundaries could not have occurred unless such boundaries, whether recorded on papyrus in an archive or informally remembered and transmitted by custom, did indeed exist.

The second point has to do with Traill's association of the rupestral texts with reorganizations.[53] Why reorganizations? Again, as noted, six of the twelve series are certainly or possibly associated with demes transferred to either Antigonis or Demetrias in 307/6. But Traill's case is further reinforced by the fact that, of the series in question, as many as three pertain to two of the six sets of *divided* demes—namely, Upper and Lower Lamptrai (no. 1) and, possibly, Upper and Lower Potamos (nos. 3 and 9). As it happens, by far the clearer evidence (with regard to the identification of the demes in question) pertains to the two Lamptrai demes, and it is

48. Traill 1986, p. 118.
49. Langdon 1985b, p. 9 with notes 13 and 14.
50. Traill 1986, p. 118. Traill here is specifically concerned with the intervals between (rupestral) *horoi*, where no exposed flat natural rock was at hand.
51. As suggested by Langdon 1985b, p. 10.
52. Stanton 1984, pp. 299, 304–305. Besides the general point, Stanton attempts to add to the record of markers explicitly linked with a specific deme the texts from the Thiti ridge, which he identifies as *horoi* of (the deme) Pambotadai (pp. 300–301). For the difficulties with this reading, however, see Langdon 1988b, p. 49, note 26 (pp. 49–50).
53. Traill 1986, p. 118.

in connection with this series that Traill, in his 1982 publication, made his initial case for the reorganization hypothesis.[54] The claim is that the reallocation of Upper Lamptrai to the new phyle Antigonis would have necessitated the marking of the boundary between it and Lower Lamptrai, which remained in Erechtheis. To do justice to the case, Traill's own words must be cited: The markers, he writes, are located "where a question of territorial jurisdiction could easily arise." With the transfer of Upper Lamptrai, again, "the tribal discrepancy of the two sections may well have caused local problems." After the creation of the new phylai and the deme transfers, "it was felt necessary, perhaps because of a local boundary dispute, or for whatever reason, to define precisely the topographical division between the Erechtheid and Antigonid Lamptrai."[55]

I wish to question the *limitation* of the function of the *horoi* to just this—or to any other such—reorganization. My objections may be illustrated by reference to Traill's own key example, the Lamptrai demes, the rupestral *horoi* from which are reproduced in Fig. 2.1. For one thing, in contrast with an assumption latent in Traill's argumentation, it is evident from Eliot's discussion of these settlements that a need to define the boundary between the two demes would have been present from the time of their creation (entailing, necessarily, their division), presumably by Kleisthenes in 508/7. The deme communities situated at modern Lambrika (identified as Upper Lamptrai) and Kitsi Pigadi (identified as Lower Lamptrai), Eliot argued, were the result of a division of a *single* settlement, which had once dominated the entire area.[56] The pre-Kleisthenic unity of the settlement would of course account for the sharing of a single name by the two demes. But even with the splitting of the community, the line dividing them remained, socially speaking, ill-defined as a consequence not only of their shared name but also of their close proximity and easy mutual communications. Most graphically, the need for a boundary is pointed up by the fact that even after the division had been accomplished, citizens of the two demes were not regularly distinguished as hailing from one or the other, rather both groups were simply called "Lamptrians."[57] Such conditions could well have necessitated the definition, and marking, of the boundary between the two demes on an on-going basis, quite apart from the fallout of any reallocation of one of the two to a different phyle, and, indeed, whether at any time they belonged to the same or to two different phylai. Yet, on Traill's reconstruction, the people of the two communities would have waited for two centuries after the creation of the democracy to mark their common boundary.

54. Traill 1982, pp. 162–171; cf. 1986, pp. 116–118. Earlier, the group of texts was published by Eliot 1962, pp. 63–64 and map, fig. 5, p. 57. For a possible seventh inscription, see Traill 1982, p. 168, note 22.

55. Traill 1982, pp. 165 (first quotation), 168 (second and third quotations).

56. Eliot 1962, pp. 53–55. For the "single settlement," see p. 55; and, for a later visit to the sites, Pritchett 1965, pp. 138–140. Eliot's assignments (which have been generally accepted by scholars) were challenged by Lauter, who placed Lower Lamptrai, not at Kitsi, but at Vari (where most scholars had situated Anagyrous) (Lauter 1982, pp. 299–315). But the traditional assignments have been defended in detail by Langdon 1988a, pp. 43–54 and esp. 47–50.

57. Eliot 1962, p. 53. See also Traill 1982, pp. 164–165, 166; and Whitehead 1986, p. 21, note 72. Two notable instances of documents wherein the "Lamptrians" are not distinguished as belonging to one or the other deme are *IG* II² 1204 (fin. s. IV), lines 2–3 and 15–17; and 2967 (med. s. IV), line 1.

Figure 2.1. Rupestral inscriptions from demes of Upper and Lower Lamptrai. After Traill 1982, pl. 21, courtesy the American School of Classical Studies at Athens.

Traill (and Langdon[58]) may yet be proved right, but the position must be supported by argument showing that a reorganization created *a special need* for boundary markers. No such need appears forthcoming. The "transfer" of a deme from one phyle to another existed only "on paper" (or, in the ancient case, papyrus or stone); it was an event of no practical significance or consequences where boundaries were concerned. True, demesmen of Upper Lamptrai will have found themselves marching in a new phyletic regiment, serving with a different board of prytaneis, and so

58. Langdon (1988a, p. 50) offered the same explanation with respect to the two markers, one published by Lauter (*SEG* 32.230), the other discovered by Langdon himself, on the ridge separating the territory of Halai Aixonides from that of Vari (traditionally identified as Anagyrous).

on, but I see no basis for the sorts of "local problems" or "boundary disputes" hypothesized by Traill. Administratively speaking, if the silence of the epigraphic record tells us anything, demes and the trittyes and phylai of which they were components seem to have had little, if anything, to do with each other. Why, then, upon the transference of a deme from one phyle to another suddenly label a previously unlabled boundary?

The positive effect of this negative argument is, finally, to underscore the more enduring need of precise boundaries for the demes with reference not to phylai but to each other. The six sets of divided demes, in particular, may well have been in special need of the formal demarcation of their borders.[59]

Localizing Properties with Reference to a Deme. Not infrequently, locations are specified in Athenian inscriptions with reference to the name of a deme, often in the locative case. Thompson, while acknowledging the phenomenon and admitting it as evidence that "[t]he demes were unquestionably local units,"[60] denied that the listing of a piece of property localized in this fashion proved that the deme in question had "exact boundaries."[61] Langdon took the opposing view, remarking that, in the absence of such boundaries, the habitual references to land by deme locations would be "meaningless and open to disputes."[62] Now, it is important to realize the respect in which Langdon's brief statement is true—and therefore confirms the theory of exact boundaries. His discussion concerns *land*, and a piece of land will of course often lie well outside the nucleated settlement of the deme, inevitably on occasion somewhere in the uninhabited spaces lying between it and neighboring demes. Accordingly, the specification of such a property's location *at* (or *in*) *Halai*, for example, would indeed be lacking in meaning and disputable were there no boundaries. But, in fairness to Thompson's judgment, it is likewise true that the same argument would *not* apply to a building or other property within or adjacent to the village center proper.

The Enktetikon. In further support of his position, Langdon adduced *IG* II² 1214 (ca. 300–250), a decree of the demesmen of Peiraieus honoring a citizen of another deme, Cholleidai. The honors include exemption from paying the ἐγκτητικόν (lines 25–28), a tax imposed on land within the deme owned by nondemesmen. Langdon argued[63] that, unless the demes had been defined by official boundaries, circumstances might arise in which it would not be clear to which deme a given piece of property belonged and so which deme was entitled to collect the tax. What if a parcel of land lay equidistant between the village centers of two different demes? The inference appears unavoidable.

---

59. See Traill 1975, pp. 123–128, app. D, "The Homonymous and Divided Demes." Whereas the two demes of each homonymous pair had, according to Traill, no geographical connection, the divided demes in three of the six known cases were "obviously very closely related geographically" (p. 123). Besides the two Lamptrai demes, the others were Upper and Lower Paiania and Upper and Lower Potamos.

60. Thompson 1971, p. 72 with note 1.

61. Thompson 1971, p. 73, note 3.

62. Langdon 1985b, p. 8.

63. Langdon 1985b, p. 8.

But there is more to be won from this text. No deme other than Peiraieus is known to have imposed just this tax. Of course, if the truth were known, it could be that all demes collected the *enktetikon* and that it is only by accident of preservation that we learn of its existence at Peiraieus. Yet the tax could also for all we know be peculiar to Peiraieus, a possibility quite in keeping with the marked particularity of the Attic demes as a whole.[64] If this were so, there could be significance in the fact that it is from just this deme alone that we have a boundary marker in the form of a *horos* monument (*IG* II² 2623, discussed above). Peiraieus, let me suggest, erected this *horos* (and probably others like it) precisely in order to enforce the collection of a uniquely Peiraic tax on properties owned by non-*demotai*. A great many Athenians had migrated to the port town to seek their fortune,[65] and the demesmen may have been alert to the possibility of exploiting this potential source of public revenue. The Peiraieis would thus have had a special reason to *mark* their boundaries but obviously could not have done so unless Peiraieus, and therefore all the demes, were already defined by precise boundaries.

With this fresh look at evidence already adduced by others in support of the deme as a block of territory, let us turn to additional, thus far unexploited material bearing on the question.

Isolated Farms and Unassigned Nucleated Settlements. The notion of the "nucleated" village as the precursor to Kleisthenes' demes is essential to Thompson's theory that no boundaries were needed for the demes, since only if all Athenians lived in such settlements would it have been possible for the reformer simply to order each citizen to proceed to what he (and others) knew to be his "home" village and to register.[66] The compact village model would also be a necessary requirement for the ongoing stability of a Thompsonian deme without boundaries following the new organization's creation. For if citizens of a given deme lived, not in a recognized deme center, but near the lands of neighboring demes, questions of various kinds would inevitably arise where the properties of the members of two or more demes met. Thompson himself, however, did not make the case for the nucleated deme settlement. Rather that task was to be taken up by Robin Osborne in his 1985 book *Demos: The Discovery of Classical Attica* and, that same year, in a companion article devoted to an examination of the evidence, chiefly epigraphic, for isolated buildings or other structures in the ancient Greek countryside. The book affirmed the existence, and predominance, of the nucleated village; the article concluded that, although isolated structures were to be found in the Greek (and specifically, the Attic) countryside, they were generally not occupied by their owners.[67]

64. This possibility has already been broached by Whitehead 1986, pp. 76, note 38, and 150.

65. As an index of the migration of citizens into Peiraieus, one could adduce what evidence survives of the presence in the deme of metics, themselves by definition migrators from elsewhere (or their descendants). According to Whitehead 1986, pp. 83–84, of the 366 metics of known deme affiliation, 69, or almost 19 percent of the total, are affiliated with Peiraieus. This is a very high number, second only to the 75 of Melite, an urban deme situated within the city circuit wall.

66. Thompson 1971, p. 74: "If living conditions in archaic Attika resembled those of modern times, then almost all the rural folk lived in villages; only a few farms and estates were isolated."

67. Osborne 1985b, ch. 2, "The Pattern of Settlement of Classical Attika," pp. 15–46; Osborne 1985a, with p. 126 for the conclusion.

Despite the initial attraction of the model (for one thing, it conforms to the predominant settlement pattern of modern Greece), it is fair to say, I think, that the case has not been well made. To be sure, many, probably most, rural Athenians did live in villages, but the conflicting indications are too numerous to accept Osborne's conclusions without qualification. Some potentially nonconforming evidence is cited, while subjected to interpretation minimizing its significance, by Osborne himself.[68] But the most telling counterarguments have been set out by Langdon, whose succinct statement on the farm in classical Attica convincingly reviews and (in answer to Osborne) reinterprets the lexical, epigraphic, literary, and archaeological evidence confirming the existence of isolated farmsteads.[69]

Langdon's critique does not link his finding with the problem about the existence or nonexistence of precise boundaries, but it is obvious that it has pertinence to that problem, above all with reference to the procedure followed by Kleisthenes upon the creation of the new public organization. Given occupied farmsteads scattered (even if only thinly) over the Attic countryside, *some* mechanism would have been necessary in order to assign one farmer to this deme and his immediate neighbor to another. No more attractive candidate for such a mechanism has been proposed than a system of exact boundary lines.

The Metics. For the last I have reserved an item of special significance for our topic, the metics. According to generally accepted opinion, metics, free persons of foreign origin or extraction officially domiciled in Attica, were not, like Athenian citizens, in any sense members of a deme association. Rather, in the place of the *demotikon,* metics were officially designated as οἰκῶν (or οἰκοῦσα) ἐν (name of deme), that is, not with reference to an hereditary affiliation with a deme association but with reference to their place of residence in a deme. Most scholars, including the author of the latest comprehensive account, David Whitehead, have maintained that, as the formulation "living in . . ." suggests, this affiliation was meant to be literally significant and that, consequently, if a metic changed residence from one deme to another, the affiliation changed accordingly.[70]

This is where boundaries of the demes come in. Were demes not defined by precise boundaries, how could the metic or anyone else have known with certainty to which deme he or she belonged? The question was not without practical conse-

---

68. Some of this evidence emerges in his detailed overviews of archaeological explorations of two specific regions, that in and around modern Vari and Vouliagmeni and that of the demes Sounion and Thorikos (1985b, pp. 22–36). The remainder is collected in an appendix to his book, the evidence falling into two classes: (A) "Isolated farms in classical and Hellenistic Athens" and, under (B) "Remains of nucleated settlement in Attika," a subsection entitled "archaeological remains indicative of nucleated settlement but which cannot be surely identified with any ancient deme" (1985b, pp. 190–191, 194–195). To the latter group could be added such tiny hamlets as Thyrgonidai, Titakidai, and others, which, having failed to acquire separate status as independent demes, evidently marched with their much larger neighbor, Aphidna (see Whitehead 1986, p. 24 with note 83; Traill 1975, pp. 87–91, under "The Late Roman Demes," "[a] Association with Aphidna").

69. Langdon 1990–1991, pp. 209–213.

70. On the question, see Whitehead 1977, pp. 72–74; cf. 1986, pp. 82–83. However, despite the plausibility of the inference, there is not a single conclusive instance of the phenomenon. An early dissenter from the *communis opinio* was Wilamowitz, followed in part by Clerc: see Whitehead 1977, p. 73.

quences. Enrollment of some kind in one deme or another was probably required,[71] but which deme? Metics paid a poll tax, possibly to a deme,[72] but (again) to which deme? Similarly, metics served in the military, but with which demesmen, if any, would they be mustered?[73] And much to the point here, at least one deme, Skambonidai, expressly allowed for participation by metics in its religious celebrations.[74] This implies, as Whitehead noted, that that deme had some method of determining which metics were (or were not) eligible for such participation.[75] What was that method?

Exact boundaries, perhaps but not necessarily marked by monuments of some kind, would have decided every such question about affiliation, since every metic, as implied by the formula "living in . . . ," presumably maintained a residence.[76] Thus boundaries would have been required wherever metics dwelled, particularly if in areas lying midway between village centers or, more to the point (since most metics were urban dwellers), in the densely populated urban area. Since the *asty* within the walls was partitioned among no fewer than five demes, the limits of a given deme would have to be determinable with precision. Fortunately, this requirement has been met by Langdon's persuasive reconstruction of the intramural deme boundaries, which he believes were formed by the city walls, the Akropolis, the Agora, and streets (including the Panathenaic Way).[77] The second main concentration of metics was in Peiraieus. Again, we think of that solitary *horos* stone. Is its survival a mere accident, or is it to be connected with a special need to define the limits of Peiraieus's obligation to, or claims upon, its large resident alien population?

If I am right, metic participation in a deme was organized not, as in the case of the citizen *demotai*, on a personal basis with reference to descent, but on a territorial basis with respect to place of residence within the precisely defined spatial limits of the deme.

71. Rolls of metics, whether, at the deme level, incorporated into the citizen *lexiarchikon grammateion* or separate from it or, at the state level, in the form of a central register (perhaps housed in the office of the polemarch, as Diller thought), are usually assumed, but there is no direct evidence. See, for discussion, Whitehead 1977, p. 75.

72. See, on the *metoikion*, Whitehead 1977, pp. 75–77. The procedure for the payment of the tax is unknown. Metics may have paid in their demes or at some central point. Whitehead favors "a central payment and record point" (p. 77).

73. See, on metic military service, Whitehead 1977, pp. 82–86. But the organization of demesmen, not to mention the metics resident within a given deme, for military purposes is far from clear. With regard to hoplite service, Whitehead in his later book favored Wyse (1904, p. 268, on Isaios, 2.42) in assuming that "members of the same deme were kept together as far as was practicable" (1986, p. 225). But no subdivision of the Athenian army based on, or called after, the deme is attested. Nor, with regard to the navy, is a role for the deme, official or otherwise, indicated (1986, pp. 133–134). Accordingly, my point, that metics resident in a given deme were in some way organized alongside citizen military personnel of the same deme, is admittedly conjectural. Another complicating factor is the "segregated units" of metics championed by Whitehead (1977, p. 83), but even this arrangement would not absolutely preclude a connection with the demes.

74. *IG* I³ 244 (= I² 188), ca. 460, lines C 6–9.

75. Whitehead 1986, p. 81.

76. The implication of the existence of a residence is not of course precluded by the prohibition on *ownership* of "land and house."

77. Langdon 1985b, pp. 11–13.

It remains to consider briefly two indirect categories of evidence. Both afford slight contributing indications in support of the theory of the territorial deme.

Evidence of Prehistoric Antecedents. The Linear B tablets, as noted above, prove that the word *damos* occurred in the Mycenaean dialect of Greek. Whitehead, exploring the uses of the word before Kleisthenes, speculated that the Attic technical term "deme," in the sense of "a local community living on its own land," had descended from the Mycenaean word. To support this claim he cited the glossary definition from Ventris and Chadwick, *Documents in Mycenaean Greek* (2d edition, Cambridge 1973): "an entity which allocates holdings of land, probably a village community."[78] Already, however, Chadwick, in a work first published in 1976, anticipating (in reverse form) Whitehead's suggestion, had specifically noted the Attic sense of *demos* as a local administrative district and (partly on this basis, thereby deriving the prehistoric from the classical meaning) had proposed that Mycenaeans at Pylos had already used the term to designate the sixteen administrative districts of the Pylian kingdom (and, hence, the people of such a district collectively).[79] Admittedly, to use Chadwick's formulation as a basis for establishing the nature of the Kleisthenic deme would involve circularity of the most obvious kind. But the fact remains that, if these Pylian "districts" were geographical entities, and if the Mycenaean word *damos* was used to designate them, then that term, if transmitted to the Athenians of the historical period and used by Kleisthenes, may likewise have denoted a territorial entity, whatever other qualities an Attic deme may have possessed.

Non-Athenian Contemporary Public Organizations. Outside Athens, the term "deme" enjoyed a wide distribution as a public unit.[80] It is exported, first, by the Athenians to their cleruchies (and possessions), but these are not new demes but mere extensions of the Athenian home units brought about by the relocation of Athenian citizens to overseas sites.[81] So in these several cases the question of a "boundary" did not of course arise. Elsewhere, secondly, the term is attached to units of mostly independent local origin, but, despite links in several instances with villages or other topographical features, it is again not possible on present evidence to point to a single instance of the term "deme" designating a well-defined block of territory. The total absence of surviving *horoi* in all these states is particularly striking.[82] No support, in short, can be found for a strictly territorial Athenian deme in those non-Athenian organizations making use of "deme" as a technical term.

But "deme" is, of course, not the only Greek word that might be used to denote

---

78. Whitehead 1986, p. 367.

79. Chadwick 1976, pp. 76–77. Whitehead (loc. cit.) acknowledges this discussion, but puts it to a use quite different from mine.

80. For a list of the states known to have possessed demes, with references to my discussions, see Jones 1987, index I. A. 3 (p. 387).

81. For the cleruchies and possessions, see the reference in note 38 above to my index entry in *Public Organization*, where the particulars will be found under "Athens."

82. See my discussion at 1987, p. 6.

a territorial segment of a city-state. Eight, possibly nine, others seem, according to the apparent literal significance of the word, to indicate the existence of territorial units in organizations outside Athens.[83] These include ἄμφοδον (compound of *amphi*, "around," and *hodos*, "street"), τόνος (based on *teinein*, "extend," presumably with reference to boundaries), and χῶρος ("place"), among others.[84] What was possible at Smyrna, Tenos, or Eretria was certainly possible at Athens.

Finally, it will become clear by the end of chapter 4 that, if my reconstruction of the sources is correct, the full emergence of the territorial deme and its eventual domination over the "personal" constitutional deme were the end product of a lengthy process of development that did not reach its climax until the Hellenistic period. It is appropriate to note, accordingly, that inscriptions of the Roman era from Nikomedeia and Nikaia in Bithynia preserve formulas, attached to personal names (and, interestingly, paralleling the designation of metics in Athens), of the form "residing in the phyle Sebastê" (Nikaia).[85] So, by this late date, citizens could be enrolled in a public unit membership in which was determined by place of residence. The question is whether or not the beginnings of this process of territorialization can, as I am suggesting, be traced to the classical age in Athens.

From this wide-ranging array of evidence, it is fair to conclude that the case for a territorial deme, when "deme" is understood as a block of territory defined by precise boundaries (whether ever marked or not), has been well made. Nor, it may be added, does any of this evidence, or any other evidence not considered here, in any way militate *against* such a territorial deme.[86] Silence (i.e., the general absence of physical remains of markers), in particular, is easily accounted for. Again, the boundaries may have been set out and a record of them entered in a local or centralized register.[87] Cairns could easily have disintegrated or been dismantled when no longer useful. Formal *horoi* may have been reused or burnt for lime; and some may, as Langdon perceptively speculated, survive undetected among the several markers, inscribed simply ὅρος, that were discovered and brought to Athens without record of their provenience.[88] Any number of markers may remain to be discovered. But the positive indicators just reviewed speak clearly and emphatically. The existence of the territorially bounded deme may be taken as assured.

83. For the list, see Jones 1987, index I. B. 2, p. 388.

84. For the states at which the units are found, with full discussion of sources, chronology, etc., see Jones 1987, index I. A, s.v., pp. 387–388.

85. See Jones 1987, ch. 8, secs. 3 and 4, pp. 350–352; cf. introd., p. 5, number (iv).

86. Two literary passages, much discussed in the context of the present topic, Strabo 1.4.7 [65] and a scholion on Aristophanes, *Birds* 997, do indeed imply the absence of *markers* but in no way suggest that demes were not defined by boundaries. See, for discussion, Thompson 1971, pp. 73–74, with note 13 [74]; and Langdon 1985b, p. 13.

87. The scholion on Aristophanes, *Birds* 997, with reference to the question of the identity of the deme in which the area behind the Long Stoa was situated, appeals to "The *Horismoi* of the Polis." Langdon takes this as evidence that "written records were kept of *urban* deme boundaries" (Langdon 1985b, p. 13; italics mine). But the use of the term *polis* (rather than, say, *asty*) leaves open the possibility that the boundaries of all the demes, urban *and* rural, were so recorded.

88. Langdon 1985b, p. 9. Examples can be found among *IG* I² 874–896.

The Territorial Deme

"The Residents"

If indeed a "territorial" deme, distinct from the personal hereditary constitutional deme, was formally recognized, we should expect to find some trace of its existence or functioning in the official records of the deme associations. What do I mean by "trace"? The boundaries, marked or otherwise, by themselves tell us very little. If they were used only to mark the location of parcels of land, mines, buildings, etc., their significance for the organization of the population of Attica would be, as I stated above, practically nil. Nor would our awareness of the mere presence (or activity) of some of the members of the putative deme within those boundaries tell us anything, because that presence (or activity) may not for all we know have been a function of membership in that deme. My claim in fact involves much more than simply a spatially bounded deme or the accidental presence or activity of people within it. To wit, it will be argued here, and again in chapter 4, that this second "territorial" deme was a fully fledged association, coexisting side by side with its counterpart, the Kleisthenic deme of the *demotai* defined by descent. Now, if this were all true, surely the facts would have betrayed themselves somewhere in the more than 150 documents at our disposal. Happily, this is, I believe, the case.

The evidence to which I refer is, in the first instance, the use on several occasions in our documents of the comprehensive phrase "the residents," οἱ οἰκοῦν-τες. The occurrence of the phrase in close context with the doings of the constitutional deme at once raises the possibility that those persons enjoyed a significant relationship with that deme. As will become apparent, explicit or implicit acknowledgment is usually made of the fact that "the residents" are distinct from the citizen *demotai* of the deme in two critical respects. First, and obviously, because they are residents of a particular deme and not another, they differ from others like themselves with respect to deme of domicile. Secondly, and to the present point, because in the context of the document-producing deme they are expressly distinguished from the *demotai* (Eleusinioi, Rhamnousioi, et al.), they differ in respect to their status. My specific reasons for supposing that "the residents" were so different will emerge from the discussion of the several instances of the formula below. But for now let it be noted that the term "the residents" itself provides an obvious, more general clue. For it immediately brings to mind the metics, since they were officially designated, as we noted, not by the *demotikon* reserved for citizens, but by the participial phrase οἰκῶν/οἰκοῦσα ἐν . . . .(name of deme). The metics of a given deme might therefore be collectively, and appropriately, included among a non-*demotai* population termed οἱ οἰκοῦντες. So, it is probable, on these as well as on the more detailed grounds argued below, that at least some of these non-*demotai* were resident aliens. But not all of them. Several of the texts discussed below specify that "the residents" are *politai*, that is, citizens of other demes resident in the deme in question.

Nonetheless, despite the variation, the formula remains constant, and in this fact we have a hint that we are dealing with an official statewide policy, emanating from the central government and transcending the particularistic practices of any of the few demes for which the formula is attested.[89] Let us review a selection of examples.[90]

The Texts

Ikarion: IG I³ 254 (= I²187) (ca. 440–415?), lines 3–4. Near the beginning of this decree of the Ikarians, the fragmentary Greek text appears to call for the selection(?) of two *choregoi* from the *demotai* and from another group at Ikarion, in both cases from among those who had not previously served in the *choregia.* Regrettably, the crucial words of the text in lines 3 to 4 identifying the second, non-*demotai* group are almost entirely lost. Lewis, accepting the restoration of Wilamowitz reproduced in *IG* I², printed the critical words as follows: [..⁵..]ι τὸν δεμοτὸν καὶ τὸν Ἰκα[ριοῖ οἰκόντ]/[ον δύο] τὸν ἀχορεγέτον . . . . , with the evident meaning "two (*choregoi*) from among the *demotai* and from among those residing at Ikarion who had not served as *choregoi* previously."

Whitehead understandably takes the non-*demotai* people "residing at Ikarion" to be Athenian citizen residents.[91] But this conjecture is somewhat undercut by the fact that the one other known instance of a non-*demotes choregos* is a foreigner, namely, the Theban who bankrolled two choruses (boys' and men's) for Eleusis a century later (*IG* II² 1186, lines 1–35). Supporting Whitehead's position, however, is the fact that the names of later Ikarian *choregoi* appear without either *demotikon* or *ethnikon,* from which he inferred that they were in fact Ikarieis, that is, citizens.[92] Another point (one not made by Whitehead himself) that militates against the identification of the non-Ikarieis as foreigners is the fact that not a single resident of Ikarion can be identified among the known metics.[93] The location of Ikarion, the site of which is illustrated in Fig. 2.2, in the rural region beyond Pentelikon may have rendered it unattractive for settlement by *metoikoi,* who overwhelmingly preferred to establish residence in the urban sectors of the city center or port town of Peiraieus.[94] Whitehead's conjecture, in sum, appears well justified. These ["residents"], if the restoration is correct, would be citizen non-*demotai* domiciled in Ikarion.

The two-deme model may also, in this particular case, help clear up a longstanding difficulty of interpretation connected with a second decree of the deme, *IG* II² 1178 (ante med. s. IV). Following the injunction to praise Nikon the demarch, the decree calls for the herald "to announce that the Ikarieis are crowning Nikon and that the Demos of the Ikarieis (is crowning) the demarch" (lines 1–6). Why are there *two* honoring parties, and what is their identity? According to Kirchner's note, Buck, the original editor, had found a distinction between *gentiles* and *demotae;*

89. The distinction is well discussed by Whitehead 1986, pp. 56–63 under the rubric "Methodology."
90. I consider here only texts offering some clue as to the composition of "the residents." Additional texts containing the phrase will be considered in the review of the decrees of Eleusis and Rhamnous in "The Garrison Demes Eleusis and Rhamnous," in chapter 4.
91. Whitehead 1986, p. 152, note 11.
92. Whitehead 1986, p. 216.
93. For a tabulation by deme of metics of known deme affiliation, see Whitehead 1986, pp. 82–85.
94. See Whitehead 1986, pp. 83–84. Almost 61 percent of the metics with known deme affiliation are from urban and suburban Athens and almost another 19 percent from Peiraieus.

Figure 2.2. Site of deme of Ikarion. [Top] After excavations of 1880: Junction of walls E and F and choregic inscription. [Bottom] After cleaning in 1981: Pythion from the northwest. *Hesperia* 51 (1982), pl. 2a and 6b, both courtesy the American School of Classical Studies at Athens.

and, along these same lines, Lewis suggested that the Ikarieis were a phratry and stood to the Demos of the Ikarieis as the (on his interpretation, phratry) Dekeleeis stood to the deme Dekeleia.[95] But our reading of *IG* I³ 254 opens up a new possibility, that the two groups are in fact the territorial and hereditary constitutional demes, respectively. Appropriately, the herald will announce that the constitutional deme crowns its *demarch* (as in the fragmentary *IG* II² 1179), while to the non-*demotai* residents he will be known simply by his given name (lines 4–6). If I am right, this text represents the sole official explicit acknowledgment of the proposed two-deme organization of Attica.

However this difficulty is resolved, the earlier text from Ikarion is of crucial importance for my argument, because, if (again) Wilamowitz's restoration continues to be accepted, it establishes the official recognition by a deme of non-*demotai* "residents" prior to the first recorded establishment of garrisons on Attic soil beginning late in the fifth century. These garrisons, whose encampments were sometimes placed within the boundaries of one deme or another, on several occasions, and with increasing frequency, joined with their host *demotai* in authorizing decrees in the name of the deme. (Eventually, as we shall see in chapter 4, the troops will issue decrees in their own names, without reference to the deme organization.) The problem is that all the remaining documentary examples of our phrase οἱ οἰκοῦντες κτλ. derive from just two of those few demes—namely Eleusis and Rhamnous—in which such garrisons are known to have been stationed. The suspicion arises, accordingly, that those "residing" in the deme are in fact soldiers and that therefore we are not dealing with a general feature of deme life and procedure across all or most of Attica, but with an atypical set of circumstances created by the extraordinary imposition of large numbers of nondemesmen or even foreign noncitizens upon a deme population.

But in opposition to any such conclusion let me offer, preliminarily to my discussion of the relevant texts themselves, the following considerations supportive of my position:

- The fact that in the following texts the phrase "the residents" occurs in contexts certainly or probably unrelated to any discernible military matter
- The existence of a relatively large number of known metics not otherwise identified as soldiers at Eleusis (but not at Rhamnous), a fact that opens up the possibility that "the residents" may in fact be these nonmilitary resident aliens
- The usual (though not invariable) designation of acknowledged *soldiers* in these (and other) inscriptions not (so far as we can tell) by the phrase "the residents" but by such formulaic phrases as "the men stationed in the fort"
- Decisively, I think, in the Eleusinian decree *IG* II² 1305 (fin. s. III?), lines 2–4, the juxtaposition of, and evident contrast between, two distinct decreeing parties, το[ῖς] τε[τ]αγμένοις Ἐλευσ[ῖ]νι κτλ (i.e., the soldiers) and τοῖς ο[ἰ]κοῦσιν τῶμ π[ο]λ[ιτῶ]/[ν] Ἐλευσῖνι (i.e., resident citizen non-*demotai*). The distinction in evidence here, to wit, between soldiers on the

95. Lewis 1963, p. 32, note 93. Buck (1886–1890, pp. 7, 101–102) in styling the "Ikarians" a "gens," had anticipated Lewis's comparison with the Dekeleian case.

one hand and mere residents who are not soldiers on the other, was strangely rejected by Pouilloux, but on insufficient grounds.[96]

Eleusis: IG *II²* 1186 (med. s. IV), lines 1–5. "Since Damasias, son of Dionysios, of Thebes [the Theban just mentioned above], while residing at Eleusis (οἰ[κ]/[ήσ]ας Ἐλευσῖνι, cf. lines 37–38), has continued being civic-minded and is well-disposed . . . toward all those residing in the deme (πάντ/[α]ς τοὺς ἐν τõι δήμοι οἰκοῦντας, lines 4–5)." Possibly the fact that the honorand was himself a foreigner inclined him toward the generous treatment of other outsiders. But this assumption brings us no closer to identifying "all those residing in the deme." One clue, however, is at hand from another quarter. Ten metics from Eleusis are known—the eighth highest figure for the 139 demes.[97] Possibly the Sanctuary of Demeter and Kore and its well-attended Mysteries, which undoubtedly offered commercial opportunities for the enterprising, prompted non-Eleusinians to relocate to the deme. So here, and in the Eleusinian decrees that follow, our phrase may represent the presence of substantial numbers of non-*demotai*, not necessarily only Athenian citizens but perhaps including metics and even foreigners as well.

Note, furthermore, the emphasis in this text on the element of residence in the deme—twice with reference to Damasias (and to his fellow Theban Phrynichos) and a third time with reference to the beneficiaries of his largess. I take this phenomenon as a sign of the emerging ascendancy of territorialism over the erstwhile prevailing principle of descent. Damasias's residence in the deme (as opposed to, say, residence in Thebes) elevates him to membership in the community. The beneficiaries are the residents of the deme, including presumably non-*demotai* and excluding Eleusinian demesmen resident elsewhere. This is a community based on propinquity of domicile, not upon inherited constitutional identity irrespective of locale.

Eleusis: IG *II²1191* (321/0 or 318/7), lines 19–20.This decree of Ἐλευσ[ινί]ων [τῶι δήμωι] / [κα]ὶ Ἀθηναίο[ι]ς [τοῖς ἐν τῆι φυλ]/[α]κῆ[ι] honors a nondemesman, Xenokles, son of Xeinis, of Sphettos[98] (line 10), for benefiting parties who are resident in the deme but who are not necessarily to be identified as *demotai*. To wit, elected epimelete of the Mysteries, Xenokles, among other good deeds, constructed at his own expense a stone bridge "in order that the rites—as well as the festival of Greeks arriving at Eleusis and at the sanctuary—be conducted well and safely, and in order that the people residing in the suburb (οἱ τὸ προάστ/ιον

96. Pouilloux 1954, p. 121 on no. 8 (= *IG* II² 3467, Rhamnous). His first point, that elsewhere the "residents" are expressly identified as soldiers (see below, and chapter 4 of this work, for references and discussion), is invalid, since usage elsewhere, whether at Eleusis or (needless to say) in another deme (viz., Rhamnous), does not dictate the meaning of the phrase in the text under discussion. The other, contrasting occurrences of the phrase merely show that it had more than one possible use or referent. His second point, that the formulation "the residents of the citizens" is, without further qualification, too vague to bear the sense of "civilian residents," both ignores the present context and is unnecessarily subjective.

97. For the figures, see Whitehead 1986, p. 83.

98. For the identification, see *PA* 11234; *IG* II² 1191, commentary; Davies, *APF*, pp. 414–415; and Ch. Habicht, *Hesperia* 57 (1988) 323–327.

οἰκοῦν[τ]ε[ς] and the farmers be secured" (lines 15–21). Who were the people "residing in the suburb?" To consider the seemingly obvious possibility, might they be *demotai* and only *demotai*? This is highly unlikely. If this were so, we should expect "the Eleusinians residing in the suburb." Such phrasing would seem required in view of the fact, just mentioned, that not a few metics are known to be residents of the deme and since the "Athenians in the garrison" (partly restored) who join the Eleusinians in authorizing the decree (lines 3–5) must include non-Eleusinian Athenian citizens. Clearly, given a mixed population such as this, "the people residing in the suburb" could not be assumed necessarily to be Eleusinian *demotai*.

Besides, nothing else about Xenokles or his benefaction suggests a narrow focus upon the constitutional deme, strictly defined as the *demotai*. The reference in lines 23–24 to δ[η]μόσι/α . . . χρ[ή]ματα pertains, not to the deme, but to the Demos of the Athenians whose funds, the decree states, he handled "with justice" in the past and so handles now (i.e., evidently with reference to the bridge, his own expenditure presumably being only an advance against future reimbursement, lines 22–23). Without question, the cult of the Two Goddesses and the Mysteries (lines 11–12) are pan-Athenian; and the law cited in lines 7–10 calls for the addition to the decree of the honorand's benefactions to the *polis* (i.e., *not* to the particular segment of the state involved in conferring the honors, the deme of Eleusis). In such a context, an exclusive concern with the Eleusinian demesmen would not be expected. These "residents," therefore, almost certainly include persons other than Eleusinian *demotai*.

Eleusis: SEG 22.127 (IG II² 1219 + 1288) (ca. med. s. III), lines 13–14, 22. This acephalous decree (line 24) of the "Eleusinians and those of the Athenians residing at Eleusis" cites the honorand's efforts to ensure the "safety of the territory" (line 12, entirely restored) and "of the citizens living in it" (τῶν οἰκούν[των ἐν αὐτῶι πολιτῶ]/ν, lines 13–14). Near the end of the preserved text, the so-called manifesto clause, as restored, terms the honoring parties [. . .᾿Ελευσίνιοι καὶ]/ οἱ οἰ[κ]οῦν- τες ᾿Ελε[υσῖνι ᾿Αθηναίων . . .] (lines 21–22). Thus, as expected, the beneficiaries and the honoring parties are one and the same. Significantly, however, the phrase in lines 13–14 compresses into a single expression the two complementary and mutually exclusive components identified in the "manifesto," namely, the Eleusinians (the *demotai*) and the resident Athenians from all the other demes. The phrase "those of the citizens living in it" (i.e., the deme) thus partially embodies the two conceptions of the deme, personal and territorial, that I am advocating, but only partially since the latter component excludes noncitizen residents such as metics and foreigners. Again, we note a movement away from the descent group, strictly defined, and in the direction of a community defined by common residence.

Eleusis: SEG 25.155 (236/5), lines 13–14. See below.

Eleusis: IG II² 1305 (fin. s. III?), lines 2–4. On the juxtaposition of, and contrast between, the two decreeing parties, "the men encamped at Eleusis" and "those of the citizens residing at Eleusis," see above. The stone is from Eleusis, but by this late date the constitutional deme is no longer in the picture. The triumph of the principle of territoriality is now complete.

Rhamnous: IG *II²* 3467 *(s. III/II; Pouilloux 1954, no. 8)*. One of the *tituli magistratuum*, this inscription from Rhamnous, honoring an epimelete from the deme Aithalidai, is in the name of the "Rhamnousians and those of the citizens residing at Rhamnous" (lines 1–3: Ῥαμνού[σιοι καὶ οἱ]/ οἰκοῦντες τῶ[ν πο]/λιτῶν Ῥαμνο[ῦντι]).

Rhamnous: PAAH *(1984) A [1988], pp. 206–207, no. 135 (ca. 220; SEG 38.127)*. This fragmentary decree is in the name of Ῥαμνουσίοις καὶ τοῖς οἰκοῦσι τῶν πολιτῶν Ῥα[μνοῦντι] (line 5; cf. lines 3–4, where the same formula occurs but without the qualifying "of the *politai*" in the second member).

Rhamnous: PAAH *(1991) [1994], pp. 34–35, no. 8 (225/4 or 214/3; SEG 43.40)*. This decree of soldiers encamped in Rhamnous honors a general who "took care of the garrison advantageously τῶι / [δήμωι καὶ τοῖς] οἰκοῦσιν ἐν Ῥαμνοῦντι, ... (lines 5–6).

Rhamnous: SEG *25.155 (236/5), passim*; SEG *15.112 (225), passim*. Both texts are, loosely speaking, decrees of the deme of Rhamnous. But in contrast with the mostly straightforward language of the preceding examples, these two texts present a far more complicated situation. So complicated in fact that three successive commentators, Pouilloux, Whitehead, and, most recently, R. Osborne, have written in various ways of the "confusion" manifested by one or the other or both texts.[99] The confusion allegedly relates to the identity of the decreeing party (or parties).

With this assessment I wish to take exception. On general grounds, it is inherently unlikely that any group (or groups) that have gone to the trouble to meet in a formal assembly, to formulate a motion, to vote a decree, and then incur the expense of engraving and erecting a permanent and publicly visible copy of that decree should be "confused" about such a fundamental matter as the identity of the decreeing body (or bodies)—about the identity of *themselves*. Because, therefore, of the inherent improbability that the actual state of affairs has been correctly portrayed, I am undertaking a fresh analysis of these two, the most problematic of the texts at issue. In the end, it will be seen that the application of my model of twin demes, one hereditary, the other territorial, will go far toward clearing up most if not all of this alleged "confusion."

Let us take the relatively simpler, somewhat later *SEG* 15.112 (= Pouilloux 1954, no. 17) first. This text honors Menander, son of Teisander, of Eitea for his services as trierarch (line 3, cf. lines 19–20) to those under his command. The decree itemizes these benefactions in some detail: he took good care of the ship's equipment (lines 4–5), meeting the demands of those under him at his own expense (lines 5–7); he supplied olive oil to the *neaniskoi* to ensure their maximum effectiveness (lines 7–9); he sacrificed to Zeus Soter and to Athena Soteira "for the health, safety, and concord" of all sailing with him (lines 9–11), providing entertainment out of his own

---

99. Pouilloux 1954, p. 131 (on *SEG* 25.155): "la rédaction du décret atteste une confusion juridique"; Whitehead 1986, p. 406: "some decrees show an *intrinsic* confusion in their voting constituency"; "[a]s with Eleusis, any general principles which may at the time have been seen to govern which body enacted which decree are now unfathomable"; Osborne 1990, p. 283: "But why were those who passed these decrees so confused as to their own identity?"

pocket (line 13); he crowned the rowers for their competitive energy toward each other (lines 13–15); he paid the dues for guarding the ship from his personal funds (lines 15–16); and, arriving at Rhamnous, he sacrificed to Nemesis, supplying sacrificial victims and wine (lines 16–19). The point is that all these acts of munificence immediately benefited a single group—the sailors on the ship (οἱ συνπλεύσαντες [ἐν τῶι ἀφράκτωι]). It is for this reason that it is precisely these who are identified in the main body of the text at lines 21-22 (and again in the summary statement within the wreath at lines 33–34) as the authors of the decree. (It is to them as well that the reflexive pronouns refer in lines 15, 25, and 28). Naturally enough, to launch our analysis with confirmation of un intuitive truth, it is the beneficiaries of the honorand's good deeds who, in turn, take primary credit for the bestowal upon him of the honors authorized by the decree. Why, then, if this is so, is the decree at its opening couched in the names of the "Rhamnousians and those of the citizens residing at Rhamnous" (lines 1–2)?

The text itself appears to provide the answer, or at least the beginnings of an answer. At lines 11–12 express acknowledgment is made of the *ultimate* beneficiaries of Menander's sacrifices to Zeus and Athena: "in order that they [i.e., his fellow sailors], of like mind, and secured from danger, also in the future prove useful τῶι δήμωι." Only the deme of Rhamnous can be meant. Where the reference is to "Athenians," the text is explicit (lines 22, 33).[100] Furthermore, the honors conferred point to the deme. Praise and crown (lines 23–24), to be sure standard fixtures of state honorary decrees, are also routinely included among the honors awarded by individual demes.[101] The third (and final) item, ἀτέλεια τοῦ πλοῦ (line 26), has been much discussed, but whatever its specific referent, such a privilege would fit in well with the attested granting by demes of exemptions from liturgies or local taxes.[102] Thus there is merit to Pouilloux's suggestion that the reference in our decree is to duties imposed on trade by sea *by the deme*.[103] If the deme was in fact so empowered to collect revenues (and there is no good reason to doubt that it was), it is hardly an objection to declare, as Osborne does, that "permission to trade without paying dues at the tiny harbour of Rhamnous would have been a pretty otiose privilege for a rich trierarch like Menander."[104] Yes, otiose perhaps, but that is not the question. The question is, could the deme (in some sense of that term) be the conferring party, and nothing rules out the possibility that indeed it was. The privilege may, it is true, have been redundant or, for a dignitary of the honorand's stature, of trifling significance. The deme wishes to honor its benefac-

100. Osborne's translation, "for the *demos*" (1990, p. 293), if by the italicized word he intends the People of Athens, is accordingly mistaken.

101. The attested examples are too numerous to require citation. On the crowns awarded by the Athenian demes, see Whitehead 1986, pp. 162–163 with notes. For the award of "praise" and/or "crown" by public units of states outside Athens, see Jones 1987, index III. F. 2. g and p (pp. 399 and 400).

102. See, for example, *IG* II²1185, lines 4–5; 1186, lines 25–26; 1187, lines 16–17; 1188, lines 29–30 (all Eleusis); 1204, lines 11–12 (Lower Lamptrai); 2496, line 13 (Kytheros); 2497, lines 4–9 (Prasiai); 2498, lines 6–7 (Peiraieus). Exemption from liturgies is several times conferred by Athenian phylai: *IG* II² 1140, lines 12–15 (Pandionis); *AE* 1965, pp. 131–136 (i), lines 1–2 (Akamantis); *IG* II² 1147, lines 9–11 (Erechtheis).

103. Pouilloux 1956, pp. 55–75, at 67.

104. Osborne 1990, p. 282.

tor and of necessity its efforts to that end are limited by its material and financial capacities.

But there is still another problem. The decree culminates with the formulaic phrase ordering that the expenses incurred be charged τῶι κοινῶι (lines 29–30). Osborne queries "but what *koinon*?"[105] Only one answer appears possible: the "Rhamnousians and those of the citizens residing at Rhamnous" in whose name the decree was introduced (lines 1–2). The apparently innocent use of the colorless term *koinon* is arguably pointed. It formalizes, at least for the purposes of this constitutional act, and reifies a *combined* organization comprising the constitutional deme *and* those citizens residing within that deme's boundaries. The use of the term makes the point that this "association" did not otherwise exist.

To continue with the analysis, the immediate beneficiaries of the good deeds of the honorand, who is not a demesman of Rhamnous, are, as we have seen, his "fellow sailors," who are of unknown deme affiliations though certainly Athenian citizens (line 22). At the more immediate level, accordingly, it is appropriate that they pass the decree (lines 21–22, 33–34) and that from them be selected the three people, who turn out to be non-Rhamnousians, charged with the implementation of the decree (lines 28–29, 30–32).[106] But this group lacks everything that under the classical democracy (and later) was needed to make possible a formal bestowal and implementation of the decreed honors—praise, crown, and the exemption from maritime tariffs. I refer of course to a suitable meeting place, a developed set of parliamentary procedures, a person or persons expert in documentary language and formulas (for the *epainos*), access to a supplier of the crown, and control over the collection of harbor dues. The deme could provide all of this (for one thing, we know this deme possessed a theater to use as a place of assembly[107]), and it was the deme that figured as the locus of at least some of the honorand's benefactions, for, as I suggested, it was to the benefit of "the deme" that his performance of sacrifices on behalf of the sailors was ultimately designed to accrue. The deme of Rhamnous, since it alone in this vicinity possessed the appropriate institutional machinery and since it alone was among the demes or other entities favorably impacted by Menander's activities, represented the natural, indeed the only possible, choice.

There is thus no "confusion" in this text, regarding the identity of either the honoring or decreeing party or any similar matter. Nor is there a rivalry, as Osborne would have it, between competing organizational principles, since, so far as this text informs us, Menander's "fellow sailors" possessed no organization. If there is a conflict of organizational principles, it is the one built into the deme's self-representation as "Rhamnousians and those of the citizens residing in Rhamnous" (lines 1–2). In terms of traditional categories, which permit only a single conception of the deme, namely the constitutional association based strictly on descent, such formulation might reasonably strike one as "confused" or "confusing." But the present thesis offers a way out. For the formulation in lines 1–2 incorpo-

---

105. Osborne 1990, p. 282.

106. The three belong to the demes Oe, Erchia, and Hamaxanteia—none even of the same phyle as Rhamnous (IX Aiantis).

107. *IG* II² 1311, line 7.

rates, according to my argument, *both* models of the deme—the personal corporation of the deme *politai* and the territorial inclusion of all other *politai* dwelling within the deme's boundaries.

It is just this distinction that underlies, and is largely responsible for, the "split of identity" and "confusion" that Osborne associated with the earlier decree, *SEG* 25.155 (= Pouilloux 1954, no. 15). It, too, is an honorary decree, and the honorand is again a nondemesman, one Dikaiarchos, son of Apollonios, of Thria. As, too, in the preceding text, the benefactor's accomplishments are set out in rich detail. Our interest, again, is initially in the beneficiaries of these accomplishments. Dikaiarchos, had, like his father, displayed good will toward "the Demos of the Athenians and the *koinon* of those stationed at Rhamnous" (lines 3–4). When King Antigonos set him over the fort, he took good care of "the detachment of the fort and those residing in it" (lines 7–8). (Similarly, when his father was at Eleusis, he [his father] was praised and crowned by the "Eleusinians and the other Athenians residing in the fort" [lines 12–14].) Stationed at Panakton, Dikaiarchos took good care "of the detachment of the fort and of the rest of the countryside of Attica" (lines 15–17). Now, placed by King Demetrios on the headland of the Eretrians, he continues to be well disposed toward "the Demos of the Athenians," a statement supported by a lengthy catalog of particular acts involving Athenian citizens (lines 17–27). Moreover, he has offered victims for sacrifice to Nemesis and to the king out of his own pocket, "in order that it be well with the goddesses for the Rhamnousians" (lines 27–30). (Note here, at the climax of the catalog in line 30, the dative Ῥαμνουσίοις, following a single blank space, in emphatic position!) The decree proper goes on to cite Dikaiarchos's "excellence" and "loyalty" toward "King Demetrios and the Demos of the Athenians and the *koinon* of those residing in Rhamnous" (lines 32–35).

Looking back over this welter of detail, one is first impressed by its apparent incoherence. But in fact, to consider our first variable, Dikaiarchos's beneficiaries are easily enumerated: King Demetrios, the Demos of the Athenians (i.e., the *politai*), the "Rhamnousians," and the people residing in the territory of Rhamnous or its fort. It is of course only with respect to the last two that the Rhamnousians, as the decreeing party, have become involved with this grant of honors. And it is manifest that these two entities correspond, respectively, to my "constitutional" and "territorial" conceptions of the deme.

The same fundamental distinction between the group defined by descent and the group defined by residence, furthermore, is observed in the two other decrees alluded to in our text (in each instance, with the implication that the "residents" in question were or, at least, included military personnel of some kind): the earlier grant honoring Dikaiarchos issued at Rhamnous in the names of the "Rhamnousians and those of the Athenians residing in the fort" (lines 10–11); and the earlier grant honoring Dikaiarchos's father issued at Eleusis in the names of the "Eleusinians and the other Athenians residing in the fort" (lines 13–14).

With these two formulas in mind, we may revisit the phrasing of the present grant, which is, again, expressly in the name of the "Rhamnousians" (line 1) and (in the resumption) the "Rhamnousians and the other Athenians [i.e., resident non-*demotai*] and those residing in Rhamnous [i.e., resident noncitizens]—all of them" (lines 30–32). Why, in this instance (but departing from the pattern evidenced by the other two decrees), are the resident noncitizens added to the roster of honoring parties? The text itself draws attention to the departure through the addition of the word that ends the formula in lines 30–32, πᾶσιν. It, as indicated by its emphatic position, marks the point that the final group, namely, the resident *non*citizens, is, in contrast with the practice observed in the two other, earlier, grants, included as well. For this reason, pace Pouilloux,[108] there is no need to delete the καί linking "the other Athenians" and "those residing in Rhamnous." The final, emphatic "all of them," in other words, reflects the otherwise unexpected addition of this third group.

At all events, in each case the honors are expressly identified as the joint act of the *demotai* and of the residents of the deme, either other Athenian citizens or, as in the third example, both these and *non*-Athenian residents as well.

Again, however, as in *SEG* 15.112, to come to our final difficulty, full responsibility for the passage, expense, and (in this case, but not in the other) implementation of the decree devolves upon the *demotai* alone. At the opening, the decree stands in their name alone (line 1); the mover of the decree is a Rhamnousian (lines 1–2); the demarch of the Rhamnousians (with the military *epimeletai*) is charged with the engraving of the stele (lines 36–38); the *tamias* of the Rhamnousians is to apportion the funds for the manufacture of the stelai and the inscription of the decree (lines 41–43); an account is to be rendered to the *demotai* (line 43); and the five men chosen to implement the decree are all demesmen (lines 43–47). Once more, I conclude that it was the deme alone that could provide the institutional means for the composition, promulgation, and implementation of such a decree. Why, then, the reader will ask, does the summary enclosed in the wreath below the decree cite as the honoring party not the "Rhamnousians" but "those of the citizens residing at Rhamnous" (lines 48–50)?[109]

An answer is at hand. Wreaths, of course, typically in cases like these *summarize* the action taken in the decree. If the decree is honorary, the wreath will enclose, as here, the name of the honoring party (in the nominative) and sometimes as well, again as here, that of the honorand (in the accusative) in the most abbreviated form possible. Where, still again as here, there is more than one honoring party (the familiar instance is "the Boule and Demos"), more than one wreath may be used, one for each party. Since, on my analysis, there are essentially two such parties, the "personal" constitutional deme and the "territorial" deme comprising non-*demotai* residents (Athenian or otherwise), we should find not a single large wreath enclosing both, but *two* wreaths.

Now, are we, as Pouilloux, Whitehead, or Osborne would have it, dealing with a form of "confusion" or "split identity"? Before resorting to so pessimistic a conclusion, let us try another approach. Perhaps one should try to discover a reason why there is only *one* wreath and, given that there is only one, why it is that it is

---

108. 1954, p. 131.

109. It goes without saying, I think, that the third and last component of the decreeing group, the resident noncitizens, would not enjoy the privilege of possessing their own wreath, much less the sole wreath inscribed. If this omission, however, is viewed as a problem, a remedy might be sought in the deletion of the καί introducing "those residing in Rhamnous," thus reducing the decreeing parties to two, namely, the *demotai* and the resident non-*demotai* citizens. See above, with the preceding note.

"the residents" who get it. For both questions there is a single answer. Because, as a result of the decline of the *demotai* as a corporate body, the actual (citizen) inhabitants of the deme, conceived as a territorial entity, had come to acquire greater importance or higher status, and for this reason had a stronger claim to represent themselves as the *sole* authors of the decree.

We began by reaffirming and strengthening the traditional view, most recently and persuasively championed by Langdon and Traill, that the Attic demes were formally defined by precise boundaries. But the acceptance of the territorial deme gives rise to an unsettling problem. The Kleisthenic "constitutional" deme was a descent group membership in which was absolutely determined by inheritance of affiliation in the male line without reference to place of domicile. This is an incontestable fact. But this fact, in combination with our finding, means that there were in effect *two* demes. The uses of the Kleisthenic deme are well known. But what was the territorial deme good for?

The beginnings of an answer are afforded by the occurrences, in the context of the official documents of the constitutional demes, of various perturbations of the formula "the people residing in the deme." The occurrences of this formula mark, I have argued, the formal acknowledgment of the residents of the deme in explicit or implicit contrast with the constitutionally defined descent group of *demotai*. The principal claim of this chapter is that the body of "the residents" is to be associated with the network of precise territorial boundaries that now seem to be established beyond question. These boundaries existed in part, in other words, in order to delimit or define the membership of a given territorial deme's body of "residents."

When, and under what circumstances, did this second, territorial deme come into existence? Presumably with the creation of the deme boundaries; and Langdon, with great sensitivity to the topographical features and diversity of classical Attica, has removed any obstruction to believing that it was Kleisthenes himself who in short order carried out the necessary surveys and recording of the official boundaries so determined.[110] But there is no reason to suppose that the territorial deme hypothesized here ever achieved a corporate existence or authority independent of its constitutional namesake. Quite the contrary. If the analyses of the final two documents from Rhamnous are accepted, it is clear that it was the constitutional deme of the *demotai* which, at least initially, provided the physical apparatus and organization for the formal decreeing activity of "the people residing in the deme of Rhamnous."

Finally, in our analysis of the decrees from Ikarion, Eleusis, and Rhamnous, signs have been detected of an evolutionary process involving the gradual domination, and eventual replacement, of the constitutional deme by its territorial counterpart. When, in chapter 4, we address again the social composition of the territorial deme of "residents," we shall return to this evolutionary process, and to its more detailed examination.

110. Langdon 1985b, pp. 5–7.

THREE

The Isolation of the Demes

From the previous chapter it will be clear that the Kleisthenic deme was bounded in two different ways: by the rule whereby membership was determined by descent (the constitutional deme) or by declared and possibly marked boundaries (the territorial deme). It is natural to ask, next, whether, and to what degree, these social and physical boundaries served to separate a given deme from other demes or from the outside world of Attica generally. Did the deme turn in upon itself? Or was it an extroverted organization, its members regularly venturing beyond its limits? While the problem is notoriously bedeviled by the portability and inheritability of the *demotikon*, study of the many tombstones bearing the names of Athenians has, as noted in the preceding chapter, begun to provide some answers.[1] Simply put, the question comes down to the agreement, or lack of agreement, between the deme of the deceased's affiliation and the place where he or she was buried. One study published in 1988 concluded that, in general, while (as always known) considerable migration from the countryside to urban areas occurred, there was "little migration between the rural districts themselves" and "very little migration from town to country."[2] Within the parameters of such a global characterization, however, it is be-

---

1. Methodological issues are of course involved. For a preliminary investigation of the data provided by sepulchral monuments with relation to social class, see Nielsen et al. 1989, pp. 411–420. The authors conclude (p. 420) that the inscriptions "may well represent a cross section of the Athenian citizen population," rather than (as previously believed) being biased toward the upper class. For a wider-ranging discussion of the use of funeral inscriptions as historical sources, see Damsgaard-Madsen 1988, pp. 55–68; and, for demographic aspects, Hansen 1990, pp. 25–44.

2. Damsgaard-Madsen 1988, p. 66.

coming apparent that, as Osborne's recent work has shown, findings may differ dramatically from one deme to another.[3] So, while the overall pattern of movement, or stability, is coming into focus, understanding of the particular case remains well beyond our reach.

Pending outcome of this ongoing research, perhaps progress can be made on the basis of other kinds of evidence. Naturally, our attention will focus upon the constitutional deme, for concerning it alone do we have any relevant indications. In chapter 4, however, a different set of concerns will allow us to return to the territorial deme.

Pankleon, Dekeleia, and the Isolation of the Rural Demes

In a short speech attributed to Lysias, *Against Pankleon,* the speaker accuses the defendant of falsely representing himself as an Athenian citizen, when in fact (it is alleged) he was metic (23.2). According to the brief, this person, one Pankleon, among other acts of misrepresentation, pretended to be a member of a deme, namely Dekeleia (§2), a claim that, if true, would of course by itself establish his citizen status. The speaker relates how he put this particular claim to the test: he approached the Dekeleians who habitually congregated at the barber shop on the Street of the Herms (§3).[4] That this establishment was located in the heart of Athens will presumably have been well known to the Athenian jury.[5] As it turned out, none of the Dekeleians questioned by the speaker had ever heard of Pankleon, and the speaker is quick to exploit this point as decisive proof that in fact the accused was not a member of the deme.

These details are ripe in implications for our subject, implications that are in no way nullified by our uncertainty whether it is the speaker or the accused who is telling the truth. If Pankleon's self-representations are true, then his personal circumstances, including his membership in the deme Dekeleia, will explain, as we shall see, how he might have been falsely accused. If he is lying, and the accuser's claims are true, then, again as we shall see, his falsehoods may have been invented

3. See Osborne 1991, pp. 239–249: 241, where statistics for Kerameis, Kephale, and Rhamnous are compiled and evaluated. For Kerameis (an urban deme), 62 percent of those demesmen commemorated (with demotic) by an engraved tombstone were found to have been buried in or near their ancestral deme. For Kephale (a distant coastal deme), the percentage is only 28 percent; for Rhamnous (another distant coastal deme), a very high 76 percent. From these figures alone, it is evident that no uniform pattern applicable to all situations is likely to be uncovered.

4. An additional reference to a place (or places), "where(ever) the Dekeleians meet in the *asty*" occurs in the decrees of the Demotionidai, *IG* II² 1237 (396/5), face B, lines 63–64 (cf. lines 122–123). The decrees were found at the royal palace at Tatoi, a site identified with certainty as that of the ancient deme Dekeleia. Additionally, and in contrast with the view taken below regarding the centralization of deme business in the deme itself, the decrees specify this location (i.e., "in the *asty*"), rather than a location in the deme itself, for the posting of a notice "on a whitened board" (further on this point, see "Regional Distribution and Relation to the Urban Center," in chapter 7). The reason(s) for this atypical departure from what I believe was the standard practice will emerge in the following discussion.

5. For ancient testimony on "The Herms," see *Agora* 3, nos. 301–313 + 203 (pp. 103–108) and 14, pp. 94–96 passim.

with a view to their intrinsic plausibility. Either way, valuable light will be shed on
the question of the relative isolation of the rural demes. But to simplify the argument, let us precede on the premise undergirding the speaker's brief—that Pankleon's claims are false.

To get right to the heart of the matter, if Pankleon was really a metic, why did
he choose to pass himself off as a *demotes* of just this deme, Dekeleia? We may conjecture that, if he is lying, the overriding concern will have been to escape detection.
In that case, Dekeleia would have been a choice favored by history. Since it was the
site of a Spartan military base during the final stages of the Peloponnesian War,
more precisely from 413 to 404, it would have been natural to suppose that the
whole or part of the population had taken refuge elsewhere for this period.[6] Such an
assumption would help explain why Dekeleians, as indicated both by Lysias and
the Demotionid decrees,[7] are found habitually congregating in the distant *asty* in
the decade or so following the end of the war. After fleeing to Athens, they never
returned to the home village. For our purposes, it would also explain why Pankleon
picked this deme: he may have believed (erroneously, it turned out) that, due to the
dispersal of the Dekeleians, few if any *demotai* would be around to contradict his
claim or have calculated that, if challenged, he could argue that, as a result of the
confusion resulting from the Spartan occupation, records or other evidence of his
affiliation—such as the *lexiarchikon grammateion*—had been lost.

Other attractions of Dekeleia, ones independent of its more recent wartime fortunes, may also be considered. Dekeleia had a bouleutic quota of four, a not particularly small number, since 93 of the 139 demes had a quota of three or fewer, but certainly not large either. To falsely claim membership in a tiny deme would have an
obvious disadvantage in that all the *demotai*, at least those still resident in the deme,
would be likely to know each other, making it difficult to escape detection. For this
reason, a very large deme, since it would offer a degree of anonymity, would have
been far more attractive. Why not, then, one wonders, Acharnai (quota 22, if split or
not) or Aphidna (quota 16)? Obviously, he was not thinking along these lines. Since,
while avoiding the smallest demes, he neither selects any of the 38 with a quota
larger than four, it is evident that, if he was lying, size was not the basis for his
choice. But a glance at Traill's maps of Kleisthenic Attica suggests a far more attractive feature of Dekeleia: the deme's remote location at the foot of Mt. Parnes,
far from the fuller's shop, presumably located in the town, where Pankleon worked
(§2). He may have reasoned that only few Dekeleians would visit the city and so be
in a position to unmask his misrepresentation. The implication for our study would
be that, in Pankleon's estimation, citizens of this distant inland deme, and inferentially of others like it, only rarely visited the *asty*.

Congruent with my suspicion that Pankleon is lying, is his parallel claim, likewise supporting his putative citizenship, that he was of Plataian descent (§1). By a
well-known extraordinary decree of the year 427, some of the people of this small
Boiotian town had received the Athenian citizenship.[8] So, for Pankleon, to claim to

6. On the site, see C. W. J. Eliot, "Dekeleia," *PECS,* p. 261.

7. See above, note 4.

8. [Demosthenes] 59.104.

be Plataian would possess, if he were ever challenged, a decided advantage: as a naturalized citizen (or his descendant) from a foreign state, he would easily be able to explain why, in Athens, he was not recognized by other Athenians. But, in addition to this general consideration, recent history might have favored this maneuver in still another way. The city had been razed to the ground by the Spartans in 427 and was not restored until about 380, only to be destroyed again, this time by the Thebans, before 374/3.[9] We do not have independent evidence for the date of composition of Lysias's speech, but the fact that all his datable surviving works fall within the period between 411 (perhaps later, but before the end of the war in 404) and 382 (or possibly 384/3)[10] suggests that at the time Pankleon was (mis)representing himself as a Plataian the city was not in existence. As with Dekeleia, Pankleon may have hoped that the dispersal of population or the destruction of records or general confusion would have allowed him to carry off his fraud undetected. The claim that he was of Plataian origin (or descent) in combination with the claim of membership in the remote deme of Dekeleia must have seemed, whether the claims were true or false, a watertight, impregnable line of defense.

As it happened, members of the deme of Dekeleia regularly congregated at a prearranged location (or locations)[11] in the city. This is a fact. If Pankleon was telling the truth, the finding that none of the Dekeleians at the barber shop recognized his name might still, however, be explicable. Perhaps an ancestor (a naturalized Plataian resident in Dekeleia) had migrated from the deme to the city with the result that his descendant Pankleon had not established contact with either the home community or with those members of that community (whether residents of the deme or urbanites) accustomed to gather in the *asty*. That such a migration in the case of a particular deme, and a small deme at that, had occurred, however, is notoriously difficult to establish.[12] Nonetheless, it could have happened, however remote such a possibility.

9. See "Plataiai," in *KlPauly* 4 (1972) coll. 893–894; and, more fully, E. Kirsten, "Plataiai 1)," *RE* 20:2 (1950) 2255-2332, at 2307–2311. A more recent account is N. Bonacasa's article "Plataiai," *PECS*, p. 717.

10. See Dover 1968, pp. 28–46, especially 44.

11. The plural is required in view of the uncertainty whether the barber shop on the Street of the Herms mentioned by the speaker of Lysias's speech and the meeting place (or places) of the Dekeleians in the *asty* where a notice is to be posted on a whitened board attested by the decrees of the Demotionidai (see above, note 4) are the same place. Would such a posting be found in or near a barber shop? The attested use of commercial establishments in and around the Agora for noncommercial purposes would suggest that it would. Lysias 24 *On the Question of Not Giving Money to a Handicapped Man* §20, a passage that will figure in the ensuing discussion, mentions the Athenians' general practice of frequenting shops in the Agora. Sokrates is reported by Xenophon, *Memorabilia* 4.2.1 and 8, to have visited a rein-maker's shop; and, according to Diogenes Laertius, 2.13.122–124, he frequented the establishment of a cobbler named Simon. To the point of the present discussion, barbershops are identified as places for gossip or socializing by Aristophanes, *Ploutos,* lines 337–339, and by [Demosthenes] 25 *Aristogeiton* I, §52. According to Plutarch, *Nikias* 30.1–2, word of the disaster in Sicily was first brought by a customer in a barbershop in Peiraieus.

12. Gomme 1933, pp. 44–45, undertakes to document the rate of urbanization from the country by compiling a tabulation of tombstones in which the demotic of the deceased is preserved, with respect to their place of discovery. Our attention is focused on table B, containing figures on 23 coastal and inland demes. Of the total of 377 items, 201 or 53.3 percent were discovered in or near Athens or Peiraieus, while only 61 or 16.2 percent were found near the site of the deme of the deceased's affiliation. Since it may be reasonably assumed that a person was buried near the place of residence at the time of death,

But the odds favor the assumption that Pankleon is lying, primarily because of the extraordinarily coincidental conjunction of his claims to have been a member of two small communities both of which had suffered enemy occupation or destruction in recent decades. If he is lying, furthermore, the Dekeleians' practice of meeting at the barber shop on the Street of the Herms (or elsewhere in the city) could easily have been unknown to him at the time when the plaintiff accosted him at the fuller's shop and summoned him before the Polemarch on the assumption that he was a metic (§2). Plataian and Dekeleian origins provided the opportunity to argue the excuses of destroyed records, death of friends and relatives, etc., but surely, he must also have thought, Athenian citizens from so distant a deme would not be found in town in appreciable numbers under any circumstances. Thus it is the assumption of a lying Pankleon which seems to entail the consequence that demesmen from a remote inland or coastal deme were unlikely to be found in the city and which, if generalized, would favor a case for the relative isolation of the extra-urban demes.

Admittedly, an alternative approach remains open and must be acknowledged. One could, irrespective of the truth or falsity of Pankleon's claims, place greater emphasis on the fact of the presence of Dekeleians in town and, furthermore, suppose that this was not an unusual case but rather typical of the practice of the memberships of those same extra-urban demes. But a complication frustrating this line of argument has already been aired: the special circumstances surrounding Dekeleia that might explain why the members of just this deme were found in the *asty*. Driven from their ancestral home, they had established permanent residences in the urban center. It is also germane to observe that no other rural deme, remotely located or otherwise, is recorded to have established such an urban location for the regular congregation of its members.

The Extra-Urban Deme as Independent Administrative Center

More abstractly put, the problem posed implicitly by Lysias's 23d speech is whether the deme had maintained its integrity as a local community or, as illustrated by the gatherings of the Dekeleians in town, had suffered a significant degree of disintegration, above all as the result of the movement of demesmen and their families to the urban center. Naturally, to the extent that we are dealing with the territorially based "alternative" deme (the existence of which I hope to have satisfactorily established in chapter 2), this question does not arise. By definition those who continue to reside in the deme, whatever may have been the impact of emigration (or, for that matter, immigration), constitute that local community at any given moment. But our

---

these figures indicate a high rate of movement out of the home demes into the urban areas. For Dekeleia, Gomme gives a total of seven items, of which four were found at or near the site of the deme, one in or near Athens or Peiraieus, while for two the provenience was not known; but it is obvious that no significance can be attached to numbers so small. For Kirchner's texts of Dekeleian epitaphs, see *IG* II^2 5980–5987.

present concern is with the more narrowly defined "constitutional" deme, the survival of which had been rendered vulnerable from Day One by the decision to make the *demotikon* both portable regardless of place of domicile within or outside the deme and inheritable in the male line in perpetuity. Was this deme association firmly rooted in its nucleated settlement? Or was it, as Lysias's evidence about Dekeleia might suggest, subject to the centripetal pull of the city? I hope to contribute to the resolution of the problem, if only at the institutional if not at the demographic (or the individual's) level, by looking at some of the details of the literary and epigraphic record in a rather different light.

Agorai

To mention but the most obvious item of evidence that bears directly on the matter, there is the question of the venue of the deme's *agorai* or meetings. At first glance, the question might seem easily answered since four different demes are found decreeing that the inscribed text of the decree be placed in its (the deme's) *agora*.[13] But can we be sure that the *meeting* out of which came that decree had also transpired on that site?

Strangely, over the two centuries of the demes' viable existence, during which each of the 139 (or 140) deme associations presumably convened its *agora* on a regular basis, only a single mention of or reference to such a meeting preserves an indication of that meeting's location. Demosthenes' brief *Against Euboulides* (57), delivered by one Euxitheos, places an assembly of the Halimousians in 346/5 somewhere (the exact location is not specified) in the *asty* (§10). According to Demosthenes' text, Halimous, though a deme of the city region (of the phyle Leontis), lay on the coast 35 stades — about 4 ½ miles — due south of the city walls. By no means could Halimous, though belonging to a city trittys, be considered, by us or by the Athenians themselves, a "city" deme in any literally significant sense of that term. Is this detail not, in the absence of any conflicting evidence, a strong indication that, contrary to the position to be argued here, the locus of activity of the extra-urban demes had shifted to the urban center?

It would seem to be at first. Yet Whitehead, in a convincing discussion, has set out the reasons for resisting the conclusion that, as formulated by Ste. Croix, a change in venue from the home deme to Athens had followed in the wake of the migration of "a fair proportion of the members of some country demes."[14] Needless to say, no one would lightly suppose that each year (if we are to generalize from the case of Halimous — perhaps a risky maneuver) the city should have played host to hundreds, perhaps thousands, of such meetings. How could one assume, in the absence of positive indications, that the members of the deme associations should have purposely and repeatedly inconvenienced themselves to such an extraordinary degree, given the difficulty and loss of time involved in travel to and from the putative meeting site? At the same time, it is *not* an effective argument against Ste.

13. See below, note 26, for references.
14. Whitehead 1986, p. 88, citing G. E. M. de Ste. Croix, *The Origins of the Peloponnesian War*, London 1972, app. 47 (pp. 400–401).

Croix's position, as Whitehead believes, that, had there been so many meetings of rural demes in the city, we should expect to find traces of them in our record, when, in fact, except for Demosthenes' text, we find none.[15] For one thing, every reference in a deme document to an *agora,* indeed every deme document itself might, though lacking any explicit reference to the location of the meeting, constitute such evidence. For another, there is no good reason to suppose that all, many, or even a significant minority of the business transactions of the deme *agorai* were recorded. The surviving texts on stone overwhelmingly comprise decrees bestowing honors upon benefactors, financial documents such as leases, or *leges sacrae* (they too of an essentially financial nature) that naturally commended themselves to inscription in a permanent form. Surely not all the doings of a typical meeting of a deme were of such moment. Many a meeting of a rural deme in the city could well have left no trace of either a documentary (or literary) nature.

It is, therefore, a better argument simply to note Demosthenes' speaker's own assertion that "the greatest number" (τῶν πλείστων) of the demesmen (still) resided in the deme (§10). If the majority ruled, and if "the greatest number" had wished to meet in the deme, they would have done so. Some special circumstances, accordingly, must have obtained such as to persuade the "greatest number" of the membership to impose such an onerous inconvenience upon themselves.

Whitehead responded to this challenge by suggesting two—actually three— candidates for such *special* circumstances.[16] Perhaps the most convincing one is prompted by the text itself: the possibility (implicit in βουλεύων at §57.8) that the demarch (Euboulides) was at the time of his tenure in that office *also* a representative of his deme on the Council of Five Hundred and that, since he was presumably obliged as a councillor to spend much of his time in Athens, he used his authority as demarch to convene the deme's *agora* in the *asty.* Secondly, and without specific support from the text, since the matter with which the speech deals, to wit, an extraordinary scrutiny of the deme's membership rolls, presupposes the prior malfunctioning of the organization's usual procedures, perhaps, as Whitehead suggests, it was decided on this occasion to seek out a neutral setting well away from the normal place of meeting. (But, one feels compelled to ask, would not such a need have been satisfied by finding an alternative location *within the deme*, without forcing the entire membership to travel to town?) Thirdly, least persuasively and possibly overlapping with either of the other two suggestions, many of the demesmen may have just happened at this time to be present in the city for reasons not known to us (Haussoullier had suggested "quelque fête publique"). Any of these circumstances, with due acknowledgment of their varying degrees of plausibility, would help us to understand why a deme whose "greatest number" of members lived in the deme had on this one known occasion met in the *asty.* But the crucial point is that these were special circumstances, peculiar to the particular case of this single deme. What about the extra-urban demes in general? One can only agree with Whitehead that general probabilities favor the surmise that it is "overwhelmingly likely" that the *agora* of the deme normally took place within the

---

15. Whitehead 1986, p. 88.
16. Whitehead 1986, pp. 88–90.

boundaries of the deme in question.[17] Let us now see if concrete evidence can be adduced in favor of this surmise.

Stelai

Luckily, the conclusion that the official life of the deme—not only of Halimous but of the demes generally—was centered in the deme itself does not depend solely upon this admittedly tenuous argument. Abundant, positive indications are at hand. The surest of these is afforded by the documents, more precisely the decrees, of the demes themselves. In 39 instances (of a total of at least 110 preserved decrees[18]) the text contains instructions for the erection of a stele in a specified location. These clauses are richly informative. The place so specified is, first, either ascertainably situated within the deme[19] or may, in the absence of conflicting indications, be presumed to be so located. In no instance, to make the vital point, is the place identifiably in the *asty* (in the case of extra-urban demes) or elsewhere outside the deme in question.

Negative evidence strongly reinforces this conclusion. In question are injunctions contained in decrees calling for the erection of two stelai bearing the text, one at the association's home base, the other in the *asty*. One of the phylai provides a clear example. A decree of Hippothontis, *IG* II² 1163, enjoins the erection of two stelai, one (as would be expected) in the Hippothontion in Eleusis (where the surviving text was discovered), the other in the Asklepieion, on the southern slope of the Akropolis. As I shall argue in chapter 5, this case illustrates the possibility of an extra-urban association, while maintaining its local integrity, establishing a presence in the *asty* by the erection there of copies of its official acts. A second example is provided by the Marathonian Tetrapolis based at Marathon;[20] a third by the phratry (?) Demotionidai based in Dekeleia.[21] With regard to the demes, it is true that there are two examples of decrees calling for multiple stelai: a *locatio* of Aixone, discovered *[i]n Aexonensium demo*, *IG* II² 2492, is to be promulgated in two copies, one in the shrine of Hebe, the other "in the *lesche*" (lines 20–23); and, from Rhamnous, *SEG* 25.155 will be engraved on two stelai, one to stand in the shrine of Dionysos, the other in the Nemesion (lines 40–41). But, despite the fact that other associations observed such practice, no trace is to be found of the advertisement of the acts of an extra-urban deme in or near the civic center. It may be inferred that the demes did not view themselves as maintaining a presence in the urbanized areas.

Another corroborating indication, if one is needed, is that none of the (single) stelai of the extra-urban demes, irrespective of the instructions contained in the

17. Whitehead 1986, p. 90.

18. For the roster of deme documents on which these (and some of the following) numbers and tabulations are based, see below, note 54.

19. In not a few instances, for example, the stele is to be set up in a shrine of which the identification and situation within the deme in question have been established with certainty: *IG* II² 1187, of Eleusis, near the Propylaia of Demeter and Kore (lines 25–27); *SEG* 22.116, of Melite, in the shrine of Artemis (lines 25–26); *SEG* 22.120, of Rhamnous, in the shrine of Nemesis (lines 8–9); and several others.

20. See "Regional Associations," in chapter 8.

21. See "Regional Distribution and Relation to the Urban Center," in chapter 7.

text itself, is securely recorded to have been found in situ either in the *asty* or else-where outside the limits of the deme in question. The telltale parallel evidence, highlighting the significance of this fact, is provided, again, by the phylai. Virtually all of no fewer than 48 decrees (plus other documents) were discovered in or near the area of the Akropolis and Agora.[22] Therefore, if the extra-urban demes had regularly been erecting stelai in the *asty*, some trace would certainly have survived. Plainly, the extra-urban demes did not display the texts of their official acts, at least not in the form of inscriptions on stone, anywhere near or about the Agora or Akropolis.[23]

Still more progress can be made. The location within the deme specified for the placement of the stele is usually spelled out in detail, sometimes with implications for the character of the deme's associational activity. In most cases (about 30 de-crees from 18 demes, by count), the location is a shrine or other cultic site.[24] In a mi-nority of others, the decrees specify, in the case of four decrees from two demes, the theater;[25] and, in the case of four decrees from four demes, the *agora*.[26] Why, first, should a deme have erected a stele in a shrine? Again, the parallel experience of an-other association, the phyle, points to an answer. As we shall see in chapter 5, the decrees of the phylai were often erected in or near the shrines of the eponymous he-roes. Furthermore, in one instance, a *meeting* of the phyle is known to have taken place in the vicinity of the shrine of its eponym.[27] That is, to combine these two in-dications, the locus of the meeting resulting in the enactment of a decree was evi-dently held to be the natural site for that decree's formal publication. Perhaps the same applied regarding the erection of stelai in theaters and *agorai*. The advantages of accommodations for seating and of wide, flat open spaces are self-evident. (And, after all, why is the meeting of a deme called an *agora*?) It would seem to be fully justified to infer that the meetings of demes occurred at or near where the decrees produced by those meetings enjoined the stelae to be placed—in shrine, theater, or *agora*.

Nevertheless, it is clear that, in the case of at least some demes, there is more

22. For the proveniences, see chapter 5, "The Disposition of the Phyle Organization."

23. Again, note, in contrast with the general trend, that the Demotionidai, based in distant Dekeleia, call for the posting of a notice on a whitened board in the *asty*, "where(ever) the Dekeleians meet," *IG* II² 1237, face A, lines 63–64, cf. 122–123. But, as we argued, extenuating circumstances applied in the case of Dekeleia. See above, with note 4.

24. Acharnai: *IG* II² 1206; *AE* 1992 (1994) pp. 179–193 (*SEG* 43.26A and B); Aixone: *IG* II² 1199; 2492; Athmonon: *IG* II² 1203; Cholargos: *IG* II² 1184; Eitea: *SEG* 28.102; Eleusis: *IG* II² 1186; 1187; 1299; *SEG* 28.103; Gargettos: *MDAI(A)* 67 (1942) 7–8, no. 5; Halai Aixonides: *AD* 11 (1927–1928) 40–41, no. 4; *MDAI(A)* 67 (1942) 10, no. 8; Halai Araphenides: *AE* 1925–1926, pp. 168–177; *AE* 1932 Chron., pp. 30–32; Halimous: *SEG* 2.7; Ikarion: *SEG* 22.117; Kydathenaion: *Agora* 16, no. 68 A and B; Kytheros: *IG* II² 2496; Melite: *SEG* 22.116; *Hesperia* 11 (1942) 265–274, no. 51 (restored); Myrrhi-nous: *IG* II² 1182; Peiraieus: *IG* II² 1177; 1214; Rhamnous: *SEG* 22.120; 25.155; 31.112; Teithras: *SEG* 24.151 and 153.

25. Aixone: *IG* II² 1197; 1198; 1202; *MDAI(A)* 66 (1941) 218–219, no. 1; Eleusis: *IG* II² 1185.

26. Eleusis: *IG* II² 1188 (restored); Halai Aixonides: *IG* II² 1174, lines 13–14 and 17–18; Peiraieus: *IG* II² 1176 + *CSCA* 7 (1974) 290–298; Sounion: *IG* II² 1180.

27. See "The Shrine of the Eponymous Hero," in chapter 5. The case in question is that of the phyle Kekropis. The shrine of the eponym almost certainly stood on the Akropolis; and it was on the Akropo-lis, according to *IG* II² 1141, that a vote of the *phyletai* was taken (lines 5–7).

involved than simply this natural linkage of meeting and publication. For in a few cases the purpose underlying the direction to erect the stele in a certain location is stated explicitly. Texts from Aixone (the theater),[28] Eleusis (the "best location"),[29] and possibly Melite (a shrine)[30] declare (or suggest) in different ways that the reason for so locating the stele was in order to inform the public (inferentially both demesmen and others). In other words, it was at such locations that the greatest number and/or the most important of the potential readers would be expected to be most likely to view the stele. Therefore, it is difficult to escape the conclusion that it was the deme itself, not the *asty* or other location, that was regarded as the natural center of activity of the deme association.

Announcements

Yet another line of argument serves to buttress my position, although it involves an apparent complicating piece of evidence. I refer to the fact that a total of eight demes append to their honorary decrees a clause calling for the announcement of the crowning, etc. on some formal occasion *distinct from* the assembly at which the honors were presumably originally voted by the *demotai*.[31] The demes in question are Acharnai, Aixone, Athmonon, Eleusis, Halai Araphenides, Ikarion, Peiraieus, and Rhamnous. Of the 12 such texts, 11 specify that the announcement is to take place at an *agon*, usually during the competition in tragedy at the Dionysia. In the twelfth case, *IG* II²1178 (ante med. s. IV), from Ikarion, no occasion for the announcement is mentioned, but since another decree from that deme, *SEG* 22.117 (ca. 330), calls for the announcement of the crown "at the tragedies of the Dionysia" (lines 8–9), we may infer the same for the earlier decree as well. Furthermore— and this is the crucial point—for each of the eight demes in question, save one (Athmonon), there is evidence, contained in the clauses themselves or independent of it, for the existence of a *theater* within the boundaries of the deme at the time that the honors, and with them presumably the provision for their announcement, were passed. The conjunction of the fact that the announcement was to occur at an *agon* or Dionysia with the existence in those same demes of a theater hardly leaves any doubt that the theater was in fact the scene of that announcement. Here follow the particulars on the eight theaters:

28. *IG* II² 1198, lines 18–28: "and that the demarch Dorotheos engrave this decree on a stone stele and place it in the theater, in order that those on each occasion going to serve the Aixonians as *choregoi* know that the deme will honor those acting energetically on their behalf"; *MDAI(A)* 66 (1941) 218–219; no. 1, lines 10–12: "and that the *tamiai* engrave this decree on a stone stele and place it in the theater, in order that the Aixonians always put on the Dionysia in the best manner possible."

29. *IG* II² 1193, lines 27–31 (partly restored): "and that the demarch Isarchos engrave this decree on a stone stele and place it wherever it seems to be in the best place." (Cf. *IG* II² 1218, line 15.)

30. *AD* 19 (1964) 26–36, lines 23–27 (partly restored): "and that the demarch engrave this decree and place it in the shrine of Artemis in order that the others also be energetic toward the *demotai*."

31. Acharnai: *AE* 1992 (1994) pp. 179–193 (*SEG* 43.26), B, lines 12–14; Aixone: *IG* II² 1202, lines 14–16; Athmonon: *IG* II² 1203, line 17; Eleusis: *IG* II² 1186, lines 19–21; 1187, lines 9–11; 1189, line 10; 1193, lines 13–17; 1299, lines 76–77; Halai Araphenides: *AE* 1932 Chron., pp. 30–32, lines 13–15; Ikarion: *IG* II² 1178, lines 3–4, 10–11; *SEG* 22.117, lines 8–9; Peiraieus: *IG* II² 1214, lines 28–36; Rhamnous: *SEG* 22.120, lines 6–7.

- Acharnai: For the theater, see *IG* II² 1206, lines 6–7. For a grant of *proedria*, see *AE* 1992 (1994) pp. 179–193 (*SEG* 43.26), B, line 20.
- Aixone: For the theater, see *IG* II²1197, line 21; 1198, line 22; 1202, lines 15–16 and 20-21; *AM* 66 (1941) 218–219, no. 1, lines 5 and 11. For a grant of *proedria,* see *IG* II² 1197, lines 9–11.
- Athmonon: No theater has been discovered or is otherwise attested. Since the deme site has been identified with certainty (Traill 1986, p. 135), it is unlikely that an edifice as large as a theater, at least one of stone construction, has escaped the attention of archaeologists and topographers.
- Eleusis: For grants of *proedria,* see *IG* II²1185, line 4; 1186, line 24; 1187, lines 17–20; 1189, lines 11–12; 1192, line 10; 1193, lines 21–24; and *Hesperia* 8 (1939) 177–180, lines 17–19.
- Halai Araphenides: For a grant of *proedria,* see *AE* 1932, *Chronika,* pp. 30–32, lines 20–24.
- Ikarion: For the theater, see Biers and Boyd 1982, pp. 1–18 at 12–14.
- Peiraieus: For the remains of the theater, see *AD* 22B.1 (1967) 143; and Wycherley 1978, pp. 263–264. For written references, see Thucydides, 8.93.1; Lysias, 13.32 and 55; Xenophon, *Hellenika* 2.4.32; *IG* II² 1035, line 44; 1176 (+ *SEG* 19.117, 21.521; and R. S. Stroud, *CSCA* 7 [1974] 290–298, no. 3) (324/3), *passim* (with references to *proedria*); *IG* II² 1214, lines 19–30 (with references to *proedria*).
- Rhamnous: For the theater, see *IG* II² 1311, line 7. For *proedria,* see *SEG* 22.120, lines 5–6. For discussion, see Pouilloux 1954, pp. 73–78.

Thus, as with the erection of stelai, announcements of honors took place within the deme itself. But before we proceed further, let us pause to consider another feature of these announcements. Since every announcement is scheduled, where an indication is given, to take place at a festival of some kind (again, the sole exception is provided by the one decree from Ikarion mentioned above), it is obvious that the announcement did not duplicate or coincide with the passage of the decree itself in the deme's *agora*. Hence the announcement potentially reached an audience of different or wider composition than that out of which the decree conferring the honors had emanated. This suggestion is consistent with the evidence for the inclusion of women (and children?) in the Rural Dionysia, the festival with which the decrees are presumably concerned. To put the question in negative, contrary-to-fact form, if the idea was *not* to reach a wider or at least different audience, what was the point of proclaiming to the *demotai* the content of a decree that they themselves had already passed? To express the result in terms of one of the central claims of this work, whereas the decree had been the product of the constitutional deme, its announcement appears to have been directed to the more inclusive membership based not on citizenship but on residence (or at least temporary presence) within the deme.

But there is a troubling complication. In a speech delivered in the year 330, Aischines mentions a decree of the state prohibiting both phylai and demes from announcing their awards of crowns "at the tragedies" (3.41–45). "The tragedies" can only be those of the City Dionysia staged in town. What are we to do with this evidence? Why, if the position taken here, that the demes, and particularly the distant rural demes, were isolated and self-contained associations, is correct, do we find those associations (with the phylai, already based in the *asty*) flocking to the urban center? Plainly, first, with Whitehead,[32] there is no reason to doubt that, in the period before this decree went into effect, such announcements in the city merely supplemented, but did not *replace,* the announcements in the demes themselves. Nonetheless, the question remains: why any announcement *at all* in the city? Some general instrumental purpose might be thought of, one, say, with a view to advancing the interests of the deme (or phyle) in the central government.[33] But in the absence of specifics regarding the grants (for example, the identity of the movers of the decrees or, especially, of the honorands, their offices or other positions, if any, and their service to the deme)—and of course Aischines provides none—any such speculation would be fruitless.

Alternatively, it is at least as likely that the purpose, or part thereof, was, in keeping with the honorific character of the crown, to enhance the honors still further by their promulgation before a much larger, not to mention more urbane, wealthier, and generally more "important" audience. There was a world of difference between a rural *agora* or—at the deme's own local announcement—its Rural Dionysia and a packed Theater of Dionysos on the slopes of the Akropolis. Besides, the effects of increased exposure would undoubtedly have redounded to the benefit of the bestowers of the honors (that is, the person charged with the actual announcement and the other *demotai* as well, present or not) as well as of the honorand himself. Such an announcement afforded an opportunity, difficult to resist, for performance before a wider public, however brief or routine that performance may have been. It is easy to imagine how such a practice, potentially earning great rewards for very little expenditure of effort, could have gotten out of hand, given the existence of 10 phylai and 139 demes. The decree mentioned by Aischines may have been necessary to prevent the overwhelming of the tragic competitions. But the point here is that such grandstanding is not to be viewed as a regular or necessary part of the deme association's normal functioning. Rather, it was a superfluous redundancy artificially grafted onto the procedures of an otherwise locally based and self-contained organization.

These articles of evidence, therefore, point unambiguously to the conclusion that, so far as we are informed by the official acts of the deme assemblies (and their aftermath), the deme association was firmly rooted in the deme itself. It is easy to see how this point may have gone undetected, or even how an investigator might have come to a quite different conclusion. For our three most explicit and (to the general ancient Greek historian) visible testimonies—Lysias's mention of the congregation of the Dekeleians at the barber shop on the Street of the Herms, Demosthenes' account of the meeting of the Halimousians in the *asty*, and, finally, Aischines' report of the demes' announcements in the Theater of Dionysos—seem to betray a decidedly urban orientation of the associations' internal affairs. But we have seen not

32. Whitehead 1986, p. 257, note 8.
33. Compare my speculations regarding possible underlying purposes of the decrees of the phylai at "The Phyle Association as Instrument of Representation," in chapter 6.

only that this evidence can be given a rather different interpretation but also that, more importantly, its real or supposed troublesome implications are overwhelmingly contradicted by the demes' own amply documented procedures.

Determinants of the Isolation of the Extra-Urban Demes: General Considerations and an Hypothesis

That the *demotai,* in their collective doings, tended to remain close to the village center might be thought intuitively evident once the texts have been cleansed of their (only apparently) conflicting indications. Since the organization consisted of *demotai* and only *demotai,* and given the continuing residence of the majority in the ancestral village, then its meetings and other functions should, all else being equal, take place in the deme. This was the normal case. Only extraordinary factors, such as those evident in Demosthenes' account of the *agora* of the Halimousians, could override the natural inclination not to venture beyond the organization's boundaries. If nothing else, one must acknowledge the inherent absurdity of the members of, say, Phaleron, staging a deme function in, say, Kydathenaion—of one organization formally congregating within the domain of some other (competing) organization. (The only alternative would have been to seek out a location in one of the neutral areas of town, such as the Akropolis or Agora, that belonged to no deme at all.)

But our present concern is with the more tangible inhibiting factors, above all those posed by the difficulties involved in travel to and from destinations outside the home deme. The principle involved is neatly encapsulated in a remark by the speaker of Lysias's speech *On the Question of Not Giving Money to a Handicapped Man.* He seeks to defend himself against the charge that his shop is a place of congregation of undesirable people with the argument that such visitations are the practice of *all* Athenians: "For each of you [i.e., the jurors] is accustomed to paying such visits, one man to a perfumery, another to a barber shop, another to a shoemaker's, or wherever—and most (visit) those people set up nearest to the Agora, the fewest those most distant from it" (24§20). Since the speaker is speaking before a courtroom physically situated in the Agora, it is self-evident that he views the Agora as the natural starting point of any such journey. True, the speaker himself is an invalid who requires the use of two canes and who must travel on horseback when venturing any significant distance (§10–12), but the statement just quoted is couched in generalizing terms with reference to others', not his own, movements. It thus possesses a general, normative value. And as such, it may be taken, pending a full investigation of the subject of travel in ancient Greece, as the basis for the formulation of an hypothesis regarding the practice of Athenians in respect to attendance at meetings, or to travel for any purpose, outside the home deme. If we may take Lysias's speaker's words verbatim, they suggest an inverse relation between the distance to be traveled and the demesman's willingness to travel that distance. People would undertake a journey, but in decreasing numbers and frequency as the distance increased.

This simple model, however problematic may be its application to individual cases, has an obvious relevance to the problem of the deme associations' relations with the urban center. It speaks directly to the question of the incidence of travel for a constitutional—or for any other—reason beyond the limits of the deme. But what demes are we talking about? And with what destinations of such travel are we concerned? An extramural deme, to be sure, might cultivate a relationship with another, especially a neighboring, extramural deme, and some undoubtedly did so on occasion.[34] Nonetheless, it is clear that the overwhelming attraction was directed centripetally toward the *asty*. The urban center was the scene of economic transactions involving, among others, a large segment of the agricultural population; it was the site of the seat of a central government in which all citizens were eligible to participate; it was the venue of a full calendar of religious and other public functions open to all Athenians. These were attractions that, theoretically, exerted their pull on all Athenians irrespective of their place of domicile. But the passage from Lysias suggests the hypothesis that Athenians were variably willing or able to visit the urban center in accordance with the distance of a citizen's domicile from the *asty*.

So my hypothesis, put baldly, would hold that the deme furthest from the urban center would experience the highest degree of insularity. Given a politicized citizenry, insularity, in turn, would foster, or at least provide an opportunity for, the robust development of the association's internal organization. Remote demes should, all else being equal, be relatively active.

At the opposite extreme, the deme situated within the *asty* region itself would be most affected by the magnetic pull of the big city. Such attraction would cover the entire spectrum of public (and, in some instances, private) life. A demesman of Melite, Koile, or Skambonidai—demes located within the city enceinte—could with very little exertion engage in Athenian public life on a daily basis. If so, we should expect in these cases, as a corollary to the hypothesis, a correspondingly lower degree of participation in the deme organization inasmuch as the need for a public life could have been fulfilled by participation in central institutions. Accordingly, one would predict for these urban demes a disproportionate incidence of weakened or, except for compulsory centrally mandated functions, even entirely inactive associations.

The hypothesis that involvement in the public life of the civic center varied proportionately with the distance of a citizen's domicile from the *asty* is, given what we know of the realities of ancient Greek communications and travel, intuitively true. Distances to the most remote rural demes ranged from 15 to 20 miles or so. People of modest means, and of course the poor—that is, the vast majority of the population—would have been compelled to travel by foot. It is therefore difficult to imagine that a demesman farmer, already obliged to dedicate his physical and mental resources to agricultural tasks, could find the time or (especially) the energy to undertake such lengthy, time-consuming, and exhausting journeys. If a layover for a night in town was required (as well it might), otherwise avoidable expenses for food and lodging might be incurred as well. And what for? To sit (and vote) as one of up to 6,000 attendees at a meeting of the Ekklesia? Or to vote under similar conditions in an *ostrakismos*? Or, as a member of the pool of 6,000 dicasts, to present

---

34. For the indications, mostly negative, on this head, see "Deme versus Deme Relations" in this chapter.

oneself in the hope of being allotted to a jury panel on that day but with a very real possibility of not being so selected?

But to assume that such a trip into town would have only a single such purpose is, perhaps, unrealistic and unfair. Alternative, less objectionable, scenarios can be imagined. Specifically, Hansen has suggested that a citizen coming into town from a remote location may have combined constitutional participation with attendance at religious festivals and trading in the market.[35] But the suggestion, though attractive at first, is open to unsettling, even fatal, objections.

Religious Festivals. It is true, as Mikalson showed, that the major Athenian state festivals (excepting those primarily involving women and families) were not duplicated in the demes, with the result that, if a demesman wished to participate, he had no choice but to come to the city.[36] But where is the evidence that they did so in significant numbers? And from distant demes? Besides, as is well known, the demes were well endowed with their own rich calendars of local cultic events.[37] According to a recent study of the deme sacrificial calendars, the demes had retained their religious independence from the city in agrarian, hero, and domestic cults; and, while, admittedly, the deme calendars made allowance for the Dionysiac festivals in the city (by scheduling the sacrifices to be held in the demes either immediately before or after the city festival), it remains true that Dionysos is the most popular deity in the calendars and that the Rural Dionysia was at all events celebrated only in the demes.[38] Another study, while acknowledging that demes or groups of demes were obligated to provide victims for several festivals confined to Athens, reminds us of the festivals confined to the demes themselves and argues that those festivals celebrated both in Athens and in at least some of the demes were the product of independent origin dating to the remote time when the demes were autonomous communities.[39] Local celebrations, to generally characterize the situation, were both numerous and for the most part conducted independently of the central authority. Thus the option to remain at home was a viable and meaningful one. And that option was, it is clear, regularly exercised. For, to put the point negatively, in contrary-to-fact form, unless demesmen had participated in local cults in significant numbers and on a regular basis, sacral calendars on the order of magnitude of that of the small deme of Erchia,[40] to select a particularly striking example, could not have been maintained. Nor would the People object, for epigraphic records seem to indi-

---

35. Hansen 1983, p. 236.
36. Mikalson 1977, pp. 424–435, at pp. 428 and 431.
37. The evidence is collected and evaluated by Whitehead 1986, ch. 7, pp. 176–222.
38. Henrichs 1990, pp. 260–264.
39. Parker 1987, pp. 137–147.
40. *SEG* 21.541 (text). To mention only a single detail by way of illustrating the fullness of the Erchian calendar, the surviving text calls for a total of *fifty-nine* sacrifices. For the editio princeps, see G. Daux, "La Grande Démarchie: un nouveau calendrier sacrificiel d'Attique," *BCH* 87 (1963) 603–634. Among subsequent discussions, particularly valuable are M. H. Jameson, "Notes on the Sacrificial Calendar from Erchia," *BCH* 89 (1965) 154–172; S. Dow, "The Greater Demarkhia of Erkhia," *BCH* 89 (1965) 180–213 and "Six Athenian Sacrificial Calendars," *BCH* 92 (1968) 170–186; and Whitehead 1986, pp. 199–204.

cate the central authority's interest in maintaining cult activity in the demes.[41] Thus the onus of proof rests on the scholar who would imagine significantly numerous and frequent journeys from the hinterland to the urban center for the purpose of joining in statewide cultic celebrations.

Trading in the Market. All are agreed that Athenians were dependent upon the city for manufactured goods, but Hansen states that, in addition, imported grain was "sold to citizens, metics, and slaves *coming from all over Attica*" (italics mine).[42] Hence, if Hansen is right, even residents of distant rural demes will have been forced periodically to visit the Agora (or Peiraieus) to purchase some of the necessities of life. But the position is open to objection. For whom, first, were the admittedly very large shipments of foreign grain destined? The large metic and slave populations were, in accordance with certain very reliable indications, with high probability concentrated in the urban center and Peiraieus.[43] Furthermore, neither

41. Two examples will suffice. (1) From Marathon, a decree dated by its editor to shortly after 490, *Hesperia* 11 (1942) 334–337, calls for the celebration of the Herakleia on an impressive scale. Since the text enjoins the *athlothetai* to make appointments *from each tribe* (lines 5–6), it is reasonable to infer that the decreeing party is the state. (2) A decree with cultic content of the intramural deme of Kollytos is immediately preceded by a decree of the state, *Hesperia* 63 (1994) 233–239 (post 327/6), incorporating *IG* II² 1195. Did the (now very fragmentary) state decree provide guidance for the drafting of the deme's answering enactment?

42. Hansen 1983, p. 236.

43. For the metics, the surest indication is the distribution of identified resident aliens among the demes. According to Whitehead's count (1986, pp. 83–84), of the 366 metics whose deme of residence is known, 223, or almost 61 percent, resided in demes of urban and suburban Athens, plus another 69, or almost 19 percent, in the deme of Peiraieus.

For the slaves, there are two indications, one positive, one negative. Positively, relatively large numbers of slaves worked in *ergasteria* known or presumed to have been located in urban areas: (1) the shield factory of Lysias and his brother employing 120 slaves (Lysias 12, *Against Eratosthenes*, §8, 12, and esp. 19; (2) the two establishments owned by Demosthenes' father, one, a sword factory employing 32 or 33 slaves, the other, a couch factory employing 20 slaves (27, *Against Aphobos*, I §9); and (3) the shield factory of the freedman Pasion, which had an income of one talent per annum (i.e., twice the income of Demosthenes' father's shield factory with its 32 or 33 slaves, Demosthenes, 27§9) (Demosthenes 36, *For Phormio*, §4, 11). To my knowledge, in no instance can any of these workshops be assigned to a specific locale. But the physical evidence for significant industrial activity in and around the Agora is impressive (see *Agora* 14, pp. 185–191), while no trace of such activity outside the urbanized region has been reported. Besides, one would expect an *industrial* workforce to be situated (1) near the source of raw materials (in Athens's case, primarily the port at Peiraieus) and, if items were being manufactured for export, (2) near the point of exportation (again, in Athens's case, Peiraieus).

Negatively, the case has yet to be made in favor of large numbers of slaves engaged in labor beyond the limits of the *asty*. The only sizable numbers of slaves known with certainty to have been engaged outside the urban areas were the gangs employed in the mines in the Laureion region. Farming represents an enormous potential for servile labor, but scholarly opinion remains divided regarding the magnitude of agricultural slavery. Among modern discussions, Jameson supported the proposition that in the classical period "the addition of some slave help to the farmer's own capacity was essential for all but the richest and the poorest" (1977/78, pp. 122–141, with quotation at p. 125), while an opposing position has been taken by Wood (1983, pp. 1–47).

An additional line of argument, one pointing in the same direction, has been advanced by Osborne in his study of the manumission records of the later fourth century, *IG* II² 1553–1578 (Osborne 1991, pp. 231–252). His analysis shows that manumitted slaves tended to gravitate toward Athens, a tendency

metics nor slaves could own land;[44] and, to compound their predicament, the production of citizen farmers, even if one were to include the harvests from the *chora* outside the immediate urbanized regions, was far from adequate to sustain the noncitizen population as well.[45] A large urban noncitizen populace unable to feed itself and without access to the production of the landowning class provides therefore the obvious and most plausible candidates for consumers of the imported grain. But do we really know that *citizen* farmers from Oinoe, Dekeleia, Marathon, or Sounion were likewise dependent on imports and consequently compelled to visit the markets of the city and Peiraieus?

Thus it is not so easy after all to imagine, with Hansen, the operation of multiple motivations for long journeys to the urban center that, in combination with each other, would justify such an expenditure of time and effort. If government service is considered in isolation, prospects for regular participation by country folk are even dimmer. Not even Hansen argues that a meeting of the Ekklesia or the prospect of assignment to a jury panel would *by itself* motivate an Athenian to devote the better part of a day to travel to and from the centralized venues. Paradoxically, however, he does entertain the possibility of a citizen from the country making a far greater commitment to the Council of Five Hundred, if not for the entire year of his membership, then for that one-tenth of the councillior year when the members of his phyle sat as the board of *prytaneis*. Board members were on duty every day, and one-third of the board was required to remain in the Tholos during that period.[46] Hansen suggests that councillors from outside the city took up temporary residence with relatives or fellow demesmen domiciled nearer the seat of government.[47] But against the assumption that Athenians willingly disrupted their personal and working lives on such a scale is the point that absenteeism in the Council, which, for all we know, involved *prytaneis* as well as ordinary *bouleutai*, is suggested by fourth-century witnesses.[48] Notoriously, any number of councillors with extra-urban de-

---

that may also have had implications for "landless citizen artisans at Athens" (p. 246). Obviously, whatever demographic or environmental factors applied to skilled (freed) slaves and to citizen artisans will have applied to nonmanumitted metics as well. Simply put, only the urbanized centers offered opportunities for residents not tied to the land.

44. This is implied by the clause in Athenian citizenship decrees bestowing upon the honorand the privilege of "land and house," with the implication that only citizens were legally capable of such ownership. For the standard treatment of the subject, see Pecirka's 1966 study of the formula of the grant of *enktesis*.

45. So much is implied by the probable size, and resulting yield, of the typical Athenian farm. Burford calculates that "most farms were in the range of 60 *plethra* and less" (1993, p. 68). The yields of such farms, she writes, "would have been adequate in a good year but never princely" (p. 67). It is fair to infer that surpluses were not normally expected or, if expected, forthcoming.

46. *AthPol* 43.1–3; 44.1.

47. Hansen 1983, p. 237.

48. See Rhodes 1972, p. 39, citing Demosthenes 22, *Against Androtion*, §36–38, with Plato, *Laws* 6.758b. Rhodes further notes the later increases of membership of the Council to 600 and 650 without accompanying enlargement of the New Bouleuterion. On the critical point of absenteeism of *prytaneis* versus that of regular *bouleutai*, Demosthenes, the one relevant source here, implies nothing regarding any special obligation on the part of the former to be in attendance.

motics may actually have been town-dwellers. Besides, the existence of a regulation recorded by Aristotle that an Athenian could serve no more than twice in his lifetime,[49] in combination with the fact that the number of Athenians known actually to have served twice seems to have been relatively small[50] shows that, even if satisfactory attendance had been maintained, service on the Council represented at best a temporary departure from a citizen's normal routines. No other governmental body, board of magistrates, or constitutional function, let it be added in conclusion, made any such demands upon Athenian citizens.

The threshold of resistance to travel was undoubtedly very high. To be more specific, the question, again, comes down to the matter of *walking*. Preliminary to a thorough study of the subject, it may be noted here that many farmers were already committed to repeated ploughings of their fields, a routine that necessitated following draft animals mile after mile.[51] All the more reason to look with suspicion upon Hansen's arguments in support of a high degree of mobility. He adduces the fact that "people in pre-industrial societies commonly walked long distances almost daily," specifically instancing (1) European workers, as late as ca. A.D. 1900, walking as far as fifteen kilometers to, and fifteen kilometers from, their place of work; and (2) in agricultural societies, peasants walking "similar" distances between dwelling and field.[52] Yet both of Hansen's categories of evidence are characterized by the element of *necessity*. These workers and farmers had no choice in the matter. In contrast, nothing *compelled* an ancient Athenian citizen to participate in the functioning of the Athenian government. Such participation was nothing more than a purely *voluntary* addition to an already existing schedule of manual agricultural labor. The case for an ambulatory Athenian demesman remains to be made.

One other factor militating against the assumption of the routine presence of citizens from distant demes in the urban center and Peiraieus still awaits acknowledgment. I refer to the question of rural attitudes about the city, city dwellers, and urban lifestyle and values generally. Ehrenberg's classic treatment, based on the plays of Aristophanes, well brought out the distrust, even the hostility, that farmers harbored toward the city, its residents, and its culture.[53] Pending a thorough modern study of the phenomenon, it will perhaps be legitimate to venture that such negative feelings about the "big city" likewise, along with the factors just mentioned, served to inhibit travel to the *asty* or Peiraieus from extra-urban demes. Again, the effect of this argument will be to place the burden of demonstration upon those who believe in the existence of a significant degree of rural-urban mobility.

49. *AthPol* 62.3.

50. Among competing calculations, in a 1988 publication Hansen defended the proposition that "in any year, about a fifth to a fourth of the councillors served for the second time, i.e., ca. 100–125" (1988, pp. 67–69, with quotation at p. 68).

51. Burford finds that three plowings were required (spring, summer, and fall) (1993, p. 121), a finding later increased to "three or four" (p. 125).

52. Hansen 1983, p. 235.

53. Ehrenberg 1951, with pp. 82–89 devoted to consideration of town-country relations and attitudes.

Testing the Hypothesis: Documents of the Demes

Can the hypothesis under review here be tested? Two distinct, separable claims are involved, and each might conceivably be evaluated in the light of the available evidence. First, the hypothesis posits a higher degree of participation in the central government in proportion to the proximity of a citizen's residence to the urban center. Accordingly, one might search for signs by which to measure participation in the government by deme or, for those no longer resident in the ancestral deme, by place of residence. But, to my knowledge, no such signs, direct or indirect, are recoverable. Alternatively, the second claim, the corollary to the hypothesis, is that participation in the home deme organization by resident demesmen increases in proportion to the distance of a citizen's residence from the seat of the central government. Now, this corollary does seem to be testable. To be sure, no *particular* aspect of that activity is sufficiently documented to permit such a test. We cannot compare from deme to deme, say, the frequency of the convening of the *agora*, or the numbers or popularity of deme cults, or, less concretely, the relative degree of solidarity among demesmen. But a rough index of the organizations' *overall* vitality could, it would seem to me, be provided by a more comprehensive measurement— by the number of surviving epigraphic texts promulgated in the names of the demes. The approach is initially encouraged by the fact that 48, or just over one-third, of the demes are represented by at least 157 documents.[54]

One thinks first of those few demes situated within the city circuit, where, on

---

54. My roster of deme documents, which totals 145 items assignable to 48 specific demes plus 12 others not so assignable, is constituted as follows:

Whitehead's list of deme documents (1986, app. 3, pp. 374–393) compiles 129 texts certainly or probably assignable to a specific deme from a total of 45 demes, with his entry for Lamptrai including examples from both the Upper and Lower demes. With Traill 1986, p. 132, *IG* II² 1183 should be reassigned from Myrrhinous (*IG*) to Hagnous, a deme previously lacking a deme document.

From the similar list in Jones 1987, pp. 67–72, add from Prasiai the dedication *Hesperia* 31 (1962) 54, no. 137 (fin. s. IV).

Published since the latest citations in Whitehead's *Demes* (for which the most recent *SEG* volume cited in the index is number 31) are: (1) the decree of Kydantidai and Ionidai of 331/0, *Horos* 7 (1989) 7–16 (*SEG* 39.148, 41.71); (2) a decree of *demotai* dated ca. 350–300 from Philati, perhaps to be assigned to Sphettos, *AncW* 13 (1986) 3–5 (*SEG* 36.187); (3) a decree of the Thorikioi dated ca. 400, *Thorikos* VII (Ghent 1984), pp. 175–177, no. 75 (*SEG* 34.107, 36.180); (4) a second decree of the same deme of the fourth century, *Thorikos* IX (Ghent 1990), pp. 144–146, no. 83 (*SEG* 40.128); and (5–6) two decrees from Acharnai of 315/14, *AE* 1992 (1994), pp. 179–193 (*SEG* 43.26).

Rhamnous, as we shall see, poses a difficulty because of the complicating presence of military personnel which unquestionably account for a large proportion of the many inscriptions from the deme. For the statement that the total number of inscriptions had reached 330, with brief descriptions of new, as-of-then unpublished material, see B. C. Petrakos, *PAAH* (1988) [1991], p. 14 (*SEG* 41.248). By a conservative calculation, the many Rhamnousian texts appearing in the *Supplementum Epigraphicum Graecum* since the closing of Whitehead's list include the following nine certain or probable decrees of the deme association (7–15): *EAH* 1993 (1994), p. 7 (303/2; *SEG* 43.27); *PAAH* (1990) [1993], pp. 31–32, no. 15 (ca. 262/1-256/5?; *SEG* 41.74); op. cit., p. 26, no. 5 (300–250; *SEG* 41.73); *PAAH* 1991 (1994), pp. 27–28, no. 2 (ca. 250; *SEG* 43.31); *PAAH* (1989) [1992], pp. 31–34, no. 15 (236/5; *SEG* 41.75); *PAAH* (1984) A [1988], pp. 206–207, no. 135 (ca. 220; *SEG* 38.127); *PAAH* (1985) [1990], p. 25, no. 6 (s. III; *SEG* 40.129); op. cit., p. 24, no. 4 (s. III; *SEG* 40.143); and *PAAH* (1990) [1993], pp. 32–33, no. 18 (s. III; *SEG* 41.76).

my hypothesis, we should expect to find relatively little trace of deme associational activity. The expectation is not, however, entirely borne out by the record. For the five intramural demes identified by Traill,[55] seven documents are known: Kollytos (II city): one decree;[56] Kydathenaion (III city) (unless the deme, the name of which is only partly preserved, is actually Kydantidai of the inland trittys of II Aigeis): two decrees on a single stone;[57] Skambonidai (IV city): one *lex sacra;*[58] Melite (VII city): three decrees and one catalog;[59] and Koile (VIII city): none. If the one doubtful case is settled (as it seems it must) in favor of Kydathenaion, seven documents for five demes yields a ratio approximating that for the 139 demes of the system as a whole. But this is hardly a conclusive result. The number of intramural demes, five, is so small that these data may not after all reflect a larger pattern, in agreement or not with my hypothesis, should such a pattern exist. It is clear that, if a significant result is to be obtained, we must count our documents according to a broader regional division of Attica.

In order to widen the scope of the inquiry, one might be inclined to appeal to the threefold regional partition of the demes among the city, coast, and inland regions, but such an approach is open to a complicating complexity of the organization, which has only recently, thanks to Traill and others, been fully appreciated.[60] Not a few demes were at some point detached from their neighbors and assigned to trittyes located in some instances at a considerable distance. Thus Diomeia, situated near the Diomeian Gate, just outside the city wall, marches with the coastal trittys of Aigeis;[61] and remote coastal Rhamnous, with its copious dossier of deme documents, is paired with Phaleron to form the city trittys of Aiantis.[62] Perusal of Traill's map will quickly reveal several other, in some cases no less dramatic, examples.[63]

Documents certainly or probably to be assigned to a deme but for which the specific deme is not identified are nos. 130–138 from Whitehead's list, pp. 391–392; and, from Jones's list, p. 72, the dedications *IG* II² 2965 (ca. 400–350) and 2843 (319/18) and the fragment of a decree, *Hesperia* 32 (1963) 12–13, no. 10 (ca. med. s. III; *SEG* 21.521).

55. Traill 1986, map at end.

56. *IG* II² 1195 + *Hesperia* 63 (1994) 233–239, lines 25–39 (post 327/6).

57. *Agora* 16, no. 68 (ca. 350–330 B.C.) (not yet published; *per litt.* Dr. Marian McAllister). The only internal evidence for the identity of the deme (cf. the reference to "the *demotai*" preserved in the second decree, at line 6) is in the first decree, at line 6: Κυδ[------]. The discovery of the stone in the Agora of course favors ascription to the known intramural deme Kydathenaion. Against the candidacy of Kydantidai, this deme belongs to an inland trittys (of Aigeis) and is assigned by Traill to a site at Mendeli at the southern foot of Pentelikon, far from the find-place of our stone (Traill 1986, p. 128, with map at end).

58. *IG* I³ 244 (= I² 288) (ca. 460).

59. *IG* I³ 243, frag. 10 (480–450); II² 2394 (340/39 or 313/2); *AD* 19 (1964) 31–33, no. 1 (ca. 330); *Hesperia* 11 (1942) 265–274, no. 51 (ca. 200–150).

60. The point is illustrated by the variations between the "trittyic" organization of Attica presented by Traill in his 1975 publication and that presented eleven years later in *Demos and Trittys*. As Traill himself noted, the more recent work reflects 27 changes in deme locations and 35 in trittys assignments (Traill 1986, p. 123). More abstractly, consider his statement: "The idea of the trittys presented here [in Traill 1986] is significantly different from that presented in 1975" (loc. cit.).

61. Traill 1986, p. 128, with map at end.

62. Traill 1986, p. 138, with map at end, and cross-reference to *Hesperia* 47 (1978) 103.

63. Traill 1986, map at end.

Accordingly, I have regrouped the demes in line with a tripartite regional division that, since it adheres closely to the general contours of Kleisthenes' Asty, Paralia, and Mesogeion, is not entirely without a historical basis: Figure 3.1 reproduces Traill's assignments of demes to sites on which my three "zones" are based.[64]

- *Inner zone:* the region defined by Aigaleos and Hymettos and the coast between them. Virtually all the demes of this area were assigned in antiquity to city trittyes. It is to be kept in mind that many of these demes, of which the large majority lie outside the city walls, were of an entirely rural character.[65]
- *Middle zone:* the territories surrounding the city area from the northwest clockwise to the southeast and corresponding in large part to Kleisthenes' inland trittyes. To the north, the zone is limited by the foothills of Parnes and Pentelikon. To the northwest, I have included Eleusis and Thria and neighboring demes, despite the fact that they belong to coastal trittyes; as the crow flies, they lie no farther from the *asty* than the demes of the inland trittyes to the east.[66]
- *Outer zone:* all remaining demes, from the more northern locations on Parnes (including Hippothontid Oinoe and Azenia? to the far west) to the region of Rhamnous in the northeast to the distant eastern coast and the southernmost extension of Attica. Most of these demes march with coastal trittyes.[67]

64. Throughout I have followed the "Conspectus of Deme Quotas and Locations" of Traill 1986, pp. 125–140, and as illustrated by his map at the end of this volume. No attempt has been made to deal with those demes for which the location is not known, despite the identification of the trittyes in several cases since, as just emphasized, in the case of an enclave or detached deme, the trittys assignment may not correspond even roughly to the actual location. Aithalidai and Hybadai of coastal Leontis, however, although listed by Traill among the demes of unknown location at the foot of his map, I have counted with the middle zone since both are associated with the same site near the Tatoi airport and since both, in fact, are named at the corresponding position on the map itself. No attempt, finally, has been made to incorporate more recent assignments by other scholars, e.g., S. G. Miller, "Pambotadai Found?" *BCH* 117 (1993) 225–231.

My scheme is similar to Hansen's tripartite breakdown constructed according to radii drawn from the urban center. His regions are labeled "Asty," "12 km.," and "18 km." (Hansen 1983, p. 236).

65. The 40 demes are: Upper Agryle, Lower Agryle, Alopeke, Upper Ankyle, Lower Ankyle, Bate, Boutadai, Cholargos, Daidalidai, Diomeia, Eiresidai, Epikephisia, Erikeia, Eroiadai (Hippothontis), Euonymon, Halimous, Hermos, Hestiaia, Kedoi, Keiriadai, Kerameis, Kettos, Koile, Kollytos, Kolonos, Korydallos, Kydathenaion, Lakiadai, Leukonoion, Lousia, Melite, Peiraieus, Perithoidai, Phaleron, Upper Potamos, Lower Potamos, Ptelea, Skambonidai, Thymaitadai, and Xypete.

66. The 42 demes are: Acharnai, Aigilia, Aithalidai, Aixone, Anagyrous, Athmonon, Elaious, Eleusis, Erchia, Eupyridai, Gargettos, Hagnous, Halai Aixonides, Hybadai, Ionidai, Iphistiadai, Kephisia, Kikynna, Konthyle, Kopros, Kothokidai, Kropidai, Kydantidai, Upper Lamptrai, Lower Lamptrai, Oai, Oe, Upper Paiania, Lower Paiania, Paionidai, Pallene, Pelekes, Upper Pergase, Lower Pergase, Philaidai, Phlya, Prospalta, Sphettos, Sypalettos, Thorai, Thria, and Trinemeia. (Note that both Aithalidai and Hybadai are associated by Traill with the same site south of the Tatoi airport: see Traill 1986, pp. 130–131, s.vv.)

67. The 40 demes are: Amphitrope, Anakaia, Anaphlystos, Angele, Aphidna, Araphen, Atene, Azenia, Besa, Deiradiotai, Dekeleia, Eitea (Antiochis), Halai Araphenides, Hekale, Ikarion, Kephale, Kolonai (Leontis, city trittys), Kolonai (Leontis, inland trittys), Kytheros, Marathon, Myrrhinous, Myrrhinoutta, Oinoe (Hippothontis), Oinoe (Aiantis), Oion Dekeleikon, Phegaia, Phrearrhioi, Phyle, Plotheia, Poros, Potamos Deiradiotes, Prasiai, Probalinthos, Rhamnous, Semachidai, Sounion, Steiria, Teithras, Thorikos, and Trikorynthos.

First, to proceed with the analysis, if we count demes represented by at least one document, the tabulation according to the above regional scheme yields the following result:[68]

Inner Zone: 12 of 40 demes or 30.0 percent
Middle Zone: 19 of 42 demes or 45.2 percent
Outer Zone: 16 of 40 demes or 40.0 percent

In view of the relatively small numbers of texts assigned to individual demes (of which several, represented by only a single text, figure in our calculation only by a lucky chance of survival, while many others, lacking that single text, are, possibly by an equally fortuitous mischance, not counted), this result, though in agreement with the prediction, can hardly be said to confirm it.

It remains to attempt to calculate the *intensity* of associational activity by region. My theory would predict not only that proportionately more demes engage in such activity the greater the distance from the urban center but also that a given deme's activity is more intense in proportion to that distance. Again, the surviving inscriptions seem to be sufficient in quantity and distribution to yield a meaningful result.

But, unlike in the previous case, there is a major complicating factor that threatens to compromise any such calculation. I refer to the fact that the count of texts for the middle zone is swollen considerably by the large fund of inscriptions of the deme Eleusis (23 texts or over one third of the total) and that of the outer zone by that of Rhamnous (25 or fully one half of the total). The reasons for these anomalies are not far to seek. Eleusis and Rhamnous were remarkable among the demes in the same two respects. Both, first, were the sites of major cult centers of dimensions transcending the narrow confines of the host deme itself: at Eleusis, the sanctuary of Demeter and Kore; and, at Rhamnous, the classical shrines dedicated to Themis and Nemesis. Since the cults, the Eleusinian one in particular, attracted visitors from outside the deme, it is easy to imagine ways in which the deme organizations might become more active in response to outsiders, with money to spend, within their domains. Surprisingly, however, there is little evidence that this happened, at least insofar as we can judge from the record of deme documents defined *stricto sensu*. The Eleusinian demesmen honor a hierophant of Paiania in a decree of the mid-fourth century, IG II² 1188; and among the dossier of Rhamnousian texts is *IG* I³ 248, an accounting of the finances of the cult of Nemesis between about 450 and 440. That is all. Either the enhanced activity did not materialize or, if it did, it failed to lead to the creation of permanent records in the name of the deme.

The other distinguishing feature of Eleusis and Rhamnous (along with a few others, notably Phyle and Sounion) is their roles as so-called garrison demes. From the late fourth through the third centuries they serve as bases for the encampment, first, of ephebes (under the system instituted around 335/4), later, of soldiers, both Athenian and foreign. As will become apparent in chapter 4, the presence in these demes of encamped military personnel is to play an instrumental role in the trans-

---

68. I omit from consideration the nine texts assignable with varying degrees of probability to a deme of unknown or uncertain identification listed by Whitehead 1986, pp. 391–392, nos. 130–138.

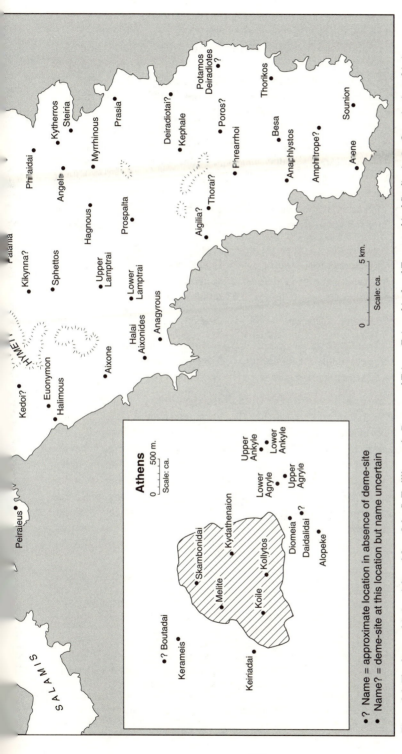

Figure 3.1. The demes of Attica. Adapted from John S. Traill's map in *Demos and Tritys: Epigraphical and Topographical Studies in the Organization of Attica* (Toronto, 1986). The following demes are of unknown location and accordingly do not appear on the map: Acherdous, Auridai, Cholleidai, Eitea (Akamantis), Epieikidai, Eroiadai, Hamaxanteia, Hippotomadai, Krioa, Oion Kerameikon, Otryne, Pambotadai, Phegous, Pithos, Sybridai, Themakos, and Tyrmeidai.

• ? Name = approximate location in absence of deme-site
• Name? = deme-site at this location but name uncertain

formation of the deme from an association based on descent (the "constitutional" deme) to one based on residence (the "territorial" deme). For present purposes, it is sufficient to note that the military presence—whether ephebes, soldiers, or a commanding officer—does, unlike what we have just noted in the case of the pan-Attic cult centers, palpably vitalize the deme associations, to the extent that vitality can be measured by the survival of texts in the name of the association inscribed on stone. By my count, at least 9 of the 23 texts from Eleusis[69] and at least 13 of the 25 texts from Rhamnous[70] are attributable to the military presence, whatever form it may have taken. Since to include these texts in my calculations would indicate that they were the product, not of the presence of ephebes, soldiers, or a commander but rather of the deme's distant remove from the *asty* (which is obviously not the case), they must be deleted.

Two different measures of the evidence may now be taken. First, the average number of documents for those demes with at least one surviving document by zone:

Inner Zone: 21 documents for 12 demes: 1.75 documents per deme
Middle Zone: 56 documents for 19 demes: 2.95 documents per deme
Outer Zone: 45 documents for 16 demes: 2.81 documents per deme

Second, the average number of documents for all demes by zone:

Inner Zone: 21 documents for 40 demes: 0.53 documents per deme
Middle Zone: 56 documents for 42 demes: 1.33 documents per deme
Outer Zone: 44 documents for 40 demes: 1.10 documents per deme

Again, both results are consistent with the truth of the hypothesis, but to claim confirmation would be to go too far. Perhaps the one secure inference is a negative one. No one could possibly maintain that deme associational activity was positively correlated with nearness to the seat of the central government; that somehow local activity constituted a sort of reflex of engagement in city political life and that remoteness from the seat of government had fostered apathy. Perhaps the best-founded impression would be one of a wide scattering of active deme associations with a discernible small increase in the extra-urban regions. While, too, 29 of the 48 document-producing associations are known by only one inscription, a few centers, Peiraieus (inner zone, 7 inscriptions), Eleusis (middle, 14), Aixone (middle, 9),

69. *IG* II² 1156, lines 45–51 plus 64 (334/3; honors for ephebes); 1189 (334/3; honors for ephebes); Pouilloux 1954, no. 2 (ca. 330; honors for ephebes); *IG* II² 1191 (321/0 or 318/7; decree of Eleusinioi and soldiers); 1187 (319/8; honors for general); 2971 (ca. 315/4; honors for Demetrios of Phaleron); 1193 (fin. s. IV; honors for peripolarch); 1280 (ante 266/5; decree of Eleusinioi and soldiers honoring Antigonos Gonatas); and 1299, lines 51–80 (236/5; honors for general).

70. Pouilloux 1954, no. 2 (ca. 330; honors for ephebes); *SEG* 43.27 (303/2; honors for general); *SEG* 24.154 (268/7 or 265/4; honors for general); *SEG* 31.110 (med. s. III?; honors for officer[s]); *IG* II² 3467 (ca. 256/5?; honors for officer); *SEG* 43.31 (ca. 250; honors for general); *SEG* 22.120 (med. s. III; honors for commander of garrison); *SEG* 25.155 (236/5; decree of Rhamnousioi and soldiers); *SEG* 15.112 (225/4; honors for trierarch); *IG* II² 1313 (fin. s. III; honors for officer and his men); *SEG* 31.112 (fin. s. III; decree of Rhamnousioi and soldiers honoring officer and his men); *PAAH* (1990) [1993], pp. 32–33, no. 18 (s. III; *SEG* 41.76; honors for general); and *PAAH* (1985) [1990], p. 25, no. 6 (s. III; *SEG* 40.129; honors for general).

Halai Aixonides (middle, 9), and Rhamnous (outer, 12), produce over one third of the dossier of assigned documents. But the fact remains that, even given the uncertainties prompted by the vagaries of the epigraphic record, greater frequency and intensity are discernible in the outlying regions and that it is in those regions that four of the five best-represented demes (all save Peiraieus) were situated.

Testing the Hypothesis: The Demes in Comedy

If the thesis under examination is correct, then the isolation of the extra-urban demes from the city centers should have left its mark on the culture (broadly conceived) of classical (and later) Athens. After all, the more or less sustained estrangement of the greater part of a citizen population from its own political, social, commercial, and ceremonial hub would be a sociological point of major proportions. But the expectation of an immediate discovery of telltale and corroborating effects of the phenomenon is sadly disappointed. The deme associations, above all the smaller, rural ones, proved not to be the sorts of entities that easily left traces of any description in the physical, documentary, speculative, or imaginative productions of the ancient Athenian people. Nonetheless, there is a possible significant exception. I refer to the comedies of the Attic stage. The true-to-life topicality, whether that topicality is of a political or domestic orientation, of an Aristophanes or a Menander, occasions the relatively frequent mention of the demes in a variety of contexts. The accumulated references are of sufficient bulk as to give rise to the hope that something might be learned, positively or negatively, about the merits of the thesis under consideration.

Before setting out the evidence, however, a thorny methodological difficulty besetting the enterprise must be acknowledged. The problem concerns a variable conditioning the evaluation of the particulars of the comedic record, namely, the composition of the audience—the very matter on which the significance of the present discussion will hinge. This factor is obviously bound up with the understanding of the point or meaning of the playwright's text, since it is self-evidently true that, in the case of comedy, the playwright's creation will be shaped, even determined, by his expectation of what will amuse, disgust, edify, or otherwise entertain his audience. To get right to the point, was the audience mainly urban, mainly rural, or some combination of the two? It is clear that the mention of a remote deme (remote, that is, with respect to the Theater of Dionysos) located in an agricultural region will get varying reactions in accordance with the composition, urban or rural, of the spectators. To judge from recent discussions in the literature, no secure, independently founded (that is, independently of the texts soon to be under review) description of a typical audience, whether during the Peloponnesian War or at any other time, can be constructed.[71] Nor is an *assumption* one way or another permissible in the context of the present argument, since any assumption concerning the presence or absence of rural Athenians in the *asty* would inevitably involve the argument in circularity (if their absence is assumed) or refute it (if their presence is assumed). Some

---

71. Certainly, the failure after repeated efforts by several scholars to determine whether or not women attended the theater does not offer encouragement.

fraction of the audience, however, *must* of course have consisted of urban dwellers. At the same time, too, it is appropriate to recall that some of the land within (as well as just outside) the walls was given over to farming and that, in the time of Aristophanes' "war" plays, large numbers of extramural residents of Attica crowded into the areas—the *asty*, Peiraieus, and the space between the Long Walls—protected by the city fortifications. At all times, and particularly during much of the war, Athenians of rural residence and presumably rural attitude were within easy traveling distance of the Theater.

My solution to this problem has been to regard the factor of the audience as a hypothetical contingency. To spell out my method in the form of a question: on the assumption that the purpose of comedy is to entertain (not exclusively, of course, through the medium of humor), do the many references to the demes achieve this goal, or achieve it more successfully, if the audience is assumed to be basically urban, basically rural, or a combination of the two? Any answer to this question will accordingly tend to confirm, or to refute, my thesis that the extramural deme associations were absent from city life in direct proportion to their distance from the *asty*.

Because the material about the demes in comedy has already been treated thoroughly—and insightfully—by Whitehead,[72] it will not be necessary to undertake an exhaustive compilation of the scattered particulars. Whitehead's chapter stands ready as a resource for the curious—and the skeptical. What justifies another discussion is the fact that Whitehead did not ask of the record the question that I am asking. He was not testing, or even incidentally considering, an hypothesis concerning the interrelation between rural demes and urban center. But we are, and for that reason we are entitled to reconsider that portion of the record relevant to this question. Nonetheless, despite the highly focused presentation, it will become clear, I hope, that even an exhaustive rehearsal of the evidence would not yield a result significantly at variance with that reached in the ensuing discussion.[73]

Old Comedy

No overall assessment of the deme in Old Attic comedy is possible. Perhaps what would have been the most illuminating material is lost, for later sources preserve a memory of Hermippos's *Demotai*,[74] and of Eupolis's *Demoi*.[75] But Aristophanes' *Acharnians*, which does survive, tells us little of the deme qua deme, if only because, for one thing, the setting of the play is not the deme itself. If Whitehead is right (as I suspect he is), the same was probably true of other comedies, now lost, of

72. Whitehead 1986, ch. 11, pp. 327–345. Earlier, a good start, with some telling points, had been made, first, by Haussoullier 1883, pp. 196–202; and, later, by Edwards 1916, pp. 24–30.

73. Throughout my discussion of Old Comedy, references to the intact plays of Aristophanes pertain to the Oxford Classical Text, *Aristophanis Comoediae*, 2d edition by F. W. Hall and W. M. Geldart, 2 vols., Oxford 1906 (vol. 1) and 1907 (vol. 2). All remaining texts are cited according to the edition of R. Kassel and C. Austin, *Poetae Comici Graeci (PCG)* and, where *PCG* has not yet appeared, Kock, *CAF*, or Edmonds, *FAC*.

74. *PCG* V, Hermippus, 3–22.

75. *PCG* V, Eupolis, 99–146. Cf. Edmonds, *FAC*, vol. 1, pp. 978–994, appendix, "The Plot of the *Demes* of Eupolis."

which the titles were based on the name of a deme or on a demotic—Strattis's *Potamioi*,[76] Eupolis's *Prospaltioi*,[77] Magnes' *Man of Titakidai* [78] (a hamlet probably belonging to the deme Aphidna), and Aristophanes' *Anagyros* [79] (i.e., the eponym of the deme Anagyrous). Generally, the deme in question, Whitehead argued, provided only the background but little of the substance of the action or other content of the drama.[80] Nonetheless, for our purposes it may be significant that these demes fit into our tripartite geographical classification as follows: inner zone (1?): Potamioi?;[81] middle zone (3): Acharnai, Prospaltioi, Anagyrous; outer zone (2?): Titakidai (i.e., Aphidna), Potamioi?[82] Apparently, demes providing the titles of works of Old Comedy were, generally speaking, relatively far removed from the urban center. We must remain alert to the possible significance of this fact as we briefly rehearse some of the material about the demes contained in the actual surviving texts.

To begin our investigation, it will be noted that the seemingly casual and non-pointed use of demotics, demes as place-names, or similar expressions reveals a conspicuous pattern when the examples are considered in relation to our three regions. I will illustrate by citing the several instances according to deme and zone. From the inner zone (6 examples): Cholargos (*Acharnians*, line 855), Kolonos (Pherekrates, *PCG* VII, *Petale*, 142), Kydathenaion (*Wasps*, lines 895 and 902), Leukonoion (Phrynichos, *PCG* VII, *Monotropos*, 22), Melite (Plato, *PCG* VII, *Laios*, 65), and Skambonidai (*Wasps*, line 81). From the middle zone (10 examples): Aixone (*Wasps*, line 895), Athmonon (*Peace*, lines 190 and 919), Cholleidai (*Acharnians*, line 406), Gargettos (*Thesmophoriazousai*, line 898), Kikynna (*Clouds*, line 134), Konthyle (*Wasps*, line 233), (Lower) Lamptrai (Aristophanes, *PCG* III 2, *Amphiaraos*, 27), Paionidai (*Lysistrata*, line 852), Phyla (*Wasps*, line 234), and Sphettos (*Clouds*, line 156). To this point, none of these uses of the demotic or mentions of a character's deme, save two, involves obvious humor or ridicule of the person (or deme) concerned. Rather they are part and parcel of the fabric of incidental detail that helps create the aura of verisimilitude required by Old Comedy's topicality. It is under such conditions alone, I wish to suggest, that as many as six of the examples pertain to the demes of my inner zone, including the downtown Athens of Aristophanes and other Old Comedy poets, of the Theater of Dionysos, and (hypothetically) of their audiences. No member of an audience from an urban deme would have found anything offensive or off-putting in any such use of his own demotic. But the last example from the middle zone, in contrast to the prevailing prosaic char-

76. *PCG* VII, Strattis, 38–40.

77. *PCG* V, Eupolis, 259–267.

78. *PCG* V, Magnes, 6, Πυτακίδης ("Τιτακίδης Bernhardy, prob. Meineke et Kock").

79. *PCG* III 2, Aristophanes, 41–66.

80. Whitehead 1986, p. 330, with the following discussion through p. 338.

81. There were three demes called Potamos, Upper and Lower (both city IV Leontis), placed by Traill (1986, p. 130) east of the *asty* at the foot of Hymettos, and Deiradiotes (coast IV Leontis) placed by Traill (1986, p. 132) in southeastern Attica near the coast north of Thorikos. The former pair of demes march with my inner zone, the third with my outer zone. Unfortunately, as Whitehead realized (1986, p. 292, note 7), the sources for Strattis's play do not distinguish among the three demes.

82. See the preceding note.

acter of the others, may, Dover suspected, make a pun on Greek *sphex*, "wasp,"[83] and
to it may confidently be added Kinesias's self-representation, with obvious sexual
double entendre, as a Paionides. Likewise, from the outer zone, of the three examples, one, Phyle (*Acharnians*, line 1028), is without evident point, but the two others,
Steiria (Kratinos, *PCG* IV, *Ploutoi*, 171, line 67) and Teithras (Hermippos, *PCG* V,
Moirai, 43), may convey the notions of contempt and pedantry, respectively.[84]

The conclusion that comedic handling of the demes may express judgments of
varying kind proportionally with the distance of the deme in question from the
urban center is not to be separated from the well-known pattern of deme affiliations
of the major invented protagonists in Aristophanes. Where determinable, *all* belong
to the middle zone: Athmonon (Trygaios), Cholleidai (Dikaiopolis), and Kikynna
(Strepsiades). (The location of Krioa, the deme of Euelpides in *Birds*, line 645, is
unknown, though Traill assigns the deme to a city trittys [of Antiochis].)[85] Aristophanes' heroes (and not a few lesser figures) are in the main rural types, even if, as
in the case of Strepsiades, transplanted to the city. Naturally, therefore, the affiliations tend to be with neither the urban centers nor the distant maritime or mountain-
ous regions. Farming lands sufficiently removed from the noxious effects of the city
are the natural home communities for Aristophanes' invented characters, major or
minor.[86] This was the positive dimension of the complex, alternately sympathetic
and demeaning, portrayal already partially suggested by the mildly negative plays
on the names of extra-urban demes.

Nor are Old Comedy references to the demes limited to the affiliations of
dramatis personae by any means. So miscellaneous are these references in character
that no easy classification is possible. Edwards's list of "reasons" for the mention of
demes in Aristophanes will, however, give an idea of the situation: (1) for characterization; (2) with reference to some local cult or custom; (3) with reference to
some local peculiarity or accident of location; (4) to recall the glories of the Persian
Wars; and (5) "to make a hit of some kind, mostly at the expense of the demes."[87]
Study of this material, and of the fuller dossier of passages assembled by Whitehead, has for the most part unveiled no striking patterns with regard to the geographic location, urban or rural, of the demes in question. But two possible exceptions may be noted, and an attempt may be made to explain them.

The first exception to the apparent lack of *Tendenz* in the deme affiliations is with
respect to food items. In both Aristophanes and other writers of Old Comedy, edibles,
as represented by six examples, are invariably associated with extra-urban demes.[88]
Self-evidently, agricultural (or maritime) produce will be linked to its expected places

83. K. J. Dover, *Aristophanes: Clouds*, Oxford 1968, on line 156. (I owe this reference to Whitehead
1986, p. 333, note 43.)

84. For Steiria, see *PCG*, loc. cit., commentary; for Teithras, Whitehead 1986, pp. 331–332.

85. Traill 1986, p. 139. The point may be moot, since Euelpides is represented as living in Halimous
(*Birds*, line 496).

86. Cf. Edwards 1916, p. 24; Whitehead 1986, pp. 332–333.

87. Edwards 1916, pp. 27–28, with some paraphrase on my part.

88. Nuts from Phegaia (*PCG* IV, Cratinus, *Kleoboulinai*, 93), red mullet from Aixone (*PCG* IV, Cratinus, *Trophonios*, 236), perch from Anagyrous (*PCG* VII, Plato, *Syrphax*, 175), tub-fish from Anagyrous
(*PCG* II, Archippus, *Ichthyes*, 27), and figs from Teithras (*PCG* VII, Theopompus, *Eirene*, 12). See, on

of origin. But there may be more at work here than this banal truism. Might these bits of incidental detail not strike an audience as exotic, quaint, or picturesque, provided that that audience was dominated by urban residents long removed from the ways of an active agricultural (or maritime) life? Or, to put it the other way around, if the audience hails from the very demes which are the sources of these foodstuffs, what is the entertainment value of their mention for the poet of Old Comedy?

Still more striking (and meaningful) instances of the phenomenon are afforded by the *humorous* references to the demes—coinciding in part with the "hits" of Edwards's fifth category of "reason." Some are good clean fun, such as the mention of a "headland" in punning reference to the deme Kephale [89] and, less obviously, the allusion to Pallene embedded in the chorus of Acharnians' pronouncement that, in order to stone (*ballein*) Dikaiopolis, they will search for him in Ballene.[90] Possibly of a similar character is the seeming pun on the demotic of Teithras in a production of Hermippos.[91] But a play on words could take a more serious turn, as when Demosthenes remarks that Kleon's mind was "in Klopidai," with Whitehead probably to be taken as a distortion of the deme name Kropidai designed to suggest theft or embezzlement (cf. *klopeuein*, etc.).[92] Similarly, a use of the demotic of Steiria by Kratinos very likely conveyed an expression of contempt.[93] Still more seriously, several mentions of demes are founded on vulgar, usually punning, associations. Scatological or grossly sexual humor is expressly involved in references to Acherdous (defecation),[94] Kopros (defecation),[95] Paionidai (copulation),[96] Anagyrous (stinking smells),[97] and Anaphlystos (masturbation).[98] Of these ten demes, four (Kephale, Teithras, Steiria, and Anaphlystos) march with the outer zone, five (Pallene, Kropidai, Kopros, Paionidai, and Anagyrous) with the middle zone, and one (Acherdous), while unplaced, has been tentatively assigned to an inland trittys (of VIII Hippothontis).[99] Not a single instance of such humor can be linked to a deme of the inner zone. How are we to interpret this pattern in the distribution of the demes?

---

this material, Whitehead 1986, p. 331, with notes 22–26. To these add sprats from Phaleron (Aristophanes, *Acharnians*, line 901; *Birds*, line 76; *PCG* III 2, *Tagenistai*, 521) and vinegar from Sphettos (Aristophanes, *Ploutos*, lines 720–721). See, on these two examples, op. cit., p. 334, with notes 48 and 51. Of the demes, Aixone, Anagyrous, and Sphettos belong to my middle zone; Phegaia and Teithras to the outer zone. Phaleron marches with the inner zone demes, but its maritime orientation renders its products exotic in the view of the landlocked city-dwellers of the *asty*.

89. Aristophanes, *Birds*, lines 475–476.

90. Aristophanes, *Acharnians*, line 234.

91. *PCG* V, *Moirai*, 43, with Whitehead's discussion at 1986, pp. 331–332.

92. Aristophanes, *Knights*, lines 78–79. See, for his comment, Whitehead 1986, p. 336, with note 59, where he acknowledges the existence of a real hamlet Klopidai (attached to the large deme Aphidna: see Traill 1975, pp. 90–91).

93. *PCG* IV, *Ploutoi*, 171, line 67, with commentary.

94. Aristophanes, *Ekklesiazousai*, lines 361–362, with Whitehead's remarks at 1986, p. 336, with note 61.

95. Aristophanes, *Knights*, line 899 (cf. *Ekklesiazousai*, line 317).

96. Aristophanes, *Lysistrata*, line 852, with Whitehead 1986, p. 335 and note 55(b).

97. Aristophanes, *Lysistrata*, lines 67–68, with Whitehead 1986, p. 335 and note 56.

98. Whitehead 1986, p. 335, with note 55(a).

99. Traill 1986, p. 137.

Whitehead allows that the demesmen of Anaphlystos and Paionidai (to cite his two examples) "laughed as heartily as anyone at such simple wit,"[100] but I have my doubts. If the audience had no objections to humor at their own expense, why are there not jokes about the close-in demes? About the demes many of whose members must have been in the Theater? And, to pose a more fundamental question, is self-deprecation an ancient Greek (as well as a modern Western) attitude or disposition of mind? Were the people of Kopros or Paionidai incapable of being insulted, or at least demeaned, on the undoubtedly endlessly reiterated and tiresome point of the comic potential of their deme names? This is a traditional society; the subject is a person's *patridha*. Better to conclude that we are dealing with urban—and urbane—humor at the expense of a largely absent Athenian rural population.

Middle and New Comedy

Although mentions of demes are not as abundant as in Old Comedy, sufficient material survives as to suggest the possible continuation of some of the trends just noted. Again, some of the passages are neutral or incidental to the humor, innocently dropping the demotic of a real or fictional character[101] or providing a geographical reference.[102] Occasionally, however, a poet alludes to a well known fact or a reported characteristic of a deme[103] and, significantly, wherever that fact or characteristic is satirically or otherwise critically portrayed, the deme tends to be an outlying one, as in the cases of Aixone, Potamioi?, Sounion, and Trikorynthos, versus the single innocuous characterization of urban Peiraieus as "a hollow nut."[104] But, for the most part, as in Old Comedy, no discernible pattern emerges.

With greater potential significance for our study, Whitehead collects eight titles incorporating or otherwise reflecting names of demes, four from Middle, four from New, Comedy.[105] All four of the former group (*Thorikioi*[106] and *Man from*

---

100. Whitehead 1986, p. 335.

101. E.g., Acharnai: Anaxandrides, *PCG* II, *Protesilaos*, 42, line 18; Timokles, *PCG* VII, *Dionysos*, 7, line 1 and *PCG* VII, *Ikarioi Satyroi*, 18, line 6, with Whitehead 1986, p. 339, note 80. Eleusis: Menander, *Sikyonios*, lines 187–188. Euonymon: Menander, *Kitharistes*, lines 96–97. Halai: Antiphanes, *PCG* II, *Tyrrhenos*, 209, line 1. Skambonidai: Menander, *Sikyonios*, lines 346–350. To the inner zone belong Euonymon and Skambonidai; to the middle zone, Acharnai, Eleusis, and Halai (Aixonides); to the outer zone, Halai (Araphenides).

102. E.g., Cholargos: Menander, *Dyskolos*, lines 32–34. Halai: Menander, *Heauton Timoumenos*, frag. 140 Edmonds, lines 3–4. Paiania: Menander, *Dyskolos*, lines 407–409. Cholargos is inner zone; Halai, middle (Aixonides) or outer (Araphenides) zone; Paiania (Upper or Lower), middle zone.

103. E.g., Aixone ("Aixonian through both parents"): Menander, *Kanephoros*, frag. 256 (cf. on calling a person an "Aixonian," Plato, *Laches* 197C, with Whitehead 1986, p. 342, note 107). Peiraieus ("a hollow nut"): Philiskos, *PCG* VII, unknown play, 2. Potamioi (improper deme registration): Menander, *Didymai* (apud Harpokration, s.v. Ποταμός, with Whitehead 1986, p. 342). Sounion (again, improper deme registration): Anaxandrides, *PCG* II, *Anchises*, 4, lines 3–4. Trikorynthos (a "queenly demeswoman"): Menander, unknown play, frag. 907. For references to food items, see below, with notes 118–120.

104. While Peiraieus and perhaps Potamioi (if not Deiradiotes) belong to the inner zone, Aixone marches with the middle zone, and Sounion, Trikorynthos, and perhaps (again) Potamioi (Upper and Lower) all march with the outer zone.

105. Whitehead 1986, p. 338.

106. *PCG* II, Θορίκιοι ἢ Διορύττων, 105.

Phrearrhoi[107] by Antiphanes; *Ikarian Satyrs*[108] and *Marathonioi*[109] by Timokles) belong to the outer zone. Therefore, wherever the action was set (and in each case this is unknown), the plays may, as a consequence of the remoteness of these demes, have had an otherworldly aura about them—again, on the hypothesis that few demesmen actually resident in such distant locales would be present in any significant numbers at these productions in the Theater of Dionysos. The four New Comedy examples represent the inner zone (*Lakiadai* by Philippides[110]), middle zone (*Man of Anagyrous* by Diphilos[111] and *Erchieis* by an unknown author[112]), and the outer zone (*Halaieis* [Araphenides] by Menander[113]). Lakiadai, though (on my geographical definitions) nominally urban, was situated outside the city walls[114] and presumably no less rural than other extramural demes. New Comedy also boasts a *Demotai* by Posidippos,[115] echoing the comedy of the same name by his Old Comedy predecessor Hermippos.

Unlike the case of Aristophanes, none of whose surviving plays was placed in a specific Attic deme, later productions, Menander's in particular, sometimes are known to have been set in a specific, textually identified deme. Five instances are registered by Whitehead (with varying degrees of probability): Acharnai or Halai Araphenides (*Epitrepontes*), Eleusis (*Man of Sikyon*), Halai Araphenides again (*Halaieis*), Phyle (*Dyskolos*), and Ptelea (*Heros*).[116] The last-mentioned deme belongs to the inner zone, but Traill places it far outside the walls under Aigaleos.[117] Acharnai and Eleusis march with the middle zone, Halai Araphenides and Phyle with the outer. When Menander wished to recreate the ambience of a deme, he, like his Middle Comedy forerunners, ventured far outside the immediate environs of the site of his productions on the slopes of the Akropolis.

Demes in later Comedy were not (so far as we know) vividly depicted or characterized, except in one area: once more, food. Examples are Aixone (fish), Phaleron (fish), Otryne (gobies), and Dekeleia (vinegar).[118] Aixone is a deme of the middle zone, and distant Dekeleia marches with the outer zone. Phaleron belongs to the inner zone, but the old seaport is topographically distinct from the inland *asty* and so culturally, if not geographically, "distant." Otryne is not yet located (though conjecturally assigned by Traill to a city trittys [of II Aigeis]).[119] Again, as with Old

107. *PCG* II, *Phrearrhios*, 222.
108. *PCG* VII, *Ikarioi Satyroi*, 15–19.
109. *PCG* VII, *Marathonioi*, 24.
110. *PCG* VII, *Lakiadai*, 13–14.
111. *PCG* V, *Anagyros* or *Anargyros*, 11.
112. *IG* II² 2323, line 98 (= *SEG* 25.194, line 81).
113. Kock *CAF* III, nos. 13–37 (pp. 7–14); Edmonds *FAC* vol. 3B, pp. 552–553.
114. Traill 1986, p. 133, with map at end.
115. *PCG* VII, *Demotai*, 10.
116. Whitehead 1986, pp. 341 and 344.
117. Traill 1986, p. 133, with map at end.
118. Whitehead 1986, p. 339, with notes 83–85 (pp. 339–340). The primary references are: Aixone: Nausikrates, *PCG* VII, *Naukleroi*, 1, lines 7–11. Phaleron: Euboulos, *PCG* V, *Orthannes*, 75, line 4; and Sotades, *PCG* VII, *Enkleiomenoi*, 1, line 30. Otryne: Antiphanes, *PCG* II, *Timon*, 204, lines 4–8. Dekeleia: Alexis, *PCG* II, unknown play, 286, line 3.
119. Traill 1986, p. 127, with map at end.

Comedy, there is a perceptible tendency for demes identified as sources of co-mestibles to be removed from the urban center. As with Old Comedy, I find here too the quaint or picturesque, reflecting an essentially urban sensibility. Nor were these (hypothetical) urbanites incapable of reflecting upon *their own* condition. The Kerameikos, just outside the city walls, was associated by Alexis with the "slick life."[120] If this quality was meant to extend to the deme in which the Potters' Quarter was located, Kerameis, it is relevant here as a possible comedic stereotyping of urban life, and implicitly so in contrast with the quite different qualities so often ascribed by comedy to the rural demes.

At the outset acknowledgment was made of our uncertainty concerning the composition of the audiences that witnessed the original productions of Attic comedy. While keeping this complicating factor in mind, I have nonetheless in the discussion above considered, *as an hypothesis*, the possibility that in various respects these plays were, paralleling their physical urban setting, urban (and urbane) in their treatment of the Attic demes. So evaluated, the mentions of the rural demes seem to suggest a foreign world removed from the everyday experience of the audience. That world could be the source of an heroic protagonist on a mission to correct the misdeeds of a demagogic city politician, but it could also produce a ridiculous figure like Strepsiades, hilariously inept in his failure to adjust to an urban setting. Rural demes could be put to work, through association with their distinctive products, to evoke images of the exotic, quaint, or picturesque. The same demes, and demesmen, could serve as the butts of punning, sexual, or scatological silliness. All of this, I am suggesting, makes the most *comedic* sense on the assumption of a predominately *urban* audience, or at least of an audience with an urban outlook and attitude. That city folk were present in large numbers is incontrovertible. The question concerns rural demespeople. My general contention that the extramural demes were generally isolated from the *asty* would suggest that only relatively few were present. It seems that the treatment of the demes on the comic stage would tend to corroborate this contention.

The "demes" of Attic comedy were, therefore, quintessentially extramural and rural. An additional, negative reason for my believing this is based on a conspicuous pattern of silence. The five intramural demes, Koile (bouleutic quota 3), Kollytos (3), Kydathenaion (11),[121] Melite (7), and Skambonidai (3), though, as indicated by their quotas of members in the Council of Five Hundred, comprising at least 5 or 6 percent of the total citizen population and surely contributing a large fraction of the theatergoing public, are scarcely heard of in comedy, Old, Middle, or New. And when these demes do receive mention, it is in a way incidental to the humor of the passage.[122] To Aristophanes, Menander, and the other comedic playwrights, the

---

120. Alexis, *PCG* II, *Pyraunos*, 206, lines 1–5, with Whitehead 1986, p. 339, note 82.

121. On the vacillation of Kydathenaion's quota between 11 and 12, see Traill 1986, p. 129.

122. Koile: no occurrences; Kollytos: no occurrences; Kydathenaion: one occurrence (Aristophanes, *Wasps*, lines 895 and 902, demotic of Kleon); Melite: four occurrences (Aristophanes, *Frogs*, line 501, toponym; *PCG* III 2, *Georgoi*, 119, "house of Meliteis"; *Geras*, 149, wild boar of Melite; Plato, *PCG* VII, *Laios*, 65, demotic); Skambonidai: two occurrences (Aristophanes, *Wasps*, line 81, demotic of Nikostratos; Menander, *Sikyonios*, lines 347 and 350, demotics).

word or notion of "deme" evidently awakened associations with the "sticks" or "boondocks," especially (at least in Old Comedy) rural (rather than maritime) districts. This restriction in the application of the term recalls the usage of Herodotos, who, when he records events of Athenian history before Kleisthenes, occasionally speaks of "the demes" in opposition to the *asty* (e.g., 1.60.5, 62.1). Isokrates, too, may in some confused way preserve a memory of such a use of the term when he writes of the division in some cities between the *polis* "by *komai*" and the *chora* "by *demoi*."[123] Very possibly, then, to add a final point, the aforementioned comedic titles "Demes" (Eupolis) and "Demesmen" (Hermippos, Posidippos) would prove, if the truth were known, to have reflected this idiosyncratic narrowing of the term and concept.[124]

Deme versus Deme Relations

Even if distant rural demes were relatively isolated from the urbanized centers, it does not follow that such demes were similarly isolated from other communities as well. We must approach with an open mind the possibility that the rural demes cultivated reciprocal relations of exchange, if not with far-flung associations, then at least with those conveniently within the reach of available modes of communication and transportation. Among the various possible such contacts, the first and most obvious relates to other units on the same tier of organization—other demes.

If we begin by restricting our investigation, in line with the purpose and methods of this book, to the level of institutions, inspection of the documentary record at once reveals a decided paucity of positive indications. No more than four clearcut examples can be adduced. Around 330, the Rhamnousians, Eleusinians, and Phylasians join the Boule and Demos in honoring the Pandionid ephebes, *MDAI[A]* 67 (1942) 21–22, no. 24 (= Pouilloux 1954, no. 2). None of the three demes, of course, belongs to Pandionis. But the demes' locations along the northern frontier of Attica and the fact that they are evidently by this time serving as sites for the stationing of troops point up the extenuating circumstances.[125] That is, these garrison demes share the distinction of having played host to the ephebic military trainees of the third phyle. About the same time, the phyle Kekropis, the Boule, and two demes, Eleusis and Athmonon (the latter of Kekropis), jointly honor in separate decrees engraved on a single stone the Kekropid ephebes of the year 334/3 and their *sophronistes,* of Athmonon, *IG* II² 1156. The Eleusinians are grateful for the ephebes' attention to the *phylake* (lines 45–51, plus 64), while the Athmoneis are motivated by

123. *Areopagetikos* 46.

124. For speculations concerning the content of Eupolis's *Demes*, see Whitehead 1986, p. 330, note 17. In the end, the significance of the play's title remains "obscure." The point that the play probably had to do with the country demes was made long ago by Edwards (1916, p. 25), but with little or no supporting argument.

125. For the epigraphic testimony relating to the garrison demes, see Whitehead 1986, appendix 6, "The Garrison Demes," pp. 401–407: at 403 (Phyle), 404–405 (Eleusis), and 405–406 (Rhamnous). For the archaeological remains (in the form of "A Provisional Corpus of Fortified Military Camps in Attica"), see McCredie 1966, part II, pp. 17–87.

appreciation for their fellow demesman, the *sophronistes* (lines 32, 52–63, plus 64). Thus the two demes share a debt of gratitude to the selfsame entity, the Kekropid class of ephebes. They do not, however, enjoy geographical propinquity or other discernible commonality. Two demes that do share a boundary are Eleusis and Thria, the two principals of a lease document from the end of the fourth century, *IG* II² 2500. According to the very fragmentary text, it appears that the Eleusinians are renting an *agora* from the Thriasians. Presumably the square was physically contained within the boundaries of the owner deme but was in less demand there than by its more populous neighbor.[126] The prospect of material advantage plainly undergirded the arrangement on both sides. Possibly contiguous, too, were the demes Kydantidai and Ionidai which combine to issue a decree dated 331/0 honoring the priest of Herakles and the *kolokratai* for their tendance to the (presumably joint) festivals of Herakles, *SEG* 39.148 (= 41.71).[127] Shared involvement in the festivals (possibly belonging to the Kydantidai, since all three honorands share their demotic) and perhaps a desire to economize by jointly bearing the expenses incurred by the decree may suffice to account for this unprecedented example of a joint act by two demes.

So, from these positive examples it is clear that cooperation between deme associations was possible. Nonetheless, given the existence of 139 demes and of a relatively copious epigraphic record, the positive cases are strikingly few. One might, for example, expect to find dedications of various sorts jointly composed and erected in the names of two or more demes.[128] But the record is virtually blank. The only remaining signs of deme-and-deme coordination involve encamped soldiers in the aforementioned garrison demes.[129] Maybe there is more than at first meets the eye to the late report that families from the demes Pallene and Hagnous did not intermarry.[130] Cooperation was by far the exception rather than the rule.

The introversion of the deme with respect to other demes appears to be a development of the post-Kleisthenic period. Before the democracy, village communities *did* enter into formal cooperative constellations, in each known case based on a cult. We know this because their names, and evidently something of their organization, survived into the later, classical era: the Marathonian Tetrapolis, the Trikomoi, perhaps a second Trikomoi, the Tetrakomoi, Mesogeioi, and the League of Athena Pallenis. Precisely because of the threat posed by the social and political cohesion among the communities that comprised these constellations, Kleisthenes, as Lewis argued in a classic paper,[131] while institutionalizing those communities as constitutional demes, attempted to weaken some of the old organizations by assigning their constituent demes to different trittyes and even different phylai. For example, the

126. Thria has seven *bouleutai* in comparison with Eleusis's eleven (?). But this is of course only part of the story. The "national" sanctuary of Demeter and Kore will undoubtedly have attracted a large permanent or seasonal noncitizen population. Thus Whitehead counts ten metics from Eleusis but none from Thria (1986, pp. 83–84).

127. Editio princeps at *Horos* 7 (1989) 7–16.

128. None surfaces at least among the dedications published in *IG* II² 2965–3016.

129. E.g., *IG* II² 1299 (post 236/5), lines 1–50. The phenomenon is not uncommon.

130. Plutarch, *Theseus,* 13.3–4

131. Lewis 1963, pp. 22–40: 30–34.

four demes that, as villages, had comprised the Marathonian "Four Towns," would not, with the separation of Probalinthos from the other three, be able to carry that solidarity over into the constitutional apparatus of the public organization.[132] Nonetheless, at least some of the old cult structures—demonstrably, five of the six just mentioned—survived into the fourth century and beyond.[133] The inclination to maintain the old ties of cooperation was evidently a strong one. All the more reason for our puzzlement with the general absence of formal cooperation among the Kleisthenic demes during the period of the democracy. Before Kleisthenes, and even after, villages could cooperate for cultic purposes, but these same (and similar) communities, qua constitutional units, seem to have gone their own separate ways.

132. According to Traill's most recent table of demes and their trittys and phyle affiliations (1986, pp. 125–140, "Conspectus of Deme Quotas and Locations"), the regional cult associations, with their deme components (plus trittys and phyle affiliations), are as follows:

Marathonian Tetrapolis: Strabo, 8.7.1 (383) records the names of the members: Oinoe (coast IX Aiantis), Marathon (coast IX Aiantis), Probalinthos (city III Pandionis), and Trikorynthos (coast IX Aiantis).

Trikomoi I: Steph. Byz. (s.v. Εὐπυρίδαι) attests Three Villages comprising Eupyridai, Kropidai, and Pelekes. Traill places the demes in a line extending from the eastern end of Aigaleos to the southern slopes of Parnes (see Traill 1986, map at end). After Kleisthenes, all three demes belong to inland IV Leontis, and so under the democracy remain constitutionally as well as geographically unified.

Trikomoi II: Bicknell 1976, pp. 599–603, posits a second Three Villages comprising Erchia (inland II Aigeis), Konthyle (inland III Pandionis), and Kytherros (coast III Pandionis). Despite their proximity along a northwest-southeast line east of Hymettos (see Traill 1986, map at end), under Kleisthenes they belong to three different trittyes from two phylai. None of the trittys assignments is unnatural, but then again nothing had prevented Kleisthenes from drawing his trittys boundaries in such a way that the three villages marched together in a single trittys. (The combined bouleutic quotas of the three demes were no greater than 10: Erchia, 6/7; Konthyle, 1; Kytherros, 2: Traill 1986, pp. 127, 129, 130.)

Tetrakomoi: The Four Villages attested by Pollux 4.105 are: Peiraieus (city VIII Hippothontis), Phaleron (city IX Aiantis), Thymaitadai (city VIII Hippothontis), and Xypete (city VII Kekropis). Thus the villages were assigned to three trittyes belonging to three phylai. But these four neighboring settlements in the harbor area could easily and naturally have been fit into two, rather than three, trittyes (not one, because their combined bouleutic quotas is around 26); and Phaleron's pairing with Rhamnous (Traill 1986, p. 138) in the city trittys of Aiantis severely compromises the territorial integrity of the old cult association.

Mesogeioi: According to Lewis 1963, p. 34, note 112 (cf. Schlaifer 1944, pp. 22–27), the likely member demes are: Bate (city II Aigeis), Diomeia (coast II Aigeis), Kydathenaion (city III Pandionis), and Kerameis (city V Akamantis). Kleisthenes assigns the demes to four trittyes in three phylai. Though all were certainly or probably situated in the city region (Bate's location, however, remains uncertain: Traill 1986, p. 127), the four demes are not in particularly close proximity to one another (see Traill's map at end). Diomeia's dislocation and inclusion in the coastal trittys of Aigeis is nonetheless conspicuously violent.

The League of Athena Pallenis: As argued by Lewis (1963, pp. 33–34, with additional note at p. 39), the League comprised Gargettos (inland II Aigeis), Acharnai (if [with Traill] split, city VI Oineis and inland VI Oineis), Pallene (inland X Antiochis), and Paiania (inland III Pandionis). (Reexamination of the inscription on which Lewis's reconstruction was based, MDAI[A] 67 [1942] 24–29, no. 26, by Stanton has reaffirmed and strengthened this conclusion: see Stanton 1984, pp. 292–298, esp. 297–298). Why are these demes assigned to four trittyes in four phylai? While the trittys assignments of Gargettos and Paiania seem natural enough, the unnatural grouping of Pallene with Aigilia and Thorai, both conjecturally located on the distant southwestern coast (Traill 1986, pp. 139–140), may reveal a desire to weaken the League by dislocating one of its members. Acharnai's case, because of the deme's unusually large size, is too anomalous to permit speculations of this kind.

133. For the full references to the relevant epigraphic testimony, see "Regional Associations," in chapter 8.

Perhaps, however, this was not what the reformer had intended. Both the trittyes and, at the topmost tier, the phylai were after all assemblages of demes. What did Kleisthenes have in mind for these assemblages? Precious little of the internal organization of the trittys survives, but it is enough to establish that an attempt had been made to launch a trittys association—and that that attempt had failed.[134] True, often a deme or two of a given trittys were separated by some distance from the main cluster, but nothing precluded the contiguous members from carrying the organization. Where, in the case of Aphidna (inland IX Aiantis), a single large deme constituted its own trittys, the deme might have represented itself instead as a trittys, but there is no sign that this happened.[135] Apparently, a trittys, in its capacity as an association, proved to be an entity of no consequence. Meanwhile, at the uppermost tier of organization, the phyle, despite its tripartite regional design, nonetheless *did* develop a modicum of organizational cohesion and purpose. In particular, if the thesis argued in chapter 6 is right, the phyle organizations served as instruments of representation whereby members could transmit their concerns, and advance their interests, in the arena of the central government. But our present focus is upon the interaction of deme with deme. Did demes, qua demes, cooperate with one another in order to further any such representative functions of their phylai? No evidence to that effect survives. The phyle association seems to have been dominated by urban residents acting without discernible reference to their deme affiliations. No trace survives of the joint cooperation within the phyle of its constituent deme associations. Nor, in the vertical dimension, is there a trace of cooperation between a deme and the associations of either the trittys or the phyle of which it was a component, for purposes of representation or for any other reason.

So far we have considered the question at its institutional level, and, still more narrowly, in terms of interaction between deme organizations. Obviously, there remain other possibilities. One involves the possible exchange between deme A and an *individual* in deme B. Fortunately, a record of many such exchanges, involving both member and nonmember honorands, has been preserved in the form of the honorary decrees of the deme associations. Typically, by a vote of the assembled membership, the honoring deme bestows praise, crown, and perhaps other honors upon a single, or occasionally two or more, benefactors. By Whitehead's count, between 113 and 116 individuals are so honored by the inscriptions (and in a few cases by other types of sources).[136] Of these, 23 are persons who are not members of the honoring deme.[137] What can we learn from this minority of the decrees? Many, as it turns out, might be described as special cases inasmuch as they reflect the presence in the deme of a military commander or troops or ephebes certainly or probably engaged in activity on behalf of the entire state of Athens. It is not a matter, that is, of the particular honoring deme's exclusive relationship with a particular individual

134. For the few traces, see Jones 1987, ch. 1, sec. 1.33, pp. 60–61.

135. Admittedly, no document of the deme association of Aphidna survives that might have confuted this claim.

136. Whitehead 1986, pp. 238–239. The few additional deme documents discovered since Whitehead wrote do not materially affect these numbers or the inferences drawn from them.

137. Not counted here are the Theban nationals honored by Eleusis in the two decrees *IG* II² 1185 and 1186 (both med. s. IV).

from outside that deme. By my count, 13, possibly 14, cases fall into this category, all but two from the garrison demes Eleusis and Rhamnous.[138] (And, to illustrate my point about particularity, of these dozen or so inscriptions, three—from Aixone, Eleusis, and Sphettos—honor the same person, Demetrios of Phaleron.)[139] Two other honorands are priestly officers of the "pan-Athenian" religious center at Eleusis.[140] Here, once more, the honorands, while in fact serving all of Athens, merely happen to do so within the territorial confines of the honoring deme. Similarly, another is the wife of a *demotes* of Melite (and therefore, technically speaking, not a member of the deme association) honored for her services to various cults—not all, significantly, necessarily cults of the deme itself.[141] Three texts are too fragmentary or vague to allow us to ascertain the nature of the benefactor's service to the honoring deme.[142] The remaining four honorands—from three texts—may be briefly described:

Lower Lamptrai: IG II² *1204 (fin. s. IV).* An Acharnian is acknowledged to have been "energetic in the sacrifices and *ta koina* to which he has access in the deme" (lines 4–7). Besides praise, he is granted *ateleia* and a portion of meats at the sacrifices of the *demotai* "just as for the Lamptrians" (lines 8–17).

Peiraieus: IG II² *1176+ (324/3).*[143] The deme crowns the four lessors of the deme's theater, namely, two *demotai,* one Lamptrian, and one man of Pelekes (lines 30–33).

Sounion: IG II² *1181 (med. s. IV).* A citizen of Erchia appears to have been honored for his performances of sacrifices.

These cases, though few, do tell us something. On occasion non-*demotai* citizens performed services for other demes and were accordingly rewarded. To better understand the relationship, one would like to know if the honorand was *resident* in the honoring deme at the time of his services. A clue is provided by the fact that in no instance where both demes are identifiable are the demes contiguous—or even

138. Aixone: *IG* II²1201 (317–307; honorand of Phaleron); Eleusis: *IG* II² 1156 (334/3; honorand of Athmonon), lines 45–51 plus 64; 1187 (319/8; honorand of Hagnous); 2971 (ca. 315/4; honorand of Phaleron), cf. fragment *k*; 1193 (fin. s. IV; honorand of Kephale); 1299 (post 236/5; honorand of Leukonoion), lines 51–80; Rhamnous: *SEG* 24.154 (post 268/7; deme of honorand unknown: see Whitehead 1986, p. 453, no. 362); *IG* II² 3467 (ca. 256/5?; honorand of Aithalidai); *SEG* 25.155 (236/5; honorand of Thria); 15.112 (225/4; honorand of Eitea); 22.120 (med. s. III; honorand of Melite); *PAAH* (1984) A [1988], pp. 206–207, no. 135 (ca. 220; honorand of Cholargos); Sphettos: *SEG* 25.206 (315/4; honorand of Phaleron); deme not identifiable: *IG* II² 1212 (fin. s. IV) (military? [see line 6]). For the reason for thinking that one of the two honorands in the last-mentioned decree is *not* a member of the honoring deme, see Whitehead 1986, p. 249, note 123.

139. See the preceding note: Aixone: *IG* II² 1201; Eleusis: *IG* II² 2971; Sphettos: *SEG* 25.206.

140. Eleusis: *IG* II²1188 (med. s. IV; honorand of Paiania); 1191 (321/0; honorand of Sphettos: see Whitehead 1986, p. 450, no. 340).

141. *Hesperia* 11 (1942) 265–274, no. 51 (ca. 200–150).

142. Eleusis: *IG* II²1192 (fin. s. IV; honorand of Phyle); Gargettos: *MDAI[A]* 67 (1942) 7–8, no. 5 (ca. 350–300; honorand of Acharnai: see Whitehead 1986, p. 416, no. 56); Peiraieus: *IG* II² 1214 (ca. 300–250; honorand of Cholleidai).

143. For the new fragments added to the text since Kirchner's edition, see R. S. Stroud, *CSCA* 7 (1974) 290–298. Since these additions do not concern the passage quoted, I have continued to use Kirchner's line numbers.

within comfortable walking distance of each other.[144] This finding comes close to proving that the honorand was a resident of the honoring deme at the time of his benefactions. This inference, in turn, permits a guess concerning his attitude. Although officially an outsider, the honorand preferred limited participation in the host deme to either inactivity or the prospect of long journeys to and from the ancestral deme. But—the point to be kept in mind—that participation was most definitely limited, as expressly acknowledged by the qualifying clause in the decree from Lower Lamptrai specifying those activites in the deme "in which he has a share": . . . ὧν μέτεστι/ν αὐτῶι ἐν τῶι δήμωι, . . . (*IG* II² 1204, lines 6–7). It is unlikely that life in a foreign deme was ever as attractive, where formal associational activities were concerned, as that in the deme of one's affiliation.

But significance is also a matter of quantity. Alongside these few positive examples of formal interdeme cooperation are at least ninety in which the deme honors *its own demotes* (-*ai*). Again, one is drawn to the conclusion that, institutionally speaking, there was little interaction between deme associations and members of other demes.

The implications of this conclusion must not be overstated. The conclusion concerns the deme *association* only. Nothing is implied (or suggested) regarding other forms of potential interaction between the various communities of Attica. Quite the contrary, the evidence for the regional integration of the Athenian population is abundant and multifaceted. Much excellent work, as it happens, has already been done in this area. To impart an idea of what is now known, it will be sufficient merely to allude to some of the more important findings.

Residence. It is well known that *demotai* from outside the urban center(s) often maintained temporary or even permanent residences in or near the *asty* or Peiraieus.[145]

Landholding. R. Osborne has charted the prevalence among upper-class citizens of multiple, fragmented landholdings.[146] Necessarily, such holdings would serve to engage the owner in communities outside the home deme.

Intermarriage. R. Osborne found that marriages outside the deme outnumber those within it, links with more distant demes being preferred to those with nearby

144. In fact, in each case but one the honoring deme and the deme of the honorand are removed from one another by considerable distances. The exception is Peiraieus (honoring) and Lamptrai (honorand) (*IG* II² 1176, line 32), but even they are far from being neighbors. Regarding the three doubtful cases (see above, note 142), in two instances the two demes in question have been securely placed by Traill: Eleusis and Phyle (*IG* II² 1192) and Gargettos and Acharnai (*MDAI[A]* 67 [1942] 7–8, no. 5). For both pairs, the distance between is about one kilometer as the crow flies. (As for the third pair, Peiraieus and Cholleidai, *IG* II² 1214, the latter deme remains unplaced.)

145. Whitehead's discussion of the phenomenon will be found at 1986, pp. 353–356. Page 353, note 14 (pp. 353–354) collects a dozen examples of migrators from the country to the town, including several owners of houses in Athens town or Peiraieus.

146. Osborne 1985b, chapter 3, pp. 47–63, "The Pattern of Land-Holding in Classical Attika." For the fact that the available evidence relates only to the wealthy sector of citizen society, see p. 60. Pages 60–63 ("A view of the whole patchwork") sum up the findings of his analysis of literary and epigraphic sources.

demes. Naturally, the relatively wealthy families overrepresented in Osborne's data undoubtedly enjoyed a higher degree of mobility than their less prosperous fellow citizens.[147] At the same time, even the small-holder will have seen attractions in a marriage tie with a distant community, as Gallant's study of subsistence farming has so persuasively shown. Access to farmland in a distant location (with commensurate variations in climate, contour, soil type, etc.) will have afforded "subsistence crisis insurance" against a catastrophic loss or decline in production at home.[148]

Cult Associations. Above, mention was made of the well-known archaic cultic associations of neighboring demes. Since the demes in question were often contiguous (or nearly so), the common cult could serve as a focus of attention and loyalty transcending a particular deme's boundaries, physical and social.

Mining Leases. R. Osborne found that the "mining demes" (comprising 15.8 percent of all demes) account for only 34 percent of the owners of the mining operations located within their boundaries. (Even less overrepresented by the mining demes were found to be those Athenians who own and lease or who lease only.)[149] For our study, the point to be made is that about two-thirds of the citizens involved in silver mining were members of demes outside the mining region.

Routine Travel between Different Areas of Attica. Among other motives, such travel occurred for commercial reasons, particularly in the case of rural dwellers visiting the Agora or Peiraieus and their environs. On a presumably less frequent but still periodic basis, Athenians from all regions journeyed to the pan-Athenian cult centers in town, at Eleusis, Brauron, and elsewhere.

The integrative effect of these interdeme involvements is undeniable. But another statistic noted by Osborne gives one pause: more Athenians (to judge from the evidence of tombstones available at the time of his writing) are buried in the deme of birth (by which he must mean the deme of the inherited Kleisthenic affiliation) or into which they were married than elsewhere.[150] While more recent study of the sepulchral material has shown, if anything, that practice differed from deme to deme, it remains true that those demespeople who erected a monument bearing a demotic generally were interred in or near the community of their affiliation.[151] Scattered landholdings, the need for a city residence, business interests, shopping expeditions, or religion might temporarily remove one from the home base, but in the final analysis, apparently, the ultimate, overriding loyalty was to one's *patridha.*

As the final word of the preceding paragraph suggests, it is perhaps germane to

147. See Osborne 1985b, pp. 127–138. For the tabulations on which the generalizations are based, see pp. 130–131. For the bias of the evidence toward wealth, see p. 130. For the conclusion that marriages outside the deme appear to have been "more normal" than marriages within it, see p. 131 (but note the qualifications that follow). For an exploration of the strategy of marrying daughters into an outside deme, see Cox 1988, pp. 185–188.

148. Gallant 1991, pp. 154–155.

149. Osborne 1985b, pp. 118–123, with p. 119 for the percentages.

150. Osborne 1985b, pp. 130–131.

151. For references to the findings of recent research, see the head of the present chapter, with notes 1–3.

think of modern rural Greece and of the relocated urbanites who faithfully return to the ancestral village for *paniyiri*, Easter, and family events.[152] Applied to the ancient case, the modern practice invites the positing of a kind of "homing instinct." Perhaps the deme association, while defined constitutionally in such a way that *demotai* might enjoy unlimited mobility while not surrendering or compromising their nominal membership, developed a solidarity sufficient to counteract a multiplicity of disintegrative forces, not the least of which was the attraction, economic if not cultural, of the city. That solidarity is much in evidence in literary texts and reaches such an intensity that the word for "demesman" and the word for "friend" experience (to use Whitehead's phrase) a "semantic overlap."[153] Such bonds of amity, reinforcing the perception of the deme as the "home base" from which one made forays, social, economic, and cultural, into other communities, and to which one subsequently returned (if only to be buried), may, as much as any repelling xenophobic tendencies on the part of potential host demes, have contributed to the general absence of contact between deme associations and individuals from outside the community.

Solidarity could also be expressed (to return to the deme association) in the formal acts of the association's *agora*. On those few occasions when the *demotai* did decide to confer honors upon a non-*demotes*, the decree sometimes explicitly draws attention to the fact that the honorand will enjoy a privilege (or privileges) normally reserved for *demotai* alone.[154] This is the same exclusivity evidenced elsewhere in prohibitions regarding access by outsiders to the deme's corporate functions or facilities.[155] In all these cases, finally, it is important to note that what is at issue is not the upholding of the law, certainly not the law of Athens. It is rather a question of attitude, the attitude of exclusion bred by the combination of the inheritable *demotikon*, isolation, and the emergence of the deme as the counter to the integrative tendencies of classical Athenian society.

152. For a discussion, see Ernestine Friedl's study of the village of Vasilika, 1962, pp. 100–103, with p. 104.

153. Whitehead 1986, pp. 231–232, with p. 231 for the quotation.

154. Hagnous: *IG* II² 1187 (med. s. IV), lines 20–23; Lower Lamptrai: *IG* II² 1204 (fin. s. IV), lines 12–17; Peiraieus: *IG* II²1214 (ca. 300–250), lines 11–17, 19–25, 25–28.

155. Lower Lamptrai, *IG* II² 1204 (fin. s. IV), lines 6–7; Peiraieus, *IG* II² 1177 (med. s. IV), lines 2–12. From Kephisia, *AD* 24 (1969) 6–7 (ca. 350–300) relates that the honorand, among other benefactions, fenced off the fountain house ὥ[στε----μὴ εἰσι]/έναι εἰς αὐτὴν (lines 8–9). If, as seems likely, the remainder of line 8 and the beginning of line 9 stated that the honorand's actions had benefited *the deme* (. . . καὶ τἆλλα φι[----] / τὸν δῆμον τὸν Κ[ηφισ]ιέων . . .), it is a natural inference that those not permitted to enter were precisely non-*demotai*. However, for a restoration of the text involving not humans (as I have suggested) but animals, see *SEG* 36.188, citing J. and L. Robert, *Bull. Ep.* 1971, no. 286. Another doubtful case is the decree of the Sounians *IG* II² 1180 (med. s. IV), which calls for the creation of a new *agora*. The space is to be large enough for the Sounians "and for anyone (else) who wishes" (lines 12–15). The underlying assumption would seem to be that in the normal case the facilities of a given deme are accessible only to the *demotai*.

FOUR

The Demes

Expansion and Decline

The Women of the *Demotai*

Thus far, the phenomenon of exclusion, initially broached in chapter 2, has been considered only in respect to people situated outside the community of the *demotai*, broadly defined. But the constitutional deme also harbored a large population of "outsiders" within itself, within the households of its members and within its territorial boundaries. Among these "outsiders" were first and foremost the womenfolk of the *demotai*, principally their wives and unmarried daughters.

Participation by Women in the Cults of the Demes

The general exclusion of women from the constitutional deme is an uncontested fact. Only males were admitted to formal membership in the organization and only the names of males were entered on the *lexiarchika grammateia*. Only a citizen male normally bore the *demotikon* in unaltered form and transmitted it to the next generation, while his wife and, until her marriage, his daughter bore (as shown by its grammatical form) not her own *demotikon* but his—despite the fact that the two affiliations were one and the same.[1] Only male members are known to have functioned as officers of the deme organization or to have figured as the principals—

---

1. Whitehead 1986, pp. 77–79. Occasionally, a married woman was identified by the demotics both of her father and of her husband. For the few, and mostly late, surviving examples of feminine demotics, see p. 78.

proposers or, in the case of laudatory decrees, honorands[2]—or voting members in the deme's *agora*. If, as many have asserted, the deme, in its role as a microcosm of the greater Athenian polity, was constructed in the image of that polity, it is evident that the modeling extended *inter alia* to the exclusion of females from membership and from virtually all the activities of the deme tied to that membership.

Yet the exclusion, as I have just hinted, was not complete. There did exist in fact a well-circumscribed pocket of female activity. Naturally, in keeping with the stated guidelines of this study, our attention must be confined to the formal, organized functioning of the deme associations. Merely to catalog incidents of female interaction with *demotai* within the territorial or other limits of a deme would contribute nothing to the accomplishment of our goals. Given such a limitation, as previous investigators have realized, all such documented female participation is confined to various aspects of the practice of religion within the deme organizations. While there is some indication of a general inclusion of females in ritual activities, the preponderance of references to women—and, in fact, *all* the references to particular female members of the demes—concern occupants of priestly offices. Let us begin by reviewing the epigraphic record in chronological order:

IG I³ 250 (ca. 450–430). Discovered at Liopesi and assigned to Lower (rather than Upper Paiania on internal evidence (see Whitehead 1986, p. 385, no. 83), this *lex sacra* twice mentions a priestess, once in broken context, the other time as recipient of emoluments (lines 5 and 33).

IG II² 1356 (init. s. IV). This fragmentary *lex sacra* specifies sacrificial perquisites for a series of priestesses. Although no textual reference to a deme survives, commentators assign the stone to Halai Aixonides on the basis of the provenience (see *IG*). References to six different priestesses are preserved, and in five cases the name of the divinity can be read in whole or part: the Heroine (line 5), Dionysos (line 9), Hera (lines 11–12), Demeter Chloe (line 16), and [- - -]/ας (feminine genitive singular; lines 19–20).

SEG 21.541 (ca. 375–350). The Erchia cult calendar from Spata, while never once referring to a priest, does specify the sacrificial perquisites for no fewer than four priestesses: of the Heroines (A 17–22, E 1–9), of Semele (A 44–51), of Hera (B 37–39), and of Dionysos (Δ 33–40)

IG II² 1175 (ca. 360). This decree of the *demotai* (lines 2–3) is assigned to Halai Aixonides on the basis of a prosopographical link (lines 5–6) in combination with the provenience. At lines 21–24, "the priestesses" are called upon to take an oath with the demarch, the *tamias*, and the priests.

IG II² 1184 (med. s. IV). In this document of the Cholargeis mention is made of the priestess in connection with the festival of the Thesmophoria. Whether this festival (and with it its priestess) belonged to the deme or was in fact the well-documented statewide celebration of the same name is not readily determinable.[3] But the two *ar-*

---

2. A single female honorand is recorded, Satyra, wife of Krateas of Melite: *Hesperia* 11 (1942) 265–274, no. 51, lines 2 and 8–9. But the late date of the text, viz., first half of the second century, renders it irrelevant to the present discussion.

3. O. Broneer, *Hesperia* 11 (1942) 265–274, at 270–273.

chousai who are charged with supplying the priestess with grain, figs, olive oil, etc. (lines 3–18) are certainly, since this is a decree of the demesmen (cf. lines 19–20), officers of the deme. An illuminating parallel is provided by the text of Isaios. The speaker mentions certain women of the deme Pithos undertaking cultic duties in the Thesmophoria (8.19–20); since they are said ἄρχειν (§19) in this capacity, it is highly probable that they too were entitled *archousai*.

IG II² 1177 (med. s. IV). Two references to "the priestess" occur in this decree of the Peiraieis concerning the administration of their festival of the Thesmophoria (lines 1 and 7); see further below.

SEG 22.116 (*AD* 19 [1964] 31–33, no. 1) (about 330). This decree, found at a site identified with near certainty as the temple of Artemis Aristoboule established by Themistokles in the vicinity of his residence in Melite, honors a member of that deme. Appropriately, the decree is dedicated to Artemis and is dated by the tenure of Chairylle as priestess (line 5).

SEG 23.80 (ca. 330–270). These sacrificial *fasti* (a new edition of *IG* II² 1363 by Dow and Healey) instance perquisites or emoluments for "the priestesses from Eleusis" (I, lines 15–16) and "the priestess of Plouton" (I, lines 23–24).

IG II² 1199 (320/19). The third of these decrees of a deme (identified as Aixone by the stone's provenience) records honors for three parties including "the priestess of Hebe and Alkmene" (lines 24–25).

IG II² 1207 (fin. s. IV?). This fragmentary opening of a decree of the *demotai* from Menidi (hence, as the mover's demotic already indicates, the Acharneis) identifies as the honorand "the priestess" who had made dedications to (Athena) Hippia (lines 2–4).

IG II² 1213 (s. IV). This small fragment preserves the words "the deme" in line 7; its findspot "[i]n vico Spata" (*IG*) settles the identification of the deme in favor of Erchia. The reference in line 3 to ταῖς ἀρξούσαις occurs in a general cultic context, so these female "officers" will have exercised religious duties of some kind. See above, *IG* II² 1184.

Hesperia 39 (1970) 47–53 (med. s. III). This *lex sacra* of the Phrearrhioi, concerned (according to its editor, Eugene Vanderpool) with "the rites of the Eleusinian goddesses, Demeter and Kore, and their associates" (p. 49), refers once to "the priestesses" (line 11), once to a single priestess (line 20), each time in broken context.

Hesperia 11 (1942) 265–274, no. 51 (init. s. II). This decree of the demesmen of Melite honors one Satyra, wife of a demesman (line 2), for her services as the priestess of the Thesmophoroi (lines 1–2, 8; cf. [12]). But the full significance of her appointment is not certainly ascertainable since, again (see above, *IG* II² 1184), it is uncertain whether this deme's Thesmophoria is or is not a local deme association festival.

A simple pattern is manifest throughout. Each priestess is attached, where an indication is preserved, to a female divinity, save for Dionysos, the female orientation of whose cult is too well known to require documentation, and Plouton, patently a surrogate for Mother Earth. This practice would seem, if (again) we subscribe to the familiar paradigm of the unit modeling itself after the exemplar of the state, to be an imitation of, or at least to have paralleled, the tendencies in evidence at Athens itself in this regard. As Athens's cult of her patron Athena Polias, or of that of the same goddess under her title Nike, resided in the custody of a priestess, so were the womenfolk of *demotai* charged with the maintenance of the demes' cults of their female divinities.

If, furthermore, females could hold priestly offices within the deme, it is natural to suppose that these same demes also maintained cults participation in which was open to the rank and file female membership as well. Mikalson's exploration of Athenian popular religion in respect to its centralized and more localized dimensions suggests that such participation, though not documentable in detail, was in fact widespread and frequent enough to have significantly impacted the communal life of the deme associations. For some of the major Athenian festivals, he found, the *demotai*—by which I understand him to mean male citizens exclusively—traveled from the home deme (if it was other than the place of the celebration) to Athens (or Eleusis) to participate. These festivals included the Panathenaia, the Mysteries of Demeter and Kore, Anthesteria, Pyanopsia, Stenia, Haloa, Thargelia, and Lenaia. Meanwhile, the home deme itself in these cases provided *no* additional local celebration of the festival whatever. (The case of the City Dionysia was somewhat different in that Dionysos enjoyed great popularity in the demes, as evidenced above all by the Rural Dionysia.)[4] What, then, was going on in the demes? Not all major festivals, Mikalson found, followed the pattern of the Panathenaia, Mysteries, and the others. Rather, those festivals which were concerned with the family or which were celebrated primarily by women were found to have been held *locally* as well as in Athens. Documented examples include the Theogamia, Skira, and Thesmophoria.[5] (The last-mentioned, the Thesmophoria, is recorded for six, possibly seven, demes, although, again, it is debated whether the festival was a deme celebration *per se* or merely a local version of the statewide event.)[6]

The reason for this pattern is a matter for speculation. For most children and some women, certainly, travel over any distance by foot will have been difficult, if not hazardous, and presumably avoided if at all possible. Another contributing factor was undoubtedly the well-established tendency to confine at home females of the citizen class. Yes, such women, particularly of the lower economic and social stratum, are known on occasion to have ventured into public, but the cultural ideal of female confinement does not seem to have been abandoned, however frequent these violations.[7] Probably the *kyrios*, if it was at all possible, preferred that his mother, wife, or unmarried daughter not venture far from the home. Naturally, if a religious event called for a relaxation of his custody, it was the deme that provided an obvious well-defined and narrowly circumscribed venue for female public activity.

The existence of priestesses and the celebration *in the demes* of state religious festivals involving women together suggest the regular participation by females in

---

4. Cf. Henrichs 1990, pp. 260–264.

5. Mikalson 1977, p. 429.

6. On the question, see Whitehead 1986, p. 80.

7. See, recently, on female seclusion, Just's study of women in Athenian law (1989), ch. 6, pp. 105–125. To counter the uncontested instances of the presence of women of the citizen class in outdoor, public places, Just underscores the recognition and effects of the maintenance of "social distance" insulating these females from strangers (see especially pp. 118–125).

cultic activities under the formal auspices of the deme association. Luckily, this conclusion finds partial verification in a scattering of sources. Twice the Erchia calendar
(*SEG* 21.541) specifies that on Elaphebolion 16 the goat is to be handed over to the
"women" (sacrifice to Semele: A, lines 44–51; to Dionysos: Δ, lines 33–40)—with
the addition of the prohibition against carrying off of the meats (οὐ φορά) guaranteeing the continuing presence of the women at the scene of the celebration. From
Peiraieus, the decree *IG* II² 1177 calls upon the demarch (acting in cooperation with
"the priestess") to take care that certain cultic activities not transpire "without the
priestess, other than when the festival of the Thesmophoria and the Plerosia and Kallamaia and the Skira (take place) and if on any other day the women come together
in accordance with ancestral custom" (lines 1–12). Besides the two statewide festivals already recognized by Mikalson (the Skira and Thesmophoria), two apparently
local Peiraic celebrations are added by name,[8] and the final clause opens up the possibility of a more general participation by demeswomen in this deme's cults. Attica-
wide, participation by women as well as men is thinly documented for the most popular deme festival of all, the Rural Dionysia. That documentation is provided by a
memorable scene in Aristophanes' *Acharnians* (although, in keeping with the apparent convention of Aristophanic and Old Comedy generally, no specific deme is identified as the setting of the celebration).[9] Elsewhere, but without attestation of the
presence of females of the citizen class, the festival is at present recorded, by sources
literary as well as epigraphic, in as many as fourteen demes.[10] To add the crucial
point, the mention of the Dionysia or allusions to the cult of Dionysos are so common in the decrees of the demes as to leave no doubt concerning its official status as
an authentic corporate activity of the deme association.[11] Finally and less certainly, a
fragmentary decree of a deme, significantly (I think) Peiraieus, the same deme that
produced the richly informative *IG* II² 1177 just discussed, *Hesperia* 3 (1934) 44–46,
no. 33 (init. s. III), reads in line 11: . . . αὐτῶν καὶ γυναικῶ[ν---] and again in lines
12–13: οἱ ἄλ]/λοι δημόται μετὰ τ[ῶν---]. For the latter passage, may I suggest
τ[ῶν γυναικῶν---]? Since the editor links the text on strong internal evidence with
"the financing of some public work of construction,"[12] it is tempting to suggest that
both the demesmen *and their wives* were envisioned by the decree as having access
to, or otherwise making use of, such construction at some future date. That any such

8. For a discussion of religion at Peiraieus, see Garland 1987, ch. 3, pp. 101–138, with app. 3, pp.
228–241. For the Plerosia, a rite of ritual ploughing, see p. 110. However, I find no reference to the
Kallamaia? in either the text, appendix, or index of Garland's book.

9. Lines 237–279. Specifically, the poet depicts the procession as headed by Dikaiopolis's daughter
carrying a cake upon which she pours porridge with a ladle. For a general treatment of the deme festival,
see Pickard-Cambridge 1968, pp. 42–56. Admittedly, additional direct evidence of female participation
in the Rural Dionysia is not forthcoming, at least not from literary or epigraphic sources. For the observation that no surviving specimen of Old Comedy is set within a particular, named deme, see Whitehead
1986, p. 332. For a recent examination of the perennial problem of the place of women in the Great
Dionysia, see Goldhill 1994.

10. Whitehead 1986, pp. 212–213, with note 212 [p. 213]. The demes in question are Acharnai, Aigilia, Aixone, Anagyrous?, Eleusis, Halai Araphenides, Ikarion, Kollytos, Myrrhinous, Paiania,
Peiraieus, Phlya, Rhamnous, and Thorikos. For a possible celebration at Lamptrai?, see *IG* II² 1161, lines
3–5, with "The Agorai...Location and Schedule," in chapter 5, with notes 27–28.

11. For the cult of Dionysos in the demes, see Whitehead 1986, pp. 220–222, with note 268 (p. 221),
which assembles the evidence for the cult above and beyond that for the Rural Dionysia.

12. Op. cit., p. 46.

"construction" was devoted to a religious function, though not explicitly indicated in our text, is highly probable.

Women and the Official Designation of Public Status

If the position of women of the citizen class in the demes was a function of the constitutional status of their male *kyrioi*, however, it does not follow necessarily that such a position had no existence independent of that status, that wives and daughters were mere appendages of their demesmen fathers and husbands.[13] Their substantive role in religion and cult would seem to demand some form of formal recognition above and beyond mere acknowledgment of significant natal or affinal relationships with males.[14] Accordingly one looks to the most likely source of insight on the matter, to the technical (or quasi-technical) terminology used to address uniformly or differentially the males and females of deme society. As it happens, such terms are sparse and uncommunicative to the extreme, but we may get some help from the analogous terms employed at the higher level of the state of Athens.

An "Athenian" went by various designations, depending upon the aspect of that affiliation under consideration: *Athenaios, Attikos, astos,* and *polites.* Some, but not all, of these terms, although a grammatically feminine form existed for each, were regularly used to denote females of the citizen class. To select a particularly perplexing example, while an Athenian man was normally called an Ἀθηναῖος, an Athenian woman was called not an Ἀθηναία but an Ἀττικὴ γυνή. Why? Philological work done by Patterson offers an explanation for the difference.[15] The adjective *Athenaios,*[16] she argues, pertained to the constitutional roles of a member of "the politically sovereign body" and as such was applied only to males, with one exception. Athenian women could, as we have seen in the case of the demes, gain access to public priesthoods and in such a capacity, in at least one documented instance, be referred to officially as "Athenians."[17] But *Attikos,* by its attested uses revealed to be a more general term, denoted, she argues, "a native member of the traditional Athenian community of Athenian families" and so was normally used to denote females as well as males.[18] Much the same distinction operates in the case of the second pair of

13. Whitehead 1986, p. 79, comes close to such a characterization when he writes that "the association of a woman with a deme or demes was through her menfolk."

14. As indicated, for example, by the *demotikon.*

15. Patterson 1986, pp. 49–67. Much of this same material was previously treated in the same author's study of the citizenship (1981), app. 1, "Citizenship Terminology in Athens," pp. 151–167.

16. Throughout this discussion, for the sake of simplicity, I refer to these denominators by their so-called dictionary form, that is, the masculine nominative singular. Nothing is hereby intended regarding any possible priority, formal or substantive, enjoyed by the masculine forms of any of the terms.

17. Patterson 1981, p. 163, citing what is now *IG* I³ 35 (ca. 448) (= *IG* I² 24; M–L 44), the decree concerning the appointment of the priestess of Athena Nike ἐχς Ἀθεναίον hαπα[σō]/[ν (lines 5–6). The restoration of the final word as feminine gender, if correct, proves that Athenian women could, in an official context, be collectively termed *Athenaiai.* Less confidence can be placed in Patterson's second example, Plutarch's statement (*Perikles* 37.3) that, according to Perikles' citizenship law, the prospective citizen had to be born "from two Athenians" (ἐκ δυεῖν Ἀθηναίων). The phrasing may be loose, or the construction or word appropriate to a female may have been assimilated to the more familiar masculine term. The question is reopened at Patterson 1986, pp. 50–53.

18. Patterson 1986, pp. 50–53 (with both quotations on p. 53).

opposed terms, *astos* and *polites*. Like *Attikos*, the substantive *astos*—the word used to denote both the male and female "citizen" parents in Perikles' law of 451/0—may be, and often is, applied to females. Patterson, again, provides a plausible explanation, in this case in contrast with our final item, *polites*. On the standard view, whereas *polites* was applied almost exclusively to male citizens and so denoted those possessing full political rights, *astos* and *astê* were extended more broadly to embrace all those endowed with "civil" rights, that is women and minors as well as adult males. According to Patterson's reconstruction, however, while *polites* continues to refer to the political community (with its public and competitive associations), *astos* (and *astê*) she connects, in line with its literal derivation from *astu*, with "a more communal meaning" of "insider" (as opposed to *xenoi* or "outsiders").[19] Hence, the word's use, to revert to our example, in Perikles' law. Yet, as with the previous brace of seeming synonyms, a problem is presented by the ostensibly more restrictive companion term. Analogously with the feminine form of the public "citizen" denominator *Athenaios*, a feminine form of *polites*, namely, *politis*, existed. What was its meaning? Its implications for the status of women in the state? It is here, with the case of the demes in mind, that we can profitably direct our attention.

The rarity of the feminine *politis* in classical Athenian contexts is remarked by Patterson,[20] but frequency of occurrence decides nothing, since in this case it may merely reflect the manifest truth that the public arena was dominated by men. Besides, because *gynê* ("woman") seems to have enjoyed a quasi-technical status as a denominator for citizen females,[21] *politis* may well have been a less preferred term and have been avoided when possible. At all events, it is evident that when the feminine form of "citizen" *is* used, initially in poetic texts[22] and later exclusively in (non-documentary) prose sources, more often than not the author is trying to express the meaning "female citizen" or "female of the citizen class," without implying that such a "citizen" necessarily possessed any of the rights or privileges of her male counterparts.[23] In a minority of the examples, literary or rhetorical factors may be at work,

19. Patterson 1986, pp. 54–57. This same ground was previously covered at Patterson 1981, pp. 151–174.

20. Patterson 1986, p. 55.

21. Cf., for example, Aristotle, *Politics* 3.3.4 (1278a), where mention is made of descent ἐκ πολίτιδος, but shortly later (§5) the sons of such unions (i.e., between a foreigner and a "citizen" woman) are called τοὺς ἀπὸ γυναικῶν. Obviously, the meaning is not merely "women" but, more specifically and (I suggest) technically, "women of the citizen class." It is also relevant to note that, as is well known, the word for "wife" is not some special vocabulary item but, again, "woman." At Athens, the emergence and crystallization of *gynê* as a *terminus technicus* may have been accelerated by the general reluctance to mention respectable women by name in public (with the significant exception at Athens, noted by Patterson 1986, p. 53, of the public priestess). By default, and since adult women (statistically, the females apt to be so mentioned) were married (i.e., were *gynaikes*), there would have been no alternative but to call them by this term. On naming conventions, see D. Schaps, "The Woman Least Mentioned: Etiquette and Women's Names," *CQ* 27 (1977) 323–330.

22. Speakers address female choruses as *politides* at Sophokles, *Electra* 1227, and at Euripides, *Electra* 1335.

23. (1) At Demosthenes 23, *Against Aristokrates*, 213 (352 B.C.), the speaker observes that the town of Oreus on Euboia did not pursue the enfranchisement of one Charidemos "whose mother was a *politis* there" (i.e., at Oreus). Obviously the term *politis* draws attention to the fact that her "citizen" status was relevant to Charidemos's potential eligibility for citizenship. (2) At Demosthenes 57, *Against Euboulides*, 43 (345 B.C.), the plaintiff argues that Protomachos, by reason of his earlier marriage to his (the plaintiff's)

especially where the masculine and feminine forms, *polites* and *politis*, or the pair of near feminine synonyms *astê* and *politis*, are conjoined in a parallel construction.[24]

But not all recorded uses of the term may be characterized as merely verbal or rhetorical. Two examples show, in one case the possibility, in the other the historical reality, of substantial content for the term *politis*. The speaker at Plato, *Laws* 7.814C, in the course of setting out the guidelines for his ideal Cretan state, declares that there should be a law requiring "all the *politai* and the *politides*" to concern themselves with military matters. Evidently, to the Greek (and Athenian) philosopher, the notion of involvement in the military naturally prompts the assumption of the possession of some measure of citizenship. If a woman is to be a soldier in this utopian community, then she must first be a citizen of it. In a speech of Demosthenes, *Against Euboulides*, the speaker, defending his claim to citizenship in the face of the allegations of his prosecutor, alludes, with reference to his mother (who he insists at §43 was a member of the citizen class), to a law making liable to prosecution anyone denigrating the employment in the Agora "of *politai* and *politides*" (§30). Here, substantial content, namely a legal protection, is linked with the status of a *politis*, so identified. Had the term been in general use (in place of the quasi-technical *gynê*), we should undoubtedly be drawn to conclude that there was indeed such a thing as a female Athenian citizen.[25]

At all events, it will not do, with Whitehead, to dismiss such usages as "meta-

---

mother, showed "by his actions that she was an *astê* and a *politis.*" From the following observation that the witnesses to this point, including children of this marriage, were all *politai* (§44), it is clear that his meaning is that the marriage, and the children that marriage had produced, satisfied the conditions of the Periklean citizenship law requiring the parents to be *astos* and *astê*. *Politis*, then, in this instance, may be taken as a rhetorical repetition and amplification of *astê*, with no significant distinction in sense. (3) At [Demosthenes] 59, *Against Neaira*, 107 (between 373 and 339 B.C.), the plaintiff assails the defendant "whom neither the ancestors left (an) *astê* nor the People made a *politis.*" Again, membership in the citizen class is in question, with two different words for "citizeness." Rhetorical amplification may account for the repetition of terms, but much could also be said for Patterson's distinction between the natural community (*astê*) and constitutional eligibility (*politis*). (4) At §112 of the same speech the fear is expressed that, if prostitutes (like Neaira) are permitted to name anyone they choose as the fathers of their children (thereby legitimizing them), the daughters of such unions will be able to compete for husbands with females of the citizen class. "So take care," he continues, "for the *politides* in order that the daughters of poor men not go unbetrothed." Again, the intent is merely to denote females of the citizen class. (5) Isaios 8 *On the Estate of Kiron* 43 (ca. 383–363 B.C.): "For if you are deceived [into thinking] that our mother was not a *politis*, then neither are we [citizens]. For we were born after the archonship of Eukleides." This is a patent reference to the Periklean law on citizenship, with *politis* glossing the word used in the law, *astê*. (6) At Isokrates, *Plataikos* 51 (between 373 and 371 B.C.), the speaker, a Plataian, declares to the Athenian listeners: "For on account of the grants of intermarriage made by you [Athenians], we [Plataians] were born ἐκ πολιτίδων ὑμετέρων" (i.e., our Plataian fathers married Athenian women). The reference is to females produced by marriages satisfying the Athenian citizenship law. (7) Aristotle, in the *Politics* (no earlier than 336 B.C.) remarks, at 3.1.9 (1275b), that, when determining eligibility for citizenship, it is impossible to apply to the original colonizers or founders of a state the rule of descent from a citizen father and citizen mother (τὸ ἐκ πολίτου ἢ ἐκ πολίτιδος). (8) At *Politics* 3.3.4 (1278a), he remarks again that, under many constitutions the law recruits citizens from foreigners, for "in some democracies the man born ἐκ πολίτιδος is a πολ–ίτης." In both passages, yet again, our term serves merely to signal membership in the citizen class.

24. Consider, among the examples assembled in the previous note, numbers 2, 3, 7, and 8.

25. Among other possibilities, one could give additional meaning to such female citizenship by adducing the civil rights possessed by Athenian women: see Lacey 1968, pp. 138–139, 151–153, and 151–176 passim; Harrison vol. 2, 1971, pp. 84, 136–137 and 145; and MacDowell 1978, pp. 84–108 passim.

phors."[26] The substantive denotations of the term are not merely imaginative derivations of analogous male rights or privileges; they are real: to wit, descent from citizen parents; the capacity, within the context of marriage to a citizen husband, to transmit citizen status to one's children; the privilege of playing various official roles in the state's (and deme's) religious cults and ceremonies; and the protections exemplified by the single item preserved in Demosthenes' text just mentioned. Even on the basis of this limited record, it is clear that we are dealing with more than mere figurative speech.

The importance of this conclusion for our subject is that a parallel term, *demotis*, seems to have existed in the case of the deme. True, it never occurs in a documentary—or even forensic or other prose—source, its sole classical Athenian occurrence being confined to a passage in Aristophanes' *Lysistrata*, produced in 411. At lines 319–351, when Lysistrata and her female supporters are about to be burned out of their encampment on the Akropolis by the semi-chorus of old men, the remaining portion of the chorus, consisting of old women, arrives, carrying pitchers of water on their heads with which to quench the fire. They are bringing the water, they say (in the first person), "for my burning *demotides*."[27] What is the referent of our term? Whitehead takes the usage to be "very loose," suggesting "comrades" (or the like) as a rendering.[28] The reason or reasons for this conclusion are not given, although elsewhere Whitehead comments on the "semantic overlap" between *demotai* and *philoi*.[29] But there is no reason to deny to the term its surface, literal denotation: women of the same deme. True, the chorus (or its leader) speaks in the first person, but these words represent the thinking of each individual member of the entire semi-chorus and, similarly, refer to the several individuals in the mixed multitude of Athenian demeswomen on the Akropolis. The leader's speech, in other words, is to be taken as each woman's addressing her own fellow female villagers. Finally, even if the word *demotides* were to be regarded (with Whitehead) as nontechnical in this particular context, that is no reason why it should be similarly nontechnical elsewhere (any more than the occasional "loose" use of the masculine form implies anything regarding its many strictly constitutional appearances in the documents).

But why, to anticipate another objection, should the term, if indeed it is a bona fide *terminus technicus* and not merely a comic formation of Aristophanes', not be found outside this single suspect context? Again, the person or persons denoted by the word are not often the subjects of surviving classical Greek discourse. Furthermore, the general absence of the term may be made comprehensible by a passage in Isaios where, when the speaker wants to refer to the women (i.e., wives and perhaps unmarried daughters) of the *demotai,* he says not *demotides* but "the women of the *demotai"* (3.80). Perhaps, then, as I have already suggested with respect to the allied word *politis,* and indeed with respect to the word "woman" itself, the phrase "woman of the *demotai"* enjoyed a quasi-technical status[30] and, as such, drove or

26. Whitehead 1986, p. 77.

27. Lines 332–334: . . . ταῖσιν ἐμαῖς / δημότισιν καομέναις / φέρουσ' ὕδωρ βοηθῶ.

28. Whitehead 1986, p. 77, note 44.

29. Whitehead 1986, pp. 231–232. However, he stops short of suggesting that the term *demotes* was ever used "loosely" of "friends" who were demonstrably or likely *not* members of one's deme.

30. Cf. the text discussed above, *Hesperia* 3 (1934) 44–46, no. 33 (init. s. III), with its two possible references to the *demotai* and their "women."

kept out of use the seemingly more natural and expected feminine form of *demotes*. In that case, the Isaian formulation, like the Aristophanic *demotis*, would indicate the formal acknowledgment of a class of "demeswomen."

Again, the category is not metaphorical; nor, to instance another of Whitehead's characterizations, was the position of women in the demes "vicarious,"[31] if by that is meant that the position of a male demes*man* was any less dependent upon the status of significant relatives. Admittedly, a woman was officially known as the daughter or wife of a citizen father or husband; and the demotic accompanying her name (say, on her epitaph) was not normally, as mentioned earlier, hers, but his.[32] But the male citizen's status and deme affiliation were no less dependent—at the naming ceremony, upon his entry into phratry and deme, and thereafter—on the facts of his descent. Witness, again, Euxitheos's defense of his citizen status which requires him to demonstrate rigorously the descent of both his father and mother (Demosthenes 57, passim; see above). At no point did a citizen's status cease to be derivative, to be a function of the statuses of his father and mother. If a woman's status in her deme was "vicarious," then so was, to no less a degree, that of any of its male members.

As a result, again, we seem to have constructed an alternative deme of larger scope than its narrowly defined "constitutional" counterpart. But these two demes are not that contrasting pair, defined alternatively by descent and residence, which are the principal subject of chapter 2. Rather we are dealing here with two categories of descent, corresponding to Patterson's "double-stranded bond" that constituted the membership of the classical Athenian *polis*. The one comprised the constitutionally defined body of male *demotai*; the other, though centered on, and limited by, the constitutional deme, extended beyond it to embrace "traditional family relationships,"[33] including especially the womenfolk—wives and unmarried daughters—and minor male children of the *demotai*. My position differs from hers in that it places more emphasis on the substantial public roles made possible by, or reflected in, membership in this larger organization,[34] and from Whitehead's in that I place a positive and independent valuation upon the status of the *demotis*, eschewing its characterization as either metaphorical or vicarious.

In view of the fully conscious and deliberate exclusivity of the male *demotai*, it is problematic how we should conceptualize, in relation to that exclusivity, the status of "the women of the *demotai*," which we have just attempted to elucidate. The fact that active female participation in the deme (as opposed to the mere possession of "civil rights") seems to have been confined to cult functions and activities suggests that in some sense religion was bracketed or regarded as a special case of public life. Although Athenian public life was not subject to any rigid dichotimization between "church" and "state," the sacred sphere was nonetheless sufficiently well-

31. Whitehead 1986, p. 77.
32. See above, with note 1.
33. Patterson 1986, p. 50 (for both quotations).
34. In both her discussions, Patterson repeatedly emphasizes that her goal is to shed light upon the "social reality" denoted by the terminology (see especially 1986, p. 50), and in one place or another she adduces and discusses most of the evidence under review here, but at no point does she take the final step of positing a substantial female Athenian "citizenship" and nowhere does she acknowledge the existence of the Aristophanic *demotides*.

defined with respect to the secular sphere[35] to permit the controlled entry into it of the female segment of citizen society. Some of the factors conditioning or justifying the split of cult from other public activity and its partial allocation to females, whether at the state or deme level, are easily enumerated. For one, the existence of prominent female goddesses and the operative roles played by females in popular sacred narratives would have facilitated the emergence of females in the arena of cult. Much of Greek religion, too, leaving divinities and myth out of it, was fundamentally preoccupied with fertility or nurturing, spheres of concern traditionally assigned to females in this agricultural society. One could also remark upon the domestic nature of the temple and the functions carried out within it. the temple was literally the house of the divinity, its occupant (embodied in the cult statue) to be draped with sacred garments (i.e., clothed), anointed (i.e., bathed), and offered animal sacrifices (i.e., fed) by its caretakers. All this represents a natural extension of the homely tasks of the Athenian citizen woman. It was perhaps inevitable, then, that at the state level religious duties be assigned to *politides*, and in the demes to *demotides*. Since cult was no less than government a fully fledged segment of public, citizen life, what was needed was that a portion—but only a portion—of the *politeia* be opened up to females of the citizen class. But even for this perhaps unexpected maneuver, there was, or would soon be, a precedent: the granting to foreigners of a single isolated privilege otherwise enjoyed only by citizens, for example, the right of ownership of "land and house."[36] Yet here the similarity with foreigners ends. Athenian women—Patterson's "natives" and "insiders"—were, unlike *isoteleis*, bona fide members of the "communal family" of the *polis* of Athens. It has been the burden of the present discussion to show that that membership, as evidenced by women's roles and official designations, extended, no less in the demes than at the level of state organization, to a partial (though not, for that reason, less genuine) share in the *politeia*.

The Rise of the Territorial Deme

The Big Picture

For our present purposes, the upshot of the foregoing discussion is that the recognition of the official status of "the women of the *demotai*" demands that we acknowledge an alternative definition—and specifically a widening—of the formal delineation of the deme. The significance of this finding must not be underestimated. Wives and daughters of demesmen had been on the scene since Day One of the Kleisthenic democracy. To put the matter in legalistic terms, a female could both be a member and not be a member at the same time; according to her constitutional status, she was an outsider, but, societally speaking, she enjoyed some of the benefits

35. As illustrated by verbal distinction between ἱερός and βέβηλος or (more commonly) ὅσιος: see *LSJ*[9], s.v. ἱερός, II.2, and ὅσιος, I.2. For an exploration of the "sacred" and the "secular" in classical Athens, see Connor 1988. His theory (p. 164) that the two terms represent, not an antithesis (as Durkheim postulated), but "parallel and co-ordinate realms" would seem to be consistent with the apparent parallel relationship between the secular male and sacred female spheres of deme association activity.

36. The point is made at Patterson 1981, p. 167, but with no obvious reference to any substantial citizen privileges, including access to public cults, enjoyed by Athenian *women*.

of membership, including the privilege of participation in the religious activities of her guardian's deme. Thus from the beginning a precedent had been established for the significant enlargement of the deme organization through the inclusion of, or association with, people who, like the female connections of the *demotai*, could never become members in a constitutional sense.

Even with the incorporation of wives and unmarried daughters of *demotai* into the life of the deme association, a large mass of the human population still remains unaccounted for, namely, the metics and slaves.[37] No place, officially defined or otherwise, in the constitutional deme was available for either of these noncitizen orders.

In chapter 2 we attempted to establish the existence of a second deme, one based upon well-defined and officially maintained physical boundaries. It is now perhaps time to consider to what uses such territorial units might have been put. One such use has always been in evidence—the localization of buildings, plots and lands, mining leases, etc. with reference to a deme. Such formulations as Ἁλῆσι, "at Halai," if the existence of the territorial deme is granted, would relate, not loosely to a village center, but with precision to a defined and possibly marked tract of territory. But our concern is with the human element and, to get right to the point, with the possibility that metics, and conceivably even slaves, were in some sense "members" of such territorial entities.

With regard to the metics, the appropriateness to a territorial partition of Attica of the designation of resident aliens as "residing" in this or that deme has already been observed in chapter 2. Place of residence, given the existence of a territorial deme, could have been determined without possibility of ambiguity or disagreement. Besides providing the metic's official affiliation, the place of residence will have determined one's affiliation with this or that deme, the military unit in which a metic soldier possibly trained and fought, and the identification of the local treasury to which the resident alien paid any taxes imposed by a deme association.[38] Absent a membership in a unit of some sort, it is difficult to imagine how the official career and duties of metics could have been determined. But the formula οἰκῶν / οἰκοῦσα ἐν . . . ("residing in . . .") strongly invites the conclusion that the locus of any such membership was in fact our territorial deme.[39]

Slaves are of course still more poorly understood. All is guesswork. But one such guess may be worth mentioning. According to the only preserved record of a census of ancient Athens, an official "investigation" undertaken during the regime of Demetrios of Phaleron (317–307) revealed the presence in Attica of 400,000 slaves.[40] Although the specific figure has generally been regarded as far too high, the fact of the number reveals that a count of some kind had taken place.[41] May I suggest that the *lexiarchika grammateia,* the deme registers, the only known rosters

37. For the moment I omit from consideration non-*demotai* citizens resident in the deme. These figured in our discussion of "the residents" in chapter 2 and will soon occupy our attention later in the present chapter.

38. See, for fuller discussion with references, "The Territorial Deme: The Case for Precise Boundaries," in chapter 2, with notes 70–77.

39. This conclusion may be assessed against the background of the status of immigrant communities in the classical city-state. For a wide-ranging overview of the subject, see Whitehead 1984.

40. Athenaios 6.272c, citing the third book of Ktesikles' *Chronicles, FGrH* 245 Stesikleides (Ktesikles) of Athens F 1.

41. The census is well discussed by Westermann 1943, pp. 451–470 (= Finley 1960, pp. 73-92). At p. 454 (p. 76, Finley), note 2, he observes that the word of Athenaios's usually rendered "census" is

of Athenian citizens,[42] would have afforded a convenient basis for such an Attica-wide tabulation? To each register, presumably physically located at the seat or administrative center of each deme, would be appended the names, numbers, and other data pertaining to the slaves actually resident in the deme in question. (The alternative plan, that slaves would have been counted under the name of each *demotes*, irrespective of his residence within the deme or elsewhere, though possible, would have been less useful, in that no impression could be formed of the distribution of the slave population over the land of Attica.) I offer this scenario, not as a serious suggestion of something that actually happened, but as a speculative example of the uses to which an organization of Athenian slaves according to territorial deme units might have been put.

These speculations, if accepted only in principle, help us to understand how the constitutional deme system might have come to terms with the social reality that the great majority of the population stood outside the exclusive registers of *demotai*. Inclusion, even if only a quasi-constitutional or partial *de facto* inclusion (as in the case of females of the citizen class) or in the form of an alternative (yet still dependent) membership made possible by the existence of the deme's territorial boundaries, would have the effect of rendering the deme a body more representative of the community's actual composition. With this idea in mind, let us now turn to the demes, and to their associations, and see if we can uncover the mechanism or mechanisms whereby such an enlarged "inclusive" community might have come into existence.

The Garrison Demes Eleusis and Rhamnous

We have just discussed the constitutional deme's exclusive posture with regard to the most visible of these non-*demotai*, its womenfolk. Into relation with this enlarged hereditary organization based on descent we have, as a next major step, brought the deme in its second, alternative mode of existence, namely, as defined by its *precise territorial boundaries*. It has been suggested that metics, and perhaps even slaves, would be found, had we more information from antiquity, to have formally or informally counted as, in some sense, "members" of this territorial entity. But the alternative deme's "membership" did not end here. The discussion in chapter 2 of the referents of the recurrent phrase οἱ οἰκοῦντες acknowledged that, in view of the fact that all but one of the documents in which the phrase occurs come from demes known to have served as "garrisons" for the encampment of ephebes and Athenian or foreign soldiers, "the residents" probably included—though were not necessarily limited to—military or related personnel physically present in the deme at the time of the document yet not, as the mere existence of the category of "residents" implies, members of that deme. Indeed, such evidence as the twin references in a decree of Rhamnous, *SEG* 25.155, to "Rhamnousians and those of the Athenians residing in the fort" (lines 10–11) and to "Eleusinians and the other Athenians residing in the fort" (lines 13–14) hardly permits any other conclusion.

ἐξετασμός, meaning rather "investigation." Nonetheless, even an "investigation" would require some method of counting in order to arrive at an estimate expressed as a number.

42. The one other possible candidate would seem to be the poorly attested registers of the phratries: Demosthenes 44, *Against Leochares*, 42, and Isokrates 1, *Peace*, 88.

Although these formulations do not imply either that all "residents" were soldiers[43] or that such "residents" were found only in these demes, they do unambiguously link the category of "residents" with the garrison. So any consideration of the question of the origins of the inclusive territorial deme must again bring into play the case of the "garrison" demes.

The demes is question have already received considerable attention from earlier investigators. Two levels of organization may be distinguished. At the more basic level of "fortifications or camps," McCredie identified some two dozen sites, of which Whitehead isolated six as falling within the territory of identifiable demes, namely Anagyrous, Anaphlystos, Aphidna, Atene, Besa, and Trikorynthos.[44] Evidently more substantial and less impermanent were the "established forts and garrisons" (again, to use McCredie's terminology). In this category McCredie placed nine sites, but, on Whitehead's showing, of the nine for only three could the fort or garrison in question be shown (a) to have been near a deme center and (b) to have had an impact upon that deme center.[45] The three are Eleusis, Rhamnous, and Sounion; and of these three, one, Sounion, is insufficiently represented by surviving inscriptions to shed any independent light upon either the deme, its garrison, or the topic here under discussion.[46]

To launch our analysis, let us briefly state where the matter was left by the most recent treatment, Whitehead's *The Demes of Attica*.[47] Chronologically, the record spans something over a century, from the late fourth through the end of the third. The "soldiers" in question are, furthermore, a group of evolving composition. Early on, presumably beginning with the establishment of the Ephebic College around 335/4, they included Athenian ephebes assigned, in accordance with the description in the Aristotelian *Constitution of the Athenians*, to duty in the frontier forts on the borders of Attica.[48] Soon thereafter, the garrisons frequently comprise regular Athenian military personnel or troops of foreign origin. Potentially, the difference between an Athenian citizen (whether ephebe or enfranchised soldier) and a foreigner might have been significant, particularly where relations with the citizen constitutional deme were concerned. But my study of the documents has not brought to the surface any such significance, and so it is likely that what counted, in the final analysis, was whether a given soldier was or was not a *demotes* of the deme of his encampment, irrespective of his Athenian or other citizenship or origin.

The presence in the deme of significant bodies of non-*demotai* is most visibly reflected in the composition of the party or parties issuing decrees in the deme's

43. The equation of the "residents" with encamped soldiers was argued by Pouilloux at 1954, p. 121. For my response, see chapter 2, with note 96.

44. McCredie 1966, ch. 3, Plate 1 (Map of Attica Showing Location of Sites) displays the threefold classification "established forts and garrisons," "fortification or camp," and "tower." For Whitehead's discussion of the "fortifications or camps," see 1986, app. 6, pp. 401–407, at pp. 401–402.

45. Whitehead 1986, pp. 402–404.

46. Whitehead 1986, pp. 406–407. Whitehead's catalog of deme documents lists only three items for the deme, one of which is doubtful (pp. 389–390, nos. 117–119). Not under consideration here, of course, are documents from the deme produced by the troops alone.

47. Whitehead 1986, app. 6, pp. 401–407.

48. *AthPol* 42.3–5. The patrols of the countryside and encampments at the guardposts took place during the second year (§4).

name or, absent a reference to the *demotai* per se as the decreeing authority, in decrees authorized by other parties identified as physically present at or near a deme's administrative center. Whitehead's analysis of the record of our two demes, Eleusis and Rhamnous, resulted in the positing of three different categories of decree: (1) "normal" decrees (i.e., decrees of the *demotai* alone); (2) decrees of the deme plus the garrison; and (3) decrees of the troops alone.[49] Beyond recognition of these types, however, the analysis fails to make significant progress, and particularly on two crucial heads. First, nowhere does Whitehead's discussion, although consistently revealing awareness of the established or suggested dates of his material and especially the inscriptions, venture to suggest that the three categories stood in any *significant* chronological relation to each other. Secondly, no explanation could be found for the variations in the composition of the decreeing bodies (or, to use Whitehead's own terms, the variations in "the constituency . . . enacting any particular decree"[50]). It will be the goal of the remainder of this section to make some progress on these two heads and to incorporate these findings into a general account of the rise of the territorial deme.

To begin with the matter of chronological significance, it is patent that Whitehead's three categories conform to a rough temporal sequence. It is not of course a question of one mode of decree entirely replacing the previous mode to hold the field until it itself is replaced by still another mode. To the contrary, the application of my two-deme model, since constitutional and territorial deme coexist, would not require the monopoly of a single category of decree. Decrees of different types may be issued at or about the same time, depending on the activity of different decreeing bodies. And, to make the fundamental point, it is the application of my model that endows with significance what is otherwise an inexplicable sequence of documentary formulas.

Eleusis

The detailed particulars of that sequence may, as a prelude to discussion of its underlying causes, be set out, first with respect to the less well documented of our two demes, Eleusis.

Decrees of the Demotai Alone. Whitehead's "normal" decrees commence as early as 319/8 (*IG* II² 1187) and continue at frequent intervals down to "fin. s. IV" (*IG* II² 1193).[51] Whitehead adduces as an additional example from the third quarter of the third century (the exact date is "post 236/5") *IG* II² 1299, lines 51–80, honoring the general Aristophanes of Leukonoion.[52] Yet this decree is appended to a preceding joint decree of the citizens stationed at Eleusis, Panakton, and Phyle and mercenary troops stationed at Eleusis (lines 20–22), surely indicating that the deme's decree was not necessarily an independent undertaking of the *demotai*. With greater justice,

49. Whitehead 1986, pp. 404–405 (Eleusis), 405–406 (Rhamnous).
50. Whitehead 1986, p. 405.
51. For the decrees, see Whitehead's list of deme documents, with the Eleusinian texts at 1986, pp. 377–379, nos. 20–42. The documents in question are collected at p. 405 (i).
52. Whitehead 1986, p. 404.

this decree would be placed with the joint decrees of the *demotai* and the garrison (see below). (Much the same may be said of a still later decree not mentioned by Whitehead in this connection, *IG* II² 949, lines 30–38 [with the summary at lines 24–29, center column], dated by the archon's name to 165/4. It too is appended to another, preceding decree, in this case of the Boule and Demos.)

Joint Decrees of the Demotai and the Garrison. Joint decrees begin early in 321/0 or 318/7 with "the surprise of *IG* II² 1191."[53] A fragment dated to the beginning of the third century, *IG* II² 1274, was restored as the preamble of a decree of the Eleusinians and of the Athenians stationed at Eleusis and Panakton (lines 2–4). But the only other unambiguous example is *IG* II² 1280 (ante 266/5), honors decreed by the "Eleusinians and those of the Athenians stationed at Eleusis" (lines 2–4). Additionally, as just explained, we should add the two decrees inscribed on a single stone, *IG* II² 1299 (no earlier than 236/5), the one (lines 1–50) in the name of the Athenian and foreign soldiers stationed at Eleusis and elsewhere (lines 20–22), the other (lines 51–80) in the name of the Eleusinians (line 74). Taken together, the two decrees have the effect of a single decree of the two groups acting jointly. If this assignment of texts to categories is accepted, the period of joint enactments may extend beyond the later decrees of the *demotai* acting alone by about two-thirds of a century.

Decrees of the Garrison Alone. Deme-less decrees begin in the 260s and continue through the end of the century.[54] In this case, the overlap with the foregoing category is substantial, with the acts of the soldiers decreeing alone appearing midway through the joint reign of the *demotai* and the garrison and then paralleling the joint decrees down to the end of their record and beyond to ca. 200.

Thus far I have followed (with significant modifications) Whitehead's schema in order to bring out a point—namely that his categorization obscures the existence of the class of people at Eleusis vital to the representation of the deme in this book, the "residents" of the deme. Two of the texts belonging to this category, *SEG* 22.127 (*IG* II² 1218 + 1288) (med. s. III) and *SEG* 25.155 (236/5), are both subsumed under the rubric "deme-plus-garrison decrees," apparently on the assumption (shared by Pouilloux) that "the residents" were in fact soldiers. My reasons for disputing this assumption (or conclusion) should by now be sufficiently clear. In the former (acephalous) example, though the preamble is lost, references to "those of the citizens residing in it [i.e., the deme]" (lines 13–14, partly restored) and to "those of the Athenians residing at Eleusis" (line 22, partly restored) leave little doubt that they, the "residents," are the decreeing party, acting in joint cooperation with the Eleusinians (if, as is likely, the restoration of the plural *demotikon* in line 21 is correct). The other, nominally a decree of the Rhamnousians (line 1), cites in lines 12–14 the praise and crown conferred on the honorand's father "by the Eleusinians and the other Athenians, the ones residing in the fort."[55] Finally, perhaps at the end of the third century, the preamble of *IG* II² 1305 preserves the names of the decree-

---

53. Whitehead 1986, p. 404.

54. From the corpus: *IG* II² 1272, 1279?, 1285?, 1287?, 1288 (see *SEG* 22.127), 1299 (lines 1–50), 1303, 1304, 1304b, 1305, 1306, and 1307?

55. For the analysis of this complex text, see "The Territorial Deme," in chapter 2.

ing parties as (according to the partly restored text) the Athenians stationed at Eleusis, Panakton, and Phyle and those of the citizens residing at Eleusis (lines 2–4). Thus οἱ οἰκοῦντες ("the residents"), whether acting alone or in conjunction with the deme, comprise a fourth, and distinct, "constituency" within the deme community. Chronologically, these texts march with the decrees of the soldiers acting alone, commencing in the 260s.

Taken together, the Eleusinian documents reveal a progression from (1) the exclusive reign of the *demotai*, to (2) the sharing of their decreeing authority with the garrison, to a period of perhaps a half century at the lower end of our record (ca. 260–200) when (3) the troops, simultaneously with the joint operation of deme and garrison, and (4) the "residents," independently or jointly with the deme association, issue decrees in their own names.

Rhamnous

Whitehead offers a typology similar to that of the Eleusinian decrees just discussed, but with the acknowledgment of the presence of increased "juridical complexities." To mention but one complicating indicator: all three types of decree, "normal," deme cum troops, and troops acting alone, turn out to be in evidence at about the same time (namely, around the middle of the third century). Nonetheless, these complexities will prove, I think, to be largely illusory once we have attempted to understand them in terms of the operation of what were essentially two different deme organizations. Let us begin again by following Whitehead's typology.

Decrees of the Demotai Alone. Acts of the demesmen begin with a decree from Rhamnous in the name of the Rhamnousians on Lemnos dated ca. 500–480[56] and resume at mid-century with the well-known accounts of the shrine of Nemesis.[57] All told, some 18 texts are with certainty or conjecturally assigned to the deme association, with the last securely identified example, *SEG* 25.155, dated internally to 236/5 and others epigraphically to as late as ca. 220.[58]

Joint Decrees of the Demotai and the Garrison. Two examples survive. *IG* II² 2849 (= Pouilloux 1954, no. 25), a dedication of the late fourth century by the priest of the founding hero, records the dedicator's [praise] and crowning by the Boule, the *demotai*, and "the soldiers."[59] Ca. 200, honors for the *xenagos* are decreed (as re-

56. *Ergon* 1984, p. 54.

57. *IG* I³ 248 (ca. 450–440) (= Pouilloux 1954, no. 35; M–L 53).

58. For a roster of deme documents of the deme of Rhamnous, see Whitehead 1986, pp. 387–389 (nos. 100–115). For another, more comprehensive listing of Rhamnousian documents, see Osborne 1990, where app. A, pp. 287–289, entitled "Decisions of corporate bodies published at Rhamnous," usefully collects not only acts of the deme but, as well, those of *isoteleis*, ephebes, soldiers, *paroikoi*, and others. A total of 52 items, some of which will figure in the following discussion, are assembled. Among more recent finds, documents from Rhamnous certainly or probably issued in the name of the deme association are collected at chapter 3, note 54.

59. Whitehead, however, observes that it is possible that the crowns were awarded separately by Boule, deme, and soldiers (1986, p. 405). But even if this were true, the mere decision to bring the decrees together on a single stone would speak for a measure of cooperation, notably between the deme and the soldiers.

stored) in *SEG* 31.112 by "the Rhamnousians and the soldiers encamped in the garrison" (lines 1–4).[60] Although the crucial opening letters of the name of the first decreeing party are missing, it is difficult to imagine, since the stone was found in the excavations at Rhamnous, how else the lacuna could be filled.

Decrees of the Garrison Alone. Ephebes (with the *sophronistai* and *kosmetai*) confer a crown in or soon after 331/0 (*IG* II² 4594a) and, about 320, "the soldiers" crown the general and the *peripolarchos* (*IG* II² 2968 = Pouilloux 1954, no. 4). From these beginnings down to the early second century, a flood of documents from Rhamnous have surfaced in the names of ephebes, encamped soldiers, *isoteleis*, and *paroikoi* but without any trace of recognition of the deme association's formal apparatus.[61]

To Whitehead's three categories, however, must again, as with Eleusis, be added a fourth and distinct group of documents associated with the "residents," specifically joint decrees of the *demotai* and the residents of the deme. Two examples survive, which, again, as with Eleusis, were placed by Whitehead (mistakenly, I have suggested) with the joint decrees of the *demotai* and soldiers. The two texts are, first, *IG* II² 3467 (= Pouilloux 1954, no. 8), dated ca. 256/5, a summary of honors in the name of the "Rhamnousians and those of the citizens residing at Rhamnous" (lines 1–3). Shortly later, in 225, *SEG* 15.112 (= Pouilloux 1954, no. 17), records honors by the "Rhamnousians and those of the citizens residing at Rhamnous" (lines 1–2).

The Expansion of the Deme Community

This relatively full record of material from Eleusis and Rhamnous makes possible a rough reconstruction of the later history of the deme association, at least in its formal, constitutional dimension. The initial question to be answered is, Which of the competing groups—encamped soldiers or "civilian" residents—was the first to challenge the existing monopoly of the decreeing function enjoyed by the *demotai*? Considerations of chronology would appear to favor the candidacy of the soldiers, and more particularly of young soldiers in training, the ephebes.

At Rhamnous, the ephebes (with their *sophronistai* and *kosmetai*) are crowning a demesman in or soon after 331/0 (*IG* II² 4594a). The date falls no more than a few years later than the conjectured date of the creation of the Ephebic College in the 330s[62] and with it, evidently, of the tour of the border forts mentioned by the Aristotelian *Constitution of the Athenians* (42.3–5). These young Athenians are natural candidates for such a quasi-constitutional innovation. Although their acquisition of full citizenship still lay a year or so in the future, it is precisely the anticipation of the assumption of the right of participation as voting members of the Assembly— and, at the same time, in their own phyle or deme *agorai*—that may have prompted

60. Lines 1–4: [----- εἶπεν· ἔδοξεν τοῖς Ῥα]/[μνου]σίοις καὶ [τοῖς στρα]/[τιώτ]αις τοῖς τε[τ]/αγμέ/[νοις τ]ῶι φρουρίωι, . . .

61. For the principal references, see above, note 58.

62. For Epikrates' conversion of the traditional *ephebeia* into a program of national service for prospective Athenian citizens, see Rhodes 1981, pp. 493–495, with the secondary literature cited there.

them to assemble to vote decrees in imitation of the practice of both the Athenian legislature and of the voting bodies of the state's segmental public associations. Thereafter, as noted above in connection with Whitehead's third category of "constituency," military personnel of all types, apparently acting independently of the deme apparatus, issue official documents, mostly decrees, in their own names. The practice continues for about a century and a half all told.

But it is the slight, though unambiguous, evidence for the *cooperation* of military personnel with the deme association that now commands our attention. Why should they have cooperated? Why should they not have remained independent of the local deme apparatus? An established feature of the physical placement of the fortifications within their respective demes, already adduced by Whitehead, certainly provides part of the answer. At both Eleusis and Rhamnous, the only two demes from which joint decrees of the *demotai* and troops (or ephebes) survive, the deme center (i.e., presumably including the *agora* or other venue of the deme assembly) lay within part of the fortifications.[63] So a meeting of troops in these demes would naturally have brought the assembled into close contact with the official deme apparatus. In significant contrast, from Sounion, where deme center and garrison were distinct, come decrees either of the *demotai* or of the troops but none of the two groups acting jointly in authoring a single decree.[64] But above and beyond the fact of mere physical contiguity there are the more substantial procedural factors discussed in the course of the analysis of the two troublesome decrees from Rhamnous in chapter 2. It was the deme organization, now in existence for upward of two centuries, that could provide the expertise, contacts, and general know-how required to conceive, formulate, and publish in permanent form a text, and particularly a laudatory decree, that, in comparison with the polished efforts of the state or of the deme associations themselves, would do honor to its recipient. Often the soldiers did (so far as we are informed) proceed on their own, but sometimes cooperation apparently seemed the more sensible course.

Military personnel were not, however, the only non-*demotai* issuing documents in their own names from within the confines of a Kleisthenic deme, and sometimes in cooperation with that deme. The existence of an officially recognized body of "residents" of the deme has not, until now, been recognized by scholars, but the documents, as we have seen, leave no alternative. In chapter 2 we reviewed a number of the instances in deme documents of the phrase οἱ οἰκοῦντες κτλ., beginning with the earliest (restored) instance in a decree of Ikarion dated ca. 440–415 (?). At Eleusis, "the residents" figure in decrees of the mid-fourth century (*IG* II² 1186) and 321/0 or 318/7 (*IG* II² 1191), but not as the (or a) decreeing party. That function is documented at the middle of the third century (*SEG* 22.127) and in or soon after 236/5 (*SEG* 25.155). At Rhamnous, the "residents" as the issuing authority are first in evidence in 256/5(?), when the *demotai* and "those of the citizens residing at Rhamnous" bestow honors on a military epimelete (*IG* II² 3467 = Pouilloux 1954, no. 8), and later, ca. 236/5 and again in 225, when they join the demesmen in decreeing honors (*SEG* 25.155 and 15.112 = Pouilloux 1954, no. 17). Whitehead, as

63. Whitehead 1986, p. 406, citing McCredie 1966, pp. 91–92.
64. Whitehead 1986, pp. 406–407.

we saw, subsumed this evidence for "residents" as a decreeing party under the more amply documented examples of the deme acting in conjunction with soldiers. Yet (once again) it is evident both from the more comprehensive uses of the phrase examined in chapter 2 and, in the present context, from the decree of Eleusis *IG* II² 1305 (fin. s. III), which juxtaposes as the decreeing parties the encamped soldiers and the citizens residing at Eleusis, that (as repeatedly already noted) these sometimes could be, and in fact were, two distinct groups of people.[65]

These considerations favor the following sequence of agglutinative phases in the evolution of the deme community: *demotai*, ephebes (alone or in cooperation with *demotai*), military personnel (alone or in cooperation with *demotai*), and the "residents" (sometimes, yet again, in cooperation with the deme). Since the deme at one time or the other entertains the involvement of all these outsider groups, it is fair to broadly characterize the process as one of the *enlargement* of the community of the deme. But what forces drove this process of enlargement? Thus far we have (with Whitehead) noted as an immediate contributing factor the spatial propinquity of deme center and garrison; and, following our speculations in chapter 2, the attraction to a body of decreeing soldiers (or other non-*demotai* residents) presented by the formal apparatus and accumulated experience of the long-established constitutional deme organization. What other factors can be identified?

Undoubtedly more than one factor was involved. What was the probable impact, for one thing, of the presence of a substantial body of military personnel on a deme community? First, and obviously, if such personnel were present in large numbers, their expenditures of public moneys, or such expenditures made on their behalf, could only have benefited the local (i.e., *demotai*) population. To exclude these residents from the public life of the deme would under the circumstances, therefore, hardly seem prudent. Accordingly, the economic dimension of their temporary residence in the deme might have been translated into a constitutional form through their inclusion in the association's *agora*. A second, contributing consideration brings into play the eligibility of these personnel to play such a constitutional role. Specifically, those of the soldiers who were citizens yet not, say, Rhamnousians (certainly, of course, the vast majority) will, as long as they were encamped at Rhamnous, have been cut off from the public life of their home demes, where alone they were full-fledged members. So participation in the assemblies of Rhamnous would have afforded them a degree of public governmental activity. Whether such a practice could have originated in the deme itself, or was the result of a directive from Athens, is not on present evidence determinable. But, either way, it was a natural development once we acknowledge the existence of the spatially defined deme. If a soldier was encamped in the fort of Rhamnous, he was a "Rhamnousian" by virtue of his physical (even if temporary) presence within the territorial limits of that deme. For this reason alone, his participation in the decreeing activities of the constitutional deme was rooted in an institution probably as old as the democracy itself.

With civilian "residents," due to the dearth of relevant material, it is less easy to imagine the motivating factor(s). But a natural source of illumination would be those decrees passed by the "residents" in which they honor some benefactor for the

---

65. See "The Territorial Deme," in chapter 2.

good deeds done them. From Eleusis, *SEG* 22.127, while honoring a military officer, praises him for securing "the safety of the place" (line 12, wholly restored in this stoichedon text), suggesting (if the restoration is correct) benefits bestowed not only on soldiers under his charge but also as well on the general population, including the "residents."[66] From Rhamnous, *SEG* 15.112, though lengthy and preserved entire, reveals no explicit indication of the motivation prompting the decision by the "Rhamnousians and those of the citizens residing at Rhamnous" (lines 1–2) to pass a decree recording the conferral of honors by a ship's crew (lines 21–22) upon their trierarch. But there are some hints. Acknowledgment is made of intended benefit "to the deme" (line 12) and, more specifically, of sacrifices to Nemesis (of course, with reference to the sanctuary in the deme) involving personal expenditure on victims and wine (lines 17–19). Even his expenditures on the crew (lines 2–19, passim), provided they were domiciled in Rhamnous, may have materially benefited the local population, whether directly or indirectly. On this basis, it may be conjectured that, when an honorand's benefactions impacted not merely the resident *demotai* but some or all of the remaining resident free population (Athenian or otherwise) as well, it was felt to be only natural to include "the residents of the citizens" (or the like) among the decreeing parties.

Admittedly, these findings conflict with Whitehead's observation of a few instances of a lack of concinnity between the "constituency" (i.e., the decreeing party) and the type of honorand identified by the decree in question.[67] But the fact is, among the numerous honorary decrees under review here, on several occasions the honorand's benefactions had impacted a wider group than the narrow circle of *demotai*, and those beneficiaries are identifiable among the decreeing authorities. Whitehead's (perhaps only apparent) exceptions remain, but they are clearly not sufficient to call into question the mechanism proposed here for the enlargement of the deme communities.

The Decline of the Constitutional Deme

With the rise of the territorial deme went hand-in-hand the decline of its constitutional counterpart. For it is a fact that, to judge from the quantity,[68] if not the inter-

66. Compare *IG* II² 1200, lines 1–50 (post 236/5), a decree from Eleusis of the encamped Athenian soldiers and mercenaries. At lines 11–12 (partly restored), the honorand is credited with inviting "all the citizens" to a sacrifice.

67. Whitehead 1986, pp. 405–406. From Eleusis, the examples are *IG* II² 1193 (a *peripolarchos* honored by the demesmen alone) and 1272 (a secretary honored by the soldiers alone); and, from Rhamnous, *SEG* 22.120 (a garrison commander honored by the demesmen alone). Fuller information, however, might of course make these combinations of honorand and "constituency" perfectly comprehensible.

68. To support this inference, it will be sufficient to present a tabulation of the surviving deme documents according to the dates assigned by their editors. For the roster of documents on which this tabulation is based, see chapter 3, note 54. Three texts, all *horoi*, are not dated (Whitehead's nos. 58, 69, and 92). The rest I have tabulated by fifty year periods, interpreting, e.g., "ante 266/5" as soon before that date, "fin. s. IV" as between 350 and 300, and, where an assigned date bridges two categories (e.g., ca. 400 or 365–322), counting it in the lower of the two. For assignments to an entire century (e.g., "s. IV")

nal content,[69] of surviving deme inscriptions, the Attic deme qua association suffered after the end of the fourth century an increasing loss of function, until it disappeared altogether on the eve of Greece's absorption by Rome. The fate of the deme is but one facet, of course, of the general decline of public institutions, including all public associations, at Athens and elsewhere in Greece during this era.[70] The subject merits renewed and detailed examination here because some of the findings of the preceding discussion will, I believe, throw new light on the process and because, after a review of existing theories, it may be possible to deepen our understanding of the process of decline.

Existing Theories

First, a word or two concerning previous work in this area. The "Conspectus" entitled "The Demes and History," the final chapter of Whitehead's study, in particular, attempts to isolate some of the principal determinants of the deme's eventual demise.[71] This discussion shall be our point of departure.

At the elemental level of abrupt historical discontinuity, there are first the disastrous effects of the Peloponnesian War on the rural districts of Attica, especially the immediate and lingering consequences of the repeated enemy invasions of Athenian territory and the enforced confinement of the rural population within the city walls. The invasions and their aftermath are graphically illustrated by our ancient sources, beginning with Thucydides, but the *degree* of impact upon the rural demes and, above all, upon their associational apparatus is difficult to judge. One obvious—or initially so—index is the presence or absence of documentation ema-

---

or to the middle of a century (e.g., "med. s. IV") I have thought it best simply to preserve the editor's assignment without further interpretation. For the sake of simplicity, in those few instances where a single entry in Whitehead's catalog actually records two decrees on a single stone, I have counted such entry only once.

500–450:   4 texts
450–400:   8 texts
"s. V":   none
400–350:   16 texts
"med. s. IV":   15 texts
350–300:   71 texts
"s. IV":   3 texts
300–250:   13 texts
"med. s. III":   4 texts
250–200:   10 texts
"s. III":   8 texts
post 200:   3 texts

69. For example, the three latest deme documents concern the following subjects: Acharnai: thank offerings to Ares and Augustus (*IG* II² 2953); Eleusis: honors for the demarch (*IG* II² 949, lines 30–38; 165/4); and Melite: honors for a priestess, wife of a demesman (*Hesperia* 11 [1942] 265–274, no. 51; ca. 200–150). None of these texts could be regarded as exceptional or unusual if compared with the routine, and mostly honorific, subject matter of the documents of the earlier periods.

70. For an account of the decline of public associations across Greece, see the Introduction to my study of the public organizations, 1987, pp. 22–24.

71. Whitehead 1986, pp. 349–363.

nating from the deme organizations. Whitehead addresses this point. Correctly noting that no simple correlation obtains between the presence of documentation and
communal vitality, at least where the fifth century is concerned, he nonetheless ventures the opinion that "the necessarily adverse effects of the war upon deme life and
activity may go at least some of the way toward explaining the surprisingly slow
reappearance of deme documentation in the fourth century."[72] Reappearance? Only
four deme documents have been dated to the half-century 500–450, only eight to
the later half 450–400. By comparison, no fewer than 71 have been assigned to the
prolific record-producing years 350–300. Granted that virtually no epigraphic
traces remain of the war years themselves (namely, 431–404), it is more likely that
the epigraphic record.tells us little or nothing about the *after effects* of the war simply because the impulse to inscribe on stone the acts of a deme association had not
yet reached its full expression.[73]

Likewise, when Whitehead specifically instances as a factor delaying the resumption of associational activity the work of physical reconstruction and repair in
the immediate aftermath of the war,[74] we must proceed with caution. Any assumption of an interval of forty or fifty years to achieve rebuilding seems excessive on
the count of scale. Such an interval is implied by this argument if the intent is to
close the gap between the end of the war and the onset of substantial surviving lapidary texts ca. 360–350. Surely, if the rural *demotai* were determined, as they evidently were, to escape a disease-ridden, suffocatingly cramped, and (to a farmer)
hostile city and to reestablish their former way of life, it would not have taken them
a half century to do so. The farmlands awaited, unworked, the return of their owners. My suspicion is that the exodus out of the city was made without delay and that
reconstruction and repairs were accomplished posthaste, but that certain inhibiting
factors, possibly psychological, had to be overcome before the *demotai* could
plunge with fervor into the business of running—and publicizing the acts of—their
associations. At all events, the recovery, when it did come (again, to judge from the
epigraphic record) around the middle of the following century, was complete, perhaps bringing the deme associations to a pitch of development surpassing even their
prewar condition. If so, the beginnings of the eventual decline (as prefigured by the
sharp falloff of surviving documents commencing a century or so later) are evidently not to be traced to any deleterious effects wrought by the Peloponnesian War.
The war had proved to be only a temporary, even if not quickly reversed, discontinuity in the careers of the deme associations.

Nor must a second major (but only apparent) discontinuity (or series of discon-
tinuities) in the career of the Athenian demes be viewed as a significant factor in
their decline. I refer to the reorganizations of the phylai in 307/6, 224/3, 201/0 (and,
under Roman rule, A.D. 124/5), which resulted in the addition to, or subtraction
from, the original phylai created by Kleisthenes. Since (with the sole exceptions of
the creation of Berenikidai in 224/3, of Apollonieis in 201/0, and of Antinoeis in

---

72. Whitehead 1986, pp. 358–359.

73. Some of the factors bringing about this awakening are well portrayed by Whitehead 1986, pp.
359–360.

74. Whitehead 1986, p. 359.

A.D. 130) no new demes came into existence in conjunction with these reorganizations, new phylai could be created and old ones dismantled only through the reallocation of demes from one phyle to another. Effects upon the demes, if only indirect, were suspected by Whitehead with respect to the reorganization of 307/6,[75] but I fail to perceive the basis for any such claim. It is one of the striking features of the Kleisthenic organization, as I have previously emphasized, that its organizational components—phyle, trittys, and deme—have, as associations, very little to do with each other. No deme association is ever found cooperating in any discernible official way with either the trittys or phyle of which it was a component. To be sure, if your deme was moved from Erechtheis to Antigonis in 307/6, you will join a new group of *phyletai* in the Council of Five Hundred, you will be mustered in a different contingent of ephebes, you will represent a different unit on a board of ten, and so on. But life in your deme, and its association, so far as we are informed, will go ahead unchanged. Nor is even this disclaimer strong enough. There was a persistent tendency, and very likely an actual governmental policy, based on Solon's law on associations,[76] to leave to themselves, undisturbed by the doings of the central government, all associations including the associational organizations of the Attic demes. So not only observed practice but probable governmental policy as well strongly suggest that adjustments in the upper tiers of the organization went undetected at the level of the village association.

Still another factor arguably impacting on the vitality of the deme association remains, and that is migration of demesmen out of the ancestral deme. Such movement must of course have been a factor from the beginning. Dispersal or other loss of members, all else being equal, could weaken the association in two different, contrasting ways, depending how the term "deme" is defined. If the deme is defined as a natural, resident community, then, if those citizen *demotai*, through emigration or other cause, decrease in absolute numbers while the remaining non-*demotai* population of the deme remains stable or grows, the remaining, resident citizen association will be weakened on the count of relative numerical strength. At the same time, on the orthodox "constitutional" definition of a deme, to the extent that the membership is conceived as the sum total of living *demotai*, including nonresidents, the organization is weakened by the de facto absence of some of its membership. An association cannot be said to be thriving if an increasingly large proportion of its members are unable to participate in its functions.

To move one's residence to a distant location meant the surrender of valuable rights and privileges. But emigration occurred nonetheless, since any such considerations were undoubtedly outweighed in many cases by various forms of political, social, and economic advantage or necessity. That, by the classical period, many citizens (and their families) no longer resided in the deme of their affiliation is an unquestioned fact. But to go beyond this vague generalization and to attempt to quan-

---

75. Whitehead 1986, p. 360: "[Y]et the creation of the two new tribes Antigonis and Demetrias may well have been unsettling in an indirect way, at least for the thirty demes which found themselves unceremoniously hoisted out of the tribes of which they had formed part for two hundred years and allocated afresh."

76. See "Solon's Law on Associations," in chapter 1.

tify the phenomenon, whether generally for Attica as a whole or specifically with respect to movement from the rural demes to the urban center or, needless to say, in connection with a particular deme or demes, is notoriously difficult, given the state of our evidence. Since Gomme's pioneering study,[77] however, recently renewed attention to the sepulchral monuments in particular has begun to yield some definite, albeit self-contradictory and not fully understood, results.[78] Damsgaard-Madsen's critique of the use of funeral inscriptions as historical sources, for one, issued in the preliminary result that in classical times there occurred considerable migration from the countryside of Attica to the urban areas; little migration between the rural districts themselves; and very little migration from town to country.[79] But this Attica-wide characterization, to judge from the results of Osborne's 1991 study of gravestones from three demes, Kerameis, Kephale, and Rhamnous, obviously did not apply uniformly in particular cases.[80] For the time being, we must be content with the global characterization of mobility with respect to town and country districts.

Notwithstanding the lamentable state of our present understanding, two aspects of the phenomenon particularly germane to our present concern with the deme associations may profit from attention.

To begin, while there is little doubt but that the main thrust of extra-deme migration was directed toward the urbanized areas, we must bear in mind that *any* relocation out of the deme, even to a neighboring extra-urban deme, is relevant to our present question. Such relevance, furthermore, embraces both the effects upon the home deme out of which the migration has occurred and the effects upon the deme that is the destination of the migration. Despite our uncertainties about the detailed demographic picture, the documentary record of the demes does justify fairly secure observations regarding the effects of both types of change upon the deme associations.

In the case of in-migration, it is clear that the host deme, in its institutional aspect, suffered little, if any, disturbance. To appeal to the content of the honorary decrees, the records of the deme associations, as we saw, reveal only scant acknowledgment of the existence, much less the active involvement in their affairs, of non-*demotai*.[81] The language of the typical deme decree is the language of exclusivity, designed to deny the presence of, or even to repel, outsiders. If the impact of the movement of *demotai* is to be measured in terms of the impact on the deme associations of their destinations, it is likely that those associations, by virtue of their assiduously cultivated isolation, remained relatively unaffected.

But there yet remains the matter of any debilitating or other effects upon the deme *out of which* such movement of *demotai* had occurred. The question was

---

77. Gomme 1933, pp. 37–48.

78. For two (apparently independent) preliminary methodological explorations undertaken in advance of major studies of the inscribed grave monuments, see Damsgaard-Madsen 1988, pp. 55–68, and Nielsen et al. 1989, pp. 411–420. See also now Hansen 1990, pp. 25–44.

79. Damsgaard-Madsen 1988, pp. 55–68, with conclusion at p. 66.

80. For example (as already noted at the head of chapter 3), Osborne found that 62 percent of the demesmen of Kerameis commemorated (with demotic) on gravestones in the fourth and third centuries were buried in or near their ancestral deme, while for Kephale the percentage is only 28 percent and for Rhamnous a very high 76 percent (Osborne 1991, pp. 231–252, apud *SEG* 41.258).

81. See "Deme versus Deme Relations," in chapter 3.

broached in Whitehead's aforementioned "Conspectus." He cites the work of Jim Moore, who, taking a position against the supposition of the movement of "a large proportion of the population," maintained that (in the words of Whitehead's approving paraphrase) there could not have been such movement for "otherwise the internal organization of the demes themselves would have broken down."[82] Naturally, this formulation borders on a self-evident truism in that obviously there must of necessity be a point beyond which loss of members would have crippled the deme organization. So, whether a given deme association survived or expired came down to numbers, to the percentage loss of membership. That said, and to attempt to mount a response to Moore's reported position, it may be ventured here that one must be careful not to underestimate the resiliency of these organizations. After all, their corps of officers were very small (even in comparison with a small membership), with the demarch and a few other loyal "activists" probably carrying the organization's administrative load.[83] No known quorum of the *agora* was required for the taking of the action by the association; indeed, one rural deme association, the Halimousians, went so far as to convene its *agora* in town despite the fact that "most" of its members still lived in the deme—and so presumably for the most part could not be counted on to be present at that meeting.[84] The raising of revenues through various means and mechanisms was not dependent upon the maintenance of residence within the deme by the deme's members.[85] The existence of full calendars of religious rites seems to imply, as we noted, an active membership, but not all such participants need have been *demotai* or in any case actual residents of the deme: for one, "the women of the *demotai*," as we saw, were among any non-*demotai* persons involved in the association's rites. In short, while Moore's contention, as a purely theoretical postulate, is undoubtedly valid, it is doubtful whether in actual practice that out-migration often, or ever, reached the point at which the deme association could no longer be sustained.

Finally, one additional "theory" (if it may be called that), already widely aired, demands mention. This is the plausible notion that somehow the decline of the internal organizations of the segments of the state was caused or at least precipitated by the general decline of the Athenian statewide government itself. Against this at first seductive hypothesis, however, is my position in chapter 3 that precisely the *reverse* relationship obtained between the degree of participation in the city democracy and the degree of participation in the local deme associations. Removal from the arena of city government, in other words, went hand-and-hand with greater intensity of involvement in the "little democracy" of the deme. If this synchronic relation obtaining in the classical period is applied in the diachronic dimension to the decline of free government in Athens and its effect on the local deme associations, the implication would clearly be that, if anything, the vitality of local associations would have been enhanced. Again, it is evident that the cause or factor we are in search of is not likely to be found here.

---

82. Whitehead 1986, pp. 356–357, with quotation on p. 357.

83. For a full account of the deme officers, see Whitehead 1986, pp. 121–148.

84. Demosthenes 57, *Against Euboulides*, 10.

85. For the various forms of income, chiefly taxes and liturgies, rents, loans, see Whitehead 1986, pp. 150–160.

But the fact remains that the Kleisthenic deme association did go into a de-cline—indeed, by about 200 B.C. it may fairly be said to be no longer in existence.[86] Yet we seem to be no closer to understanding the root causes of that decline and eventual extinction. The reason for this state of affairs, I wish to suggest, is that in-sufficient attention to this point has been given to the deme's—I mean the constitu-tional deme's—relations with other persons residing within its boundaries.

A New Hypothesis

As already noted, the variety of types of decreeing party at both Eleusis and Rham-nous manifests a rough chronological progression. Taken as wholes, each dossier of documents illustrates an original ascendancy of the demesmen giving way to part-nerships with outsider groups, the partnerships in turn giving way to decrees of sol-diers encamped in the deme that betray no trace of the deme association's presence. One way, a negative way, of characterizing this process would be to label it the de-cline of the deme association.

Several underlying factors conditioning or accelerating this decline may be iso-lated. For one, it may be noted that the Kleisthenic citizen deme association, as a consequence of the mandatory portable and inheritable *demotikon,* was doomed, if not to extinction, then to a gradual dissipation over time.[87] Members could, and did, leave, thereby diminishing the numbers of resident *demotai.* At the same time, the recruitment of new members from outside the deme organization was a legal impos-sibility. (Adoption and naturalization, again, at best contributed only negligible ad-ditions to the deme registers.) Furthermore, once a demesman had permanently re-located, it was doubtful whether he would remain active in the deme association of his affiliation. In the most frequently occurring case of the citizen migrant to the city or Peiraieus, especially if the home center lay on the distant periphery of Attica, say, at Dekeleia, Trikorynthos, or Atene, the factor of distance rendered the demes-man de facto inactive. Paradoxically, at the same time, once settlement in the new deme had occurred, the displaced Trikorynthian, say, was, as we saw in chapter 3, debarred from meaningful participation in his new deme of residence, say, intra-mural Koile or Skambonidai. Rather, the fact of his presence within the boundaries of the deme was acknowledged, if at all, by his inclusion among οἱ οἰκοῦντες, "the residents." True, in this capacity his presence might now be recognized in the offi-cial acts of the demes and he might even join with the *demotai* in the passage of de-crees, but his formal exclusion from membership in the deme association was per-manent, extending even to his lineal descendants in perpetuity. Nonetheless, such a

---

86. For the incidence of deme documents by period, with a sharp falling off around the end of the third century, see above with the tabulation in note 68.

87. I am concerned here only with the loss of members to the local deme association, not with the al-lied but different phenomena of the decline (or growth) of either the number of Athenian citizens actu-ally resident in Attica at any one time or of the total numbers of Athenian citizens irrespective of resi-dence. These latter topics are addressed by Hansen at 1982, pp. 172–189. Consistently, however, with my arguments, Hansen proposes "that the Athenian citizen population after the introduction of Perikles' citizenship law was doomed to be stationary or to decline, and that any significant increase in the num-ber of citizens living in Attica was ruled out" (p. 172).

second-class existence as this might have been thought to compensate for the de facto loss of full participation in the deme association of his affiliation.

Nor were the "residents" limited to these displaced non-*demotai* citizens. As I have argued, they with certainty also included the metics, οἱ οἰκοῦντες (or αἱ οἰκοῦσαι) par excellence. Whether slaves were ever registered, counted, or otherwise acknowledged by their deme of residence will probably never be known. In all these instances, it was the *territorial* deme, the deme defined by precise boundaries, that had made the emergence of such a category of residents, complementing the Kleisthenic personal deme based on descent, possible. So, in sum, if the full truth were known, we might find that the alternative deme had potentially created a semblance of a structured and enduring associational existence for a majority that otherwise would have stood completely outside the only fully legitimated public organization of the city of Athens.

Such temporizing measures as these, however, could not forever forestall the decline, and eventual extinction, of the constitutional deme. Certainly in the major garrison demes, and possibly (though not demonstrably) in others as well, the non-*demotai* population continued to grow, not only numerically but in significance as well—economic, social, and political significance. Meanwhile, the numbers of the *demotai* were not able to increase, not only because recruitment was not legally possible, but also, more fundamentally, to the extent that the population of *demotai* was limited by the amount of arable land within the territorial boundaries of the deme. Many sons of *demotai*, once the ancestral farm had been reduced to the dimensions of subsistence production, unless unoccupied land was available elsewhere in the deme, would have had no choice but to emigrate if they intended to farm. Normal, undivided inheritance would allow for the replacement of a smallholder *demotes* by a single new *demotes* in the next generation but no more. The likely political consequence of this fact is that a stagnant or dwindling caste of resident *demotai* could not keep up the fiction that it spoke or acted for even the citizen community of Oe, Sypalletos, or Potamos Deiradiotes, as undoubtedly they once had done in 508/7 when all the members actually resided in the deme of their affiliation.

It is this combination of non-*demotai* growth (or abrupt addition of residents, as in the case of the garrisons) and stable or shrinking citizen membership that spelled the demise of the local constitutional association. In the end, when presumably the imbalance had reached a certain (but of course unknown) critical point, encampments of soldiers (and, for all we know, other non-*demotai* as well) began to bypass the deme association altogether and issue decrees in their own names. Expressed in the negative terms in which the discussion has thus far been couched—the terms appropriate to the point of view of the Athenian citizen class—this development marked the final chapter in the process of decline. But if, alternatively, one were to observe the process from the perspective of these extra-deme constituencies (above all the metics and soldiers), it would perhaps be apt to characterize this final stage in positive terms as the triumph of the *natural* community of the Athenian deme.

FIVE

The Phylai

Disposition, Meetings, and Solidarity

The demes, in both their constitutional and territorial modes, were able, by virtue of their physical remove from the urban center, reinforced by the deliberate cultivation of isolation from other deme associations, to maintain a vigorous solidary community independent from life in Athens. And it was in this community that, I am arguing, resided a distinctive "response" to perhaps the most limiting characteristic of the central government of Athens, to wit, the physical confinement of the organs and processes of government to the urban center. In the case of the phylai, however, it is obvious that no such model is applicable. To mention only the most obvious relevant factor, the fact that one of the three trittyes of a given phyle consisted of demes assigned to the urban region made any such disengagement from the *asty* impossible on the face of it. Nonetheless, we shall find in the phylai a very different mode of response to another striking characteristic—and, in the estimation of some, limitation—of the democracy—the principle of direct rule.

Introduction

Recent decades have witnessed a veritable explosion of publications devoted to various aspects of the democratic constitution of Athens after Kleisthenes. Not a few of

This and the following chapter together represent a virtually unchanged version of my article "The Athenian Phylai as Associations: Disposition, Function, and Purpose," which appeared in *Hesperia* 64 (1995) 503–542. For a brief postscript acknowledging a relevant discussion of the cults of the eponyms by Emily Kearns, see the end of the present chapter.

these publications concern the framework of that constitution, the network of phy-lai, trittyes, and demes through which the various responsibilities and privileges of government were theoretically equally apportioned over the citizen population. The functioning of these segments of the state was by no means limited, however, to the distribution or administrative management of the business of the democracy, for all three sets of units were simultaneously internally organized as more or less self-contained and autonomous *associations* devoted to the pursuit of activities possess-ing little or no connection (or so it has seemed) with the operation of the organs of the central government. It is in regard to this second, arguably no less vital, aspect of the constitutional framework that my statement about the "explosion" of publica-tions requires some qualification. Not until 1986 was Haussoullier's venerable study of the Attic demes[1] finally superseded by Whitehead's penetrating and exhaustively detailed book *The Demes of Attica 508/7–ca. 250 B.C.*, and even it appeared under the subtitle *A Political and Social Study*.[2] The trittyes, although they have played an important role in attempts to understand the political motivations behind, and the originally intended or actual later functioning of, Kleisthenes' new organization, have not left sufficient traces of their internal arrangements to support even the most rudimentary attempt at description.[3] That leaves the phylai, about which, as will be seen, considerable documentation survives. Except, however, for a brief summary description in my own *Public Organization in Ancient Greece,* that documentation has gone largely unexamined.[4] It is the purpose of the present study to make good this deficiency.

The plan of my discussion, which is of necessity constrained and shaped by the availability of only certain kinds of evidence, requires a few words by way of intro-duction. Briefly, it begins with a review of the indications for the location of the "seats" of the phyle organization, with a view to establishing the point that their concentration in the town (a fact that has never been contested) was not an accident but the result of deliberate, and continually reaffirmed, choice. At or near that seat, furthermore, were held the *agorai* or meetings of the phylai, which I shall argue were devoted in significant part to managing the finances of the organization with a view, I shall further suggest, to acquiring the funds necessary to support the most frequently documented phyletic activity, the conferring of honors upon the benefac-tors of the organization. Against this positive finding must be set, by contrast, the negative observation that there is little evidence of solidarity among *phyletai* and that, therefore, the primary purpose of the phyle organization was apparently not to promote community among its members. At the beginning of chapter 6, a lengthy discussion of the personnel of the phylai (officeholders, proposers of decrees, and honorands) will help us to understand just what that purpose might have been.

1. Haussoullier 1883.

2. Whitehead 1986.

3. For what little documention there is, see Jones 1987, ch. 1, sec. 1.33, pp. 60–61.

4. Jones 1987, ch. 1, sec. 1.32, pp. 58–60. Earlier accounts, brief as they are, may be mentioned: C. Lécrivain, "Phyle," *DarSag*, vol. 5, pp. 450–454, especially 452–453; Gilbert 1895, pp. 200-203; H. Swoboda in Busolt and Swoboda 1920–1926, vol. 2, pp. 974–975; and K. Latte, "Phyle," *RE* 20 (1941) cols. 994–1011, especially 1008–1009. To these accounts, little or nothing is added by the comprehen-sive treatises of Szanto 1901 and Roussel 1976.

While officeholders of a phyle seem often to have been citizens of substance yet at the same time men without ambitions beyond the phyle organization itself, the proposers of that same phyle's honorary decrees may have seen this role, I will suggest, as a means of promoting their present or future careers in the political life of the city. But it is the record of the people honored by a phyle that yields the most telling clues, for not only their current positions in the central government but also, even more revealingly, the reasons given by the phyle for so honoring them suggest strongly that the purpose of these decrees, and indeed of the organization as a whole, was to promote the advancement of the phyle's interests in the context of the public life of the city of Athens. Thus, I shall conclude at the close of chapter 6, we may understand the urban situation of the seat and the preoccupation with the bestowing of often costly honors especially upon *phyletai* with official appointments of one kind or another in the city: the associations of the *phyletai* had evolved, to sum the situation up in a single word, into organs of *representation*.

Before we proceed, a few words concerning our sources of information. By far the most abundant and informative indications are provided by inscriptions[5] comprising decrees of individual phylai (the overwhelming majority) plus an assorted miscellany of other texts. All ten Kleisthenic phylai except Oineis are represented by at least one decree; of the five post-Kleisthenic units we *may* have a single decree of Ptolemais; and not a few texts, though not assignable to a specific unit, are recognizably authorized by a phyle. Chronologically, the vast majority of the inscriptions fall within the fourth century; only a very few texts, namely, the herm of Aigeis (before 415) and a dedication of Pandionis (fin. s. V), are likely to antedate the year 400,[6] and only a scattering of others demonstrably postdate the dismantling of the democracy under the Macedonians. Similarly, what literary references we have to *phyletai* in their capacity as members of a phyle association range, as we shall see at the close of this chapter, from an Aristophanic use of *phyletes* in the *Birds* (produced in 414) down through the orators Andokides, Lysias, and Demosthenes in the later fourth century. But such literary sources are surprisingly few, a fact to which I shall attach a significance vital to my position.

Archaeological evidence is another matter. As will be seen, the destroyed or so far undiscovered (but epigraphically attested) shrines of the eponyms severally served as the focal points of the *individual* phyle organizations. But much of the rest of the physical record would seem to require a quite different interpretation. The depiction of the eponyms on the east side of the Panathenaic frieze (partially reproduced in Fig. 5.1),[7] the monument of the Eponymous Heroes in the Agora,[8] and the epigraphic record of ten *kylikes* "of the Eponymoi" dedicated by the Boule

5. For the reader's convenience, I have supplied in appendix 3 a corrected and amplified version of the list of the inscriptions of the phylai published in Jones 1987, ch. 1, sec. 1.4, app., pp. 65–67.

6. For a probable fifth-century attestation of Aiantis's board of *epimeletai* (this term does not actually occur in the text), see *IG* I³ 377 (= I² 304 B) (407/6), lines 21–22 (with Traill 1986, pp. 79–80, no. 1[b]).

7. For the interpretation of the figures on the frieze as the eponyms, see Kron 1976, pp. 202–214, and Harrison 1979, pp. 71–85. More recently, the identification has been opposed by I. D. Jenkins 1985, pp. 121–127.

8. On the monument, see *Agora* 3, nos. 229–245, pp. 85–90; 14, pp. 38–41; Shear 1970, pp. 145–222; and Kron 1976, pp. 228–236.

Figure 5.1. Plaster cast of slab VI, figures 43–46 (the so-called eponymous heroes of the phylai), from east side of the Panathenaic frieze of the Parthenon. Bibliothèque Nationale, Paris, apud Kron 1976, Tafel 31, no. 2.

in the name of "the Hero"[9] all bespeak the *collective* representation of the eponyms by the state. Some scholars have favored in this connection the notion of a common cult of the ten heroes.[10] Yet, not only is such a notion not otherwise supported, but also, on the hypothesis argued here, it is no longer necessary. If I am right, the purpose imposed upon the phyle organization by its active members was to promote the interests of that organization beyond the phyle *in the wider context of the city of Athens.* The frieze, the monument, and the *kylikes* may, on such a reconstruction, all be regarded as the state's response to this trend: while an individual phyle might promote itself at the expense of the remaining nine-tenths of the state, the state itself by these collective representations of the heroes asserted both the *unity* of the state and *its own suzerainty* over the individual parts of the state. None of these physical remains should be confused with the acts or arrangements of the phylai themselves, whether individually or collectively.

9. Rotroff 1978, pp. 196–209.

10. So, most recently, Rotroff in her publication of the inscription mentioning the "ten *kylikes* of the Eponymoi" (Rotroff 1978, pp. 207–208). In the end, on the basis of this text, she comes down in favor of "a common cult of the ten Eponymoi in Athens in the 4th century B.C." (p. 208). Earlier, Kron, to whom the inscription was not known, had concluded that the existence of such a cult remained merely a possibility (Kron 1976, p. 228).

The Disposition of the Phyle Organization

The Nature of the Problem

At the heart of Kleisthenes' new partition of Attica was a geographical division into three regions: the city, coast, and inland. Over these regions were scattered the units of the organization, probably exactly 139 in number and, once institutionalized by Kleisthenes, known technically as "demes." Some of these were formed on already-existing rural villages, others the reformer carved out of the more or less continuous sprawl of the urban center. The demes, in turn, Kleisthenes grouped in the clusters called trittyes, ten clusters to each region, numbering thirty in all. Each of the ten phylai was constructed of three trittyes of demes, one trittys from each of the three regions. Thus the organization comprised three tiers of units—phyle, trittys, and deme—each of which was theoretically capable of providing the territorial basis for an independent "association" of the type found in numerous Greek city-states.[11]

In two of the three cases, the creation and maintenance of such an organization was probably a relatively straightforward, uncomplicated affair. For many of the demes, especially the rural ones, a nucleated settlement already existed, and even in the densely packed urban center more or less natural "neighborhoods" may have been defined by streets or other built or topographic features. Not surprisingly, therefore, the record of associational life in the deme is relatively copious, for (to select an easily calculated index) of the 139 units we have epigraphic documents of one kind or another (but usually decrees) in the names of nearly fifty.[12] The case of the trittys was somewhat more complicated. Not all trittyes (despite my use of the term "cluster" above) were compact, contiguous aggregates of constituent demes; in a number of instances an individual member deme might lie at a considerable distance from the main body of the trittys. Obviously, the physical separation of some of the members of the trittys from each other could only impede the internal functioning and associational life of the organization, were such an organization to be formed. Among other problems, one would have been in which member deme or demes to situate any institutional structures, such as a town hall or communal shrine, or, if such structures were to share a common location, the "seat" of the trittys. But we shall never know how this or any other related problem was solved since, although just enough evidence survives to indicate that the trittys did develop internally, that evidence is too slight to permit meaningful generalization.

With the phyle, of course, the problems of the physical separation of the membership and of situating the "seat" acquire far greater urgency. It is one thing when one or two demes of a trittys lie at some remove from the main cluster. It is quite another when the unit—the phyle—falls into three more or less equal (in population, if not in territory or numbers of demes) and usually noncontiguous segments

---

11. For the recorded examples, see Jones 1987, index III ("Internal organization of public units"), pp. 396–403.

12. See the list of deme documents in Jones 1987, ch. 1, sec. 1.4, app., pp. 67–72; a similar, annotated list may be found in Whitehead 1986, app. 3, pp. 374–393. More recent documents are listed at chapter 3, note 54, of the present work.

situated in three topographically and demographically distinct regions.[13] Nor is it simply a matter of the political question of how to decide the problem of which trittys will enjoy the privilege of possessing the seat, important as that question would have been. For the location of the seat would (and, in the event, undoubtedly did) go far toward determining the composition and so the character of the organization since, given the realities of ancient transportation and communications, only *phyletai* living in close proximity to the seat would have acceptably convenient access to the phyle's meetings, cultic celebrations, and other functions. In which of the three regions, then, would the seat be located? Or would there be more than one seat, perhaps one in each region? Evidently because, as we shall see, virtually all the available evidence has pointed to the urban center, no one (so it seems to me) has bothered to come to grips with this question. To mention only the most obvious item of that evidence, nearly every relevant inscription (the very few exceptions are discussed below) was, where a provenience is known, found either on the Akropolis or in or near the Agora. Not unnaturally, therefore, the situation of the seat in the town might be taken as a given of the phyle organization.[14] Yet, I shall argue, this outcome was the product of a choice, or series of choices, and the perception of the basis for that choice or those choices will provide an important ingredient in our ultimate characterization of the function and purpose of the internally organized phylai.

The Shrine of the Eponymous Hero

Some commentators (at least those who express or imply a view on the matter) believe that it was at the shrine of the eponymous hero that the *phyletai* focused their associational activities.[15] This belief is not without merit. The Aristotelian *Constitution of the Athenians* states (21.6) that Kleisthenes appointed ten eponymous heroes for the phylai, chosen by the Pythian priestess from a preselected list of one hundred founders (*archegetai*). That the tradition of instituting a hero continued after Kleisthenes with the later additions (totaling five) to the original ten phylai is demonstrated by the phases of construction of the monument of the Eponymous Heroes in the Agora: as a new phyle was added to, or an old phyle subtracted from, the organization, statues of the corresponding eponyms were tacked on to, or removed from, the monument. Shrines are another matter; the recognition of a hero need not necessarily imply the existence of a shrine. So, the first order of business, prior to asking whether a shrine, if it existed, functioned as the "seat" of its phyle, is to determine the existence, then the location, of that shrine. Of course much attention has been given already to these questions, most fully by U. Kron in her 1976

---

13. For cartographic representations of the affiliations of demes, trittyes, and phylai, see Traill 1975, maps 1–3, at end; and, for an improved version, Traill 1986, map at end.

14. For the reasoned position of Swoboda, however, see below, with note 19.

15. Such is the assumption underlying my own statement in Jones 1987 that "several, if not indeed all, of the phylai were headquartered on or near the Akropolis" (p. 58). This statement was based, although not explicitly so, on my further observation that "Each eponymous is known (or can be assumed) to have possessed a sanctuary, with a concentration on the Akropolis, where three, possibly four, of the shrines are believed to have been situated" (p. 60).

monograph cited earlier,[16] so there is no need to go over once again this already much-worked ground. For our purposes, however, since we are opening up a question about the phylai previously believed to be answered (or not worth asking), it is important to observe a distinction regarding the evidence on the basis of which the determination of the location of the shrine (given its existence) is made. Some of this evidence, such as a notice in Pausanias, is independent of the documents under review here. But to what extent is the evidence of the inscriptions, including above all the record of their proveniences, admissible in this connection? If, on the one hand, as in the case of Pandion, some of the decrees of the phyle Pandionis (as restored) call explicitly for the stele to be erected "on the Akropolis in the shrine of Pandion," and if (as is the case) a number of such stelai are found in that very location, namely, the Akropolis, the conclusions that, first, the (thus far undiscovered) shrine of Pandion was located in this vicinity and that, second, this shrine was of some importance for the administration of the phyle Pandionis are both unobjectionable. But we cannot assume, on the other hand, that the provenience of a phyle inscription containing no such injunction to erect the stele in the shrine of the eponym (or any other mention of the hero or his cult) necessarily indicates, should the existence of that shrine be established, the location of that shrine, for that would be to beg the question regarding the location of the phyle's seat. The seat, in other words, may have been situated elsewhere than in or near the shrine. In the end, happily, only the case of Erechtheis is affected by this consideration, and that is the one phyle for which not only the existence but also the location of a shrine of the eponym is beyond all doubt. Nonetheless, it may be helpful to rehearse briefly (with the help of Kron, McLeod, and Rotroff)[17] the key indications, and above all the epigraphic testimony, bearing on our question.

I Erechtheus. The building on the Akropolis visited by Pausanias (1.26.5) and incontrovertibly identified as the Erechtheion can only have been the shrine of the eponymous hero of the phyle. The decrees of the phyle, although in three instances found on the Akropolis (*IG* II² 1146, 1150, 1165), do not preserve an injunction to set up the stele in the shrine.

II Aigeus. An *heroon* of Aigeus is recorded by Pausanias (1.22.5) but without indication of its precise location. H. G. Lolling, *MDAI (A)* 11 (1886) 322–323, placed the shrine at the western base of the Akropolis. Consistently with this placement, Agora 15, no. 69, identified as a decree of the phyle, was discovered *in arce* (see on *IG* II² 656). Perhaps pertinently, too, an inscription identified by its editor as a joint decree with Aiantis, *Hesperia* 56 (1987) 47–58, was discovered near the western entrance to the Agora Excavations (op. cit., p. 47). While the editor regards the stone as Aiantis's copy (op. cit., p. 51), I think it equally likely, in view of the difficulties involved in locating the latter phyle's shrine (see below), that we have the copy of Aigeis.

III Pandion. Pausanias (1.5.4) saw a statue of the hero on the Akropolis, and several inscriptions of the phyle enjoin that the stele be placed (as restored) "on the

16. Kron 1976.
17. Kron 1976, passim; McLeod 1959, pp. 125–126; and Rotroff 1978, pp. 205–206, note 46.

Akropolis in the shrine of Pandion" (*IG* II² 1144, 1148, 1152; *Hesperia* 32 [1963] 41, no. 42) or simply "in (the shrine) of Pandion" (*IG* II² 1138, 1140, 1157). All these inscriptions were found "*in arce*" (the *IG* texts) or "near the Eleusinion" (*Hesperia*). For discussion of the shrine's possible precise location, see H. R. Immerwahr's publication of a dedication by Pandionis (evidently the phyle), likewise found on the Akropolis, *Hesperia* 11 (1942) 341–343, no. 1; and, for the probable original erection of the stelai at the shrine, see D. M. Lewis, *ABSA* 50 (1955) 17–24, no. 25.

IV Leos. The honorary ephebic decree of Leontis, *Hesperia* 9 (1940) 59–66, no. 8, dedicated [τῶι ἥ]ρωι (line 1) and to be placed "in the shrine of the hero" (col. I, lines 31–33) or simply "in the shrine" (col. II, line 5), was discovered in the northeast part of the Agora. As Rotroff notes (1978, pp. 206–207), the *lex sacra* of Skambonidai (a deme of Leontis), *IG* I³ 244 (= I² 188), is recorded to have been discovered "Athenis ad Theseum," that is, near the Hephaisteion northwest of the Agora. She concludes that Leos's shrine, if such existed, may have stood near the north side of the Agora. Alternatively, she adds, Leos may have shared the shrine of his daughters, the Leokoreion, again situated on the north side of the Agora. On the Leokoreion, see *Agora* 3, nos. 317–338 (pp. 108–113); *Agora* 14, pp. 121–123; Wycherley 1978, pp. 63–64 (northwest corner of the Agora). Further afield, McLeod (1959, p. 126) conjectured the existence of a shrine of the hero near the present Daphni ("perhaps in the inland trittys of Leontis"), the provenience of a dedication by the *epimeletai* of Leontis τῶ[ι Λεῶι . . .], *IG* II² 2818 (357/6). Traill, while passing no judgment on the shrine (although it had already been rejected by Kron 1976, p. 200), has argued that Daphni belonged to the deme Kettos in the *city* trittys of the same phyle (1986, p. 81, note 7), so on constitutional grounds McLeod's proposal remains a possibility. The original situation of a similar dedication to the hero, however, in this case in the name of the *prytaneis* of the phyle, *IG* II² 1742, is not recorded.

V Akamas. *IG* II² 4983, an altar of the third century dedicated to Zeus Herkeios, Hermes, and Akamas, was found "In ore Dipyli" and, according to the editor, in situ: U. Koehler, *MDAI (A)* 4 (1879) 288. He also noted that the deme in which the Dipylon Gate was situated, Kerameis, belonged to the phyle Akamantis. With this rather good evidence the remaining indications are in conflict. Two decrees, the second explicitly of Akamantis, *ArchEph* 1965, pp. 131–136, call for the stele (as restored) to stand "in the shrine of Akamas" (I, lines 10–11; II, lines 22–24). The find spot is recorded as the neighborhood of Kallithea, understood by the editor to fall within the deme Xypete of the phyle Kekropis (op. cit., p. 136); Traill places this deme in the city trittys of the phyle (1986, p. 134). Obviously, if there was a shrine of Akamas in this location, it could not have been the headquarters of Akamantis. Similarly, the ephebic dedication of the phyle published by McLeod 1959, pp. 121–126, was discovered in the fortress at Rhamnous, but this deme belonged to coastal Aiantis, so even if the editor's restoration of "the hero" in line 1 is correct, it would be difficult to posit the existence of a shrine belonging to Akamantis in that location.

VI Oineus. No evidence for existence of a shrine. The marker of the tomb (ὅρος σήμ[ατος]) of one Oineus found in the Agora and published by W. K. Pritchett,

Hesperia 11 (1942) 240–241, no. 45 (s. IV), is unlikely, as he says, to have had anything to do with the phyle's eponym.

VII Kekrops. The decrees *IG* II² 1156 and 1158, both found on the Akropolis, order (as restored) that the stele be placed "in the shrine of Kekrops." *SEG* 2.8, "at Athens . . . formerly *in arce* . . . of uncertain origin," contains (on the original editor's restoration and interpretation of the fragmentary text) two separate decrees. The one, an honorary decree (of the Boule and Demos?) is to be set up "on the Akropolis" (line 2); the other (a decree of the phyle Kekropis) sets aside a *topos* for the honorary statue "in the shrine of Kekrops" (lines 10–11). It is a tempting, but of course by no means compelling, inference that the shrine stood *in arce. IG* II² 1141, of unknown original provenience, records a vote "on the Akropolis" (line 7).

VIII Hippothoon. Pausanias (1.38.4) testifies that the hero's shrine stood in or near Eleusis—under the Kleisthenic organization, a deme of the coastal trittys of Hippothontis. Two decrees of the phyle, *IG* II² 1149 and 1153, were found in Eleusis; the former (as restored) calls for an announcement of the honors "in the Hippothontion." *IG* II² 1163 enjoins the erection of *two* stelai bearing the identical text, one in the Asklepieion (on the southern slope of the Akropolis), the other in the Hippothontion. The decree's findspot "between the theaters of Dionysos and Herodes" (*IG*, ad loc.) indicates of course that it is the former of the two copies. As McLeod noted (1959, p. 125, note 12 [p. 126]), a priest of Hippothoos is mentioned in the accounts *from Eleusis, IG* II² 1672, lines 290-291.

IX Aias. The decree *Hesperia* 7 (1938) 94–96, no. 15, found in the Agora, calls for erection of the stele "in the Eurysakeion." Eurysakes, of course, was the son of Aias. Harpokration (s.v.) places the Eurysakeion in the deme Melite [of the phyle Kekropis and located a short distance west of the Agora: Traill 1986, p. 134]; Pollux (7.132–133) states that the Kolonos Agoraios was "beside the Eurysakeion" (similarly, the second hypothesis to Sophokles, *Oedipus Coloneus*). Postclassical inscriptions from the Agora—not, however, connected with the phyle Aiantis— call for their placement "in the Aianteion" (*IG* II² 1008 [118/7], line 87; *Hesperia* 24 [1955] 220–239 (128/7), lines 140–141). Since other decrees inscribed on these same stones instruct that the stele be set up in the Agora (*IG* II² 1008, line 42; *Hesperia,* loc. cit., lines [43], 99, [113], 127), Wycherley concluded that the Aianteion was situated in the Agora and suggested, furthermore, that it was not necessarily distinct from the Eurysakeion "on the Kolonos Agoraios" (*Agora* 3, p. 91, col. i; Wycherley 1978, p. 97). Rotroff, however, argues from the find-spots of the latter two inscriptions ("at the southeast corner of the Agora, near the south end of the Stoa of Attalos") for "a separate shrine [of Aias] somewhere in this area" (Rotroff 1978, p. 206).

X Antiochos. The only evidence for the existence or location of a shrine is provided by one of three decrees of the phyle (or of components thereof) found on the bank of the Ilissos near the shrine of Herakles at Kynosarges, *SEG* 3.115–117; the decree of "the phyle of the *hippeis*" (no. 115) calls for erection of the stele "in the shrine of Antiochos" (lines 22–23).

    Mention must also be made of the five post-Kleisthenic phylai, since in one instance an honorary decree, if correctly assigned to its phyle, preserves an injunction vital to my line of argument. The heroes of these phylai were not studied by Kron.

Antigonos. No evidence for existence of a shrine.

Demetrios. No evidence for existence of a shrine.

Ptolemy. An honorary decree of a phyle from the Agora, *Hesperia* 32 (1963) 14–15, no. 13 (init. s. II), enjoins erection of the stele "in the Eurysakeion." The name of the phyle was wholly restored by Meritt (*ibid.*) as Ptolemaiis in line 9 on the ground that the deme of the honorand, Aphidna, belonged to that phyle at the time of the inscription. On the Eurysakeion, see above under IX Aias. Meritt (op. cit., p. 15) speculated that the phyle inherited from Aiantis "a close association with the sanctuary and its attendant privileges."

Attalos. No evidence for existence of a shrine.

Hadrian. No evidence for existence of a shrine.

   Thus, of the fifteen phylai, ten, including all but one (Oineus) of the ten Kleisthenic phylai, are known to have possessed, or to have had access to, a shrine of an eponymous hero. Of these ten, three (possibly four) are assigned to the Akropolis (Erechtheus, Pandion, Kekrops, possibly Aigeus), three to the Agora (Leos, Aias, Ptolemy), two to the city but outside the Agora (Akamas, Antiochos), and one to Eleusis (Hippothoon). The five others remain entirely unattested and so may or may not have existed (Oineus, Antigonos, Demetrios, Attalos, Hadrian). Again, the concentration in the urban center is striking and must, in view of the tripartite regional disposition of the phyle, be given an explanation. Now, some of the shrines of the ten Kleisthenic eponyms were probably already in existence at the time of Kleisthenes' reforms. A degree of recognition in any case is implied by the fact the heroes had already achieved status as "founders" when the names of the one hundred *archegetai* were submitted to the Pythia at Delphi. So the location of the *shrine* will probably already have been predetermined in at least some cases. And even if a shrine of an eponymous hero were to have been founded later than the reforms, the chances that it would have been located outside the urban center are remote. The eponyms had been selected (with the known exceptions of Aias, a hero of Salamis, and of Hippothoon, closely linked with Eleusis) from among the *archegetai* of the city of Athens, not of the formerly independent communities of the countryside of Attica. Must, then, to proceed to the next step, the shrine *also* have become the headquarters or "seat" of its phyle?[18] Swoboda came close to such a conclusion. Since, he reasoned, the phylai, divided into three distinct regions, possessed no "Bezirksvororte" (territorial center), the shrine of the eponym became by default the "Versammlungsplatz" (place of assembly).[19] Shortly, we shall examine the evidence

18. The one other *monumental* structure that might be considered a candidate is the tomb of the eponymous hero. Pritchett, in the course of dismissing the possibility that the *horos* of the grave of Oineus pertains to the eponymous hero, cited evidence for such tombs of Erechtheus and Kekrops: *Hesperia* 11 (1942) 241, note 40.

   19. H. Swoboda, in Busolt and Swoboda 1920–1926, vol. 2, p. 974.

for the place of assembly of the phylai. But concerning the location of the head-quarters, or "seat," the testimony under review here is unambiguous. In the cases of seven of the nine known shrines of the ten Kleisthenic eponyms at least one decree calls for the stele to be erected "in the shrine of the eponymous" (or the like), and this, despite the fact that in each instance the content of the decree in question is not related to the hero, to the functioning of the shrine, or to any discernible religious matter. That is, there is no apparent reason for the stelai to be set up in these locations, unless the shrines were in some sense the administrative centers of the associations.

Yet, there are two discernible, and I think telltale, variations from this otherwise neat and tidy picture. First, all three of the heroes assigned to the Agora (Leos, Aias, Ptolemy) are certainly or possibly linked by the phyle documents with a shrine *other*, strictly taken, than that of the hero himself (respectively, the Leokoreion, Eurysakeion, and Eurysakeion again), despite the fact that in one instance (Aias) a shrine of the eponymous (the Aianteion) is independently attested. In principle, therefore, the seat of a phyle was not unalterably wedded to the ancestral shrine of the eponymous. That is to say, those headquarters that *were* so located were placed in their eventual locations as a result of a conscious decision. Secondly, another sign that we are dealing with deliberate choice is afforded by the inscriptions of Hippothontis. That phyle's shrine and administrative center (as shown by the find-spots of two of its decrees) were situated in Eleusis, a coastal deme, yet, as noted above, a third decree calls for a second stele to be erected in the Asklepieion *in town*. The conjunction of the unparalleled extramural situation of the phyle's shrine and of the unusual provision for a second decree to be erected in a different location cannot be accidental. Again, it appears that, although the connection between shrine and headquarters was admittedly a strong one, it was not preordained to the extent that it could not be contravened. The location prescribed for the second stele shows that the inclination to focus the phyle in the urban center could override, or at least successfully compete with, whatever propensity existed to house the seat of the association at or near the ancestral shrine of the eponymous hero.

The *Agorai*: Location, Schedule, Agenda, and Purpose

Location and Schedule

If a decree of a phyle was regularly placed in the shrine of its eponymous, it is natural to begin here—in or around the shrine—our search for the place of the meetings of the *phyletai*, namely, the *agorai*, to which our inscriptions make several references and at which most or all of the formal business of the phylai was demonstrably or presumably conducted.

Let us first review the exasperatingly few scraps of direct evidence. The term *agora* itself might be thought to provide a clue about location or a type of location, but the word's derivation from ἀγείρειν suggests that it denoted simply a gathering of people, without any necessary allusion to the *place* of assembly, much less to any *particular* place of assembly (such as was originally, presumably, the Agora of

Athens).[20] As it happens, there is only one direct indication of the location of these meetings, but it is a good one: an inscription of Kekropis (*IG* II² 1141) records the taking of a vote ἐν Ἀκροπόλει (line 7), where, in fact, as noted above, the shrine of Kekrops is to be located with high probability. Thus the *agora* of at least this phyle will almost certainly have been convened in or near the Kekropeion "on the Akropolis."

What remaining epigraphic clues there are relate largely to other aspects of the *agora*, yet they are not entirely without implications for its venue. The meetings were convened by the chief officers, the *epimeletai*, for they are the only possible subjects of the clause ὅταν ἀγορὰν ποιῶσιν embedded in the decree of Erechtheis *IG* II² 1165 (ca. 300–250), line 34. (In *SEG* 3.115 [ca. 330], however, the subject of the parallel clause ὅταν ἀγοράζει [line 18] is manifestly "the Antiochid phyle" mentioned in the immediately preceding phrase.) In lines 7–9 of the Erechtheid decree Wilhelm restored [sc. and he saw to it] ὅπως . . . [. . . κα]ὶ ἀγοραὶ γίγνωνται ὑπὸ τ[ῶν φυλετῶν κατὰ μῆνα κατὰ τὰ γεγρα]μμένα κτλ., but the bracketed words are unfortunately not entirely supported by the other phyle documents. Besides the problem about the identity of the convener(s), monthly meetings, while not in themselves unthinkable, are unlikely, since a somewhat earlier decree of Pandionis, *IG* II² 1140 (386/5), is prefaced by the words "in the *agora* after Pandia" (lines 4–5). If the meetings of a phyle were monthly, why do we not find a reference to a specific month? At all events, since, to build upon this last phrase, the Pandia was shown by Mikalson to have occurred on Elaphebolion 17, following directly upon the City Dionysia on the 10th through 16th of the same month,[21] it is a tempting speculation (with T. Mommsen) that the meeting was timed in order to take advantage of the probably large numbers of *phyletai* in town for the two festivals; conceivably, the meeting was held late in the day of the 17th prior to the departure of the *phyletai* to their homes that same evening.[22] Thus the date might be taken as an (admittedly weak) argument for an urban setting for the meeting.

Whatever may be thought of this argument, the *agora* "after Pandia" need not have been the *only* meeting of Pandionis during the year. The slightly later decree of Kekropis already cited, *IG* II² 1141 (376/5), mentions a secret vote of the *phyletai* on the Akropolis τῆι κυρίαι ἀγορᾶι (lines 6–7).[23] The implication is that, parallel with the practice at the state level, there were other meetings that were not

20. Whitehead notes, however, in connection with the deme assemblies, for which the term *agora* was also used, that "[s]ometimes its sense is almost purely locative" (1986, p. 87 with note 6).

21. Mikalson 1975, p. 137.

22. Thus the speaker of Demosthenes 57 (delivered in 345?), in his account of a meeting in the city of the demesmen of Halimous, relates how, before the proceedings had actually been brought to a close, the older *demotai* had already returned to their farms, "for in the case of our deme, men of the jury, being thirty-five stades from the *asty,* and since the greatest number lives there, the majority had gone back" (§10). For Mommsen's speculation (based on a slightly different set of dates), see Gilbert 1895, p. 202, note 4.

23. Part of line 6, as indicated by the editor's subscript lines, depends entirely upon the testimony of Fourmont. But, except for the first letter of the definite article, the phrase "the *kyria agora*" was clear on the stone when republished by Pritchett, *Hesperia* 10 (1941) 263–265, no. 67.

thus *kyriai*. [24] If so, the distinction between "ordinary" and "extraordinary" might refer to the time (or even the place) of assembly or to the agenda or to both. An example of meetings of both extraordinary timing and subject matter is provided by a motion made in the Assembly by Demosthenes in the year 337 that *agorai* of the phylai be called for the second and third days of Skirophorion in order to select superintendents and treasurers for work on the walls (Aischines, 3.27, 330 B.C.). More vaguely, the previously cited phrases "whenever (the *epimeletai*) convene an *agora*" and "whenever (the Antiochid phyle) convenes an *agora*" might be taken to suggest extemporaneous meetings devoted to some irregular or unforeseen item of business.

A possible distinction between different kinds of meetings may also be detected in one of the Eleusinian decrees of Hippothontis, *IG* II² 1149 (ante med. s. IV). It calls for the *epimeletai* to "announce" a crowning "in the Hippothontion" (lines 5–6 as restored).[25] The term ἀνειπεῖν is technical in this sense in the deme documents and in the documents of public units of other states,[26] but, I think significantly, has only one other use in the phyle decrees despite the very frequent mention of crownings. (That one other use is in the somewhat later *IG* II² 1161 [fin. s. IV], on which see below.) Given its rarity, in other words, there must be a point in the addition of the announcement to the act of crowning itself. I suggest that, again, the explanation is to be found in the unusual, that is, extramural, location of the shrine of Hippothontis. Possibly the crowning and its announcement were to be carried out in two different locations. Since the text enjoins that the announcement take place (in Eleusis) at the shrine, it is at least worth suggesting that the *agora* at which the crowning was actually performed had taken place in the city, where it might be witnessed by a larger number (or at least different set) of *phyletai*. This interpretation is consistent with the likely import of the decree of an unknown phyle just mentioned containing the other attestation of an "announcement," *IG* II² 1161. Although the stone was found on the Akropolis, the text reads in lines 3–5: [. . . ἀν]/ειπεῖν Λαμπ[τρᾶσι------ Δι]/ονυσίοις τὸ[ν στέφανον. . . . In this case, on the reasonable assumptions that we have the only copy of the decree, that it was erected in the general vicinity of the place of its passage, and that the crowning was part of the agenda of that meeting, the crowning will have taken place on or near the citadel, with the announcement assigned, apparently on the occasion of the celebration of the Rural Dionysia,[27] to a place called Lamp(trai?). Both demes named Lamptrai—Upper and Lower—belonged

---

24. Similarly, a *kyria agora* is attested for the deme Aixone at *IG* II² 1202, lines 1–2. Yet, it is surprising that, if the phrase indicates regular procedure among all or even a large number of the demes, it is found in no other deme decree, the single possible additional example being the restored phrase in a lease from Rhamnous, *IG* II² 2493, lines 14–15. See, further, Whitehead 1986, pp. 90–91. For practice in the city *ekklesia*, see Aristotle, *AthPol* 43.4.

25. [. . . ἀ]νειπεῖν ἐν τ/[ῶι Ἱπποθωντί]ωι, ...

26. For examples, see Jones 1987, index III "Internal organization of public units," F.2.b ("announcement of honors"), p. 399. Occasionally, the synonymous nominal term *anagoreusis* and others are used outside Athens.

27. However, I find in Whitehead's detailed discussion of the Rural Dionysia (1986, pp. 212–222) no mention of either Lamptrai.

to the phyle Erechtheis[28] and to the coastal trittys. Thus in both texts the effects of the regional diversity of the Kleisthenic phyle would be in evidence: the crowning will take place in the urban trittys, its announcement in the coastal trittys.

Nor is this the only significance to be found in these texts. Presumably, it was the act of crowning itself, the *stephanosis*, that was regarded as the more important event of the two. Presumably, as I have suggested, it was at the *kyria agora* that the crowning took place, since, to judge from the frequency of mention of crowns in the decrees, this was an item of regular business. If, then, in these two examples, the actual crowning transpired in the city, while the less important subsequent announcement was relegated to the coastal trittys, we are entitled to speak of a prioritizing of the urban *phyletai*. This was the more important audience. Some confirmation is provided by a passage in a roughly contemporary forensic text. Aischines mentions a decree of the state prohibiting both phylai and demes from *announcing* their award of crowns "at the tragedies" (sc. in town) (3.41–45: 330 B.C.). Obviously, since we are here dealing with an announcement not before a meeting of *phyletai*, but before a general audience, the matter goes beyond normal phyletic procedures. Nonetheless, the underlying idea may be the same. The state's decree aimed to curb the efforts of the associations to publicize their acts, specifically their crownings of their benefactors, by staging announcements in front of a captive urban audience at the well-attended tragic productions on the slopes of the Akropolis. Aischines is explicit on the point that the phylai and demes were engaging in unfair competition with the state; the persons crowned by them, he says, were receiving greater *timai* than those crowned by the People (§43). Just as (on my argument) the phylai Hippothontis and Erechtheis seem to have favored the city trittys by holding their crownings in the "ordinary" meeting in town, so those phylai checked by the decree mentioned by Aischines had pursued that same tendency still further. Not satisfied with a *stephanosis* conducted in town before their own *phyletai*, they sought to publicize their acts further by gaining access to the urban members of *all* the phylai. The prioritizing of the town had been carried to its ultimate extreme.

Agenda and Purpose

With these findings in mind, we may now consider the evidence for the business of the assemblies. Some of this evidence concerns alleged central governmental functions, of which one in particular, if accepted, would go far toward providing the raison d'être of the phyle's *agora*. Whitehead has suggested that the selection of *bouleutai* (and of the five hundred *phrouroi*) was conducted, not at the deme level as always thought, but in the "tribal" assemblies.[29] The question turns on the interpretation of a vexed passage in the Aristotelian *Constitution of the Athenians*. At §62.1

28. If the deme? in question is Upper, not Lower, Lamptrai, the phyle may after all be Antigonis, since the stone is dated "fin. s. IV" (*IG*) and since that deme belonged to Antigonis under the XII phylai (307/6–224/3) and XIII phylai (223/2–201/0): see Traill 1975, p. 111, no. 83.

29. Whitehead 1986, p. 269. His statement of the position at pp. 269–270 is somewhat more guarded: "My suggestion is, then, that the actual process of sortition which resulted, after necessary adjustments, in the final tribal complements of fifty councillors and an appropriate number of deputies was conducted at tribal level by special meetings (or at least special deliberations) of the tribal assemblies."

it is stated that at one time some of the sortitive magistracies, including the nine archons, used to be allotted "from the whole phyle," while the others, allotted in the Theseion, were distributed among the demes. But, the text continues, when the demes began to sell the magistracies, they allotted the latter group as well "from the whole phyle," with the exception of the *bouleutai* and *phrouroi*, "which they [still] turn over to the demes." Now, the mention of "whole" phylai certainly opens up the possibility that at the *agora* of each phyle the assembled membership conducted the selection of its apportioned quota of state officers. Whitehead's point, however, concerns the demes. He proposes, with reference to the allotment by the demes in the Theseion of the councillors (and guards), that the meetings in question were in fact the ten "tribal assemblies." His principal arguments, in the absence of any reference to such assemblies in the text, are ones of economy. He finds it difficult to believe that all 139 demes met separately and individually for this purpose in the Theseion; and there are logistical problems involving fractions of *bouleutai* (or their alternates) that could be handled more elegantly at the level of the phyle.[30] But Whitehead's proposal, whatever its merits, entails a difficulty — the fact that Aristotle places the earlier allotments by the demes (and presumably, but not necessarily, the later as well) in the Theseion. Indeed, Aristotle may have been mistaken in limiting that venue to the sortitions of the demes, since Aischines (3.13), writing in 330 and so with reference to the later procedure,[31] appears to place both classes of sortition (that is, by "whole" phylai as well as by the demes) in the Theseion, on which point he is followed (contra Aristotle) by Rhodes who supposes that "A.P. has been careless in his phrasing."[32] So, it is quite likely that all the sortitions, both early and late, took place in this single location. That is the problem. It would help, of course, if we knew more about the Theseion, but the design of the building and its location, except for the fact that it was situated somewhere in the general vicinity, probably to the east, of the Agora, remain an enigma.[33] Even so, whatever the structure's disposition or location, the sortitions were manifestly conducted by *all* the phylai in a *single* place; that they were also conducted at a *single* time must, however, remain, at least on Aristotle's (and Aischines') evidence, a mere unverified possibility. It follows, in any case, that the sortitions could not possibly have coincided with the several *agorai* of the individual phylai. Even the scanty evidence reviewed above shows that the latter were convened at different locations (including in at least some instances the several shrines of the heroes) on separate schedules and at the behest of "the phyle" or its officers, acting (so far as we are informed) individually, not to mention the fact that none of the phyle documents so much as alludes to either sortitions or the Theseion. We must, I think,

30. Whitehead 1986, pp. 266–270.

31. For the suggestion that the later procedure indicated by Aristotle was instituted with or prior to the introduction of the division of the phyle into ten sections, A–K, early in the fourth century, see Rhodes 1981, on §62.1, pp. 690–691. By ca. 370 the use of *kleroteria* had been extended to magisterial appointments; and the associated bronze *pinakia* (magisterial as well as dicastic) show each phyle divided into the ten sections.

32. Rhodes 1981, on §62.1, pp. 689–690.

33. See *Agora* 3, nos. 339–362, pp. 113–119; *Agora* 14, pp. 124–126 (with p. 125 for the location to the east); Rhodes 1981, on §15.4, pp. 210–211.

rule out the possibility that the sortitions at any period, whether by "whole" phylai or demes, coincided with, or were elements of, the *agorai* of the phylai formally attested in our inscriptions.

Even so, it must be admitted that the *agora* was not entirely without central governmental roles. As previous scholars have suggested, it is reasonable to assume that the selection of the holders of liturgies (*gymnasiarchia, trierarchia, choregia*, and others) and of the members of the extraordinary statewide boards of *taphropoioi, teichopoioi*, and *trieropoioi*, all apportioned *kata phylas*, was conducted by each phyle in its *agora*.[34] Elsewhere, I have suggested that it was at these meetings that the fathers of each year's ephebic recruits assembled *kata phylas*, took oaths, and selected from those over forty years of age three men "the best and most suitable" to take charge of the ephebes. (From these candidates the Demos elected by show of hands a *sophronistes* for each phyle and, from the other Athenians, a single *kosmetes* to preside over the whole class.)[35] Along the same lines, it has been suggested that the *agora* might be put to ad hoc uses by the state, but the putative cases of such uses known to me are neither numerous nor compelling. A passage in the *Athenaion Politeia* (48.4) containing a reference to ταῖς ἀ[γορ]αῖς was once thought to allude to the assemblies; if so, the text would be saying that the (state's) *euthynoi* and their *paredroi* were compelled, at or during the *agorai*, to sit at the statue of the eponymous hero of each phyle (to hear charges brought by citizens against the magistrates). But a more attractive rendering "in the market hours" was championed by Wilamowitz, followed by Rhodes.[36] Andokides, in a speech of 399 (1.97), records a decree of the Assembly ordering all Athenians to take an oath "by phylai and by demes." Whitehead interprets this to mean not that the oath was taken twice over by each citizen both in his deme and phyle but "that the demesmen took it, by demes, at the tribal assemblies,"[37] a reasonable, but unverifiable, suggestion. The state, in sum, seems to have made only very limited use of the administrative apparatus of the internally organized phylai.[38]

What, then, was the function of these assemblies? To judge from our inscriptions, virtually all the business transacted by the *phyletai* was concerned with the internal affairs of the association. These will have included, of course, the selection of the phyle's officers (on which, see chapter 6), although such elections lack explicit attestation. What the inscriptions do attest is that on a seemingly regular basis, and without visible prompting from the central government, the *phyletai* assembled to vote, bestow, and perhaps announce various honors for a wide range of benefactors. Among these, by far the best known are the boards of *prytaneis* or other councillors

34. For details concerning the liturgies, including the evidence for their representation of the phylai, see Jones 1987, ch. 1, sec. 1.27, pp. 48–51; for the extraordinary boards, see sec. 1.26 (p. 47: *taphropoioi* and *teichopoioi*) and sec. 1.29 (p. 57: *trieropoioi*).

35. Jones 1987, ch. 1, sec. 1.29, p. 54, and sec. 1.32, p. 59, citing Aristotle, *AthPol* 42.2.

36. Rhodes 1981, on §48.4, pp. 561–562. As Rhodes says (p. 561), "Some indication of time is needed, since the place is specified in what follows."

37. Whitehead 1986, p. 109.

38. We must, therefore, reject or severely qualify the statement of Swoboda (in Busolt and Swoboda 1920–1926, p. 975) that "Die Phylenversammlungen hatten sich aber auch mit staatlichen Angelegenheiten zu beschäftigen."

upon whom the *phyletai* sometimes conferred formal honors.[39] But, irrespective of the identity of the honorand(s), if the sheer bulk of documentation provides even the most approximate index of frequency, the conferring of honors represents the principal business of the *agorai*. Even if the (few) bouleutic texts are set aside, of the 51 remaining decrees, 48 or 94 percent are recognizably honorary in character. Nor is it merely a matter of frequency. Granted the possibility that the engraving on stone of certain types of documents and not others has skewed the record (and honorary texts will have enjoyed a strong claim to both public and permanent display), it is plain that the bestowal of honors drew heavily upon the financial resources of these organizations. One need only consider the value in drachmas attested for some of the crowns [40] How, then, we must ask, was the association able to finance such a costly activity?

The residue of isolated particular items of business from the inscriptions provides the answer. Several allude in different ways to measures taken to bring funds into the organization. A simple example is provided by the decree of Akamantis threatening to fine any person (i.e., member) who contravenes its terms.[41] But for the point, vital to my argument, that it was the *agorai*, that is, the memberships as a whole, that managed the financial affairs of the association, there are three straightforward articles of evidence. A brief attributed to Demosthenes charges that a member of Leontis, Theokrines, had been found at his *euthynai* to owe 700 drachmas to the Eponymous (i.e., to the phyle). To demonstrate that Theokrines had acknowledged the debt and that he had made arrangements with the *phyletai* for its payment, the speaker adduces the decree that one Skironides had moved "among the

39. Of the 56 inscriptions of the period of the original ten phylai published in *Agora* 15, all but 12 are certainly or probably dedications or decrees set up by individual phylai acting in their own names. But of these 44, at least 15 cite the praise and/or crown by the Boule, the Demos, or the Boule and Demos, so they, and undoubtedly many others, were presumably prompted by prior action at the state level. Nonetheless, evidence of independent action by the phylai can be found. In no. 5 (= *IG* II² 1142; init. s. IV), a board of pytaneis is honored in a decree of an organization of unknown identity; Meritt and Traill express the opinion that the text belongs to the dedication of a phyle. From a later period, no. 69 (= *IG* II² 656+; Dow 1937, no. 2) is printed by Meritt and Traill as a decree of Aigeis, but the key reference to the phyle in line 10 is wholly restored (note, however, the possible mention of the *epimeletai* in lines 15–16). No. 33 (= *IG* II² 3202; 344/3), a dedication of an unknown phyle, preserves several wreaths, of which two read "the *phyletai*" (lines 6 and 9). From the Macedonian era, similar wreaths or citations of "the phyletai" are found in *Agora* 15, no. 58 (=Dow 1937, no. 1; 305/4; Akamantis), lines 86, [92], [98]; no. 67 (init. s. III; unknown phyle), line 3; no. 76 (279/8; Pandionis), lines 47 and 53; no. 84 (256/5; Antigonis), lines 81, 89, 92, 95, 100; and no. 95 (s. III; unknown phyle), face A. In one instance, *Agora* 15, no. 38 (= *IG* II² 1749; 341/0; Aigeis), the inscription, while acknowledging the crowning of the prytaneis by the Boule and Demos (lines 1–3), appends three decrees, of which the first (lines 74–77) and second (lines 78–81), honoring the *tamias* of the phyle and "them" (i.e., the prytaneis themselves), were passed by "the *phyletai*."

40. Thirty-six crownings are attested by the decrees (or consequent dedications by the honorands). In six cases, the text is sufficiently preserved to show that the type of crown was not specified; in one other, it is too damaged to allow one to determine whether the type was specified or, if it was specified, what the type was. Of the 29 others, 10 are stated to be of olive and 19 of gold. Of the 19 gold crowns, while five are not given a specific value and in three other cases the number or numeral is not preserved, eight are recorded (or the text is so restored) to have been of 500 drachmas and three (or so the text is restored) of 1,000. For the references to the gold crowns of stated value, see chapter 6, note 51.

41. *ArchEph* 1965, pp. 131–136 (i), lines 6–8.

phyletai" (58.14–15; 17–18). The reference here can only be to the phyle's *agora*. Similarly, the two other examples, both epigraphic records of decrees, must be the products of formal meetings of the *phyletai*. A decree proposed by Antisthenes of Erechtheis (to be discussed in detail in chapter 6) called for the biannual inspection of properties under lease from the phyle.[42] No less concerned with financial matters is the decree of an unknown phyle setting out the terms of the lease of certain of its properties, *IG* II²1168 (s. III?).[43] That the terms of a lease in particular should have been promulgated in the form of a decree is proof that the memberships, while concerned frequently with the bestowal of honors, were simultaneously engaged in the raising of the substantial funds required for the crowns, sacrifices, exemptions, etc. in which these honors consisted.

In support of this general conclusion regarding procedure may be marshaled a miscellany of particular examples, in some instances culled from decrees of the phylai (but often incidental to the decree's principal content), of the financial dealings of the phyle: the above-mentioned imposition of a fine and pursuit of funds owed to the Eponymous; the recovery by Aiantis at a state auction of 666 2/3 drachmas owed by a former *epimeletes* who had failed to turn over "the sacred money of Aias" which he had collected;[44] the lending of funds by Kekropis on the security of a plot of land;[45] the leasing (again) by Erechtheis of its lands and by an unknown phyle of properties of uncertain identification;[46] the evident ownership of other lands abroad (at Oropos and on Lemnos) by Antiochis and at Oropos by all the phylai jointly holding the properties in pairs;[47] and the attestation of accounting procedure in a decree of Hippothontis.[48] More or less formal references to "revenues" or "money" appear in the inscriptions of several different phylai.[49]

Plainly, funding was a topic of considerable concern to the memberships. To be

---

42. *IG* II² 1165 (ca. 300–250), lines 17–22.

43. That the text belongs to a phyle is shown by the reference to "the *epimeletai* of the phyle" in lines 9–10; that it is a decree (and so the product of an *agora*), by the words τόδε τὸ ψήφισμα in line 20.

44. *Hesperia* 5 (1936) 393–413, no. 10 (346/5), lines 153–185.

45. *IG* II² 2670, line 5 (Kekropidai). Cf. the decree of Erechtheis, *IG* II² 1165, lines 21–22, where mention is made of mortgage stones (*horoi*) placed on the properties of the phyle.

46. *IG* II² 1165 (ca. 300–250), lines 17–22, credits the honorand with moving a decree calling upon the *epimeletai* to make regular inspections of the properties (*ktemata*) to ascertain whether the lands (*choria*) were being farmed in accordance with the leases (*synthekai*). The lease of the unknown phyle is *IG* II² 1168.

47. *SEG* 3.117 (303/2; Antiochis), lines 6–17. The acquisition by Athens in 338 of lands at Oropos and their division among pairs of phylai were mentioned by the orator Hypereides in his speech (IV) in defence of Euxenippos (§16). A badly damaged inscription dated ca. 330, Agora Inv. No. I 6793, is believed by its editor to be "very probably" (p. 51) a joint decree of Aigeis and Aiantis concerning their portion of the lands: see Langdon 1987, pp. 47–58. Langdon identifies the stone as the one of two copies belonging to Aiantis. Since publication of Langdon's *editio princeps,* lines 2–16 have been improved by Walbank 1990, pp. 95–99. Inter alia, Walbank establishes two points broached by Langdon but not confirmed by his readings, namely, that the text is a *decree* of the two phylai and that there were originally *two* stelai (lines 4–5).

48. *IG* II² 1163, lines 26–28.

49. Erechtheis: *IG* II² 1165, lines 4–5, 11; cf. 1146, line 9; Kekropis?: *IG* II² 1158, lines 8–9; Antiochis: *SEG* 3.117, line 20. The new decree of Aigeis and Aiantis published by Langdon and improved by Walbank (above, note 47) seems in lines 9–10, according to Walbank's readings, to direct that the costs of publication be met out of the "common monies" of the phylai (Walbank 1990, p. 97).

sure, the probability that matters affecting the financial well-being of the organization enjoyed a particularly strong claim to be permanently recorded on stone may distort our perception of the volume and frequency of such transactions. Nonetheless, even if such dealings were infrequent, the sums involved were in some cases demonstrably substantial. Nor are the uses to which such moneys would be put difficult to imagine. By such means the phylai would have been able to support any otherwise nonfunded cultic and other associational activities of their organizations (presently to be discussed), but most importantly, as I have suggested, they would have been able to sustain thereby the considerable expense involved in their frequent and sometimes lavish bestowal of honors upon their benefactors.

The Solidarity of the Phyle as Association

Since the phylai give every appearance of functioning as internally organized, self-sufficient associations, it would be natural to expect to find traces of some degree of solidarity among the members of a phyle when measured against their actions toward or feelings about other Athenians who were not members. To begin, were occasions available for meaningful interaction among *phyletai*? Naturally, a suitable venue, large and centrally located, would be needed. The shrines of the eponyms (and just possibly their tombs[50]) are likely candidates. It is most plausibly at the shrine that the *thysia* (sometimes stated to have been offered in the name of the eponymous hero) attested for Erechtheis, Pandionis, and Akamantis should be situated.[51] These sacrifices might have been of a frequency and dimension that, if we had more information, would impress us. As it is, our only clues are, with regard to magnitude, the attestation (twice) of 50 drachmas as the sum awarded to a benefactor in order to allow him to carry out such a *thysia*,[52] hardly enough to fete even a small fraction of only the city residents of a phyle. With regard to frequency, the restoration ἐν τῆι ἐπιθέτω[ι θυσίαι . . .] at *IG* II² 1146, line 11, suggests a regular calendar to which an addition might on occasion be made.[53] Somewhat differently, since (as with all liturgies) the state was involved, one could add the *hestiasis,* or banqueting of the phyle, an annual liturgy borne by individuals nominated by their phylai and attested for both the Dionysia and the Panathenaia.[54] But, except for

50. See above, note 18.

51. Erechtheis: *IG* II² 1146, line 7 (restored); 1150, lines 4–5; 1165, lines 5–6; Pandionis: *Hesperia* 32 (1963) 41, no. 42, line 5; *IG* II² 1152, line 8; Akamantis: *IG* II² 1166, lines 4–5 (sacrifices performed by honorand in his capacity as [state] *hieropoios*). In the inscription of Aigeis and Aiantis concerning their holdings at Oropos discussed above (with note 47), Walbank conjectured in line 4 a reference to a sacrifice ordered by the joint decree (Walbank 1990, p. 97).

52. Both texts belong to Pandionis: *Hesperia* 32 (1963) 41, no. 42, lines 4–7; and *IG* II² 1152, lines 7–9. In both cases the number, though partly restored, appears to be the only likely candidate.

53. At line 7 of the decree of Erechtheis, *IG* II² 1165, the editor offered a restoration likewise suggesting a calendar of sacrifices: . . . ὅπως ἂν θύωνται ἐν τοῖς [καθήκουσι χρόνοις . . .] (". . . that they sacrifice at the [appropriate times . . .]").

54. Jones 1987, ch. 1, sec. 1.27, p. 49. It is perhaps to these banquets that we should refer τὰ φυλετικὰ δεῖπνα said by Athenaios (*Deipnosophistai*, 5.185d) to have been "ordained" by "the lawgivers" (viz., of earlier times).

these cultic events, there is very little trace of significant interaction among *phyletai* qua *phyletai*. The qualification is vital for my position. Two members of the same phyle might associate with one another on the basis of blood relationship, marriage ties, proximity of residence, occupation, deme or phratry affiliation, or other factor. Only if that relationship can be shown to be a function of membership in the same phyle to the exclusion of all other factors will it count toward establishing a case for "tribal" solidarity.

As it happens, the epigraphic testimony offers a single instance: Erechtheis, in addition to the usual praise and crown, honors its member Antisthenes by calling upon the *epimeletai* to care for the needs of his daughter whenever she, upon her father's death, should become legally defined as *epikleros* (*IG* II² 1165, lines 30–38). Apparently, we have here a suggestion of the sort of camaraderie one might expect to find in a tightly knit organization, with the membership going so far as to play a role otherwise normally confined to the context of closely related blood or affinal relatives. But by no means can this episode be regarded as anything but atypical. This extraordinary measure had been prompted by the equally extraordinary benefactions of Antisthenes, themselves unparalleled in our corpus of phyle inscriptions.[55] It is an isolated datum without significance for the day-to-day functioning of these organizations.

Literary sources might be expected to add more, but their positive evidence, when measured against the quantity of potentially relevant texts in which such indications might be expected to appear, is meager. Osborne asserted that Athenians felt "closer links with tribesmen than with the mass of the citizen body;"[56] and Whitehead, responding to Osborne, cited a number of passages from the orators and Aristophanes, observing that "there is ample evidence for bonds between men of the same tribe."[57] Examination of these passages, however, fails to support the hypothesis of intraphyle solidarity.[58]

Demosthenes, for example, in his brief against Meidias, asserts that his adversary, in attacking him, the *choregos* of his phyle Pandionis, at the Dionysia, "thought fit to act insolently not only against me and mine but also against the *phyletai* through me" (Demosthenes 21, *Against Meidias*, §81); and, again, that not only was he, Demosthenes, injured, but also, because Meidias's misdeeds were directed against the chorus, the phyle, the tenth part of the citizenbody, as well (§126). The point here is that, since the *choregos*, and hence the chorus, of the phyle had been publicly humiliated, such humiliation could only extend to the

---

55. For the case of a phyle undertaking to regulate the marriage of its "heiresses" (*epikleroi*) at Gortyn, see *Inscriptiones Creticae* vol. 4, Gortyn no. 72 (med. s. V?), with Jones 1987, ch. 5, sec. 29, pp. 224–225. The conferral of honors upon benefactors by the phylai will be taken up in detail in chapter 6.

56. Osborne 1985a, p. 90.

57. Whitehead 1986, p. 248, with note 119.

58. I confine myself to the passages adduced by Whitehead (note 57 above). Limitations of space do not permit an exhaustive examination of the literary record at this time. (The final item in Whitehead's note, i.e., Demosthenes 29.33, incidentally, is a misprint for 29.23, treated below.) Significantly, however, regarding the prospects of discovering previously undetected evidence of such solidarity, Lécrivain (*DarSag*, vol. 4, s.v. ""Phyle," p. 453 with note 11) adduced in support of his alleged "des liens de solidarité entre les membres des tribus" two of the same passages appearing in Whitehead's list (viz., Andokides 1.150 and Demosthenes 23.206) plus the Erechtheid decree concerning Antisthenes' daughter.

phyletai represented by that *choregos* and chorus. But such reactions or feelings do not by themselves amount to the "links" or "bonds" that characterize a cohesive, interconnected community. Andokides' exhortation (1, *On the Mysteries*, §150), closely paralleled by the sentiment expressed by Demosthenes in 23, *Against Aristokrates*, §206, that the *syndikoi* chosen from his phyle express a favorable opinion of himself before the court is ambiguous in that it leaves open the possibility that such fellow tribesmen are in fact kinsmen, affines, or personal friends. It is, in any case, an exhortation, not a statement of fact. Besides, both texts are explicit on the point that the *syndikoi* had been *chosen* to represent their fellow tribesmen; accordingly, it cannot be inferred that *any* member under *any* circumstances would automatically be expected to come to the aid of his *symphyletes*. Polystratos is said by the speaker of [Lysias] 20 *For Polystratos* to have been chosen by his *phyletai* as one of the Four Hundred by reason of the soundness of his views "concerning his fellow demesmen and concerning the citizen body." Yet, he continues, his enemies accuse him of disloyalty to this very citizen body, even though he had been chosen by his *phyletai*, "who can best judge the character of this or that person among them" (§2). These last words might in isolation be taken to indicate solidarity, but, plainly, the reference here to *phyletai* is prompted, indeed required, by the previous reference to his selection as one of the Four Hundred "by his *phyletai*;" and, still more decisively, this previous reference goes on to attribute to Polystratos sound views concerning not his *symphyletai* (as we would expect, if there were such a thing as intraphyle solidarity) but, in addition to the citizenry as a whole, his fellow *demesmen:* a small, tightly knit "natural" community with whose members an individual might indeed possess some real familiarity. The speaker of Lysias's speech *On a Charge of Taking Bribes* mentions that the officer staff of his ship had included Alkibiades, who he would have much preferred had not sailed with him, since Alkibiades was "neither friend nor kinsman nor *phyletes*" (21.6). Here, the absence of an expected reference to fellow demesmen in place of the use of the term *phyletes* suggests that the latter term appears for a reason not necessarily having anything to do with solidarity. Namely, that Alkibiades' presence on board with the speaker would normally be the result of their common membership in the same phyle, as was true of the Athenian military organization generally,[59] but in this case, exceptionally, was not. Special significance also appears to be attached to common membership in the same phyle at Demosthenes 29, *Against Aphobos* III §23, where the speaker exploits the fact that Phanos is "a friend and *phyletes*" of the accused, from which he concludes that it was not enmity that had motivated Phanos to give testimony injurious to Demosthenes' adversary. Closer attention to the affiliations of these two individuals, however, reveals Demosthenes' probable motive in singling out just the phyle, and not some other association, for mention. Phanos's deme was Kerameis,[60] of the city trittys of Akamantis; Aphobos's deme was (according to Davies) almost certainly Sphettos,[61] of the inland trittys of that

---

59. For the dominating role by the phylai (vs. trittyes and demes) in the military organization of Athens, see Jones 1987, ch. 1, sec. 1.29, with pp. 56–57 for the naval arrangements.

60. Davies, *APF* 14079 = 14080.

61. Davies, *APF* 3597, VI, p. 120.

phyle. Demosthenes would undoubtedly have liked to say, but could not, that the two men were of the same deme, or even of the same trittys. So, in desperation he pins his argument on the common phyle affiliation. We come, finally, to the conjunction of "kinsman" and *"phyletes"* in Aristophanes, *Birds*, line 368, where the context seems to suggest that both terms bespeak solidarity. But Aristophanes' own text proves, as Sommerstein realized, that the poet could not have intended the latter word to be taken literally.[62] Accordingly, if *phyletes* means in this context something other than "member of a phyle," the passage necessarily loses all value for the present discussion.

Possibly, to add a single item to the texts cited by Whitehead, one could strengthen the argument by adducing from Aristotle the notice that the ephebes συσσιτοῦσι . . . κατὰ φυλάς ("dine by phylai") (*AthPol* 42.3). But is this not merely an instance of the enforced association of Athenians within military units based on the phylai in their primary role as administrative entities, whereas it is with the *voluntary* interaction between *phyletai* that we are concerned in this context?

Given, again, the large volume of contemporary written sources, if *phyletai* qua *phyletai* enjoyed close relationships, we should expect to learn more of them. The decree of Erechtheis shortly to be discussed in chapter 6, *IG* II² 1165, which twice implies the ignorance on the part of the *phyletai* of their own affairs (lines 9–10, the calendar; 17–18, properties), may be more representative of the actual situation. It seems that we are being drawn to the conclusion that the phylai did not in fact maintain a particularly intimate associational life.

Postscriptum

Since the completion of my analysis in this (and the following) chapter, I have become aware of the discussion by Emily Kearns of the cults of the eponyms of the phylai (Kearns 1989, pp. 80–92). I am happy to see that the findings of her far wider-reaching exploration of this subject are in general agreement with my own assertions. With the exception of Aias (from Salamis) and Hippothoon (from Eleusis), she states that the other heroes seem to be chiefly from Athens itself (p. 80), although some have possible additional links with other parts of Attica as well (p. 80, with note 2; and compare, at pp. 88–89, the extra-Athenian connections of some heroes both within and outside Attica). However, her statement that "[t]he hero's shrine acted as a kind of centre for the whole tribe" (p. 80) must be assessed in the light of the complicating factors discussed above. Against my position, at the same time, she has a point when she observes that the explanation for the erection in town at the Asklepieion of the second copy of the decree of the phyle based in Eleusis,

---

62. The words are addressed to the birds by Tereus, who inquires why they are about to tear apart the two men Peisetairos and Euelpides, since they are "kinsmen and *phyleta* [dual number] of my wife." The point of the joke is that Tereus's wife, Prokne, is the daughter of Pandion and so is naturally a member of Pandionis! But when Euelpides gets around to mentioning his deme, it turns out to be Krioa (line 645), a deme not of Pandionis but Antiochis. Perhaps, as the scholiast suggested, Aristophanes had in mind for Tereus's meaning something like "compatriots." See Sommerstein's commentary on line 368 (1987, pp. 220–221).

Hippothontis, *IG* II^2 1163, is that the honorand was a priest of Asklepios (p. 83). Even so, the copy remains evidence for the urban orientation of an extra-urban association. My reasons for opposing the assumption of a "collective cult" of the eponyms (see p. 83) were set out at the head of the chapter, though I would agree with her to the extent that it is patent that the state, for its own reasons, did make collective representations of the ten *eponymoi*.

SIX

The Phylai

Instruments of Representation?

The Officers of the Internally Organized Phylai

If *phyletai* did not regularly fraternize or feel or express strong bonds of attachment with each other qua *phyletai*, it does not follow that the organization was entirely without vitality or purpose. In fact, the phylai will emerge as vigorous, purposeful organizations thanks in large part to the ambitions and energies of a relatively few individuals, usually but not demonstrably in every instance their officers. What do we know about these *phyletai*?

Epimeletai *and Other Officers*

The board of *epimeletai*, it is no exaggeration to say, for the most part monopolized the formal administrative leadership of the phylai throughout the period of our evidence.[1] Since the *epimeletai* are attested for most of the phylai, and in the absence of any competing title, their presence in all may be assumed with surety. The offi-

---

1. Besides the very brief accounts or mentions in the works listed at chapter 5, note 4, the *epimeletai* of the phylai have been studied by J. Oehler, "Epimeletai," *RE* 6, 1907, cols. 162–171: 168–169; H. Swoboda, in Busolt and Swoboda 1920–1926, vol. 2, pp. 974–975; and, most recently, Traill 1986, chapter 4, "The Epimeletai of the Phyle," pp. 79–92. Among other contributions, Traill seeks to identify the *epimeletai* with the trittyarchs appearing in inscriptions dated between 301/0 and 295/4 (pp. 89–90).

cers served for one year[2] and were normally three in number (never demonstrably more or fewer), invariably in our records one from each of the three *trittyes* of the phyle, as shown by Traill.[3] As a *collegium*, the *epimeletai* will have possessed the manpower and, presumably, variety of experience and competence to cover effectively a wide range of duties. A multiplicity of duties might in any case be expected in view of the nondescript generality of the title *epimeletes*, or "caretaker." Not surprisingly, therefore, the documented tasks of the officers reflect a variety of competencies. Legally, they could represent the phyle's interests before the state, as shown by Demosthenes' account (21.13) of a meeting of the Athenian Assembly when the *epimeletai* of Pandionis engaged the archon in a dispute regarding the phyle's failure to appoint a *choregos*. In the cultic domain, they were charged with the holding of sacrifices for the association, according to a decree of Erechtheis.[4] Several examples, too, are found of a financial capacity. From a decree of an unknown phyle concerning the lease of certain of its properties, *IG* II² 1168, we learn that the board (with the *tamias*) was charged with the receipt of rents (lines 9–10) and was (again with the *tamias*) to take possession of the securities in the event that the lessees failed to pay in accordance with the contracts (lines 11–13). Similarly, we find a single (?) *epimeletes* of Aiantis entrusted with the collection of "the sacred money"; and, when this officer failed to turn the money over to the phyle, the same inscription records that the (three) current *epimeletai* laid a claim against him in a state court.[5] Antisthenes of Erechtheis, also, we shall see momentarily, assumed, probably qua *epimeletes*, a variety of (mainly financial) functions.

But the great bulk of attested acts of the *epimeletai* have as their setting the phyle's assembly. A clause in a decree of Erechtheis indicates that it was they who convened the *agora*,[6] and from this it is a likely inference that they also presided over all such meetings. Accordingly, their attested business, reflecting the content of our decrees, has to do almost entirely with the passage and implementation of honorific grants: the announcement of the honors;[7] the engraving of the stele (meaning, of course, the commissioning of a mason);[8] its erection in a suitable place (such as the shrine of the eponymous);[9] the necessary payment to the party(ies) contracted to

2. *IG* II² 1165 (Erechtheis), lines 18–19: οἱ ἐπιμελεταὶ / οἱ αἰεὶ καθιστάμενοι κατ᾽ ἐνιαυτὸν . . . . ("the *epimeletai* appointed each year") (and, again, in lines 31–32). A similar reference to a board serving κατ᾽ ἔτος ("by year") was wholly restored by Kirchner at *IG* II² 1164 (init. s. III; unknown phyle), lines 6–8.

3. Traill 1986, pp. 79–92.

4. *IG* II² 1150, lines 4–5.

5. *Hesperia* 5 (1936) 393–410 (346/5), lines 161–163 and 176–179 (the collection); 167–171 (the claim).

6. *IG* II² 1165, line 34.

7. *IG* II² 1149 (Hippothontis).

8. *IG* II² 1147 (Erechtheis, restored); 1138, 1139, 1140, 1157 (all Pandionis); *ArchEph* 1965, pp. 131–136 (i) (Akamantis; restored); *IG* II² 1163 (Hippothontis); *Hesperia* 7 (1938) 94–96, no. 15 (Aiantis); *Hesperia* 4 (1935) 41–42, no. 9 (unknown phyle; restored).

9. The instruction to erect the stele is often conjoined with the order to inscribe. See *IG* II² 1144 and 1157 (Pandionis); *ArchEph* 1965, pp. 131–136 (i) (Akamantis; restored); *IG* II² 1163 (Hippothontis); *Hesperia* 7 (1938) 94–96, no. 15 (Aiantis); *Hesperia* 4 (1935) 41–42, no. 9 (unknown phyle; restored).

execute the stele;[10] the disbursal to the honorand of a sum of cash (the attested amount is fifty drachmas) for a (one-time?) sacrifice;[11] and the responsibility for the appropriate accounting of the expenses.[12] Since no other officer is assigned such tasks, it is evident that when a phyle acted to bestow honors, it was upon the *epimeletai* that the primary responsibility regularly devolved. Whether still other duties beyond these just mentioned fell to the board, however, must remain an open question. Since stone stelai are our sole source of information on these matters and since the surviving stelai are overwhelmingly honorific in character, it is quite possible that these indications do not actually represent the full range of their activity. Not all official acts of course had necessarily to be recorded and those that were, not necessarily on stone. In the case of an honorary text, the object of a lapidary inscription may not have been so much documentary as to enhance an honorand's sense that the accolade had been appropriately, that is, publicly and permanently, promulgated. A stone stele, in other words, can hardly be regarded as a necessary condition of an official act by a phyle, or by any of its officers. We may, therefore, be ignorant of much of these officers' duties and functions.

As it happens, we are lucky to have a possible indication of a far more substantial role for the epimelete in a decree of Erechtheis of the first half of the third century, *IG* II² 1165, honoring its member Antisthenes, son of Nikandros, of (Upper? Lower?) Lamptrai (*PA* 1198). Unfortunately, the case is of uncertain significance for this discussion because we cannot be sure of Antisthenes' status at the time of his meritorious services. Nor must an office necessarily be assumed, since three decrees certainly or probably of Kekropis honor individuals who are not identified by any title whatsoever.[13] The repeated use of the verb *epimeleisthai* (lines 1, 3), on the other hand, suggests the office. So does the fact that one of his acts is the authorship of a decree calling for future boards of *epimeletai* to carry out certain inspections of phyle properties (lines 17–22). However, if he was an epimelete, since this magistracy comprised more than a single officer, as the text proves (lines 18, 31–32), the fact that he *alone* is honored by this decree opens up the possibility—indeed, it borders on a probability—that Antisthenes' accomplishments fell outside the normal run of magisterial duties. If not, why is there no trace of his two colleagues?

Whatever their roles, if any, a large part of Antisthenes' services to the phyle was financial, not surprisingly, in view of the probable fact that Antisthenes' father, Nikandros, served as *tamias* of the goddess in 343/2.[14] The fragmentary opening

---

At *Hesperia* 32 (1963) 14–15, no. 13 (Ptolemais?), lines 10–12, as restored by Meritt, the location for the erection of the crown and statue is to be approved by the *epimeletai*.

10. *IG* II² 1148 (Pandionis); *Hesperia* 9 (1940) 59–66, no. 8 (i), col. II, lines 5–7 (Leontis; restored); *IG* II² 1161 (unknown phyle; restored).

11. *Hesperia* 32 (1963) 41, no. 42 and *IG* II² 1152 (both Pandionis). At *Agora* 15, no. 69 (Aigeis; 284/3), Meritt and Traill print a restored text calling for the *epimeletai* to advance a sum to the *bouleutai* of Aigeis for a sacrifice, but the number of drachmas is not preserved (lines 14–17).

12. *IG* II² 1163 (Hippothontis).

13. *IG* II² 1141 (= *Hesperia* 10 [1941] 263–265, no. 67), 1143, 1145.

14. *PA* 10688 citing *IG* II² 1443, line 6.

lines refer to his receipt of funds (the use here of the technical term for such re-ceipts, παραλαμβάνειν, which normally indicates a succession of officers or boards, is an additional hint that he is not merely a *privatus*) and to the balance (at the end of his year of office?) of more than 3,000 drachmas (lines 4–5). At an inter-val follow (again, fragmentary) references to (disbursals?) "from the common rev-enues" (line 11) and to "four drachmas" (restored, lines 11–12). Although the inter-vening lines mention in broken context his evident efforts to regularize the schedules of (?) "the sacrifices to Erechtheus" (lines 6–7) and "the *agorai*" (line 8), it is not clear at all what Antisthenes did to promote these activities, in particular whether personal expenditures or other extraordinary effort on his part were in-volved. But the object of his effort was that something "be preserved" (line 16, plural) "for all time" (line 15) and in a manner "advantageous to the phyle" (lines 16–17, restored). So far, however, except for the fact that he has acted without a colleague (a fact of significance, of course, only if he is an epimelete), Antisthenes' stewardship, though not paralleled in the body of evidence under review, is hardly extraordinary when measured against the larger background of internally organized Greek public units.

What follows is otherwise. Antisthenes authored a decree to ensure that all the Erechtheidai be informed about their properties (*ktemata*), to which end (the Greek construction, however, is paratactic) the *epimeletai* in office each year would "walk" the properties twice during the year to ascertain whether the fields were being worked in accordance with the contracts (i.e., with the phyle) and whether "they" (the lessees) had planted the mortgage stones similarly in compliance with those contracts (lines 17–22). Again, finances are to the fore and Antisthenes has acted alone. Much, too, is made of the fact that Antisthenes carried out his benefactions "neither for his own benefit nor placing any one's interests before those of the phyle nor receiving a bribe from anyone; rather, he has continued speaking and acting in the manner best for the phyle, presenting himself blameless *to all the phyletai* (my emphasis)" (lines 22–26). These last words echo two previous references to *all* the members: in line 9 in uncertain context but with explicit reference to Antisthenes' ef-forts to make something known (καὶ εἰδότες πάν[τες) and, again, in line 18 with reference to the membership's hoped for knowledge about the phyle's properties (εἰδῶ[σιν ἅπ]αντες).

Taking these details together, and particularly with the final point in mind, I suggest the following reconstruction: Antisthenes had found the organization in disarray and, most importantly, while returning its finances to a condition of sol-vency, took measures to ensure the future predictable and orderly conducting of its meetings and sacrifices and in each area saw to it that the organization's arrange-ments come under the scrutiny of all its members. Thanks to his efforts, the phyle could now function in a more financially secure, open, and democratic fashion con-ducive to the interests of the entire association.

If an epimelete (or, less likely, it now appears, a *privatus*) could play so far-reaching a role, it stands to reason that there would have been little need for an ex-tensive corps of subordinate officers. And, indeed, we learn only of a secretary, treasurer, and herald, each bearing a common Greek generic descriptive title (γραμματεύς,[15] ταμίας,[16] κῆρυξ[17]) and, where recorded, performing predictable and appropriate tasks. Probably such duties were too bothersome or time-consuming to impose upon a person qualified and willing to assume the onerous responsibilities of "caretaker," or they required specialized knowledge or skills. Exceptionally, a small residue of responsibility is assigned in three instances to ad hoc boards[18] rather than to an additional officer or officers bearing a distinctive, specialized title, possibly differing (as with the demes) from phyle to phyle. Again, as I observed in connection with the *epimeletai*, it is difficult to escape the conclusion that Erechtheis, Pandionis, and the others were equipped with similarly titled staffs of just these few officers and, furthermore, that, given the relative abundance of our records, we now possess the full complement of these titles.[19] Such uniformity undoubtedly reflects, in contrast with the often remote and isolated situation of the demes, a shared concentration of headquarters and of active magisterial personnel and members in the urban center.

The Rewards of Holding Office in the Phyle

The holding of such offices, despite the sometimes onerous work and significant responsibility involved, was not without its rewards. For some individuals, certainly, simply to bear an official title was sufficient reward in itself, since a title allowed a citizen to stand out amidst the uniformity imposed by the prevailing egalitarian ethos. Beyond that minimal return, such formal (or informal) powers as these officers possessed at the same time afforded opportunities for the pedaling of influence in connection with the various departments of phyletic business; that is, the powers of the office could be used in such a way as to assure future payoffs from the beneficiaries of such use. And with the expiry of one's term of office, even a modest achievement on the phyle's behalf could easily, and sometimes did, result in a highly public conferral by vote of the *phyletai* in the *agora* of honors of various type and value (on which, see further below). The question to be asked (and answered) now is, Was this all? In particular, one would like to know whether tenure in an office of a phyle was a prelude to some higher level of attainment. Still more particularly, was such an office in fact, or at least perceived as, a stepping-stone in some sense to office or other prominence in the city of Athens?

15. *Hesperia* 9 (1940) 59–66, no. 8 (Leontis) (i), col. II, line 4; *ArchEph* 1965, pp. 131–136 (ii) (Akamantis), line 23 (restored); *IG* II² 1158, lines 11–12 (restored); and *SEG* 2.8, line 4 (restored) (both Kekropis). For very late attestions (after 166) of a [γραμμ]ατεὺς ἱππάρχοις φυ[λετῶν] and of a [γραμμ]ατεὺς φυλει, both allotted, see *Hesperia* 3 (1934) 42–43, no. 31, lines 14–17, but these secretaries may not belong to the assocation per se. Likewise, I assume that the secretaries occasionally mentioned in bouleutic inscriptions pertain to the Council and to the boards of *prytaneis* in particular.
16. *IG* II² 2824 (Aigeis); 1158 (Kekropis?; restored); 1168, lines 9 and 12–13 (unknown phyle). Again, as with the secretaries, I omit the officers associated with the personnel of the Council.
17. *IG* II² 1145, lines 7–8: [. . . τ]/[ὸν κή]ρυκα (Kekropis?). The relation of these words to the larger context is uncertain.
18. *SEG* 2.8, line 5? (Kekropis); *SEG* 3.115, lines 15–23 (Antiochis); *Hesperia* 32 (1963) 14–15, no. 13, lines 12–14 (Ptolemais?).
19. Momentarily, however, I shall consider the possibility that the existence of another, previously unattested board of three is implied by the text of *IG* II² 2824.

This question is by no means a new one. A century ago, Haussoullier, to be followed until recent times by a number of others, maintained that the typical Athenian political career was launched at the local level, where apprentice politicians learned the ropes, so to speak, of democratic politics and built the power base which was to undergird their attempts to achieve appointment to the higher elective city offices. By "local level" (my term) the author of *La Vie municipale en Attique* had in mind of course the demes. But this model, however plausible its original or later formulations, was decisively exploded by Whitehead in his 1986 study. True, Whitehead concedes, an individual might through participation in deme politics acquire a degree of practical know-how applicable to city politics and, within the safe confines of his home community, harmlessly undergo the trials and errors of political activity as a preliminary to the more hazardous risk-taking in the urban arena. But the building of a clientele, the forging of links of patronage, the acquisition of a political reputation, to the extent that these were intended to be transferable to politics in the big city, were another matter altogether. In any case, to put the matter in empirical terms, had successful careers in the central government indeed been launched in the demes, we should now, with more than one hundred deme decrees in addition to literary evidence at our disposal, be able to find traces of such a progression from home community to urban center. Yet Whitehead's prosopographical investigation revealed that the "overlap" between citizens active at the deme level and those active at the city level is "strikingly small."[20] These were, he concluded, two different groups of people. What, then, we may now ask, of the phylai? Were their offices or, more generally, political activity of any kind within the phyle in any sense a prelude to similar activity in the city of Athens?

Since little trace survives of the workings of the political life of the internally organized phylai (such as we have, for example, in the case of the demes), we are entirely dependent upon the prosopographical record of *phyletai* serving as officers in their phyle organizations. That record consists of about thirty names preserved in whole or part in epigraphic sources. To answer our question, two aspects of each officer's biography must be considered: wealth (as indicated principally, following Davies's work, by membership in the liturgical class) and the holding of governmental office (or political activity) in the urban center. As it happens, in all but nine instances no information about membership in the liturgical class or governmental or political activity of any kind has come down to us regarding the officer himself, his father, or any determinable near ancestor or other family connection. The remaining harvest of positive instances may be quickly reviewed. A decree of Pandionis honors three of its members, on the basis of which number they were identified by the editor as the *epimeletai*. Meritt restored the third name as Meidokrates, son of Meidokrates, of Probalinthos; if the restoration is correct, he may be the councillor of that name ca. 336/5 or his father, the former alternative being preferred by Traill on chronological grounds.[21] The second name was restored by Traill as Antis-

20. Whitehead 1986, pp. 313–326, especially 317 (for the quotation) and 319. For the original formulation of the theory, see Haussoullier 1883, pp. i–ii.

21. *Hesperia* 32 (1963) 41, no. 42 (ante med. s. IV), lines 2–4. For the councillor, see *Agora* 15, no. 42, line 165; and, on the chronology, Traill 1986, p. 87.

thenes, son of Antisthenes, of Kytherros, a man of documented wealth and service in public liturgies.[22] Three other candidates are provided by the three honorands crowned by Pandionis at the end of the fourth century and, again in view of their number, presumably *epimeletai*. The first was restored by Kirchner, followed by Davies, as Pheidippos (II), son of Pheidon (II?), of Paiania; if the restoration is correct, he may be identified as a member of the liturgical family of Chairephilos, the salt-fish seller.[23] Traill restored the second as Aristodamas, son of Kallisthenes, of Myrrhinous; while this Aristodamas is otherwise unknown, the father he identified with the Kallisthenes who was councillor for Myrrhinous in 336/5.[24] The third, Nikomachos, son of Θρα[σ.....], [Κυ]/[δα]θην, may be a descendant (a grandson?) of the Kalliades, son of Nikomachos, of that deme named in a *diadikasia* about 380.[25] Next, Chairimenes, son of Lysanias, of Deiradiotai, one of the three *epimeletai* of Leontis who dedicate *IG* II² 2818 (357/6), might be a descendant of Chairimenes of Leontis, the foreman of the *prytaneis* in a decree of 410/09, *IG* I³ 101 (= I² 108), line 5;[26] and another, Philoneos, son of Gnathios (III), of Leukonoion, was assigned by Davies to the liturgical family of Apollodoros (II), son of Thrasyllos (II).[27]

Two further names may be added from a dedication, *IG* II² 2824 (313/2), erected in the names of the *tamias* (preserved fully in lines 1 and 3) and, as once thought by some following the restoration by Koehler in lines 1 and 4, the *epimeletai*. A reference to the board here is made attractive by the fact three, and just three, names follow. Traill's reexamination of the stone, however, has shown the restoration to be impossible on grounds of spacing.[28] Even so, it is clear that the three names comprise a board of officers of the phyle Aigeis, for the following reasons: (a) their presence alongside the assured officer, the *tamias;* (b) the fact that the two preserved demotics (Ἀλαιεύς, lines 4, 5, sc. Halai Araphenides) as well as that of the *tamias* (Ἰκα/[ριεὺς . . .], lines 3–4) belong to the same phyle; and (c) the fact that the remains in line 1 [-- ca. 5 1/2 --]αι must, since they immediately precede καὶ ταμίας, denote such a college. Pittakys had proposed λογισταί, which, as Traill observes, is correct for the spacing, although, as we have seen, it is without parallel in our dossier of documents. Another suitably short word, not mentioned by commentators, ὁρισταί, is found in a decree of the deme of Peiraieus, but its perti-

---

22. Traill 1986, p. 86. For his wealth and public service, see Davies *APF* 1194 = 1196 = 1197.

23. *IG* II² 1152, lines 5–6. For Davies's reconstruction of the family, see *APF* 14162 with the cross-reference to 15187, especially p. 567.

24. Lines 6–8. Traill 1986, p. 88. For the councillor, see *Agora* 15, no. 42, line 179. While I follow Traill's argument in favor of his restoration of the *nomen*, I fail to see the basis for his statement that Aristodamas "should be a son of either the prytanis or the property lessee in the poletai record," since these people belong not (so far as we know) to the epimelete's family but to another family of Myrrhinous to which he appeals for his onomastic parallels.

25. Lines 8–9. Thus Davies *APF* 10951 with the cross-reference to 7794; for the *diadikasia*, see *IG* II² 1932, line 19 (with Davies's date).

26. *PA* 15232. For other possible family connections, see Traill 1986, p. 82.

27. Davies *APF* 1395 = 1429 (see p. 43; stemma on p. 46). For probable ancestors of this epimelete, see Traill 1986, p. 82.

28. Traill 1986, pp. 90–92.

nence to the dedication is entirely a matter of conjecture.[29] Nonetheless, officers they must be. Of the three, Philagros (patronymic and demotic not preserved) may, following Davies, be identified with the syntrierarch of that name from Halai in 322.[30] Secondly, the son of Nikokrates of Halai, again following Davies, may be associated with a branch of the family of the Nikostratos of that deme who was syntrierarch in the 370s and again before 356.[31]

Nor can this roster be extended by enlisting the preserved names of the other phyle officers—secretary, treasurer, or herald. Only a single name is sufficiently preserved to allow even a tentative identification.[32] If officers of the Ephebic College were included, perhaps a few others might be added, but since these officers (*sophronistai*, ephebic *taxiarchoi*, and *lochagoi*) functioned, qua officers, outside the phyletic organization, they are not really relevant to our present concern.[33]

Thus, to revert to the first of our two criteria, we are left with a total of six certain or possible members of wealthy families (Antisthenes, Pheidippos, Nikomachos, Philoneos, Philagros, and the son of Nikokrates). The number, though small, represents about a fifth of the total and is, accordingly, significant given the fact that, on Davies's estimate, the liturgical class comprised no more than 2 or 3 percent of the citizen population in the fifth and fourth centuries.[34] Wealth, inferentially, characterized the class of phyle officeholders. None, however (to address the second criterion and the question raised by Haussoullier and Whitehead), except for a single (nonelective) councillor (Meidokrates), is expressly recorded to have *himself* engaged in the political life of the city. Obviously, it would be difficult on this basis to argue that an office in one's phyle served to pave the way to prominence or high elective position in the democratic central government.

More likely, these phyletic offices were in fact, and regarded as, political dead ends. Secretaries, treasurers, and heralds were charged with doubtless petty specialized tasks that neither necessitated nor allowed significant contact with people of power or wealth and so afforded no opportunity for political ladder-climbing. Somewhat differently, the duties of the epimelete, as I suggested above, probably ex-

29. *IG* II² 1177 (med. s. IV), line 22. If, as remains possible, all three officers (other than the *tamias*) were of the same deme, namely Halai Araphenides (on which point, however, see Traill, loc. cit.), it is conceivable that the board had been involved in a dispute regarding the deme's boundaries and that they, along with the treasurer, were honored by the phyle for their meritorious service.

30. Davies *APF* 14208*bis*, at p. 535, citing *IG* II² 1632, line 192.

31. Davies *APF* 11019, at p. 411; for the syntrierarchies, see *IG* II² 1605, lines 38–39 and 1622, line 266. Ca. 370, one Nikokrates, son of Nikodemos, of the deme was councillor: *Agora* 15, no. 492, line 64; since, on the basis of script and orthography, Traill favors the later date, i.e., 313/2 (rather than 340/39), for no. 2824, identification is plainly impossible.

32. Namely, the *tamias* in *IG* II² 2824, lines 3–4, Gorgiades, son of Mnesikleides, of Ikarion (*PA* 3062). Mnesikleides Γο[ργιάδο] of the same deme, councillor ca. 370, *Agora* 15, no. 492, line 72, is probably an ancestor.

33. For the known members of the liturgical class, however, see below, note 91.

34. Davies 1981, pp. 27–28, estimates the size of the two classes of men who performed the liturgies, i.e., the trierarchy and the agonistic or festival liturgies. Each numbered, he calculates, about 300 men. Together, they will have comprised about 2 percent of a population of 30,000 in the fifth century and about 2.8 percent of the 21,000 citizens counted by Demetrios of Phaleron late in the fourth.

tended far beyond the perfunctory responsibilities necessitated by the execution and implementation of honorary decrees and so known to us from stone inscriptions. After all, no other major office is known, and the minor officers were certainly confined to the functions indicated by their titles. It was probably upon the *epimeletai* that most tasks not assigned to their more specialized colleagues devolved, and, indeed, it was doubtless upon them that ultimate responsibility for the health, if not the survival, of the organization rested. If this were true (and the case of Antisthenes, whose father almost certainly was the Nikandros who was *tamias* of the goddess in 343/2 and so a member of the Solonian class of *pentakosiomedimnoi*,[35] suggests that it is), we could then appreciate the relative preponderance of officers with liturgical connections. Their wealth was needed in order to sustain the organization. At the same time, however, it is obvious that a burden of such magnitude will have held little attraction for a man not only of wealth but of talent and ambition as well and intent upon a career in city government. The *epimeletai*, by contrast, were, while often prosperous, more likely men of modest aspiration, fully conscious of any limitations of capacity, happy to be a big fish in the little pond of their phyle's organization, and, by no means a negligible factor, perhaps at the same time a trifle intimidated by the well-known dangers of Athenian political life.[36]

The Proposers of the Decrees

To identify the officers as the chief sustainers of the organization leaves unanswered of course the question of whose interests were actually served by that organization beyond satisfying the limited ambitions of those content to venture no further than the boundaries of their own phyle. For the beginnings of an answer we turn to a second category of *phyletai* identifiable by name, the movers of the decrees.

Of the twenty-three wholly or partially preserved names, for nine (moving ten decrees) there is an indication of wealth or service, or both, on the part of the proposer himself or some member of his family, in the central government. One Moschos, of Anaphlystos, mover of a decree of Antiochis, is the son of Antiphanes (I), syntrierarch in 356, and Moschos's own son, in turn, is recorded to have been a councillor in 304/3.[37] Demokrates, son of Demokles, of Aphidna, the proposer of a decree of Aiantis of 327/6, was remembered inter alia for his pro-Macedonian political activity; he is assigned by Davies to a cadet branch of the family of Harmodios and Aristogeiton, the Gephyraioi, which, according to Davies's discussion, sustained its prominence in public affairs from the mid-fifth to the late third century.[38] Onetor (VIII), son of Kephisodoros (I), of Melite, mover of a decree of Kekropis of 376/5, belongs to a wealthy and powerful family of his deme.[39] Pandaites (II), son of

35. For Nikandros, see above, with note 14. For the census class of the *tamiai*, see Aristotle, *AthPol* 8.1 and 47.1 with the comment of Rhodes 1981, pp. 147–148.

36. On these dangers, see Sinclair 1988, ch. 6, pp. 136–162.

37. *SEG* 3.115, lines 3–4. See Davies *APF* 1227. For the syntrierarch, see *IG* II² 1612, line 106; for the councillor, *Agora* 15, no. 61, line 312.

38. *Hesperia* 7 (1938) 94–96, no. 15, lines 2–3. See Davies *APF* 12267, especially pp. 472 and 475.

39. *IG* II² 1141, line 8. See Davies, *APF* 11473 and, for Onetor [VIII], son of Kephisodoros [I], p. 425.

Pasikles, of Potamos, proposer of a decree of Leontis of 333/2, is the son of a niece of the syntrierarch (and councillor) Alkisthenes, son of Alkibiades, of Cholleidai.[40] Kirchner found the father of Polynikos, mover of a decree of Hippothontis, in Phokiades of Oion, a treasurer of Athena in 425/4.[41] Just possibly to be associated with Kallikrates, son of Kallikrates, of Paiania, proposer of two decrees of Pandionis, is another Kallikrates (I) of that deme, who, according to the Aristotelian *Constitution of the Athenians* (28.3), brought about the abolition of the *diobelia*.[42] Kallikrates, son of Glaukon, of Aixone, the mover of a decree of Kekropis of 334/3,[43] is honored by a decree of his deme of 313/2;[44] perhaps, as Whitehead suggests, the deme is commemorating his *choregia*, for four years earlier his father (or son [?], so Whitehead), Glaukon, son of Kallikrates, had been honored by the same deme, in this case explicitly for his service as *choregos*.[45] Proxenos (II), son of Pylagoros (II), of Acherdous, proposer of a decree of Hippothontis, was identified by Kirchner as the grandson of *PA* 12271, a *grammateus kata prytaneian* in 335/4.[46] A very strong candidate for Philton, mover of a decree of Erechtheis of the mid-fourth century, is the homonym (no patronymic is preserved, but the name is very rare) of the Erechtheid deme of (Upper? Lower?) Lamptrai who was *tamias* in 346/5.[47] Despite points of uncertainty, the cumulative effect of these associations is, again, significant. Wealth, indicated in four instances (Moschos, Onetor, Pandaites, and Kallikrates of Aixone), is, to be sure, only slightly less frequently encountered than in the case of the officers. But, if family members may be counted as well as the proposers themselves, in seven cases or nearly one-third of the total (Moschos, Demokrates, Pandaites, Polynikos, Kallikrates of Paiania?, Proxenos, and Philton), there are possible indications of participation in city government, or city politics, or both, and in three instances the mover himself is indicated to have been so active.[48] Above, I speculated about the rewards, chiefly psychic, of service as an officer of a phyle. What, may now be asked, was so alluring to a man of governmental or political aspirations about moving a decree in the *agora* of that same association?

Some general considerations may be mentioned at the outset. First, all the decrees (except Philton's, *IG* II² 1146) moved by these men are honorary; that is, they, by proposing their decrees, are publicly pronouncing judgment on the merits of the individual(s) so honored. Now, what is the likely status of a man who would presume publicly, first before his assembled fellow *phyletai* and later, with the erection

---

40. *Hesperia* 9 (1940) 59–66, no. 8 (ii), col. III, lines 10–11. See Davies, *APF* 11572, with cross-reference to no. 643 and stemma on p. 24. For the councillor, see *Agora* 15, no. 13 (370/69), lines 40–41.

41. *IG* II² 1153, lines 2–3. See *PA* 15066 citing, for Phokiades, *IG* I² 241, line 101.

42. *IG* II² 1159 (303/2) and 1160 (ca. 300). For Aristotle's Kallikrates, see *PA* 7975.

43. *IG* II² 1156, lines 26–35.

44. *IG* II² 1202.

45. *IG* II² 1200 (317/6), lines 2–7. See Whitehead 1986, p. 419, no. 86.

46. *IG* II²1163 (ca. 288/7), lines 2–3. See Kirchner, *PA* 12271, citing *Agora* 15, no. 43, line 227.

47. *IG* II² 1146 (ante med. s. IV), line 2. For the *tamias*, see *PA* 14790, citing Michel no. 832 (from Samos; 346/5), line 2.

48. Compare the results of Whitehead's parallel study of the movers of the decrees of the demes (1986, p. 318): of the 59 known proposers, only eight, or 14 percent, could be identified as participants in central government, or city politics, or both.

of a stone stele, before all his fellow Athenians in perpetuity, to pronounce such judgment? Plainly, a person of high station, at the very least at or near the same rank of the person receiving the accolade. Men of wealth or ambition, accordingly, will be found among their number. Furthermore, whatever the formal or understood requirements, the job of proposer was probably also viewed as possessing certain attractions. No particular effort was involved; only a brief and accurate speech (*epainos*) needed to be composed. There was presumably little risk, provided that the honorand was not controversial and the mover ventured no inflammatory opinions in his speech. Positively, the role was highly visible, played out before potentially one-tenth of the citizen population, not to mention the fact that the mover's name was to occupy a prominent position on the eventual stone stele. Nor can the possibility of a future reciprocation on the part of the honored party be ruled out. (This possibility may be illustrated by the case of Kallikrates, son of Glaukon, of Aixone, mentioned above. He, presumably as a younger man, moves the decree of Kekropis of 334/3, *IG* II² 1156, lines 26–35, honoring its class of ephebes and, two decades later, is himself honored in turn by a decree of his deme, *IG* II² 1202 [313/2]. Was the proposer of the latter decree one of the ephebes honored by Kallikrates' phyle decree in 334/3?) Now, was this all, or can we imagine still other rewards in moving a decree, rewards peculiar to the nature of the phyle organization?

I believe that there were such rewards—rewards connected with the phyle's urban focus (whether at the shrine of the eponym or other location of its *agora*). To frame my point, let us consider by way of contrast the often remote rural situation of the demes. The probable difference between the meetings of the two organizations is instructive. The chances are that the mover of a deme decree, even when the meeting of a nonurban deme took place in the city (as we know happened at least once, in the case of Halimous: Demosthenes 57.10), spoke before a group of farmers or fishermen who only seldom visited the town. But the proposer of a phyle decree addressed an audience consisting of preponderantly city *phyletai*, since, as we saw in chapter 5, all evidence for the *agora* places it in or near the urban center. (Nothing precluded the attendance of coastal or inland *phyletai*, but why should they, all else being equal, have made a greater effort to attend than their urban counterparts?) Now, these same city *phyletai*, by virtue of such residence, could be expected to vote in statewide elections in greater relative numbers than their rural *symphyletai*, since the elections of course took place in the town. Accordingly, a speech (comprising the motion plus the laudatory *epainos*) before the phyle's *agora* afforded the proposer an opportunity to display his political wares to a large group of potential voters and possible supporters of his own candidacy in some future election. Herein, I think, lay the attraction for the politically ambitious of the job of mover of a phyle decree.

The Honorands of the Decrees

The one other identifiable class of people preserved in our records is the honorands named in the laudatory decrees. Such texts, again, comprise 45 or 94 percent of the total of 48 decrees preserved. Typically, the decree identifies the honorand, specifies in what capacity the meritorious conduct was accomplished (although in a small minority of cases, no office or official position of any kind is mentioned),[49] characterizes that performance by laudatory language (usually adverbs or a prepositional phrase), mentions the party (self, phyle, or state) benefited (or not) by the honorand's actions, and finally indicates the honors to which he or they are entitled. These honors, while admitting some variation, always (with one possible exception) include praise[50] and a crown of olive or gold, in the latter case of a value, when stated, of either 500 or 1,000 drachmas;[51] in two instances, discussed above, the crowning is to be officially announced.[52] Anomalous honors are the exemption from liturgies for two[53] or three[54] years or for life[55]; the award on two occasions of 50 drachmas for a sacrifice;[56] a statue[57] or, following upon the voting of a statue by the Boule and Demos or the phyle itself, possibly a place (*topos*) in which to erect it;[58] and, finally, the privilege of setting up a dedication in the shrine of the hero.[59] Plainly, some of these honors were of considerable value and must have taxed, in the absence of any other information about fiscal resources, the income from fines, rents, and so on reviewed in chapter 5. It is legitimate to ask, accordingly, what motivated the *phyletai* to commit their resources so frequently and on occasion in such a lavish manner. Together, the honorary decrees preserve the names of quite a few honorands. Perhaps the answer to our question is to be found in the prosopographical record of these men?

Not surprisingly, first of all, the phyle honors its own members with only a single exception. The exception is an ephebic decree of Leontis of 333/2, *Hesperia* 9

49. The three certain cases, all from Kekropis, are given in note 13 above. The doubtful case of Antisthenes of Erechtheis was discussed above at length, without certain result.

50. Twenty-nine instances are preserved. The possible exception is *IG* II² 1149 (ante med. s. IV; Hippothontis), which, though only fragmentarily preserved, with certainty opened with the injunction to crown. Elsewhere, mention of the praise precedes that of the crown.

51. As with praise, the crown is never demonstrably absent. *IG* II² 1142 (init. s. IV; unknown phyle) hardly counts as an exception, since here the phyle (?) is evidently honoring (with praise alone?) an entire board of prytaneis. For the total number of crownings and the recorded types (olive or gold), see chapter 5, note 40. For the 500 drachma crowns, see *IG* II² 1152 (partly restored) and 1157 (both Pandionis); *Hesperia* 9 (1940) 59–66, no. 8 (i) (Leontis), col. I, lines 28–30; *IG* II² 1141; 1156, lines 26–35 (*bis*; once restored); 1158 (all Kekropis); and *Hesperia* 4 (1935) 41–42, no. 9 (unknown phyle; restored). For the 1,000 drachma crowns, see *Hesperia* 9 (1940) 59–66, no. 8 (i) (Leontis), col. I, lines 16–17; (ii), col. III, lines 15–16 (restored); and *Hesperia* 7 (1938) 94–96, no. 15 (Aiantis).

52. *IG* II² 1149, lines 5–6 (Hipponthontis); 1161, lines 3–4 (unknown phyle).

53. *IG* II² 1147 (Erechtheis; number restored).

54. *ArchEph* 1965, pp. 131–136 (i) (Akamantis), lines 1–2 (number restored).

55. *IG* II² 1140, lines 13–15 (Pandionis; partly restored).

56. *Hesperia* 32 (1963) 41, no. 42 (number and numeral restored); *IG* II² 1152 (both Pandionis). At *Agora* 15, no. 69 (= *IG* II² 656+; 284/3), Meritt and Traill print a restored text calling for the *epimeletai* to grant to the honorands, the *bouleutai*, a sum for a sacrifice (lines 14–17). The number of drachmas is not preserved.

57. *Hesperia* 32 (1963) 14–15, no. 13, lines 11–14 (Ptolemais?; both references to the [bronze] *eikon* are wholly restored).

58. *SEG* 2.8 (Kekropis): first decree ("the setting up of the *eikon*"; partly restored), second decree ("to provide a place in the shrine of Kekrops"; reference to the *topos* wholly restored). As the *SEG* editor observes, both decrees, in the estimation of Hiller and Kirchner, were passed by the *phyletai*.

59. *Hesperia* 9 (1940) 59–66, no. 8 (i) (Leontis), col. I, lines 31–33 (largely restored).

(1940) 59–66, no. 8, which honors, besides the phyle's own ephebes and their officers, two "*didaskaloi* of the phyle" (as restored), one an Athenian citizen of the
deme Pallene (phyle Antiochis), the other a foreigner from Methone ([i], col. I,
lines 33–38). Presumably, these were skilled professionals unobtainable from
within the phyle's own membership. That they should be mentioned in a document
otherwise concerned only with the phyle's own members is best explained as a requirement of the subject matter of the text (that is, if any ephebic officials are
named, they must all be named).[60] The exception accounted for, we may proceed
with the classification of the great bulk of the honorands. Predictably, the phyle
sometimes honors its own internal officers. Perhaps not so predictable is the relative
infrequency of such cases. The subordinate officers (secretary, treasurer, herald),
despite the fact that their duties were undoubtedly both tiresome and vital to the
smooth functioning of the organization, are never so honored in our surviving
texts.[61] No less surprisingly, in only a maximum of eight instances can a case be
made that the honorands are in fact the board of (three) *epimeletai*. *IG* II² 2818
(357/6), a dedication by the three *epimeletai* of Leontis, records the phyle's crown
(cf. no. 2842 [321/0 or 318/7]; phyle unknown); and, in the next century, *IG* II² 2861
preserves two (of an original total of six?) crowns enclosing the names of *epimeletai*
of Antigonis and Demetrias.[62] The three honorands of the decree of Aiantis of the
mid-fourth century, *IG* II² 1151, were understood by Koehler to be the board of
epimeletai, and he offered a similar interpretation for the somewhat later laudatory
decree of Pandionis, *IG* II²1152 (fin. s. IV). Similarly, the identification of the three
honorands in another decree of Pandionis, *Hesperia* 32 (1963) 41, no. 42, depends
solely upon their number. (The rubric "curatores Erechtheidis honorantur," however, is open to question in the case of *IG* II² 1150, since, in the absence of any precise indication of the number of honorands, it rests entirely upon the plural words in
lines 5 and 6.) We have already examined Erechtheis's accolade of Antisthenes, *IG*
II² 1165, in which, as we saw, the identification of the honorand as epimelete is not
quite certain. Given, then, the survival of nearly fifty honorary decrees (plus a number of dedications), nearly all of which preserve some indication of the identity of
the honorand(s), this is a rather small harvest.[63] Plainly, these phylai were not introverted groups content to reward their own for merely carrying out the day-to-day
administrative responsibilities required to keep the organization afloat. Who, then,
are these honorands, and why are they so honored?

Perhaps unexpectedly, all remaining honorands, although their services in various capacities are recorded to have benefited the honoring phyle in one way or an-

60. For additional examples of *didaskaloi* of a phyle, some known not to be members of the phyle,
see Rhodes 1981, on §42.3, pp. 506–507.

61. Again, as stated above with notes 15 and 16, I do not include in the present discussion the secretaries and treasurers honored by phylai (or by the state) in bouleutic inscriptions on the grounds that in
all probability they are specific to the Council and not officers of the association per se.

62. For the phyle affiliations, see appendix 3, under these phylai.

63. I assume that the *dedications* by the *epimeletai* acknowledging the conferring of honors upon
them by their phylai just mentioned imply the existence of *decrees* no longer extant and so must accordingly be included in this enumeration. For a decree authorizing the erection of such a dedication by the
honorand, see *Hesperia* 9 (1940) 59–66, no. 8 (i) (Leontis), col. I, lines 31–33 (as restored).

other, performed their benefactions not while holding an office in the organization itself but rather in a position or capacity that, though dependent upon appointment by the phyle itself or by the state *kata phylas,* involved the honorand in the statewide activities of the city of Athens. The attested cases fall into four more or less well-defined clusters, with a small residue of isolated or problematic items. Four of the men honored by decrees with certainty, and possibly as many as six, are identifiable as *choregoi;* and nine others can be added from the list of subsequent awardees of Pandionis in *IG* II² 1138.[64] The Ephebic College is represented on eight occasions in the persons of the officers the *kosmetes?,*[65] the *sophronistes,*[66] the ephebic *taxiarchos,*[67] *lochagoi,*[68] and (exceptionally, on one occasion) the ephebes themselves.[69] As a third group we may instance those few so-called prytany inscriptions in which the party initiating the accolade is recognizably not the Boule and/or Demos but the phyle itself.[70] The fourth cluster comprises five certain attestations (and one probable) of a *thesmothetes* allotted from the honoring phyle.[71] Isolated are the (phyle's) priest of the eponymous hero of Pandionis;[72] the (state's) priest of Asklepios;[73] the (state's) priest of Asklepios and Hygieia (restored);[74] a (liturgical) gymnasiarch charged with the training of a team of *lampadephoroi;*[75] a *phyletes*

---

64. *IG* II² 1147 (Erechtheis); 1138 = 1139 (+*Hesperia* 22 [1953] 177, no. 1); *IG* II² 1157 (both Pandionis); 1158 (Kekropis); *Hesperia* 4 (1935) 41–42, no. 9 (unknown phyle; status as *choregos* uncertain). Besides the immediately foregoing inscription, another problematic item is *IG* II² 1144 of Pandionis, which, as restored in lines 9–11, calls for the engraving of the name of the archon and of the "victors" by patronymic and deme, with evident reference to a catalog of succeful *choregoi* (cf. no. 1138, also of Pandionis).

65. *ArchEph* 1965, pp. 131–136 (ii) (Akamantis), line 15. The word is wholly restored; for the editor's justification, see p. 133. The decree of Leontis, *Hesperia* 9 (1940) 59–66, no. 8 (i), dedicated "to the hero" by the *sophronistes* and the taxiarch upon their crowning by the Boule and Demos and the phyle (lines 1–2, partially restored), appends the name of the *kosmetes* (col. II, lines 12–13), but he does not figure among the phyle's ephebic honorands.

66. Besides the honorand in the decree of Leontis just cited (above, note 65), line 1; (i), col. I, lines 4–5, 14–15; col. II, lines 13–14; (ii), col. III, lines 11–12, the *sophronistes* of Kekropis is honored at *IG* II² 1156, lines 31–32.

67. Again, besides the honorand of the decree of Leontis (above, note 65), line 1; (i), col. I, lines 20–22 and col. II, 15, Kekropis honors its taxiarch at *IG* II² 1155, lines a2 and b7–12.

68. Yet again, the honorands of the decree of Leontis (above, note 65) include the *lochagoi* at lines col. I, lines 22–28; col. II, lines 16–22.

69. Finally, the decree of Leontis (above, note 65) cites the ephebes beginning at col. II, line 22.

70. For the references, see chapter 5, note 39.

71. *IG* II² 1148 (Pandionis); *Hesperia* 15 (1946) 189, no. 35 (Leontis or Aiantis); and *Hesperia* 7 (1938) 94–96, no. 15 (Aiantis). At *IG* II² 1163 (Hippothontis; ca. 288/7), lines 8–10, the reference to the honorand's tendance of "the sortition of the courts" suggested to Koehler that the man, who is otherwise identified only as priest of Asklepios (lines 3–4), had simultaneously served as thesmothete. Two additional instances are preserved in dedications. The phyle (Kekropis) joined the Boule, Demos, the honorand's fellow demesmen and colleagues in the archonship in honoring one Kleonymos, son of Kleemporos, of Epieikidai, according to his dedication, *IG* II² 2837 (329/8); similarly, an unknown phyle, Boule, and Demos in no. 2843 (319/8).

72. *IG* II² 1140 (Pandionis).

73. *IG* II² 1163 (Hippothontis).

74. *IG* II² 1171 (unknown phyle). The injunction in line 14 to stand (the stele?) "beside the eponymous" strongly favors the ascription of the decree to a phyle.

75. *IG* II² 1250 (Aiantis).

who had served as judge at the Thargelia;[76] a phylarch of the cavalry;[77] another person, undoubtedly a phylarch too, who had led his *phyletai* to victory in the *anthippasia;*[78] and a *syndikos* (acting) "on behalf of the *temenos* on Lemnos."[79] In the problematic category are a *hieropoios* (a member of one of the state boards designated by this name?) conjecturally restored in a decree of Akamantis;[80] and an honorand of unknown identification who will render his *euthynai* and who therefore must be an officer of the state.[81]

The decrees themselves leave no doubt why these various *phyletai* are being so honored. In the carrying out of their duties, they had, we learn, benefited the phyle in some way. By my count, in no fewer than 36 instances (of a total of 45 honorary decrees, some of which are fragmentary) attention is drawn, explicitly or implicitly, to this fundamental fact. In no intact (or nearly intact) decree, moreover, is such acknowledgment absent. What is perhaps somewhat surprising is that, despite the fact that in each instance the honorand had been concerned with duties or responsibilities at the state level, on only seven or eight occasions does the decree appear to acknowledge comparable benefits to the city of Athens, and in each instance this point supplements, but normally does not replace, the still-present mention of the phyle's interests.[82] Thus the impression left by the decrees as a group is that the phyle is honoring a member or members who, in the exercise of a city office or (as with the liturgies) a post operating at the city level, had nonetheless in some way benefited his (or their) own phyle, to the exclusion, necessarily, of the remaining nine-tenths of the state.

We could learn more if the decrees were more specific about the nature of such benefits, but characteristically their language is vague or merely laudatory. External evidence must be brought to bear. To consider only our four principal categories, a choregic victory of course meant good publicity for the liturgist's phyle, first in the theater itself, later in the form of sometimes impressive monuments inscribed in the name of the phyle.[83] (A similar argument applies to the phylarch's victory in the *anthippasia* and to the gymnasiarch's coaching of the torch-runners.) The well-being

---

76. *IG* II² 1153 (Hippothontis).

77. *SEG* 3.115 (Antiochis).

78. *Hesperia* 9 (1940) 111–112, no. 21 (unknown phyle).

79. *SEG* 3.117 (Antiochis), lines 7–8. No title is associated with his services, described in lines 12–19, in connection with certain properties at Oropos.

80. *IG* II² 1166 (Akamantis), line 2. Whatever the title, a statewide religious post of some kind is indicated by the context.

81. *IG* II² 1164 (unknown phyle), line 6.

82. A generous list, giving the benefit of the doubt in fragmentary passages, would include *IG* II² 1150 (Erechtheis), lines 3–4; 1148 (Pandionis), lines 9–10; 1167 (Pandionis), lines 4 and 9; 1163 (Hippothontis), lines 7–8 and 19–20; 1151 (Aiantis), line 8 (?); 1142 (=*Agora* 15, no. 5; unknown phyle), line 8 (with reference to a board of *prytaneis;* not necessarily a decree of a phyle); *Hesperia* 9 (1940) 111–112, no. 21 (unknown phyle), lines 6–8. At *IG* II² 1141 (Kekropis), lines 8–9, the text "since Pyrros has proved good concerning the phyle and *ta koina*" was improved by W. K. Pritchett, *Hesperia* 10 (1941) 263–265, no. 67, to read "concerning the phyle and *ta koina* of the phyle." Mention is not made of any benefit to the phyle in either *IG* II² 1142 or 1167, but both these texts are too fragmentary for any significance to be attached to this fact.

83. For the details, with references to the epigraphic texts, see Jones 1987, ch. 1, sec. 1.27, pp. 48–51.

of the ephebes—young men about 18 and 19 years of age—will have been a topic of some concern, since these teenagers, probably often away from home for the first time, were being entrusted to the care of older adult males, a relationship to which Greeks were notoriously sensitive. This must be at least part of what Aristotle is getting at when he writes that, after the scrutiny of the cadets, their *fathers* (my emphasis)[84] meet *kata phylas* and select on oath three men over forty years old whom they regard as "the best and most suitable" to take charge of the cadets. (From these the Demos was later to elect one man from each phyle as *sophronistes* and from all the Athenians one *kosmetes* over all [*AthPol* 42.2]). It is presumably in part the ephebic officer's success in living up to the standard of "the best and most suitable" that has motivated the accolade of the home phyle, no doubt largely at the prompting of the fathers of the cadets. As for the *prytaneis*, no obvious explanation is at hand, but there is a strongly suggestive parallel in a decree of the demesmen of Teithras, who honor their *bouleutai* (note, not their *prytaneis*) "since they well and energetically took care of the sacrifices and everything else that the *demotai* bid."[85] Here, explicit acknowledgment is made of the serving by members of the Council of the interests not of the state, but of their home community. The case of the *thesmothetai*, finally, is quite unclear. A decree of Aiantis mentions the honorand's attention to the allotment of offices, to the staffing of the courts, and to "everything else that concerns the Aiantid phyle." In the "manifesto" that follows, the hope is expressed that future *thesmothetai* will be similarly zealous on behalf of the phyle;[86] but the connection between the state office and the benefiting of the phyle is not made explicit, nor is it easy to imagine. Certainly public acknowledgment of favoritism toward one's *phyletai* in connection with either the magistracies or the courts would be hard to accept as an explanation. It is to be suspected, accordingly, that the honorand's benefactions, though no less the result of his use of the office, are in fact masked by the vague reference to "everything else that concerns the Aiantid phyle" (lines 10–12). A similar opacity marks the honors by Leontis or Aiantis of its thesmothete for his attention to [---τῶν πε]/ρὶ τὴν φυλὴ[ν κατὰ τοὺς] / [νό]μους ("matters concerning the phyle in accordance with the laws") in a decree of about the same date.[87]

The practice of the phylai, then, will have fallen midway between two extremes. At the extreme of self-promotion, an officeholder might use his powers for

---

84. Cf. *IG* II² 1159 (Pandionis), lines 11–14, where "the fathers of the ephebes" are recorded to have testified to the *sophronistes'* praiseworthy performance.

85. *Agora* 15, no. 45 (= *Hesperia* 31 [1962] 401–403, no. 3; 331/0 or 330/29), lines 7–12: ἐ]πειδὴ κ/[αλῶς καὶ φιλ]οτίμως / [ἐπεμελήθησ]αν τῶν θ/[υσιῶν καὶ τῶ]ν ἄλλων / [ὅσα ἐκέλευσ]αν οἱ δη/[μόται. . . . Note, importantly, that nothing is said or implied here regarding the *location*, whether the town, the deme itself, or elsewhere, at which either the sacrifices or the other services were carried out. Whitehead, however, assumes without argument that the duties in question were undertaken "within the deme" (1986, p. 266, note 40), with a view to supporting his contention that the *bouleutai* of Teithras did *not* function as representatives of their deme. As a matter of fact, nothing precludes or even lessens the probability of my view that these councillors had acted, on order from their *demotai*, to advance the interests of the deme in the arena of the city of Athens.

86. *Hesperia* 7 (1938) 94–96, no. 15, lines 5–12, 21–27.

87. *Hesperia* 15 (1946) 189, no. 35, lines 5–7.

personal benefit, hence the decrees on occasion praise the honorand for carrying out his duties "well and justly and *without taking bribes*."[88] At the other extreme, in this case a praiseworthy attitude but one (as we saw) hardly recognized, the honorand is stated to have served the interests of the entire city of Athens. But the great bulk of our material specifies neither self nor state, but the phyle of the honorand as the proper recipient of his benefactions. Such actions are customarily characterized with laudatory language (e.g., "well", "well and energetically") and often, too, by a prepositional phrase ascribing to the honorand "excellence," "justice," "moderation," or the like, but such verbiage is beside the point when measured against his benefaction to the phyle. Sometimes, too, to drive the point home still further, the decree ends with a formulaic element (of varying construction) expressing the hope that others, incited by the present honorand's award, may similarly benefit the phyle in the future.[89]

That the reason for the bestowal of honors resided in the honorand's official position and in his use of that position to the advantage of the phyle is, I think, the most likely but not the only possible interpretation of the record. Alternatively, it might be argued that the office itself is incidental to the award of honors, that it merely provided an occasion or excuse for a decree, and that the real, underlying reason was the honorand's use of his wealth or influence to the benefit of the phyle above and beyond the narrowly circumscribed range of his duties in office or liturgy. To be sure, such a view garners some plausibility from the presence among the honorands of the liturgical *choregoi* [90] as well as from several indications of wealth or significant political service at the state level in the persons or families of some of the others.[91] But against this line of reasoning are the several explicit statements

88. The word is ἀδωροδοκήτως: *IG* II² 1148 (Pandionis), lines 4–5 (partly restored); 1153 (Hippothontis), lines 4–5. So also, more fully, Antisthenes' accolade by his phyle Erechtheis, *IG* II² 1165, lines 22–24.

89. *IG* II² 1159 (Pandionis); *Hesperia* 7 (1938) 94–96, no. 15 (Aiantis); *Hesperia* 32 (1963) 14–15, no. 13 (Ptolemais?); *Hesperia* 9 (1940) 111–112, no. 21 (unknown phyle); *IG* II² 1171 (unknown phyle).

90. The honored *choregoi* are: Saurias, son of Pythogenes, of Lamptrai (Erechtheis), *IG* II² 1147 (Davies, *APF* 12612); Nikias, son of Epigenes (I), of Kydathenaion (Pandionis), *IG* II² 1138 (and 1139) (*APF* 10807); [--10--]δωρου of Kydathenaion (Pandionis), *IG* II²1157 (*APF* A85); lost name (Kekropis?), *IG* II² 1158; lost name (unknown phyle), *Hesperia* 4 (1935) 41–42, no. 9; lost name of possible *choregos* (Pandionis), *IG* II² 1144. The final three examples are not listed in *APF*'s "lost names," D1–22, pp. 592–595. From the catalog of victors of Pandionis come the nine additional names: *IG* II² 1138, lines 17–32: Andokides (IV), son of Leogoros (II), of Kydathenaion (*APF* 828, especially p. 31); Euripides, son of Adeimantos (I), of Myrrhinous (also at *IG* II² 2812, lines 1–3; *APF* 5949=5955=5956, especially p. 204); Demon (III), son of Demoteles, of Paiania (*APF* 3737); Charmantides (II), son of Chairestratos (I), of Paiania (*APF* 15502); Philomelos (II), son of Philippides (I), of Paiania (also at *IG* II² 2812, lines 4–7; *APF* 14670); Apemon, son of Pheidippos, of Myrrhinous (*APF* 1350); Xenopeithes (I), son of Nausimachos (I), of Paiania (*APF* 11263); Kleomedon (I), son of Kleon (I), of Kydathenaion (*APF* 8586); and Antisthenes (I), son of Antiphates, of Kytheros (*APF* 1194=1196=1197). For the name of the gymnasiarch honored by Aiantis in *IG* II² 1250, see *SEG* 40.124.

91. For the certain or possible members of liturgical families among the phyletic officers (most of them, where a determination is possible, as it turned out, *epimeletai*) honored by the decrees, see above, "The Rewards of Holding Office in the Phyle." To these may be added five others: Nikandros of Lamptrai (*PA* 10688), *tamias* of the goddess in 343/2, is the father of Antisthenes, honored by Erechtheis, *IG* II² 1165; Demon (I), son of Demomeles (I), of Paiania, priest of Pandion, honored by Pandionis, *IG* II² 1140, belongs to a liturgical family (Davies, *APF* 3735); Epikrates, son of Peisianax, of Sounion, ephebic *lochagos*, honored by Leontis, *Hesperia* 9 (1940) 59–66, no. 8 (i), col. I, lines

that the honorand, by fulfilling the duties of his post, did so to the enhancement of his phyle's interests,[92] plus the fact, already noted, that at least one phyle, Kekropis, on two or three occasions honors a *phyletes* for whom no post of any kind was indicated.[93] This latter practice implies that no need was felt to name an office simply to satisfy some perceived prerequisite to the bestowal of praise or crown. We can be sure, then, that the benefactions had been delivered through the medium of the honorand's office or liturgy.

The Phyle Association as Instrument of Representation

What Kleisthenes originally (or, in later times, other reformers) intended, if anything, for the associational role of the phylai we shall never know. But a few recorded or highly probable features of the nascent phylai would seem to have encouraged, or at least to have opened the door for, such a development. The new phylai were given eponyms selected from among the "first founders" of the Athenian state which might, by virtue of their high antiquity, be cast in the role of fictive common ancestors. These eponyms were already, or soon thereafter became, the objects of formal cults organized around a shrine, thereby providing potential foci of religious activity. Although each phyle fell into three quite disparate segments, each segment was extensive enough to embrace a great many already existing familial or associational units in toto. That is to say, many of the new *symphyletai* found themselves already related to each other in a number of different ways. And, as a consequence of the usage imposed by Kleisthenes upon the demes, membership in the phylai, of which the demes were components, was to be transmitted hereditarily from father to son irrespective of the place of domicile. Thus the conditions were from a very early date ripe for the emergence of an association of the *phyletai,* quite apart from any reformer's intentions. But that this would happen was by no means certain. Internally organized public units are rather infrequently attested among the 200 or so city-states for which some trace of a public organization has survived.[94] The development of an association depended upon the presence of certain needs to which the resulting organization would constitute the response. What some of these needs were in the case of Athens can, I think, be deduced from the record of evidence that we have just reviewed.

24–25; col. II, lines 17–19, belongs to a liturgical family (*APF* 9688, IX, pp. 378–379); Pandaites, son of Pasikles (I), of Potamos, ephebic *lochagos,* honored by Leontis, *Hesperia* 9 (1940) 59–66, no. 8 (i) col. I, line 23; col. II, lines 16–17, belongs to the family of a syntrierarch (and councillor) (*APF* 11572; see 643, with corrected stemma on p. 24); [Δημοκλῆς Φιλ]ιστίωνος Ἀφιδ[ναῖος] (PA 3496), ephebic taxiarch, honored by Ptolemais?, *Hesperia* 32 (1963) 14–15, no. 13, "belonged to a family prominent over many years" (op. cit., p. 15). (I omit the half dozen or so certain or probable cases in which an honorand or his relative is merely known to have served as councillor.)

92. Where the text is preserved reasonably intact, not a single decree honoring any of the nonphyletic officers or liturgists under review here fails to indicate in some fashion the honorand's service to his phyle.

93. See above, note 13.

94. For a convenient synopsis of the record, see Jones 1987, index III "Internal organization of public units," pp. 396–403.

Plainly, to begin with a negative point, the explanation is not to be found in any administrative demands placed upon the phylai by the central government. We saw in chapter 5 that there are few indications that state business of any significance was conducted in the phyletic *agorai;* and that, in particular, there is little to favor the suggestion that the sortitions of the councillors (or of the guards), or of any government officials, were actually conducted in meetings (special or otherwise) of the "tribal assemblies." By no means could these assocations be imagined to have been sustained by the bureaucratic requirements of the central government.

Nor, equally clearly (and leaving the central government out of it), as we also saw in chapter 5, did they develop in response to a need for an organization characterized by close ties of solidarity. Of course, the integration of the *phyletai* of city, coast, and inland was perhaps never a viable possibility. Still, *phyletai* of a single regional block of demes might have formed a cohesive group had conditions been right. That of the three such blocks, the one (the urban trittys) for which we might expect our evidence to preserve traces of such a development evidently did not is probably to be ascribed to a surfeit of competition from other organizational entities, beginning with the state itself and extending down through the trittys and deme, the phratry, the genos and other religious associations, clubs of various kinds, and the family in its conjugal and more extended forms. What need was there, in other words, for still another focus of allegiance or activity?

An alternative, and far more likely, suggestion is that a need was felt by some for a relatively small-scale forum for political activity, leadership, and achievement. At the level of the central government, the opportunities to hold a significant (i.e., for the most part, elective) office, to make a speech before the Assembly or Council, or to receive public honors were few and far between, being reserved for those of exceptional talent, ambition, and courage. How much better one's chances would be in an organization only one-tenth that size! But this factor too, however well founded, explains only part of the record. It fails, first, to explain why the phylai were headquartered in the town, when the same organizational ends could be achieved equally well in either the coastal or inland regions. It fails, too, to account for the most striking feature of the record, the pronounced tendency to bestow honors not upon the most natural candidates, the associational officers, but upon holders of statewide posts with a context of operations outside the phyle in the city of Athens.

To account for these facts we must entertain still another variety of need. I have in mind the need felt by ambitious individuals to facilitate their entry into, or continuing success within, the politics of the city; and, at a grass roots level, a need on the part of the membership as a whole to maximize their influence within the central government, at least insofar as the acts of the central government affected their own lives. To meet these needs, however, an important condition had to be satisfied: the seat or headquarters, and above all the place of the meetings, of the phyle had to be situated in the urban center. The mover of an honorary decree who hoped, by means of an eloquent or persuasive laudatory *epainos,* to obtain political support among his *phyletai* would obviously prefer to speak to urbanites likely to vote in city elections or plebiscites. Such men will have seen to it that the phyle's seat be established, or remain, in or near the area of the Akropolis or Agora. But the rank-and-file membership certainly had its own agenda as well. They might utilize the resources of the organization to subsidize the bestowal of honors upon those of their number whose official position provided an opportunity to represent their (the membership's) interests in the arena of Athenian public life. Again, the urban setting was essential. It was in the town that the preponderance of politically active *phyletai,* my hypothetical attendees and voters in the phyle's *agora,* were likely to reside (at least those residing far from the urban center were less likely to be so active). It was in the town also that the *choregoi,* ephebic officers, *prytaneis,* and *thesmothetai,* among others, were frequently and of necessity present in order to carry out some or all of their official duties. Thus the holding of the phyle's meetings in the town would bring together the interested parties among the membership and those individuals, the state officers and liturgists selected from their phyle, whom those interested parties hoped to influence by holding out the prospect of the bestowal of coveted or valuable honors.[95]

Hence the phyle organizations as we find them in our admittedly fragmentary evidence do appear to have ended up, whatever intent may have prompted their creation, serving as instruments of *representation.* Some scholars have denied the existence of representative government in ancient Greece,[96] but I think there can be lit-

---

95. If in fact, as I am suggesting, urbanites tended in proportionately greater numbers to engage in the associational life of the phylai, we might expect to find some trace of the tendency in the preserved deme affiliations of the personnel just reviewed. But the data for the officers, first, are rendered valueless by the fact that nearly all of those known by name are demonstrably or probably *epimeletai,* who were normally drawn one from each of the three trittyes of the phyle (see above, "*Epimeletai* and Other Officers"). The sole exceptions are confined to the members of Aigeis named in *IG* II² 2824: for the treasurer from Ikarion (inland trittys), see note 32; for the board of three of uncertain identification but certainly not *epimeletai,* at least two (and possibly all three) of whom belong to Halai Araphenides (coastal trittys), see above, with notes 28–31. Second, while the figures for the honorands (including those whose crowns are attested by dedications) are generally more meaningful, some of the *epimeletai,* with their mandatory regional distribution, are numbered among them. My count is: city, 15; coast, 23; inland, 21. For the proposers, finally, the distribution of recorded demotics is city, 4; coast, 6; and inland, 6. Obviously, these figures do not reveal the disproportionate imbalance in favor of the town demes that one, on my theory, might have been led to expect. But two alternatives remain open. (1) The fairly even distribution among the regions might be explained on the assumption that the extra-urban *demotai* in question in fact were residing in the town. (2) If the honorands and proposers did not reside in the town but in the demes of their affiliations, they (and perhaps the officers as well, including the coastal and inland *epimeletai*) might be assumed to have been willing to traverse the sometimes considerable distances from home to urban meeting place. Certainly there was no lack of rewards: for the honorands, the public bestowal of praise and crown; for the movers of decrees, as I have argued, an opportunity to address a potentially important audience; for the officers, the inducements and payoffs that I have discussed at length above. For parallel explorations of the problem of participation in city politics by citizens residing outside the town, see Harding 1981, pp. 41–50 and Hansen 1983, pp. 227–238. Both favor the notion that citizens from outlying areas would travel considerable distances in order to partake in the public life of the city. However, I am prepared to endorse their views only to the extent that lengthy journeys were compensated with substantial rewards. For my reasons for doubting that ruralites regularly walked to the town for routine participation in government, see "Determinants of the Isolation of the Extra-Urban Demes," in chapter 3.

96. Thus Finley 1983, p. 74 with note 16, with reference to the Council of Five Hundred. Whitehead's position against representation, however, is far more sweeping: "The democratic *politeia* neither consisted of nor even anywhere contained a body or bodies of mandated delegates; it was, nonetheless, a *politeia* designed to reflect—and so 'represent' in that sense—the entirety of the citizen body" (1986, p. 265). See also above, note 85, for his interpretation (in fact, I believe, misinterpretation) of one of the

tle doubt that these state officials and liturgists, all known to have been selected "by phylai," were given strong incentives to regard the phyle from which they had been selected as a kind of constituency and to represent the interests of that constituency in the various fora of Athenian city life.[97] An organization as large and heterogeneous as an Athenian phyle was likely of course to cater to a multitude of purposes and concerns, but it is in the need for *representation* of the membership in the life of the city that we can identify perhaps the principal driving force.[98]

---

few possible explicit documentary illustrations of my position, the decree of the deme of Teithras honoring its *bouleutai*, *Agora* 15, no. 45.

97. This formulation may be evaluated in the light of the generalizing statement with which J. A. O. Larsen commenced his exploration of "representative government" in the Greek and Roman worlds: "Representative government, for the purposes of the present study, can be defined as government in which the ultimate decisions on important questions are made by representatives acting for their constituents and having authority to makes such decisions according to their own best judgment." These citizens, he continues, are "true representatives and not messengers merely recording the will of their constituents" (Larsen 1955, p. 1). In the present case, while our evidence is not such as to allow us to decide whether we are dealing with representatives independently exercizing their own judgment or (as is far more often the case in modern democracies) passive message carriers, the simple fact of the existence of representation of some kind is, I believe, beyond doubt.

98. My thesis may help to explain two otherwise puzzling and seemingly unrelated silences in the ancient Greek writers on government, above all Aristotle, namely, on the one hand, concerning the internally organized phylai (as well as the trittyes and demes) and, on the other, concerning the phenomenon of representation. In fact, the two silences may be organically related. Because the writers did not care to notice the phyle (or trittys or deme) in its role as an association, they consequently failed to observe the operation of representation as it functioned within that association. For discussion of Aristotle's evidence, see "Ancient Sources for the Associations of Classical Athens," in the Introduction. For the place of this finding within the larger context of government-associations relations, see chapter 10.

SEVEN

The Phratries

The Public Role of the Phratries

Superficially, the phratries[1] resembled the internally organized segments of the public organization in that they were open only to citizens and in that all citizens seem to have been eligible for admission.[2] As, too, with the demes and (as an automatic consequence) the larger groups of which the demes were components, the phylai, membership in this or that phratry was determined exclusively on the basis of descent, with the father obligated to demonstrate his son's legitimate birth to the satisfaction of his fellow *phrateres*.[3] Given, then, the extension of membership only to the legitimate male offspring of existing citizen members, it is not surprising that we encounter signs in the documentary record of the phratries of that same exclusivity

1. Early accounts of the Athenian phratries include Ferguson 1910; Busolt and Swoboda 1926, vol. 2, pp. 958–964; Guarducci 1937, vol. 1, pp. 11–57; and Hignett 1952, pp. 55–60. Study of the subject has now, however, been put on a more secure footing by Hedrick's work, especially his edition and commentary on the decrees of the Demotionidai (1990), and by Lambert's comprehensive account of the Athenian phratry (1993). Lambert's app. 1, pp. 279–370, lists all the inscriptions under review in this chapter. Wherever appropriate, I shall provide his "T" numbers for these documents alongside the conventional epigraphic references.

2. See, on phratry membership and Athenian citizenship, Lambert 1993, chapter 1, pp. 25–57. Shortly, however, I shall contest Lambert's thesis regarding the respective roles played by the phratry and the deme in determining access to the citizen body.

3. See, on the principle of descent, Lambert 1993, pp. 35–40, 237, 381–383.

that so strikingly characterizes the deme.[4] It was an exclusivity, furthermore, that by definition pertained not merely to general phratry status but as well to membership in a *particular* phratry. Nevertheless, at the same time, as will be emphasized, all Athenian citizens were linked by a common bond of phratry membership that crossed the boundaries of the individual associations, in marked (and, as we shall see, significant) contrast with the particularity cultivated by the deme associations.

Since all citizens actually or potentially belong to a phratry, and since the individual phratry organizations seem to have carefully monitored the admission of new applications to membership, it has always been obvious that the phratries could have performed a useful service in this area on behalf of the central government. Because admission to the phratry preceded admission to the deme, a young Athenian whose father had successfully secured his son's entry into his brotherhood would ipso facto have already satisfied one of the deme's dual criteria of age and legitimacy. By the latter term I refer to the Aristotelian *Constitution*'s citation of birth "in accordance with the laws," namely the Periklean law requiring as a precondition of citizenship descent from an Athenian father and a "duly betrothed" Athenian mother.[5] And surely it was legitimacy so defined, rather than the more easily ascertainable factor of age, that might have proved problematic. So, in this one area, it is widely believed or assumed, the otherwise "private" phratry may have performed an exceedingly valuable "public" function on behalf of the state.[6] The principle operated both negatively and positively. If an aspirant to deme membership (and hence to citizenship) had previously failed entry into his putative father's phratry on the grounds of legitimacy, this must have been an adversely prejudicial indication in the eyes of the *demotai* assembled to consider his case. If, on the other hand, he had successfully cleared that first hurdle, a strong presumption now existed favoring his admission to the deme on the ground of birth "in accordance with the laws."[7]

Twin, redundant tests of legitimate descent (and age), given the notorious sources of uncertainty regarding paternity in particular, make perfectly good sense on procedural grounds alone. But there was more at stake than membership in a phratry or deme, or even membership in the citizen body. On the question of legitimacy also depended the legal capacity to inherit.[8] A youth whose eligibility for citi-

---

4. Take, for example, the list of names headed by the title οἵδε φράτερες, *IG* II² 2344 (init. s. IV). For the analysis of the names as comprising at most eight families, see Hedrick 1989, pp. 127–133. Such limitation of membership to a few groups of close relatives strongly suggests exclusion, although Hedrick (p. 130) leaves open the possibility that not all members of the phratry are necessarily listed. Arguments for "a full phratry," however, are set out by Flower 1985, pp. 232–235.

5. *AthPol* 42.1–2. For the leading modern study of the law and its operation, see Patterson 1981.

6. For full discussion, see Lambert 1993, pp. 31–43.

7. Admittedly, it is true, as noted by Lambert 1993, p. 41, that there is no positive indication in the sources that demes were systematically obliged to examine "the phratry credentials of candidates before admission." But this is not the sort of datum that would have to be recorded, much less inscribed on stone. Nor is the silence of Aristotle or other sources on the matter good reason to entertain suspicions. As recognized by Lambert himself, and argued here, phratries were strongly linked to deme centers, and so many of the *phrateres* who had voted on a candidate's admission to phratry would also be present when that same candidate came before his father's deme. The relevant evidence and the outcome of the earlier deliberations would be common knowledge and probably known to all concerned.

8. Harrison 1968, vol. 1, p. 130; MacDowell 1978, pp. 92–95.

zenship had been undermined by phratry and/or deme on the grounds that his puta-tive parent(s) were not in fact his parent(s) was in effect legally disinherited, with the consequent likely opening up of the field to a new claimant or claimants to an estate. Even among the politically apathetic, consequently, it is easy to imagine that considerable interest was awakened whenever an Athenian citizen sought, through the medium of his phratry and deme associations, to establish the constitutionally defined legitimacy of the young man he claimed as his and his wife's son. Two hear-ings on the matter were certainly none too many.

However plausible, the notion of redundant tests by phratry and deme was called into question by Lambert in his recent synoptic study of the Athenian phratry. To reduce his position to its essentials, Lambert maintains that "the phratry was of particular significance where matters of descent were concerned" and that "[i]t was the phratry, not the deme, that bore the onus of controlling the implementation of that principle."[9] This view, it seems to me, is ill-founded. Naturally, as we have just seen, it is not difficult to make the case that the phratry was positively concerned with the matter of descent, if only for the purpose of monitoring its membership. There is also justice in his conclusion that the phratry was "a structure *par excel-lence* for the formation and maintenance of the natural relations that existed among persons connected to each other by kinship or proximity of abode, the relations among citizens."[10] The phrase "natural relations" reflects his general characteriza-tion of the phratry as a "natural community."[11]

But this characterization may be overdrawn, if only because the alleged "natu-ralness" of the phratry is far from evident. For one thing, although, as soon to be emphasized, phratries were generally localized around a deme center, their mem-berships could also become dispersed, as the case of the Medontidai graphically il-lustrates.[12] Moreover, for all we know, phratries might well in some cases have been quite large associations, and, to the extent that they were, they may have dwarfed the many tiny demes whose commensurably tiny assemblies were meeting to pass on the admission of new members. A probable specific instance of an association, almost certainly to be identified as a phratry, both geographically distended and rel-atively large is provided by the organization of *thiasoi* very likely centered in the large deme of Alopeke but including members from the surrounding, smaller demes of the immediate neighborhood.[13] In this case the phratry was a rather widely ex-tended organization embracing a plurality of village settlements. Which was the

9. Lambert 1993, p. 35.

10. Lambert 1993, pp. 42–43.

11. Lambert 1993, p. 14.

12. The relevant evidence is collected at Lambert 1993, pp. 319–320. Note, too, in this case that, contrary to the process of fission at work elsewhere (and duly emphasized by Lambert), the Medontidai did not, so far as the preservation of the original name in several locales indicates, undergo a splitting of the membership.

13. See *IG* II² 2345, with the analysis of Humphreys 1990, passim. Walters (1982, pp. 4–5, with map, p. 30), building upon the analyses of Ferguson (1910, pp. 270–273) and of Andrewes (1961, p. 10), attempts to extend the geographical distribution of the organization in service of his case against the re-gionalist interpretation of archaic Athenian politics. But his conclusion, that the *genos* Salaminioi and, with the *genos*, all its various *demotai*, were members of the phratry? documented by *IG* II² 2345, is conjectural to say the least.

more "natural" entity, the phratry or the deme? Congruent with the obvious implications of this example is the typically relatively small size (in terms of citizen population) of the majority of the demes. To adduce a handy quantification, 72 or just
over one-half of the 139 demes had a bouleutic quota of two or fewer. So, on
grounds of size alone, the typical deme will probably have had a stronger claim to
"naturalness" than many a phratry.

Nor is size the only relevant factor. As we saw in chapter 2, the settlement of
the Athenian countryside was highly nucleated, with the result that the members of
a given deme typically resided in close proximity to one another. At issue here, let
us remember, are such matters as the entry of strangers into houses, the movements
of women, and the observation of pregnancies. Secrecy or deception will have been
difficult under the cramped circumstances evidently prevailing in such tiny, closely
clustered hamlets. Proximity of residences apart, many demesmen will have of
course been related to each other by blood or marriage, not to mention less intimate
ties of obligation or reciprocity. Probably most demes (or at least their members still
resident in the village center), therefore, could satisfy any reasonable criterion of
"naturalness," when it came to questions of parentage. Not surprisingly, to mention
only one telling indication, in courtroom trials a litigant occasionally appeals to the
supporting testimony of his *demotai*, in order to establish a point regarding descent,
adoption, wills, etc.[14] To be sure, Lambert correctly notes the general absence among
the deme documents of texts expressly concerned with the question of "membership
control,"[15] but we have already seen in chapters 2 and 3 the considerable evidence
establishing beyond doubt the deme association's preoccupation with the maintenance of exclusivity of membership and privilege. Besides, vigilance in the matter
of ascertaining legitimacy is not the sort of activity that one would expect to leave
its mark on the documentary record, if only because the great majority of applicants
were probably routinely admitted to membership without incident.

Another alleged distinction undergirding Lambert's attack on the notion of an
equally weighted, redundant scrutiny by phratry and deme regards the public roles
played or not played by the two organizations. To the deme Lambert ascribes substantial statewide importance and roles: "the mass of political, financial, and military
privileges and responsibilities associated with citizenship was connected, conceptu-
ally and legally, with membership in a deme and was organized in practice on the
basis of the deme/trittys/phyle structure."[16] Again, and even more forcefully: "Certainly the deme functioned as a local community, but central to its purpose was the
fact that it was the structure by and through which the functions of the state were organized."[17] This characterization of the deme's statewide roles goes well beyond the
evidence. The truth is that in post-Kleisthenic Athens, as generally throughout
Greece, statewide functions were highly concentrated in the upper tiers of the public
organization, particularly the phylai.[18] Segmental units such as the deme play only a

14. See, on the demesman as witness, Whitehead 1986, pp. 227–228.
15. Lambert 1993, p. 36 with note 50.
16. Lambert 1993, p. 40.
17. Lambert 1993, p. 43.
18. As I noted at *Public Organization*, 1987, p. 18. I shall return to the significance of this striking
fact in chapter 10.

few, minor discernible roles in public administration; and, at Athens, the political, financial, and military functions ascribed by Lambert to the "deme/trittys/phyle structure" are in fact, with very few exceptions, confined to the phylai and least of all involved the demes.[19] Where the deme does come into play, it is usually through the medium of the demarch, who serves as an "agent" of the central government, implementing central government policies.[20] But the deme association's own active roles in statewide administration, qua *demotai*, are minor, even trifling, at best.

If, then, the relative responsibilities exercised by the two associations have been misrepresented by Lambert, what is to be our final verdict regarding the place of the phratry in Athenian public life? To look beyond Athens for a moment, my examination of the Greek public organizations resulted in the finding that in the cases of a dozen cities the phratries can be observed playing a public role, in nearly every instance such role being signaled by the inclusion of the phratry among the units in which newly enfranchised citizens were eligible to be enrolled.[21] The presence of the phratry clearly reflects the part played by the association in determining eligibility for citizenship. Because phratry membership and citizenship were inseparable, the phratry naturally joined the roster of units specified in the enrollment clause. At Athens, the importance of this gatekeeper function is further reflected in statutes preserved in Krateros[22] and Philochoros[23] regulating admission to the Athenian phratries, whether or not, as Lambert argues, the two measures should be associated with Perikles' law on citizenship, perhaps even as actual extracts from the text of that law.[24] Krateros's text penalized the entry into the phratry of foreigners; Philochoros's mandated the admission of eligible Athenians. It is difficult to escape the conclusion, to return to our point of departure, that the central government looked, at this first stage of the determination of eligibility, to the phratry to perform an initial screening of those aspiring to entry into the Athenian citizen body. The "brotherhood" may have been a "private" association, but its monitoring of legitimacy, even if not formally recognized by the state, thrust it willy-nilly into the limelight of public life. So, to this extent, we may follow the *communis opinio*, though not at the cost of diminishing the equally—indeed, as I have argued, even more—crucial custodianship in the matter of descent entrusted to the demes.

19. For the scattering of public statewide functions of the Athenian demes, see Jones 1987, ch. 1, sec. 1.2, pp. 31–57, with the summary at p. 38. Much of the relevant material is brought together by Whitehead 1986, pp. 109–111, under the rubric "other aspects of state administration performed by demes."

20. The evidence is collected and discussed by Whitehead 1986, pp. 130–139.

21. For the list, with references to my discussions, see Jones 1987, index I, A.30, p. 388 (Andros, Argos, Chios?, Corinth, Delos, Ilion, Megalopolis?, Miletos, Syracuse, Tenos, Theisoa). Of course, this does not purport to be a complete list of states with phratries but only of those states whose phratries performed some public function. Since the publication of *Public Organization*, I have reexamined much of this same material, including the case of Athens, in a study of the enrollment clauses in Greek citizenship decrees, 1991, pp. 79–102.

22. *FGrH* 342 Krateros F 4. The fragment descends from the fourth book of the collection of Athenian decrees. Lambert suggests book 4 may have included the year of Perikles' legislation, 451/0 (1993, p. 45).

23. *FGH* 328 Philochoros F 35a. For the book number, four, see fr. 35b. Again, Lambert's suggested chronological span for the book would cover the year of the citizenship law (1993, p. 46).

24. Lambert 1993, pp. 45–47. Still valuable in this connection is Andrewes's 1961 study of the Philochoros fragments (Andrewes 1961).

Regional Distribution and Relation to the Urban Center

In comparison with the segments of the public organization, we have very little general idea of the phratry associations in the aggregate. While only nine or so different phratries have been securely identified by name, their actual total numbers have been set or estimated from as few as twelve (*AthPol*, frag. 3) to about 30 in the fourth century (Lambert) on up to the number of the demes, 139 or 140.[25] Since all citizens seem to have been eligible for phratry membership, with any variation in the number of units there would naturally be commensurably mild or violent variations in the numbers of members of each association. So we have no idea of the size—minimum, average, modal, or maximum—of a phratry, either.[26] Nor is it possible, on the basis of our rather meager documentary record, to discern the sorts of distinguishing idiosyncratic characteristics that may have set one phratry apart from the others after the fashion of the far better documented deme associations. But there is one area relevant to the concerns of this study on which we are significantly, if only minimally, informed—the spatial distribution of the phratries over the expanse of Attica.[27]

At once the phrase "spatial distribution" calls to mind some of the ambiguities and uncertainties that bedeviled our examination of the phylai in chapter 5. There we wrestled with the problem of how to define and, once defined, to identify the "seat" of the tripartite regional principle units of the Kleisthenic organization. Various competing indicators of such a "seat" came into play, especially the known or presumed original places of the display of phyle inscriptions, the locations of the shrines of the eponyms of the phylai, and the places at which the memberships met to pass decrees and conduct other associational business. Fortunately in the case of the phylai, it turned out that these competing indicators were in substantial agreement with one another, but even so by no means could one assume such consistency in advance of the analysis. If, with this caution in mind, we turn to the case of the phratries, we at once find that, unlike the phylai with their nearly uniform concentration of functions in the vicinity of the Akropolis and Agora, the various kinds of evidence for their location strongly tends to associate them with ancient settlements, with those settlements in nearly every case turning out to coincide with an established nucleated center of a Kleisthenic deme. (The major exceptions link the phratry association with the Agora or Akropolis, neutral areas that belonged to no particular deme—a point of significance to which I shall presently return). So, by way of launching our investigation of the spatial distribution of the phratries, let us begin by setting out the evidence *by deme* in the following table.[28]

---

25. See Lambert 1993, pp. 18–19.

26. See Lambert 1993, pp. 19–20. For an attempt to show that *IG* II² 2344 indicates that the phratry whose members it allegedly catalog numbered only twenty, see Flower 1985, pp. 232–235. For an opposing interpretation, see Hedrick 1989, pp. 127–133.

27. The territorial character of the phratry has long been recognized. See, for example, the remarks of Hignett 1952, p. 57. What is at issue here is the specific configuration of the phratry's regional distribution and orientation. Recent work includes the brief gathering of some of the evidence by Lambert at 1993, p. 12, note 42, with the maps at pp. 352–353 as well as the full treatment of the record for regional affinities by Hedrick 1991. But because my reconstruction differs from those of previous scholars, Hedrick's in particular, it has proved necessary to rehearse some of that record once again.

28. No such tabulation exists in the literature and, since my argument will depend upon the geograph-

Deme	Phratry	Notes
1. Aigilia?	phratry? Pyrrhakidai	epigraphic evidence[29]
2. Alopeke?	name?	demotics[30]
3. Anaphlystos?	name?	demotics[31]
4. Aphidna	Titakidai and Thyrgonidai	literary evidence[32]
5. Boutadai	name?	literary evidence[33]
6. Dekeleia	Demotionidai/Dekeleieis	findspots/center[34]
7. Erikeia?	Medontidai	findspot[35]
8. Kephale	Achniadai	findspot/shrine[36]
Kephale	phratry? Medontidai	findspot[37]
9. Kephisia	phratry? Elasidai	shrine[38]
Kephisia?	name?	findspot/*phratrion*[39]

---

ical location of the demes in question within Attica (as well as of certain of their properties), I take the liberty of supplying one here. For the detailed references, with discussion (with not all of which I agree by any means), I reference the catalog *by phratry* of Hedrick (Hedrick 1991, with his numbers) and that of Lambert *by document* (Lambert 1993, with his T numbers from the appendix on phratry documents).

29. Lambert 1993, p. 368, on T 33, adduces two round monuments dated ca. 400 from Delos bearing the inscriptions reading, in one instance, Τριτοπάτωρ / Πυρρακιδῶν / Αἰγιλιῶν. He cites P. Roussel's view, *BCH* 53 (1929) 178, that the final word refers to the deme Aigilia. Lambert queries "were all the Pyrrhakidai members of this deme"? Perhaps the word was meant to identify the deme center alone, without implying thereby that all members of the phratry (?) were *demotai* of that deme. For the Pyrrhakidai as *genos*, see Bourriot 1976, pp. 1161–1171.

30. The identity of the deme rests on Humphreys's analysis of a list of names, *IG* II² 2345, in combination with its findspot (see Humphreys 1990, passim). On the identification of the list as a phratry, see Lambert 1993, pp. 82–84 (where the question is left unsettled) and on the deme affiliations, pp. 369–370, on T 35 (where Humphreys's view that all persons whose demotics are not given are from Alopeke is called into question).

31. The provenience of *IG* II² 2723, the marker of a *prasis epi lusei* (to, among others, various *phrateres*), is not securely known (the stone was reported to the original editor to have come from the Agora). Of the creditors, a single individual is affiliated with Leukonoion; two others whose names identify groups of *phrateres*, with Anaphlystos. See Hedrick 17 and Lambert T 21. Anaphlystos is securely located in deep southeast Attica. But Traill assigns Leukonoion to city IV Leontis and locates the deme at Peristeri northwest of the city under Aigaleos (Traill 1986, p. 130, with map at end), while acknowledging (note 22) the evidence for a placement in southern Attica (nearer to Anaphlystos). See also Lambert 1993, p. 283, on T 2.

32. See Hedrick 10 and Lambert T 15. For the postclassical demes going by these names, see Traill 1975, pp. 88 and 122, with the comment of Parker 1996, p. 325.

33. See Hedrick 19, citing Aischines 2.147 and other sources.

34. *IG* II² 1237 (Lambert T 3) and 1242 (Lambert T 4). See Hedrick 3.

35. *IG* II² 1233 (Lambert T 9), found at Kypseli. See Hedrick 9.D.

36. Findspots at Keratea: *IG* II² 2621 (Lambert T 1) and 4974 (Lambert T 2). The latter marks the *hieron*. See Hedrick 1.

37. Findspot, at Keratea, of *IG* I² 872 (Lambert T 8). The word [h?]ιερόν signifies not a shrine but a dedication. For the possibility that the Medontidai may not be a phratry, see Lambert's discussion. See Hedrick 9.C.

38. *IG* II² 2602 (Lambert T 29), found at Kephisia, is the marker of a *temenos* of Apollo. See Hedrick 5. Parker 1996, p. 322, regards the status of the group, whether phartry or genos, as indeterminable.

39. The inscription *IG* II² 1240 (Lambert T 20), found in Rangabe's garden in Kephisia, could of course have come from anywhere. But if the demotic Χο[λ] in line 2 is referred to the deme Cholargos, situated by Traill to the north of the city, an original provenience somewhere in the area becomes a possibility. See Hedrick 6.

10. Melite?	Therrikleidai	findspot/shrine[40]
11. Myrrhinous	Dyaleis	findspot/property[41]
12. Paiania (Lower?)	name?	findspots/demotics[42]
13. Perithoidai? (Phlya?)	phratry? Philieis	literary evidence[43]
14. Skambonidai	individual phratry?	altar in situ[44]
15. Thymaitadai	Thymaitis	name/shrines?[45]
16. site at Kato Charvati	name?	findspot/*phratrion*[46]
17. unknown provenience	name?	*oikia* ("house")[47]

At once it is clear from the notes in the right-hand column that there are multiple indications on the basis of which an investigator might decide that a given phratry was "located" in this or that deme. Not all these indications, obviously, carry equal

40. My tentative assignment to Melite rests on the fact that *IG* I³ 243, reconstructed from fragments found in the Agora, includes among other elements, according to Meritt's interpretation, a decree of this deme on face D, while face B of the same inscription was found by Meritt, followed by Hedrick (1983, p. 301 with Hedrick 7), to preserve a mention of "the Therrikleion" (lines 30–31), i.e., the shrine of the Therrikleidai. Tending somewhat against the assignment is the provenience in the Agora of the more recent inscription assigned to the Therrikleidai by Hedrick 1983 (restoring τοῖς Θερρικ]/λείδαις at lines 9–10, but with admission of a difficulty with syllabic division at p. 301). (The findspot of *IG* II² 4973, a marker of the shrine of Apollo Patroios of the same phratry, however, is not recorded.) Hedrick 1983, p. 301, concludes that the fact that both the new inscription and the fragments of *IG* I³ 243 were found at various locations in the Agora suggests that the phratry "had some connection with this part [viz., the southeast corner] of the Agora." I continue to attribute greater significance to the presence of a decree of the deme Melite. Of the hundred or so preserved decrees of demes, *not one* can be shown to have been erected in the Agora or indeed at any location outside the deme center itself.

41. *IG* II² 1241 (Lambert 5), a lease from Menenda, ancient Myrrhinous, mentions land, a house, and vines, but no shrine. See Hedrick 4.

42. *SEG* 3.121 (Lambert T 17), of unknown original provenience, was once stored in the museum at Liopesi; this fact, in combination with the probable deme affiliations of the honorands, supports the assignment to Paiania. The inscription has been reexamined by Hedrick 1989, pp. 133–135. *IG* II² 2344 (Lambert T 18), a list of *phrateres* found near the site of the deme, is thought by some to name only Paianieis (see Hedrick 1989, pp. 127–133, with pp. 131–132 for speculation that all the *phrateres* listed belonged to the deme of Paiania). See also Hedrick 12. In the former inscription, the reference to "the temple" (lines 6–7, partly restored) and to Zeus Phratrios and Athena Phratria (lines 7–8, partly restored), the recipients of the honorand's endowment, need suggest nothing about any shrine in the deme itself. Likewise, the heading of the list, "Of Zeus Phratrios and of Athena Phratria" (line 1), may well refer to a national cult in the urban center rather than to a cult (or shrine) in the deme.

43. For the lexicographical evidence, Harpokration s.v. Κοιρωνίδαι, see Hedrick 11 and Lambert T 32. For the possible association of the phratry with the similarly named deme Phlya, see Lambert 1993, p. 368.

44. No specific phratry is named on the inscribed altar *Hesperia* 7 (1938) 615–619 (Lambert T 22). For Hedrick's interpretation, not followed here, see Hedrick 14 and Hedrick 1991, pp. 256–259.

45. The two texts attesting the phratry, *IG* I² 886 (Lambert T 13) and *Hesperia* Supplement 9, p. 11, no. 21 (Lambert T 14), were discovered in the region of the Pnyx and Areopagos, respectively, but neither in situ. The first certainly, the second according to a plausible restoration, marked the location of a *hieron*. Despite this evidence for an urban seat, Hedrick and others associate the phratry with the nearly homonymous deme. Thus Hedrick 1988c, p. 85: "Because of its name, it is likely that this phratry originally had some ties with the deme of Thymaitadai. I would suggest that the phratry's original, traditional seat was located in the neighborhood of its homonymous deme." See also Hedrick 8.

46. *IG* II² 1239, found at Kato Charvati southwest of Pentelikon, records honors, with the preserved text including instructions to erect the stone stele "in front of the *phratrion*" (lines 26–27, restored). No mention is made of a shrine. See Lambert T 19 and Hedrick 13.

47. *IG* II² 2622 (Lambert T 23). See Hedrick III.1.

weight, although none, under the right circumstances, is entirely without significance. Take demotics. If, as in the case of the phratry? associated with Alopeke? (item 2 above), a roster of known or probable members reveals a heavy concentration of deme affiliations in or around a particular area, that is patently strong evidence for a regional orientation. At the same time, however, there is always the possibility that a given phratry predates the determination of the original deme affiliations by Kleisthenes in 508/7; in that case, if a *phrater* had, prior to that time, relocated to a distant deme and so acquired an affiliation with that deme, then obviously his demotic, should it show up in one of our documents, would have no value for determining the "location" of the phratry. Similarly, with properties. Land or structures held corporately by the association (see item 11) are ipso facto evidence of some sort of regional concentration. But an individual's ownership of property in this or that place may reflect the vagaries of gift, sale, dowry, or inheritance and so tell us nothing about the phratry to which he belongs. Far more reliable, by contrast, is any evidence for the findspots of an association's stone inscriptions. A stele is unlikely to have been placed far from the place of the composition of the text that it bears and—the real point—from a place at which it would be most accessible to the main body of the association's membership.[48] Likewise, another reliable indicator is the situation of a phratric shrine or other cultic structure. Any such facility, particularly if dedicated to the eponym, can only have been a focus of associational activity of a significant kind and on a regular, calendric basis.

But even a shrine, contrary to the impression left by some recent scholarship, may not tell the whole story. After all, just what is a *temenos* (of the Elasidai in item 9) or *hieron* (in items 8, 10, and 15), architecturally speaking? It may very well be nothing more substantial than an altar surrounded by a low wall or other barrier. That meant that, if the phratry were to hold a meeting (as they evidently frequently did, in order to pass decrees[49]), either that meeting would take place out of doors in the "shrine" or, if an indoor location were sought, somewhere else. Here resides, I suggest, the reason for the occurrence in two documents of a *phratrion* (items 9 and 16) and in one other of an *oikia* (item 17). To these may be added from *IG* I² 871, a marker found at the entrance to the Akropolis, a (restored) attestation within the urban center of an *agora* of the Medontidai.[50] Surely significantly, in none of the sources for these latter installations is there a trace of a shrine or other cultic facility. A strong presumption arises that shrine and "phratry house" may, if both were to be possessed by a single phratry (a plausible but unexampled possibility), have been situated in two different places, perhaps quite distantly removed places. An ancient phratry might have maintained a shrine at an ancestral rural center, while at some later time have undertaken the construction of a phratry house in the city of Athens. Another, more fundamental ramification is that, again in contrast with one

---

48. That these inscriptions, rather than serving a merely archival purpose, were actually meant to be *read* is strongly suggested by the addition of clauses in honorary decrees advertising the association's intention to similarly award any future benefactors. See, for an example from a decree of an unidentified phratry, *IG* II² 1239 (T 19), lines 22–24

49. E.g., *IG* II² 1237 (T 3), 1241 (T 5), 1242 (T 4), and others.

50. For the restoration [ἀγο]/ρᾶς, see Hiller's apparatus, where he compares a more surely restored marker of an *agora*, *IG* II² 896.

of the guiding assumptions of recent scholarship, if the "seat" is identified with the phratry house and if this house does not coincide with a shrine, we are no longer compelled to continue to view these associations as primarily cultic organizations, even though (of course) like all known *koinoniai* of the classical period, no phratry would be entirely without a religious dimension.

Even with the recognition of these difficulties, the tabulation of phratries by deme set out above may be taken as fairly secure.[51] And what does this evidence tell us? A glance at Traill's most recent map of Attica at once reveals that the preponderance of the demes with which an individual phratry is specifically associated—in fact, on my count, twelve of the fifteen—lay far from the urban center (clockwise from north to south to west): Thyrgonidai and Titakidai in Aphidna (inland IX Aiantis), Demotionidai/Dekeleieis in Dekeleia (inland VIII Hippothontis), possible phratry Elasidai or phratry subgroup in Kephisia (inland I Erechtheis), unnamed phratry at an unidentified site at Kato Charvati south of Pentelikon (item 16),[52] unnamed phratry in Upper or Lower Paiania (inland III Pandionis), Dyaleis in Myrrhinous (coast III Pandionis), Medontidai in Kephale (coast V Akamantis), Achniadai in Kephale (coast V Akamantis), unnamed *phrateres* in Anaphlystos (coast X Antiochis), possible phratry Pyrrhakidai in Aigilia (inland X Antiochis), Thymaitis in Thymaitadai (city VIII Hippothontis), and a possible phratry at Perithoidai (city VI Oineis). According to the regional categorization of the demes adopted in chapter 3, two of the above demes (Perithoidai[53] and Thymaitadai) march with the inner zone, five (Aigilia?, Kephisia, Kydantidai, Lower or Upper Paiania, plus the unidentified site at Kato Charvati) with the middle zone, the remaining five (Anaphlystos, Aphidna, Dekeleia, Kephale, and Myrrhinous) with the outer zone. But however grouped, it is clear that none of these twelve demes (or sites) represented in any practical topographical sense a "city" or "urban" community.[54]

Over against this evidence may now be set the minority of indications of an urban setting of the phratries. Some of these testimonies, it will now be seen, can either be explained away or be given quite different interpretations. The *horos*, just mentioned, marking the [χό]/ρας or [ἀγο]/ᾶς of the Medontidai discovered at the entrance of the Akropolis, *IG* I² 871—even conceding the correctness of either sug-

---

51. I have omitted as excessively problematic *IG* I³ 247, found at Spata, which may at once refer to a phratry (of uncertain name) and a deme (possibly Kydantidai, so Jameson and Lewis). See Lambert T 36 for the references. For the suggested association of the phratry Philieis with the similarly named deme Phlya, see Lambert 1993 on T 32, p. 368. For the earlier deme assignment of Kato Charvati (no. 16), see the following note.

52. This site (at Kato Charvati) was originally tentatively identified by Traill as Kydantidai (Traill 1975, p. 41), but more recently he has moved Kydantidai to Mendeli (Traill 1986, p. 128), leaving Kato Charvati without a deme assignment.

53. If the deme affiliation of no. 13 proved in fact to be Phlya (inland VII Kekropis), this item would move from the inner to the middle zone.

54. At this point it is appropriate to note that Hedrick has collected the evidence for "phratries with unallocated shrines but attested demotics" (1991, pp. 248–249). The demes indicated by that record reveal the following distribution by my three regions: inner zone: 7, middle zone: 4, outer zone: 3, demes of unknown location: 3. The tendency of the sources, particularly of the literary sources that constitute the basis of much of Hedrick's information, to deal with the urban population (and urban-based individuals) may account for this unexpected (and conflicting) pattern of distribution.

gested restoration—may pertain only to an urban segment of this multicentered phratry.[55] The evidence of another document of the Medontidai, a fragmentary decree found at a location northeast of the city, Kypseli, tentatively associated by Traill[56] with the deme Erikeia, *IG* II² 1233, is compromised by the fact that the preserved crowns enclose as codecreeing parties the Boule, Demos, and possibly the *hippeis*. That is, the provenience of the stone may reflect the physical situation of the central government as much as that of any regional center of the phratry. A *horos* "of property sold for redemption," *IG* II² 2723, of unknown provenience but reportedly coming from near the Agora, records among the creditors two groups of *phrateres*, but obviously the marker's (and the property's) location would tell us nothing necessarily about any center of the (unnamed) phratry(ies).[57] True, an honorary decree found in the excavations on the Akropolis, *IG* II² 1238, appears to be in the name of "the *phrateres*" (see lines 1, 3–4, 12), but in the absence of a preserved name, it cannot be excluded that more than one phratry was involved, with the neutral ground of the Akropolis selected for the display of their joint decree.[58] Similarly, the "*horos* of the house of the *phrateres*," *IG* II² 2622, of unknown provenience, may not have been the property of a single, specific association. And even if it was, the structure may, as already suggested, have been intended to accommodate the urban residents of a phratry actually centered in some distant rural location— the members, say, corresponding to the *phrateres* of Demotionidai/Dekeleieis accustomed to "frequent" the *asty* on a habitual basis.[59]

With the removal of these doubtful or ambivalent cases, a total of three bona fide cases of demes of the immediate urban region with an associated individual phratry remain: Alopeke (name of phratry [?] unknown), Boutadai (name of phratry unknown), and Melite (phratry Therrikleidai). With reference to our table of the spatial distribution of the phatries, I will shortly eliminate Skambonidai, the intramural deme within the probable boundaries of which the altar of Zeus Phratrios and Athena Phratria was found (item 14), by arguing that the monument has nothing to do with any individual phratry. The phratry Thymaitis, assigned above to the deme Thymaitadai (item 15), certainly possessed a *hieron* in the city, but there is no reason to suppose that the ancestral rural center ceased to remain active. Now, to the remaining three must be added a fourth candidate attested by a monument not as yet associated with any particular deme: the marker from the Agora excavations signifying the (sanctuary) of Kephisos of the phratry Gleontis, *Hesperia* 17 (1948) 35, no. 18. This case demands special attention.

The problematic matter is the peculiar character of the phratry's name. The rare

---

55. For the evidence, see Lambert 1993, pp. 319–320.

56. Traill 1986, p. 127.

57. For the provenience, see Lambert T 21 and Hedrick 1991, p. 247 note 30.

58. There is also merit to Lambert's suggestion that the honoring party wished to bestow "some sort of national prominence" on the honorand and to this end displayed the inscribed stone on the Akropolis (1993, on T 16, p. 337). Again, the actual center of the phratry(ies), if such existed, would remain unknown. Against the supposition of the involvement of more than one phratry, however, is the restoration of lines 3–4 as τὸ κοιν]ὸν [τῶν] φρατ[έ]/[ρων (Hedrick 1988a, p. 113). All else being equal, a single *koinon* should indicate a single association. But the restoration is far from assured.

59. *IG* II² 1237 (Lambert T 3), face B, lines 63–64.

adjectival formation Gleontis has naturally encouraged speculation that it is connected in some way with the Old Attic phyle Geleontes. As of Lambert's publication in 1993, however, the nature of the connection remained obscure.[60] Nonetheless, I wish to argue that the record of public organization outside Athens suggests a new and, in the present context, attractive approach. My *Public Organization* documents no fewer than four cities where one or more of the four inherited original phylai of the Old Attic division (or its two "Ionian" supplements) have been demoted to a lower tier of organization: Thasos (*patra*),[61] Samos (*chiliastys*),[62] Ephesos (*chiliastys*),[63] and Kolophon (*chiliastys*, by restoration).[64] Probably such demotion was normal practice whenever an existing inherited organization was replaced or was overlain by a new one. Significantly, too, in three of the four cases (the exception, undoubtedly by accident of preservation, is Samos) the units in question include Geleontes. If this name, evidently meaning something like "the resplendent ones," had something to do with nobility,[65] it may have possessed a certain advantage in survival value over other obsolescent units of organization. And in fact, the phyle Geleontes *did* survive at Athens, for it (with its constituent trittys Leukotainioi) figure as the recipient of sacrificial perquisites according to a fragment of the Athenian state calendar dating to the period immediately following Nikomachos's revision in 403/2.[66] But if the Geleontes were to survive at Athens after 508/7 as a phyle alongside the fully empowered new phylai created by Kleisthenes, it would have to be as a phyle with greatly diminished administrative, and probably exclusively ceremonial, status. Hence their sole recorded classical appearance in the sacrificial calendar, and the equally isolated function of the *phylobasileis* (along with the King Archon) as judges of lifeless objects and animals reported by the *Constitution of the Athenians* (57.4). But demotion to the status of phratry would perhaps have been perceived as opening up new opportunities for the all-but-defunct phyle association.

I propose that this was exactly what happened. Linguistically, the name Gleontis reveals the syncopation of the inherited form of the name already in evidence in the above-mentioned calendar of sacrifices.[67] The adjectival form of the name Γλεοντίς (sc. φρατρία) may be a compressed way of expressing the idea "the

---

60. Lambert 1993, on T 6, p. 308: "It is possible that there was, or had been, some organizational link between the two groups, though we can scarcely guess what."

61. Thasos 5§1, pp. 184–186. Of the four Old Attic phylai, only Geleontes appears among the attested *patrai*.

62. Samos 5§13, pp. 195–202. The phyle in question is Oinopes, one of the two so-called "Ionic" additions to the original "Old Attic" quartet.

63. Ephesos 7§11, pp. 311–315. Of the six Old Attic-Ionic phylai, a total of five (all except Hopletes, surely by accident of preservation) appear among the *chiliastyes* of the Greek organizations or its Imperial additions.

64. Kolophon 7§10, pp. 310–311. With the preserved name of Geleontes, I restore the term *chiliastys* in a single clause of enrollment from a citizenship decree.

65. Hesychios, s.v., glosses γελεῖν as λάμπειν, "to shine." For references to the secondary literature, see Rhodes 1981, pp. 67–68.

66. *Hesperia* 4 (1935) 5–32, nos. 1 and 2, at p. 21, no. 2, lines 35–37.

67. See Threatte, *GAI,* vol. 1, p. 398, s.v., for the "likely" syncopation.

Gleontid phratry descending from the Geleontes (phyle)."[68] If the phratry itself had been named "Geleontes," its simultaneous coexistence with the phyle of the same name would be unsettling, but the adjectival expression would help diminish any such duplication of name. Just possibly, too, such a demotion may in some unrecoverable way lie behind the otherwise unexampled identification of the "three parts" of the Old Attic phyle as *phratriai* (and *trittyes*) preserved in fragment 3 of the *Constitution of the Athenians*.[69]

But the crucial point to be made here is that, if the phratry Gleontis is in fact a relic of an Old Attic phyle, and if that phyle, as its name would seem to suggest, was in some substantial way associated with the "nobility," then the urban center, and in particular the civic hub of the Agora, will have been a natural locus of its activity. That the leisured elite maintained residences in the *asty* is well known. But we also saw in chapter 5 that all available evidence indicates that the "seats" of the Kleisthenic phylai were likewise established in the civic center. Might the same have been true of their predecessors, the Geleontes included?

With this point established, we may now approach the remainder of the positive record for the location of phratries in the urban center (which I have deliberately withheld up to this point). That evidence is of a quite different character from anything acknowledged so far. Three of the so-called phratry documents are in question: *Hesperia* 7 [1938] 612–625 (= T 22; Hedrick 14), *Hesperia* 6 [1937] 104–107 (= T 24; Hedrick 15), and *IG* II² 4975 (= T 25; Hedrick 16), the first discovered in situ in the northern part of the city (and possibly to be associated with the deme Skambonidai), the others in the Agora. The first two are altars, the third a marker (actually an inscribed broken marble roof tile), all in the name of Zeus Phratrios and Athena (Phratria). Crucially, none of the texts, though seemingly intact in each case, bears any trace of an association with a *specific* phratry. Accordingly, the excavator of T 22 and T 24, Homer Thompson, assigned the altar T 24 to a small building in the Agora, which he identified as a central Athenian sanctuary of Zeus Phratrios and Athena Phratria.[70] Hedrick, however, has argued for the association of these monuments with individual phratries, a conclusion reflected, incidentally, in his consistent use of the phrase "anonymous phratry" in connection with them.[71] But the case is a difficult one to make, above all because each of the texts presents no obvious opening for the restoration of a proper phratry name. If an altar or

68. Already, Hedrick 1988c, pp. 83–84, has suggested that the adjectival form was designed to distinguish the phratry from another group (namely, the phyle) with a similar name. (This point was prompted by a similar speculation regarding the relation of the phratry Thymaitis to the deme Thymaitadai.) But he does not consider, as here, the possibility that the phratry literally descended from the phyle through the process that I have labeled "demotion."

69. *AthPol*, OCT, ed. Kenyon, 1920, under the *fragmenta deperditae partis primae*. The possibility that the phratry was a subgroup of the phyle is taken up by Lambert 1993, pp. 14–17.

70. *Hesperia* 6 (1937) 77–115: 104–107, on the "Sanctuary of Apollo Patroos."

71. Hedrick 1991, pp. 255–256 ("the physical appearance of the phratry shrine"), pp. 256–259 ("an Athenian phratry shrine") and, for a straightforward statement of his position, p. 260: "At least two, possibly three anonymous phratries kept shrines in the vicinity of the Agora..." (he then goes on to mention the three texts, his numbers 14, 15, and 16). The use of the formulation "anonymous phratry" occurs throughout in conformity with this interpretation.

marker did in fact pertain to a single phratry and not to the others, surely that fact would have to have been signified (precisely as it was, on Hedrick's own representation, in the case of the Therrikleion).[72]

Due attention must also be given to the powerfully significant negative evidence. No monument or text linked with the Athenian phratries but demonstrably (as in the above cases) *not* to be associated with any particular phratry has been found in, or is to be associated with, the extra-urban regions of Attica. Furthermore, the failure of the epigraphic record to attest more named phratries in and around the Agora and Akropolis must be taken as significant. After all, as we saw in chapter 5, the presence of as many as seven of the ten Kleisthenic phylai, which evidently *were* based in the urban center, is documented by inscriptions from the Akropolis or Agora. Therefore, it is difficult to understand why, if larger numbers of individual phratries were in fact based in the *asty*, or even if rural-based phratries had established branch centers in the city, so few traces of such presence have come to light.

The apparent evidence for the presence within the walls (but not outside them) of "generic" monuments seemingly accessible to all *phrateres* and for the general absence in urbanized areas (but proliferation in relatively distant country locations) of orthodox individual phratry associations[73] cannot be due to accident of preservation or discovery. Furthermore, the "generic" installations were situated not only within the walls but on neutral ground—the Agora in particular—as well, ground that belonged to no one particular deme. It is difficult to escape the inference that the state, as in so many other areas, is here actively involved in the promotion of associational life in the public interest. By providing these "generic" altars, we may conjecture, the central government could make participation in phratry life accessible to urban-dwelling *phrateres* cut off from their ancestral (and hereditary) phratric centers. Thereby, too, at a deeper level, the government could sustain the health of associational life in Athens by ensuring the survival of rural phratry organizations that stood to fall into decline should their members migrate to town and thereafter cease to participate in phratric functions altogether.

Therefore, if a phratry may be said to have possessed a center (and it may), that center was just as likely, indeed far more likely, to be outside the city than within it. Naturally, this is not to say that *phrateres* based in the country did not establish contacts with the urban center. The Medontidai, above and beyond the natural and expected gradual dispersal of members over time, were multicentered, as indicated by various sites of properties, concentrations of residences of members, or inscribed stone inscriptions.[74] But it is the famous decrees of the Demotionidai, *IG* II² 1237,

72. Thus at 1991, p. 255, Hedrick draws attention to the fact that these shrines, the putative installations of individual phratries, went by the "generic" terms *hieron* or *hiera*, while the sanctuary of the Therrikleidai, also situated (according to his theory, Hedrick 1983, p. 301) in the Agora, he acknowledges, was called the Therrikleion, but attempts no explanation for these mutually contradictory facts.

73. For my arguments, contra Hedrick, against the assignment of the Therrikleion to the Agora, and in favor of the (admittedly, intramural) deme Melite, see the list of phratries by deme above, item 10 with note 40.

74. See Lambert 1993, pp. 319–320, for the evidence.

Figure 7.1. Decrees of the Demotionidai, *IG* II² 1237. [Left] face A (neg. 83/579). [Right] face B (neg. 83/582). Photographs courtesy of the German Archaeological Institute, Athens.

pictured in Figure 7.1, that alone shed specific light upon town-and-country relations among the members of a given single phratry.

These three decrees, as their provenience and internal content unmistakably indicate, were passed by the assembled membership in or near the center of the distant deme of Dekeleia. At five points in the texts, provision is made for the posting or publication of the texts produced by the decrees: (1) At the close of the decree of Hierokles, the priest is called upon to give notice on a whitened board "at whatever place the Dekeleieis frequent in the city" (face B, lines 61–64). (2) Immediately following, the priest is ordered to inscribe the decree and the priestly dues on a stone stele before the altar at Dekeleia (face B, lines 64–68). (3) At the close of Menexenos's brief motion, the phratriarch is instructed to write up the text and to display it "at whatever place the Dekeleieis frequent" (face B, lines 121–123). (4) Meanwhile, the priest is to post the same text on a whitened board in the shrine of

Leto situated in the deme of Dekeleia[75] (face B, lines 123–125). (5) Finally, where the text fails at the end of the decree of Menexenos, just enough is preserved to indicate an injunction to erect a stone stele, but no clue as to that stele's intended location is preserved (face B, lines 125–126).

The pattern is obvious. Although the meeting had taken place in the deme center at Dekeleia, where one stone stele (2), very possibly another (5), and a whitened board (4) were to be erected, provision has been made for the nonparticipant *phrateres* domiciled or otherwise present in the city (1, cf. 3). But if, as Hedrick has suggested by way of explaining the evidence for a supposed splitting of a phratry between a rural home base and the urban center, town-dwelling *phrateres* on a regular basis returned to their ancestral phratry centers in the country,[76] why were the postings in the *asty* necessary? They would not have been necessary. The postings in the *asty* could only have been carried out in the expectation that the urban members of the phratry would *not* visit the phratry center in the foreseeable future. After all, the stone inscription(s) erected in Dekeleia were obviously intended to stand for quite some time—certainly long enough to accommodate even infrequent visits by town-dwelling *demotai*. This is my main reason for thinking that while, indubitably, there is evidence of phratric presence in the city and while, again indubitably, rural phratry associations enjoyed established ties with the *asty*, the phratries under the democracy remained disproportionately extra-urban organizations more or less cut off from any urban satellite colonies of members. The urban-rural ties existed, but they did not involve the movement of people. This conclusion, furthermore, comports well with the other, positive signs that this phratry in particular strove to maintain its regional integrity by limiting certain of its functions to those *phrateres* actually resident in the home deme of Dekeleia.[77] Evidently, the association felt it necessary by such measures to counteract the centripetal forces of urbanization that stood to threaten the survival of many such locally based rural organizations.

Such a reconstruction seems far preferable to that offered by Hedrick. For Hedrick, the installations in the Agora belonged, as we have seen, to individual phratries, yet not only to urban phratries but as well to phratries *with a rural home base*. Naturally, there can be no a priori objection to the notion of an urban phratry, provided that the case can be made for identification with a specific association. However, Hedrick's case for dual rural and urban shrines or other installations belonging to a single named phratry, with the possible exception of Thymaitis, is groundless. Two dimensions of these supposed town-and-country relations are in question. On the one hand, his shrines of the "anonymous phratries" served, he suggests, as ad hoc meeting places for the town-dwelling members of individual rural phratries.[78] At the same time, on the other, his relocated urban *phrateres* must make a "trek" back to the ancestral shrine in the country for initiations, sacrifices, and

75. For Leto at Dekeleia, see *IG* II² 1242 (with Lambert T 4 for the text), at line 2.

76. Hedrick 1991, p. 267.

77. E.g., *IG* II² 1237 (Lambert T 3), lines face A 52–54, on the conducting of *meia* and *koreia* to the altar "at Dekeleia;" and 1242 (T 4), lines 4–5, a fragmentary reference to (as restored) "five men residing at Dekeleia."

78. Hedrick 1991, p. 261.

business.[79] Both contentions, as we have seen, are difficult to square with the evident implications of the various phratry documents here under review.

Documents apart, Hedrick's reconstruction also suffers from a distinct lack of economy of explanation. It is far simpler to imagine that urban and rural *phrateres* generally remained in the close vicinity of their residences except under the most compelling circumstances and that, as I have argued, relocated rural *phrateres* resident in town were served by pan-phratric installations situated on neutral ground within the walls.[80] City residents did not have to undergo, as Hedrick would have it, a time-consuming and exhausting journey to a distant rural ancestral phratric center merely in order to celebrate a festival that could just as well be held, and (I believe) was in fact held, in town. Such a strategy made all the more sense since, as commentators are agreed in recognizing, individual phratries, and particularly their cult practices, were linked by strong commonalities. The city version of the Apatouria, to mention the "central event in the phratry calendar," may have differed in no substantial way from its simultaneous celebration in the many ancestral phratry centers situated throughout extramural Attica. Thereby deracinated *phrateres* could, without leaving town, keep alive a sense of belonging to the ancestral brotherhood based at the rural deme center of their demotic affiliation.[81]

The Relations of the Phratries and the Demes

It appears, then, that *phrateres* domiciled in or near the ancestral phratry center and their co-*phrateres* now relocated in the town may have been in the main generally isolated from one another. This should not be taken to mean that urbanites never ventured to the extra-urban center of the phratry; it only means that, overall or on the average, the Apatouria or other phratry function was not sufficient to bring about a general exodus of extra-urban *demotai* out of the town and into the countryside. Since all citizens belonged to a phratry, and since significant numbers of rural dwellers had permanently relocated to the town, bringing their hereditary phratric affiliations with them, there can be no question but that large numbers of Athenians were potentially involved. Note, too, negatively, that these town-dwelling rural *phrateres*, if the example of the Demotionidai is representative, had not split off from the parent organization and formed a new, urban phratry, not even one bearing the same name as the ancestral phratry in Dekeleia. They remained, in other words, deracinated members of an association in whose functions they were de facto un-

---

79. Hedrick 1991, pp. 261–262.

80. My theory superficially resembles Hedrick's suggestion (1991, pp. 261–262) that members of rural phratries now relocated in the city made use of their "urban shrines." To the credit of this reconstruction, the model would apply in the case of the Thymaitid phratry, if correctly assigned to a base in the deme Thymaitadai, since this phratry did indeed possess a shrine in the *asty* (see table above, no. 15). But Hedrick, as I have indicated, does not acknowledge the existence of "generic" urban phratric installations.

81. See, on the festival, Lambert 1993, pp. 152–161, with p. 143 for the quotation. For the likelihood of separate ceremonies in individual phratries coinciding with the festival staged in the city, see p. 154. For the celebration of the festival by all phratries on the same day, see p. 157 with note 80.

able to participate. Again, it is easier to suppose that these urban dwellers repaired to a shrine or altar of Zeus Phratrios and Athena Phratria in or around the Agora.

This conclusion, however, leaves unsettled the predicament of rural Athenians still resident in the ancestral phratric center. In particular, since every known such center is associated with a settlement, and since nearly every such settlement has turned out to be the known or probable village nucleus of a Kleisthenic deme, we would like to know just what relationship, if any, a phratry enjoyed with respect to the deme of its seat. *Some* sort of exchange seems a priori likely, given the close proximity within the village of the two citizen organizations. But positive hints to this effect are not forthcoming. None of the phratry documents reveals any aware-ness of a deme association, and in none of the documents of the demes associated with a phratry center is there a trace of the presence of the phratry. What makes this situation all the more surprising is that, if Hedrick's plausible arguments are (as I think they must be) accepted, there was a very substantial overlap in membership between a phratry and its host deme association.[82] Yet it appears that the two orga-nizations were, at least so far as we are informed by the official records of their business, totally insulated from one another.

Even so, the linkage between phratry and deme does not appear to have been the product of chance. For one thing, pace Hedrick,[83] the presence of a phratry in a deme seems to be significantly correlated with the deme's size. The bouleutic quotas afford the telltale clues. The average quota of all 139 demes (counting Acharnai, as throughout this discussion, as one deme) is 3.59 councillors. Now, according to the tabulation of phratries by deme in the previous section, individual phratries can be associated with some confidence with about fifteen different known specific demes (including the unassigned site at Kato Charvati). The average quota of the fourteen named demes is 6.77 councillors, indicating that, on the average, demes with a known phratry are almost twice as large as the average deme. But the global aver-age masks an even more pronounced pattern. Of the fourteen demes with a phratry, nine, or 64 percent, have a bouleutic quota of six or more: Aigilia (6), Alopeke (10), Anaphylstos (10), Aphidna (16), Kephale (9), Kephisia (6), Melite (7), Myrrhinous (6), and (Lower) Paiania (11). Yet of the 139 demes, only 29, or 21 percent, have quotas of six or more. While it is true, to be sure, that in a few cases a phratry is found associated with a small deme (Boutadai [1], Erikeia? [1], Perithoidai? [3], and Thymaitadai [2]), these demes represent a decided minority. Still more significantly, these few small demes tend to be situated near the urban center, that is, it may be suggested, near a large concentration of population from which they might draw ac-tive members. That is, under normal circumstances so small a deme as Boutadai could not sustain a phratry on its own. By contrast, nearly all the more distant demes with an associated phratry are of considerably more substantial size.[84]

82. For the probable membership of *phrateres* in the local deme of Paiania, see Hedrick 1989, pp. 126–135, esp. 131–132; and, in general, Hedrick 1991, pp. 262–263.

83. Hedrick 1991, p. 260: "There is no pattern to the locations of the various shrines, nor to their as-sociations with the various demes. In some cases phratries are associated with very large demes . . . in others they are linked to very small demes."

84. Only distant Dekeleia, with a quota of 4, fails to conform to this pattern, but even its quota is not particularly small.

Now, it might be objected that part of the explanation for this pattern is to be found in the fact that the size of a deme is positively correlated with the production, survival, or discovery of stone inscriptions. But the available data do not sustain such an objection. In comparison with the average quota of all demes of 3.59 councillors, the average quota of the 48 demes from which at least one epigraphic document is preserved is 5.42.[85] So, admittedly, there is a definite tendency for larger demes to be better represented in the epigraphic record. But the tendency does not fully account for the higher average of the 14 named demes with a phratry, 6.77 councillors, nor, and equally to the point under discussion here, for the fact that none of the smaller demes concerned were situated in far-flung rural locations.

Did phratries, then, tend to be founded or, once founded, survive, in especially large demes? A possible model that springs to mind would be that of a phratry center situated in a largish deme and serving the members of immediately surrounding smaller communities. To judge from the deme affiliations of its members preserved in an inscribed list of names, this may well have been the case with a phratry (?) of unknown identification almost certainly based at Alopeke (bouleutic quota 10).[86] But this simple model is complicated by the evidence, first, for a single phratry linked with two or more demes[87] and, second, for two phratries in a single deme.[88] Nonetheless, the pattern of linkage of phratries with rather larger demes remains, despite the overall untidiness of the distribution of the phratries over the demes. The explanation may simply be that these organizations needed a substantial number of active members in order to sustain themselves. It is undoubtedly true, too, that a larger deme was more likely to supply those few wealthy individuals or families on which, so far as we are informed, all classical Athenian associations depended for material support. So, over time, if tiny demes ever enjoyed the exclusive presence of a phratry, these phratries may well have withered on the vine.

At all events, in the case of those demes that were blessed with a phratry center, it is not hard to imagine why the two organizations have so little to do with each other. The deme, at least the extra-urban deme, as we saw in chapter 3, was an introverted community, and with that introversion went hand-in-hand a pronounced particularity. Deme membership did not encourage contact, or exchange, or a sense of camaraderie, with other demes; the demes beyond the boundaries of one's own community belonged, in a very real sense, to an alien world. But phratries were linked by commonalities. Unlike the demes with their particularistic traditions, phratries shared common cults, and celebrated the Apatouria, if not together at a single site in the city as once believed, then at their own shrines, though still per-

85. For the full roster of deme documents on which this calculation is based, see chapter 3, note 54. The quotas used throughout are those of Traill 1986, pp. 125–140. (Where alternative quotas are given by Traill, I have always taken the first number of the two.)

86. *IG* II² 2345, with the interpretation of Humphreys 1990, passim. The other demes represented are: Agryle (six names), Paiania (two), Euonymon (one), Kedoi (one), Kephisia (one). On her analysis (p. 243), only the members from Kephisia and Paiania are "outliers."

87. Viz., Medontidai: see, again, Lambert 1993, pp. 319–320, and the list of phratries by deme above, items 7 and 8.

88. Viz., Kephale. See the list of phratries by deme above, item 8.

haps on a single day.[89] Phratry membership meant ipso facto linkage with the members of other phratries. And outside the confines of Athens, phratry membership joined the Athenian *phrater* to his Ionian brethren in other cities. The difference between the two associations was simply the difference between introversion and particularity and extroversion and commonality. Phratry and deme simply served the individual Athenian in two very different, though mutually complementary, ways.

Subdivisions of the Phratry and Social Differentiation

But there was another difference as well that set the phratry apart from its host deme. For, despite the universalizing similarities that allowed one phratry, considered as a whole, to resemble all other phratries, each individual phratry seems to have embodied considerable internal diversity in the form of its own subdivisions of its membership. This was a feature most certainly not shared by the deme, for, notwithstanding the survival of documentation far more plentiful than that of the phratries, only a single deme subdivision (or seeming subdivision) is known by name—the *triakas* of the (in other respects) highly atypical "super" deme Peiraieus.[90] Whatever differences of class or status actually obtained within deme society, those differences were not carried over into the formal structuring of the association. But a phratry was, we shall see, anything but a monolithic body.

The evidence in question is that concerning what Lambert has loosely (and with full awareness of its limitations in the present context) labeled the "subgroups" of the phratry.[91] Sadly, as Lambert himself would be the first to admit, the matter of the relation of the phratry to its seeming "subgroups" is not as straightforward as this term might suggest. His characterization of the situation as "the untidy picture of phratry subgroups"[92] pretty well sums things up. No wholly contained segmental component of the phratry can be identified with certainty. Indeed, in a case or two the association that in one context appears to be a component of the phratry in another context seems to be wholly independent of the larger organization. At the same time, of the five associations or types of association suggested below as candidates for subgroup status, in no instance can the members of the selfsame putative subgroup association be assigned to more than one phratry. So, it appears that we are dealing with associations smaller than the phratry that sometimes were more or less segmentally related to a single phratry but not always or necessarily wholly contained by it. The subgroups identified by Lambert (with my supplementary comment) are as follows.

Genos.[93] Not every citizen belonged to a *genos*,[94] a fact that automatically identifies the "clan" as a more restrictive unit than the phratry. Its subgroup status is suggested

89. See above, note 81.

90. *IG* II² 1214 (ca. 300–250), lines 17–19.

91. Lambert 1993, ch. 2, "Phratries and Their Subgroups," pp. 59–94.

92. Lambert 1993, p. 93.

93. For discussion, see Lambert 1993, pp. 18, 46–49, and 59–74 (with pp. 64–74 devoted to analysis of the seven pieces of evidence regarding the interrelation of phratry and *genos*). Lambert concludes (p. 74): "To summarize, gene were normally subgroups of phratries."

94. Lambert 1993, p. 18.

(though not absolutely proven) by one phratry's attested sharing of its altar with a *genos*[95] and by the law preserved by an Atthidographer calling for the admission of *gennetai* by the *phrateres*.[96] No *genos* is associated with more than one phratry. Nor is a single phratry known to have contained more than one *genos*. A unique one-to-one segmental relation between phratry and *genos*, therefore, is a real possibility.

Orgeones. Two items of evidence bearing on the relation of these cultic associations to the phratries were isolated by Lambert, of which one, the Philochoros fragment regarding the necessity incumbent upon *phrateres* to admit *orgeones* as well as *gennetai* as members, suggests, though it does not require, a segmental relation.[97] This conclusion, if Lambert's arguments are accepted, is confirmed by the epigraphic evidence of the year 367/6 that seems to show that the *orgeones* of one Aischines of Melite were members of the phratry Medontidai.[98] But if some *orgeones* were contained by a phratry, the two associations must have remained functionally independent of one another, for neither group's documents ever mention or otherwise reveal the existence of the other organization.

Oikos. The term has but a single appearance in the Athenian phratric documents, in the form of the House of the Dekeleieis in the decrees of the Demotionidai.[99] Lambert argued that the House was "a phratry subgroup" showing "some similarity to the genos."[100] The reference, then, would be to a "house" in its human dimension of the "household." Hedrick, however, adducing parallel evidence from both within and outside Athens, made a case for associating the term with the physical building in which the "corporation" met and not with "any putative familial relationships amongst its members."[101] But this promising approach is carried too far, for I cannot endorse Hedrick's ensuing argument that, since the name Dekeleieis is securely attested only as the demotic (i.e., of the deme Dekeleia), and since the incontrovertible deme of Melite seems to have possessed an *oikos*, the House of the Dekeleieis must be a name for "the assembly of demesmen."[102] For one thing, the only term attested for the meeting place (or the meeting itself) of a deme is *agora*.[103] For another, Hedrick's own sources for the House of the deme Melite identify the structure as (1) a house rented out as a hotel and (2) a house used as a rehearsal place by tragedians[104]—neither of which approximates an assembly of the members of the

95. Aischines, 2.147.

96. Philochoros, *FGrH* 328 F 35a.

97. *FGrH* 328 F 35a, with Lambert 1993, p. 75. The other text, the claim of Isaios's speaker that he was enrolled in his father's *orgeones* as well as in his phratry and deme (2.14, cf. 15–17 and 44–45), does not speak to the present point.

98. Lambert 1993, p. 77, with commentary at pp. 314–320 on *Hesperia* 10 (1941) 14–27, no. 1 (= Lambert T 10), lines 16–35.

99. *IG* II² 1237 (Lambert T 3), face A, lines 32–33, 42.

100. Lambert 1993, p. 78.

101. Hedrick 1990, pp. 47–52, with p. 51 for the quotations.

102. Hedrick 1990, pp. 51–52: "I am strongly disposed to regard the οἶκος Δεκελειῶν as a name for the assembly of demesmen."

103. See Whitehead 1986, pp. 86–87.

104. Hedrick 1990, pp. 50–51, citing Zenobios II, 27 (hotel) and Hesychios, s.v. Μελιτέων οἶκος (rehearsal place).

community owning such a structure. Absolutely nothing recommends this peculiar interpretation.

External evidence suggests an alternative approach. Among the more than 200 known public organizations, there is a single state where the House plays a quasi-public administrative role. From Karthaia on Keos, citizenship decrees of the third century call for the enrollment of honorands in the phyle and *oikos* of their choice.[105] This public acknowledgment of the House naturally suggests an affinity with the other associations of the private sphere known to have played such a role in city-state administration—notably the *genos* and phratry, to select the two candidates appropriate to the case of Athens.[106] While this is not the place to open up once again the question of the interrelation of the Demotionidai and the Dekeleieis (which remains a question, even if it is granted that only the demesmen of Dekeleia are otherwise known to have gone by the latter name), it is still worth observing that if, as many have argued, the Demotionidai are a phratry, the House of the Dekeleieis might then be, following an old line of interpretation, an association of some kind based on descent. Viewed this way, the House would conform to the parameters implicit in the observations above regarding the relation of phratry and genos. And since an association based on descent might well possess a physical house, the results of Hedrick's discussion of the possible referents of *oikos* could continue to stand.

The Horos IG *II² 2723*. This marker for a *prasis epi lusei* records among the creditors the "*phrateres* with Eratostratos of Anaphlystos" and the "*phrateres* with Nikon of Anaphlystos" (lines 5–8, 11–13). A similar marker of 319/8, *PAAH* (1992) [1995] 36–38, no. 7 (*SEG* 43.56), records as creditors "*phrateres* with Antiphilos." I concur with Lambert that such formulations denote, not whole phratries, but rather groups within a single phratry. The shared demotic (in the case of *IG* II² 2723) suggests that a single phratry is in question; and the absence of a specific term such as *genos* or *oikos,* that these groupings were not identical with any of the others here under review.[107] Yet for these very reasons, and particularly in view of the manifestly ad hoc and temporary nature of the transaction, it is doubtful that partnerships of this kind were sufficiently structured or enduring to qualify as "associations" in the same sense or to the same degree as more formally titled organizations.[108]

Thiasos. This term enjoyed a wide currency over a lengthy period of Athenian history and reflected a variety of associational structures. Among other uses, the Greek word *thiasos* could denote a band of revelers, a cultic association, or, less specifi-

---

105. Jones 1987, Karthaia ch. 5, sec. 16, p. 206, citing *IG* XII 5(1), nos. 528, 540, 541, and 5(2) no. 1061, with supplements.

106. See Jones 1987: *genos:* Erythrai (ch. 7, sec. 8), Kolophon (ch. 7, sec. 10), Pygela (ch. 7, sec. 12), and Samos (ch. 5, sec. 13); phratry: Andros (ch. 5, sec. 17), Argos (ch. 2, sec. 7), Athens (ch. 1, sec. 1), Corinth (ch. 2, sec. 2), Delos (ch. 5, sec. 20), Ilion (ch. 7, sec. 2), cf. Miletos (ch. 7, sec. 16), Tenos (ch. 5, sec. 18), and Theisoa (ch. 3, sec. 4).

107. Lambert 1993, pp. 78–79.

108. For a more enduring mode of organization, compare the formula οἱ περί + nomen. The phenomenon is discussed by Dow 1960, pp. 395–406.

cally, any kind of group or association.[109] To our immediate question, that of the relation of the *thiasos* in any of its permutations to the phratry, there is no simple answer. Lambert's lengthy analysis of the record illustrates well his remark about the "untidy picture" left by the phratric subgroups.[110] There is but one instance of a *thiasos* figuring as a subgroup within a phratry, *IG* II² 1237, where *thiasoi* appear as subgroups of the House of Dekeleieis (but not, significantly, directly as subgroups of the presumable phratry Demotionidai).[111] Elsewhere, the relation of the *thiasos* to any phratry, segmental or otherwise, dependent or otherwise, is not secure.[112] Nonetheless, despite the murky and confusing indications, Lambert finds that the term was probably pressed into service whenever, in more recent Classical times, *phrateres* wished to form a subgroup of the organization that did not coincide with the old institutions *genê* and *orgeones*. They were, he concludes, "created either by the phratry as a whole for its own purposes or by groups of citizens associated in their capacity as phrateres."[113]

The existence of such a multitude of subdivisions, whether wholly contained or not, within the phratry brings us back to the question of the difference between a phratry and a deme. That is an important question. Once the regional, deme-based character of the phratry is established, with the prevailing pattern being a one-to-one correspondence between a phratry and a (generally somewhat larger than usual) deme, it is natural to wonder why these two associations coexisted in close spatial proximity with each other for as long as they evidently did. Their memberships are the same —citizens and only citizens. Both their orientations are essentially communal, for we saw at the beginning of this chapter that there is scant evidence for positing a public deme concerned with state business in contrast with a private phratry. True, as noted, demes tended to be introverted and particularistic, phratries pan-Athenian, even pan-Ionian, in their outlook, but this alone cannot account for the survival of two large redundant organizations within the confines of a single and (by modern standards) small village community.

It is in the subgroups of the phratry that the answer is to be found. The deme, or rather the constitutional deme, as we saw in chapters 2, 3, and 4, was a highly exclusive body, generally intolerant of penetration by outsiders. The same could be said with justice of the phratry if viewed as a single, unified organization. Only the legitimate sons of existing *phrateres* could aspire to membership in the association. Female connections of a male member were not, according to scholarly consensus, bona fide members of the association of the phratry in their own right, their participation being confined to special circumstances regarding inheritance or a wedding ceremony involving a member.[114] No non-Athenian is ever recorded as a *phrater;*

---

109. Lambert 1993, pp. 81–82, with note 103 [p. 81] for modern secondary sources and note 104 [pp. 81–82] for a selection of primary sources on the use of the term.

110. Lambert 1993, pp. 81–93.

111. *IG* II² 1237 (Lambert T 3), decree of Nikodemos, face B, lines 68–113, passim.

112. Lambert 1993, p. 90.

113. Lambert 1993, pp. 92–93 (with p. 93 for the quotation).

114. The evidence is collected and acutely reviewed by Lambert 1993, pp. 178–188. For a general assessment, see pp. 36–37; for the possibility of female participation in phratry admission during the Apatouria, pp. 161–162.

and in fact the text preserved by Krateros in his book of decrees specifically made liable to prosecution a person of foreign descent acting as a phratry member.[115] The exclusion appears to have been absolute.

Furthermore, the phratry was, like the deme, an inclusive organization to the extent that it brought together (so far as we are informed) without discrimination Athenian citizens of all backgrounds, statuses, and ages. Given what we know about the stratification and class-consciousness of Athenians even under the egalitarian democracy, such an undifferentiated assemblage of people would stand little chance of developing a cohesive associational life. The differences separating the various socioeconomic components would simply have overpowered any tendency to flock together on the flimsy basis of shared phratry membership.

Both problems were addressed through the creation and eventual flourishing of the phratric subgroups. To take first the latter phenomenon, the lack of differentiation among the citizen membership, it has long been recognized that certain of our subgroups bore the stamp of a distinctive class affiliation. For example, in the following chapter we shall allude to the evidence favoring the traditional identification of the *genos* as a predominantly aristocratic organization.[116] The *orgeones* were once thought to be an underprivileged set (in contrast with the aristocratic *gennetai*), whose rights to phratry membership were expressly protected by the law preserved by Philochoros, but were more recently typified by Andrewes as a "fairly small and relatively obscure upper class minority."[117] The House of the Dekeleieis, to the extent that it may, as above, be compared to an aristocratic *genos*-like group based on descent, would also naturally be associated with such a minority. It goes without saying that creditors named, with express reference to a shared phratry membership, on a "mortgage" stone, were men of substance. Except for the last-mentioned item, all these characterizations have been much debated and questioned, but it is unlikely that all of them are misguided. Unlike the deme which played host to the phratry's shrine or other center, the phratry itself does seem to have allowed for internal differentiation in response to the socioeconomic diversity of citizen membership. Through these subgroups opportunities were opened up for *phrateres* to interact on a more realistic basis reflecting shared background and interests.

The problems created by the exclusion of noncitizens from the organization were also addressed through the network of subgroups. What I wish to suggest is that the segmental relation of subgroup to phratry was a loose one and that in fact admission to or participation in the activities of the subgroup was tolerated in the cases of persons who would not qualify as bona fide *phrateres*. Two such groups of concerned outsiders can be identified, female connections of the *phrateres* and non-Athenians.

Females are listed among the *thiasotai* conferring crowns in an inscription dated "post med. s. IV," *IG* II² 2347, lines 31–33 (Hesychia, Erotis, and Aitherion). (For two possible similar such lists, see nos. 2348 [fin. s. IV], line 7 [Soteris], and

---

115. *FGrH* 342 F 4.

116. Contra Lambert 1993, pp. 61–62.

117. Andrewes 1961, p. 2. At p. 15, the *orgeones* are characterized as "small groups of relatively wealthy non-gennetai who had achieved their independence by Solon's time."

2349 [s. IV], line 1 [Myrtaso], though in neither case is the term *thiasos* or *thiasotai* preserved.) True, no. 2347 was discovered on Salamis, which, as an Athenian possession rather than Attic territory *stricto sensu,* did not fall within the deme system; nor is any reference made to a phratry or *phrateres.* Still, the identification of the names as *thiasotai* is assured (lines 1, 5, and 6) and on its basis we may postulate indirect female membership in the phratry through the medium of its component, or affiliated, "segment." The hypothesis, furthermore, might help explain an otherwise anomalous passage in the fragmentary decree from Rangabé's garden in Kephisia, *IG* II² 1240 (fin. s. IV?; T 20). The preserved injunction to erect the stele "before (?) the *phratrion*" (lines 10–11) appears to identify a phratry as the decreeing party. But what about the nearly contextless mention of a γυνή in line 5—the only reference to a female in a surviving phratry decree? On the basis of the manifest cultic content of the decree, Lambert suggested that the decree is that of a phratric subgroup rather than of a whole phratry, but it is obvious that the corpus of phratry documents is not nearly large enough to permit such an argument from silence.[118] Nonetheless, the possibility of female membership in phratric *thiasoi* remains attractive.

An analogous argument might be thought possible in the case of noncitizen foreigners. Non-Athenian *thiasotai* are honored by their associations in several decrees of the early third century: *IG* II² 1263 (300/299; honorand from Olynthos, proposer from Salamis); 1271 (298/7; honorand from Herakleia [on Latmos?]); and 1273 (281/0; first decree, honorand from Troizen, proposer from Herakleia; second decree, honorand from Herakleia.) But the argument is complicated again, first, by the absence of any expressed connection with phratries, secondly, by the fact that all three stones come from Peiraieus. The provenences, in combination with the post-Macedonian dates, immediately invite comparison with the *orgeones,* for which the simultaneous coexistence of citizen and noncitizen groups in Hellenistic times is beyond question, the latter invariably based in the port town.[119] Nonetheless, even the mere sharing of the term *thiasos* (and *thiasotai*) with noncitizens may have been a point of some significance. An Athenian *terminus technicus* as old as Solon and, as the Demotionid decrees show, indubitably linked with bona fide citizen *phrateres,* must have had the ring of in-group respectability. Perhaps the participation by these foreign *thiasotai* was only vicarious, but it would be a form of participation even so.

Thus, I am suggesting, the phratry, if only through its putative subgroups, served to promote integration, at least institutionally, in the case of females, within its own local community and, just possibly, in the case of non-Athenians, with persons situated outside that community. The Athenian democracy had been founded upon the principle of minority rule by an elite of adult male citizens to the exclusion of both their own family members and of all those others born outside the citizen

118. Lambert 1993, p. 347: "Inscriptions of whole phratries the main subject of which is the regulation of religious cult are rare, possibly nonexistent.... It is possible, therefore, that this is the decree of a phratry subgroup."

119. In the case of no. 1273, the parallelism is further strengthened by the association's cultivation of the Mother of the Gods (lines 23–24, 31–32), a nontraditional divinity also worshipped by certain Peiraiean *orgeones.* For a similarly skeptical view on the identification of these *thiasoi* as phratric subgroups, see Lambert 1993, p. 90, with note 142. The *orgeones* will be discussed in chapter 8.

caste. It may be that it was through the phratry's associational structure that, in marked contrast to the system of exclusive constitutional demes, the people of Athens were eventually able in part to mount their response.

That "response to democracy" was, it has turned out, multifaceted. Scholars have long acknowledged, albeit with minor variations, the (indirect) gatekeeper role played by the phratry through its admission procedures. To this extent, the state had, paralleling its use of the family for various instrumental purposes in the interests of the wider Athenian community, appropriated a function of a "private" association for essentially "public" purposes. But our principal goal in this chapter has been to ferret out those less obvious features of the phratry's territorial distribution and internal organization that, it now seems, appear to have served to compensate for some of the democracy's most glaring inadequacies—its urban bias, its enforced egalitarian leveling, and its uncompromising exclusivity. The "response," we have found, took the forms, respectively, of thriving rural phratry organizations, of internal differentiation among the membership, and of the integration of outsiders through their entry into the phratry's nominal subgroups.

We may turn to the record of the remaining "private" associations, associations that differed from the phratry, however, in their more "voluntary" and largely self-selected memberships. Were their design and structure in any sense fashioned in response to the character of the Athenian government?

EIGHT

"Clubs," Schools, Regional, and Cultic Associations

Classical Athenian "Voluntary" Associations

By way of introducing the present chapter, it will be useful to review briefly what we have accomplished up to this point. In chapters 2 through 6, sustained attention was given to the relevant aspects of the internally organized segments of the Kleisthenic public organization: the demes (chapters 2, 3, and 4) and the phylai (chapters 5 and 6). The immediately preceding chapter was devoted to an association independent of that public organization, the phratry, but one rendered quasi-public in function by the bestowal upon it of an indirect "gatekeeper" role with respect to admission to the Athenian citizen body. What deme, phyle, and phratry have in common is the fact that all were statutorily open to all male members of the citizen class upon the demonstration of attainment of the requisite age and of legitimate descent from Athenian parents as defined by Perikles' law of 451/0. Now, with the present chapter, our study takes a new turn. Our concern will be with those groups to which access was not (so far as we know) granted statutorily to all Athenians (or to any other segment of the population). Furthermore, there is no reason to suppose that the decision to join such a group was anything but entirely voluntary, whereas, in the cases of the internally organized segments of the public organization and of the phratry, the fact that participation in the democracy depended upon such membership left the prospective enrollee with hardly any choice. These two sets of groups fall well toward the opposite ends of the voluntary versus nonvoluntary scale.

Before we embark upon the examination of the "voluntary" associations, however, it will be well to comment briefly, for the sake of completeness of coverage, upon those groups which, on the basis of their inclusion in Solon's law or in Aristotle's epitomizing account of *koinoniai*, might potentially belong to such a discussion but which cannot, for want of sufficient evidence, be adequately characterized. Let us begin with the law, in accordance with the emended version analyzed in chapter 1.[1] The deme and phratry have, as noted, already been selectively treated with respect to their relation to the central government and their place within the whole of Attica. While the *orgeones* will receive full attention here under the rubric of "cultic association," no further consideration will be given to the similarly cultic *thiasotai* beyond their brief acknowledgment as components of the phratry in chapter 7. As stated in the Introduction and justified in appendix 1, the independent *thiasos* association appears to be a phenomenon of the post-Macedonian era. My restoration of the *naukraria* has reference to the pre-Kleisthenic public organization still in existence in 594; but since no associational role is ascribed to the naukrary under the democracy, it will not figure in the following account. Solon's *syssitoi* are also unexampled in the records of classical Athens, save for the possibility of the referral of the term to either ephebes or soldiers encamped in various locales of Attica, including the demes (the latter having been examined in this connection in chapters 2 and 4).[2] Associations of "pirates" and "traders," as observed in appendix 2, if they ever existed, have left no traces whatever in our classical records. The text's mention of *homotaphoi*, reasonably glossed as "burial societies," is paralleled in the classical period only by a fleeting phrase in a brief of Demosthenes.[3] Such societies might prove, if we knew something about them, to be excellent candidates for voluntary associations, but, even if so, we could only guess, given their likely small size and probable age profile, what sort of "response" they might have mounted to the democratic central government.

As for Aristotle, the need for agreement with the roster of particular associations treated in our study is less pressing for the simple reason that the great bulk of the material he provides comes from writings that are not expressly described as— nor are in fact likely to have been—descriptions of his own city of residence. The one work that is so described, the *Constitution of the Athenians*, besides predictably acknowledging the existence of the units of the pre-Kleisthenic and Kleisthenic public organizations (though, significantly, only rarely in their associational mode), otherwise adds only the baffling remark that Kleisthenes allowed each Athenian to keep his *genê* and phratries (21.6). The phratry is the subject of chapter 7, while the units once thought to be "clans" will, in the present chapter, be found (following recent opinion) likely to have been something quite different. This leaves the reference in the synchronic half of the *Constitution* to suits concerning *eranoi* and *koina*.[4] But the former term may well refer to "friendly loan" arrangements lacking any associational status[5] and the latter of course could embrace associations of any de-

1. For the text of the law, see appendix 2.
2. For further speculations regarding the use of the term by Solon, see appendix 2.
3. 57 *Against Euboulides*, §67. For the interpretation, see appendix 2.
4. *AthPol* 52.2: ἔτι δ᾽ . . . ἐρανικαὶ καὶ κοινωνικαὶ (sc. δίκαι).
5. On this point, see my discussion of the *eranistai* in appendix 1.

scription. All remaining Aristotelian comment on associations derives from more general theoretical works, especially the *Eudemian* and *Nichomachean Ethics* and the *Politics*. A listing of those groups relevant or potentially relevant to the Athenian case was assembled in the Introduction. Some of those associations will be taken up now, but only obviously on the strength of evidence specifically linking them to democratic Athens.

The subject matter of the present chapter is the *hetairiai* (glossed in the title as "clubs"), the philosophical schools, the regional associations, and two major cultic associations, the *genê* and *orgeones*. Again, the basis for inclusion is in each case incontrovertible contemporary documentation from the classical city. That, in the majority of cases, the association in question is absent from one or both of our programmatic texts—Solon's law and the epitomizing passage from Aristotle's *Nichomachean Ethics*—means that a necessary component of the discussion of the associations affected will be an attempt to explain or understand such silence.

"Clubs"

By the use of the English term "clubs" I quite deliberately allude to the title of George Miller Calhoun's University of Chicago dissertation, published in 1913, *Athenian Clubs in Politics and Litigation*[6] The Greek term around which Calhoun's clubs tend to converge is *hetairia*, an ostensibly nondescript neutral word meaning something like association or company, with its byforms *hetairoi* (the collective plural) and the neuter *hetairikon*. But Calhoun's net is cast widely enough to embrace as well the *synomosia* (collective plural *synomotai*), a conspiratorial group of persons bound by oath; "friends" (*philoi, epitedeioi*), where such terms illusively or euphemistically denote political unions in particular; and groups denoted by the idiomatic use of a phrase constructed around the name of a leader in the form οἱ περί τινα ἑταῖροι or the like. To these more or less explicitly labeled groups, finally, he added evidence for a great many combinations or instances of cooperative activity not associated with any of this, or with any comparable, terminology.[7]

Were these groups studied by Calhoun, whether going under the name of *hetairia*, or one of the other formulations, or no title at all, "associations"?

The failure of any such term to occur in Solon's law on associations, in either its transmitted or emended form, is an initial, negative indication. Silence in this instance may be significant, for Herodotos (5.71.1) mentions the existence of an *hetairia* led by Cylon at the time of his abortive coup d'état a full generation earlier than the traditional date of Solon's archonship. If the *hetairia* was a genuine association at the time of the lawgiver's legislation, then, why does it not appear in the

---

6. Calhoun 1913. For more recent work, see Sartori 1957, passim; Connor 1971, pp. 25–29; and Welwei 1992, pp. 481–500. Given the nature of my investigation, however, it is convenient to continue to cite the well-articulated and richly documented older study.

7. For discussion of these terms, with references, see Calhoun 1913, pp. 4–9. For several passages in the dissertation where significant claims are made regarding the clubs in the absence of a specific ascription, see my discussion below, with note 21.

law's roster? The possibility always exists of course that Herodotos has unwittingly retrojected a term familiar in his own day but which, if the truth were known, might prove quite anachronistic in a late seventh-century setting. So, such groups may in Cylon's time have gone by another name, but, even if they did, the fact remains that none of the terms preserved in the law bears even a remote resemblance to such an organization. Accordingly, the possibility should be considered that "clubs" of such kind did not exist at this early date. After all, the accounts of the factional strife that rocked Athens in the generation following Solon attest regional loyalties, dynastic marriage between the leading families, and a personal bodyguard strong enough to seize the Akropolis[8]—a profile of the organization of political activity sufficient, I think, to account for the recorded developments of the period, including the tumultuous course of the Peisistratid tyranny. The emergence at historical Athens of the *hetairia* as a noteworthy presence may, therefore, have come at a later time. The inference is encouraged by the fact that it was apparently not until later that the Athenian state expressly outlawed any *hetairikon* formed for the purpose of overthrowing the democracy.[9] Obviously, had the *hetairia* been included in a (hypothetical) original uncorrupted text of Solon's law, the later statute would have been redundant, since the Solonian text explicitly prohibits associational activity in conflict with "written statutes of the People."

Aristotle's epitomizing account of *koinoniai* (*Eth. Nic.* 8.9.4–6: 1160a), exploited in chapter 1 as a source for the definition of "association," does not specifically mention the *hetairia* by name either. But, apart from the fact that Aristotle's examples of particular *koinoniai* are not represented by the author as a complete, definitive list, the references in the passage to "social intercourse" as a purpose of certain associations and the mention of "gatherings" and of "leisure activities (combined) with pleasure" all, as we shall see, have obvious pertinence to groups of this kind. Nor is it irrelevant that the *hetairia* receives occasional mention in the *Politics*.[10] If, as I have urged, Aristotle's conception of the *koinonia* (once those of the Gemeinschaft-style familial or purely affective type are eliminated) may be taken as defining what we mean by an ancient Athenian "association," there can be no doubt, as the next paragraph will show, that Calhoun's "clubs" satisfy that definition.

With these preliminaries in mind, we are at liberty to briefly characterize the "club" with reference to Calhoun's full rehearsal of the historical record. Nominally, *hetairiai* were private societies of upper-class males devoted to purely social activity among themselves. That the "clubs" were a preponderantly or exclusively urban phenomenon cannot be demonstrated, but the emphasis upon elegant "dinner-party" gatherings tends to point in that direction. The normal setting of such activity was the private home, a circumstance that points to a relatively restricted and intimate circle of members.[11] The inference is supported by several bits of evidence,

8. *AthPol* 13 (between Solon and Peisistratos), 14–19 (the tyranny of Peisistratos). Rhodes's commentary provides a full exposition of the parallel sources (1981, pp. 179–240).

9. Hyperides 4, *In Defense of Euxenippos* (ca. 330–324), 8. Although the phrase referring to the overthrow of the democracy follows the preceding citation of simple meetings, it is stylistically legitimate, I believe, to understand it with the mention of the formation of an *hetairikon* as well.

10. E.g., 5.5.5 (1305b), 5.5.9 (1306a), 5.9.2 (1313b).

11. Calhoun 1913, pp. 26–27, with note 5 [p. 26] and p. 29, with note 4.

collected and interpreted by Connor, that suggest "relatively small numbers."[12] Literary texts, furthermore, identify commonality of age and of (aristocratic) social status as the underlying basis of membership in a club.[13] Such shared fundamental points of likeness help account for the extraordinary cohesion and solidarity of these groups evidenced by the copious record of their political activity. But political though they may have become, the preserved names of one well-defined class, the so-called hell-fire clubs, reveal a basically religious or cultic orientation: Autolekythoi,[14] Ithyphalloi,[15] Kakodaimonistai,[16] and Triballoi.[17] As Parker explains, these were inversions of legitimate and expressly cultic organizations commonly named after the day of the month on which the membership celebrated the rites of the patron divinity, to wit, Noumeniastai, Tetradistai, Hebdomaistai, Dekadistai, and Eikadeis.[18] Admittedly, the "hell-fire" names contain elements of obscenity, parody, or other evidence of the antisocial or iconoclastic mind-set of their (sometimes demonstrably) youthful members, but at least two of the four are ostensibly ritualistic in some respect.[19] Such an orientation would have provided an appropriate context, even if the group's purpose was parody or sacrilege, for the oaths and rites of initiation abundantly attested by our sources.[20] Again, the striving for, and maintenance of, group solidarity is very much in evidence.

It will be recalled that the passage from the *Ethics,* above and beyond its specific

12. Connor 1971, pp. 27–28, with note 43 [p. 28], citing the archaeological report of O. Broneer at *Hesperia* 7 (1938) 228–243. Connor astutely conjectures (op. cit., pp. 25–26, 27–28) that the fourteen persons [so identified by analysis of their "hands"] responsible for the inscribing of the cache of 191 ostraka all but one bearing the name of Themistokles found in a single deposit in the Agora "was perhaps not far from the average size of a *hetaireia*" (p. 28). Although we do not know how these 14 "hands" came together, the obvious political complexion of their activity favors, at the very minimum, its ascription to an oligarchical, and perhaps aristocratic, organization of some kind.

13. Calhoun 1913, pp. 27–29. Herodotos, 5.71.1, with regard to Cylon's *hetaireia*, adds that it consisted of "men of the same age."

14. Demosthenes 54, *Against Konon*, 14, 16 . For the meaning, see Carey and Reid 1985, p. 87; they find that the term expresses "contempt for social norms."

15. Demosthenes 54, *Against Konon*, 14, 16, cf. 17. According to Carey and Reid (1985, pp. 86–87), the word has "connotations of sexual potency, of unrestrained language and behavior, and perhaps verbal abuse."

16. Lysias, speech LXXIII, no. 53.2 Thalheim. The members of this club made a point of dining on days of ill-omen. On the "desire to shock" evident here (as with the Ithyphalloi), see Carey and Reid 1985, pp. 86–87.

17. Demosthenes 54, *Against Konon*, 39. See again the illuminating comment of Carey and Reid (1985, pp. 100–101): "properly a Thracian tribe, notorious in Athens from the fifth century for their barbarous tongue and character . . . ; also used as a term for idlers and wastrels." For an earlier discussion, with pertinent testimonia on the tribe, see the excursus at Sandys 1886, pp. 229–230.

18. Parker 1996, pp. 335–337. Compare, with Parker, the discussion of O. Murray in Murray 1990, pp. 149–161.

19. The name Ithyphalloi is associated with fertility ritual (Carey and Reid 1985, p. 86); and Kakodaimonistai are expressly concerned with (evil) spirits (cf. op. cit., pp. 86–87). As for the Autolekythoi, notwithstanding Carey and Reid's assertion that the *lekythoi* in question were oil flasks used for bathing (1985, p. 87), I see no a priori reason for excluding the well-known use of these vessels in connection with ministrations to the dead. But the fact remains that the abundant lexicographical material quoted by Sandys in his excursus on the word contains no trace of the funereal or other cultic usage (Sandys 1886, pp. 227–228).

20. Calhoun 1913, pp. 34–35 (oaths and pledges), 35–37 (initiations).

content, also afforded the basis for the construction in chapter 1 of a more fundamental definition of "association" based on four scales, with reference to which it is possible to measure or gauge the more important aspects of our *koinoniai*. Given the problematic status of the "clubs," it might be appropriate at this juncture to assess the *hetairia*, in the light of the above profile, with respect to these four dimensions of associational organization. Measured against the private versus public continuum, clubs were wholly private, with no discernible direct or indirect public roles to play. With respect to voluntary versus nonvoluntary orientation, the clubs were wholly voluntary. There is no reason to think such membership was required or even expected of men of aristocratic social class, qua aristocrat. Self-evidently, not every person of exalted pedigree was temperamentally inclined to the sorts of extracurricular activities, whether deviant and antisocial or political and hazardous, in which the clubs sometimes engaged. With regard to the urban street violence, the speaker of Demosthenes' *Against Konon,* in anticipation of his opponent's counterarguments, singled out youth and male gender, in combination with good breeding, as characteristic of the participants (54.14). Duration is an imponderable factor, but the formulations οἱ περί τινα κτλ. prompt the inference that in some cases the club did not survive its leader or, if it did, only with a new moniker and possibly new orientation.

But the crucial item for our study is the fourth, and final, scale measuring expressive versus instrumental orientation. Acknowledgment has been made of the well-documented social purposes and functioning of Calhoun's clubs. With these innocent "expressive" goals, it is customary to place in diametric, mutually exclusive opposition the equally well documented political activities of these very same associations. The record begins with Cylon's *hetairia* late in the seventh century and culminates with the overthrow of the democracy at the end of the fifth, an episode in which, according to Thucydides (8.54.4), conspiratorial societies played a crucial role. Nonetheless, though the facts cannot be gainsaid, this portrayal of an innocuous social group temporarily subverted to serve some external "instrumental" political end may perhaps be overdrawn. For one thing, as already hinted, the long narrative of litigious and political activity compiled by Calhoun and ascribed to the "clubs" appears to a significant degree to rest on quicksand. At several places in his account, claims of this kind are made in the complete absence of a mention of an *hetairia* or "club" of any description.[21] In actual fact, it may be that the organization in question (if, indeed, an organization of any description was involved) was less formal, not connected with social activities, and lacking the pretense of cultic interests. Another objection is that the antithesis between innocent socializing and subversive conspiratorial political machination may be a false one.[22] Given the predominately oligarchic ideological tendencies of the aristocratic elite, how likely is it that

21. E.g., Calhoun 1913, pp. 56 (with reference to *antidosis*: "There is no direct evidence that clubs were concerned in this case"), 63 (with reference to assassination: "There is no mention of clubs in these cases"), 75 (with reference to improper influencing of the jury: "There is no direct statement that clubs or cliques were concerned in the cases of bribery which have been studied"), and 93 (with reference to obtaining information regarding one's opponent's case: "While there are few specific allusions to this proceeding, . . .").

22. The characterization of the *hetairia* by Connor 1971, pp. 26–27, approaches such a polarization but stops short of the admitted caricature to which I am addressing my remarks.

these clubs were ever at any time or in any sense nonpolitical? Quite the contrary, a shared ideology may well have been a large part of the community of interest that had brought these men together in the first place. Viewed this way, the clubs are perhaps more reasonably characterized as embodying instrumental alongside expressive goals from the very beginning.[23]

To what extent could the clubs be said to be a "response to democracy"? Subversion of the central democratic government, or its threat, is the clearest possible example of such a response.[24] But such purposive political activity must be viewed from the perspective of its wider context. The *hetairia*, like the symposium and a host of other upper-class lifestyle traits, may be referred to the "defensive standard" of the aristocratic elite so convincingly described and explained by Walter Donlan.[25] To the extent that the aristocratic lifestyle in general was, as Donlan demonstrates, a response to an egalitarian ideology, so was the particular phenomenon of the aristocratic *hetairia* more specifically a "response" to a democratic government. After Athens lost the war, some aristocrats, as is well known, withdrew from Athenian public life.[26] But it is an equally valid observation that, from the very beginnings of the democracy, aristocrats, or at least some of them, had been in a permanent condition of emotional and ideological withdrawal. If the *demokratia* could not be fairly said to have created the clubs, at the very least it provided them with a powerful reason for their continuing existence.

Philosophical Schools

Until the early seventies, it could be maintained, on the basis of widely held opinion buttressed by the authority of the great Hellenist Ulrich von Wilamowitz-Moellendorff, that the philosophical schools were in fact, and were recognized by the Athenian state as, *thiasoi*. By the term *thiasos*, which, as we noted in chapter 7, enjoyed a rather wide range of specific meanings, Wilamowitz intended something like a religious brotherhood dedicated, in the present case, to the worship of the Muses. But the year 1972 saw the publication of John P. Lynch's *Aristotle's School*, a much needed study that, among other contributions, decisively exploded the Wilamowitzian theory.[27] It is merely the most elementary of Lynch's counterarguments

23. Not all agree, however, that the *hetairiai* were predominately, much less uniformly, oligarchical. See, for example, Connor 1971, p. 26 with note 40.

24. For the law prohibiting the formation of an *hetairikon* for the purpose of such subversive activity, see above, with note 9.

25. Donlan 1980. For the "defensive" standard, see p. xiii. For the association, see p. 168, where mention is made of "the aristocratic phenomenon of the drinking club (*hetairia*)."

26. For an estimation of the phenomenon from the perspective of a theme in Lysias's courtroom speeches, see Lateiner's treatment of "the man who does not meddle in politics" (Lateiner 1982, pp. 1–12, with an adumbration of the historical background at pp. 11–12).

27. Lynch 1972, pp. 108–127. At p. 127 he concludes: "There is no substantial evidence for believing with Wilamowitz and many after him that the Peripatos and other Athenian schools of higher learning were organized either internally or externally as *thiasoi* devoted to the cult of the Muses." Wilamowitz's views were set out in his study *Antigonos von Karystos*, to which was appended an excursus entitled "Die rechtliche Stellung der Philosophenschulen" at 1881, pp. 263–291. Among other studies antedating Lynch, much of the subject matter of my discussion is well treated by Wycherley 1961 and 1962.

that the Academy, Lyceum, and the others are never called *thiasoi* in the sources, their students never called *thiasotai*, the leader never called a *thiasarchon*. Rather, these institutions went by quite different terms, revealing no hint of a sacred orientation, such as *scholê* and *diatribê*.[28] Terminology apart, the schools, except for their undeniable maintenance of sanctuaries of the Muses,[29] emerge as essentially secular institutions devoted to the pursuit of purely secular ends. It is clear that the Wilamowitzian position mistakes the superficial sacral trappings characteristic of virtually all ancient Athenian organized groups for the focus or core of interest around which such groups were formed and sustained. The religious concerns of these organizations, as Lynch perceived, were only incidental to their dominating central doctrinal and educational purposes.

If it were still possible to regard the philosophical schools as *thiasoi* and their students as *thiasotai*, they would immediately qualify as associations since this particular *koinonia*, the *thiasotai*, as we saw in chapter 1, happens to occur in both the Solonian law and in Aristotle's programmatic passage in the *Nichomachean Ethics*. But it is not, as we have just seen, possible. Nonetheless, the case for their associational character can still be made, indeed it can be made with some assurance.

Why, to confront the first of two obvious and pressing questions, is neither a *scholê* nor *diatribê* (or other suitable term) included in Solon's roster of associations? The answer is simple. Even if any of the gymnasia in which three of the philosophers eventually settled had been standing in 594, none of the schools themselves is known to have been in existence earlier than the probable dates of the foundations of Isokrates' school around (perhaps shortly before) 390[30] and of Plato's Academy in or around 387.[31] Less easily explained is Aristotle's silence on the matter, especially since he himself was of course the founder and head of his own philosophical educational institution. The absence of an appropriate term in his summary statement about the *koinoniai* that comprise the *koinonia* of the *polis* might in fact be thought to be a fatal objection to the characterization of the schools as "associations." But all is not lost. At least twice in the *Ethics* Aristotle uses the verb corresponding to the noun *koinonia* of those participating in philosophical activity.[32] This assertion of the communal nature of the speculative process recalls Plato's similar insistence on *synousia*;[33] and at a later date Theophrastos, Aristotle's successor, is to use the phrase *hoi koinonountes* of the "community" of the Lyceum.[34] Plato's own

28. Lynch 1972, pp. 109–110.

29. For the *mouseia* in the Athenian philosophical schools, see Lynch 1972, pp. 113–116.

30. See Lynch 1972, p. 52 with note 25.

31. For the date, see Lynch 1972, p. 65. For a slightly later estimate "um 385," see *KlPauly* 1 (1964), s.v. "Akademeia," col. 211.

32. *Eth. Nic.* 9.1.7 (1164b): on the subject of remuneration for performance of services: "and so it seems [i.e., that payment should be made] also with regard to those who deliver instruction in philosophy (οὕτω δ᾽ ἔοικε καὶ τοῖς φιλοσοφίας κοινωνήσασιν)"; 9.12.2 (1172a): "whatever represents existence for a man or that for the sake of which he lives, this he desires to do with his friends; hence some men drink or gamble together, others exercise or hunt or do philosophy together (ἢ συμφιλοσοφοῦσιν), . . . for wishing to live together with their friends, they do these things and share in these things (καί τούτων κοινωνοῦσιν) as best they can."

33. See, on Plato's *synousia*, Lynch 1972, pp. 42–44 (with note 18 on p. 42), 63, 85–86, and 88.

34. See Theophrastos's will preserved in Diogenes Laertius, V 51–57, at 53.

Symposium, of course, merely affords the best known instance of group philosophical activity among several in his dialogues. When it is remembered that Aristotle, in contrast with the impression of inclusiveness left by Solon's text, is not claiming in the *Ethics* (either in our passage or elsewhere) to be providing his reader with a full roster of known *koinoniai*, it is clear that no basis remains for denying that the schools do indeed, at least on verbal grounds, satisfy any Aristotelian definition of a *koinonia*. [35]

It is this conclusion, it may be noted, that justified our treatment of the schools in chapter 1 in connection with the attack upon them by Sophokles of Sounion. In 307, the Athenians approved Sophokles' bill making it illegal for any philosopher to be appointed head of a school without the appointment first having been authorized by the Council and Assembly. Following the departure of the philosophers from the city, a pupil of Aristotle's named Philon successfully indicted Sophokles on the charge of making an illegal proposal. My suggestion, made in the context of a general consideration of "validating" legislation on associations, was that Sophokles' decree proved to be illegal on the point of its conflict with the law of Solon, which guaranteed the validity of the arrangements of associations provided that those arrangements were not in violation of "written statutes of the People."[36] Obviously, the argument is valid only if it can first be established that the schools were in fact associations and so protected under the terms of the law.

An association, by definition, has members. Who were the "members" of a philosophical school? Besides its leader, its students, obviously—in fact, no other candidates are at hand. This might be thought at first to present a problem, when one considers the matter of the duration of membership. Members of demes, phylai, and phratries, once enrolled, normally remained so for life. But the engagement of the student "member" of a philosophical school might range between the length of a single lecture to a more or less lifelong discipleship. Even if Isokrates' statement that his students stayed with him for three to four years (and even so, he adds, they left with regret and tears)[37] is taken as indicating a typical tenure in one school, the fact that a person could join or separate himself or herself from the "association" at

---

35. Against my position, Lynch declines to accord any such status to the schools, but for reasons that do not strike me as compelling. At 1972, p. 111, he quotes (in part) our programmatic passage from Aristotle's *Ethics* (8.9.5: 1160a), with the comment that the author, while speaking of *thiasoi* and *eranoi*, does not do so in a way that suggests that, as a member of the Academy, he himself belonged to a group of this kind. He adds that Aristotle does not attribute any educational purpose to *thiasoi* and *eranoi*. But, clearly, this argument stakes all on two specific types of *koinoniai*, when in fact the schools, if *koinoniai*, may have been of another type. Again, it will be remembered that the roster of examples provided by the text is not represented by Aristotle as exhaustive but only as illustrative. At pp. 62–63, Lynch suggestively notes the existence of "clubs" in the fifth and fourth centuries and the early formation of trade, professional, and religious organizations, adding that "[g]roups such as these might have suggested points of organization which Plato incorporated into his school" (p. 63). But the conclusion that the schools were, or became, such clubs or organizations themselves is not drawn.

36. Any connection with the law of Solon is implicitly denied by Lynch, who doubts that the schools possessed any "official status" at all (1972, pp. 128–129). Ultimately, his reason for doing so is his apparent conviction that the schools were not associations and, since they were not, could not come under the terms of the law. See the immediately preceding note.

37. Isokrates 4, *Antidosis* 86–88.

will adds a new element to the profile of the Athenian *koinonia*. But we must remember that the model of the association under review in this book is one prompted by the Athenians themselves, in particular Aristotle. His evidence, reflected in the construction of one of our four scales in chapter 1, justifies a fluid perception of the duration of a *koinonia*, with the temporary cooperation of traders or sailors at one extreme, the ongoing permanence of the state segmental division, the deme or phyle association, at the other. Now, if a genuine *koinonia*, for Aristotle, may be either transitory or enduring, then certainly his perception of an association would accord member status to the temporary as well as to the lifelong *participant*. As for the schools themselves, there can be no question regarding their capacity to survive any particular cohort of leaders or members. The schools' survival was ensured by the permanence of their physical surroundings, by the arrangements made the scholarchs (by will or otherwise) for succession upon their deaths, and by the lasting appeal of their philosophical doctrines. Isokrates' school had evidently died with him,[38] as probably did Antisthenes' at Kynosarges,[39] but the Stoa, Academy, and Lyceum, among others, were to enjoy exceedingly long lives.

Another attribute of associations repeatedly to the fore in the preceding chapters is *place*. Demes, phylai, and phratries were, as stressed through much of our discussions, either defined by boundaries or, failing that, at least centered at some headquarters or seat. To what extent is it appropriate to seek the "place" of a philosophical school? And, if we do seek it, what do we find? Sokrates had engaged in philosophical activity in a variety of locales—at a cobbler's,[40] in a rein-maker's shop,[41] in the market,[42] by the Tables,[43] in the Stoa of Zeus,[44] and near the Stoa Basileios.[45] Despite this mobility, and significantly, I wish to suggest, in each case the chosen venue was in the area of the Agora in the heart of urban Athens. After Sokrates' time, furthermore, the practice of Plato's teacher was to prove exemplary, for the stoas, and especially the Poikile, were to become the more or less permanent meeting places, and in one case the namesake, of the adherents of two major philosophical doctrines, the Cynics[46] and of course the "people of the stoa," the Stoics.[47] With this development, the schools did come to resemble some of the other *koinoniai* in respect to their more or less enduring situation in a single, fixed locale. Obviously, for the purposes of the present study, special significance resides in the fact that this early activity of Sokrates', as well as that of the later permanent schools

---

38. Lynch 1972, p. 54.

39. Lynch 1972, p. 50.

40. Diogenes Laertius, 2.13.122 and 123.

41. Xenophon, *Memorabilia* 4.2.1 and 8.

42. Plutarch, *de tranquillitate animi* 10 (470–471); Aelian, *Varia Historia* 2.1.

43. Plato, *Apology* 17c, *Hippias Minor* 368b; Aristeides 46.134.

44. [Plato], *Eryxias* 392a, *Theages* 121a; Xenophon, *Oikonomikos* 7.1.

45. Plato, *Euthyphro* 2a, *Theaitetos* 210d.

46. For the Cynic Krates' frequenting of a stoa (probably the Poikile), see Apuleius, *Florida* 14 , with *Agora* 3, no. 52, p. 33; and for Menippos the Cynic's remark about the Poikile, Lucian, *Icaromenippos* 34, with *Agora* 3, no. 75, p. 38.

47. For the use of the Poikile by the Stoics, see Apuleius, *Florida* 14; Diogenes Laertius, 7.1.5, 14, 22; Hesychios, s.v. στωικοί; Suidas, s.v. Ζήνων; and other ancient and modern authorities compiled at *Agora* 3, p. 31, under "Poikile."

housed or at least centered in the Stoas, converges upon the Agora. To this extent, the physical location of the seat of the democratic central government (and of public activity generally) and the hub of speculative exchange and education approximately coincided. Still, this fact by itself is not, given the wider context of uses to which the civic center, and especially the Agora, were put, particularly noteworthy. If a space could simultaneously be used for constitutional, political, social, commercial, theatric, athletic, and artistic purposes,[48] why should particular significance be found in the presence there of the philosophers?

But, in fact, the general congruity of location between civic center and philosophical school was to prove only a temporary phenomenon. Already around 390, within a decade of the execution of Sokrates, the school founded by Isokrates is reported, according to our single surviving and exasperatingly vague report, to have been situated "near the Lyceum"—perhaps, as Lynch speculates, in the founder's own house.[49] Soon thereafter, or perhaps even before this time, began the trend whereby three other schools, including the two that were to prove the most influential, were founded in the nominally cultic exercise facilities called *gymnasia* on the outskirts of the city. Antisthenes the Cynic at some unknown date, probably soon after Sokrates' execution and in any case long before his own death around 365, founded a school at Kynosarges, southeast of Athens on the south bank of the Ilissos in front of the Diomeian Gate.[50] In or around 387, Plato, Sokrates' pupil, shifted the focus of his master's work from the Agora to the Academy to the northwest outside the circuit wall in the outer Kerameikos.[51] Aristotle, after his return from Macedon to Athens in 335, established the Peripatos at the Lyceum, now securely placed

48. The massive and varied evidence is assembled in *Agora* 3 and 14 passim. For a brief account, see Jones 1997, pp. 63–68.

49. Lynch 1972, p. 53, citing the *Anonymous Life of Isokrates* 108–109, p. 257 Westermann.

50. For the date, see Lynch 1972, p. 50. On the gymnasium and school at Kynosarges, see Travlos 1971, "Kynosarges," pp. 340–341; Lynch 1972, pp. 50–51; and Wycherley 1978, pp. 229–231. While Wycherley's discussion leaves the site of the gymnasium unresolved, it remains true that both the site mentioned (favored by Travlos) and the second candidate, removed farther to the southeast toward Phaleron (favored by Wycherley), were outside the city circuit wall. A more recent discussion is Billot 1992, pp. 119–156.

51. For appreciations of the Academy and its school, with citation of bibliography, see Travlos 1971, "Akademia," pp. 42–51; Lynch 1972, pp. 54–63; Wycherley 1978, pp. 219–226. For the evidence for the "Peripatos," a structure of the fourth century with associated architectural remains of the sixth located to the northeast of the later gymnasium, and the possible site of Plato's ambulations, see Wycherley's discussion at 1978, pp. 224–225. Since Wycherley's writing, an already inconclusive epigraphic record has deteriorated still further. *SEG* 13.28, an inscribed list of four names (the first three fragmentary) found at the site of the Academy originally dated ca. 300 and interpreted as a list of Platonic dialogues, later improved and downdated to the second century (*SEG* 21.638), has now been read as a list of names of schoolboys from Platonic dialogues: see Brumbaugh 1992, pp. 171–172. The so-called Academy Tablets (i.e., *SEG* 19.37; 22.61), found to the northwest near the circuit wall, alleged by their discoverer Stavropoullos to be schoolboys' work originating in a school active in the Academy area during the fifth century, have been reinterpreted by Lynch, who concludes that the tablets are "probably little more than discarded materials from an ancient building project of the second century A.D. or later" and that "no even remotely plausible connection has been established between the tablets and the workings of the Academy in any period" (Lynch 1983, pp. 115–121, with pp. 120 and 121 for the quotations). For the texts and a case (against Lynch) for a date "by the end of the 5th century," see Balatsos 1991, pp. 145–154, with p. 154 for the date.

by Lynch immediately outside the southeast section of the ancient city wall.[52] To be sure, the use of these new suburban locations for intellectual purposes was not entirely without precedent. For Plato, the gymnasium or palaestra or their environs serve as the mise-en-scène for several of his *Dialogues*. The Lyceum in particular had already been a haunt of philosophers, as witnessed by early visits by Sokrates himself[53] and, later, as already noted, by the proximity of Isokrates' instructional facility. But the fact remains that a major shift of associational activity had occurred, from the urban center to the perimeter (or, in the case of the Academy, to a little beyond the perimeter) of the urbanized center of Attica. Why?

It would be helpful if, first, we were able to recover why the Agora had been the preferred venue of philosophical activity in the first place. At the most basic level, it might be argued that, given the multifarious uses to which the Agora had long been put, any public (or publicly conducted) activity involving a sizable number of persons would naturally gravitate to the square. There were, or were perhaps at first believed to be, no viable options. More particularly, as we saw, philosophical exchange was by definition a group activity; and if a *philosophos* or *sophistes* had set himself up as a teacher, he would need students. Obviously, a heavily settled residential district or a public square, like the Agora, frequented by a large segment of the Athenian population would provide a large pool of potential interlocutors or pupils. But there were drawbacks as well—drawbacks, furthermore, that were not confined to the easily imagined high noise level, excessive crowding, and, unless (as often) recourse was made to an enclosed or semi-enclosed space like a stoa, inclement weather. To wit and famously, Sokrates had made himself unpopular by reason of verbal exchanges that had occurred mostly, if not entirely, in the Agora and its environs. The popular jury of Athenians that eventually convicted and sentenced him undoubtedly contained a great many citizens who, far from intending to pursue any speculative interest, had simply by accident found themselves in the vicinity of Sokrates and been irritated by some aspect of his activity. To continue in such a venue, it must have been plain from the year 399 on, would be risky.

What was needed was to move away from the Agora, without going so far as to cut oneself off from the necessary supply of listeners or interlocutors, doctrinal adherents, and pupils. The gymnasia would seem to have fit the bill. They were popular places, but the clientele was self-selected to the extent that a good walk was required to reach Kynosarges, the Lyceum, and particularly the Academy, given a point of departure from the Agora. Those who were there were there for a reason, rather than being mere passersby engaged in some quite unrelated constitutional, commercial, or other business. The three gymnasia represented points of equilibrium between the congested urban center and the sparsely populated countryside.

---

52. On the physical setting of the Lyceum, see Travlos 1971, "Lykeion," pp. 345–347; and Lynch 1972, pp. 9–31 (with app. A, "Inscriptions and the Location of the Lyceum," pp. 209–212, and map following at p. 216). For the founding of the Peripatetic school, see Lynch 1972, pp. 68–105, and Wycherley 1978, pp. 226–229. More recently, the question of the exact location of the Lyceum has been reopened by Ritchie (1989, pp. 250–260) who, principally on the basis of the dedication *IG* II² 2875, places the gymnasium south of Syntagma Square in the area of the National Gardens, yet still, in agreement with Lynch, outside the city walls (see *SEG* 39.197 and 203).

53. E.g., Plato, *Lysis* 203a.

Their modest remove from the Agora would tend to filter out those nonphilosophically inclined parties who, if inadvertently exposed to doctrine or eristic debate, might visit the offending party or his adherents with a repetition of Sokrates' fate. At the same time, however, they would still be within reach of the *asty*, given a moderate degree of motivation.[54] To put the matter in the terms of the primary theme of this study, the schools, so far as concerns their geographical situation, may be viewed as having evolved in response to the dominant egalitarian ideology, and resulting societal ambience, of the classical democracy.

This reconstruction could receive some corroboration if we could demonstrate a fit between the composition of the philosophical sets and the already existing clienteles of the gymnasia. As it turns out, such a demonstration is not easily accomplished. A gymnasium, and particularly one equipped with a palaestra, should, in the light of well-established realities of Athenian culture, be dominated by male members of the Athenian elite.[55] At Athens, only boys and men engaged in wrestling and in athletic activity generally. Within the male population, only the leisured had the time or energy to devote to such nonproductive pursuits. And, to narrow the field still further, contemporary literary witnesses leave no doubt that these leisured males were predominately or typically members of the aristocratic upper stratum of Athenian society.[56] Such a profile, however, does not comport uniformly with what we know about the composition of the philosophical schools and followings. True, the Sophists had catered only to those who could pay their hefty fees, and Sokrates, notoriously, had appealed to some prominent upper-class young men; but there is no reason to think that this trend, if it were ever a trend, prevailed throughout the philosophical community. Sokrates' own confrères included the proprietors of a cobbler's[57] and of a rein-maker's shop[58] and, to illustrate the point by simply citing a single, better-documented case, Plato's Academy is recorded to have played host to a farmer, magi, and a woman disguised as a man.[59] So, while it is likely that the schools drew upon a captive audience of habituees of the gymnasium, many other disciples must have been outsiders who had found their way there from elsewhere.

The model of movement away from urban center to suburban periphery should not be overdrawn. As we noted earlier, some philosophers had frequented the gymnasia in the fifth century, long before the formal establishment of the "schools." In the case of at least one sect, the Epicureans, withdrawal was evidently more a mat-

54. Lynch, at 1972 p. 30, is correct when he asserts that the three schools "were all in fact anything but isolated suburban retreats." It is not a question of isolation but rather one of establishing a degree of insulation from casual, and potentially hostile, traffic unconcerned with the business of philosophical discourse.

55. For some specific sources bearing on the people actually known to have visited the Lyceum, see Lynch 1972, pp. 30–31. Some of this evidence, however, applies to a period later than that addressed by the present study.

56. See Donlan 1980, pp. 156–157, citing Aristophanes, *Knights* 188–193, 579–580, and *Frogs* 727–729, with Ehrenberg 1951, p. 99.

57. See above, note 40. According to Diogenes' report, the cobbler himself, one Simon by name, took to recording his conversations with Sokrates in the form of dialogues.

58. See above, note 41.

59. For the evidence, see Lynch 1972, pp. 57–58. Lynch adduces these examples in support of "the open character of the Academy" (p. 57).

ter of philosophical doctrine than of adverse reaction to a hostile urban setting. Others, such as the Stoics, seemed to have circulated from one base to another, never settling upon a permanent home. And in Hellenistic times, with the construction of the Ptolemaion and Diogeneion, the city became once again the primary center of organized intellectual instruction and exchange.[60] But the fact remains that during the latter half of the period of the free democracy under review in this study, extramural gymnasia became the permanent seats of philosophical schools. Among these was the intellectual dynasty begun by Sokrates in or about the Agora but latterly relocated to the Academy and Lyceum.

The philosophical school represented a unique blend of the private and the public—a private school housed in a public space, whether Agora, or stoa, or gymnasium.[61] As Lynch has noted, this fact—the use of a public space—in and of itself gave the central government a powerful source of leverage over the philosophers, for they could be expected, even required, to conform, more narrowly, to the regulations governing that space and, more generally, to the will of the People of Athens.[62] After all, the setting of a stoa or a gymnasium no less than the open space of the Agora could only have exposed teacher and pupils to the gaze of the Athenian public, even granting, in the case of a gymnasium, the relative isolation provided by a suburban location. These are undoubtedly the conditions underlying Sophokles' attack on the schools, which, even though later demonstrated to be illegal, could not have been carried off initially without considerable political support—and widespread popular antipathy toward the philosophers. But the same public that attacked the schools could, through its institutions, afford them relief from persecution. And in the end it was not the mere accident of the use of a public space but the more fundamental matter of a school's classification as a *koinonia* that, if my arguments are accepted, brought the schools under the umbrella of protection—and regulation—embodied in the Solonian law on associations.[63]

Regional Associations

Beyond the city walls and the gymnasia which, in the three instances just considered, housed philosophical schools, stretched the countryside of Attica. In earlier chapters (2, 3, and 4) we examined various aspects of the deme associations around

60. For the evidence supporting these broad-brush characterizations, see Wycherley 1978, pp. 231–235.

61. Not only was the school a "private" institution but the school's leader might, while using the gymnasium as his base of operations, also make additional or subsidiary use of his own personal properties. For Plato's (private) house and garden and their proximity and probable relation to the (public) Academy, see Diogenes Laertius 3.5 (cf. 3.7), with Lynch 1972, p. 61, and Wycherley 1978, pp. 220–221; a more recent discussion is Dillon 1983, pp. 51–59. Similarly, Theophrastos, Aristotle's successor at the Lyceum, owned, in the vicinity of the gymnasium, a private garden, a *peripatos*, and buildings adjacent to the garden, all of which he bequeathed to this friends in order to promote their pursuit of philosophy (Diogenes Laertius, 5.52–53, with Lynch 1972, pp. 98–102, and Wycherley 1978, p. 227).

62. Lynch 1972, pp. 130–134.

63. For Lynch's account, see 1972, pp. 104 and 117–118. However, he does not, as here, adduce Solon's law on associations in connection with this episode.

which the public and communal lives of many extra-urban citizen residents of this countryside (and their households) seem to have been centered. Given the isolation and intense inward focus that we found to be characteristic of these village communities, they might be thought to have provided sufficient opportunity for associational activity, however complete a citizen's estrangement from the city of Athens. And if not, then surely the phratries, which, as we saw in chapter 7, were in several cases regionally focused upon some of the larger rural demes, would, over and above their purely local dimension, have sufficed to cater to any complementary, outreaching needs of the Athenian people, since the phratry, in contrast with the deme associations, seems to have promoted a sense of connectedness with one's fellow Athenians or even with other Ionian Greeks. It is thus mildly surprising to discover that well into the classical period (and beyond) there is documentary evidence for the continuing existence and functioning of several archaic regional associations that, in all but one instance, were demonstrably centered in extramural regions of Attica—the very regions seemingly dominated by rural demes and phratries. Not only is the need for such seemingly redundant organizations not immediately apparent, but, on the widely accepted theory advanced by David Lewis, Kleisthenes had designed his new system of demes, trittyes, and phylai in precisely such a way as to weaken these very regional constellations.[64] But before we turn to consider the explanation for their survival, let us summarily review the evidence for their activity under the democracy.[65]

Marathonian Tetrapolis. The Tetrapolis comprised the demes Oinoe, Marathon, Probalinthos, and Trikorynthos (Strabo, 8.7.1: 383; Steph. Byz., s.v. Τετράπολις). The associational activity of the organization is documented by the sacred calendar *IG* II² 1358 (ca. 400–350), which preserves material pertaining to Marathon (lines 1–53) and Trikorynthos (lines 54–56);[66] by the dedication of the Tetrapolees *IG* II² 2933 (med. s. IV); and by the decree of the Tetrapolis *IG* II² 1243 (med. s. III). The last-mentioned document, concerned with the monitoring of the association's funds,

64. For the evidence on this point with respect to the regional associations here under review, see chapter 3, with note 132.

65. Included here are only those entities for which clear evidence survives of formal organization as an association. Thus I omit the Epakreis attested by two documents: the one, a decree assigned to the deme Plotheia, *IG* I³ 258 (= II² 1172; 425–413), line 30; the other, a fragment of an honorary inscription of some unspecified deme association, *AE* 1980, pp. 94–95 (ca. 350–300; *SEG* 32.144), line 1. The former records Plotheia's contribution to Epakreis, the latter connects the group with an *archon* for the Apollonia (evidently a festival) under the words "the *demotai*," possibly Hekale or (with Parker 1996, p. 330) Semachidai. Since Traill (1986) places these three demes in close proximity to one another a short distance northeast of Pentelikon, the possibility of a regional "association" is opened up: hence Parker 1996, p. 330, favors "a pre-existing religious association" from which the Kleisthenic trittys-name was borrowed (on which, see Traill 1986, pp. 105–106). Earlier, Solders (1931, pp. 120–121) had associated the Epakreis with the regional following of Peisistratos called the Diakrioi. But whatever communal solidarity these Athenians may have possessed, it is not known to have been institutionalized in the form of an enduring organization. See now, on the "local religious associations," Parker 1996, app. 3, pp. 328–332.

66. For interpretation of the content of the calendar, see Mikalson 1977, pp. 426–427; Whitehead 1986, pp. 190–194; and the unpublished 1971 Harvard University dissertation of Gerald M. Quinn, *The Sacrificial Calendar of the Marathonian Tetrapolis*, briefly summarized in *HSCP* 76 (1972) 299.

reveals the existence of *archontes* and formal decreeing and auditing procedures. Despite its relatively late date, there is no reason to doubt its pertinence to the association under the classical democracy.[67]

Of great interest for our subject is the fact that the decree *IG* II² 1243 calls at the end of the preserved text for the engraving and erection of two stelai, one in the shrine of Dionysos at Marathon, the other "in the *asty*" (lines 20–22, partly but convincingly restored).[68] The surviving text was found "[i]n arce" (*IG*). Again, as I have speculated regarding the similar practice of the phratry organization centered in the distant deme of Dekeleia,[69] the implication is that the members of the association now living in town would not normally have occasion to visit the home-base in the Marathon area, so for their benefit a second copy had to be placed in the urban center. And, too, as with the case of the phratry, I conclude that the Four Towns, as was true of the demes that constituted its components, remained relatively isolated and particularly so from the region of the *asty*.

Another piece of the puzzle is provided by the fact that the sacred calendar, *IG* II² 1358, calls for the *demarch* of the Marathonians to perform certain sacrifices (col. II, lines 23–26, cf. lines 1–4 [restored]). At the minimum, the point illustrates the interplay between the Tetrapolis and at least one of its constituent members, significantly the home-base village, Marathon. At a higher level, since the demarch, as Whitehead has convincingly demonstrated, served as an "agent" of the central government,[70] it is apparent that the democracy in Athens may well have played a role in the functioning of the organization. We shall return shortly to the question raised here regarding state-association relations.

"The Demes around Hekale." Plutarch, *Theseus* 14.2, records that "the demes around about" (οἱ πέριξ δῆμοι) used to gather in order to sacrifice the Hekalesia to Zeus Hekalos and to honor Hekale.

Trikomoi I. The three villages were Eupyridai, Kropidai, and Pelekes (Steph. Byz., s.v. Εὐπυρίδαι). No evidence of the functioning of the association survives.

Trikomoi II. According to Bicknell's arguments, this second organization of three villages comprised Erchia, Konthyle, and Kytheros.[71] Given the correctness of this theory, the association will have been responsible for *IG* II² 1213 (s. IV), a fragmentary honorary decree found at Spata, the site of ancient Erchia. Evidence preserved here of a formal organization includes "the altars" (line 2), female officers called *archousai* (line 3), funds (line 5), and "the *trikomarchos*," evidently the chief officer (line 6). It is unclear whether the isolated words "the demos" (in the accusative

---

67. Finally, with Schlaifer 1943, p. 35, note 2, I concur that the inscription from the Marathon area concerning the Herakleia published by Vanderpool (1942, pp. 334–337, shortly after 490) may pertain to the deme alone. Vanderpool's suggestion, that the festival was probably, prior to the Persian Wars, celebrated chiefly by the people of the Marathonian Tetrapolis (pp. 335–336), though attractive, is neither supported by the text nor necessary.

68. ἀναγράψαι δὲ τόδε τὸ ψήφισ[μα ἐν στήλαιν δυοῖν καὶ τὴν] / μὲν μίαν στῆσαι ἐμ Μαραθ[ῶνι ἐν τῶι ἱερῶι τοῦ Διο]/νύσου, τὴν [δ]ὲ ἑτέραν ἐν ἄ[στει].

69. See "Regional Distribution and Relation to the Urban Center," in chapter 7.

70. Whitehead 1986, pp. 130–139.

71. Bicknell 1976, pp. 599–603.

case) preserved in line 7 refer to a constituent deme or to the Demos of the Athenians, but the fact that the association comprised not one but *three* demes would tend to favor the latter alternative and so to reinforce the point about state-association relations made with regard to the Tetrapolis: the People were somehow involved in the functioning of this regional organization.

Tetrakomoi. The four villages are Peiraieus, Phaleron, Thymaitadai, and Xypete (Pollux, 4.105). Documentation survives in the form of two agonal dedications, *IG* II² 3102 (med. s. IV) and 3103 (330/29), and the dedication by *epimeletai,* no. 2830 (med. s. IV), all found in Peiraieus. The former agonal text records a victory by the Phalereis in the names of several individuals grouped under the wholly restored title *komarchoi* (lines 1–2); the latter, a similar victory by the Xypetaiones in the names of the *archon,* four *komarchoi,* and five *komastai.* The dedication by the *epimeletai* seems to have carried four names, of which two, a Peiraieus (lines 2–4) and a [Thy]maitades (lines 8–10), are preserved; the two names presumably representing the other two villages are almost entirely lost. Evidently the contest took place among the members of the four villages competing against each other.[72]

Mesogeioi. According to Schlaifer's arguments, the likely member demes were Bate, Diomeia, Kydathenaion, and Kerameis.[73] All four demes were certainly or probably situated in the city region, but even so were not particularly near to each other.[74] The association is documented by a series of honorary decrees: *IG* II² 1244 (fin. s. IV?), 1245 (ca. 251/0), and 1247 (med. s. III).[75] The epigraphic dates are rather late for our purposes, but no. 1244 may just catch the tail end of the democracy. In any case, the cults of the association may, with Schlaifer, date from at least the sixth century.[76] Taken together, the texts reveal a full and formal organizational structure with a cultic focus.

   Not at all so straightforward is the regional disposition of the organization. It has long been noted that, despite the apparent import of the name "the people of Mesogeia," the various indications—find-spots, cult center, and deme affiliations— all point to an engagement with the city. Schlaifer concluded that "the association as such had no connection with the Mesogea."[77] Certainly the deme affiliations leave this impression. Kydathenaion was situated within the walls; Kerameis just outside the walls to the northwest; Diomeia just outside the walls to the southeast. Bate is assigned by Traill to a deme site at Ambelokipi, again outside the city walls, in this instance to the northeast.[78] If the association maintained a center, perhaps it is indi-

---

72. For the additional complexities of interpretation, see Parker 1996, pp. 328–329.

73. Schlaifer 1944, pp. 22–27. For a more recent discussion, see Parker 1996, pp. 306–307.

74. See on this point, chapter 3, note 132.

75. Two additional decrees, nos. 1246 (med. s. III?) and 1248 (med. s. III), were assigned to the association by the editor of *IG* II². For the disqualification of no. 1246, see Schlaifer 1944, p. 22, note 1 (reporting the then-new readings of S. Dow); for the disqualification of no. 1248, see p. 23, note 15 (pp. 23–24). At a later date, Dow and Gill characterized the case for attributing 1248 to the Mesogeioi as "very doubtful" (1965, p. 113).

76. Schlaifer 1944, p. 25.

77. Schlaifer 1944, p. 25.

78. Traill 1986, p. 127.

cated, as Schlaifer thought, by the find-spots of two of the documents, nos. 1245 and 1247, about a mile outside the Acharnai Gate due north of the enceinte, possibly at or near the site of the chief sanctuary of the Mesogeioi, the Herakleion, where the decrees call for the stelai to be erected (no. 1244, lines 2–3; no. 1247, line 27).[79] Given the generally northerly outlook of the member demes, and their scattered locations, the choice of this sanctuary might have been a sensible attempt at compromise.

Thus far, in accordance with the definition set out in chapter 1, I have labeled the Mesogeioi an "association." Schlaifer, however, raised, on exceedingly dubious grounds, the question of the formal identity of the group, in the end limiting the field to either *genos* or *oikos*, between which alternatives he was not in the end able to make a clear choice.[80] The "dubious grounds" to which I refer concern the unfilled lacuna at *IG* II² 1244, lines 7–8, where, in the context of an expression meaning "the measures decreed by the Mesogeioi," a *terminus technicus* denoting the organization seemed to have been lost by damage to the stone.[81] The *IG* editor had restored the nine-letter phrase τῶι κοινῶι to the eight-stoichos gap in the stoichedon inscription, and Schlaifer accordingly objected on grounds of spacing. The only two words he could find of the required length were γένει and οἴκωι, but even Schlaifer, writing in an article published in 1944, could see some of the difficulties entailed by either of these restorations. Besides, it is clearly easier to assume that, in accordance with occasionally observed epigraphic practice, the mason had inscribed one of the two iotas of the phrase favored by the *IG* editor in the same stoichos with another letter.[82] It is also germane to note that at *IG* II² 1245, lines 2 and 10, and at 1247, lines 5, 10, and 15, the associates call themselves simply Mesoge(i)oi. May I suggest that an association of villages (or of constitutionalized Kleisthenic demes) could refer to itself only by a neutral term such as *koinon* (or *koinonia*) or by a noncommittal collective moniker such as "Tri-Villages" or "Midlands," but certainly not by a specialized cultic or familial word like *genos*, *oikos*, or *thiasos*?

Schlaifer notes the presence among the attested names of several men from among the "substantial and prominent citizens."[83] Such members, I suspect, sufficed

79. Schaifer 1944, p. 23 with note 13.

80. Schlaifer 1944, pp. 25–27.

81. According to Schlaifer 1944, p. 25, the text at lines 7–8 reads: . . . τὰ ἐψ[ηφισμένα. . . .⁸. . . . τ]/ῶι Μεσογεί[ων. . . . (This appears to be merely a reproduction of the version printed in *IG*.)

82. This point is made by Dow and Gill in their discussion of the text (and of Schlaifer's analysis), but in the end they prefer to restore a reference to "the *genos*," which they regard as "all but certain." No mention is made, however, of Schlaifer's second candidate, *oikos*; and still a third candidate, *thiasos*, suggested by Dow and Gill's own text, is, like *koinon*, dismissed on the grounds that the restoration would be one letter too long (although, as they noted, two final iotas would again be available to share a stoichos with another letter) (1965, p. 114). Note: 1245 is a misprint for 1244. More recently, the candidacy of "genos" has found favor with Parker 1996, pp. 306–307.

83. Schlaifer 1944, p. 26. For Amynomachos, son of Philokrates, of Bate, proposer of *IG* II² 1245, see *PA* 742 (an heir of the philosopher Epicurus). For the choregic family connections of Epigenes, son of Metrodoros, of Kydathenaion (*PA* 4809), honorand of *IG* II² 1247, see *PA* 10807. This decree's proposer, Prokleides of Kerameis (*PA* 12201), is the grandson of a mover of a decree of the People (*PA* 12200). Kirchner (but oddly, not Schlaifer) identifies the honorand of *IG* II² 1245, Polyeuktos, son of Lysistratos, of Bate (*PA* 11940), as the father of a priestess of Athena Polias (*PA* 9585). However, Schlaifer's association of these persons with *genê* (evidently on the assumption that these were exclusive aristocratic organizations) is, as we have seen, without textual basis.

to sustain the organization. No hint, in any case, is found of governmental interest or intervention in the association.

League of Athena Pallenis. By this traditional title I refer to an association of villages fundamentally similar to those already reviewed. The sole primary documentation is the list of *archontes* and *parasitoi* originally published by Peek and more recently reexamined by Stanton, who assigns to it a date in the 350s.[84] According to Stanton's analysis, the association comprised the Kleisthenic demes Gargettos, Acharnai, Pallene, and Paiania.[85] Stanton further established, on the basis of the two lists of *archontes* preserved in lines 4–7 and 38–40, that on both occasions the four officers had been provided by the same four demes, from which he concluded that these demes controlled the association. (By contrast, the preserved demotics of the numerous *parasitoi* reveal a wide scattering over all of Attica, possibly reflecting the drawing power of a high-status position rather than the regional disposition of the organization.)[86] At all events, as noted in chapter 3, the fact that these four demes ended up in four different phylai justifies the inference (again with Lewis) that Kleisthenes had deliberately intended through these assignments to weaken the power of the association.[87]

All else depends on reconstruction and combination. Schlaifer's 1943 study of the Cult of Athena Pallenis is concerned with a passage in Athenaios (*Deipnosophistai* 6.234c–235c) preserving information, compiled from three different primary sources, about cult personnel called "parasites." Although Schlaifer did not know of the inscription (it was not to be published until eight years later, in 1951), it is evident that these are the selfsame *parasitoi*, for two of the three authorities cited, Polemon and Themison, say something about "Pallenis." Polemon mentions a certain dedication by the *archontes* and *parasitoi* (who had been crowned in the archonship of Pythodoros in 432/1) preserved ἐν . . . Παλληνίδι, with reference either to a temple of Athena Pallenis or simply to Pallene.[88] Similarly, the passage in Themison's work excerpted by Athenaios is attributed ἐν Παλληνίδι, with uncertain meaning but most likely, again, as with Polemon's citation, referring to either a temple or a toponym.[89] But a problem is posed by the demes of the three dedicators

84. W. Peek, *MDAI[A]* 67 (1942) [1951] 24–29, no. 26. For Stanton's new edition, see Stanton 1984, pp. 292–298, with p. 296 for the date. The purpose of the inscription is obscure, but it may have been a list of the colleges of officials on different occasions (Stanton 1984, p. 293).

85. Stanton 1984, pp. 297–298.

86. On this point I concur with Stanton against Walters 1982, p. 10 (with map, p. 31), who finds in the deme affiliations of the *parasitoi*, by combining them with those of the *archontes*, evidence of the "extensive" geographic spread of the League itself.

87. Chapter 3, with note 132. Stanton 1984, pp. 296–298.

88. 234f: frag. 78 Preller, pp. 114–123 (= *FHG* III 137–138). Preller took the words to mean "in the temple (of Athena) at Pallene," but Gulick, who cites Preller's interpretation, translates simply "And at Pallene . . ." (Loeb, vol. 3, p. 57). Jacoby, arguing against the suggestion that the words indicated a book title, likewise finds in them a reference to a place: *FGrH* III B, commentary on §374, Themison, p. 149, with note 12.

89. 235a: *FGrH* 374 Themison 1. Against the supposition of a book title, I follow Jacoby's judgment, IIIB, commentary, p. 149. According to Gulick in the Loeb edition (vol. 3, p. 58), Wilamowitz had taken the words to refer to "an ordinance in the temple at Pallene." Ronald Stroud, whose study of the *kyrbeis* involved examination of Polemon's citation of such objects at 234e–f, states that the Greek scholar's text

whose demotics are preserved in Polemon's fragmentary text: they are Gargettos, Pithos, and Gargettos again. While Gargettos is one of the four demes figuring in the list published by Peek, Pithos demonstrably is not. Nor does it help that Pithos remains unplaced topographically.[90] Accordingly, the link between the list and the information preserved by Athenaios remains questionable, certainly where the member demes of the "League" are concerned.

Both Themison and the third source, Krates, cite in connection with the *parasitoi* "the law of the king," presumably with reference to the Athenian state magistrate the archon basileus.[91] This law, too, Schlaifer concluded partly on the basis of the reference to Themison's *Pallenis*, had dealt with the cult of Athena Pallenis.[92] As reconstructed by Schlaifer, it called for the selection of the *parasitoi* "from the demes" (I, line 3 [Krates]; III, lines 10–11 [Themison]).[93] The demes in question can only have been the member communities of the association of four demes attested by the mid-fourth-century list. Presumably, as with the *poleis* and *komai* that were the demonstrable forebears of the Kleisthenic demes comprising the other regional associations, these "demes" had once been independent entities functioning beyond the reach of the central government now physically located in the distant city of Athens. As Schlaifer emphasized, the fact that the cult of Athena Pallenis was now subject to regulation by "the king's law" reveals that any earlier independence enjoyed by the four communities had been lost and was by this time replaced by "public supervision."[94] At all events, much later, under the democratic regime described by the Aristotelian *Constitution*, the powers of the archon basileus included the management of "all the ancestral festivals" (57.1). According to the text of Athenaios (who is excerpting Plutarch, who is in turn excerpting Polemon), it was written "in the laws of the king" that "the *parasitoi* of Acharnai are to sacrifice to Apollo" (234f). Acharnai, again, was one of the four demes of the League. It follows that under the classical democracy this erstwhile autonomous association, as represented by its member deme Acharnai, had become subject to intervention by the central authority.[95]

A final feature of the cult preserved in the extracts and potentially touching these deme communities is worthy of note. According to Themison, the king's jurisdiction extended to the old men and women still married to their first husbands. Schlaifer inferred that "the privilege of participating in certain rites" had been extended to these parties, but in fact Athenaios's Greek calls for the old men and wives to join in *administering* the cult, not merely to participate in it.[96] However in-

---

appears to have been copied directly from "inscribed physical objects" (1979, pp. 24–25). Autopsy could be reconciled with a visit to either the deme Pallene or to a temple, but would obviously be inconsistent with the assumption that "Pallenis" was a book of some kind.

90. Traill 1986, p. 135, note 34 (p. 136).

91. 235a–c: *FGrH* 362 Krates 7.

92. Schlaifer 1943, pp. 39–40, 59–61.

93. Schlaifer 1943, pp. 60–61 (the reconstructed text of "the king's law").

94. Schlaifer 1943, at e.g., p. 35.

95. The connection between the notice in the *AthPol* and the reference to the laws of the king in Athenaios is drawn by Rhodes at 1981, p. 639, but without comment with regard to the League. See, further, on the competence of the archon basileus, Harrison 1971, vol. 2, pp. 8–9.

96. 235a: ἐπιμελεῖσθαι δὲ τὸν βασιλέα τὸν ἀεὶ βασιλεύοντα . . . καὶ τοὺς γέροντας καὶ τὰς γυναῖκας τὰς πρωτοπόσεις, with Schlaifer 1943, pp. 37, 61 (text); pp. 50-51 (interpretation).

terpreted, this detail may be evaluated against the background of our discussion of the inclusion of womenfolk in the cultic functions of the Kleisthenic deme in chapter 4. Since what was true of the League may well have been true of that League's components, it provides valuable further evidence, I suggest, for my alternative "enlarged" deme community advanced in that discussion.

These nominally cultic and, so far as we are informed, voluntary associations were in each case, as we have seen, based upon, indeed comprised, three or more of the demes erected by Kleisthenes. But in several instances it is certain or likely that the association was already in existence prior to the year 508/7. Among other indications, the constituent communities' earlier status as "villages" (komai) or "towns" (poleis) was preserved in the formal titles by which some of them still went in much later times. With the creation of the democracy, those communities were institutionalized and, with that institutionalization, the associations of which they were components were, as a consequence, themselves inevitably incorporated within the fabric of the Athenian state. Thereafter, as demonstrated by the case of the Marathonian Tetrapolis, the central government could act through its "agent" to implement policy at the regional associational level. While the reference to "the demos" in a document of Trikomoi II remains enigmatic, a clear positive illustration of the phenomenon, provided we follow Schlaifer's arguments, is afforded by the subjection of the League of Athena Pallenis to the law of one of the chief archons, the basileus. We may not be able to demonstrate that such intervention was a frequent occurrence,[97] but these examples may nonetheless be indicative of a more widespread pattern.

This finding must be evaluated in the light of another demonstrable or likely feature of these associations—their relative isolation from the urban center. All the associations, with the sole exception of the Mesogeioi, were situated at a fairly distant remove from the asty. The practical consequences of this peripheral, outlying orientation are perhaps illustrated by the decision of the Tetrapolis to erect a second stele bearing its decree "in the asty." Again, as I have already suggested in two other contexts, the provision for the display of a second copy of the decree in town seems to reflect the assumption that members of the association resident in the asty would not normally be expected to visit the ancestral home-base in the foreseeable future.[98]

Now, it is at least worth suggesting that the facts of governmental intervention and of rural isolation are organically connected. That, in line with the central theme of this study, the urban central government undertook, through the "agency" of the demarch and (speculatively) through the validating and regulating powers afforded by Solon's law on associations, to sustain these organizations in order to enhance the communal life of these de facto disfranchised communities. Accordingly, it is here, perhaps, that we may find at least part of the explanation for what Whitehead terms the "stubborn survival" of these archaic cult organizations.[99] Indeed, as noted

97. As ventured by Schlaifer 1943, p. 35.

98. For the provision of a second stele in town called for by a decree of the phyle Hippothontis headquartered at Eleusis, see chapter 5, "The Shrine of the Eponymous Hero;" for that of the phratry headquartered at Dekeleia, see "Regional Distribution and Relation to the Urban Center," in chapter 7.

99. Whitehead 1986, p. 184.

at the head of this section, their survival does need explanation, and it is in the central government's interventions that we may well be able to find it.

Since these regional constellations comprised *koinoniai* (or "associations") of *demotai*, it is legitimate to term them, as I have done from the beginning, "associations" themselves. The equation of the regional association with its constituent deme associations has another welcome consequence as well. It explains why no separate reference is made to any of our organizations in either the law of Solon (in whose time certainly some of the regional associations were in existence) or in those writings of Aristotle (under whom they continued to function) adduced in the Introduction and chapter 1.[100] In fact, they *are* present in those sources, in the Solonian statute citing the δῆμος, and wherever Aristotle, as in the epitomizing passage from the *Nichomachean Ethics*, writes of δημόται.

Genê

Among the various groups (or claimants to group status) considered as possible "associations" in this work, by far the most problematic is the *genos*. To anticipate the conclusion of my discussion, it has become apparent from a review of the more recent literature that in fact the entities called *genos*, so far as can be known from the contemporary sources for classical Athens, do not, with a single exception (to be noted in due course), meet even the very generous requirements of associational status set out in chapter 1. Nonetheless, the candidacy of this widely known group (if, and when, it is indeed a group) may strike some readers as self-evidently probable, so a few words will be devoted to briefly characterizing the present rather surprising state of affairs.

Until the 1970s it was customary for ancient Greek historians to think of the *genos* as a well-defined and organized extended kinship group resembling the far better understood Roman *gens*. At least in the Anglo-American academic tradition, this conception of the genos is perhaps best illustrated by the profile constructed long ago by George Grote in his history of Greece and faithfully reproduced by others for over a century. According to Grote, the Greek *genos*, comprising a number of constituent families all claiming descent from a common ancestor, expressed its communal solidarity by common religious ceremonies; by use of a common burial place; by observance of mutual rights of succession to property; by acknowledgment of reciprocal obligations of help, defense, and redress of injuries; by observance of certain rights and obligations with regard to marriage; by the communal ownership of property; and, finally, by the selection of magistrates or officers to administer the organization.[101] Among more recent scholarly works, this model underlay the efforts of MacKendrick to reconstruct the membership of the Athenian aristocracy[102]

100. In this connection, one may also well keep in mind my discussion regarding the terminology used (or not used) to denote the Mesogeioi.

101. George Grote, *A History of Greece,* London 1884, vol. 3, pp. 54–55. For the sake of clarity and simplicity, I have paraphrased and expanded Grote's formulation of the model.

102. MacKendrick 1969, p. vii.

and was even cited in extenso in the exploration by Connor of the "new politicians" of fifth century Athens.[103] But the year 1976 witnessed the simultaneous publication of two major studies, apparently executed independently of one another, by Bourriot and Roussel, which were devoted in whole or part to the demolition of the Grotian paradigm. To judge from the reviews and other responses of historians, the negative outcome of these studies has met with a generally favorable reception.[104] Grote's model, if nothing else, now appears to be lacking in evidential basis,[105] although, as more recent publications continue to show, old ideas die hard.[106] The question to be confronted here is whether anything remains of the societal phenomenon going by the name of "genos" that might merit inclusion in a comprehensive study of the associations of classical Athens.

To reach their largely destructive conclusions, the two French scholars were required to sift through an enormous mass of material, beginning with Homer, in which the not uncommon Greek term *genos* or related words are found.[107] To boil that sifting down to its essentials, their research established, first, that the word *genos* is frequently used in various ways that have absolutely nothing to do with "clans," associations, or any other type of organized group such as imagined by Grote. Rather the term may, and often does, signify such phenomena as lineage, ethnic group, a caste, a type, and so on. The absolutely crucial point, for our purposes, is that a person may be said to be a member of a certain lineage, ethnic group, etc. without implying or even suggesting that that body of persons constitutes an organization characterized by varying degrees of private or public orientation, voluntary or nonvoluntary membership, temporal or ongoing duration, or expressive or instrumental activity.[108] These instances of the term *genos*, to invoke the customary trite image, exist only on paper; they do not necessarily denote, or correspond to, solidary, purposeful organizations. *Genos* in these senses may refer to something as nebulous and ill-defined as one's "background," "pedigree," "family tree," or "relatives." Once this finding is accepted, as I believe it must, a vast array of erstwhile candidates for associational status at once vanishes into thin air.[109]

---

103. Connor 1971, pp. 11–12.

104. Among other notices, I will instance N. R. E. Fisher's review of Bourriot (Fisher 1979) and Richard C. Smith's appraisal of the impact of both Frenchmen's work (Smith 1985).

105. For a succinct, and devastating, critique, see Smith 1985, pp. 52–56. For a critical review of the "historiography" of the *genos,* see Bourriot's penetrating and illuminating discussion, 1976, pp. 29–198. Some of the specific "attributes" of the *genos* ascribed to it by Grote's model are exhaustively weighed against the evidential record by Bourriot 1976, pp. 712–1179 (number of families per *genos*; and gentilicial property, "fiefs," so-called family tombs, and religion). The subject of family tombs and tomb cult has more recently been explored by S. C. Humphreys, 1993, pp. 79–134 (= 1980, pp. 96–126), with largely negative results.

106. Thus Walters's 1982 study of "geography and kinship as political infrastructures" reveals little awareness of the scholarship of the previous decade (see especially pp. 2–4).

107. For Bourriot's exhaustive examination of the sources, see 1976, pp. 236–339 (archaic), 340–389 (fifth century), and 390–711 (fourth century).

108. For the establishment of these four scales, by which I have proposed various groups be distinguished from one another, see "Aristotle on *Koinoniai* and a New Definition," in chapter 1.

109. For discussion of some of these nonassociational meanings, see Bourriot 1976, pp. 25–26, 199–235.

But this is not to say that at no time or in no place does a *genos* ever constitute an organized group of some kind. Several types of group called *genos* remain as potential candidates for associational status, with various degrees of plausibility. Perhaps least relevant are the military unit called *genos* recognized by Roussel[110] and the *genos* as "royal family" described by Bourriot[111]—neither possessing any relevance to the society, public or private, of Athens under the democracy. More promising by far are those *genê* organized around a cult, if only because, if we may take a hint from Parker's synoptic study of Athenian religion, such orientation clearly lay at the heart of the indubitable Athenian *genos* associations.[112]

Genê of this type, which might be styled "sacerdotal families" in English, were extensively examined by Bourriot and Roussel.[113] A brief discussion, with particular attention to the epigraphic record, will have to suffice here, given the enormous dimensions of the subject. The best known examples are the Kerykes and Eumolpidai based at Eleusis and associated with the sanctuary of Demeter and Kore. Although of far more remote origins, from the late fourth century we find them epigraphically represented in their own names as relatively highly organized and, like the bona fide associations with which this study is concerned, issuing formal honorary decrees in the customary style.[114] But the Kerykes and Eumolpidai are merely the best-known of the "sacerdotal families." Among "les corporations religieuses dites génè," Roussel admits the following:[115] (1) *genê* organized around families whose chiefs had taken charge of sanctuaries, including both the well-known Lykomidai[116] and Gephyraioi[117] and the "obscure" Thyrgonidai and Titakidai;[118] (2) *genê* in custody of the *theoi poliades*, namely the Eteoboutadai, Bouzygai, Amynandridai,[119] Praxiergidai, Thaulonidai, and Hesychidai; and (3) *genê* arising from religious brotherhoods or guilds, both Eleusinian (the Philleidai,[120] Krokonidai,[121] Koironidai, and Eudamenoi, as well as the Eumolpidai and Kerkyes) and non-Eleusinian (the Euneidai, Phreorychoi, Poimenidai, Chalkidai, and Aigeirotomoi). To these may be added, since it is epigraphically attested, the *genos* Theoinidai, which is recorded to

110. Roussel 1976, pp. 79–88. Cf. the objections of Bourriot, who does not recognize this type (1976, pp. 460–491).

111. Bourriot 1976, pp. 522–525.

112. Parker 1996, ch. 5, pp. 56–66.

113. Bourriot 1976, pp. 526–547, with 1180–1346, 1349–1361; Roussel 1976, pp. 65–78bis.

114. *Hesperia* 29 (1960) 2–4, no. 3 (incorporating *Hesperia* 10 [1941] 42, no. 10) (ca. 334–326; Kerykes); *IG* II² 1230 (fin. s. IV; Kerykes); 1231 (fin. s. IV; Eumolpidai; *SEG* 30.98, 39.151, 41.81); 1235 (ca. 274/3; Kerykes and Eumolpidai; *SEG* 29.134); 2944 (s. III; Kerykes and Eumolpidai); 1236 (ante med. s. II; Kerykes and Eumolpidai; *SEG* 36.197); 2959 (med. s. II p.; Eumolpidai); and 2340 (ca. 200 p.; Kerykes; *SEG* 12.40).

115. Roussel 1976, pp. 65–78bis, at pp. 67–68.

116. The Lykomidai, along with the (*phyletai*) Kekropidai and the (*demotai*) Phlyeis, are recorded as creditors on the *horos IG* II² 2670.

117. *Hesperia* 9 (1940) 86–96, no. 17 (incorporating *Hesperia* 8 [1939] 80–81 and *IG* II² 1096) (ca. 37/6; *SEG* 30.85).

118. For the classification of these two bodies not as *genê* but as phratries, see Lambert 1993, pp. 332–334.

119. *IG* II² 2338 (27/6-18/7; *SEG* 30.120).

120. *IG* II² 2954 (s. I p.).

121. *IG* II² 1229 (post med. s. IV; *SEG* 32.148).

have honored a priestess of Nymphe in a late Hellenistic inscription of unknown provenience published by Vanderpool.[122] For a complete and up-to-date catalog, I refer the reader to Parker's detailed checklist where 47 "certain and probable gene" and 33 "uncertain and spurious gene," with extensive citation of primary and secondary sources, will be found.[123]

Although a thorough examination of the record on which these categorizations and assignments are based is obviously not possible within the confines of the present work, it is patent that the *genos* qua association generally conforms to the model of a *koinonia* implicit in the examples cited by Aristotle in the passage from the *Ethics* adduced in chapter 1 in support of our definition of "association." To further define the "sacerdotal families," one might score them according to our four scales, whereby they would be typified as "private" (though subject to governmental intervention regarding the admission of members[124]); nonvoluntary to the extent that membership was strictly hereditary (though, again, subject to a law ordaining the admission of *orgeones* and *homogalaktes*[125]); generally characterized by enduring permanence; and, along with their presumable expressive activities, "instrumental" to the extent that some at least (especially category [2] above) served the central government through their maintenance of Athenian state cults and priesthoods. If there is a problem, it is the failure of *gennetai* of this type to receive mention in Solon's law.[126] But an explanation is suggested by still another category of the use of *genos*, the "aristocratic family." This category embraces those politically important families of the later fifth and early fourth centuries that called themselves *genê* in order to create for themselves a (not necessarily true) association with the patriotic and religious traditions of the past.[127] The outstanding example is provided by the Alkmaionidai, in the fifth century known as an *oikia* but late in the fourth styled *genos* by the author of the *Constitution of the Athenians*.[128] It seems that the semantic change that *genos* underwent with the enlargement of its meaning from "sacerdotal family" to include the "aristocratic" or "noble" family was the product of ahistorical politically motivated retrojection. At all events, however defined or labeled, the "aristocratic families," in accordance with my remarks in chapter 1, more nearly resembled Tönnies's Gemeinschaften than Gesellschaften to the extent that their members were related by ties of consanguinity or marriage and so were characterized by purely affective bonds. And it is this fact that may help explain why Aristotle, who might well be expected to have mentioned *gennetai* qua "sacerdotal fam-

---

122. Vanderpool 1979, pp. 213–216 (= *SEG* 29.135). The text is known only from a copy in a sketchbook executed in Athens between 1810 and 1813. As Vanderpool noted (p. 215), the *genos* Theoinidai, attested only by a brief notice in Photios, had previously not been included among the Attic *genê*. (It was missing, for example, in the pioneering study of Toeppfer 1889, pp. v–vi.) Vanderpool acknowledges that the restoration of the incompletely preserved name of the *genos* was first suggested by S. Humphreys.

123. Parker 1996, app. 2, pp. 284–327.

124. Philochoros, *FGrH* 328 F 35a.

125. Philochoros, *FGrH* 328 F 35a.

126. For Wilamowitz's suggested restoration of γεννῆται to the *Digest*'s text, see appendix 2.

127. Bourriot 1976, pp. 548–559, 694–711, 1365–1366; Roussel 1976, pp. 39–50, 51–61, 62–64.

128. *AthPol* 20.1, 28.2. For full discussion of this case, see Bourriot 1976, pp. 10–12, 549–559; Roussel 1976, pp. 62–64; and Parker 1996, pp. 318–319.

ily," that is, as a true *koinonia*, does not. He may have assimilated all forms of the *genos* to the one he knew well, the "aristocratic family," and relegated them all to the Gemeinschaft end of the associational spectrum.

Not obviously fitting into any one of these categories of "clans" were the Salaminioi, a self-styled, divided *genos* abundantly documented by three surviving contemporary inscriptions. But the quite uncertain nature of the organization in combination with the apparently unique circumstances of its historical origins hardly permits our using this isolate as the basis for mounting a discussion of the "association" of the *genos*.[129] Nonetheless, one aspect of the case demands our attention here: the division of the *genos* into two branches, οἱ ἐκ τῶν Ἑπταφυλῶν and οἱ ἀπὸ Σουνίου. The former Ferguson referred to seven of the ten Kleisthenic phylai, with the implication that members of this branch were relatively widely dispersed. But of the other branch Ferguson could assert that in 508/7, when the deme system was created, the forebears of the members represented by the much later inscriptions lived "compactly" in the district which was organized as the deme of Sounion.[130] Might we now, on the strength of this one securely documented example, posit a general tendency for the *genê*, however defined, to be concentrated in or associated with a particular region? It does not appear so. For present purposes, it is sufficient merely to cite the results of the two revisionist monographs. For one, with regard to the linkage of confirmed or doubtful *genê* with various localities within, or even outside, Attica, the available evidence is far from unequivocal. Some groups classified as *genê* seem to possess geographical names, but only three of the apparent examples—Salaminioi (again), Kephiseis, and Kolieis[131]—will withstand scrutiny.[132] Conversely, some of the demes possess patronymic names, but in no case, according to Roussel's analysis, does such a deme correspond to a genos qua association attested for the historical period.[133] It thus appears unlikely on the face of it

129. For the epigraphic documents of the Salaminioi, see *IG* II[2] 1232 (fin. s. IV) and Ferguson 1937, pp. 1–74, no. 1 (363/2) and no. 2 (ca. 250). Interpretations include Nilsson 1938; Young 1941, pp. 163–165; Bourriot 1976, pp. 574–594; and now Parker 1996, pp. 308–316.

130. Ferguson 1937, pp. 12–15, with p. 14 for the quotation.

131. A marker of a piece of property (*chorion*) of the Kolieis was published by Raubitschek (1974, pp. 137–138), but the fact that its provenience is unknown removes any value it might have had for localizing the group. We remain dependent upon Hesychios's notice, s.v. Κωλιεῖς· γένος ἰθαγενῶν, ὅπερ ἐκ τῆς Κωλιάδος, in combination with remaining literary and physical evidence for the site.

132. For the evidence, with discussion, see Bourriot 1976, pp. 570–594. Besides the three examples just mentioned, he evaluates the candidacy of Titakidai and Thyrgonidai (possibly, in fact, phratries: see the list of phratries by deme in chapter 7, with note 32) and of Dekelieis, Ikarieis, Ionidai, and Semachidai. But all, or almost all, of these are probably to be disqualified as genuine *genê* in any bona fide sense of the term.

133. Roussel 1976, p. 71. The conclusion conflicts with the statement of Traill 1975, pp. 100–101, that a number of deme names "are identical with, or closely related to, well-established Athenian *gene* with long pre-Kleisthenic histories." He offers as examples Philaidai, Paionidai, Ionidai, and Boutadai, and adds that "there would undoubtedly be more, were our knowledge greater concerning the early Athenian *gene*." Whitehead 1986, pp. 24–25, endorses "the usual and surely correct view," that "the name of another, older type of organization—most obviously a *genos*—was appropriated for that of a deme." As an example, Whitehead adduces from Lewis 1963, p. 26, the naming of the deme Boutadai after the homonymous genos. But against this position it may be observed that there exists no other similarly persuasive example of the phenomenon.

that the typical *genos* enjoyed a particularly strong association with a specific place or region.

Similarly dispersed, according to fourth-century evidence, were the members of the *genos* Brytidai, for Demosthenes records seven members from six different demes—three from the inner zone (Eroidai, Lakiadai, Phaleron), one from the middle zone (Aigilia), and two from the outer zone (Hekale, Kephale).[134] By Roman times, with the artificial restoration of the antique classical associations, the memberships are so scattered that catalogs of *gennetai* are, seemingly following the classification of the Salaminioi "of the seven phylai," arranged according to the principal Kleisthenic units. The catalog of the Amynandridai, for example, registers 51 *gennetai* from 25 demes spread widely over city, interior, and coastal regions.[135] If nothing else, these archaizing institutions (or at least the documents that preserve the memory of them) may reflect, however approximately, the historical reality of dispersed memberships in the classical era. All told, it is difficult to imagine that *gennetai* ever enjoyed significant territorial solidarity. And the absence of such solidarity is another point against their alleged associational integrity.[136]

To place these negative characterizations on a broader-based footing, perhaps the most convincing refutation of the Grotian model of the aristocratic clan is the one derived by Smith from prosopographical data. The argument is founded upon an examination of the 779 Athenians collected by Davies in his study of the propertied families between ca. 600 and ca. 300 B.C. To put it simply, Smith found in the recorded links between these individuals little support for the nineteenth-century conception of a Roman-style political "clan" dominating Athenian society.[137]

Above, it was observed that Aristotle's discussion of *koinoniai*, and indeed his writings generally, fail to mention any association of *gennetai*. But there is a potential exception to this observation, one that expressly concerns the city of Athens. The much discussed fragment 3 of the *Constitution* asserts that Aristotle wrote (with reference to the pre-Kleisthenic regime) that there were four phylai, each comprising three parts (called trittyes and phratries), and that there were thirty *genê* to each part, a *genos* consisting of thirty men. That these *genê* are indeed the same sorts of groups with which we are concerned is indicated by the citation as examples of the Eumolpidai, Kerykes, and Eteoboutadai. But one's suspicions are aroused by the comparison of the system to the number of seasons (the four phylai), months (the

---

134. Demosthenes, 59.60–61, with Walters 1982, p. 3. The "zones" are those introduced in chapter 3, with notes 64–67.

135. *IG* II² 2338 (between 27/6 and 18/7; Amynandridai), with Walters 1982, pp. 3–4, for the count. Cf. nos. 2339 (161/2; name of *genos*? not preserved) and 2340 (ca. A.D. 200 p.; Kerykes).

136. With this conclusion, I agree with the results of Walters's brief analysis at 1982, pp. 2–5, with regard to associations of *gennetai*. However, I cannot endorse his general case against the regionalist analysis of archaic Athenian political history.

137. Since the outcome of any such examination will obviously be determined in part by the assumptions made and the methods used, and since Smith does not clearly indicate what those assumptions and methods are, it is best simply to quote his conclusion verbatim: "only one family, the Kerykes, have the requirements that would qualify them as a genos in relationship both to operation of a cult of some type and a family heritage going back into the early archaic period in terms of information presently available from all periods of Athenian history. Yet the majority seem to have considered themselves 'well-born' in the aristocratic sense as well as wealthy" (1985, p. 58).

twelve trittyes or phratries), and days (the 360 *genê*) in a year. Not unreasonably, the fragment's specific information has been rejected by many scholars.[138] But it is the underlying assumptions that are of interest here: namely, that all Athenian citizens were members of a *genos* and that the *genos* constituted a wholly contained segment of the public organization.

Notwithstanding the arguments of some scholars in favor of accepting these ramifications of the fragment, I must demur, pending the (admittedly unlikely) recovery of corroborating evidence. Meanwhile, it may well be wondered, if the *Constitution*'s information about early Athens is false, just what the basis of this false report might have been. To account for the specific *numbers* in the text, it may be conjectured that Aristotle worked back from round number estimates: for example, a population of about 10,000 citizens in combination with the assumption that a *genos,* or at least its male heads of households, numbered 30 (*AthPol*, frag. 3) would yield a total of 333 *genê*—an adequate basis for the "calendric" 360. With regard to the text's *substance*, a somewhat different approach to a reply may be suggested. For one thing, the *genos* does indeed make an appearance elsewhere in Greece as a public unit: at Erythrai (enrollment of new citizen in *genos*; classical date),[139] Kolophon (enrollment in *genos*; late classical and Hellenistic dates),[140] Pygela (enrollment in *genos*; ca. 310–290),[141] and Samos (enrollment in *genos*; in or after restoration in 322 or 321).[142] The chronology of this non-Athenian material is sufficiently early as to suggest the possibility that Aristotle, the putative author of 158 Greek *politeiai*, may have attempted to reconstruct the undocumented Ur-organization of Athens on the basis of contemporary parallels.[143] Such material might have supported the inference that a *genos* could be a segmental component of a public organization, which entailed in turn the consequence that all citizens were *gennetai*.

To resume the line of our investigation of associations, such *genê,* if internally organized, would, like the phratries they would then resemble, constitute indubitable examples of associations as defined by and exemplified in this study. But the fact remains that, pace fragment 3, there is no good reason, apart from the text of the fragment itself, for thinking that any such universal segmental organizations ever existed in ancient Athens.[144]

Having mentioned the phratry, it might be illuminating to compare with this bona fide association the *genos* as we now understand it in the wake of the revisionist work by our two French scholars. Generally speaking, it is clear that the two or-

138. For a review of the scholarship on this text, see Bourriot 1976, pp. 15–17, 460–491; Roussel 1976, pp. 79–87.

139. Jones 1987, ch. 7, sec. 8, pp. 303–306, citing *ZPE* 44 (1981) 45–47, no. 1.

140. Jones 1987, ch. 7, sec. 10, pp. 310–311, citing *AJP* 56 (1935) 377–379, no. 3 (ca. 334) and *BCH* 39 (1915) 36–37 (ca. 250–200).

141. Jones, ch. 7, sec. 12, p. 315, citing *JÖAI* 23 (1926) Beiblatt 73–90.

142. Jones 1987, ch. 5, sec. 13, pp. 195–202, citing numerous citizenship decrees (see pp. 197 and 200). The Samian case is discussed in depth by Roussel 1976, pp. 87–88.

143. Of the four states just mentioned, the surviving fragments of the *Politeiai* include (from Rose's collection) the Kolophonians (no. 515, Rose 1886, p. 324) and the Samians (nos. 570–578, Rose 1886, pp. 353–357).

144. For a far more accepting and positive viewpoint, however, see Oliver 1980, pp. 30–56. Cf. also Sakardy 1978, pp. 3–8, on "gentilicial forms" in the early *polis* organization of Athens.

ganizations bore no significant similarities. For one thing, while the phratries were essentially "private" organizations at least to the extent that they were not components of the statewide administrative structure, they also played, as acknowledged in chapter 7, a conspicuous public role. Meanwhile, the Athenian *genos*, except for the latent public involvement of the "sacerdotal families" in statewide cults and priesthoods, evidences no such public orientation. The phratry's enrollment procedure, in particular, seems to have served as a preliminary hurdle for those aspiring to citizenship, but no comparable importance is known to have been attached to the enrollment processes of the *genos*.[145] Newly enfranchised citizens, also, are normally permitted to enroll themselves in a phratry as well as in a phyle and deme;[146] the *genos*, in contrast to the non-Athenian examples just cited, makes no such appearance at Athens. Finally, the phratry may figure, as Drakon's law on homicide illustrates,[147] in Athenian legal arrangements; but the *genos* is not mentioned in any surviving Athenian statute.[148] These points of difference clearly separate the *genos* from the phratry and strongly suggest that, whenever the former constituted in any sense an "association," it lacked visible and direct involvement in the administration of the Athenian state. Had the *genos* resembled a phratry (or a deme or phyle association), such lack of involvement would be difficult to understand, given the obvious utility of such a group to a central government clearly prepared to deploy the resources of the private sector in the service of its own public administrative ends. Again, we are driven to place this association well toward the Gemeinschaft pole of Tönnies's spectrum.

Orgeones

Unlike the *genos*, the cultic society known by the collective plural *orgeones*, or "ritualists," makes an appearance in the Solonian law on associations, given the acceptance of a very likely textual emendation justified in appendix 2. However, despite the probable existence of the association as early as the time of Solon, it is not heard of again until the middle at the fifth century, and throughout the lifetime of its documentation virtually all the explicit attestations by name are provided by surviving epigraphic texts.[149] Nonetheless, the *orgeones* will be seen, even on the basis of the following highly selective and focused discussion, to have been a societal phenomenon of the first importance—and one that will bear importantly upon the acceptance of the thesis argued in this book.

According to a much discussed fragment of the Atthidographer Philochoros, the historian recorded a regulation requiring "the *phrateres* to accept the *orgeones*

145. For discussion of the significance of the phratric enrollment, see "The Public Role of the Phratries," in chapter 7. References in the orators to enrollment in a *genos* include Andokides, 1.127; and Isaios, 7.13, 15, 17, 26, and 43.

146. For the texts, see Jones 1991, pp. 80–81; for discussion of the role played by the phratry (including its absence in Athenian block enrollments), see pp. 91, 93, and 102.

147. *IG* I³ 104 (409/8) (= I² 115 ; M–L 86), lines 18 and 23, reproducing the text of Stroud 1968, pp. 5–6.

148. Roussel 1976, p. 43.

149. A notable exception is the reference at Aristotle, *Eth. Eud.* 7.9.3 (1241b).

and the *homogalaktes*, whom we call *gennetai*."[150] The text was assigned by Lambert to Perikles' law on citizenship of the year 451/0.[151] Whatever the setting or specific meaning of the original statute, it is at least clear that by mid-century the central government had intervened in the affairs of the phratry, apparently to the immediate benefit of the *orgeones* (as well as of the *gennetai*[152]). The context of this intervention is beyond recovery, but the regulatory powers implicit in the Solonian law on associations should at least be kept in mind as a possibility.

At all events, the *orgeones* first enter the light of history, documentarily speaking, at the time of Perikles' law and are sporadically attested by inscriptions at wide intervals thereafter. Paralleling our study of the later deme in chapter 4, however, we shall follow some of the epigraphic testimony down into the later Hellenistic age in the hope that the abundantly documented postclassical forms of the association will shed further light upon the question of the relations between associations and the central government.[153]

It is our good fortune that the Athenian *orgeones* have already been the subject of detailed and discerning study by W. S. Ferguson.[154] To organize his analysis, Ferguson divided the inscriptions, and so the associations of *orgeones* corresponding to those inscriptions, into two classes, which he designated "A" and "B."[155] Class A *orgeones* consist exclusively of citizens and, to judge from the findspots of the relevant inscriptions, were centered in and around the *asty*. These *orgeones* were devoted to the maintenance of the cults of a hero or heroine, and, organizationally, were characterized by a single, noncollegial officer, the *hestiator* or "host."[156] By

---

150. *FGrH* 328 F 35a. Among the enormous literature on this text, special mention may be made of the incisive discussion of Andrewes 1961 and, a brief but recent discussion citing the principal literature, Lambert 1993, pp. 74–77.

151. Lambert 1993, pp. 46–47.

152. With reference to the immediately preceding discussion, it is noteworthy that Philochoros's words, taken at face value, imply nothing regarding any possible *associational* status of the *gennetai*.

153. My policy, in line with the coverage of this book, has been to include those *orgeones* known to have been in existence prior to the end of the classical democracy. Throughout, the two major publications of W. S. Ferguson, 1944 and 1949, have been my guide with reference to attribution, chronology, etc. Accordingly, attention has been given to the *orgeones* of the hero Echelos and the heroines (Ferguson 1944, no.1); of Amynos, Asklepios, and Dexion (no. 7); of Bendis (no. 13); and of the Mother (no. 14). For the reader's benefit, I list here the groups omitted (with Ferguson's number and page references): (2), 1944 pp. 79–81, hero Egretes (*IG* II² 2499 [306/5]); (3), pp. 81–82, "god" Hypodektes (no. 2501 [fin. s. IV]); (4), pp. 82–83, *orgeones* (*Hesperia* 10 [1941] 56–57, no. 20 [ca. 300]); (5), p. 83, *orgeones* (*Hesperia* 10 [1941] 14–30, no. 1, lines 30–35 [367/6; *poletai* record]); (6), pp. 84–86, *orgeones* (*IG* II² 1289 [init. s. III]; (8), pp. 91–92, *orgeones* (of Asklepios?) (no. 2355 [s. III?]); (9), p. 92, *orgeones* (*IG* XII 8, nos. 19 [314/3] and 21); (10), p. 93, *orgeones* (*IG* II² 1246 [med. s. III?] plus Dow and Gill 1965, pp. 104–114); (11), pp. 93–94, *orgeones* (no. 1294 [s. IV/III]); (12), pp. 94–95, *orgeones* (no. 2947 [s. III/II]) plus Ferguson 1949, pp. 162–163; (15), pp. 115–119, *orgeones* of Dionysos (nos. 1325 [185/4], [i], lines 1–33; [ii], lines 34-39; 1326 [176/5]; and 2948 [init. s. II]); and (16), pp. 119–121, *orgeones* of Hagne Aphrodite (no. 1337 [97/6] plus Ferguson 1949, p. 163). A few additional texts published since Ferguson's time are cited below.

154. Ferguson 1944 and 1949.

155. Ferguson 1944, p. 73. Here Ferguson merely characterizes type A *orgeones* as concerned with heroes and heroines, type B *orgeones* as devoted to higher deities of foreign origin. My statement above reflects his subsequent analyses and findings.

156. For the class A documents, nos. 1–12, see Ferguson 1944, pp. 73–95.

contrast, class B *orgeones* consistently include noncitizen members and are regularly localized in or about the port town of Peiraieus. Their cults are centered not on
heroic figures but rather on full-fledged divinities, often of non-Greek origin, thus
confirming the observation that "clubs" of the classical period often serve a hero or
god not yet recognized by the state.[157] Organizationally, type B *orgeones* were governed not by a single host, but by rather sizable corps of officers.[158]

Ferguson's two categories, as noted, correspond roughly to urbanized Attica,
the *asty* and port town, respectively. Were *orgeones*, then, exclusively urban in orientation? It does not seem so. Despite its classification under class A, an inscription
from Keratea dated s. III?, *IG* II² 2355, carries a dedication to Asklepios by "the
orgeones." The catalog of sixteen names below, which is apparently complete, is
headed by the rubric Prospaltioi, the plural demotic of Prospalta, a deme of the inland trittys of Akamantis and assigned by Traill to a site a short distance north of
Keratea. As Ferguson observed, the names reveal that they belong to a small group
of closely interrelated families; perhaps, as he speculates, they constituted the full
complement of members.[159] This inference, in combination with the findspot, suggests strongly that the association was wholly contained within the deme community of Prospalta. Additional such evidence may be forthcoming with the full publication of *SEG* 41.84, reported to be a decree preserving part of a catalog of
orgeones, seven from Phlya and two from Probalinthos. The proposed locations of
these two demes point to a base in the vicinity of Pentelikon, although the discovery of the stone in a sanctuary in Athens will, on such a theory, obviously require
explanation. But the fact remains that the text from Keratea opens up the prospect
of a wide distribution of these associations throughout Attica.

Orgeones *of the Hero Echelos and Heroines*

The earliest direct evidence for *orgeones* of class A—and for *orgeones* of either
class—is provided by "the ancient decrees" mentioned and, in two instances,
quoted verbatim in a decree of "the *orgeones*" found on the Areopagos and dated
by its editor, B. D. Meritt, to the early years of the third century, *Hesperia* 11
(1942) 282–287, no. 55. The first of the two *psephismata*, eventually restored
more or less in its entirety, was dated ca. 450 by Ferguson on the basis of internal
verbal evidence.[160] Later, Meritt, following Ferguson's 1944 publication, returned
to the text, and the several improvements were published by Ferguson in his 1949
study. The improved text of the decree (lines 12 through 23) reads in translation as
follows:[161]

> Decreed by the *orgeones*. The *hestiator* is to perform the sacrifice on the 17th and
> 18th of Hekatombaion. He is to sacrifice on the first day to the heroines a young

157. *OCD*², s.v. "clubs, Greek," p. 254.
158. For the class B documents, nos. 13–16, see Ferguson 1944, pp. 95–121.
159. Ferguson 1944, p. 91–92.
160. For Ferguson's discussion, see 1944, pp. 73–79, and 1949, pp. 130–131. For the date, on stylistic and lexical grounds, see 1944, p. 76.
161. For the improved text (after Meritt), see Ferguson 1949, pp. 130–131.

pig; and for the hero [he is to sacrifice] an adult victim and set a table. And on the next day [he is to sacrifice] to the hero an adult victim. And he is to record whatever he spends. And he is to spend no more than the income. And let him distribute the meats to the *orgeones* who are present, and to their sons up to one half [viz. an *orgeon*'s share] and to the women of the *orgeones*, giving to the free ones the equivalent share and to their daughters up to one half and to one (female) attendant up to one half. And he is to hand over to the man the share of the woman.

Before giving out in line 24, the inscription preserves a few traces interpreted by Meritt as the beginning of a second decree and restored by him to read:

Decreed by the *orgeones*. The *hestiator*, the revenues . . .

Ferguson inferred from the first decree that the *orgeones* consisted exclusively of adult males. "They alone participate in the decree-making body and they are the principals in the sacrifice," he wrote.[162] However, amidst the mentions of women, sons, daughters, and the single "attendant" (she, too, a female), this claim requires demonstration with reference to the text. For Ferguson's position, the vital words occur in line 18, where "the *orgeones*" are set apart from all other classes of recipients of the sacrificial meats. Since the latter are, by implication, not *orgeones* themselves, and since they account for all classes of immediate family members, the conclusion appears inescapable. What, then, can be said positively about the status of "the women of the *orgeones*"? Ferguson argued, probably correctly, that this phrase is an umbrella category for all the females, embracing thereby "the free (sc. women)," "the daughters," and "the (exclusively female) attendants." The "free women," moreover, would include not only wives, but the widows and spinsters (and possibly aunts and married daughters) as well of the orgeonic families.[163] To further strengthen (and to modify somewhat) Ferguson's argument, let me adduce my interpretation of the phrase "the women of the *demotai*," which I portrayed in chapter 4 as a technical formula (the existence of which accounts for the infrequency of the expected association-specific δημότιδες). Analogously, while the *orgeones*, stricto sensu, may include only adult males, the existence of the formulation "women of the *orgeones*" at least demarcates these females from others who were not so affiliated. Noteworthy in this regard, too, is the fact that the women are to receive portions equal to those of the *orgeones*.

At the same time, there appears to be no basis for Meritt's earlier interpretation of ἐλευθέραις in line 20 as "independent," with the specific sense "women who were *orgeones* of their own right."[164] According to his revised text, in any event, the point of "free" women would of course be, not to mark their independence, but to contrast them with the following mention of the servile attendants.[165] I raise the question in order to underscore a negative feature of all the classical Athenian associations that we have examined up to this point: that there is no such thing as an "independent" female, at least where membership status is concerned.

162. Ferguson 1944, p. 77.
163. Ferguson 1944, p. 75, note 18.
164. *Hesperia* 11 (1942) 287, with note 28.
165. See Ferguson 1949, pp. 130–131.

All women, like all minors, and of course the attendants were of necessity dependent upon some *orgeon*. Indeed, only if that adult male head of a household is physically present (τοῖς παροῦσι, line 18) would it be possible for the others to receive their portions, for the decree closes with instructions to distribute a female's portion to "the man," to wit, her husband, guardian, or master, but in any case an *orgeon*.

The number of these households was, moreover, as Ferguson realized, probably small.[166] A single table (line 15) is sufficient for all; and the first day's sacrifice is confined to two victims (one of which was to be a young pig, the other an adult victim), the second day's to an adult victim alone (lines 14–16). Unless the ἱερεῖον τέλεον were an ox, the number of assembled could not have been very large. Furthermore, this inference is in accord with the explicit evidence or implications of other documents for both class A and class B *orgeones*. For example, the two *triklinia* cited as the seating capacity of an *oikia* of a sanctuary rented by an association of *orgeones* of the hero Egretes in *IG* II² 2499 (306/5) will, Ferguson calculated, represent between twelve and thirty diners, no more, no less.[167] The *orgeones* who dedicate to Asklepios according to a third century text, *IG* II² 2355, number only sixteen; and, from class B, the *orgeones* called Dionysiastai decreeing ca. 185/4, *IG* II² 1325, total just fifteen. Importantly, too, as no. 2355 illustrates, these small numbers might represent an even smaller number of families: the sixteen *orgeones* fall into only four closely related clusters of kinsmen.[168] To be sure, we are a long way from our mid-fifth-century "ancient decree," but the fact that these indications regarding the sizes of these associations converge on the same small numbers cannot, in the total absence of conflicting indications, be without significance.

With regard to the financial standing of these *orgeones*, there are some fleeting hints of a degree of prosperity. The intact "ancient decree," by restricting to one the number of female attendants accompanying each (woman?) at the sacrifices, implies, as Ferguson realized, that some, if not all, of these (few) families possessed the means to own *two or more* such attendants. A person, male or (as in the present case) female, going by the title of *akoulothos*, "follower," can only of course have been a slave. To Ferguson it was evident that these *orgeones* "did not belong to the class of the 'poor' (*aporoi*)," for it was the poor who were compelled to employ their wives and daughters to perform the services for which the well-to-do used female slaves.[169] Put in such negative terms, the conclusion is perhaps irrefutable, but it leaves unclear what degree of wealth we are dealing with. In his 1944 publication Ferguson had calculated, arguing from his restoration of a reference to an ox in line 20, that the provision of the required sacrificial animals would demand an annual income on the part of the association of not less than 90 drachmas.[170] But with the abandonment in 1949 of his restored reference to the ox, the basis for his calcula-

166. Ferguson 1944, p. 78.

167. Lines 29–30. For the calculation, see Ferguson 1944, p. 80 with note 27.

168. Ferguson 1944, p. 91, with Kirchner's commentary, citing *PA* 23 and 8816; and compare the list of *thiasoi IG* II² 2345 (with Humphreys 1990).

169. Ferguson 1944, p. 79.

170. Ferguson 1944, p. 78.

tion was decisively undermined.[171] This leaves the reference to "accruing interest" (τῶν ἐπιγενομέ[ν]/[ων . . .) in lines 24–25 of the second "ancient decree," echoed by the instruction in the third-century decree "to engrave the (names of those) owing something to the *koinonia* on a stone stele" (lines 5–6). By itself, however, this detail tells us nothing; even wealthy *orgeones* might wish to collect arrears owed to the association. We are thus brought back to the single, but unambiguous, implication that some or all the members were capable of owning two or more "attendants."

Around the middle of the fifth century, to sum up, small associations of *orgeones*, headed by adult males but including their womenfolk and minor children, were engaging in sacrificial feasts in the names of "the hero" and "the heroines." The members were presumably all citizens (like the proposer of the third-century decree) and demonstrably persons of significant means. The findspot of the third-century inscription preserving "the ancient decrees" indicates a base of operations in the urban center.

Considerable attention has been given to this document because it is by far our earliest testimony—indeed, it is one of the very earliest of all records for classical Athenian associations. With our somewhat tentative reconstruction as a point of departure, we may undertake a discussion of those aspects of the later orgeonic records relevant to our goal to investigate the relationship of contemporary associations with the democratic central government. But it will be necessary, before proceeding to the class B organizations devoted to foreign divinities and concentrated in the port town, to examine briefly one other association of class A.

Orgeones *of Amynos, Asklelpios, and Dexion*

These *orgeones* are known only from honorary decrees, *IG* II² 1252 + 999 (ca. 350–300; *SEG* 26.135; 39.149) and 1253 (post med. s. IV), both found in the ruins of their shrine at the western base of Akropolis, pictured in Fig. 8.1.[172] *IG* II² 1259 (313/2), also honors voted by *orgeones,* was found in the same location, and on that basis assigned to this same association. The proposer and the two honorands of no. 1252 all have demotics; and it is likely, following Kirchner's restoration, that the proposer of no. 1253 did as well. Since the two honorands of no. 1259 are identified as ἱστιά[τορ]/ες (lines 1–2), it is reasonable similarly to identify the two pairs of honorands in nos. 1252 and 1253.

So far, so good. The problem concerns the status, social, political, or otherwise, of the nine individual known or presumed citizens in these three records. Ferguson endorsed Koerte's view that they were (in his own paraphrase) "persons of considerable standing in the community." In his own words, "The orgeones known to us were quite respectable Athenians, preponderantly persons of the propertied classes."[173] In actual fact, the prosopographical record of these men will not bear the weight of

---

171. For . . . [ἄν ἧι β]οὺς in the earlier version (1944, p. 74, note 16) he substituted, following Meritt, [. . . διδ]οὺς in the later (1949, pp. 130–131).
172. Ferguson 1944, pp. 86–91. For the physical remains, see Travlos 1971, "Amyneion," pp. 76–78.
173. Ferguson 1944, p. 87 (for both quotations).

Figure 8.1. Sanctuary of *orgeones* of Amynos, Asklepios, and Dexion, view from west. Photograph courtesy of the American School of Classical Studies at Athens: Agora Excavations.

these characterizations. Six of the nine, for one thing, are known from no other source, at least from no source suggesting wealth or prominence. The other three are: Kleainetos, son of Kleomenes, of Melite (*PA* 8462; proposer, no. 1252) is a *diaitetes* in the catalog *IG* II² 1926 (325/4), line 122; Kalliades, son of Philinos, of Peiraieus (*PA* 7798; honorand, no. 1252) is the proposer of a decree of his deme, *IG* II² 1176 (ca. 360);[174] and Antikles, son of Memnon (*PA* 1069; honorand, no. 1259) is probably the grandson of (not, as Kirchner, followed by Ferguson, originally thought, the same man as) the person mentioned in a catalog of the mid-fourth century or a little latter, *IG* II² 2383, line 19. That is all.[175] And of these three, only one can lay claim to "considerable standing" or membership in the "propertied classes:" namely Antikles, refered by Davies to a "notable fourth-century family."[176]

It is of course no accident that the one man of wealth identifiable in these texts is thanked for his performance as host and for his tendance "of the common interests and its sacrifices" (no. 1259, lines 4–5). Furthermore, this organization twice awards gold crowns (nos. 1252 and 1253), once of 500 drachmas (no. 1252); and the

174. For the identification, see Whitehead 1986, p. 445, no. 304. For a possible relative, compare, with Kirchner, the gravestone of Kalliades, son of Kallikrates, of Peiraieus, *IG* II² 7170 (ca. 390–365).

175. I omit from consideration here the very questionable membership in these *orgeones* of Sophokles the tragedian and of his "distinguished" son Iophon, evidence on which Ferguson banks heavily in support of his characterization of the association (1944, p. 87). The identification of Sophokles with Dexion (*Etym. Magn.*, s.v. Δεξίων) and Dexion's conjunction with Amynos and Asklepios in the cult of the *orgeones* are not sufficient to establish the poet's actual membership in the association.

176. At *APF* 10652, p. 399.

standard "manifesto" clause twice invites similar benefactions, promising similar awards (nos. 1252 and 1259). This evidence suggests not a group of uniformly propertied members, but rather a more diverse membership dependent upon the largess of a few generous benefactors.

These two societies might prove, had we more information, to be typical of the cultic organizations of prosperous Athenians, at least such Athenians residing in the city. Small and devoted, in the name of a divinity, to social events centering on the performance of sacrifices, such *koinoniai* would have offered a welcome respite from the massed public gatherings of democratic Athens.

Negatively, in neither association can any involvement with the central government be discerned. To uncover any such link, clearly, evidence of a different kind would be needed. As we turn now to the class B *orgeones*, we shall find that the sources leave little question about the fact or nature of such involvement.

Orgeones *of Bendis*

At the opening of the *Republic*, dramatic date around 411, Plato's Sokrates, relating his trip to Peiraieus the day before to witness the rites of the goddess (who, at a later point, turns out to be Bendis, 1.354a), mentions the separate contingents of the Thracians and the "locals" (*epichorioi*) (1.327a).[177] It is a sensible inference that, on the assumption that the Thracians are noncitizens, the "locals" must be Athenians. The inference has obvious relevance to future developments, because ·when the epigraphic record of the *orgeones* of Bendis commences in the fourth century, the inscriptions are found to fall into two groups, "Thracian" and "citizen." Accordingly, it is tempting, although nothing is said anywhere in Plato's text about *orgeones*, to posit the existence at this time of distinct groups of citizen and Thracian devotees, if not actual *orgeones*, of the goddess.

Early on, however, such a division among those devotees is difficult to discern. According to the accounts of the year 429/8, *IG* I³ 383 (= I² 310), line 143, Bendis (Βε[νδίδος]) was at that time numbered among the "other gods" whose treasure had presumably been placed on the Akropolis by the decrees of Kallias of 434/3, *IG* I³ 52 (= I² 91/92). If, as Ferguson argued, the existence of a treasury implies a shrine, then the construction of that shrine must have antedated the year 429/8.[178] A few years later, in 423/2, the accounts of moneys loaned to the state by the Treasurers of the Other Gods, *IG* I³ 369 (= I² 324), may preserve another reference to Bendis, if Meritt's restoration of [Βενδ]ῖδος in line 68 is accepted; and, again, the implication is that a shrine is in existence. At all events, by 404/3, on Xenophon's evidence,[179] a Bendideion had been established in Athens on the hill of Mounichia in Peiraieus.

None of these sources, however, reveals the orientation, Athenian or Thracian,

---

177. Ferguson 1944, pp. 96–107; 1949, pp. 131–162. For a thorough overview and analysis of the evidence relating to the cult of Bendis at Athens, including the associations of *orgeones*, see Simms 1988. For Bendis in Peiraieus, see Garland 1987, pp. 118–122, and, for epigraphic testimonia, 231–233, nos. 37–46.

178. Ferguson 1949, p. 132.

179. *Hellenika* 2.4.10–11.

of any early shrine of the goddess. The first such indication comes much later. According to a decree of the Thracian *orgeones* in Peiraieus dated 261/0, *IG* II² 1283, the People had, in accordance with the oracle at Dodona, granted to the Thracians, "alone of the *ethnê*," the privilege of *enktesis* and *hidrysis tou hierou*, whereby they will have been enabled, though foreigners, to erect a shrine on Attic soil.[180] If this Thracian shrine is the same shrine Ferguson believed was implied by the accounts of 429/8 (and of 423/2), the grant will have preceded that date. If so, at least one shrine of the goddess, located in Peiraieus and administered by Thracian nationals, was in place by the time of Sokrates' viewing of the first Bendideia later in the fifth century.

When the two classes of *orgeones*, corresponding to Plato's citizen "locals" and "Thracian" *xenoi*, do eventually come into view, it is by virtue of a rather substantial epigraphic record. Thanks to Wilhelm, it is possible to assign most of the surviving texts to one association or the other with some assurance. On the basis of the few securely assigned texts, Wilhelm proposed a more or less formal pair of models by which to distinguish the two organizations: the organization meeting on the 2nd of the month and crowning with olive leaves is the *orgeones* of the citizens, while the organization meeting on the eighth and crowning with oak leaves is the *orgeones* of the Thracians.[181] The correspondence is far from perfect, and a few orgeonic texts fail to conform to either model, but even so the categories are sufficiently well established to provide a platform for the following brief analysis.[182]

The Thracian Orgeones. According to the decree of the Thracian *orgeones* just mentioned, *IG* II² 1283, of 261/0, the Athenians, when, at the much earlier date, granting permission for construction of a shrine, had further enacted that the Thracians "send the procession from the hearth in the Prytaneion," an injunction to which the inscription subsequently refers as a "law . . . which orders (νόμωι . . . ὃς κελεύει) the Thracians to send the procession to Peiraieus."[183] Undoubtedly, this procession is one and the same with the festival of Bendis witnessed by Sokrates.[184] But our present interest is not in these early developments, but rather in the current concerns of the Thra-

---

180. *IG* II² 1283, lines 4–6.

181. Wilhelm 1902, pp. 132–134.

182. Thus belonging to the citizen *orgeones* are: *IG* II² 1361 (post med. s. IV; meetings on the second of each month), 1324 (init. s. II?; olive crown). To these, on other criteria, Ferguson (1944, p. 98, note 43 [pp. 98–99]) adds the following two texts: 1255 (337/6; gold crown; honorands with demotics) and 1256 (329/8; gold crown, although as Simms 1988, p. 69, observes, the *duae coronae* below the text represent olive leaves).

To the Thracian *orgeones* are assigned: *IG* II² 1283 (261/0?; meetings on eighth of Hekatombaion) and 1284i (med. s. III?; oak crown) and ii (med. s. III; meetings on eighth of Skirophorion; oak crown).

A third category is comprised by three texts from Salamis in which the decreeing parties call themselves not *orgeones* but *thiasotai*:1317 (fin. s. III; meetings on second of Skirophorion; olive crown), 1317b (274/3; meetings on second of Skirophorion; olive crown [in sculpture]), and *SEG* 2.10 (med. s. III; meetings on second of Skirophorion; olive crown). See, on these devotees, Simms 1988, p. 70.

Fragments attributed to these *orgeones* but of indeterminable classification are *Hesperia* 30 (1961) 227, no. 5 (s. III) and 29 (1960) 21, no. 27 (s. II/I).

183. Lines 6–7, 10–12.

184. Simms 1988, p. 66. As she further notes, the establishment of the Bendideia may be the subject of the fragmentary inscription *IG* I³ 136.

cians who enacted our decree, *IG* II² 1283, approximately 150 years later. This text represents the earliest direct evidence for the Thracian association.

Since it is not "the Thracians" but rather "the (Thracian) *orgeones*" who express their desire to comply with the law of the People (lines 9–12), we are at liberty to conclude that by this date the Thracian participants in the procession were none other than the members of the association. Two groups of Thracians, it turns out, are in question, one in town, the other in Peiraieus. The decree, composed from the point of view of the presumably original group based in Peiraieus, acknowledges the existence of "those in the *asty* who have chosen to construct a *hieron*" (lines 7–8) and calls for cooperation with this group in a joint observance of "the law of the *polis*" (lines 10–11). By this decree, henceforth the *epimeletai* in Peiraieus are to receive their urban confrères at the Nymphaion, providing sponges, basins, water, crowns, and, "in the *hieron*, lunch—just as they provide for themselves." When a sacrifice is performed, furthermore, the Peiraic priests and priestesses, in addition to their usual prayers, are to include those in the *asty*, "in order that, once this is accomplished and all the *ethnos* is in harmony, the sacrifices to the gods and all else that is fitting take place in accordance with the ancestral customs of the Thracians and with the laws of the *polis*, and that it be well and pious for all the *ethnos* with respect to the gods" (lines 20–27).

This text is remarkable in its repeated acknowledgment (lines 10–11, 25–26 [restored]) of the central government's law (or laws) "ordering" the Thracians to stage the procession from Athens to Peiraieus. Recently, Garland, supported by Dow, has sought to dilute the force of this language by observing that the verb translated as "order" (κελεύει, line 11) in fact may sometimes possess a less peremptory meaning (as in English "bid") and by suggesting that such a meaning is appropriate here.[185] The general lexical point about the meaning of the verb may be granted. But militating against this approach with respect to the present text is the simple fact that in the first of two passages mentioning the law of the city the Peiraieus *orgeones* are said to desire to "obey" (πειθαρ/χοῦντες, lines 10–11) that law, a formulation that would be robbed of sense if mere "bidding" were in question. Some ambiguity, to be sure, does remain, for it is not clear just what is being "ordered"— whether it is the simple fact of the procession or merely its point of departure (as the text, if read strictly, might be taken to suggest). But the law, taken either way, does seem to require the participation by all of the *orgeones* of Bendis, both those in the port town and their co-nationals in the town.

At its end, the inscription, if I read it rightly, departs from the subject of the Bendideia and closes with provisions for the future interaction of the Peiraic and urban *orgeones*. Throughout, it will be noted, the decreeing organization, the Thracians in Peiraieus, seem to be dictating terms (in evident compliance with "the law of the *polis*") to the urban association. They—the urban *orgeones*—are to have the privilege of "approach after the rites;" if any so desire, they may "enter the [Peiraic] *orgeones*;" and "for life take their portion of a sacrifice . . . without paying the fee" (lines 27–32, restored). Note, importantly, that the text stops short of calling for the actual amalgamation of the two units into a single association. Rather, the dominant

185. Garland 1987, pp. 120–121.

theme is not unification but cooperation (lines 8–9, 23–24, 26), specifically with regard to the staging of the procession (lines 13–16). What we are witnessing, in other words, is the creation of a cooperative arrangement between two independent associations, one unit headquartered in each of the two components of the bicephalous urban complex that was ancient Athens. Approximately five miles, by way of the corridor between the Long Walls,[186] separated the two *koinoniai*. That they could not coalesce into a single entity may reflect a determination to maintain territorial integrity on the assumption that a membership distended by even this short distance would not be able to sustain its solidarity or schedule of activities.[187]

The Citizen Orgeones. Besides the Thracians, the citizen *orgeones* too were active participants in the festival from the beginning. If Plato's evidence is taken literally, the *epichorioi* (i.e., the Athenians) had mounted their own *pompê* (*Republic*, 1.327a), possibly as a separate contingent within the larger procession. As well, like their Thracian counterparts, the citizen group seems eventually to have established a shrine to the goddess in Peiraieus.[188] In the centuries after Plato's festival, two honorary decrees from Peiraieus, one honoring three *hieropoioi* (*IG* II² 1255, 337/6), the other a single *epimeletes* (1324, init. s. II?), credit the honorands with the sending of the *pompê* and, in the earlier text, with a distribution of meats, probably in connection with a sacrifice at the same festival. Another measure taken to ensure the success of the procession may, if Ferguson is right (as I think he is), have been the decision, recorded in a law of the *orgeones* dated epigraphically "post med. s. IV," *IG* II² 1361, to admit to the association "anyone who wishes" ([τῶι] βουλομένωι), upon the payment of a specified number of drachmas (the numeral is lost); once the payment is made, the new member will have his name "engraved on the stele" (lines 21–22). Stated explicitly, the purpose of the measure was, in the words of the decree, "in order that the *orgeones* be as numerous as possible" (lines 20–21, partly restored). By way of explanation, Ferguson adduced "the law of the *polis*" just discussed, ordering the Thracian *orgeones* to mount the procession at the Bendideia. If, as Ferguson seems to suggest, the citizens were under a similar obligation, they might well have taken this step to ensure that their numbers be equal to the task.[189]

The Bendideia apart, these measures are remarkable in two respects. First, the decision to admit new members in exchange for a payment suggests that the association may not have enjoyed the same financial health as others did, particularly those others that relied upon the benefactions of a few wealthy (and generous) indi-

---

186. The laying out of a route within the Long Walls may have been a response to the conditions of the Peloponnesian War, when the presence of the enemy army in Attica made travel outside the fortifications impossible: see Garland 1987, p. 121.

187. Garland 1987, p. 119, writes of "the formation of a splinter band of *orgeones* in the Asty for the convenience of those Thracians who were resident in Athens." The image of splintering suggests, however, the calving off of a satellite colony from the main organization. Such a suggestion is not supported by any ancient evidence. Nothing rules out the hypothesis that both *orgeones*, in the town as well as the port, arose independently of each other.

188. For the shrines at Peiraieus, see Garland 1987, p. 119 with p. 162.

189. Ferguson 1944, pp. 99–101.

vidual members. Secondly, there is the matter of the departure from the principle of hereditary succession as the sole criterion governing the admission of new members. That principle appears to have played a role in the earlier history of the organization, for the preserved text opens in lines 1 and 2 with the words (partly restored): "all who were engraved on the stele or their descendants."[190] It is to this same stele that the passage just quoted about the engraving of the names of the new members appears to refer (lines 22, 23). So, from this point on, new members will enter the association according to the conflicting mechanisms of descent and payment of a fee. Conversely, any member found to have moved, or put to the vote, a measure in conflict with the law "will no longer have a share of the *koina*" (line 14). So, again departing from recorded practice of the democratic era, a duly enrolled member could be expelled. To be sure, the old mode of recruitment has not been abandoned, but alongside it now stands a new regulation built upon a principle at odds with the exclusivity, founded on heredity succession in the male line, that has characterized associations at Athens throughout the classical period.

A larger or at least more open membership is the chief respect in which the citizen *orgeones* of Bendis visibly differ from the *orgeones* of foreigners. Probably in part as a consequence of growing numbers, furthermore, the citizen associates, in contrast with their noncitizen counterparts, sustained a remarkably sizable corps of officers: priest, priestess, *hieropoioi* (*IG* II^2 1255), *epimeletai* (1256, 1361, 1324), secretary (1361, 1324), and treasurer (1324). No doubt, some or all of these posts were functional liturgies requiring or pressuring the incumbent to spend, or at least to lend in advance of payment by the members of the association, from his own funds. The personal expenditures or advances (line 7) of the honorand, probably an epimelete (line 1, restored; cf. line 9), crowned by the *orgeones* in a decree of the early second century, *IG* II^2 1324, are a good example. The gold crowns awarded by *IG* II^2 1255 (300 drachmas) and 1256 (100 drachmas) may represent partial reciprocation for such munificence. Viewed from this angle, the growth of the officer corps may reflect a desire to increase the number of benefactors and/or to spread the burden of financial responsibility among a larger number of people. Nor was the personal expenditure by a benefactor the only mode of increasing income. A number of additional sources of revenue are attested in the later fourth-century law discussed above, *IG* II^2 1361: sacrifices by nonmembers in the association's *hieron* for which a payment in the form of sacrificial portions was required (lines 4–7); a fine of 50 drachmas for the illegal sacrifice of *parabomia* within the sanctuary (lines 7–8); rental of the *oikia* and proceeds from the sale of water (both moneys to be used toward the repair of the *hieron* and *oikia*) (lines 8–12); a fine of 50 drachmas (as well as exclusion from the *koina*) for proposing or putting to the vote any measure in conflict with the (immediately preceding) law (lines 13–14); and mandatory payment by each *orgeon* to the *hieropoioi* of two drachmas prior to the celebration of the Bendideia, failure to do so resulting in a fine of two drachmas "sacred to the goddess" (lines 17–20). Taken together, these particulars suggest the absence of an endowment and, again, of wealthy benefactors by the earnings or generosity of whom the association might perpetuate itself. Rather the impression is left of de-

190. . . . ὁπόσοι ἐν τῆ[ι στήλ]/η[ι ἐ]γ[γεγρα]μμένοι εἰσὶν ἢ το[ὺς τ]ούτων ἐκγόνους.

pendence upon a trickle of small dues and fines, with cash reserves so small that the association cannot finance its annual festival without first collecting a small fee (or equivalent fine) from its entire membership. It is perhaps here—quite apart from any desire to put on an impressive display in the procession of the Bendideia—that we may find the real, underlying reason for the abandonment of hereditary succession and the adoption of the sale of memberships to the citizen public. The change in orientation, ultimately, was brought about by the economics of their survival as an association.

Despite the impression of independence left by the internal procedures of the citizen *orgeones* of Bendis, the very real possibility of intervention by the People cannot be discounted. Perhaps, as Ferguson speculated, the citizens were under pressure to turn out in large numbers at the Bendideia. Simms has further speculated that the *hieropoioi* mentioned in the documents of the citizen *orgeones* are in fact state officials, through which the state may have maintained a certain amount of control over business affairs and even the regular meetings of the association.[191] Similarly, Ferguson had speculated that the priest and priestess of the citizen *orgeones* were actually public officials selected ἐξ Ἀθηναίων ἁπάντων.[192] When these possibilities are weighed alongside the expressed direction by the state of the activities of the Thracian *orgeones*, it is obvious that these associations, citizen as well as noncitizen, were being put to service in the public interest. Why?

Already, from at least as early as the later fifth century, as evidenced by Sokrates' report, the festival called Bendideia had provided an opportunity for the joint participation of "local" citizen and Thracian noncitizen worshippers of the goddess. Just possibly, the state's intervention is to be explained in terms of a policy designed to counteract the social segregation created by the citizen monopoly by requiring or encouraging the simultaneous participation of both groups. At the same time, joint participation need not have necessitated actual intermingling of Athenian "locals" and foreigners. Any such efforts to achieve integration seem to be confined to the enactment of "the law of the *polis*," whereby two otherwise independent Thracian associations of *orgeones*, one in the city, the other in the port town, achieved at least a temporary and ceremonial fusion.[193] It was one thing to re-unite co-nationals, quite another to break down the barriers that separated Athenians from *xenoi*.

No less graphically, the procession of the Bendideia also brought about, if only momentarily once each year, the literal and symbolic linkage between the two poles of the Athenian urban infrastructure, the town and the port. That Athens was in effect two cities was made clear to all when the city and Peiraieus were under two separate governments between 288 and 262.[194] If the proposed date, 261/0, of *IG* II² 1283, is right, then the next year saw the establishment—or reestablishment—of an official ceremonial and social link between the two Thracian populations.

191. Simms 1988, p. 71. The *hieropoioi* figure at *IG* II² 1255, lines 2–3 (partly restored), and 1361, line 16. Cf. Ferguson 1949, p. 155.

192. Ferguson 1949, p. 156.

193. For speculation that the decree of 261/0 in fact marked a revival of an already existing practice, see Garland 1987, pp. 121–122.

194. Ferguson 1911, pp. 144–187. I owe this reference to Simms 1988, p. 70, who does not, however, put the events in question to the same use as I do.

Through the Bendideia, the two cities could be made one again. This integration had been brought about by a law of the *polis*, but it is doubtful whether a result of such magnitude could have been achieved except through the already existing organizational apparatus provided by associations such as the *orgeones.*

Orgeones *of the Mother of the Gods*

The epigraphic presence in Peiraieus of the Mother of the Gods goes back to the late fourth century, the date assigned to the earliest inscribed dedication from the *hieron*, *IG* II² 4609 (fin. s. IV).[195] Early in the next century, in 281/0,[196] come two decrees of the *thiasotai* of the Mother from Peiraieus, *IG* II² 1273, but with no trace of the presence of *orgeones.* Such presence is not recorded until later in the next decade, 272/1, the archonship of Lysitheides,[197] when *IG* II² 1316 is promulgated in the name of the *orgeones* (lines 13–14). Surprisingly, however, the main body of this text is preceded and followed by a total of four coronae, each of which identifies the honoring party as "the *thiasotai.*" Why this unprecedented mixture of associational categories?[198] Ferguson, although working with a now no longer accepted date for Lysitheides' archonship, suggested that the sanctuary, earlier occupied by the *thiasotai*, had been taken over by *orgeones,* but that some of the former, with their old titles intact, had been incorporated into the new organization, hence the continued appearance afterward (as in the crowns of no. 1316) of "the *thiasotai*" in a decree of the *orgeones.*[199]

Another approach, however, was opened up two decades later when Dow and Gill published an epigraphic palimpsest theretofore concealed by the decree of the *orgeones IG* II² 1246 (init. s. III). The new text, too, proved to be a decree of the *orgeones* and was dated "fin. s. IV," but after 316/5. Surprisingly, however, the palimpsest, though expressly a decree of *orgeones* (line 1; cf. lines 2, 4, 5), calls for erection of the *dogma* "in the *thiasos*" (lines 3–4); the editors tentatively restored the same phrase in line 3 of the later decree, *IG* II² 1246. Rejecting the possibility that the unparalleled phrase "in the *thiasos*" refers to a shrine or meeting place, Dow and Gill suggested the meaning "in the presence of" or "in the midst of the association."[200] To justify this suggestion, the editors followed the theory that *orgeones*, because no corporate noun existed by which they could designate their association (such as *genos* with respect to *gennetai*), pressed into service the available term *thiasos.* In-

195. Ferguson 1944, pp. 107–115. For a recent discussion of the cult of the Mother in Peiraieus, see Garland 1987, pp. 129–131, with a listing of the pertinent epigraphic testimonia at pp. 235–237, nos. 80–98. For a decree of an association of *orgeones*, possibly of the Mother, published since Ferguson's work, see *Hesperia* 26 (1957) 209–210, no. 57, now dated ca. 200 by Habicht 1982, pp. 159–163.

196. For the date, see G. Arnaoutoglou, *ZPE* 104 (1994) 103–106; and S. V. Tracy, *Attic Letter Cutters 229 to 86 B.C.*, Berkeley 1990, p. 259.

197. For the date, see W. Dinsmoor, *Hesperia* 23 (1954) 284–316.

198. An approximate parallel is provided by the three inscriptions from Salamis preserving decrees of groups identified as the *thiasotai* of Bendis, whereas the Attic evidence would suggest the use of the term *orgeones.* But no single Salaminian document, as here, combines the two terms. For the references, see above, note 182.

199. Ferguson 1944, app. 4, pp. 137–140, at pp. 139–140.

200. Dow and Gill 1965, p. 112.

deed, they found in the palimpsest the earliest known instance of the "general, more neutral, significance" that the word *thiasos* was to acquire in Hellenistic times.[201] Thereby the simultaneous use of the two *termini technici* could be accounted for without resort to Ferguson's developmental hypothesis.

Still, the problem remains. These *orgeones* might have called themselves, as did many an association, a *koinon*.[202] What is the explanation, then, for the adoption instead of *thiasos*?[203]

Aliens and slaves

Ferguson's original position may, I wish to argue, still possess merit. The question remains one of the relation of the two decrees of *thiasotai* engraved on *IG* II² 1273 to the *orgeones*. At the minimum, both decrees, though containing no reference to *orgeones*, are expressly associated with the cult of the Mother: first decree, fine payable to the Mother of the Gods (lines 23–24), second decree, the shrine of the Mother of the Gods (lines 31–32). Some sort of link appears probable.

The speaker of the first is a Herakleian, the honorand a Troizenian; in the second, the proposer is not identified by ethnic, but the same Herakleian who moved the prior decree is, this time around, the honorand. Even if these associations were open to Athenians, it is evident that they were dominated by resident aliens. With these facts in mind, we may consider the possible constitutional status of the *orgeones* by which these *thiasotai* were seemingly (on Ferguson's theory) embodied. With only one exception, wherever an indication of status is preserved, the *orgeones* are citizens: in six texts (*IG* II² 1314, 1315, 1328i, 1327, 1328ii, 1329), the proposer has an Athenian demotic; in three instances (1316, 1327, 1329), the honorand likewise has a demotic. In the exceptional case, *IG* II² 1327, however, at the close of the text the three *epimeletai* are identified by name, the first two by nomen and demotic, the third simply by the nomen Ergasion. Not only the absence of the demotic (proving that, since the name is in parallel construction with the other two, that this person was not a citizen) but the name itself is striking. Reilly's collection of names of slaves assembles three instances from manumission texts of slaves with this name.[204] After all, what other kind of name could "Worker" be? Ferguson fails to do justice to the situa-

---

201. Dow and Gill 1965, p. 113.

202. It is not sufficient merely to dismiss (with Ferguson) the perfectly acceptable term *koinon* as "completely colorless" (Dow and Gill 1965, p. 113). Besides, since *thiasos* had previously been used (and perhaps was still being used) to denote a subgroup of the phratry (see "Subdivisions of the Phratry and Social Differentiation," in chapter 7), its adoption by *orgeones* could only lead to confusion. Some overriding, pressing, concern must be assumed.

203. I give no credence to the suggestion, made by Ferguson only to be dismissed (1944, pp. 138–139), that the inscribing of the crowns is due to the mason's error. One such error would be believable, but that the same error should have been made four times strikes me as quite unlikely. For an entirely different reason, viz., that the text is written in verse, little can be made of the mention of "your *thiasos*" in an address to Dionysos, evidently the work of the *orgeones* called Dionysiastai, *IG* II² 2948 (init. s. II), line 6. Besides, leaving *orgeones* out of it, the word possessed well-known special pertinence to matters Bacchic.

204. Reilly 1978, p. 43. The three examples are: *IG* II² 1567, lines 17–18 (Athens; fin. s. IV); *SGDI* 2011 (Delphi; 196/5); *IG* IX I, no. 676a (Physkos; 166/5). The name is not found in *Prosopographia Attica*.

tion when he calls Ergasion simply an "alien" without further discussion.[205] But the use to which he puts the name, even if it is not adequately characterized, may nonetheless be on the right track. The presence of a Herakleian and a Troizenian among the *thiasotai* of the Mother prompts the inference that, on (Ferguson's) hypothesis that the *thiasotai* had been incorporated within the *orgeones*, the slave or freedman surfaces among the otherwise citizen *orgeones* by virtue of his membership in the same *thiasotai* that welcomed free Greek non-Athenians (namely, Herakleians and Troizenians). Ferguson ventured well beyond the evidence when he went on to suggest that the *orgeones* perhaps made a regular practice of placing an "alien" on each year's board of three *epimeletai*. But one can only endorse the conclusion that the phenomenon indicates "a certain weakening, attributable to the intermingling of citizens and aliens in a religious fraternity, of deep-rooted prejudices."[206] My suspicion is that it was the absorption of an earlier alien association by a larger dominant citizen association that had provided the mechanism enabling such a profound, and perhaps otherwise unobtainable, development.[207]

Women

A cult devoted to the Mother of the Gods would be expected, in line with general Greek practice, to accord a conspicuous role to females. The expectation is not disappointed. The principal cultic official is a priestess, and the several former priestesses of the cult, as we shall see, constituted a sort of *concilium* capable of presenting a request before the *orgeones*.[208] The priestess presided at sacrifices, opened and closed the shrine on specified days, and recorded dedications and received moneys.[209] Eventually, the priestess was entitled to appoint a female *zakoros* to assist her in her duties.[210] Female "vessel-bearers" and "ladies in waiting on the Goddess" formed a cortege of the Mother, conducting her on processions through the streets and taking collections.[211]

Despite their high visibility, however, women remain figures of problematic status within the association of *orgeones*. For example, a decree of 272/1, *IG* II² 1316, honors not only Zeuxion, the priestess, but as well her husband, Agathon of Phlya (line 14, partly restored), who lacks any title. Both are credited with energetic superintendence of the sanctuary, expenditures on the *orgeones* from their own funds, the proper erection of dedications, and the responsible rendering of income accruing during "their" tenure—when, in fact, only Zeuxion occupies a formal office. Accordingly, the two pairs of coronae preceding and following the decree read "the *thiasotai* (honor) Agathon and his wife Zeuxion" (lines 1–4, 25–28). Simi-

---

205. Ferguson 1944, p. 111.

206. Ferguson 1944, p. 111.

207. While this account admittedly leaves unexplained the phrase "in the *thiasos*" in Dow and Gill's text, my theory is not thereby compromised.

208. *IG* II² 1328i, lines 16–18.

209. *IG* II² 1316, lines 6–13.

210. *IG* II² 1328i, lines 16–19.

211. *IG* II² 1328i, lines 10–11.

larly, in a somewhat later text, *IG* II² 1315 (211/0), the priestess Krateia is honored for her performance of the *eisteteria* and the remaining sacrifices, for decorating the sacred couch at the Attideia as well as providing all else well and piously, and for continuing to serve the goddesses and opening the sanctuary on the appropriate days. The decree, furthermore, is fitted out with two crowns. The one reads, predictably, "the *orgeones* (honor) the priestess Krateia," but the other, unexpectedly, "the priestess (honors) Hieronymos." The latter person was almost certainly correctly understood by Foucart to be the husband of the priestess.[212]

The same phenomenon may be in evidence in an even more extreme form in the two decrees *IG* II² 1328i and ii, dated 183/2 and 175/4. Both are concerned exclusively with women. The first, acknowledging the complaint of the earlier annually allotted priestesses that they had been subject to excessive expenses while in office, records their request for an "arrangement" whereby they may perform their liturgy in the future with "no additional expense imposed upon them" (lines 5–7). At the end, instructions are given for the appointment of the (female) *zakoros:* the incumbent priestess is to make the appointment from the past priestesses, no one serving twice until all have served (lines 16–19). Eight years later, evidently after the cycle has run its course, the second decree, noting the meritorious service of one *zakoros* Eutaxis (ii, line 43), modifies the earlier decree by providing for the lifetime appointment of Eutaxis's daughter Metrodora at the joint request of the assembled body of former priestesses. Metrodora's excellences during her initial annual term had included the point that "she gave of herself" (ἐπέ/δωκεν αὐτὴν, lines 25–26).

Although it is with the (male) *orgeones* that the decision rests (ii, lines 30, 37, 39), it is manifestly the organization's women whose past, present, and future service are under consideration. Nevertheless, the corona at the head of the stele reads: "the *orgeones* (honor) the contributors" (τοὺς ἐπιδεδωκότας), with the term denoting the honorands, though literally prefiguring Metrodora's "giving of herself," standing in the masculine gender. No other explanation is at hand than that credit for the women's meritorious service was felt (in all three inscriptions just reviewed) to belong, not entirely to the women themselves, but at least in part to the presumable ultimate sources of authority, as well as of funds—their husbands or other male connections among the *orgeones*. Indeed, we may go still further. In two places, the second decree makes reference to "the priestesses *and* the *orgeones*" (ii, lines 28 and 33). The implication is that these women were not, strictly speaking, members of the association at all, but enjoyed such privileges as they did, including the offices of priestess and *zakoros*, by virtue of their male connections' member status.

Social Welfare

The preeminence of males in this association, despite its orientation around the cult of a quintessential female divinity and the conspicuous roles played by women in that cult, is reflected not only in the association's self-advertisement but in its operation— and above all its financial operation—as well. Inevitably, as always, males fill the nonpriestly offices, which, in the particular case of these *orgeones*, go by the custom-

212. *BCH* 7 (1883) 72.

ary generic titles of Athenian associational organization: the three *epimeletai* (*IG* II²
1327, lines 30–33), the *tamias* (*IG* II² 1327, line 4), and the *grammateus* (*IG* II² 1329,
line 5). Nothing of particular note here as far as titles are concerned. But the fact is
that the occupants of these posts on at least two occasions performed benefactions,
on behalf of their fellow association members and possibly to the benefit of others as
well, that far exceed the scope or dimensions of anything observed in connection
with the associations of Athens under the classical democracy. The two individuals
are a treasurer, Hermaios, son of Hermogenes, of Paionidai, honored in 178/7 by a
decree of the *orgeones* from Peiraieus, *IG* II² 1327; and a secretary, Chaireas, son of
Dionysios, of Athmonon, honored in 175/4 by another decree of the *orgeones* also
from Peiraieus, *IG* II² 1329. Some of their benefactions, to be sure, fall within the
range of the routine. Hermaios underwrote sacrifices, advanced money from his own
funds, including moneys for certain repairs, and took the lead in the collection for the
loan fund; Chaireas "took care" of the sanctuary on several occasions, made contributions and took measures to reduce expenses, and, when necessary, lent money in
advance at no interest when the treasurer was out of town. But two exceptional—exceptional by the standards of classical Athens—items of expenditure call for special
consideration: burial expenses and charitable distributions to the poor.

Burial Expenses. According to his decree, Hermaios, "when no money was available to some of the departed, contributed to the association for their burial, in order
that they be dignified even in death" (*IG* II² 1327, lines 10–12). As nearly contem-
poraneous parallels, one may adduce with Ferguson a law and a decree of *thiasotai*,
the one from Peiraieus, the other from the area of the Pnyx, *IG* II² 1275 (init. s. III),
lines 4–7; and 1277 (ca. 278/7), lines 14–16.[213] But communal arrangements for
burial involving associations go much farther back in Athenian history. It will be recalled that Solon's law on associations attests the existence of *homotaphoi*, but no
organization dedicated to "common burial," with the exception of an organization
illusively mentioned by a fourth-century orator,[214] is recorded before the documents
under review here. The reason for the general absence of such associations, at least
under the democracy, is ascertainable. A speech misattributed to Demosthenes preserves a law of the state requiring that, in the event that no one collects (for burial)
the body of a person who has died in the deme, the demarch of the deme in question
take action. If, after serving notice to the relatives, the body is still not taken up, he
is to contract for the burial, exacting double his expenses from those liable (43
Against Makartatos §57–58).[215] Since the law applied to both free and slave, and
since the deme system accounted for virtually all the inhabited space of Attica, no
unburied bodies (unless found in the Agora or other public space) remained for a
private association to concern itself with. But with the decline of the deme system,
these procedures must have fallen into disuse. By the later third and second centuries, an area of need had opened up, and it was these *orgeones* that filled the void,
at least as far as their own memberships were concerned.

---

213. Ferguson 1944, p. 115.
214. See "Limitation of the Subject," in the Introduction. For the fourth-century text, Demosthenes,
57.67, see appendix 2.
215. For additional discussion, see Whitehead 1986, pp. 137–138.

Charitable Distributions to the Poor. Chaireas is credited with "giving attention that the *demotikoi* partake of the *philanthropa* provided by the *orgeones*" (*IG* II² 1329, lines 12–14). Who, first, were the *demotikoi*? People of the Athenian Demos, that is, citizens? Since Chaireas, and certainly others of the association, were citizens themselves, it would be odd so to identify the recipients of the distributions. Demespeople, that is, members of the deme of Peiraieus? A possibility, but *demotai* would in this case be the expected word. That leaves the meaning "relating to the people," in its politically colored sense and especially with an intimation of poverty or at least low-class orientation. Such a term would not fall unnaturally from the lips of a wealthy patron like Hermaios or Chaireas. But were these *demotikoi* also members of the *orgeones* of the Mother? As with the unburied bodies of the dead, it is not possible to answer definitively one way or the other, although the formulaic expressions at the head of our two honorary inscriptions do identify the *orgeones* as the beneficiaries (*IG* II² 1327, lines 6–7; 1329, lines 3–4).

Either way, the association is here found functioning, as with the burials, as a mechanism for redistributing the bounty of the rich among the needy. It is not hard to suggest a reason why associations under the classical democracy do not engage, so far as we are informed, in such charitable activity. Pay for participation in government, steady wages for military service, compensated labor on public works projects, emigration to overseas cleruchies, all subsidized by the tribute of an empire or then still-productive silver mines, directly or indirectly combined to relieve the suffering of the poor of Athens. But the Athens in which the *orgeones* of the Mother of the Gods found themselves was another world altogether. It is symptomatic of the inherited symbiotic relations between central government and associations that, once extraordinary and artificial sources of supply represented by empire and precious metals were exhausted, the burdens of social responsibility should have been shouldered by these private organizations.

It is clear that, by this late date, the nature of the "response to democracy" has altered its character. Under the regime of the classical democracy, it was a matter of adjusting to the peculiar features of a powerful and successful government—its egalitarian ideology, direct rule, minority citizen participation, and the exclusion of non-Athenians. Now, the response is still in evidence, but with a new direction. From the slender beginnings of which we saw only hints in the classical associations, the admission and meaningful participation (if not recognition) of women, foreigners, and possibly even slaves has dramatically increased. And, with the contraction of the government and of public spending and services due to general economic decline, we find these citizen *orgeones* stepping up in order to address the pressing needs of at least their own memberships. Perhaps it would not be going too far to imagine that the ground for a response of this nature had been prepared much earlier with the establishment of a paradigmatic dovetailing relationship between government and association under the classical democracy.

NINE

The Organization of the Cretan City
in Plato's *Laws*

Introduction

We have now completed study of the attested associations of the classical period with respect to their relation to the central government and, in the light of that relation, to their place in the greater state of Athens. Our findings must stand or fall on their own to the extent that they are supported or not by the evidentiary record for the actual design and functioning of those associations. Nonetheless, any corroboration forthcoming from other sources would be most welcome. There is in fact one such source—contemporary Athenian political theory.

In the course of reviewing the primary sources in the Introduction, we looked at the relevant writings of Aristotle and found that only scant attention is given to our subject in either the diachronic historical or synchronic contemporary sections of the *Constitution of the Athenians*. But the relevant portions of the theoretical treatises, the *Politics* and the two *Ethics* in particular, at first glance appeared more promising, since Aristotle's conceptualization of the *polis* as a *koinonia* of component parts, themselves *koinoniai*, would seem to open up the possibility that his model of the city-state approximated that being urged throughout the course of this book. Aristotle's normative *polis*, in other words, might offer support for the particular reconstruction of a particular *polis* that has been emerging from our studies in the foregoing chapters. But this expectation was found to be largely disappointed. For, by defining his "state" inclusively Aristotle implicitly rules out the possibility that his constituent *koinoniai*, over and above being merely organic components of a unified polity, are in fact engaged in a process of response to a central government—the "state" in the narrower, exclusive sense. He also imposes on his model a unified teleological *purpose* quite at odds with the intuitively possible and historically documented conflict of purpose between a central government and the associations embodied by the state in the larger sense. So, in the final analysis, except for bits of particular empirical data, Aristotle's account of the *polis* cannot be said to confirm my thesis with respect to its basic configuration and underlying dynamic. At best, Aristotle merely endorses the intuitive whole-and-part relation between *polis* and *koinonia*.

Nonetheless, as noted in the Introduction, another potential source of corroboration remains: the final published work of Aristotle's mentor, the *Laws* of Plato. And it is to that work that we now turn.[1]

In the *Laws*, Plato, in contrast with the abstract idealism of the *Republic*, characterizes his project as the attainment of a constitution approaching, yet falling short of, immortality and only second best with respect to merit (5.739e). Nonetheless, the substantive problem with which he wrestles in the later dialogue remained the same: how to create a stable commonwealth. Without stability, as events of the fifth century had illustrated, the benefits uniquely characteristic of a state society could not be secured. The author of the *Republic* had looked for the solution in monolithic unity, which was to be obtained by the removal of the sources of disunity, above all private property and the family. Plato substituted the state itself as the sole focus of loyalty; thereby, he thought, faction and conflict would of necessity be eliminated. But this solution, as the reflections of Plato's career would seem to have revealed, gave rise to another problem—rootlessness. Humans are social beings, but the utopia was to permit no affiliation other than that with the state itself. The resulting rootlessness might generate effects equally threatening to the stability of the new order.

Thus the author of the *Laws*, I will conjecture, coming once again to grips with the original problem, must unify his community without compromising its capacity to provide its citizens with the requisite allegiances. Here, I believe, resides the motivation for Plato's departure from abstract idealism, for it is just this same dilemma that, as I have argued previously, was typically confronted, and successfully dealt with, by the historical city-state.[2] The cure was found in the creation and maintenance of *associations* of citizens which at once, by virtue of their mediating relation between individuals and the state, contributed to unity and, by virtue of their own inwardly focused communal organization, served to satisfy the need for face-to-face fellowship. Plato, while readmitting private property and—the most potent focus of loyalty—the family, pursues historical practice still further by erecting just such a network of associations. The philosopher's realism, in terms of structure and function, goes right to the heart of the matter.

In line with this appraisal, I propose that we assess the organization of the city of the *Laws* in the light of the historical record. But in order to do so, we must first of course make sure that we understand, as a preliminary to comparison, the ontological status of that city. Traditionally, the matter has been discussed in terms of a

1. The following is a revised version of the original article published in *CW* 83 (1990) 473–492, under the title "The Organization of the Kretan City in Plato's *Laws*."
2. Jones 1987, pp. 17–22.

choice between the one extreme or the other of a utopia versus real-place-and-time continuum. But in fact Plato's vision combines elements of both fact and fiction. From the opening passages of the dialogue Plato vividly evokes the land and monuments of the Crete of his own day as the stage setting, as it were, for the new colony. Still realistically, he goes on to locate the site about eighty stades from the sea; it possesses, he says, fine harbors; in its variety of plain, mountain, and forest it resembles the rest of Crete; it is rich in nearly all resources, etc. (4.704b–705c). Nonetheless, despite these manifest advantages, the place has lain deserted for a good long time. Deserted by whom? By the people called Magnetes—the only inclusive name Plato provides for either the former or future inhabitants of the site. Taken together, these details have invited linkage with the persistent tradition that Magnesians from Thessaly had migrated to Crete, where they founded a city between Gortyn and Phaistos, and that later some or all of them had departed in order to participate in the foundation of Magnesia on the Maeander River in Ionia. Significantly, all three stages of the migration are recounted in a late third-century inscription from the Ionian city. The tradition, that is, can be traced to an unimpeachable source dating to no later than a century and a half after Plato's writing.[3] But exactly where in this tradition do Plato's new colony and its projected inhabitants fit in?

A complex answer is necessitated by the ambiguity of Plato's use of the names "Magnetes" and "*polis* of (the) Magnetes." On occasion, the former, departed population is meant: at 8.848d their local deities are to be paired with those of other ancient peoples whose memory is still preserved; and at 11.919d the god is said to be reerecting and refounding the Magnetes. Accordingly, it is reasonable on this basis with Morrow to associate the city of the *Laws* with the (as yet undiscovered or unidentified) place mentioned by the third-century inscription.[4] Elsewhere in the text, however, the Magnetes (to mark a distinction not adequately acknowledged by previous commentators) are also the *new* colonists (9.860e, 12.946b)—although, admittedly, in an afterthought at 12.969a (cf. 4.704a) the possibility is opened up that the god may substitute for Magnetes a different eponym, with a consequent change of name.[5] The mere fact that the retention of the old name is

3. For the literary tradition, see Konon, *FGrH* 26 F 1; Parthenios, V, pp. 48–50 Martini (following Hermesianax); Schol. on Apollonios of Rhodes, I 584, pp. 50–51 Wendel; Strabo, 14.1.11 (636) and 40 (647); Apollodoros, *Library*, p. 219 Wagner (= Tzetzes, Schol. on Lykophron, 202); and Schol. on Plato, *Laws* 9.860e, p. 344 Greene. For the inscription, see O. Kern, *Die Inschriften von Magnesia am Maeander* (Berlin 1900) no. 17 (ca. 207/6), lines 16–19; and, for the Thessalian Magnesian-Cretan connection alone, no. 20 (about the same date). For the epigram of one "Thessalos, from Crete, a Magnes by birth, son of Haimon," see Pisander of Rhodes, *Anth. Pal.* 7.304. For study of the tradition, see U. von Wilamowitz-Moellendorff, "Die Herkunft der Magneten am Maeander," *Hermes* 30 (1895) 185–186; M. B. Sakellariou, *La migration grecque en Ionie* (Athens 1958) 106–116; Morrow 1960, pp. 30–31; and Piérart 1973, pp. 9–12. On the location of the Cretan city, see Panagopoulos 1987, pp. 125–126.

4. Morrow 1960, pp. 30–31.

5. In this connection, it is germane to note that the application of the old name to the new colonists will mask the fact that they, under the leadership of Knossos, will actually be drawn, according to the text, from most other Cretan cities and from the Peloponnese (3.702c; 4.708a). (With Plato's plan compare the division of the population of the historical colony of Kyrene into three phylai, ostensibly reflecting the place of origin, viz., Therans [and *perioikoi*], Peloponnesians and Cretans, and all the islanders: Herodotos, 4.161.3, with Jones 1987, ch. 5, sec. 26, pp. 216–219.)

even considered points to *reconstruction* as the appropriate characterization of Plato's enterprise (thus 11.919d). Founded on the site of an ancient ghost town, Plato's city is rooted in reality, but at the same time, because the site has been abandoned, an opportunity is afforded for renewal on the basis of a wholly new set of principles. Morrow is reminded of Plato's demiurge whose purpose is the eventual improvement of those elements with which he has started, and of the programmatic statement (with which we began) about the "second best" constitution that merely imitates the ideal (5.739e).[6] The limitations imposed by the condition of his raw materials inevitably qualify any aspirations to ideal perfection. Plato's city thus hovers between the poles of real place and unreal utopia, without ever fully coming to rest at either.

My central interpretative claim is that the quasi-historical, quasi-ideal status of Plato's city possesses an analogous relation to the familiar everyday world of his readership. For, while an historical Cretan city is under reconstruction, virtually nothing is said about the earlier city per se. Rather, Plato draws as his raw materials authentic *Realien* from Athens, Sparta, the "Cretan constitution," and, significantly (as we shall see), Ionian Magnesia. If the analogy holds, the newly created state should amount to a rebuilding of those cities from which the *Realien* were drawn— indeed, since no predominating dependence on any one of them can be discerned, of all the cities of Greece. The visionary commonwealth will, to anticipate my detailed argument, acknowledge (and attempt to correct) the general societal dilemma that I have just adumbrated. Evidence will be seen to emerge from various quarters, including in more than one instance Plato's often subtle transformations of recognizable historical institutions, particularly those of Athens. Plato's city not only transcends the sum of its mundane components; it also in detail frequently transcends a given component in its individuality. But seldom is the transformation so drastic that the reader loses sight of the fact that this is a project of reconstruction, not of creation.

The "associations" to which reference was made at the head of our discussion will be, in the first instance, the internally organized segments of the public organization—the utopian analogues to the demes and phylai of Athens already examined in this study. It was in these public associations that Plato, I shall argue, discovered —or rediscovered—the solution to the twin problems of disunity and rootlessness. By cooperating equally and simultaneously in the carrying out of the business of government, the Cretan city's phylai and demes might confer a substantial degree of unity upon the citizen body. Concurrently, those same phylai and demes, each centered upon its own cult center, might develop a corporate cohesion and solidarity hardly possible if the seat of the central government were itself the only focal point of communal life. However, in the end, as we shall see, Plato elaborates on this basic plan by, among other innovating features, overlaying his public organization with a system of purely associational—and, as I shall argue, functionally regulatory—*syssitia* or common messes. Nonetheless, in essentials the arrangements of the Cretan city are fundamentally similar to those of the cities of the contemporary Greek world, Athens included.

6. Morrow 1960, pp. 11–12.

Evaluation of the subject in the light of this program, as opposed to the piece-meal collation of Platonic and historical institutions, will set my study apart from the existing literature.[7] Even the "piecemeal collation" will, as we shall see, be significantly advanced since none of the existing accounts, even within its stated limits, undertook the systematic comparison with the complete record of the historical public organizations. But this too, with the publication of my comprehensive study in 1987, is now within our reach, and happily so, since, as will be seen, the settling of the larger questions absolutely depends upon the proper appreciation of the details. So, with our larger purposes in mind, and with the detailed record of the historical organizations at our disposal, let us turn to the interpretation of the organization of Plato's Cretan city.

The Public Organization: Components and Disposition

At the surface level, the arrangements of the Cretan city do not consistently resemble those of any historical state—not even Plato's own post-Kleisthenic Athens. Indeed, the very situation of the city has suggested to commentators a deliberate avoidance of the characteristic geographic feature of the Athenian organization under the democracy, since the landlocked tract is to be located (as we saw) about eighty stades from the sea, thereby far removed from the noxious social and economic consequences of a maritime orientation (4.704a–705c). With the selection of this site, and after the demarcation of a sanctuary sacred to Hestia, Zeus, and Athena placed as closely as possible to its center (henceforth to be called the "akropolis"), the founder will lay out "twelve divisions of the city (the *polis*) and of all its territory (the *chora*)" (5.745b–c). There is much to recommend Golding's proposal that the boundary between the urban and rural regions was intended by Plato to be established by the functional wall of semidetached dwelling units described at 6.779a–b.[8] Furthermore, the twelvefold division will be carried out in such a way that each of the segments will be of equal value: those consisting of good land are to be small; those consisting of inferior land, larger (5.745c). Apparently, the segments

---

7. General accounts include E. B. England, *The Laws of Plato*, 2 vols. (Manchester 1921); Leo Strauss, *The Argument and Action of Plato's* Laws (Chicago and London 1975); John Ferguson, *Utopias of the Classical World* (Ithaca 1975), pp. 61–79; W. K. C. Guthrie, *A History of Greek Philosophy*, vol. 5 (Cambridge 1978), pp. 332–383; R. F. Stalley, *An Introduction to Plato's* Laws (Indianapolis 1983); and George Klosko, *The Development of Plato's Political Theory* (New York and London 1986).

The existing comprehensive institutional studies are Alston Hurd Chase, "The Influence of Athenian Institutions upon the *Laws* of Plato," *HSCP* 44 (1933) 131–192; Glenn R. Morrow, *Plato's Cretan City* (Princeton 1960); Marcel Piérart, *Platon et la cité grecque: Théorie et réalité dans la constitution des "Lois"* (Brussels 1973); and P. A. Brunt, "The Model City in Plato's *Laws*," *Studies in Greek History and Thought*, Oxford 1993, pp. 245–281.

The more recent specialized publications relevant to our concerns are Wesley E. Thompson, "The Demes in Plato's *Laws*," *Eranos* 61 (1965) 134–136; Naomi H. Golding, "Plato as City Planner," *Arethusa* 8 (1975) 359–371; Trevor J. Saunders, "Notes on Plato as a City Planner," *BICS* 23 (1976) 23–26; E. David, "The Spartan *Syssitia* and Plato's *Laws*," *AJP* 99 (1978) 486–495; and Michel Woronoff, "Ville, cité, pays dans les Lois," *Ktema* 10 (1985) 67–75.

8. Golding 1975, p. 364.

were intended to be wedge-shaped and arranged in spokelike fashion around the hub of the akropolis.[9]

Next, the founder is to mark off the 5,040 allotments, presumably in equal numbers or 420 per division. Each allotment will then be cut in half, on the plan that each citizen receive a half parcel from the city and a half parcel from the country-side. By two devices these newly combined allotments are to be rendered equal in value. First, paralleling the disposition of the twelve divisions, the undivided lots will be large or small according to the value of the land. Secondly, each combined lot is to be equal in terms of its aggregate distance from the geographical center; that is, the closest-in parcel will be paired with the most distant rural parcel, the next closest-in with the second most distant, and so on. The result will be a sort of parity of urban access or (more to the point for Plato, as we shall see) rural isolation (5.745c). Once this is accomplished, the 5,040 male heads of households may be placed on the land as follows. The citizens are divided into twelve groups, each of equal total net worth with respect to property holdings as determined by a census. By some unstated process, but presumably sortition, the twelve groups are then to be assigned to the twelve divisions of land. Each citizen must establish a residence in both his urban and his rural half-parcel. Each of the twelve divisions will be con-secrated to, and named after, one of the twelve gods and will thereafter be desig-nated by the technical term "phyle" (5.745d–e).[10]

Units below the twelve phylai are only scantily–and confusingly–indicated. At 5.746d, the Athenian calls for consideration of the manner in which the law is to fix "the elements accompanying these [phylai] and generated out of these [phylai]." Not aired by any previous commentator, the natural interpretation of these words would be "divisions cutting across and subdividing the phylai."[11] The units men-tioned immediately thereafter, if taken in order, conform to this reading: *phratriai*, *demoi*, and *komai*. Phratries, personally disposed in all historical examples from an-cient Greece, will have been constituted without regard to the boundaries of the state's territorial segments; that is, they will have cut across these segments, includ-ing the twelve phylai.[12] "Demes and villages," by contrast, should, on the basis of

9. Golding 1975, p. 364. The possibility of a "circular state" is explored in depth by Saunders 1976, pp. 23–26.

10. Everywhere I assume the identity of the phylai with the twelve "sections" (τμήματα of the city: 5.745e), "parts" ([κατὰ] δώδεκα μέρη at 12.946c), and "divisions" (see below, with notes 13 and 14). Two such twelvefold territorial divisions would not only be without historical parallel but would also be quite redundant, given the presence of the villages and various associations in the Cretan city soon to be discussed.

11. England (1921, on this passage) correctly distinguishes the personal phratry from the local deme and village but takes the interpretation no further. Morrow (1960, pp. 124–125) attempts to ease the dif-ficulty of the passage by positing the "principle of interpretation" that, where details are absent, Plato intended his readers to flesh out the picture from their own knowledge. But his discussion requires ex-clusively Athenian readers drawing upon an exclusively Athenian experience—a questionable approach on more than one count. Piérart (1973, p. 70) without argument merely characterizes all as "subdivisions des douze sections."

12. Justification is lacking for the definition of the phratry, in support of which the present passage is cited, as a "political subdivision of the φυλή" at *LSJ* [9], s.v. φρατρία, II. While Jones 1987, index I.A.30, p. 388, assembles eleven states where a public function for the phratry can be demonstrated, only at Argos (ch. 2, sec. 7) and Syracuse (ch. 4, sec. 20) is the segmental relation with the phyle indicated, and

historical usage, designate constituent parts of the principal (territorial) divisions. But if so, the question arises regarding their relation to the *additional* segmentation of each of the twelve phylai into "twelve subdivisions" called for in the following book (6.771b, d).[13] Nowhere is a recognizable technical term attached to this subdivision; and common sense hardy permits the existence of still another tier of territorial units below the phylai. Moreover, when Plato comes to speak of the functions of the demes and villages, there is no suggestion that a third such unit remains to be accounted for. Either the deme or the village, therefore, was intended to be understood as a twelfth part of the phyle. From 8.848c, it is clear that the term in question is not "deme" but "village."[14]

This conclusion leaves unresolved the matter of the mutual relationship of the deme and the village—a seemingly otiose duplication, for what is "deme" but another word for "village"? No historical city-state is known to have institutionalized both terms, though each occurs frequently in the absence of the other.[15] Possibly, to return to Plato's text at 5.746d, the words "and villages" in the series "phratries, demes, and villages" are simply epexegetic, adding (for the benefit of non-Athenian readers?) the ordinary prosaic noun for the technical "demes." But against this reading —as well as against any allegation of simply sloppy or redundant writing—is Plato's allocation to deme and village of distinct and mutually exclusive functions (see further, below): to the deme, statewide public functions; to the village, an internal associational function. The distinction, then, is one of aspect or of role. "Deme," "village," as well as "subdivision," all refer to the selfsame segment of the territorial phyle.

We are left, therefore, with a territorial system of twelve phylai subdivided, twelve units per phyle, by 144 demes (or, in their associational role, villages) and cut across by an unknown number of personally disposed phratries. What affinities with Athenian or other historical organizations are detectable?

By itself, the combination of phyle, deme, and phratry is too common to permit the identification of a specific source of inspiration. The *numbers* of units involved, however, are another matter. At Athens, the number of phylai was first increased from ten to twelve in the year 307/6,[16] forty years after Plato's death, so commenta-

---

in both cases the phylai in question are personal, not territorial, in disposition. In chapter 7 of the present work, it is argued that the Athenian phratries centered in the outlying rural regions tended to have their seats in the larger demes (see "The Relations of the Phratries and the Demes"), but this does not imply of course that any such phratry's members all came from that deme. Indeed, in more than one instance such was demonstrably not the case.

13. 6.771b: "And our entire number has twelve divisions (*dianomai*); and the number of the phyle is also twelve;" 6.771d: "twelve for the division (*dianomê*) of the phyle and twelve for the partition (*diamerismos*) of the city by itself."

14. "There should be twelve villages (*komai*), one at the center of each twelfth part; and in each village (*komê*) we must first select shrines and an agora." Thompson (1965, p. 136) refers the subdivision of the phyle at 6.771d to the deme, but Plato nowhere uses that term in association with the subdivisions of the phyle. The present (and, I think, decisive) passage is not adduced.

15. Jones 1987, index I.A.3 (δῆμος) and 11 (κώμη), p. 387. At Athens, for example, where "deme" is the technical term, "village" occurs only in informal contexts without necessitating the assumption of a second constitutional territorial entity.

16. Jones 1987, ch. 1, sec. 1.21, p. 35.

tors, forced to look elsewhere and reasonably encouraged by the general Solonian cast of the Cretan constitution,[17] have sometimes sought the exemplar in the pre-Kleisthenic organization of Athens. The one promising candidate here is the twelve trittyes that subdivided the four Old Attic phylai—promising because we know that they survived in vestigial form into the fourth century. But against the rapprochement is the likelihood that these trittyes were not territorial but personal groupings and the certainty that, in any case, Plato has implicitly rejected, as we saw earlier, the trittys-form of organization characteristic of later, Kleisthenic Athens. So why look to the pre-Kleisthenic trittyes?[18]

Plato himself declares his preference for a numerical basis for organization (e.g., 5.746d–747b), but the choice of *twelve* seems to be supported solely by reference to the Twelve Gods (5.745d). Beyond this weak motivation, might there yet be some external, non-Athenian institutional prototype? In fact there is one, and only one, attested historical organization that is known to satisfy all the necessary conditions of arrangement and chronology, that of Magnesia on the Maeander River in Ionia. Following the refoundation in 400/399, the city's phylai, documented as early as the fourth century, were with near certainty twelvefold, with each (originally) bearing the name of one of the Twelve Olympians.[19] The agreement is significant because in historical times the Ionian Magnesians, as mentioned above, claimed to be colonists of their Cretan namesakes. On that basis, Plato may have regarded their arrangements as particularly suitable to his revived Cretan "Magnesia."[20]

The city's 144 territorial units at once recall the 139 (or 140) demes of Kleisthenic Athens. Not only are the numbers very close but, as well, no other known organization has anything like so many territorial or other units.[21] Accordingly, there is a strong temptation to posit here a partial Attic prototype. Either Plato could not escape the influence of, or found attractive, the extreme fragmentation of the Athe-

17. For the Solonian elements in Plato's Cretan constitution, see Chase 1933, p. 191, where ten instances of "direct correspondence" are cataloged.

18. For the pre-Kleisthenic trittyes, see Jones 1987, ch. 1, sec. 1.1, pp. 28–31.

19. Jones 1987, ch. 7, sec. 13, pp. 315–317. The fragmentary record attests only ten names of phylai, of which eight have deities as eponyms (Apollo, Ares, Aphrodite, Hermes, Hestia, Hephaistos, Poseidon, and Zeus) and two, dynasts (Attalos and Seleukos). But since all the deities belong to the canonical twelve and since an altar and ritual of the Twelve Gods are epigraphically documented (Kern, *IMagnesia*, no. 98), I argued that the two dynastic phylai represent later replacements (or, what amounts to the same thing, renamings) of two components of the original duodecadic organization. These, and two others whose names are not attested in any form, will have been the phylai of Athena, Artemis, Demeter, and Hera. Twelvefold systems of phylai occur elsewhere, but at this early date only the Magnesian organization features theophoric names.

20. To cite possible alternative lines of approach, Morrow (1960, p. 124) speculated that Plato desired to bring the number of phylai into agreement with the number of months, thereby making possible the organization of the *prytaneia* on a monthly basis (for my own discussion of this subject, see below); and Piérart (1973, pp. 66–68) endorses those rapprochements—the twelve phratries, the twelve months, and "cosmic time" in general—that underscore the important role accorded to religion by Plato.

21. States known to have had large numbers of territorial units are Eretria (Jones 1987, ch. 1, sec. 5: in excess of fifty demes); Argos (ch. 2, sec. 7: in excess of thirty villages); Lokroi Epizephyrioi (ch. 4, sec. 12: at least thirty territorial? units); and Tauromenion (ch. 4, sec. 21: in excess of thirty territorial? units). In no instance is it likely that a total of 144 units was even remotely approached.

nian organization. (In the end I shall suggest that it was a case of attraction.) At the same time, however, neither Athens nor any other state is known to have segmented its phylai, as Plato does, by *uniform* numbers of territorial units. For Ionian Magnesia, no lower level unit whatever is recorded; indeed, there are good reasons for believing that no such units ever existed.[22] At Athens, the number of demes per phyle ranged from six (Aiantis) to twenty-one (Aigeis);[23] obviously, nominally equal artificial phylai could not contain equal numbers of preexisting "natural" villages as components. Plato's numerical first principle willfully flies in the face not only of attested practice but of common sense as well.

The preoccupation with numerical division, while extreme, does nonetheless reflect a trend in the development of historical public organizations. All over Greece, numerically designated units, fractional partitions, ordinal enumerations, and other kinds of schematization emerge from an era of radical constitutional reform. Similarly, the Cretan city's bias toward territorialism mirrors the widespread tendency, most clearly in evidence at Athens, to abandon the personal disposition of inherited social groupings in favor of various geographical arrangements. Still a third historically documented innovation, in this instance probably unique to Athens, finds its structural counterpart in the requirement that every citizen establish dual residences in both the urban and rural halves of his allotment. Reduced to its essentials, a similar town-and-country integration was the ostensible objective of Kleisthenes' use of the trittys system in order to combine segments of the city, inland, and coastal regions in each of his ten phylai. All of which is to say that, despite its unparalleled features, Plato's organization reveals the author's consciousness of, and similar responses to, the predicament of the historical Greek city-state.[24]

The Public Organization: External or Statewide Functions

With his realistic, up-to-date organization in place, Plato assigns to it functions representing a fair sample of the departments actually serviced by its historical counterparts—financial, military, religious, constitutional, and judicial.[25] Administratively, this is to be a typical Greek city-state. But below the surface there runs a consistently innovative current. Again and again, the detailed inspection of procedures reveals that the impact of the units of public organization upon the function in question will be, by one means or another, diluted. In a few instances, a precedent may be found in, for example, the loosening of strict representation of the public unit on a board of magistrates, but Plato accelerates the process beyond any observed historical case. As the full record will reveal, the object is to inhibit the transfer of the units' internal solidarity to the operation of the central government.

To take an uncomplicated instance, a financial function emerges at 12.955d, where the *phyletai* are called upon to furnish an annual record of the year's produce

22. Jones 1987, ch. 7, sec. 13, pp. 315–317, esp. 316.

23. Traill 1986, pp. 126–128 (Aigeis), 138 (Aiantis).

24. For discussion of these historical trends, with examples, see Jones 1987, Introd., pp. 11–24.

25. For the record of statewide applications of the public organization, see Jones 1987, index II, pp. 389–395.

to the *agronomoi* (on which, see further below). This may naturally be taken to mean that the records are to be compiled by phylai. For parallels, while at (distant) Messene an early Imperial document tabulates assessments and arrears by phylai,[26] more relevantly both the pre-Kleisthenic *naukrariai*[27] and the Kleisthenic demes[28] are linked to taxation. But Plato's six treasurers (the people actually handling state funds), while in Attic style drawn only from his first property class, are not explicitly linked to his utopian phylai. Meanwhile, in historical Athens, several boards with accounting and financial responsibilities continue to observe selection *kata phylas*, although some relaxation of strict representation has already been prefigured in the mode of selection of the board of *Hellenotamiai* and by the single treasurer of the military fund.[29] Plato severs the connection altogether and thereby implicitly precludes the direct influence of the phylai on financial matters. Similarly, the board of twelve *euthynoi*, or examiners, if initially constituted (as at Athens) by phylai,[30] will subsequently abandon representation entirely as new members are recruited on a wholly different principle (12.946c).

In the military sphere, Plato parallels widespread historical practice at 6.755c by organizing his foot soldiers by phylai.[31] These regiments' immediate commanders are to be the taxiarchs, whom the generals will nominate "for themselves [i.e., to command the phyle regiments], twelve in number, one taxiarch for each phyle (6.755d)." At this point, Plato is certainly following the Athenian model, since the taxiarch of the phyle is found in no other state.[32] Presumably, analogously, his phylarchs (6.755c, 756a, 760a; 8.834c; 9.880d), although not explicitly so described by the author, were intended to correspond to their Athenian counterparts who, selected one from each phyle, headed the cavalry squadrons.[33] But what authority is to oversee the Cretan city's taxiarchs and phylarchs? Three generals elected by popular vote (6.755e) and two hipparchs elected by vote of the cavalry (6.756a-b)—in neither case with any stated relation to the public organization. Meanwhile, at Athens, the generals, ten in number, continue to be elected by phyle until at least 357/6 and possibly later, while the hipparchs, though only two in number, were still in Aristotle's day set over one-half of the phylai each—that is, their sphere of duty, if not (as was true of the generals) the basis of their selection, was determined by the public organization. Plato's units, while playing an administrative role, are subordinate to the higher authority of officers appointed without reference to those units. Where the generals are concerned, Plato has responded in short order to—or, conceivably, actually anticipated—the transition at Athens to election ἐξ ἁπάντων.[34]

---

26. Jones 1987, ch. 3, sec. 8, pp. 146–148. The document is *IG* V 1, no. 1433 (time of Gaius or Claudius).

27. Jones 1987, ch. 1, sec. 1.1, pp. 30–31, citing Herodotos, 5.71.2.

28. Jones 1987, ch. 1, sec. 1.25, p. 45, citing Demosthenes, 50.8.

29. Jones 1987, ch. 1, sec. 1.25, pp. 44–45.

30. Jones 1987, ch. 1, sec. 1.25, p. 44, citing *AthPol* 48.4.

31. For the phyle regiment of Athens, see Jones 1987, ch. 1, sec. 1.29, p. 55, and, for its occurrence elsewhere in Greece, index II.L.2.m, p. 395.

32. For the Athenian evidence, see Jones 1987, ch. 1, sec. 1.29, p. 55, citing *AthPol* 61.3 plus epigraphic documentation.

33 .Jones 1987, ch. 1, sec. 1.29, pp. 55–56.

34. Ibid.

Regarding the *agronomoi* and *phrourarchoi*, each district (that is, the μόριον, to which one phyle has been allotted) is to provide five such "field administrators and guard commanders," and each of these five is to select twelve "young men" of his own phyle between the ages of 25 and 30 (6.760b–c).[35] Recalling the tour of duty of the Athenian ephebes, the men will serve two years, each group (of sixty) being assigned to a district (i.e., phyle) for a month, then moving on to the next district in a clockwise direction; for the second year, the rotation is to be reversed (6.760b–e).[36] (Just possibly, the contingents may mimic the historical 500 guards of the docks selected by lot by the demes; if, as seems likely, the bouleutic quotas were followed, each phyle will have provided fifty men apiece.)[37] But the crucial point is that these citizens, prior to assuming their permanent duties within their own phyle districts, will have spent two formative years familiarizing themselves with the remaining eleven-twelfths of the state's territory. Indeed, that is the very reason given by Plato for the rotation (6.760c–e). But why go to all this trouble, if afterward they will be confined to their own districts? My answer is that thereby they, unlike the fellow *phyletai* they have been trained to police, will have acquired a sense of loyalty to the *entire* polity that overrides any narrow allegiance to the phyle of their affiliation. Thus in still another way, administrative assignment based on the unit will not be allowed to contribute to fragmentation of the monolithic commonwealth.[38]

In the administration of religion, any sectional influence possessed by boards selected *kata phylas* will be diluted to an extreme degree. Twelve women who are to assume custody of the children and their nurses, for example, are to be drawn one from each phyle.[39] But their relationship with the unit of their origin is twice qualified: their appointment is subject to the decision of the Women in Charge of Marriages, who themselves have no stated relation with the public organization; and before they may exercise their duties they must first be assigned by the Guardians of the Laws (7.794a–b). Since, furthermore, these duties are expressly centered on a village (7.794a), the possibility is opened up that the Guardians will assign a woman to a "band" (ἐφ᾽ ἑκάστῃ sc. ἀγέλη, 7.794b) in a village, or even in a phyle, other than her own, thereby neutralizing the factor of a possible "constituency." But Plato sheds no further light on this point. With the *exegetai*, or interpreters of sacred laws, a similar possible effect will be achieved through a complex election procedure. The

---

35. My interpretation of this troublesome passage is simply stated dogmatically here. For detailed discussion, see England 1921; Morrow 1960, pp. 186–190; and Piérart 1973, pp. 260–267.

36. *AthPol* 42.3–5. The procedure is possibly to be connected with the apparent counterclockwise sequence of the urban trittyes around the Akropolis center of Athens noticed by Traill 1975, ch. 3, pp. 35–55, at 55.

37. Jones 1987, ch. 1, sec. 1.29, p. 57, citing *AthPol* 24.3 and 62.1.

38. Plato himself provides as the motive behind the rotation a desire to acquaint the men with all the districts and at various times of the year (6.760c–e). The somewhat different purpose that I have suggested, though not stated in so many words, is nonetheless latent in the procedure Plato lays out and is entirely compatible with the philosopher's explicit formulation.

39. For the board of women there is no parallel at Athens, but compare at Elis (Jones 1987, ch. 3, sec. 7, pp. 142–145) the Sixteen Women, who Pausanias at 5.16.7 states were drawn two from each of the (then-existing) eight phylai; and at Miletos (ch. 7, sec. 16, pp. 326–327) the twelve female youths who appear to represent the (twelve) phylai in a Hellenistic epitaph, *Didyma* II, no. 537 (ca. 200; partly restored).

twelve phylai are to be divided into three groups of four. Each group is to conduct an election—making three elections in all—whereby a single man will be selected from each phyle. The three (of each lot of four, thus totaling nine) with the most votes are to send the nine (with the next largest number of votes) to Delphi where the oracle is to select one from each triad (of candidates), resulting in the board of twelve (presumably, with the addition of the final three, representative *kata phylas*). In the event of vacancy, the four phylai are to elect a replacement from the phyle in question (6.759d–e). Why the groupings? England suggested that they conformed to a territorial arrangement designed to obviate the regional concentration of candidates. But Plato makes no mention of such a design. Alternatively, the text does suggest that citizens, once so grouped, would be permitted to vote for other than their own *phyletai*.[40] Again, the result would be the weakening of any emerging sense of constituency. Beyond that, even the voice of Apollo will be enlisted to limit the autonomy of the individual public unit.

Let us now turn to the composition of the Cretan city's council. The body is to comprise "thirty twelves," Plato writes, because the number 360 would be appropriate to "the divisions" (6.756b). Since he goes on to describe a partition into four groups, with ninety councillors to be drawn from each of the four property classes (6.756c), the "divisions" in question should be just these property classes. But if so, why does he say *twelve* thirties instead of "four nineties" or simply "three hundred and sixty"? On our reconstruction, a twelvefold division extending over the entire state can apply only to the phylai. At once, the historical partition of the Athenian councillior year into ten *prytaneiai*, or "presidencies," springs to mind.[41] Possibly Plato, with his twelve phylai already in place, envisioned a more "natural" sequence of *prytaneiai* that, though based on the system of phylai, at the same time corresponded to the twelve months of the civil calendar. And, sure enough, this is just what the philosopher proceeds to say with reference to an executive board of "guards" of the Council serving in rotation in good Athenian style (6.758b–d).

At the same time, the twelfth-part *segments* of each phyle that I have identified as the villages (or demes) could have been represented on the phyle's panel of thirty only by fractional or alternating integral numbers—both unlikely assumptions in the case of a numerically "ideal" system of government and in any event inconsistent with attested Athenian usage.[42] Moreover, since, as we saw, the twelfth-part villages (or demes) are equal in size, the historical Athenian system of bouleutic quotas based on the widely varying citizen populations of the demes is obviously not applicable.[43] Still worse, and departing again from the Athenian model, the ensuing text couches the procedure for selection of the councillors in terms of the prop-

40. The interpretation offered here was considered, but not favored, by England (1921, p. 568). Morrow (1960, p. 420) concludes that the procedure cannot be determined with precision. Still other analyses are assembled and critiqued by Piérart (1973, pp. 337–339).

41. Jones 1987, ch. 1, sec. 1.22, p. 40, citing *AthPol* 43.2.

42. Although, admittedly, in the case of alternating integral numbers, one could cite the "variant quotas" recognized by Traill. See the Conspectus at Traill 1986, pp. 125–146, where 16 examples of such variation are instanced.

43. Ibid.

erty classes without so much as a hint of a role for either phylai or demes (6.756c–e). It appears an inescapable inference that, despite the numerical inelegance involved, Plato intended that his twelve "presidencies" be in some way correlated with the four classes, not with the phylai.[44] This dramatic deviation from Athenian practice can only have been deliberate, for Plato, the author of the *Apology*, if anyone, understood the administrative structure of the Council of Five Hundred. In that work, Sokrates is made to cite as an example of his commitment to justice his tenure on the *prytaneia* of the phyle Antiochis when the People proposed to the Council the trial en masse of the ten generals at Arginousai (32b–c). His protests proved to be in vain.[45] Did Plato assign responsibility for this travesty of justice to the procedure by which the councillors, in particular the boards of presidents, had been selected? We cannot, in the absence of his explicit judgment, be sure. But it is a fact that had Sokrates' fellow *phyletai* followed his example, the trial would not have taken place. Reorganization on an entirely different basis, then, might in some way decrease the possibility of such malfunctions.

　　If it was a judicial proceeding of the Athenian Council that inspired the divergent composition of its Cretan counterpart, is the same tendency discernible in the court system itself?[46] For the hearing of civil cases, Plato envisions a three-tier structure (6.767a). Initially, suits are to be heard before "arbitrators and neighbors" (11.920d; cf. 6.766e). If a settlement cannot be reached, recourse might be had to the "tribal courts" which appear under a variety of designations (e.g., ἐν τοῖς φυλετικοῖς δικαστηρίοις, 6.768c). Once they are styled "villagers and *phyletai* according to the twelfth part" (12.956c); since each phyle is itself to be divided into twelve parts (6.771b), with one village per part (8.848c), the court might be understood as the internally organized tribunal of a single phyle. The alternative reconstruction, that it and the other courts were constituted on a statewide basis, drawing equally upon all twelve phylai, though admittedly favored by historical Athenian practice, is not compelling. For why, if that were Plato's meaning, would the tribunal be said to consist of "villagers" as well as of *phyletai*? Plato's vision, as we shall see, acknowledges a high degree of local solidarity centered on the village. And, if historical practice is to play a part in the interpretation, decentralization of the administration of justice finds a precedent in Peisistratos's institution of the traveling circuit judges called *dikastai kata dêmous* (*AthPol* 16.5, 26.3), while courts based on and contained within a public unit are attested for the village at Argos,[47] for the deme on

---

44. Morrow (1960, p. 173, note 50) observes (with earlier commentators) that, given twelve *prytaneiai* and so a single *prytaneia* of thirty councillors, the four property classes could not, as expected, be represented by equal numbers on the panel. Piérart (1973, p. 103) merely comments that Plato has not told us how the *prytaneia* was constituted and airs as a possibility "une négligence du philosophe."

45. Cf. also the account of Xenophon, *Hellenika* 1.7.14–16.

46. The judicial system of the Cretan city is treated at length by Chase, Morrow, and Piérart. It is principally against Morrow (1960, pp. 257–258), who draws upon his earlier, detailed discussion (1941, pp. 314–321), that I maintain with Chase (1933, p. 158) and others that the civil court of the second instance was not constituted on a statewide basis. Piérart (1973, pp. 391–393), however, agrees with Morrow in finding in the Athenian Heliaia the most likely model for this tribunal.

47. Jones 1987, ch. 2, sec. 7, p. 117. For the judicial proceedings of the Argive *komê* of Mycenae, see *IG* IV 498 (init. s. II), lines 7–8.

Kos,[48] and, again significantly, for the deme at Athens.[49] But, since the first hearing will be (as, in certain cases, at Athens) an arbitration, to shift proceedings thereafter to the city would leave no room for such a local tribunal. By contrast, Plato does foresee (9.867e) a delegation of twelve judges, who are to act on behalf of the entire state, and these would more naturally be selected one from each phyle than from the twelve parts of a single phyle.[50] But statewide panels and locally organized tribunals could certainly coexist. Thus in the final analysis there is no good reason *not* to accept the simpler interpretation of the phrase at 12.956c and to understand the intermediate phase of judicial procedure, the "tribal court," as essentially a group of "villagers" organized within a single phyle. However, in the event of a need for still another appeal, the third and final court is to comprise a mixed panel of magistrates (6.767a, c–d; 768b–c) with no expressed relationship to the public organization.

It is evident that Plato has here parted ways with contemporary Athenian procedure. *None* of the three tiers need have brought into play statewide participation by the phylai, acting individually or collectively. While, to be sure, local autonomy in judicial matters will be guaranteed by establishing tribunals, within each phyle, at the village level, no higher unit of population, regardless of disposition or orientation, will wield divisive influence in the third, and final, tier of the judicial system simply because, at that final level, no court constituted of representatives of those units will exist.

To what extent do units other than the phylai figure in statewide functions? The role of the village in the administration of justice has just been discussed. Elsewhere, selection of officials will require the submission of tablets bearing the names of nominee and nominator. To each name will be appended "the name of his father and of his phyle and of his deme to which he belongs" (6.753c). Recalling the Kleisthenic innovation of adding to the given name, in place of or in addition to the father's name, the *demotikon* (*AthPol* 21.4), the formula nonetheless requires the phyle, unnecessarily if, as our reconstruction implies, the deme was, like a Kleisthenic deme, uniquely contained by a given phyle as its constituent subdivision.[51] Either Plato did not clearly picture the interrelationship of the two units, or he is more or less consciously departing from Athenian practice by implicitly denying to his demes their historical status of primary source and guarantor of citizenship. The latter explanation is strengthened by the fact that it is the *phratry*, to the complete exclusion of the deme, which is to be the custodian of the lists of living citizens in-

48. Jones 1987, ch. 5, sec. 41, pp. 240–241. For the internal judicial arrangements of the deme Isthmos, see *ASAA* 41–42 (1963–1964) 161–163, no. 6 (s. III/II), lines A 24–38; and of the deme Halasarna, *REG* 9 (1896) 418–419, no. 6 (n.d.).

49. For the (unique) instance of the assembly of an Athenian deme (as it happens, Aixone) functioning as a court of law, see Whitehead 1986, pp. 113–114, on *IG* II² 1196 (326/5).

50. For examples of such statewide panels, see Jones 1987, index II.E.1–2, p. 390.

51. The *phyletikon* is only very rarely encountered with Athenian names, and then usually outside Athens proper. See, for example, the names of *epoikoi* of Poteidaia with Athenian *demotikon* or *demotikon* and *phyletikon* recorded on gravestones of the fifth or fourth centuries: Jones 1987, ch. 6, sec. 1, pp. 266–267, citing *TAPA* 69 (1938) 58–59, no. 11 (fin. s. V) and *AAA* 7 (1974) 190–198 (fin. s. V vel init. s. IV); and the possible cleruch on Melos, whose name, also on a gravestone, is followed by both deme and phyle affiliation: Jones 1987, ch. 5, sec. 24, pp. 214–215, citing *IG* XII 3, no. 1187 (416–404?).

scribed on a whitened wall according to the archonship (that is, the year) of birth (6.785a–b). No mention is made anywhere here of anything like the Athenian lexiarchic registers in the demes.

Taken together, the net effect of these examples is to deny constitutional supremacy to *any* of the "natural" units of this society, whether village, deme, or phratry. Instead, it is the attenuated and artificially integrated phyle that, by virtue of its near monopolization of statewide functions, will play the primary administrative role. Yet even that role, as we have continually seen, will not be permitted to be translated into a destabilizing impact upon the operation of the commonwealth.

The Public Organization: Internal or Associational Functions

The internal arrangements of the Cretan organization are characterized by the official promotion of the isolation and solidarity of the local community. Reference has been made to the localization in the village of the intermediate stages of judicial proceedings. Promotion of isolation is also implicit in the division of the craftsmen into thirteen groups, one to be assigned to the city region, the other twelve to the phyle regiments of the countryside, where their residences will be established. So distributed, Plato thinks, the craftsmen will both present the least annoyance and be of the greatest utility to the farmers (8.848e–849a). Concurrently with the deliberate fragmentation of this potentially cohesive and therefore destabilizing class, the consciousness of the phyle association—the territory of which is the scene of their confinement—is to be directed inward. Thus, for example, we may understand the statute ordering that the deliberate and unjust murder of a "tribesman" is to be punished by particularly severe penalties (9.871a). The higher valuation placed on relations among *phyletai* will cause a concomitant devaluation of others, including those based simply on membership in the state as well as in other organizations. As an Athenian historical parallel one may cite the extension of the right of self-help to *phrateres* of a murder victim by Drakon's law on homicide.[52]

Acts of outrage, Plato continues, are most serious when directed against "things public (as well as holy) or in part held in common—of *phyletai* or of some other such associates" (10.884). That is, the rites of the internally organized phylai will rank high on the list of public religious arrangements. These rites are to involve altars (and their appropriate fittings) and will require two meetings per month for sacrifices (6.771d). Earlier interpretation had held that this meant that each phyle would mount one rural and one urban festival every month, the former for the phyle as a whole, the latter for the segment of that phyle in the city proper. But Thompson, comparing 8.828b, argued for one monthly festival in honor of the eponym of the phyle, the other in honor of the eponym of the deme, meaning that every citizen (not merely urbanites) would attend two festivals reflecting his two public associational affiliations, with phyle and deme.[53] Regarding the *purpose* of the festivals, Plato is

---

52. *IG* I³ 104 (409/8) (= I² 115+; M–L no. 86), lines 13–20, reproducing the text of Stroud 1968, pp. 5–6, with discussion of the cited passage at pp. 49–51.

53. Thompson 1965, pp. 135–136.

explicit: "First, for the sake of giving thanks to the gods and all that pertains to them; secondly, concerning our own fellowship and mutual acquaintance, so to speak, and for the sake of general contact." The latter objective is illustrated by an allusion to the necessity of such communal activity for worship and successful marriage unions. Hence the meetings (*synodoi*) are to include dances (for boys and girls overseen by supervisors and controllers) (6.771d–772a). Apparently, the choice of marriage partners is to be limited to the membership of one's phyle or deme. The rarity with which we learn of historical regulations promoting "endogamy" of this kind underscores the reactionary trend of Plato's contemplated social order.[54]

Is greater precision possible concerning the actual intended settings of these communal activities? No local center of a phyle distinct from those of its constituent twelfth parts is specified in the text. Thompson's interpretation calls for recognition of "the importance of the *demes* [italics mine] in the religious life of Plato's community,"[55] but in fact the text mentions only "the division of the phyle" (6.771d). Elsewhere it is the *komê*, the village, that appears to be the "natural" rural nucleated settlement. It is the villagers who are each other's enemies (1.626c); it is the village of which one part is superior to another (1.627a). Fixtures of the village include an agora and *hiera* (8.848d), altars and *hiera* (10.910a). Children of a given village are to congregate at its shrine (7.794a; cf. 6.785a)—an unmistakable sign of an intention to establish it, not the deme, as the focus of public communal life. Where the lawgiver aims to promote the communal life of the nucleated settlement, he uses the term "village." Where one's affiliation with that same settlement will play a constitutional role, the term in use, as we have seen, is "deme."

Internal organization is, in sum, conferred upon both the phylai and the villages. But the solidarity of the phyle is plainly, as a consequence of its artificial combined urban-and-rural disposition, tenuous and obtainable only under centralized direction. Public organization apart, what, then, of the Cretan city's *social* organization, in the narrow sense of that term? Beyond the *oikos* (family or household) and *genos* (one's "relatives"?),[56] the phratry makes a constitutionally significant, however brief, appearance (see above on 6.785a), but, as we saw, its potential as a solidary social grouping is scarcely acknowledged. Rather, Plato concentrates local communal life upon a single entity—the nucleated village. Nonetheless, the village, even in the absence of all other associational contacts, could have by itself proved adequate to meet the needs of the colonists. But in the event, it apparently did not. Plato goes on to introduce and to develop the *syssition*, or "common mess," a distinctively Cretan (and Spartan) institution unknown to Athens. What is *its* place in his utopian city?

---

54. For the sole recorded instance of endogamy within a public unit (in this case a phyle), see, at Gortyn (Jones 1987, ch. 5, sec. 29, pp. 224–225), the Law Code *Inscriptiones Creticae* IV, Gortyn no. 72 (ca. 450?), lines vii 15–ix 24. At Athens (ch. 1, sec. 1.32, p. 59), the phyle Erechtheis undertakes merely to "take care of" the *epikleros*-daughter of a member, *IG* II² 1165 (ca. 300–250), lines 30–38. For the apparently weak solidarity of the Athenian phyle association, see "The Solidarity of the Phyle as Association," in chapter 5.

55. Thompson 1965, p. 135.

56. For the meaning of this term in classical Athenian contexts, see "*Genê*," in chapter 8.

The *Syssitia*

Kleinias ascribes the historical emergence of the *syssitia* on Crete to "some divine necessity" (6.780e), but elsewhere in the dialogue it is evident that this necessity pertains only to military affairs.[57] Common messes became necessary when soldiers on campaign were forced to take meals together for the sake of their own survival (1.625e). Hence, the Spartan Megillos agrees with the Athenian stranger that "the lawgiver" devised these associations "with a view to warfare" (1.633a). Conversely, the failure of divine necessity to operate *outside* the military sphere is shown, to continue our paraphrase of Plato's argument, by the fact that in these same states the *women* fail to be so organized. They, left without such organization, historically had been abandoned to their "chaotic condition." Problems, not only for themselves but for the entire (Spartan or Cretan) state, resulted because women, the argument goes, if unregulated, insofar as they are inferior in goodness to males, just so far do they affect more than (their) half of the population. Accordingly, in the city of the *Laws* it will be better to revise the institution of the common mess and in general "to deploy all arrangements for women as well as for men in common" (6.781b; cf. 6.783b). Not surprisingly, given ancient Greek historical experience, a passage in book 7 dictates separate *syssitia* for men and for female children and their mothers under the supervision of an *archon* and an *archousa* (7.806e; and note the pointed acknowledgment of women's distinctive hesitancy at 6.781c–d).

The regulatory function underlying these arrangements is variously revealed. Besides the continuing organizational benefits for the military system, common messes (as well as gymnasia) are well designed, Plato says, for fostering *andria* and *sophrosyne* (1.635e–636a). These are represented as virtues unobtainable in isolation, acquired only through training, and so necessarily best developed within an institutional framework. At the same time, the potential benefits made possible by the institution are counterbalanced by a potential for disruption, especially where alcohol and sex are involved. While "the young man" short of thirty years may drink in moderation but must abstain from drunkenness and bingeing, when he reaches forty he may feast "in the *syssitia*" and invoke Dionysos, that is, drink freely (2.666a–b). The implication is that the messes otherwise foster excessive extremes of behavior, an observation that Plato applies not only to the consumption of wine but to the choice of lovemaking partners as well (1.636b). According to Greek thinking, a male reached his *akmê* at age forty; beyond that age, inferentially, he posed less of a threat for disruption, even if drunk. The absence of any reference to females in this context, incidentally, may reflect a negative estimation of a woman's capacity, however advanced her age. The *syssitia* cannot serve the interests of the state if, through their inappropriate management, they exacerbate rather than check a human's innately destructive impulses.

---

57. To complement the following discussion, with its focus narrowed in conformity with the larger aims of this book, the reader may consult the general studies of Morrow (1960, pp. 389–398) and of Piérart (1973, pp. 77–80) in addition to the detailed and more recent article by David (1978, pp. 486–495). The *syssitia* also figure importantly in Figueira's study of mess contributions at Sparta, 1984, pp. 87–109.

If this argument is valid, it hardly matters that the *syssitia* are apparently independent to the extent that they are to receive funds directly from citizens rather than, as might have been expected on our argument, indirectly through the central government as an intermediary. At least Plato's text seems to imply that (on one of two possible plans) it is only after a payment (of "dues"?) to the *syssitia* that the state will exercise its authority to tax citizens' annual income (12.955e). To posit a true voluntarism on this basis, however, would fly in the face of the regulatory purpose manifest elsewhere in the constitution of the Cretan city. The *syssitia* came into existence, and will continue to operate, as instruments of management by the central authority with a view to maintaining security (6.780b–c with 780d–781b). As the Athenian comments (8.842b), it really makes little difference whether the specific type of dining group actually adopted is the Cretan, Lacedaemonian, or "some other that is better than either." Plato's purpose is far less antiquarian than it is ideological.

Additional regulatory aspects might be discerned were it possible to characterize the spatial disposition of the *syssitia* over the urban and rural territory of the city. The Athenian stranger calls for the establishment κατὰ ἑκάστους τοὺς τόπους of *syssitia*, "in which all must take their meals in common" (6.762a). Possibly each village is intended to have its own messes, with the result—or purpose?—that no one need travel to another village (or to town!) in order to participate in an associational gathering. Again, one suspects a self-conscious effort to ensure the isolation of the local community. For a foil, one need search no further than Athens, where probably by classical times the memberships of some of the traditional associations had become widely dispersed over Attica.[58]

Moreover (and to mention another significant point of departure from historical practice), whereas membership in historical Athenian voluntary associations was at the prospective member's initiative and thereafter conditioned by hereditary succession, Plato substitutes universal membership, extended even to women and children and, although individual affiliation (and one's accommodations) reflect distinctions of age and gender, without any stated reference to background or personal attainment. And why? Because, it may be suggested, if the state's monitoring of the citizen population is to be complete, then obviously membership must be open to all.

Paradoxically, regulation through the *syssitia* will, Plato is forced to acknowledge, create a problem of its own: the potentially divisive effects generated by the very existence of these organizations—a point made above with respect to drinking and sexual behavior. Common messes, while beneficial to cities in other respects, may (like the gymnasia) contribute to internal unrest, as they did in the case of the "young men"(παῖδες) of Miletos, Boiotia, and Thourioi, who played leading roles in the upheavals within their cities (1.636b). The "most hostile man of all to the entire city" is identified as he who (among other things) "makes the state subject to *hetaireiai*" (9.856b). This is sufficient reminder of the revolution that had over-

---

58. For a vivid postclassical illustration of such dispersal, see the lists of *gennetai* arranged by phyle and demotic: *IG* II² 2338 (between 27/6 and 18/7: Amynandridai), 2339 (A.D. 161/2: identity of group not known), and 2340 (ca. A.D. 200: Kerykes). See further on this point, "*Genê*," in chapter 8.

thrown the democracy of Plato's own Athens. Women left unregulated or drinking by underage males are but mere symptoms of the underlying organic sickness. Abstractly put, every body, in Plato's metaphysical view, contains the seeds of its own dissolution; even an individual person will be found to be at war with himself (1.626b–627a, 644c). Where the body of the state is concerned, the lawmaker's insistence upon the equitable distribution of property merely helps to eliminate the basis for charges of unfair treatment as a prelude to conflict. There will remain in Plato's Cretan city, even after the institution of minimum and maximum property holdings, the inborn instinct to enhance one's self interest at the expense of one's neighbor or of the general community.

What cure, then, is available for this all-pervading potential for self-destruction? The architect of the Cretan city sees only one possibility—autocratic, centralized management. Thus we may understand the emphasis placed upon the qualities of the leader as the factor making the difference between good and bad organizations (1.639c–641a). And that leadership role will be exercised—to return to our subject—over and through not only the *syssitia* but all those associations, phyle, deme, and phratry, admitted to the Cretan polity. The historical social clubs, like the Athenian *hetaireiai* that had created civil unrest, had been, and still were in Plato's time, independent, self-governing voluntary associations subject only to the minimal oversight made possible by such legal devices as Solon's law on associations. Plato's associations, by contrast, while lacking all visible signs of self-governance,[59] emerge as mere instruments of his central authority's regulatory apparatus.[60]

Conclusion: The City of the *Laws* and Associations

We are now in a position to fully appreciate Plato's approach to the twin problems of disunity and rootlessness. That approach took as its point of departure a model manifestly derived from historical observation: the network of associations as a mediating structure between individual citizens and the central government. By creating, then institutionalizing segments of the state as phylai and demes, the state, while acting in the name of egalitarianism, might produce a substantial monolithic unity by requiring those segments to cooperate in the performance of public business. Ample evidence of this strategy has been noted in the functions of the boards and organs of government reviewed in the foregoing discussion. At the same time,

59. For example, one of the most striking features of Plato's associations is the total absence of internally selected officers. (Plato's phylarchs are, of course, as the context of their appearance shows, statewide military commanders.) Historically, officers of internally organized public units of all types and nomenclatures are abundantly attested. Indeed, they are among the most commonly encountered administrative features of public organization: see Jones 1987, index III.C.1–9, pp. 396–398.

60. My argument calls into question a central contention of David's analysis, that "the equilibrium and stability of the socio-economic structure" had *already* been achieved by maintenance of the original number of households and by the imposition of minimum and maximum levels of personal wealth (1978, p. 493). The reading of Plato's text offered here rather suggests that it was through the *syssitia* as well as the other components of the public organization, by virtue of their use as instruments of centralized management, that such "equilibrium and stability" could be achieved, in Plato's estimation.

while again mirroring observable tendencies in contemporary cities but to a markedly accelerated degree, Plato will not permit these associations of citizens to exert disproportionate influence on the actual operation of his government. There will be no executive committee of the Council with the potential to subvert justice as the board drawn from the phyle Antiochis, on which Plato's teacher had sat, had done in the case of the Arginousai generals. And the loyalty of citizen soldiers will, prior to their assuming permanent stations in their phyle of origin, have been diluted through enforced rotation over all twelve districts. And so on. By such controls, that is, the groupings of citizens institutionalized for the sake of a centralized unity will not be allowed to undermine the very purpose of their creation.

The beauty of the model lay in the concurrent introversion of each segment of the public organization as a communally organized association. Statewide unity and local community might thereby coexist. Plato's specific strategy is revealed by the differential weighting of public external function versus the degree of internal solidarity. Statewide functions are concentrated in that unit, the phyle, which, because of its deliberately unnaturally extended disposition over town and country, has little potential for corporate cohesion. Accordingly, its associational dimension is scarcely developed. By contrast, the nucleated village, in its constitutional capacity as a deme, will not be permitted to exert even the minimal influence its counterpart had enjoyed in classical Athens. Instead, its public role will be to develop further its already present "natural" community. Absence from the seat of government and intense localized activity are complementary aspects of the Cretan city's administration.

From this characterization it is clear that Plato's reconstructed Cretan city resembles in structure and allocation of function the philosopher's own historical Athens. As we saw in chapter 5, the Kleisthenic phylai, though virtually monopolizing those statewide functions allocated to the public organization, developed very little solidarity as associations.[61] Conversely, the Kleisthenic demes, largely lacking in significant statewide public roles,[62] did emerge as bona fide, and conspicuously exclusive and isolated, communities.[63] Furthermore, the imposition upon Plato's Magnesian polity of Spartan or Cretan style "common messes," though without exact historical analogue in the arrangements of classical Athens, does recall, if my characterization of the *syssitia* is accepted, the patently regulatory purpose of the Solonian law on associations and of those other interventions reviewed in chapter 1.[64] Thus both in terms of gross structure and underlying dynamic, the political order reconstructed by Plato would tend to confirm the portrayal of classical Athens under consideration in the present work.

With this return to the matter of the state and its interventions, it is an especially appropriate time, since our individual analyses are now complete, to revisit in more explicit and connected form the theme running throughout this study—the relation of our associations to the central government of democratic Athens.

61. "The Solidarity of the Phyle as Association," in chapter 5.
62. Jones 1987, Introd., p. 18; and ch. 1, sec. 1.21, p. 38.
63. Chapter 2, 3, and 4, passim.
64. "Solon's Law on Associations," in chapter 1.

TEN

Government and Associations

"The Response to Democracy"

I

The democratic government of classical Athens, despite its well-known overt egalitarian features, imposed severe limitations upon the political aspirations of the populations of Athens and Attica. Egalitarianism itself, by definition, absolutely precluded claims to privilege based on the traditional distinctions of bloodline, background, or merit. The ideology's impact extended to all matters involving the use of sortition or decided by votes of the entire citizen body or (as in the case of the courts) of some randomly constituted and theoretically representative selection thereof. The fact that the legislature, too, was based on the principle of direct rule, rather than on the (to us) more familiar representative model, meant that little opportunity existed for individuals or groups—that is, for what we call "constituencies" —to advance their particularist interests in the arena of the central government. But the barriers to the achievement of one's aims posed by egalitarianism and direct rule were problems that existed only for those whose circumstances made possible their participation in government in the first place. And what of the others? Circumstantial factors potentially bearing positively or negatively upon participation included degree of wealth, availability of free time, and level of education. But it was the factor of the separation of one's permanent residence from the urban center that, alone of such factors, could pretty much disfranchise an entire community. All citizens, rich and poor, occupied and leisured, well- and ill-educated, were, if they resided in a distant rural deme, de facto hindered or entirely prevented from exercising their franchise on a regular basis. And, last but not least, for the great majority of residents of Attica who were not full-fledged members of the citizen caste, the question of whether one's circumstances permitted or did not permit such participation did not even arise.

It is obvious that the democratic government fell short of meeting what we know or may reasonably suppose to have been the expectations of both the citizen and noncitizen populations. To be sure, the nature of the problem would be conceptualized differently according to the rank, socioeconomic situation, and general predicament of the particular Athenian resident or group. Aristocrats believed themselves unfairly deprived of their birthright. Would-be activists or "special interest groups" among the rank and file of the voting populace must have found themselves, and their agendas, hopelessly overwhelmed in a legislative system based on a high level of participation—a Council that drew upon all 139 demes and an Assembly that required a quorum equaling one fifth or more of the entire citizen body as a necessary condition of reaching a decision. Simply put, they were outnumbered. Those with disinterested civic-minded purposes were undoubtedly frustrated by the particular schedules of the meetings of the organs of government, by the excessive amounts of time (as in the case of the Council) that participation could demand of one, by a political or juridical discourse that could shut out all but the most literate or lavishly tutored in the rhetorical arts, and, again, by accident of the place of one's birth or location of one's arable landholdings with respect to the seat of government. The spirit might have been willing, but the structure, style, or physical location of the government could make participation difficult or impossible. The *de iure* disfranchised, women of the citizen class, metics, and even those slaves who had enjoyed the benefits of citizen status in the places of their origin, must have found exceedingly arbitrary a regime that automatically excluded themselves while, equally automatically, bestowing the mantle of privilege upon all males of the citizen class meeting the minimal twin requirements of majority and legitimate birth.

What makes all this important for our study is that the population of Athens—and by "Athens" I include the whole of Attica—was highly politicized. It is sufficient to recall the received accounts of the era preceding the rise of the tyrant Peisistratos, when the leading political factions are reported to have been regionally organized around the leaders of the Men of the Plain, the Men of the Shore, and the Men from beyond the Hills. This was not a case of a divided urban populace, to which significant political rivalry was confined, while a sleepy, apathetic rural countryside passively awaited the outcome of events in town. The whole, or nearly the whole, of Attica had been brought into the picture. When, a half century later, the democracy was set up by Kleisthenes, the bestowal of constitutional rights merely formalized what was already an accomplished fact. Yes, Herodotos in a famous sentence declares that Kleisthenes had taken the Demos into his *hetairia* (5.66.2), but it would be a mistake to infer that not until that time had the wider citizen body—the citizen body beyond a narrowly circumscribed group of aristocratic factions—become conscious of its political potentialities. The creation of the deme system, the invention and general application of the *demotikon*, the institution of the Council based on the deme system according to population quotas, the broadening of the base of the Assembly, courts, and ostracism by the imposition of the quorum of 6,000—these were all merely reaffirmations of an impulse toward political activism or at least of a political self-consciousness that had been in place for some time. And, on a daily basis, the democracy's advertisements of itself in the form of highly publicized acts of "the People of the Athenians" or in the form of the sustaining of "national" cults with formally scheduled activities potentially involving the entire citizen body, or in the form of public architecture or iconography that explicitly asserted the universality of Athenian citizenship—all these could only have reminded the practically disfranchised among the citizens of their unrealized or unrealizable potentials. Even the noncitizens were, arguably, a politicized sector. By 393 Aristophanes' *Ekklesiazousai* had explicitly aired the possibility of a democratic government run exclusively by women; and political theory, above all Plato's *Republic* and *Laws,* was to explore, before an Athenian readership, the possibility of alternative ways of defining the limits of the enfranchised. Again, it would be wrongheaded to suppose that the matter of nonparticipation was not a live issue on the grounds, say, that such ideas had never occurred to anyone or still lay centuries in the future.[1]

It is the basic problem created by these circumstances that the present study has attempted to address. At the very minimum, it must be conceded that the great disfranchised majority would have sought alternative avenues to act out its constitutional or political aspirations. But there is also the matter of stability. How could such a regime as I have just characterized have remained so relatively settled and undisturbed by internal discord for the nearly two centuries of the democracy? So far as we know, no institutional remedies were taken in order to redress any imbalances imposed by the particular character of the Kleisthenic democratic central government. The seat of the government remained exclusively confined to the area of the Agora, save for a few concessions to the port town at Peiraieus.[2] No change in the deme system involving the demes themselves or their allocation to the trittyes and phylai can be associated with the nature or facts of citizen participation.[3] Sortition, if anything, was even more widely applied.[4] Direct rule, seemingly, remains in force throughout the lifetime of the democracy. No chinks in the armor of the invincible citizen caste have been detected.[5] And so on.

---

1. With this statement one may compare the assessment made by Mion in the course of his exploration of "politicization and constitutional restraints," that "[f]ifth-century Athens was characterized by an intense degree of politicization, in the sense that the political was dominant and pervasive in all areas of life" (Mion 1986, p. 225). However, Mion, while realizing the low level of attendance in the Assembly and Council (p. 227, with note 19 citing Hansen), does not seem to acknowledge that this fact, in combination with politicization, represents a problem in need of attention. See also Rahe's essay on the "primacy of politics" in classical Greece, 1984, pp. 265–293.

2. On the "duplicate city" of Peiraieus, see Wycherley 1978, pp. 262 and 264 (on the duplication of constitutional functions).

3. For such changes as did occur, e.g., the creation or abolition of phylai with the consequent movement of demes from one phyle to another, see Traill 1975, pp. 25–34, with Tables of Representation XI–XV.

4. As evidenced, for example, in the shift from the election to sortition of the archons in 487/6 (*AthPol* 22.5) and in a similar change in the mode of selection of the prytany secretary at some uncertain date (*AthPol* 54.3).

5. As a symptom of the continuing exclusivity of the People, consider the infrequency with which the legislature bestowed citizenship upon outsiders: M. Osborne 1983, vols. 3 and 4, pp. 204–209, esp. 205–206.

This book has found the answer to this conundrum in the existence and particular design, composition, and functioning, of the Athenian *associations*. The cornerstone of my argument is the law ascribed to Solon and reasonably assigned to the time of his archonship in 594—nearly a full century before the birth of the democracy. My discussion in chapter 1 (supported by my scrutiny of the Greek text in appendix 2) represents the law as a general statute on associations defining the relationship between those associations and the central government. To judge from the approach to its subject and the specific wording of the law, it finds an existing or potential conflict between the groups cataloged by name (deme, phratry, *orgeones*, et al.) and the "written statutes of the People" of the central authority. One way of resolving that conflict, a solution exemplified by late Republican and early Imperial Rome, might have been to subject the associations to exceedingly confining sanctions or simply to abolish them altogether. Instead, a formula was devised for peaceful coexistence: the members of the "associations" may make any arrangements they please regarding their proper business provided that the "written statutes"—that is, state laws and decrees—do not prohibit such arrangements. My analysis has depicted Solon's legislation as comprising two quite different forms, namely, validation and regulation. Both modes of intervention, furthermore, were found to be in evidence in several subsequent episodes dating to the classical democracy (and even beyond). Whether or not on each such occasion it was actually Solon's law that enabled the intervention is impossible to tell, but it at least became clear that governmental policy had continued along the lines of the two modes of intervention evidenced by the original law.[6]

The subtitle of this book, "The Response to Democracy," entails considerable ambiguity in that the "response" to which it refers may actually have assumed more than one form. A straightforward instance, the one just indicated, involves the actions undertaken by the central government to promote itself by alternately "validating" or "regulating" the associations—the positive and negative sides of the intervention it had reserved for itself through Solon's law. Thus the democracy could compensate for its own exclusivity or other deficits by alternately enforcing or shaping the arrangements or acts of a *koinonia* and thereby insuring its—the association's—viability and appropriate functioning.

Such intervention was, I argue, guided by the assumption that, if a citizen or other resident could not find satisfaction through participation in the central government, perhaps his situation could be ameliorated through participation in one or more associations of some form. To those removed from the seat of government by a great distance, the local association offered readier access. For those overawed by the large numbers of the Assembly or the court system, a tiny deme or phratry meeting presented far less daunting circumstances. Whereas, in town, the operation of sortition from large pools of candidates prevailed, at the local level small numbers or indifference opened up opportunities for merit or energy at much better odds. If highly educated city speakers delivered highfalutin and incomprehensible rhetoric, proceedings in one's home village were bound to be conducted in more fa-

---

6 . "Solon's Law on Associations," in chapter 1.

miliar terms. The obvious advantages in promoting the functioning of such organizations could not have escaped the attention of the people who ran the Athenian democracy. Hence the interest in "validating" the arrangements of associations.

At the same time, however, a *hetairia* turned violent and seditious or even a phyle taken to undermine the authority of the state by using the Theater of Dionysos as a forum for the uncalled-for and redundant announcements of its internal acts posed various degrees of threat to the stability of the commonwealth. Hence the concurrent interest in "regulating" the arrangements of associations. In this negative and limiting mode, as in the positive and enhancing mode illustrated in the previous paragraph, the state itself is represented as the source and author of the "response."

From an evidential standpoint, the specific events to which I refer (here and in the main body of my discussions) are well known and uncontested facts of the historical and documentary record. What is new is my referral of these interventions to Solon's law on associations and my placement of the phenomenon within a more holistic portrayal of the institutions and public life of classical Athens.

Examples of this pattern of state-association relations have emerged in various quarters. Thanks to Whitehead's insightful work, it is now apparent that the demarch served as a—indeed, *the*—vital link between the central government and the local deme association. Whitehead's evidence is collected under five heads: the compilation of inventories of property forfeit to the state, the collection of the extraordinary taxes called *eisphorai*, the conscription of military personnel, the discharging of religious responsibilities on behalf of the state, and the burial of unburied dead bodies.[7] None of these functions, on its face, even remotely resembles the validation or regulation of the deme association. Rather the pattern seems to be one of the state's familiar deployment of the segments of the state for purely bureaucratic or administrative ends. But the fact that it was this very man, so clearly marked as the state's agent, who, as the dominating deme official, likewise served as the "agent" of his deme's assembly (again, Whitehead's term) in the areas of finance, religion, and law,[8] obviously opens up the possibility that, in these ostensibly purely *associational* capacities, he was in fact simultaneously serving the interests of the central government. By definition, any action taken by the demarch to advance his association in a lawful manner would amount to the validation and regulation of its acts in accordance with our understanding of Solon's law.

Analogously, the demarch, as suggested in chapter 8, could also have played a comparable mediating role with respect to the regional associations of which the constituent members were, after 508/7, the constitutionalized villages of the democracy. If not, what is the explanation for the cultic role of the demarch of Marathon in the activities of the Tetrapolis?[9] Still another instance may be provided by the phratries, if, as I suggested in chapter 7, the installations in the Agora in the name of Zeus Phratrios and Athena Phratria were in fact pan-phratric and so accessible to the members of all phratries rather than dedicated in the name of a particular phra-

7. Whitehead 1986, pp. 130–138.
8. Whitehead 1986, pp. 121–130.
9. "Regional Associations," in chapter 8.

try, and if their purpose was, again as I suggested, to serve the needs of rural Athenians removed from the country seats of their ancestral brotherhoods.[10] My point is that the state, by providing these facilities, has deliberately undertaken to compensate for the limitations of its own governmental structures by acting to strengthen and preserve existing associations. The maintenance of the health of these predominately rural corporations could easily have been part of such a design, but obviously these phratries could not remain healthy if significant numbers of members were lost to urbanization and subsequently dropped out of the organization. Given such a representation of the situation, the provision of these centrally located "generic" facilities is easy to comprehend.

A second form taken by the response involves the association's independent use of its own mechanisms. The primary case in point is the representative function and purpose that I have attributed to the phyle associations in chapter 6.[11] Such a role is not ascribed to the phylai, or to any other segment or organ of the state, by any contemporary or even later witness. Aristotle's silence on the matter might be thought particularly troublesome, since the phenomenon of "representative" government as we know it escapes him entirely, with regard both to Athens and any other Greek state. But I have argued that difficulties with access to information may account for the conspicuous absence in his writings of any significant awareness of the internally organized units of the public organization. And, if he was not sufficiently aware of the phyle association, he could not, according to my reconstruction of the phenomenon of "representation," possibly have discerned the workings of any such process.[12] So, the silence on the public associations serves to explain the silence about representation. Rather, as it turned out, it is the documents of the phylai themselves that, upon close examination of their prosopographical content, reveal a pattern that can be explained only, or best, in terms of the association's efforts to communicate its "special interests" to the forum of the central government. Thereby, I believe, the associational network found a mechanism for countering the effects of one of the democracy's most pronounced, and, from a political perspective, crippling, characteristics—its uncompromising adherence to the principle of direct rule.

The representative purpose that I have attributed to the phyle associations in no way necessarily involves conscious planning or design on the part of the central government or Kleisthenes, much less Solon. It is indeed far more likely that the mechanism that I have reconstructed simply evolved out of procedures that were originally innocent of any such intentions. The bestowal of honors upon benefactors, and their promulgation, are among the most frequently encountered and conspicuous manifestations of associational life. All that I claim is that, over time, it was noticed that, if such honors, especially ones of significant monetary value, were bestowed upon those members of the association who held statewide offices or were holders of Athenian liturgies, it might be possible to motivate these men to advance the interests of the association at the central statewide level. On this model, the con-

10. "Regional Distribution and Relation to the Urban Center," in chapter 7.
11. "The Phyle-Association as Instrument of Representation," in chapter 6.
12. "Ancient Sources for the Associations of Classical Athens," in the Introduction.

ception, planning, and execution originated, accordingly, entirely in the associations themselves.

The third type of response is perhaps the most conjectural. It brings into play no necessary conscious deliberation or intention on the part of either the central government or the association. It is rather a question of conditions over the passage of time reaching a point of equilibrium through a process of adjustment on the part of the associations to the realities of public life. No calculation or planning, least of all on Kleisthenes' part, is to be imagined. After all, at the time of Kleisthenes' work in 508/7, a far wider range of theoretical possibilities existed for associational development than were actually realized by the period of our fullest evidence in the fourth century. The prime example is the trittys. It is clear from the exiguous remains that trittys associations had indeed been launched[13] and that, furthermore, if circumstantial evidence may be admitted to the discussion, the trittys association may in fact have been intended to be the centerpiece of the new network of public associations[14] But it did not in any event work out that way; these associations withered on the vine. Rather, the development, or failure to develop, of the various associations occurred in response to the evolving institutional environment. For example, and speculatively, if my arguments in chapter 3 are accepted, the deme associations developed differentially according to the distance of their remove from the urban center.[15] Some deme associations, in any case, clearly flourished; many others go entirely undocumented. But it was less a question of policy or plan as of the concerned Athenians, and of the concerned Athenian institutions, as it were finding their own level. Only once the point of equilibrium had been reached, I will conjecture, did the central government become involved, to the extent that it was ever involved at all, through the medium of the powers of validation and regulation bestowed upon it by the law of Solon. Any such involvement would have amounted to the maintenance of a satisfactory status quo.

II

Among the variables of ideology, wealth, free time, educational level, citizen or noncitizen status, and access, which worked to enable or inhibit an Athenian's participation in government, it is the first-mentioned, ideology, that most obviously prompted the formation, or thereafter sustained the existence of, those probably exclusively urban *koinoniai* euphemistically called *hetairiai*. That at least some of them were havens for beleaguered aristocrats is beyond cavil. This is one of the familiar facts of classical Athenian political history. But the placing of the *hetairia* within the general context of Donlan's defensive aristocratic standard helps bring these associations into relation—a reactionary relation—with the dominating egalitarianism of the central government. This way, too, the *hetairia* no longer, as specialist monographs might lead one to think, needs to be viewed as an isolated phe-

13. Introduction, with note 3.
14. Lewis 1963, pp. 34–36.
15. "Testing the Hypothesis: Documents of the Demes," in chapter 3.

nomenon but rather as but one element of a network of associations spawned in response to the *demokratia*.[16] What seems so obviously true of these aristocratic "clubs"
may also, perhaps less obviously, have applied in the cases of the archaic regional
cultic associations that survived under the democracy, the "sacerdotal families"
called *genê*, and possibly some of the small ritual groups known as *orgeones*.[17]

The notion of ideological haven has at least one other application here—to the
philosophical schools. It has not been possible within the confines of the present
work to carry out a prosopographical study of the philosophical community, much
less a complete social history of the philosophical movement. But I have reasserted
some well known facts about the teachers and the schools with respect to the topographic dimensions of their movements or locations. While, it is true, certain of the
sects remained ensconced in or about the Agora, three others, including two that
were to enjoy conspicuous success, retreated to the periphery of the urban center as
defined by the circuit wall of the city. That no fewer than three of the schools should
have undergone under the democracy what was essentially, geographically speaking, the same relocation from Agora to periphery suggests response to a common
dynamic. That dynamic was, I argued, the peculiar features of the democratic regime
at the height of the domination of which the relocations occurred. The new "suburban" locations at once insulated the teachers and their adherents from the ideologically charged atmosphere of the Agora that had contributed to the execution of
Sokrates, while at the same time not removing the schools so far from the main
population center that they would be cut off from the needed steady supply of educated and leisured listeners and disciples.[18]

In the case of the schools, as I have suggested, distance from the urban center is
the determining factor. But unlike the schools, which remained at once removed
from but still within reach of the *asty*, those other associations with which the present study has been in large part concerned—above all the demes, the phratries, and
the regional associations—were in the great majority of cases, qua associations,
more or less permanently removed from life in the bipolar urban center. Previous
scholars have sometimes taken as an a priori given that people would not voluntarily travel great distances to and from the town, but scholarly assertions to the contrary have necessitated our continued attention to this problem.[19] The result of our
investigations has in each case been that an association with an outlying rural base,
whether deme or phratry or cultic league, tended, qua association, to function more
or less independently of the town of Athens. (Demonstrably in the case of the
demes, furthermore, the associations seem to have remained more or less isolated
from other demes, including outlying ones just like themselves.)[20] The situation is
pretty well summed up by the specific instances of the phyle Hippothontis headquartered at Eleusis,[21] the *phrateres* based at Dekeleia,[22] and the Tetrapolis at

16. "Clubs," in chapter 8.
17. "Regional Associations," "*Genê*," and "*Orgeones*," in chapter 8.
18. "Philosophical Schools," in chapter 8.
19. "Determinants of the Isolation of the Extra-Urban Demes," in chapter 3.
20. "Deme versus Deme Relations," in chapter 3.
21. "The Disposition of the Phyle-Organization," in chapter 5.
22. "Regional Distribution and Relation to the Urban Center," in chapter 7.

Marathon,[23] all of which provide an example of a decree calling for the erection of a second copy of that decree in the city. In each case the fully warranted inference would seem to be that those members who had migrated to the distant urban center would not be expected to return to the home base where they might view the solitary permanent stone inscription otherwise normal in such circumstances.

It is crucially important to realize that the factor of distance is not monodimensional but actually embodies within itself a bundle of related variables. It is a matter of the manifold points of difference between the city of Athens and the scores of usually tiny rural, coastal, or montane communities that dotted the countryside of Attica. The attractions to remaining at the extra-urban home-base are not difficult to imagine. The factor of the time involved in travel between local community and town is of course recognized by everyone, but it should not be forgotten that the physical effort involved in walking great distances might have been even more critical. Yes, farmers did enjoy considerable periods when the agricultural calendar made no demands or light demands upon their time. They did have access to family members, hired hands, tenants, slaves, or others to put to work in their absence. They were in the main, as I have emphasized, politicized at least to the degree of being fully aware of their potentialities as participants in the constitutional and political processes and so not necessarily lacking in motivation. But the case has yet to be made that a man normally engaged in extremely taxing manual labor would voluntarily, and without the prospect of significant palpable reward, routinely walk great distances merely to cast a vote, sit on a jury, or serve on a sortitive magisterial board.[24]

Perhaps even more important than the obvious factors of time and effort, however, was the matter of the familiarity of one's circumstances. That the city was the favored place of residence for disproportionate numbers of wealthy (and so, often, highly educated) Athenians; that it was in large part given over to nontraditional industrial and other gainful or leisure-time pursuits; that it was a hotbed of intellectual activity often (in the case of Athens) spilling over into iconoclastic speculation; that it was disproportionately occupied by noncitizen people of foreign origin or extraction are facts too familiar to require demonstration. But it may not always be adequately appreciated that the typical rural village was almost certainly *none* of these things. Even if time and effort had not been (as they were) inhibiting factors, it is certainly by no means obvious that all or even a significant number of extramural Athenians would have *desired* on a regular, routine basis to visit what must have been to many a very foreign place. The local community—deme or phratry or regional cultic association—offered the great advantage of familiarity. That familiarity would extend of course to the specific persons and setting involved but more importantly, as I am suggesting, to the general cultural ambience. The democracy was more than simply a few well-defined organs of government. Democracy, as practiced in classical Athens, also necessarily entailed a very specific set of cultural as well as purely institutional circumstances—circumstances that for many Athenians must have been unsettling if not positively repellent.

The preceding paragraph treats the extra-urban based associations as a unified

23. "Regional Associations," in chapter 8.
24. "Determinants of the Isolation of the Extra-Urban Demes," in chapter 3.

block of organizations, but in fact they are to be distinguished from one another along some very important lines. The point applies especially with regard to the features setting apart the relatively well-understood deme and phratry. Institutionally speaking, the deme association was, as I have argued in chapter 3, an isolated and mostly introverted organization, with little interest in cultivating relations with other groups or persons outside its own boundaries.[25] This portrayal of the association is supported, as we saw in chapter 2, by the general pattern of particulars extending across the full board of its documented existence.[26] The deme association represented the ultimate expression of the homing instinct, of the prioritizing of the familiar. By contrast, the phratry possessed elements of a pan-Athenian, even a pan-Ionian orientation.[27] The phratry member who celebrated an initiation or the Apatouria in the rural extra-urban phratry center was, consciously or unconsciously, engaging in a sort of mental or spiritual communion with all other *phrateres*. No demesman, to judge from the evidence available to us, could under similar circumstances within his own deme center have experienced such feelings about the members of other Athenian demes. So, whereas the deme offered to the Athenian de facto disfranchised from participation in the central government by reason of his physical (or cultural) remoteness from the seat of that government, a substitute or replacement constitutional or political experience, the phratry organization, although no less removed from the town, made possible as well a vicarious identification with all other Athenians. Additionally, in contrast to both deme and phratry, the regional cultic associations, known or probable enduring vestiges of the predemocratic era, supplied an historical dimension by establishing and maintaining a sort of continuity or linkage with Athens's distant past, indeed with a past that undoubtedly antedated the creation of the democracy and perhaps even of Athens itself.[28]

III

Above, it was conceded that, with regard to this third species of "response to democracy," we cannot be sure of the existence of any intention, on the part of either the central government or the associations themselves, to bring about any such adjustment. But statements in the *Constitution of the Athenians* attributed to Aristotle do provide hints about possible intentions on the part of the democracy's founder, Kleisthenes. At §21.4 the author writes that Kleisthenes "made those living in each of the demes *demotai* of each other, in order that they not, by addressing each other by the father's name reveal their new-citizen status, but would rather call each other by their demes. As a result, Athenians address each other according to demes." True, the point here concerns naming conventions, but the fact remains that the innovation could only have had the effect—and so reveal part of a purpose?—of recognizing the community of demesmen and of creating a sense of solidarity within it.

25. "Deme versus Deme Relations," in chapter 3.
26. "The Deme as 'Natural Community,'" in chapter 2.
27. "The Relations of the Phratries and the Demes," in chapter 7.
28. "Regional Associations," in chapter 8.

It is likewise germane here that, in the next sentence, at §21.5, the author attributes to Kleisthenes the institution of the demarchs, later to emerge as the chief officers of the deme associations. If we could be sure about the associational status of the pre-Kleisthenic *naukrariai*, the case that Kleisthenes himself created the deme associations would be made, for the author goes on to state that "he made the demes in place of [that is, they replaced] the naukraries" (§21.5). Inferentially, if the naukraries had been associations, then in all likelihood so were Kleisthenes' new demes as well. Still another statement brings Kleisthenes into play, this time with respect to the "clans" and "brotherhoods," for the author states that "he allowed each person to keep their *genê* and phratries and priesthoods in accordance with ancestral custom" (§21.6). Regarding the *genos*, the ambiguities of this term noted in chapter 8 are such that it would be risky to assume the subject here is an association, although the "sacerdotal family" is an attractive candidate for such a role.[29] Besides, the presence in the string of three terms of "priesthoods" obviously obviates the necessity of any such assumption. But about the phratries, indubitable *koinoniai*, there can be no doubt.[30] It therefore remains arguable that the characterizations and roles of the demes and phratries offered in this work, and specifically their suggested relations to the central government and their place in the inclusively defined state of Athens as a whole, were the end products of arrangements wrought by the creator of the *demokratia* himself.

Additional, circumstantial evidence may be brought to bear upon this question. In my inclusive study of the *Public Organizations*, I observed that the record of the 200 or so known such organizations supports the finding that the overwhelming preponderance of statewide functions that were allocated to the segments of the state were concentrated in the upper tiers of these organizations, the phylai in particular. Put in negative terms, it was found that the lower level units, and especially the primary units going by various terms denoting the nucleated village, are known to have performed very few, if any, public statewide functions. The pattern obtains in the case of by far the best-documented of the 200 examples, classical Athens.[31] There is an apparent paradox here. At Athens the demes comprised all citizens and only citizens; and the few statewide public roles that they do play illustrate their potential for still greater such administrative or bureaucratic activity as segments of the greater state of Athens. But, since they demonstrably did not play such a role, why were they created? My answer in my previous work remains my answer here. They—the lower level units, and especially the demes and their non-Athenian analogs—were created precisely in order to function as internally organized public associations. It is only a small additional step to include in that original blueprint for the demes, or in Kleisthenes' institution of the *demotikon* or his decision to let each

29. "*Genê*," in chapter 8.

30. I omit from consideration here the perplexing statement in Aristotle's *Politics* (6.2.11: 1319b) regarding changes in the constitution at Athens and Cyrene. Since the author does not distinguish between the changes undertaken in the two different cities, it is not clear whether his remark about the institution of "different and more numerous phratries" applies to Athens or not. See Jones 1987, ch. 5, sec. 26, p. 218.

31. Jones 1987, pp. 17–22.

citizen keep his phratry, the sorts of compensating relations with respect to the central government being urged upon the reader throughout this study.

As a result of the emergence of a polity so constituted, whether by Kleisthenes' original design or, alternatively, as the ultimate outgrowth of a lengthy process of adjustment on the part of the associations, the phenomenon, so familiar to modern societies, of the "voluntary association" was usurped in large part by the state. Demes, trittyes, and phylai were part of the fabric of the constitutional apparatus. Provided that majority and legitimate birth could be demonstrated, membership was automatic and virtually nonvoluntary in that failure to join meant the surrender of all the constitutional rights of an Athenian. Even the "private" orientation of the phratry, if the usual representation regarding its role in the determination of citizen status is accepted, was compromised to the extent that the failure to secure membership in one's father's phratry counted heavily against success before one's father's demesmen. Moreover, as we saw in chapter 7, by the erection of "generic" phratry installations in the quintessentially public Agora, the state co-opted the role, otherwise reserved for the "private" associations themselves, of overseeing the maintenance and custody of phratric cults and gatherings.[32] Different modes of state intervention were noted in respect to the "clubs,"[33] the philosophical schools,[34] the *genê*,[35] and the *orgeones*.[36] It is obvious that the line demarcating "state" and "society" was drawn in a way, and in a place, quite foreign to the experience of modern Western societies. In fact, Athens did not stop at associations, for the state's legal and institutional interventions even in the citizen's private household were both various and determined.[37] Obviously it would be mistaken to imagine that on the grounds of some ideology of "privatism" the state—by which I mean the voting members of the Athenian citizen body—would have balked at intervening in the associational life of its citizens for the purpose of fostering the greater good of the Athenian *polis*.

The *effect* of these arrangements was, I am suggesting, stability. It is self-evidently true that, once the effect was perceived, an unintended or accidentally emerging set of conditions could have evolved into a *purpose* on the part of the governing authority. Stability, I think, was, from the perspective of this authority, the ultimate goal. Athens's own recent—and, at the end of the fifth century, renewed—record of political division and upheaval must have imprinted upon the mind of every voting Athenian citizen the abiding consciousness that such division and upheaval might be revisited at any time. Certainly among the major destablizing factors we must include the practical disfranchisement of the enfranchised, especially the already *politicized* enfranchised.

This, rather than a desire to counteract the centripetal effects of the continuing trend toward urbanization, to mention one attractive alternative, provided the dy-

32. "Regional Distribution and Relation to the Urban Center," in chapter 7.
33. "Clubs," in chapter 8.
34. "Philosophical Schools," in chapter 8.
35. "*Genê*," in chapter 8.
36. "*Orgeones*," in chapter 8.
37. See, for discussion of the phenomenon, Lacey 1968, pp. 84–99, and Jones 1997, pp. 130–132.

namic underlying and driving this aspect of the process.[38] Attractive because, after all, even Peisistratos, a half century before the creation of the democracy, had appreciated the potential for disruption should ruralites migrate to the city in significant numbers, and so took appropriate preventative measures.[39] And it is not inconceivable that such calculations played a part in Kleisthenes' (and later politicians') thinking. It may even be suggested that the object in instituting (or preserving) hereditary affiliation in deme or phratry was to inhibit urbanization, since a citizen originally resident in a distant deme relocating elsewhere would thereafter be de facto barred from participation in the deme or phratry of his membership—and, by the same token, in anyone else's. Change of residence could be undertaken only at considerable cost. The resulting braking effect could well have retarded, if not reversed, the flow into the city center. Nonetheless, urbanization, for all such efforts to counteract it, seems to have continued unabated. At all events, what really counted, I think, in the minds of Kleisthenes and others, was the level of satisfaction of those who *remained behind* in the ancestral village or other settlements. Could such satisfaction be produced, an important step toward the maintenance of political stability would have been achieved. And even in the absence of division or discord, the network of associations, as observed in chapter 1, without question served a number of valuable administrative purposes by mediating between government and the individual, by affording opportunities for upward mobility in the political/social hierarchies, and by playing important integrative roles.[40] Plainly, the government had every reason to promote, by the enforcement of the Solonian law or other means, the vitality of Athenian associations.

IV

In addition to the evidence adduced and the arguments presented at each stage in my investigation, I have attempted in chapter 9 to support my reconstruction by examining the text of Plato's final dialogue, the *Laws*, with respect to the insights it may offer concerning the author's own city, classical Athens. Briefly put, Plato's Cretan City in its overall design resembles historical Athens—and the historical Athens of my reconstruction—in several important respects. Plato, like Kleisthenes, erected a public edifice of segmental units, namely phylai and demes, alongside which were placed the private associations, likewise familiar to many Greeks, the phratries. As in historical Athens, public statewide functions are concentrated in the principal units, the phylai, while, simultaneously, the associations based on those same phylai were scarcely developed. The purpose here, I suggested, was to inhibit the emergence of solidarity among *phyletai* lest they, in the carrying out of their multifaceted public duties, have an opportunity to express that solidarity in a way that would be injurious to the commonwealth. Conversely, the demes are virtually without statewide public functions, while, in the context of their harmless

38. As suggested by Osborne 1985b, p. 184.
39. *AthPol* 16.5.
40. "Democracy and Associations," in chapter 1.

rural situation, they are allowed to undergo full development as freestanding associations. It is evident that, as for the historical classical Athens that I have reconstructed, Plato's purpose was to create arrangements that made for the maximization of stability. What is new for Plato is the overlaying of his polity by a network of *syssitia* possessing, I have argued, a basically regulatory purpose.[41] But even though the Cretan City's "common messes" are not closely paralleled by any analogous classical Athenian association, the spirit as it were of their regulatory purpose was embodied, if I am right, first in Solon's law and later in the various other interventions in classical Athenian associational life that we have identified and attempted to interpret.

V

Thus far the discussion has concerned only the citizen class—that is, legitimate adult male sons of Athenian parents. But it is self-evident that stability, broadly conceived from a societal rather than a narrowly political standpoint, could not have been a problem involving only the citizen class, if that class comprised (as it did) only a small fraction—probably less than a quarter—of the human population of Attica. True, it was citizen (or aspiring citizen) groups that had played the visible roles in Athens's revolutionary past, but it would be foolish to assume that no other potential source of dissatisfaction existed or was recognized. Throughout our studies, considerable attention has been given to this dimension of the problem. It was hypothesized in chapter 4 that in "the women of the *demotai*" an opening had been created for the redefinition and enlargement of the deme association.[42] If to women qua *politides*, that is the womenfolk of citizens, could be accorded substantial privileges or protections denied other free females resident in Attica, then, by analogy, the same applied to those same females qua *demotides*, the "women of the *demotai*." Since any such understanding would almost certainly have obtained from the very creation of the democracy in 508/7 when the demes were instituted, it follows that there had always existed a potential for the widening of the definition of the general deme community.

That potential was, as I argued at length in chapters 2 and 4, eventually realized in the creation, or more likely the gradual emergence, of a second deme association, one based upon precise territorial boundaries rather than, as was true of the constitutional deme, legitimate descent.[43] Study of the documents of the demes led to the isolation of the phrase "the residents" as a technical term denoting the persons officially or informally recognized as the "members" of this alternative, territorial deme association. At the minimum "the residents" will have included non-*demotai* citizens resident within the host deme's boundaries and, above all, the metics, the "residents" of the deme par excellence. And before the classical era was out, I argued, the ephebes and soldiers garrisoned at Eleusis, Rhamnous, and other demes were to

41. "The *Syssitia*," in chapter 9.
42. "The Women of the *Demotai*," in chapter 4.
43. "The Disposition of the Deme: People or Territory?" in chapter 2.

be included in their number.[44] Although the organizational and administrative purposes of the territorial deme are a matter of conjecture, at the very least deme "membership" would have provided these *de iure* nonenfranchised parties with a sense of identification with the Athenian state, if nothing else. To be sure, we are here in the realm of hypothesis, but it is an hypothesis made attractive by the convergence of two otherwise inexplicable bodies of evidence: (1) the indications for the existence of precise boundaries of the demes and (2) the seemingly technical and significant repetition of the phrase "the residents" in meaningful documentary contexts.

Beyond the deme associations, in the phratry, or rather its subgroups, some evidence was found, following the hints of earlier workers in the field, for the possible partial inclusion of women and foreigners.[45] The same tendencies are less ambiguously in evidence in the case of the cultic *orgeones*, once that, in the urbanized port of Peiraieus, organizations paralleling the citizen *orgeones* centered in the town were opened up to members of the noncitizen population, demonstrably including Athenian women, non-Athenian free persons, and perhaps even slaves.[46]

VI

These developments, at least as concerns the *orgeones*, were, however, relatively late in manifesting themselves. But the lower terminus of our study is the suppression of the free government by the Macedonians in 321, an event long predating the initial appearance of these more open cultic associations. Thus, before proceeding further, it will be necessary to consider what effects, if any, the end of the free democratic regime had upon associational life in Athens. For if, as I have argued, the democracy had been organically intertwined with contemporary associations, would not the sudden and severe alteration of that government have left telltale traces in the record of the existing associations or have played a part in the rise of the new associations that were to come later? A glance at the epigraphic record would at first blush suggest that it did. For one thing, as I observed in the Introduction, a wide spectrum of associations attested by surviving inscriptions following the Macedonian takeover seem *not* to have been in existence prior to that time.[47] These simple facts of chronology open up the possibility of a cause-and-effect relationship between change of government and change, whether in the form of decline or rise, in associational life. Let us attack this complex problem by alternately considering the decline of the old and the rise of the new associations in the light of any possible impact worked by the fortunes of the Athenian government.

To take the classical associations first, it has sometimes been suggested that somehow the groups that flourished under the autonomous *demokratia*, above all the deme and the phratry, partook of the character of the free government. The vi-

44. "The Territorial Deme: The Case for Precise Boundaries," in chapter 2, "The Rise of the Territorial Deme," in chapter 4.
45. "Subdivisions of the Phratry and Social Differentiation," in chapter 7.
46. "*Orgeones* of Bendis," "*Orgeones* of the Mother of the Gods," in chapter 8.
47. "Limitation of the Subject," in the Introduction, supported by appendix 1.

tality of a participatory direct democracy had invigorated the contemporary associations in some way essential for their continuing survival; when, accordingly, the central government ceased to function as before, the gradual atrophy or eventual collapse of the *koinoniai* became inevitable. Thus, to cite only one very recent expression of the theory, Lambert, in his attempt to explain the demise of the phratry, invokes "the decline of the democratic idea as an effective force in Athenian society."[48] However, precisely the opposite effect would seem to follow from the hypothesis propounded here in chapter 3: namely, that de facto disfranchisement of a politicized citizenry had led to the intensification of activity in the more remote demes in proportion to their remove from the seat of government. Applied diachronically to the present case, this line of reasoning would predict that the crippling of the democratic institutions in Athens should have resulted not in decline, but in still more vigorous activity in the local community.

Nonetheless, the evidence unmistakably points to the weakening, and eventual extinction, of virtually all the associations studied in this book, during the century following the end of the classical democracy. The telltale indicator is the dramatic falloff in surviving documents of the document-producing organizations from, very approximately speaking, the end of the fourth century. The epigraphic records of the three *koinoniai* documented in significant quantity, phylai,[49] demes,[50] and phratries,[51] all tell the same story: gradually encroaching senility culminating in effective demise around the middle of the third century. It is with reference to this phenomenon that a reflex to the fate of the democratic central government might seem (and has seemed) most attractive. Promulgation of the acts of the People had been a hallmark of the *demokratia*. With the collapse of that free regime, devaluation of the acts of the People would have undermined the importance of publicizing those acts—and the effect would have been mirrored at the associational level. But this argument overlooks the most striking feature of the documentary records of the associations: their preponderantly honorific content and, still more to the point, their mercenary (rather than political or ideological) purpose.[52] Phylai and demes, certainly, set up great numbers of decrees honoring their benefactors precisely—and explicitly—in order to generate still more benefactions.[53] When the incidence of such decrees went into decline, it was not because of Athens's loss of autonomy. Some different line of approach must be assayed.

Examination of the decline of the deme undertaken in chapter 4 pointed the way to a different model—a model that, because citizens (and only citizens) are involved, is potentially applicable to the other exclusive *koinoniai*, to wit, the phylai (of which, of course, the demes were components), the regional associations (again,

48. Lambert 1993, p. 275.

49. For the documents, with their dates, see appendix 3.

50. For the roster of documents, see chapter 3, note 54; for the chronological distribution of those documents, see chapter 4, note 68.

51. For a catalog of phratry documents, with full particulars, see Lambert 1993, app. 1, pp. 279–370.

52. For the demes, by far the best-documented association, see the Introduction, "Ancient Sources for the Associations of Classical Athens;" for the phylai, see chapter 6.

53. For examples of the so-called "manifesto" clause, see my discussion of the phyle documents, at chapter 6, with note 89.

comprised of demes), and the regionally concentrated phratries. All were governed by the rule of descent. Any such group, accordingly, was doomed to stagnation, if not gradual decline. Rural deme associations, for example, were subject in varying degrees to loss of members to relocation, especially to the urban centers. Such *demotai*, if landowners, not only no longer participated in the association of their affiliation but also, because they continued to own their land, effectively prevented another citizen from replacing them. Not that it would have mattered, since the rule of descent precluded growth through recruitment of outsiders, even if resident in the deme. Growth by propagation of the existing membership, too, was limited in farming communities by the fixed amount of arable land in combination with the acreage requirements of subsistence-level agriculture.

Meanwhile, as I argued in chapter 4, the presence of "outsiders" resident in the deme eventually resulted, if the experience of the garrison demes is in any way typical of Attica as a whole, in the emergence of counter deme associations. My territorial alternative deme was the first such counter-association, but the epigraphic records of the garrison demes show that, after a period of cooperation between "outsiders" and the official deme association, the soldiers eventually bypassed the official organization altogether. The sheer numbers involved may provide part of the answer, but ultimately, as I suggested, it came down to whether a stagnant or dwindling, and perhaps politically discredited, association of citizen *demotai* could continue to speak for the "natural" inclusive community of the deme.[54]

With these developments the rise of the "Hellenistic association" (to consider the putative "effect" of the process) need not have been related in any simple sequential, cause-and-effect way. Indeed, on chronological grounds alone it cannot, for some of the new groups—*eranistai*, independent *thiasotai*, and ethnic associations—are found flourishing long before the demise of the phyle, deme, or phratry organization.[55] While investigation of the circumstances surrounding the emergence of the new groups lies well beyond the limits of the present work, one factor in particular deserves mention by reason of its pertinence to a recurring topic in these pages—the role of cult. By and large, the associations with which we have been concerned were engaged, devotedly or peripherally, with formal religious activity. Typically, the cults in question were organized around native Greek divinities. But the introduction into Athens of foreign deities even before the fifth century was out is familiar to all students of Greek antiquity. Since in this society "religion" was generally not a solitary, "personal" affair but was invariably conducted in the context of a group, the inevitable result of the advent of a new divinity will have been the formation of an appropriate *koinonia* of some kind or another. This fundamental fact explains much. Positively, it helps us to understand the inclusion in these new associations of non-Athenian foreigners and, eventually, of women and slaves (quite apart from their ethnic or constitutional status). Non-Athenians, Greek or otherwise, slaves (themselves usually non-Greek), and women of all statuses tended to worship gods or heroes different from the divinities worshipped by the traditional "official" phratry, deme, or other associations. Negatively, it is self-evident that the

---

54. "The Decline of the Constitutional Deme," in chapter 4.
55. For the relevant documents, with their dates, see appendix 1.

emergence of the new groups that grew up in response to this hitherto unfulfilled need had nothing necessarily to do with the suppression of the free democracy by the Macedonians in 321.

Nonetheless, as the slow decline of the classical associations gathered steam, the two processes, one of atrophy, the other of growth, did become intertwined. The erstwhile domination of the "public associations" (especially the deme and the quasi-public phratry) had artificially suppressed the need for true voluntary associations. Self-evidently, the demise of these groups will, in the absence of any corrective action by the central government, have given rise to a corresponding demand for new associations of appropriate type. At the close of our study, when we pursued the development of the *orgeones* of the Mother of the Gods down into the late Hellenistic period, two specific manifestations of this transfer of function from the public to the private sphere came strikingly into view. The areas of need in question were the burial of abandoned corpses and the distribution of alms to the poor, social responsibilities that had previously, by statute or policy, fallen within the bailiwick of governmental institutions.[56] So, like their classical predecessors, these cultic *orgeones*, by rising to the occasion to meet the needs of their members, provide our final example of an association's response to the Athenian democracy.

The classical Athens reconstructed in this book is an Athens of institutions, specifically of those institutions I have called "associations" in the mode of their "response" to an exclusive and severely limiting central governmental order. But even so defined and circumscribed, these associations tell much of the story of the classical city, for to a great—and observable—extent this state was run through its institutions and not through extragovernmental or extralegal forces or groups.[57] Nonetheless, the limitation is real and must be borne in mind. My Athens is not the Athens of interpersonal relationships, where affective bonds, or marriage links between families, or ties of patronage or other varieties of mutual obligation demonstrably penetrate, or even override, the boundaries of my associations. It is not the Athens of communications or travel—an Athens at least intermittently integrated, for example, by pilgrimages to and from national cult centers in town, at Eleusis, Rhamnous, and Brauron. It is not the Athens of multiple property holdings or business interests whereby a well-positioned Athenian might entertain multiple ties of identity or interest to locales or groups lying well beyond the village or neighborhood of his birth. Were it possible to combine with the results of my study the indications of personal or familial bonds, movements of people, or geographically or socially distended vital interests, it is likely that conflicts or, to borrow from other contexts a well-worn critical term, a certain "dissonance" would result. Such an outcome, however, would not invalidate any of these ways of looking at the city of Athens, including my own; indeed, it is probably to be expected as a reflection of the multifarious and mutually conflicting forces and impulses at work in this highly developed,

56. "*Orgeones* of the Mother of the Gods," in chapter 8.
57. This fundamental point has been emphatically upheld in the writings of Mogens Herman Hansen. For discussion of the importance of institutions for the analysis of the democracy, see 1989b, pp. 107–113; for discussion of institutions and ideology in the democracy, see 1989a, pp. 137–148.

complex society.[58] But such an enormous undertaking remains well beyond the more modest aspirations of the present study. At the least I hope that I have succeeded in showing that, given a nominally inclusive and egalitarian democracy in fact dominated by an urban minority, and given that such a situation would tend to foster instability necessitating, if equilibrium was to be maintained, the presence of compensating conditions, that those conditions were created by the organized groups which Athenians called *koinoniai* and we call "associations."

---

58. At the close of my discussion of the isolation of the deme in chapter 3, "Deme versus Deme Relations," I suggested that the village association developed insularity and solidarity in response to a wide array of countervailing forces. This is one, I think convincing, way in which we could reconcile the conflicting tendencies represented by my reconstruction of "associational" Athens versus the other, more integrative dimensions of contemporary Attic society just mentioned.

APPENDIX ONE

Post-Macedonian Associations at Athens

As stated at the beginning of the Introduction, a wide range of associations do not appear, to judge from the epigraphic record, to have come into existence or, if in existence, to have engaged in significant corporate activity until *after* the suppression of the free government by the Macedonians in 321. The assumption undergirding this observation is that the production of inscriptions is a reliable index of such activity. A society of *eranistai* or *thiasotai* may have existed in some form under the classical democracy, but the creation and display of permanent records, particularly of decrees, bespeak significant organizational development in the form of meetings and the taking of votes, financial resources with which, inter alia, to obtain and inscribe stelai, and perhaps the possession of a sanctuary or other property on which to erect those stelai. The present appendix supports my position by compiling references to the published epigraphic texts pertaining to each of these associations. For the larger background of "private religious associations" at Athens, reflecting sources nonepigraphic as well as epigraphic, see now, in brief, Parker 1996, appendix 4, pp. 333–342.

Eranistai. Absent from Solon's law, *eranistai* do figure in the epitomizing passage from Aristotle's *Nichomachean Ethics* (8.9.4–6: 1160a) analyzed in chapter 1. Since Aristotle characterizes the *eranistai* as a *koinonia* and identifies as their purpose "social intercourse," it is clear that we are dealing with a genuine association rather than (to mention a quite different meaning of *eranos* and *eranistai* current at about this time) an ad hoc group of individuals formed to make friendly loans. Not so clear is the character of the entities implied by the *eranikai* (sc. *dikai*) mentioned at

AthPol 52.2, but it is likely, since suits are in question, that the reference is merely to "friendly loans."

The earliest dated epigraphic evidence of the genuine association is *IG* II² 2935 of 324/3, but no other such text antedates the end of the classical democracy in 321. Also early are the dedications *SEG* 41.171 (300/299) and *IG* II² 2940 (s. IV ?) and the decrees *SEG* 41.82 (ca. 300–280?), *IG* II² 1265 (ca. 300), 1266 (fin. s. IV?), and 1291 (med. s. III). Later documents of the association include the decrees *IG* II²1335 (102/1), 1345 (A.D. 53/4), 1339 (A.D. 57/6), and 1369 (fin. s. II p.?; *SEG* 25.175, 29.139); *SEG* 31.122 (= 36.198) (ca. A.D. 121/2); the catalogs *IG* II² 2354 (fin. s. III) and 2358 (ca. 150); the dedication *Hesperia* 32 (1963) 46, no. 64 (init. s. II; *SEG* 21.633); and the unidentified document *MDAI[A]* 67 (1942) [1951] 30–31, no. 29 (52/1; *SEG* 37.103).

Eranistai as creditors are attested by eight Athenian *horoi* collected and analyzed by Finley 1951: nos. 30 (*IG* II² 2699), 31 (2700), 32 (2701), 40 (2721), 42 (2719), 44 (2722), 70 (2743), and 71 (*Hesperia* 10 [1941] 54, no. 18A; 309/8). Add now *EAH* (1992) [1993] 3 (s. IV; *SEG* 41.127). With regard to any associational development of these groups of moneylenders, Finley caps his analysis of the *eranoi* (1951, pp. 100–106) with the statement that his study had eliminated "any form of permanent or continuing group as a significant factor in the field of hypothecation, and even in the field of moneylending generally, in Athens before the Roman era" (p. 106).

Independent thiasotai. Solon's law lists *thiasotai* (see appendix 2). Two hundred years later, *thiasoi* (or *thiasotai*) figure as subgroups in one of the Demotionid decrees of 396/5, *IG* II² 1237, decree of Nikodemos, face B, lines 68–113 passim. Aristotle's account of *koinoniai* in the *Ethics* mentions *thiasotai* in parallel construction with the *eranistai* and attributes to them the purpose of performing sacrifices (*Eth. Nic.* 8.9.5: 1160a).

But the epigraphic record for an independent *thiasos* (that is, one not, as at Dekeleia, demonstrably embedded within a larger association) includes but a single text of the fifth century, *IG* I³ 1016, a dedicatory base dated epigraphically to the mid-fifth century in the name of the *thiasos* of the Etionidai. Thereafter come a number of documents categorized by *IG* as *catalogi* and dated epigraphically to various parts of the fourth century: *IG* II² 2343 (init. s. IV; *SEG* 33.161, 35.131 and 137, 39.192), 2345 (ante med. s. IV; *SEG* 21.632)), 2347 (post med. s. IV), 2348? (fin. s. IV), 2349? (s. IV), followed by 2351? (init. s. III), 2352 (ca. init. s. III), 2356? (s. III?), and 2359? (init. s. I). (Regarding the list of names *IG* II² 2344, identified in the *Corpus* as a list of the *thiasotai* of a phratry, though expressly labeled only as *phrateres*, see Flower 1985 and Hedrick 1989.) Of these texts only *IG* II² 2347, which registers the names of persons crowned by the *thiasotai*, unambiguously indicates independent associational activity. Crownings are also commemorated in the dedications *IG* II² 2936 (fin. s. IV) and 2939 (s. IV); cf. *AD* 23A (1968) 6–7, no. 2 (s. IV or a little later; *SEG* 24.223) and *Hesperia* 15 (1946) 156, no. 13 (ex. s. III; *SEG* 21.533). The earliest decrees are the three engraved on *IG* II² 1261 (302/1, 301/0, 300/299; *SEG* 16.108), followed by 1262 (301/0), 1263 (300/299), 1271 (298/7), and about a dozen others collected in the *Corpus* under *decreta collegiorum et sodaliciorum*. More recently published examples include the decrees *SEG* 2.9 (ca. 257); 2.10 (med. s. III); *Hesperia* 30 (1961)

227–228, no. 26 (227/6); *AD* 23A (1968) 1–6 (238/7; *SEG* 24.156, 32.149); and the honors *Hesperia* 15 (1946) 156, no. 13 (ex. s. III).

For the use of the term *thiasos* in association with *orgeones*, see Dow and Gill 1965, pp. 111–112, no. 1 (fin. s. IV post 316/15), lines 3–4, and cf. p. 112, no. 2 (= *IG* II² 1246; init. s. III), line 3 (restored). For my discussion, see "*Orgeones* of the Mother of the Gods," in chapter 8, with notes 195–207.

Cultic associations. Named associations are: Amphieraistai, *IG* II² 1322 (after 229; *SEG* 33.145); Artemiastai, *IG* II² 2942 (s. III); Asklepiastai, *Hesperia* 28 (1959) 178–179, no. 4 (= *IG* II² 1293; med. s. III), *IG* II² 2353 (med. s. III) and 2960 (med s. II p.); Daitaleis, *IG* II² 1267 (fin. s. IV); Dionysiastai, *IG* II² 1326 (176/5; *SEG* 25.160); Eikadeis, *IG* II² 1258 (324/3); Heroistai, *IG* II² 1339 (57/6); Iobacchoi, *IG* II² 1368 (s. II p.; *SEG* 17.38; 25.174; 33. 254, 1570; 34.113; 35.111); Isis, *SEG* 22.114 (A.D. 37 or shortly later; *SEG* 23.77); Megaloi Theoi, *Hesperia* 30 (1961) 229, no. 28 (112/1; *SEG* 21.535) and 229–230, no. 29 (111/10; *SEG* 21.536); Men Tyrannos, *IG* II² 1365 (s. I p.) and 1366 (s. I p.; *SEG* 15.116, 25.173, 28.233, 29.138); Paianistai, *AD* 30 (1975) [1983] B, p. 42 (Roman?; *SEG* 32.232); *IG* II² 2481 (s. II p.; *SEG* 28.255, 32.220, 39.194) and 2963 (ca. A.D. 212/3); Sabaziastai, *IG* II² 1335 (102/1); Sarapiastai, *IG* II² 1292 (med. s. III); and Soteriastai, *IG* II² 1343 (ca. 37/6). Untitled cultic groups include: a list of various personnel, *IG* II² 2403 (post med. s. IV); *synthytai* of Zeus and Antha, *IG* II² 2360 (ca. 150; *SEG* 25.565, 32.219); and *mystai*, *IG* II² 2339B + 1999 (A.D.164/5; *SEG* 17.56).

Ethnic and foreign associations. Achaeans, *IG* II² 2961 (s. II p.); Dorians, *IG* II² 2415/16 (fin. s. IV); Salaminians from Cyprus, *IG* II² 1290 (med. s. III); Sidonians, *IG* II² 2946 (s. III/II); Tarantines, *IG* II² 2975 (init. s. III); and the Panhellenes, *IG* II² 2956–2958 (time of Hadrian). For lists of *peregrini*, see *IG* II² 2390–2392 (med. s. IV), 2404 and 2406 (post med. s. IV), 2420–2421 (s. IV); *Hesperia* 29 (1960) 54–55, no. 76 (*SEG* 19.173; init. s. IV) and 33–34, no. 40 (*SEG* 19.178; s. IV/III).

Professional or commercial associations. Solon's law (see appendix 2) had listed among its inclusive roster of groups "those going abroad for commerce" (οἰχόμενοι ἢ εἰς ἐμπορίαν), but no association corresponding to this description surfaces prior to the Macedonian era. From the classical period we have only the dedication by fullers (οἱ πλυνῆς), *IG* II² 2934 (med. s. IV). Later are *IG* II² 2941 (ca. 268/7), a dedication by parties "[crowned] ὑπὸ τοῦ κοινοῦ τῶν ἐργαζ[ομένων] (line 2), and 2952 (ca. 97/6), honors conferred by οἱ ἔμποροι κα[ὶ ναύκληροι].

Groups of women. IG II² 2357 (catalog of women; init. s. II) and 1346 (decree of college of women; *SEG* 21.538; ca. A.D. 100–150).

Unidentified groups. The collection in *IG* II² of *decreta collegiorum et sodaliciorum*, nos. 1249–1355, includes nearly a score of decrees of unidentified or unidentifiable groups ranging in date between "post med. s. IV" (1251) and the second or third century A.D. (1355).

None of the above texts, save the single inscribed base dedicated by the *thiasos* of the Etionidai, *IG* I³ 1016, is securely dated, even epigraphically, to the fifth century. Since, however, the *thiasos* as component of the phratry is known from an early date, and since it is notoriously difficult to distinguish among the various uses of the term, it would be unwise to erect a theory of a classical independent *thiasos* on the basis of this single text. Several other texts are given dates within the fourth century, usually the middle or the end, but, again, these dates are all, with only two exceptions, based on epigraphic criteria. The two exceptions are *IG* II^2 2935, a dedication by *eranistai*, and 1258, honors conferred by the cultic Eikadeis, both placed in the year 324/3 by their citations of the archon Hegesias. For the purposes of the present study, accordingly, I conclude that all these associations are to be viewed as essentially the products of the eras following the end of the classical democracy.

APPENDIX TWO

Solon's Law on Associations

At 47.22.4 the *Digest* preserves a passage from Gaius's commentary on the Twelve Tables. Gaius adduces in support of his comment a law of Solon's:[1]

> *Sed haec lex videtur ex lege Solonis tralata esse: nam illuc ita est*:
>
> Ἐὰν δὲ δῆμος ἢ φράτορες ἢ ἱερῶν ὀργίων ἢ ναῦται ἢ σύσσιτοι ἢ ὁμόταφοι ἢ θιασῶται ἢ ἐπὶ λείαν οἰχόμενοι ἢ εἰς ἐμπορίαν ὅ τι ἂν τούτων διαθῶνται πρὸς ἀλλήλους κύριον εἶναι, ἐὰν μὴ ἀπαγορεύσῃ δημόσια γράμματα.

In support of the general characterization of the meaning and purpose of this law offered in chapter 1, I present here the detailed reasons justifying my treatment of the transmitted text, including discussion of others' emendations and arguments favoring two new emendations of my own.[2] For my final, corrected text, see the head of my discussion of the law in chapter 1.

δῆμος. The appropriateness of this item to a law ascribed to Solon has been repeatedly questioned. Wilamowitz appears to have been the first to note the apparent anachronism of its presence.[3] When, a century later, Whitehead turned to the al-

---

1. Ruschenbusch 1966, F 76a (77), pp. 98–99.
2. Namely, the substitution of ὀργεῶνες for the transmitted ἱερῶν ὀργίων and of ναυκραρία for the transmitted ναῦται. The latter emendation has been made independently by Lambert 1993, p. 250, note 27 (pp. 250–251).
3. Wilamowitz 1881, pp. 278–279.

leged evidence for a Solonian, or even pre-Solonian, deme system, including the text preserved in the *Digest*, he concluded that that evidence was "entirely inconclusive," and on that basis rejected it.[4] By way of explaining the state of the received text, Whitehead agreed with previous scholars that the *Digest*'s version conflates (genuine) archaic elements with later ones and (following Wilamowitz) classed the mention of "a deme" with the latter.[5] This conclusion is of course in agreement with the standard view that it was Kleisthenes who first institutionalized Attica's hamlets, villages, towns, and neighborhoods for constitutional purposes and that it was he, accordingly, who first established *demos*, its plural collective *demotai*, and related words as *termini technici*. So, if the technical term is in use here, the anachronism is patent.

But two other approaches remain open. One, obviously, is that the word may not be technical. After all, the word had been in use since at least Mycenaean times, and even in the archaic and classical periods it is demonstrably put to nonconstitutional uses, usually as a common prose term for "village."[6] Besides, the suggestion of such a use here would gain support from the cumbersome locutions at the end of the catalog for "pirates" and "traders," which certainly do not correspond to any "official" language (if official language, in their cases, ever existed). The second approach, which I shall favor, is that the word is indeed technical, but in a different sense from that envisioned by Wilamowitz and Whitehead. To establish a preliminary point, the existence of an official sense of *demos* before the time of Kleisthenes is indicated by the title of the *dikastai kata demous* instituted by Peisistratos.[7] And what was the content of that pre-Kleisthenic "official sense" of the word? The argument advanced in chapters 2 and 4 of the present work has opened up an entirely new possible understanding of its meaning. I have argued that there were not one but two definitions of the deme, the narrowly limited constitutional deme and, to the point here, the wider, "natural" community embracing all persons residing inside the deme's territorial boundaries. May I suggest that Solon's law, though a century earlier than the institution of the constitutional deme (and the creation of the corresponding terminology), refers to this latter, wider, "natural" community? (Analogously, the sphere of operation of the Peisistratid *dikastai kata demous* would be not merely the Athenian citizens resident in the "demes" but rather, as the purpose ascribed by the *AthPol* to the tyrant, namely to keep the rural folk—presumably all rural folk—out of the urban center [16.3–5], would suggest, the entire resident population of each village.) My interpretation would also help ease the shock of the unexpected singular substantive in contrast with the collective masculine plurals in evidence throughout the remainder of the statute. "Village" suggests the totality of the community; "villagers" (in the masculine gender) a subset of adult males. Indeed, the failure of the transmitted text to supply the normal Kleisthenic collective *demotai* is an argument *against* the case

4. Whitehead 1986, pp. 12–14 (with p. 14 for the quotation).

5. Whitehead 1986, p. 14.

6. For a detailed discussion, with references, see Whitehead 1986, pp. 5–16 and app. 1, pp. 364–368. For an earlier discussion of the "changes and shifts" in the meaning of *demos*, see Donlan 1970, pp. 381–395.

7. *AthPol* 16.5.

for anachronism. A truly anachronistic text would have given the form in normal use in documents throughout the recorded history of the deme associations. The received word δῆμος is therefore probably authentic, and authentic in the specific sense that I have suggested.

φράτορες. Ziebarth printed without comment the familiar Attic orthography φράτερες.[8] According to *LSJ*[9], s.v. φράτηρ, the spelling preserved by Gaius is frequent in codices but, on Herodian and Eusthathios's evidence, a later form. For usage in Solon's time, one thinks first of the later copy of Drakon's law on homicide, where the "brothers" are twice mentioned. But according to Stroud's improved text of the law published in 1968, in both passages where the word has been partly restored the crucial vowel is not preserved.[9]

ἱερῶν ὀργίων ἢ ναῦται. Commentators are agreed that corruption has occurred somewhere within this stretch of text. One's suspicions are aroused, first, by the strange phrase "of sacred rites," strange because of the unexpected—and inexplicable—genitive and, more substantively, because of the otiose use of the term "sacred." *Orgia* are by definition "sacred," and *all* associations in any event are known or legitimately suspected to have had a cultic or ritualistic orientation. Something must be wrong.

Solutions vary. Early emendations recorded by Radin in his 1910 publication include the additions ἱερῶν ὀργίων θῦται ("sacrificers of sacred *orgia*," Mommsen) or μύσται ("initiates of sacred *orgia*," Caillemer),[10] to which may be added Guarducci's (συ)ν(θ)ύται ("co-sacrificers")[11] and Endenburg's κοινωνοί ("associates").[12] In each case (save the last), the supplied word has been reconstructed from the following transmitted letters, ἢ ναῦται. Though in varying degrees paleographically attractive, however, each of these solutions suffers from two defects: (1) from the absence of an early Athenian association designated by the term in question and (2), a stylistic point, from the palpable redundancy of the phrases when compared with the minimalist wording of the remainder of the text: "sacrificers," "initiates," or "associates," would, given (again) the cultic orientation of all associations, have sufficed without further specification or qualification (i.e., without the superfluous addition of ἱερῶν ὀργίων).

Are other remedies available? With little supporting argument, Wilamowitz proposed emendation of the entire stretch of text to ἢ ὀργεῶνες ἢ γεννηταὶ [sic] ("or ritualists or clansmen").[13] Later, he was followed in part by Ferguson, who, noting that Wilamowitz had left the transmitted ἱερῶν unaccounted for, suggested ἢ ἡρώων ὀργεῶνες ἢ γεννῆται ("or ritualists of heroes or clansmen").[14] If we may, for the moment, postpone consideration of the *gennetai*, it is evident that the suggested presence of *orgeones* in the law has much to recommend it. We would be rid

8. Ziebarth 1896, p. 167.
9. Stroud 1968, pp. 5–6, lines 18 and 23. Stroud's text is reproduced as M–L 86 (87) and *IG* I³ 104.
10. Radin 1910, p. 37.
11. M. Guarducci, *RFIC* 1935, p. 333.
12. Endenburg 1937, pp. 163ff.
13. Wilamowitz 1881, pp. 278–279.
14. Ferguson 1944, p. 64, with note 5 (pp. 64–65).

of the redundant phrase ἱερῶν ὀργίων, getting in its place the citation of a class of associations known, as we saw in chapter 8, to have been prominent in Classical and Hellenistic Athens. Besides, the replacement of this term by an intrusive gloss is easily imaginable, since forms of the word *orgeones* are largely confined to epigraphic texts, while the commentators on its few uses in literary texts manifestly regard it as a difficult word in need of definition or explanation.[15] As for Gaius's text, it is quite possible that an original ὀργεῶνες might have been glossed by some word or words involving ὄργια, and that the gloss has somehow been intruded in place of the true reading. (The fact that the two words may not actually be linguistically related[16] is beside the point; they would have looked sufficiently alike to satisfy an ancient scribe.) So far, then, we are at liberty to follow Wilamowitz and Ferguson. But the latter's further specification of the *orgeones* as "of heroes," while making good paleographic sense, nonetheless, as Ferguson's fellow worker A. D. Nock seems to have perceived, fails on a point of substance. Nock observed that, on Ferguson's own analysis, *orgeones* "of gods" existed alongside those "of heroes."[17] Why should the law mention only one, to the apparent exclusion of the other? It is perhaps better, then, to suppose that the phrase "of sacred *orgia*" ultimately derives from a gloss on ὀργεῶνες alone.

Thus far, no reason has been acknowledged for calling into question the words (emended in most or all of the proposed texts above) ἢ ναῦται. Yet they were deleted by Ziehen on the ground that they are a copyist's "interpretation" of the phrase that follows shortly, ἢ εἰς ἐμπορίαν.[18] But this is hardly credible, since the words "people (going abroad) for commerce" make good sense by themselves (and so would have required no gloss in the first place) and in any case would have been most inadequately—in fact, misleadingly—defined by so general a locution as "sailors." Radin, while conceding the possibility of the received text's authenticity, found the placement of the phrase within the series of terms to be "extraordinary."[19] However, this judgment looked ahead to his very questionable grouping of the associations named in the law into three internally homogeneous "classes."[20] Without that (unfounded) grouping, there is no good reason at hand for questioning even the word's placement, must less for its removal or emendation. Besides, if context is to be a consideration, *nautai* fits well immediately preceding its natural complement, the *syssitoi*.

Natural though the word may be in this setting, however, Wilamowitz, as we saw, substituted for "sailors" the familiar masculine plural *gennetai*. But the emendation fails on both formal and substantive grounds. Paleographically, the received text makes no sense either as a corruption of or conjecture for the supposed original text. For all that, it is the substantive objection that is the decisive one. Wilamowitz apparently believed strongly enough in the existence and importance of the *genos*

---

15. The relevant passages from the lexica are collected and discussed by Ferguson 1944, pp. 62–64.

16. For a detailed discussion of the linguistic problem, see Ferguson 1944, app. 1, pp. 131–132. Frisk 1970, vol. 2, p. 412, associates the two words, but compare his later remarks at 1972, vol. 3, p. 163.

17. Hence his proposal to insert ἢ θεῶν after ἡρώων in the text: see Ferguson 1944, p. 64, note 5 (pp. 64–65).

18. *Apud* Ziebarth 1896, p. 167, with note 1.

19. Radin 1910, p. 37.

20. Radin 1910, pp. 48, 50.

as an association that he regarded as necessary its presence in any catalog of associations pretending to completeness. But as a result of both Bourriot and Roussel's careful and exhaustive studies of the term *genos* and related lexical forms, it is now clear that any such belief is open to question. At this early date, the *genos*, it now appears, far from necessarily being a structured and cohesive "association," may merely be a person's family tree, descent group, relatives, or the like, with corresponding meanings for the allied collective *gennetai*.[21] Consequently, Wilamowitz's supposed "clansmen" lose any attraction they may once have possessed as replacements for the "sailors" of the transmitted text of Solon's law.

Are we, then, to retain the transmitted text? Sailors are found, beginning no later than the mid-fourth century, issuing decrees, the Paraloi,[22] "those sailing in the sacred ships,"[23] and eventually ordinary crews[24] all being attested. Since Athenian navies are known to have been active by Solon's time (in the wars with Aigina, with Megara over Salamis, and with Mytilene over Sigeion[25]), there can be no objection on chronological grounds to supposing that the term "sailors" reflects conditions in 594. What is more, πλωτῆρες figure in the passage from Aristotle's *Ethics* exploited in chapter 1 to establish our definition of "association."[26] Again, the natural conjunction of "sailors" with their land-based counterparts, the *syssitoi*, might also be thought a point in favor of the *Digest's* text. Nonetheless, the jejune and colorless ναῦται might after all be convincingly viewed as an intrusive gloss, should a sufficiently convincing candidate for the original text be found. Among paleographically or linguistically possible words, *naukleroi* springs to mind, for captains did in fact eventually form associations of a kind.[27] But with this term (unlike, as noted, with the case of *nautai* itself), we would come very close to redundant repetition of the following (so far as we can tell, secure) phrase "people (going abroad) for commerce." Though possible, it is not at all likely that *both* would have been named in so brief a text.

Alternatively, one thinks of the pre-Kleisthenic statewide units the *naukrariai*, over which were placed officers called *naukraroi*, according to the Aristotelian *Constitution*.[28] The ascription of both unit and officer to the time of Solon is explicit. Two additional possibilities for our text are thereby opened up. The case for ναύκραροι is not, however, a strong one. The *Constitution's* statement (21.5) that Kleisthenes established the demarchs, "having the same competence as the earlier *naukraroi*," suggests that the latter, like the demarchs in relation to the demes, numbered only one per *naukraria*. Since the naukraries, in turn, numbered 48 or 50,[29] a

21. See "*Genê*," in chapter 8. The result of our discussion was that, alone of the various uses of the term *genos*, only the "sacerdotal families" qualify as bona fide associations.

22. For the references, see chapter 2, with notes 16–17.

23. *IG* II² 2987 (s. II/I; *SEG* 18.68).

24. See *SEG* 15.112 (225 B.C.), a decree acknowledging benefactions bestowed upon the honorand by "his fellow sailors." For analysis of the text, see chapter 2, "The Territorial Deme."

25. Rhodes 1981, p. 151.

26. "The Definition of 'Association,'" in chapter 1.

27. E.g., *IG* II² 2952 (ca. 97/6), a dedication by οἱ ἔμποροι κα[ὶ ναύκληροι] (line 1).

28. See *AthPol* 8.3 (= Ruschenbusch 1966, F 79 [71], p. 100). For a brief review of the evidence, the reader may consult Jones 1987, ch. 1, sec. 1.1, pp. 28–31.

29. For forty-eight units, twelve per each of the four phylai, see *AthPol* 8.3; for fifty units, apparently the result of reforming activity by Kleisthenes, see Kleidemos, *FGrH* 323 F 8.

sufficiently large group would have been created to make credible "the prytaneis" ascribed to them by Herodotos in a notoriously problematic passage (5.71.2). Yet how likely is it that these officers would have formed among themselves one or more "associations"? Turning to the naukraries, however, the *Constitution*'s statement that Kleisthenes created the demes "in place of the *naukrariai* " (21.5) suggests, by associating the *naukrariai* with the demes, that the former possessed an essentially associational character. A reference here to the naukraries would, on historical grounds, be welcome, since otherwise none of the three tiers of the pre-Solonian public organization documented by the *Constitution* (8.3), phylai, *trittyes*, and *naukrariai*, would be included. Paleographically, too, the emendation is attractive in that the obsolete term ναυκραρία is sufficiently obscure and sufficiently similar in *apparent* sense to the word for "sailors" as to have given rise to ναῦται as a gloss. The one drawback is that, amidst the direct or indirect evidence linking the units with tax collection, ships, and temples, no explicit indication of an associational orientation has survived.[30]

σύσσιτοι. Besides its well-known currency at Sparta, the term *syssitos* (and related words) is occasionally found in Athenian contexts to designate soldiers' bivouacs or encampments.[31] The question is whether it also had anything to do with associations, however temporary or informal. No association under just this name is recorded, but positive hints in that direction come from three quite different quarters. First, late Classical and Hellenistic inscriptions attest, as we saw in chapters 2 and 4, the formation of organizations of ephebes or of Athenian or foreign troops encamped in certain rural or coastal demes for the purpose of passing honorary decrees. Such organizations approximate, however distantly, associations of *syssitoi*. Secondly, according to the Aristotelian *Constitution of the Athenians*, the ephebes συσσιτοῦσι...κατὰ φυλάς ("dine by phylai") (42.3). True, the Ephebic College had not come into existence until shortly before these words were written down, but the choice of language may nonetheless preserve a relic of a much earlier associational organization of *syssitoi*. Thirdly, it is possible that Solonian practice is reflected in the arrangements of the Cretan City in Plato's *Laws*, studied in chapter 9 of this book. There, as we saw, a system of phylai and demes with strong Athenian affinities is overlain by a network of *syssitia*.[32] Even allowing for the palpable Spartan or local Cretan inspiration of Plato's utopian regime, the possibility of the relevance of Plato's Cretan City to the Athenian Solonian law on associations is suggested by the striking recurrence of borrowings from Solonian Athens throughout the philosopher's visionary polity.[33] Therefore, in the absence of contrary indications, we must entertain the possibility of more or less formally organized "messes" contemporary with the law's formulation.

ὁμόταφοι. To judge from the passages cited s.v. by *LSJ*[9] (viz., Aischines, 1.149 and Plutarch, 23 *On Isis and Osiris* 359b), the term *homotaphos* should be connected

---

30. Among the voluminous literature on the subject, one may consult Thomsen 1964, pp. 119–146; Jordan 1970; Billigmeier and Dusing 1981; Rhodes 1981, pp. 79–84; Gabrielsen 1985; Lambert 1986; and Jordan 1992.

31. See, for example, Isaios, 4.18; Demosthenes, 54.4; Lysias, 13.79; and Plutarch, *Alkibiades* 7.2.

32. "The *Syssitia*," in chapter 9.

33. See Chase 1933, p. 191.

with the practice of common burial. Accordingly, the plural of the term might naturally be used technically of what is commonly called a "burial society." But, in contrast with the popularity of such organizations under the Roman Empire, Ziebarth failed to find in the sources for free Greece evidence for the collective provision, monetary, organizational, or otherwise, for the burial of the dead.[34] Later, Radin opened his discussion of the Solonian *homotaphoi* with the remark that "[f]amily organizations . . . γένη and parts of γένη, buried their dead together from immemorial custom."[35] But the only proof he offers in support of this generalization is the suggested emendation of a passage in Demosthenes 57, *Against Euboulides.* In that brief, the speaker concocts an imaginary list of *oikeioi* suitable to testify regarding the identity of his father: various relatives (cousins, sons of cousins, men married to female cousins), φρατέρες, γεννῆται, εἶθ᾽ οἷς ἡρία ταὐτὰ εἶθ᾽ οἱ δημόται (§67). Noting that no such (unnamed) group corresponding to the penultimate item in the series and distinct from the *phrateres, gennetai,* and the rest, is specifically indicated, Radin adduced chapter 28 of the same speech, where mention is made of "ancestral tombs in which share all who are members of the *genos.*" The reference here to the *genos* prompted Radin to delete from the previously cited passage the word εἶθ᾽, which separates the mention of the *gennetai* from the reference to "(those) for whom are the same tombs." Thus he could conclude that "it is in the γένος or in the οἶκος that we must primarily look for ὁμόταφοι."[36]

Needless to say, where chapter 67 is concerned, this is rather cavalier handling of the evidence. Textually speaking, his deletion is utterly without justification. It may be added that Humphreys' study of the full record, literary and archaeological, for "family tombs" yielded a largely negative result.[37] So, while chapter 28 does unambiguously ascribe common burial to all the members of a *genos,* this term, in line with our discussion in chapter 8, is probably best understood not as an association but as a descent group of some kind. As for the catalog of associations in chapter 67, Demosthenes' text, if left undisturbed and allowed to speak for itself, identifies as a body practicing interment in common graves a plurality of persons, unnamed by the speaker and, except for the negative implication that it was not close consanguineal or affinal relatives, *phrateres, gennetai,* or *demotai,* not specifically identified. It would be perverse to resist the temptation to equate such a body of Athenians with the *homotaphoi* of Solon's law and to characterize that body, since it is mentioned in parallel construction with the phratry and deme, as an association.

θιασῶται. The different usages of this rather elastic term, some of rather high antiquity, were remarked in chapter 7: a band of revelers, an organized cultic association, or a group or association of unspecified nature and function.[38] No indications are at hand, however, that would allow us to select that usage, or usages, intended by the original text of Solon's law. A second point of uncertainty concerns the relation of such *thiasotai* as Solon may have intended to another class of association

34. Ziebarth 1896, p. 17.
35. Radin 1910, p. 45.
36. Radin 1910, p. 46.
37. Humphreys 1993 (= 1980, pp. 96–126), pp. 79–134, with the conclusion at pp. 120–122.
38. Chapter 7, with notes 109–113.

mentioned in the text, the *phrateres*. It is well established by several articles of evidence that *thiasotai* might be organized as the component part of the larger body of "brothers."[39] If so, such a whole-and-part relationship between two distinct items in the *Digest's* list of associations would wreak havoc with its otherwise strictly paratactic arrangement. But there is no reason to think that *all* types of *thiasoi* were segmentally contained by phratries, and as long as the possibility exists that the two units were not in fact organically related, there is no reason to suspect the integrity of the received version of the text.[40]

ἐπὶ λείαν οἰχόμενοι ἢ εἰς ἐμπορίαν. "Pirates" and "traders" appear to be meant, but all detail, including any insight into the substantive issues with which this study is concerned, escapes us. It is unlikely, however, that in the time of Solon groups of this type were yet organized into formal, enduring associations such as the later professional guilds of merchants. With reason, therefore, Radin prefers the use of the term "partnership" to characterize these apparently temporary ad hoc associations.[41] But whatever their legal properties, the question remains why Solon sought to include in his legislation such groups as "pirates" and "traders" in the first place. After all, both were presumably engaged in activities, commercial and otherwise, that would have taken them far beyond the boundaries of Attica. What are they doing here alongside the constitutional, cultic, and social groupings that comprised the associational framework of domestic citizen society? The answer, I suspect, is to be found in connection with the lawgiver's general interest, manifested in several particular statutes and reforms, in the economic growth and health of the Athenian state.[42] State intervention in such partnerships may, in ways we can only guess, have been thought to contribute to the realization of such goals. Did Solon think that the state, by ensuring the viability of such partnerships, or by their regulation, could somehow enhance or protect the commercial health of Athens, even if, as in the case of the "pirates," grossly illegal or violent activity was involved?

With the completion of our brief review of the individual associations preserved in the *Digest's* text, it is incumbent upon us to ask, with Radin,[43] whether this list may, despite its manifest defects, nonetheless be complete. Bold though it must seem, it may, I think, be ventured that, given what little we know of Athenian associations at the time of Solon, the list is in fact without demonstrable exception a full roster. To establish the point, it is necessary only to comment briefly upon a few seeming omissions. Wilamowitz, for one, was troubled by the absence of the *genos*, and so he, as we have just seen, proposed the insertion of *gennetai* in place of the suspect *nautai*. Our reasons for denying both his guiding premise and his proposed solution to this nonexistent problem have already been given. Radin wondered why

39. See Lambert 1993, pp. 81–93.

40. Admittedly, this conclusion is in conflict with the conclusion reached in appendix 1, that the *thiasos* as independent association does not emerge until the Macedonian era. Perhaps *thiasoi* were independent in the time of Solon, only to disappear for a lengthy period prior to their resurgence under the very different conditions of Hellenistic Athens.

41. Radin 1910, p. 49.

42. See *AthPol* 5–12, with the commentary of Rhodes 1981, pp. 118–179. For a brief discussion of the major points, see Jones 1997, pp. 82–83.

43. Radin 1901, p. 51, who endeavors to explain the apparent "omissions."

the phyle—or rather the *phyletai*—were not to be found, but his answer to his question, that the "existence" of the four Old Attic phylai could only have been "vague" in Solon's time and that they (or at least their management) were confined to "the nobility," could have been exposed even in 1910 as baseless speculation.[44] A better approach would be, first, to emphasize that our question concerns not (of course) the fractional segment of the statewide constitutional framework but rather *only* the internally organized association based upon that segment; and then, secondly, with this in mind, to look to the internally organized phylai of the successor organization established by Kleisthenes for clues about earlier times. This very investigation was carried out in chapter 5, and it was found that the Kleisthenic phylai underwent very little associational development.[45] I am inclined, therefore, to retroject similar conditions to the regime of the four Old Attic phylai under Solon. An identical argument will apply to the one other potential candidate for a missing association, the pre-Kleisthenic *trittys*, the third part of the Old Attic phyle.[46] Besides, the absence of both the phyle association and the trittys association would be compensated for by the acceptance of my proposed emendation ⟨ναυκραρία⟩. Again, since on the *Ath-Pol'*s evidence the *naukrariai* were replaced by the demes (21.5), destined to be the most active associations of the Kleisthenic public organization, it would be natural to look to the *naukrariai*, the bottommost tier of the pre-Kleisthenic system, for the most active associations of the predecessor public organization.

It is fair to conclude, therefore, that, once the *Digest*'s text has been emended and understood in conformity with the above discussion, there is no omission, either originally (and deliberately) on Solon's part or as a consequence of the many hazards posed by the process of transmission. In view of this finding, all the more significance attaches to another general observation, made by more than one commentator, that, despite the evident effort to compile an exhaustive enumeration of these groupings, no single word or expression meaning "association" is to be found in the text.[47] What is the explanation? Perhaps, given the very early date of the Solonian legislation, it may be suggested that this area of Athenian law was still in its infancy, and that when Solon turned to the problem of addressing the place of the association in his reformed polity, no word embracing all such entities existed or, if it existed, had come into use in this specific sense. The *koinon* of Attic inscriptions and the *koinonia* of Aristotle's *Nichomachean Ethics* may still have lain many years in the future.

It remains only to comment upon the closing, operative words of the law, which have the general sense: "whatever arrangements these associations make are to be valid, unless the written statutes of the People forbid." While the more general import of the text is taken up in chapter 1, it is appropriate here to query, first, regarding the syntax and referent of τούτων. One commentator, Poland,[48] supplied τινές,

44. Radin 1910, p. 44.

45. "The Solidarity of the Phyle as Association," in chapter 5.

46. For what little is known of the internal organization of Kleisthenes' trittyes, see Jones 1987, ch. 1, sec. 1.33, pp. 60–61.

47. E.g., Radin 1910, p. 51, where, however, the writer's term is not association but "corporation." The point is also made by Jones 1956, pp. 162–163.

48. Poland 1909, p. 14.

yielding the sense "whatever some of these [associations] arrange." Wilhelm objected that, even without the supplement, the text could be made to give the same meaning[49] (a construction glossed by Ferguson as "a partitive genitive as subject"[50]). As an additional and, I think, more attractive possibility, let me suggest that τούτων is indeed partitive but that it is to be constructed with a word actually preserved in the text, and in close context at that, namely ὅ τι. The entities to which "these things" would have referred will have been named in the preceding, lost sentence the existence of which is signaled by the connective δέ with which Gaius's extract is introduced. We do not know what "these things" are, but, whatever they were, the effect will have been to limit the application of the law. That is to say, arrangements made by associations that did *not* concern "these things" will not have come under the state's guarantee of "validation" (for the term, see my discussion in chapter 1). My guess is that the intent was to limit validation to cases where "these things" were matters appropriate to the functioning of the association in question, for example, burials for burial societies, sacrifices for cultic organizations, contracts for trading companies.

A final point, like the preceding pertinent to my interpretation of the general intent of the law, concerns the referent of πρὸς ἀλλήλους. Ferguson commented: "I take it that the statute envisaged two sets of reciprocal arrangements, one of two or more of the groups, and another of the members of a single group."[51] Linguistically, this may be a possible reading, but the record of Athenian associations is decidedly against the former of the two modes of arrangement. Athenian associations are not often found entering into agreements with each other, whether the organizations in question are of the same or of different orders. For example, the surviving records of the phylai, demes, and phratries preserve very few traces of any "reciprocal arrangements;" and our examination of the deme associations in particular revealed the pronounced absence of formal recognition of other *demoi* or *demotai*.[52] For this reason, my discussion in chapter 1 has understood the purpose of the law to have been to "validate" a given association's internal arrangements *concerning its own membership* and has developed some of the implications of such a policy.

49. Apud Busolt 1920, p. 192, note 4 [p. 193].
50. Ferguson 1944, p. 64, note 5 [p. 65].
51. Ibid.
52. "Deme versus Deme Relations," in chapter 3.

APPENDIX THREE

Documents of the Internally Organized Phylai

The following is a corrected and amplified version of the list of the documents of the phylai published in Jones 1987, ch. 1, sec. 1.4, app., pp. 65–67. As in the previous list, I include only texts that recognizably represent acts of the phyle qua association. Thus a mere roster of ephebes arranged under the name of their phyle would not, in the absence of an indication of official action taken by the phyle, merit inclusion. For the prytany (and other bouleutic) inscriptions of the phylai, see chapter 5, note 39.

I Erechtheis. Decrees: *IG* II² 1146 (ante med. s. IV; *SEG* 25.140, 35.246, 39.144); 1147 (ante med. s. IV); 1150 (= Traill 1986, p. 83, no. 4 [*SEG* 36.178]; med. s. IV); 1165 (ca. 300–250; *SEG* 29.1730; 39.146).

II Aigeis. Decrees: *Hesperia* 56 (1987) 47–58 (joint decree with Aiantis; *SEG* 37.100, 39.145, 40.125; ca. 330); *Agora* 15, no. 69 (= *IG* II² 656+; Dow 1937, no. 2; 284/3; reference to phyle in line 10 wholly restored); *Hesperia* 29 (1960) 78–80, no. 155 (*SEG* 18.31; but see Ch. Habicht, *MDAI[A]* 76 [1961] 141–143; ca. 160). Herm dedicated by the phyle: Andokides, 1.62; Aischines, 1.125; cf. Plutarch, *Alkibiades* 21.3 (415 or earlier). For the dedication *IG* II² 2824 (313/2), once thought to be in the names of the *epimeletai* (as well as of the *tamias*) of the phyle, see Traill 1986, pp. 90–92, no. 8.

III Pandionis. Decrees: *IG* II² 1138 and 1139 (partial copy of 1138) + *Hesperia* 22 [1953] 177, no. 1 (*SEG* 12.96) + *IG* II² 2812 (fragment of still another copy of 1138: see D. M. Lewis, *ABSA* 50 [1955] 17–24, no. 25 [*SEG* 16.105]) (ca. 390–380); *IG* II² 1140 (386/5); 1144 (init. s. IV); 1148 (ante med. s. IV); *Hesperia* 32 (1963) 41, no. 42 (SEG 21.515, 34.101; Traill 1986, pp. 85–87, no. 6; 332/1, 327/6, or 324/3); *IG* II² 1152 (= II² 596; Traill 1986, pp. 87–88, no. 7; ante fin. s. IV); 1157 (326/5); 1159 (303/2); 1160 (ca. 300); 1167 (s. III). Dedications: *Hesperia* 11 (1942) 341–343, no. 1 (by the phyle; fin. s. V); *IG* II² 2812? (but the pertinence of this text to *epimeletai* was denied by D. M. Lewis, *ABSA* 50 [1955] 17–18) (init. s. IV); 2828 (by priest of Pandion and *phyletai;* med. s. IV); cf. *Hesperia* 4 (1935) 55, no. 17 (dedicator? ca. 350–300).

IV Leontis. Decrees: *Hesperia* 9 (1940) 59–66, no. 8: i, of Leontis; ii, of *lochagoi* of Leontis (333/2); *Hesperia* 15 (1946) 189, no. 35 (= *Hesperia* 3 [1934] 43–44, no. 32; ca. 325)? Dedication: *IG* II² 2818 (by *epimeletai*; Traill 1986, pp. 81–82, no. 2; *SEG* 39.202; 357/6). A literary reference to a decree moved by one Skironides "among the *phyletai*" in the year 346/5 is preserved in a speech attributed to Demosthenes 57, *Against Theokrines*, 17.

V Akamantis. Decrees: *ArchEph* 1965, pp. 131–136 (*SEG* 23.78; but see Dow 1976 [*SEG* 26.131], pp. 81–84): i (361/0) and ii (334/3 or soon thereafter [Dow]); *Hesperia* 17 (1948) 114–136, no. 68 (*SEG* 25.141; 304/3 or 303/2) (but see Woodhead 1981, pp. 357–367); *IG* II² 1166 (ca. 300–250). Honorary inscription: *SEG* 18.81 (= 21.749; s. II p.). Dedication: *Hesperia* 28 (1959) 121–126 (by taxiarch and *lochagoi*? 334/3–307/6).

VI Oineis. Tombstone: *Hesperia* 11 (1942) 240–241, no. 45 (of eponymous hero? s. IV).

VII Kekropis. Decrees: *IG* II² 1141 (= *Hesperia* 10 [1941] 263–265, no. 67; 376/5); 1143 (init. s. IV); 1145 (of Kekropis? post 353/2?); 1155, lines 7–14 + 16 (339/8); 1156, lines 26–35 + 64 (334/3); 1158 (of Kekropis? post med. s. IV); *SEG* 2.8 (two decrees, the latter of Kekropis? s. IV). Dedication: *IG* II² 2837 (by thesmothete; 329/8). Mortgage stone: *IG* II² 2670 (s. IV).

VIII Hippothontis. Decrees: *IG* II² 1149 (ante med. s. IV); 1153 (med. s. IV); 1163 (ca. 288/7).

IX Aiantis. Decrees: *IG* II² 1151 (Traill 1986, pp. 84–85, no. 5 [*SEG* 36.179]; med. s. IV); 1250 (of *lampadephoroi*; *SEG* 40.124; ante 335); *Hesperia* 56 (1987) 47–58 (joint decree with Aigeis; *SEG* 37.100, 39.145, 40.125; ca. 330); *Hesperia* 7 (1938) 94–96, no. 15 (327/6); *Hesperia* 15 (1946) 189, no. 35 (= *Hesperia* 3 [1934] 43–44, no. 32; ca. 325)?

X Antiochis. Decrees: *AD* 8 (1923) 98–100, no. 4 (of *hippeis* of phyle; ca. 330); 89–96, no. 2 (of elder *epilektoi* of phyle; ca. 330); 85–89, no. 1 (of phyle; 303/2) (= *SEG* 3.115-117; no. 1 = *SEG* 22.115; 25.142).

Antigonis. One of the two completely preserved (of an original total of six?) crowns in the dedication *IG* II² 2861 contains the name of an epimelete of Ikarion. If Kirchner's date "s.III a." is correct, the dedication belongs to the period 307/6 to 201/0, when Ikarion was a deme of Antigonis (see Traill 1975, p. 110).

Demetrias. The other preserved crown in the dedication just mentioned contains the name of an epimelete of Poros, which continuously belonged to Demetrias from 307/6 to 201/0 (see Traill 1975, p. 112).

Ptolemais. Decree: *Hesperia* 32 (1963) 14–15, no. 13 (*SEG* 21.522; init. s. II)?

Attalis. Honorary inscription: *IG* II² 1170 (of Attalis? s. II). Dedication: 2890 (by *phyletai*? aet. Rom.).

Identity of phyle unknown. Decrees: *IG* II² 1142 (init. s. IV); *Hesperia* 51 (1982) 46–47, no. 5 (*SEG* 32.140; ca. 375-350)?; *IG* II² 1154 (med. s. IV)?; *Hesperia* 4 (1935) 41–42, no. 9 (fin. s. IV); *IG* II² 1161 (fin. s. IV); 1162 (fin. s. IV); *Hesperia* 9 (1940) 111–112, no. 21 (init. s. III); *IG* II² 1164 (init. s. III); 1168 (s. III?); 1169 (s. III); 1171 (= 1124: see A. S. Henry, *ZPE* 38 [1980] 92–93, no. 3: *SEG* 30.90; s. II p.). Dedications: *IG* II² 2842 (by *epimeletai*) (321/0 or 318/7); 2843 (by thesmothete plus line 4 [the phyle in crown]; 319/8). Lease: cf. *IG* II² 1168 (s. III?).

Bibliography

The following list includes all titles cited in the body of the book that are concerned directly or indirectly with the subject of classical Athenian associations. It excludes primary texts, periodicals, dictionaries and encyclopedias, collections of inscriptions, and other basic works of reference; for my practice in the citation of these, see the Abbreviations. Throughout, titles are referenced by author's last name and year of publication; if the titles for a given year of a given author number two or more, the work is referenced in the form "Hansen 1983a," "Hansen 1983b," etc.

Andrewes, A. "Philochoros on Phratries." *JHS* 81 (1961) 1–15.

Balatsos, P. "Inscriptions from the Academy." *ZPE* 86 (1991) 145–154.

Bicknell, P. J. "Clisthène et Kytherros." *REG* 89 (1976) 599–603.

Biers, William R., and Thomas D. Boyd. "Ikarion in Attica: 1888–1981." *Hesperia* 51 (1982) 1–18.

Billigmeier, J. C., and M. S. Dusing. "The Origin and Function of the Naukraroi at Athens: An Etymological and Historical Explanation." *TAPA* 111 (1981) 11–16.

Billot, M.-F. "Le Cynosarges, Antiochos et les tanneurs: Questions de topographie." *BCH* 116 (1992) 119–156.

Bourriot, F. *Recherches sur la nature du génos: étude d'histoire sociale Athénienne, Périodes archaïque et classique.* 2 vols. Lille 1976.

Boyd, Thomas D., and Michael H. Jameson. "Urban and Rural Land Division in Ancient Greece." *Hesperia* 50 (1981) 327–342.

Brumbaugh, Robert S. "An Academy Inscription." *Ancient Philosophy* 12 (1992) 171–172.

Brunt, P. A. "The Model City in Plato's *Laws.*" *Studies in Greek History and Thought.* Oxford 1993, pp. 245–281.

Buck, Carl D. "Inscriptions from Ikaria." *Papers of the American School of Classical Studies at Athens* 5 (1886–1890) 71–108.

Burford, Alison. *Land and Labor in the Greek World*. Baltimore and London 1993.

Busolt, G. *Griechische Staatskunde*. Vol. 1 and vol. 2 (with H. Swoboda). Berlin 1920, 1926.

Calhoun, G.M. *Athenian Clubs in Politics and Litigation*. Austin, Texas, 1913.

Chadwick, J. *The Mycenaean World*. Cambridge 1976.

Chase, Alston Hurd. "The Influence of Athenian Institutions upon the *Laws* of Plato." *HSCP* 44 (1933) 131–192.

Connor, W. Robert. *The New Politicians of Fifth-Century Athens*. Princeton, New Jersey 1971.

———. "'Sacred' and 'Secular': Ἱερὰ καὶ ὅσια and the Classical Athenian Concept of the State." *Ancient Society* 19 (1988) 161–188.

Cox, Cheryl Anne. "Sisters, Daughters and the Deme of Marriage: A Note." *JHS* 108 (1988) 185–188.

Damsgaard-Madsen, Aksel. "Attic Funeral Inscriptions: Their Use as Historical Sources and Some Preliminary Results." *Studies in Ancient History and Numismatics Presented to Rudi Thomsen*. AArhus University Press 1988, pp. 55–68.

David, E. "The Spartan *Syssitia* and Plato's *Laws*." *AJP* 99 (1978) 486–495.

Davies, J. K. *Athenian Propertied Families 600–300 B.C.* Oxford 1971.

———. "Athenian Citizenship: The Descent Group and the Alternatives." *CJ* 73 (1978) 105–121.

———. *Wealth and the Power of Wealth in Classical Athens*. New York 1981.

Dillon, J. "What Happened to Plato's Garden?" *Hermathena* 134 (1983) 51–59.

Donlan, Walter. "Change and Shifts in the Meaning of *Demos* in the Literature of the Archaic Period." *PP* 135 (1970) 381–395.

———. *The Aristocratic Ideal in Ancient Greece*. Lawrence, Kansas 1980.

Dover, K. J. *Lysias and the Corpus Lysiacum*. Berkeley and Los Angeles 1968.

Dow, S. *Prytaneis: A Study of the Inscriptions Honoring the Athenian Councillors*. Hesperia Supplement I. Princeton 1937.

———. "The Athenian Epheboi: Other Staffs, and the Staff of the Diogeneion." *TAPA* 91 (1960) 381–409.

———. and David H. Gill. "The Greek Cult Table." *AJA* 59 (1965) 104–114.

———. "Companionable Associates in the Athenian Government." *In Memoriam Otto J. Brendel: Essays in Archaeology and the Humanities*. L. Bonfante and H. von Heintze, editors. Mainz 1976, pp. 69–84.

Edwards, John Bowen. *The Demesman in Attic Life*. Dissertation. Johns Hopkins University, Menasha, Wisconsin 1916.

Ehrenberg, V. *The People of Aristophanes: A Sociology of Old Attic Comedy*. Cambridge, Mass., 1951.

Eliot, C. W. J. *Coastal Demes of Attika: A Study of the Policy of Kleisthenes*. Phoenix Supplement V. Toronto 1962.

Endenburg, P. J. T. *Koinonia, en Gemeenschap van Zaken bij de Grieken in den klassieken Tijd*. Dissertation. Utrecht, Amsterdam, 1937.

England, E. B., *The Laws of Plato*. 2 vols. Manchester 1921.

Ferguson, W. S., "The Athenian Phratries." *CP* 5 (1910) 257–284.

———. "The Salaminioi of Heptaphylai and Sounion." *Hesperia* 7 (1938) 1–74. With "Additional Note on the Identification of the Property of the Salaminians at Sounion" by Homer A. Thompson, pp. 75–76.

———. "The Attic Orgeones." *Harvard Theological Review* 37 (1944) 61–140.

———. "Orgeonika," *Commemorative Studies in Honor of Theodore Leslie Shear*. Hesperia Supplement 8, Princeton 1949, pp. 130–163.

Figueira, Thomas J. "Mess Contributions and Subsistence at Sparta." *TAPA* 114 (1984) 87–109.

Finley, M. I. *Studies in Land and Credit in Ancient Athens 500–200 B.C.* New Brunswick, New Jersey, 1985 (1951).

———. ed. *Slavery in Classical Antiquity: Views and Controversies*, Cambridge 1960.

———. *Politics in the Ancient World.* Cambridge 1983.

Fischer, N. R. E. "Review of Bourriot 1976." *JHS* 99 (1979) 193–195.

Flower, Michael A. "*IG* II² 2344 and the Size of Phratries in Classical Athens." *CQ* 35 (1985) 232–235.

Forbes, Clarence A. *Neoi: A Contribution to the Study of Greek Associations.* Middletown, Conn., 1933.

Forrest, W. G. *The Emergence of Greek Democracy: The Character of Greek Politics, 800–400 B.C.* London 1966.

Foucart, P. *Des associations religieuses chez les Grecs: Thiases, éranes, orgéones.* Paris 1873.

Friedl, Ernestine. *Vasilika: A Village in Modern Greece.* New York 1962.

Gabrielsen, Vincent. "The Naukrariai and the Athenian Navy." *C&M* 36 (1985) 21–51.

Gallant, Thomas W. *Risk and Survival in Ancient Greece: Reconstructing the Rural Domestic Economy.* Stanford 1991.

Garland, R. *The Piraeus from the Fifth to the First Century B.C.* Ithaca, New York, 1987.

Gilbert, G. *The Constitutional Antiquities of Sparta and Athens.* E. J. Brooks and T. Nicklin, translators. London and New York 1895.

Goldhill, Simon. "Representing Democracy: Women at the Great Dionysia." *Ritual, Finance, Politics: Athenian Democratic Accounts Presented to David Lewis.* Robin Osborne and Simon Hornblower, editors. Oxford 1994, pp. 347–369.

Golding, Naomi H. "Plato as City Planner." *Arethusa* 8 (1975) 359–371.

Gomme, A. W. *The Population of Athens in the Fifth and Fourth Centuries B.C.* Oxford 1933.

Guarducci, Margherita. *I'Istituzione della Fratria nella Grecia Antica e nelle Colonie Greche d'Italia.* Rome 1937.

Habicht, Chr. *Studien zur Geschichte Athens in hellenistischer Zeit.* Göttingen 1982.

———. "Die Beiden Xenokles von Sphettos." *Hesperia* 57 (1988) 323–327.

Hands, A. R. *Charities and Social Aid in Greece and Rome.* Ithaca, New York, 1968.

Hansen, Mogens Herman. "How Many Athenians Attended the Ecclesia?" *GRBS* 17 (1976) 115–134 (= 1983a, pp. 1–20, 21–23).

———. "Demographic Reflections on the Number of Athenian Citizens 451–309 B.C." *AJAH* 7 (1982) 172–189.

———. *The Athenian Ecclesia: A Collection of Articles 1976–1983.* Copenhagen 1983 (= 1983a).

———. "Political Activity and the Organization of Attica in the Fourth Century B.C." *GRBS* 24 (1983) 227–238 (= 1983b).

———. *Demography and Democracy: The Number of Athenian Citizens in the Fourth Century B.C.* Gjellerup 1985.

———. "The Average Age of Athenian Bouleutai and the Proportion of Bouleutai Who Served Twice." *LCM* 13 (1988) 67–69.

———. "Athenian Democracy. Institutions and Ideology." *CP* 84 (1989) 137–148 (= 1989a).

———. "On the Importance of Institutions in an Analysis of Athenian Democracy." *C&M* 41 (1989) 107–113 (= 1989b).

———. "The Demography of the Attic Demes: The Evidence of the Sepulchral Inscriptions." *ARID* 19 (1990) 25–44.

———. *The Athenian Democracy in the Age of Demosthenes: Structure, Principles and Ideology.* Oxford and Cambridge, Mass., 1991.

Harding, P. "In Search of a Polypragmatist." *Classical Contributions: Studies in Honour of M. F. McGregor.* G. S. Shrimpton and D. J. McCargar, editors. New York 1981, pp. 41–50.

Harrison, A. R. W. *The Law of Athens.* Vol. 1 (*The Family and Property*) and vol. 2 (*Procedure,* edited by D. M. MacDowell). Oxford 1968 and 1971.

Harrison, E. B. "The Iconography of the Eponymous Heroes on the Parthenon and in the Agora." *Greek Numismatics and Archaeology. Essays in Honor of Margaret Thompson.* O. Mørkholm and N. M. Waggoner, editors. Wetteren 1979, pp. 71–85.

Haussoullier, B. *La Vie municipale en Attique: essai sur l'organisation des dèmes au quatrième siècle.* Paris 1884.

Hedrick, Jr., Charles W. "Old and New on the Attic Phratry of the Therrikleidai." *Hesperia* 52 (1983) 299–302.

———. "An Honorific Phratry Inscription." *AJP* 109 (1988) 111–117 (= 1988a).

———. "The Temple and Cult of Apollo Patroon in Athens." *AJA* 92 (1988) 185–210 (= 1988b).

———. "The Thymaitian Phratry." *Hesperia* 57 (1988) 81–85 (=1988c).

———. "The Phratry from Paiania." *CQ* 39 (1989) 126–135.

———. *The Decrees of the Demotionidai.* APA American Classical Studies. Atlanta 1990.

———. "Phratry Shrines of Attica and Athens." *Hesperia* 60 (1991) 241–268.

Henrichs, A. "Between Country and City: Cultic Dimensions of Dionysus in Athens and Attica." *Cabinet of the Muses. T. G. Rosenmeyer.* M. Griffith and D. J. Mastronade, editors. Atlanta 1990, pp. 257–277.

Hignett, C. *A History of the Athenian Constitution to the End of the Fifth Century B.C.* Oxford 1952.

Humphreys, S. C., "Public and Private Interests in Classical Athens." *CJ* 73 (1977/78) 97–104.

———. "Family Tombs and Tomb-Cult in Classical Athens: Tradition or Traditionalism?" *JHS* 100 (1980) 96–126.

———. "Phrateres in Alopeke, and the Salaminioi." *ZPE* 83 (1990) 243–248.

———. *The Family, Women and Death: Comparative Studies.* 2d ed. Ann Arbor 1993.

Jameson, Michael H. "Agriculture and Slavery in Classical Athens." *CJ* 73 (1977/78) 122–141.

Jenkins, I. D., "The Composition of the So-Called Eponymous Heroes on the East Frieze of the Parthenon." *AJA* 89 (1985) 121–127.

Jones, A. H. M., *Athenian Democracy.* New York 1958.

Jones, J. W. *Law and Legal Theory of the Greeks.* Oxford 1956.

Jones, Nicholas F. *Public Organization in Ancient Greece: A Documentary Study.* Memoirs of the American Philosophical Society. Vol. 176. Philadelphia 1987.

———. "The Organization of the Kretan City in Plato's *Laws.*" *CW* 83 (1990) 473–492.

———. "Enrollment Clauses in Greek Citizenship Decrees." *ZPE* 87 (1991) 79–102.

———. "The Athenian Phylai as Associations: Disposition, Function, and Purpose." *Hesperia* 64 (1995) 503–542.

———. *Ancient Greece: State and Society.* Upper Saddle River, New Jersey, 1997.

Jordan, Borimir. "Herodotos 5.71.2 and the Naukraroi of Athens." *CSCA* 3 (1970) 153–175.

———. *The Athenian Navy in the Classical Period.* University of California Publications: Classical Studies 13. Berkeley and Los Angeles 1975.

Just, R. *Women in Athenian Law and Life.* London and New York 1989.

Kearns, Emily. *The Heroes of Attica. BICS* supplement 57. London 1989.

Kornemann, E. "Koinon." *RE* supplement 4 (1924) coll. 914–941.

Kron, U. *Die Zehn attischen Phylenheroen: Geschichte, Mythos, Kult und Darstellungen.* Berlin 1976.

Lacey, W. K. *The Family in Classical Greece*. Ithaca, New York, 1968.

Lambert, S. D. "Herodotus, the Cylonian Conspiracy and the ΠΡΥΤΑΝΙΕΣ ΤΩΝ ΝΑΥΚΡΑΡΩΝ." *Historia* 35 (1986) 105–112.

———. *The Phratries of Attica*. Ann Arbor, Michigan, 1993.

Langdon, Merle K., and L. Vance Watrous. "The Farm of Timesios: Rock-Cut Inscriptions in South Attica." *Hesperia* 46 (1977) 162–177.

———. "The Attic *Tituli Memoriales*." *GRBS* 24 (1983) 67–70.

———. "Hymettiana I." *Hesperia* 54 (1985) 257–270 (= 1985a).

———. "The Territorial Basis of the Attic Demes." *SO* 60 (1985) 5–15 (= 1985b).

———. "An Attic Decree Concerning Oropos." *Hesperia* 56 (1987) 47–58

———. "The Topography of Coastal Erechtheis." *Chiron* 18 (1988) 43–54 (= 1988a).

———. "The ΖΩ/ΒΑ *Horoi* at Vari in Attica." *GRBS* 29 (1988) 75–81 (= 1988b).

———. "On the Farm in Classical Attica." *CJ* 86 (1990/91) 209–213.

Larsen, J. A. O. *Representative Government in Greek and Roman History*. Berkeley and Los Angeles 1955.

Lateiner, Donald. "'The Man Who Does Not Meddle in Politics': A *Topos* in Lysias." *CW* 76 (1982) 1–12.

Latte, K. "Phyle." *RE* 20 (1941) 994–1011.

Lauter, H. "Zwei Horos-Inschriften bei Vari." *AAA* 15 (1982) 299–315.

Lewis, D. M. "Cleisthenes and Attica." *Historia* 12 (1963) 22–40.

Linders, T., and G. Nordquist. *Gifts to the Gods: Proceedings of the Uppsala Symposium 1985*. Stockholm 1987.

Littman, R. J. "Kinship in Athens." *Ancient Society* 10 (1979) 5–31.

Lynch, John P. *Aristotle's School: A Study of a Greek Educational Institution*. Berkeley 1972.

———. "The 'Academy Tablets' (SEG XIX, No. 37)." *ZPE* 52 (1983) 115–121.

MacDowell, Douglas M. *The Law in Classical Athens*. Ithaca, New York, 1978.

———. *Demosthenes, Against Meidias*. Oxford 1990.

MacKendrick, Paul. *The Athenian Aristocracy 399 to 31 B.C.* Martin Classical Lectures 23. Cambridge, Mass. 1969.

McCleod, W. E. "An Ephebic Dedication from Rhamnous." *Hesperia* 28 (1959) 121–126.

McCredie, J. R. *Fortified Military Camps in Attica*. Hesperia Supplement 11. Princeton, New Jersey, 1966.

McKechnie, Paul. *Outsiders in the Greek Cities in the Fourth Century B.C.* London 1989.

Mikalson, Jon D. *The Sacred and Civil Calendar of the Athenian Year*. Princeton, New Jersey, 1975.

———. "Religion in the Attic Demes." *AJP* 98 (1977) 424–435.

Mion, Mario. "Athenian Democracy: Politicization and Constitutional Restraints." *History of Political Thought* 7 (1986) 219–238.

Morrow, Glenn R. "On the Tribal Courts in Plato's *Laws*." *AJP* 62 (1941) 314–321.

———. *Plato's Cretan City*, Princeton, New Jersey, 1960.

Mulgan, R. G. *Aristotle's Political Theory: An Introduction for Students of Political Theory*. Oxford 1977.

Murray, Oswyn, ed. *Sympotica: A Symposium on the Symposion*. Oxford 1990.

Nielsen, Thomas Heine, et al. "Athenian Grave Monuments and Social Class." *GRBS* 30 (1989) 411–420.

Nilsson, Martin P. "The New Inscription of the Salaminioi." *AJP* 59 (1938) 385–393.

Ober, Josiah. "Rock-Cut Inscriptions from Mt. Hymettos." *Hesperia* 50 (1981) 68–77.

———. "The Polis as a Society: Aristotle, John Rawls, and the Athenian Social Contract." *The Athenian Revolution: Essays on Ancient Greek Democracy and Political Theory*. Princeton 1996, pp. 161–187.

Oikonomides, Al. N. "P. Haun. 6 and Euxenos the Athenian Eponymous of 222/1 B.C." *ZPE* 32 (1978) 85–86.

Oliver, J. H., "From Gennetai to Curiales." *Hesperia* 49 (1980) 30–56.

Osborne, M. J. *Naturalization in Athens.* Vol. 1 (Brussels 1981), vol. 2 (1982), vol. 3 and vol. 4 (1983).

Osborne, Robin. "Buildings and Residence on the Land in Classical and Hellenistic Greece: The Contribution of Epigraphy." *ABSA* 80 (1985) 119–128 (= 1985a).

———. *Demos: The Discovery of Classical Attika.* Cambridge 1985 (= 1985b).

———. "The Demos and its Divisions in Classical Athens." Oswyn Murray and Simon Price, editors. *The Greek City from Homer to Alexander.* Oxford 1990, pp. 265–293.

———. "The Potential Mobility of Human Populations." *OJA* 10 (1991) 231–252.

Panagopoulos, Andreas. "Two Notes on Plato's Crete." *BICS* 33 (1987) 125–126.

Parker, R. "Festivals of the Attic Demes." In Linders and Norquist, pp. 137–147.

———. *Athenian Religion: A History.* Oxford 1996.

Patterson, C. *Pericles' Citizenship Law of 451–50 B.C.* Salem, New Hampshire, 1981.

———. "HAI ATTIKAI: The Other Athenians." *Rescuing Creusa: New Methodological Approaches to Women in Antiquity. Helios* new series 11 (1986) 49–67.

Pecirka, J. *The Formula for the Grant of Enktesis in Attic Inscriptions.* Prague 1966.

Pickard-Cambridge, A. *The Dramatic Festivals of Athens.* 2d ed., revised by J. Gould and D. M. Lewis. Oxford 1968.

Piérart, Marcel. *Platon et la cité grecque. Théorie et réalité dans la constitution des* "Lois." Brussels 1973.

Poland, Franz. *Geschichte des griechischen Vereinswesen.* Leipzig 1909.

Pouilloux, J. *La Forteresse de Rhamnonte: étude de topographie et d'histoire.* Paris 1954.

———. "Trois Décrets de Rhamnounte." *BCH* 80 (1956) 55–75.

Pritchett, W. Kendrick. *Studies in Ancient Greek Topography.* Vol. 1, University of California Publications: Classical Studies. Vol. 1. Berkeley and Los Angeles 1965.

Radin, Max. *The Legislation of the Greeks and Romans on Corporations.* Dissertation. Columbia University, 1910.

Rahe, Paul. "The Primacy of Politics in Classical Greece." *American Historical Review* 89 (1984) 265–293.

Raubitschek, Antony E. "Kolieis." ΦΟΡΟΣ. *Tribute to Benjamin Dean Meritt.* D. W. Bradeen and M. F. McGregor, editors. Locust Valley, New York, 1974, pp. 137–138.

Reilly, L. C. *Slaves in Ancient Greece. Slaves from Greek Manumission Inscriptions.* Chicago 1978.

Rhodes, P. J. *The Athenian Boule.* Oxford 1972.

———. *A Commentary on the Aristotelian* Athenaion Politeia. Oxford 1981.

Ritchie, Jr., C. E. ΦΙΛΙΑ ΕΠΗ ΕΙΣ Γ. Ε. ΜΥΛΩΝΑΝ. Vol. 3. Athens 1989, pp. 250–260.

Robertson, N. "The Attic Genos Erysichthonidai." *AJP* 105 (1984) 369–408.

Rose, Valentinus. *Aristotelis qui ferebantur librorum fragmenta.* Leipzig 1886.

Rotroff, S. I. "An Anonymous Hero in the Athenian Agora." *Hesperia* 47 (1978) 196–209.

Roussel, D. *Tribu et cité.* Paris 1976.

Ruschenbusch, Eberhard. ΣΟΛΩΝΟΣ ΝΟΜΟΙ. *Historia* Einzelschriften 9. Wiesbaden 1966.

Sarkady, J. "Gentilizische Formen in der frühen Polis-organisation Athens." *ACD* 14 (1978) 3–8.

Sartori, F. *Le eterie nella vita politica ateniese del Vi e V secolo a.C.* Rome 1957.

Saunders, Trevor J. "Notes on Plato as City Planner." *BICS* 23 (1976) 23–26.

Schlaifer, R. "The Cult of Athena Pallenis." *HSCP* 54 (1943) 35–67.

———. "The Attic Association of the ΜΕΣΟΓΕΙΟΙ." *CP* 39 (1944) 22–27.

Shear, Jr., T. L., "The Monument of the Eponymous Heroes in the Athenian Agora." *Hesperia* 39 (1970) 145–222.

Siewert, P. *Die Trittyes und die Heeresreform des Kleisthenes. Vestigia* 33. Munich 1982.

Simms, Ronda R. "The Cult of the Thracian Goddess Bendis in Athens and Attica." *Ancient World* 18 (1988) 59–76.

Sinclair, R. K. *Democracy and Participation in Athens.* Cambridge 1988.

Smith, Richard C. "The Clans of Athens and the Historiography of the Archaic Period." *EMC* 4 (1985) 51–61.

Solders, S. *Die ausserstädtischen Kulte und die Einigung Attikas.* Lund 1931.

Sommerstein, A. H. *Aristophanes, Birds.* The Comedies of Aristophanes. Vol. 6. Warminister 1987.

Stanton, G. R. "Some Attic Inscriptions." *ABSA* 79 (1984) 289–306.

Stockton, David. *The Classical Athenian Democracy.* Oxford 1990.

Stroud, R. S. *Drakon's Law on Homicide.* University of California Publications: Classical Studies 3. Berkeley and Los Angeles 1968.

———. *The Axones and Kyrbeis of Drakon and Solon.* University of California Publications: Classical Studies 19. Berkeley and Los Angeles 1979.

Szanto, E. *Die griechischen Phylen. SBWien* 144, no. 5, Vienna 1901 (=*Ausgewählte Abhandlungen* [Tübingen 1906], pp. 216–288, 419).

Thompson, W. E. "The Demes in Plato's *Laws.*" *Eranos* 61 (1965) 134–136.

———. "An Interpretation of the 'Demotionid' Decrees." SO 42 (1968) 51–68.

———. "The Deme in Kleisthenes' Reforms." *SO* 46 (1971) 72–79.

Thomsen, R. *Eisphora: A Study of Direct Taxation in Ancient Athens.* Copenhagen 1964.

Tod, Marcus Niebuhr. "Clubs and Societies in the Greek World." *Ancient Inscriptions: Sidelights on Greek History.* Oxford 1932, pp. 69–93.

———. "Clubs, Greek." *OCD²*, pp. 254–255; *OCD³*, pp. 351–352 (with S. Hornblower).

Toepffer, Iohannes. *Attische Genealogie.* Berlin 1889 [reprint New York 1973].

Traill, John S. *The Political Organization of Attica: A Study of the Demes, Trittyes, and Phylai and Their Representation in the Athenian Council. Hesperia* supplement 14. Princeton, New Jersey 1975.

———. "An Interpretation of Six Rock-Cut Inscriptions in the Attic Demes of Lamptrai." *Studies in Attic Epigraphy, History, and Topography Presented to Eugene Vanderpool. Hesperia* supplement 19. Princeton 1982, pp. 162–171.

———. *Demos and Trittys: Epigraphical and Topographical Studies in the Organization of Attica.* Toronto 1986.

Travlos, John. *Pictorial Dictionary of Ancient Athens.* New York and Washington 1971.

Vanderpool, Eugene. "An Archaic Inscribed Stele from Marathon." *Hesperia* 11 (1942) 329–337.

———. "The Genos Theoinidai Honors a Priestess of Nymphe." *AJP* 100 (1979) 213–216.

Ventris, M. G. F. and J. Chadwick. *Documents in Mycenaean Greek.* 2d ed. Cambridge 1973.

Vinogradoff, Paul. *Outlines of Historical Jurisprudence.* Vol. 2. *The Jurisprudence of the Greek City.* London 1922.

Wade-Gery, H. T. "Studies in the Structure of Attic Society, I. Demotionidai." *CQ* 25 (1931) 129–143. "II. The Laws of Kleisthenes," *CQ* 27 (1933) 17–29.

Walbank, Michael B. "The Property of Aiantis and Aigeis." *ZPE* 84 (1990) 95–99.

———. "A *Lex Sacra* of the State and of the Deme of Kollytos." *Hesperia* 63 (1994) 233–239.

Walters, K. R. "Geography and Kinship as Political Infrastructures in Archaic Athens." *Florilegium* 4 (1982) 1–31.

Welwei, Karl-Wilhelm. "Polisbildung, Hetairos-Gruppen and Hetairien." *Gymnasium* 99 (1992) 481–500.

Westermann, W. L. "Slavery and the Elements of Freedom in Ancient Greece." In Finley 1960, pp. 17–32.

Whitehead, David. *The Ideology of the Athenian Metic*. Cambridge Philological Society Supplementary vol. 4, Cambridge 1977.

———. "Immigrant Communities in the Classical Polis: Some Principles for a Synoptic Treatment." *AC* 53 (1984) 47–59.

———. *The Demes of Attica 508/7-ca. 250 b.c.: A Political and Social Study*. Princeton, New Jersey 1986.

———. "The ΚΩΛΟΚΡΑΤΑΙ of Kydantidai and Ionidai." *ZPE* 95 (1993) 159–162.

Wilamowitz-Moellendorff, U. von. *Antigonos von Karystos*. Berlin 1881.

Wilhelm, Adolf. "Inschrift aus dem Peiraieus." JÖAI 5 (1902) 127–139.

Wood, Ellen Meiksins. "Agricultural Slavery in Classical Athens." *AJAH* 8 (1983) 1–47.

Woodhead, A. G. "Athens and Demetrios Poliorketes at the End of the Fourth Century b.c." *Ancient Macedonian Studies in Honor of Charles F. Edson,* Thessaloniki 1981, pp. 357–367.

Woronoff, Michel. "Ville, cité, pays dans les Lois." *Ktema* 10 (1985) 67–75.

Wycherley, R. E. "Peripatos: The Athenian Philosophical Scene." I, *G&R* 8 (1961) 152–163. II, *G&R* 9 (1962) 2–21.

———. *The Stones of Athens*. Princeton, New Jersey 1978.

Wyse, William. *The Speeches of Isaeus*. Cambridge 1904.

Young, John Howard. "Studies in South Attica." *Hesperia* 10 (1941) 163–191.

Ziebarth, Erich. *Das griechische Vereinswesen*. Leipzig 1896.

Select Literary Passages

Select Inscriptions

IG II² (*continued*)
1202: 184
1204: 119, 120
1213: 236–237
1214: 64–65
1219 + 1288: 75
1233: 205
1237: 83 n. 4, 205, 208–210, 215, 217, 219
1238: 205
1240: 219
1243: 235, 236
1244: 237, 238
1245: 237, 238
1246: 237 n. 75, 262–263
1247: 237, 238
1248: 237 n. 75
1252 + 999: 254
1253: 254
1255: 259
1258: 310
1259: 254
1263: 219
1271: 219
1273: 219, 262, 263
1275: 266
1277: 266
1283: 43, 45, 257, 257–259, 261–262
1289: 12, 39–40
1299: 116 n. 129
1305: 73–74, 75
1315: 264–265
1316: 262, 264
1324: 259
1327: 263–264, 266, 267
1328i and ii: 265
1329: 266
1358: 235, 236
1361: 259–261
2338: 247
2339: 247 n. 135
2340: 247 n. 135
2345: 197, 213
2347: 218–219

2348: 218–219
2355: 251
2492: 89
2500: 116
2512: 59 n. 42
2617–2619: 59 n. 43
2622: 205
2623: 59, 65
2723: 205, 216
2824: 180–181, 193 n. 95
2830: 237
2933: 235
2935: 310
2965–3016: 116 n. 128
3102: 237
3103: 237
3467: 74 n. 96, 76
4975: 207
5980–5987: 85 n. 12
13246–13247: 60 n. 45

MDAI[A]
67 (1942) 21–22, no. 24: 115
67 (1942) 24–29, no. 26: 239–240

Pouilloux 1954
no. 2 = *MDAI[A]* 67 (1942) 21–22, no. 24
no. 8 = *IG* II² 3467
no. 15 = *SEG* 25.155
no. 17 = *SEG* 15.112

SEG
15.112: 76–79
21.541: 127
22.117: 91
22.127: 75
25.155: 75, 76, 79–81, 89
32.230: 63 n. 58
38.127: 76
39.148 (= 41.71): 52 n. 9, 116
41.84: 251
43.40: 76
43.56: 216

Subject Index